Illustrated Guide to
the Game Parks and
Nature Reserves of
Southern Africa

Reader's Digest

Illustrated Guide to the Game Parks and Nature Reserves of Southern Africa

Published by The Reader's Digest Association, South Africa (Pty) Limited, Cape Town

Editors: Judy Beyer, Alan Duggan
Associate Editor: Brian Johnson Barker
Cartographer: André Reinders
Researchers: Taryn James, Frances le Roux, Patricia Brennan
Consultants: Kathleen Ginn; Clive James; Gideon Louw, M Sc, Ph D; Willie Olivier; M D Picker, Ph D
Project Manager: Carol Adams
Project Coordinators: Grant Moore, Tania Petersen
Indexer: Sandie Vahl
Proofreaders: Eric Canterbury, Anne Wevell

Title page: Malachite kingfisher (*Alcedo cristata*)
Left: Cheetah (*Acinonyx jubatus*)
Page 5: Red bishop (*Euplectes orix*)

Third edition copyright © 1997
The Reader's Digest Association South Africa (Pty) Limited, 130 Strand Street,
Cape Town 8001

All rights reserved. No part of this book may be reproduced, translated, stored in a retrieval system, or transmitted in any form or by any means, electronic, electrostatic, magnetic tape, mechanical, photocopying, recording or otherwise, without permission in writing from the publishers.

® Reader's Digest is a registered trademark of The Reader's Digest Association, Inc. of Pleasantville, New York, United States of America.

ISBN 1-874912-50-5

How to use this book

This book has been divided into nine principal natural regions. These regions are listed on the contents page overleaf with their appropriate page numbers.

Each region is subdivided into particular zones, with each zone featuring a detailed map showing you the location of the reserves and the type of accommodation you will find there. The parks and reserves are all listed alphabetically within each region and, to help you while you are on the road, we have included information on distances, the best routes to follow and the condition of the roads.

Note that groups of pictures are captioned clockwise from the lower left.

Every effort has been made to ensure that the information contained in this book is accurate and up to date. However, the state of nature conservation in southern Africa is constantly changing, and we recommend that you contact the reserve you intend to visit to confirm the details. Check also on the security aspect, and take appropriate action to protect yourself and your belongings. The publishers cannot accept responsibility for mishaps that arise from consulting this book.

Contents

To find a particular area, check the page numbers on the map (opposite page), or the list on the right. Reserves within each area are listed alphabetically.

How to use this book 5

Lowveld 8
Kruger National Park 10
The Far North 31
West of Kruger 41
Swaziland 53

Highveld 58
Northeastern Escarpment 60
Bushveld Basin 76
Northwestern Highveld 94
Northeastern Highveld 106
Free State 117
Lesotho 128

KwaZulu-Natal 132
Drakensberg 134
Midlands 144
The Lakes 154
Mfolozi Valley 166
South Coast 172

Eastern Cape 180
Across the Kei 182
Northeastern Cape 188
Amatola 195
Port Elizabeth 206

Southwestern Cape 214
The Garden Route 216
Little Karoo 228
Southern Cape 233
Cape Peninsula 247
The West Coast 255

The Interior 262
Namaqualand 264
Great Karoo 269
Southern Kalahari 277
Augrabies 283
Kalahari Gemsbok National Park 288

Namibia 294
Fish River Canyon 296
The Centre 303
The Namib 308
Skeleton Coast 317
Etosha National Park 324
The Northeast 333

Botswana 342
Okavango 344
Kalahari Desert 352
Makgadikgadi 357
Chobe National Park 362

Zimbabwe 366
Hwange and Victoria Falls 368
Lake Kariba 374
Harare and the Northeast 381
The Eastern Highlands 387
The South 393
The Southwest 398

Index 402

Acknowledgements 423

Picture credits 424

Turn to the page numbers indicated for information on the game parks and nature reserves in each area.

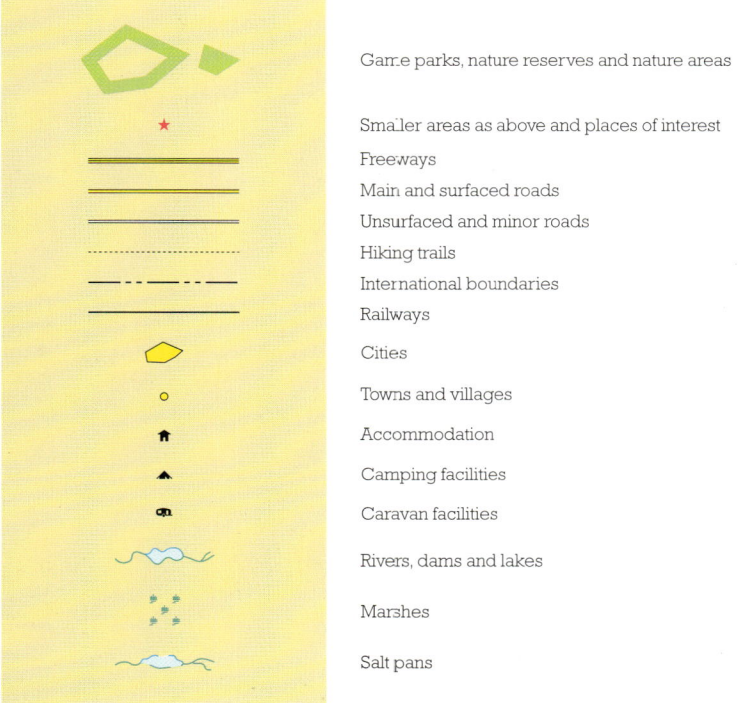

(green shapes)	Game parks, nature reserves and nature areas
★	Smaller areas as above and places of interest
═══	Freeways
───	Main and surfaced roads
───	Unsurfaced and minor roads
·····	Hiking trails
─ ─ ─	International boundaries
───	Railways
(yellow shape)	Cities
○	Towns and villages
⌂	Accommodation
▲	Camping facilities
🚐	Caravan facilities
~~	Rivers, dams and lakes
∴∴	Marshes
≈≈	Salt pans

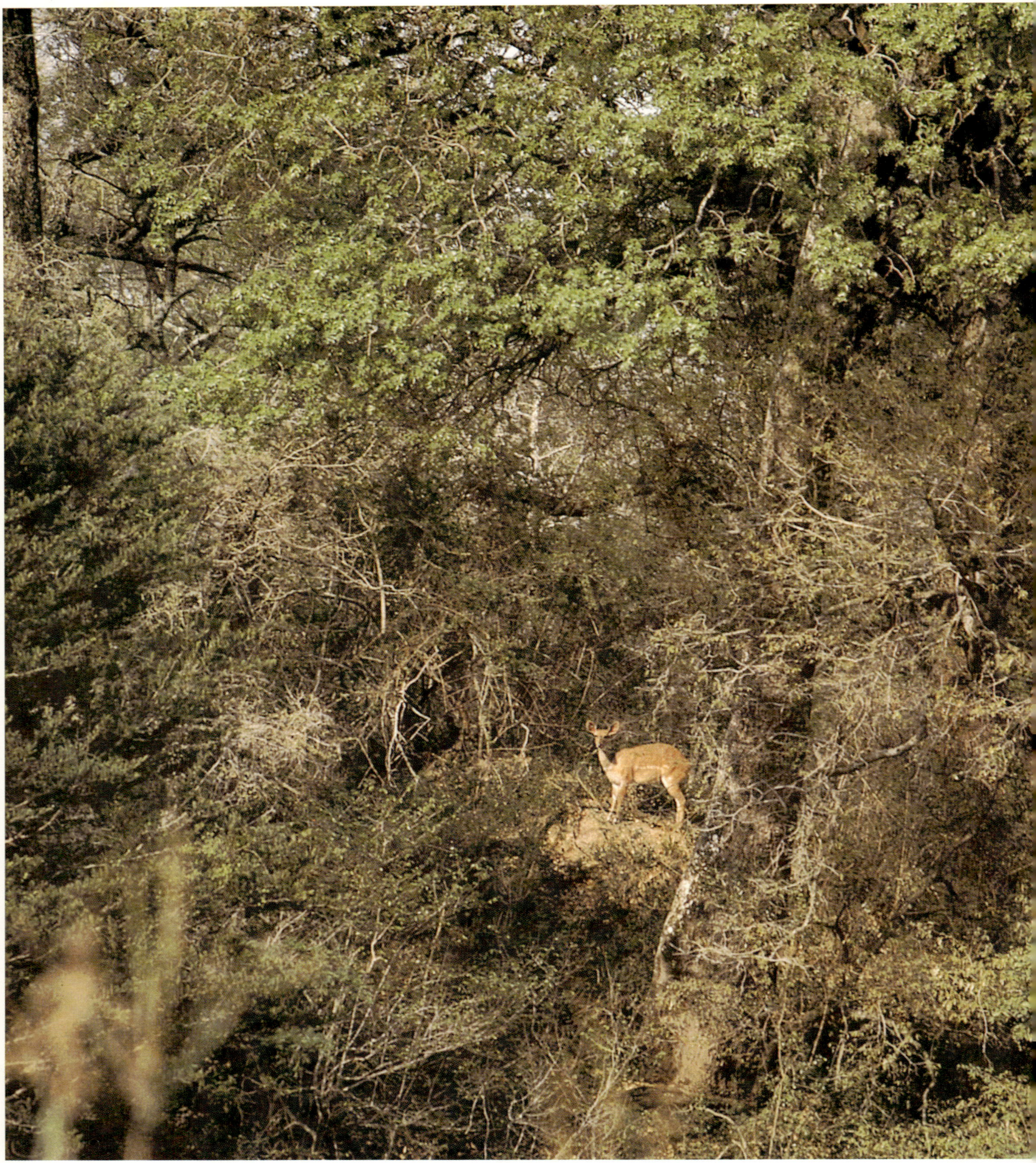

LOWVELD

The Lowveld region of Northern Province is a slice of raw Africa, a searingly hot land covered with bushwillow, acacia and mopane woodlands that stretch as far as the horizon.

It is also the home of the baobabs – ancient giants which thrust their massive branches heavenwards with a dignity achieved only by trees which have witnessed the earth's changes for more than a thousand years.

This land was once infested with tsetse fly and the rinderpest virus: then it began to recover, attracting farmers, adventurers, miners, hunters – and conservationists. Today the entire Lowveld is rich in many respects, but its richest asset by far is surely the Kruger National Park, one of the great natural sanctuaries of the world, and certainly one of the most popular tourist attractions in southern Africa. The park's 1 948 500 ha make it much the same size as Israel.

However, Lowveld wildlife is by no means restricted to Kruger Park. Some visitors prefer to stay at one of the luxurious game lodges beyond the park's western fence, from where they track game in 4x4 vehicles.

At the northern end of the escarpment, the Lowveld meets the Soutpansberg and sweeps north to the wild Limpopo. Here several nature reserves have been established to conserve the vegetation and wildlife. Further south, the Lowveld rolls into the little kingdom of Swaziland, where the authorities have assembled an impressive array of parks and nature reserves, encompassing both the country's undulating plains and its craggy mountains.

A bushbuck ewe peers guardedly from a thick tangle of bush in the Mala Mala Game Reserve, west of the Kruger National Park.

The great spaces washed with sun

Majestic in extent, rich in game, grand in its scenic splendour, the Kruger National Park is the pride of South Africa.

This almost 2 000 000 ha expanse of savannah and bush country in the northeastern corner of South Africa, bounded by the Crocodile River in the south, the Limpopo 350 km to the north, the Mozambique border in the east, and a man-made barrier to the west, is a true haven of the wild. Its game population includes 147 species of mammal, more than 500 species of bird, 114 species of reptile, 49 species of fish, 34 species of amphibian and over 200 species of butterfly.

The Kruger Park is big game country. Lion, elephant, buffalo, rhino and tens of thousands of antelope roam the sunlit plains. Leopard stalk the night; shy bushbuck hide in the riverine bush; giraffe browse on the sweet-scented acacias of the south-central region. Vultures wheel overhead, alert for kill and carcass.

In no other wildlife sanctuary in the world is so much so readily – and comfortably – accessible to the ordinary holiday-maker. The park has 2 624 km of tarred and gravel roads which take you to numerous well-frequented waterholes, tranquil, shaded picnic spots and grand viewing points. The 26 rest camps offer a range of accommodation from the rustic and rudimentary to the unashamedly luxurious and, together with the caravan sites, shops and restaurants, can cater for the daily needs of more than 3 000 visitors. For an inexpensive family holiday, the Kruger National Park is probably unrivalled.

This wildlife haven has been described as 'Africa's largest hotel', and so it might be because the rest camps and their adjuncts are run, and run very well, by a single authority. But it has little of the traditional hotel atmosphere about it. The neatly laid-out, fenced, beautifully thatched clusters of rondavels and bungalows are shady oases in a wilderness of unsurpassed magnificence.

Although the park is open throughout the year, it is especially popular during the South African school holidays. Generally speaking, the area's climate is subtropical, and the warmth of its days and the cool nights allow easy and pleasant gameviewing for most of the year. In the six-month rainy season which starts around October, though, tall grass will interrupt the view along some of the routes, and a few secondary roads may be closed to traffic for short periods.

Until quite recently the northern areas of South Africa were vast, relatively undisturbed, treasure-houses of wildlife. Then, in the late 19th century, Western man arrived. Farmers settled and white hunters brought their formidable fire power to bear on the herds, taking a devastating toll of the buffalo, wildebeest and other species.

Left: A kudu cow in the Kruger National Park. Although females also have vertical stripes, they are smaller and more slender than the males, and do not have horns. Greater kudu – the only species found in southern Africa – usually live in family groups of four or five individuals, or in small herds, while lesser kudu (a far smaller species found further north, frequently in drier country) tend to live in pairs. **Below:** The male horsefly has such large eyes that they occupy the major part of its head. Only the females are bloodsuckers: the males use their long, flexible proboscises to draw up the nectar from deep flowers.

LOWVELD: KRUGER NATIONAL PARK

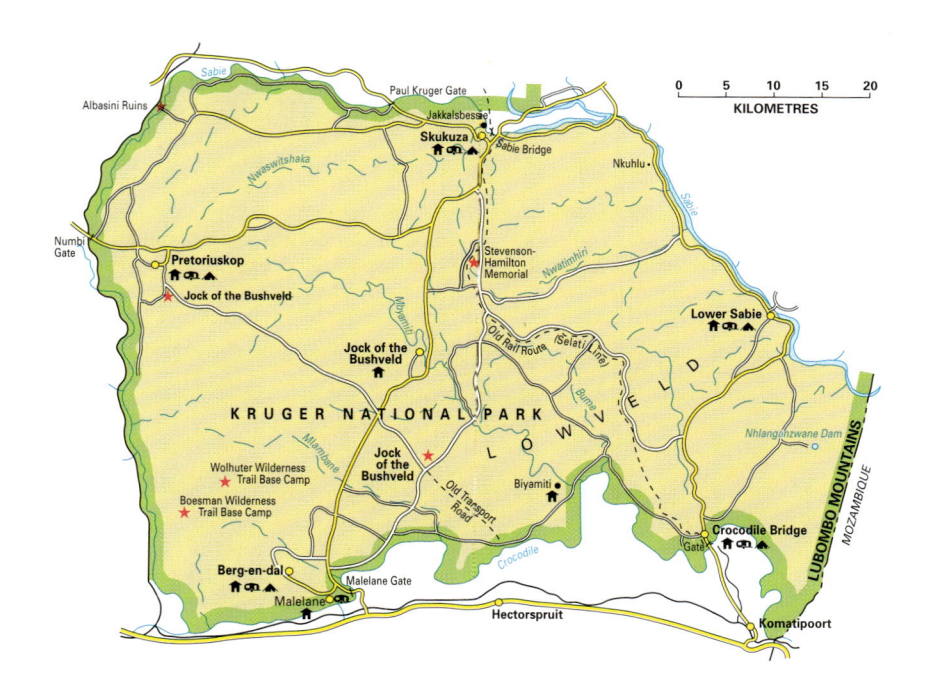

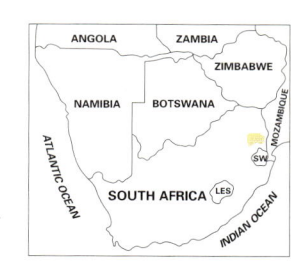

It is reckoned that over two million hides had been exported to the tanneries of Europe by the end of the 1870s – a tragic enough figure, but one which represents just a fraction of the true extent of the slaughter. For these men hunted for pleasure as well as profit: they killed indiscriminately in game drives that trapped thousands of animals, and left countless carcasses on the plains for scavengers and the bleaching African sun.

Paul Kruger, who at the age of ten travelled north with his family on the Great Trek, was a true child of the veld. Young Kruger was a good

SOUTHERN KRUGER PARK AT A GLANCE

When to go Gameviewing is easiest in winter but some connoisseurs prefer the lush vegetation of summer. April and May see the dramatic rutting of impala, wildebeest and other species, and November and December see the birth of their young.

In general, entrance gates and rest camps open at sunrise and close at sunset, and motorists travelling in the park after hours are fined. The park is open year round, but opening and closing times vary from month to month.

Reservations and information To book accommodation in a rest camp or to apply for a place on the Wolhuter, Napi or Bushman (or Boesman) wilderness trails, write to National Parks Board, P O Box 787, Pretoria 0001, or telephone (012) 343-1991, fax 343-0905; or National Parks Board, P O Box 7400, Roggebaai 8012, telephone (021) 22-2810, or fax their offices on 24-6211.

Getting there Enter at one of four gates: Paul Kruger Gate (12 km from Skukuza) and the old Numbi Gate (9 km from Pretoriuskop) are both approached from the west, while Malelane Gate and Crocodile Bridge (both of which have their own rest camps) can be approached from the south. There is an airport at Skukuza with daily scheduled flights to and from Johannesburg. Private flights must obtain clearance before landing at the Skukuza airstrip.

Accommodation There are five rest camps: Skukuza, Pretoriuskop, Lower Sabie, Crocodile Bridge and Berg-en-dal. There is also a small private camp which has to be reserved and occupied as a whole – Jock of the Bushveld (12 beds), which lies along the old transport route between Pretoriuskop and Malelane. Accommodation varies, but there is usually a choice of family cottages (two rooms with two beds in each, bathroom, toilet, kitchenette with gas stove, fridge, eating and cooking utensils; huts with shower and toilet (one room with two or three beds); or ordinary huts (available with two, three, four or five beds and a handbasin with cold water, close to an ablution block). There are caravan and camping sites at all the camps except Jock of the Bushveld. Malelane is a small bushveld camp with six rondavels and 15 caravan sites. Jakkalsbessie and Biyamiti bushveld camps offer self-catering accommodation. Most of the camps in southern Kruger cater for the physically disabled.

Eating and drinking All camps except Crocodile Bridge, Malelane and Jock of the Bushveld have licensed restaurants, and shops that sell fresh meat, groceries, beer, wine and spirits. (The small bushveld camps do not have these facilities.) There are field kitchens and braai facilities close to the accommodation and caravan/camping sites, as well as at the designated picnic places.

Getting around Main roads are tarred and secondary roads are gravelled. Speed limits vary between 40 and 50 km/hour. Once outside rest camps, visitors must remain in their cars (except at the picnic spots or designated monuments, where they may alight at their own risk). There are filling stations at all the gates, except Malelane and Paul Kruger, and at all the main camps (none at bushveld and private camps). Diesel fuel is available at Lower Sabie, Pretoriuskop and Skukuza. The Automobile Association has an Emergency Service Centre at Skukuza, with a mechanic and breakdown truck.

Twice a week, on Sundays and Wednesdays, parties of eight leave Berg-en-dal on the three-day Wolhuter and Bushman wilderness trails. (Napi trailists leave from Pretoriuskop.) Hikers sleep in bush camps in the Stolsnek area to the south and east of Pretoriuskop. Bedding and food are provided but hikers must take their own drinks.

Special attractions All rest camps except Biyamiti, Crocodile Bridge, Malelane and Jock of the Bushveld present a nightly film show (weather permitting). Berg-en-dal has a trail for the blind.

Special precautions Precautions against malaria are necessary. Because specific drugs are required to combat the various strains of malaria in particular areas, you are advised to consult your doctor.

LOWVELD: KRUGER NATIONAL PARK

hunter, and a brave one. When his thumb was shattered in an accident, he stoically severed the dangling fragments with his knife.

But even as he hunted, Kruger became uncomfortably aware that the once-limitless herds were dwindling. Others were of the same mind: in the 1850s the Transvaal Volksraad drastically curtailed the killing of elephant and forbade hunters to shoot more game than they could consume. In 1870 pit-traps and snares were outlawed, and four years later the Volksraad established closed seasons to allow game to breed. Further restrictions followed during the course of the next two decades, but it was Paul Kruger who, in the 1890s, gave real impetus to the creation of wildlife sanctuaries. The Sabie Game Reserve, between the Crocodile and Sabie rivers, was formally proclaimed on 26 March 1898, in the twilight of his presidency of the then Transvaal.

In the grim years of the Anglo-Boer War which erupted in 1899, the new sanctuary's status was, understandably, ignored. Both sides hunted to supplement rations, and the hungry black population scoured the countryside for food. But with peace came renewed awareness of the old Transvaal's unique natural heritage. James Stevenson-Hamilton, a former major in the Inniskilling Dragoons who had explored and hunted in Central Africa, was appointed

TIPS FOR VISITORS

Entry into and travel within the park is confined to daylight hours.

The speed limits are 50 km/hour on tar and 40 km/hour on gravel. You may be fined if you exceed these limits and if you feed the animals. Fines for leaving the safety of your car in unprotected areas or disturbing the animal life in any way are especially severe.

All roads within the park are well signposted, and good maps are available at the entrance gates, camps, and from the Automobile Association at Skukuza. There is a checklist of the park's trees, as well as a variety of other publications, including guides to the park's birds, fish, reptiles, small and large mammals, and butterflies. Prominent tree specimens, close to the roads, have been numbered to correspond with the listed entries, facilitating easy identification.

On the forbidden list are pets, open vehicles and motorcycles. Firearms must be sealed. Boating and fishing are also prohibited. Caravans are allowed on the tarred roads and on some of the gravel roads.

The Kruger Park is low-lying country, on average less than 300 m above sea level, and in summer the sticky, almost suffocating, daytime heat is relieved only by sudden rainstorms that roll across the veld. Most people go on their gameviewing drives early in the morning or in the late afternoon, resting during the intense heat of the day (the animals also tend to nap at this time). However, you should take warm clothing in the winter months.

Although the larger camps have restaurants, the park caters essentially for inexpensive outdoor living – braai facilities are excellent, and visitors can either stock up before departure or buy their food from the well-stocked camp shops.

Be sure to book accommodation well in advance to avoid disappointment.

Left: A reconstructed Iron Age settlement on an archaeological site near the Kruger Park's Phalaborwa Gate. **Above:** A young roan. This is the third largest antelope (after kudu and eland) and is relatively rare in the Kruger Park. **Below:** Among the most beautiful of the park's many floral species is the impala lily, with its star-shaped petals. Note the long seed pods.

12

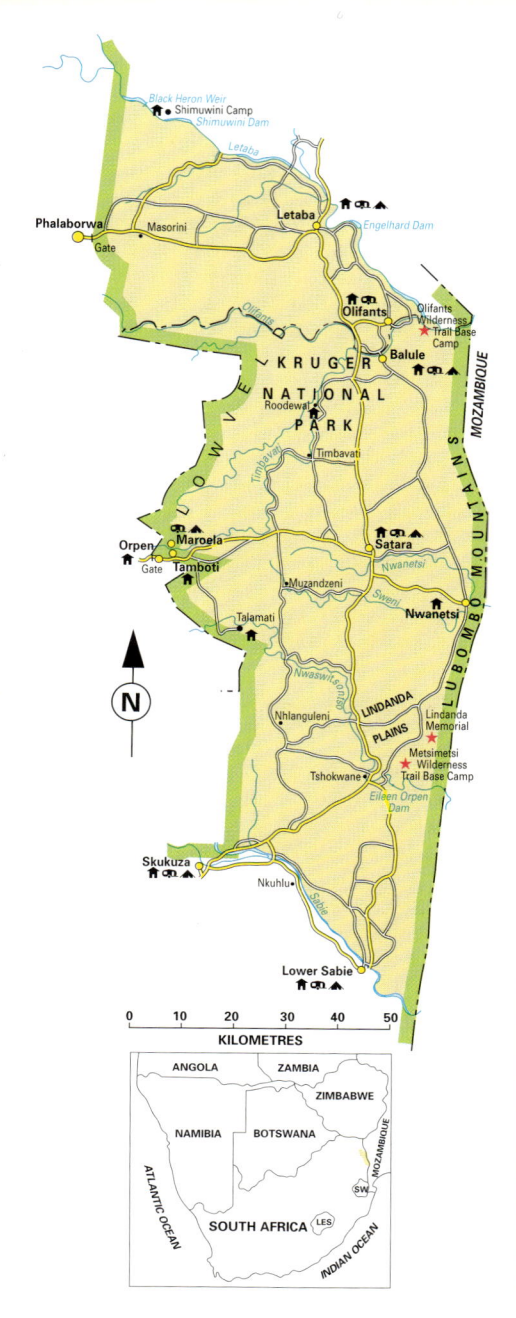

CENTRAL KRUGER PARK AT A GLANCE

When to go As in the rest of the park, the central region is open year round, but visitors should check the opening and closing times at the entrance gates and rest camps.

Reservations To book accommodation in a rest camp or to apply for a place on the Metsimetsi, Sweni or Olifants wilderness trails, write to National Parks Board, P O Box 787, Pretoria 0001, or telephone (012) 343-1991, fax 343-0905; or National Parks Board, P O Box 7400, Roggebaai 8012, telephone (021) 22-2810, fax 24-6211.

Getting there Two gates serve the camps in the central region: Orpen Gate, reached from Acornhoek, and the Phalaborwa Gate, reached from Gravelotte or the south. Phalaborwa has an airport with car-hire firms in attendance and there are daily flights to and from Johannesburg.

Accommodation The chief rest camps are Satara, Olifants and Letaba, and there is limited accommodation at Orpen and Balule, while Nwanetsi and Roodewal are private camps that must be reserved as a unit. There are caravan and camping sites at Satara, Letaba, Balule, and at Maroela, north of Orpen. Satara caters for the disabled. Tamboti, a small camp lying 4 km from Orpen on the road to Satara, offers furnished tents on wooden stilts. Talamati Bushveld Camp, 31 km south of Orpen, offers self-catering cottages.

Eating and drinking Satara, Olifants and Letaba have licensed restaurants and sell snacks. They also have shops selling fresh meat, groceries and liquor. All the rest camps offer field kitchens and braai places. There is a tearoom at Tshokwane and there are picnic spots at Eileen Orpen Dam, near Tshokwane; at Muzandzeni, east of Orpen; at Nhlanguleni, between Orpen and Tshokwane; at Mlondozi, north of Lower Sabie; at Nwanetsi; at Timbavati, northwest of Satara; and at Masorini, east of Phalaborwa.

Getting around All main roads are tarred and secondary roads are gravelled. The speed limits vary from 40 to 50 km/hour. When outside rest camps, visitors must stay in their cars (except at the Tshokwane tearoom, picnic sites and designated lookout points and monuments where they may alight at their own risk). There are filling stations at Orpen Gate and at the major rest camps, but not at the Phalaborwa Gate, Balule, Nwanetsi, Roodewal or Maroela. Diesel fuel is obtainable at Satara and Letaba. There is an Automobile Association garage at Letaba with a breakdown truck. Twice a week, parties of eight leave Skukuza and Letaba on the Metsimetsi and Olifants wilderness trails. Hikers sleep in bush camps. Bedding and food are provided but hikers must take their own drinks.

Special attractions The Masorini Museum, east of Phalaborwa, is a reconstructed Iron Age village which is well worth a visit. The lookout point west of Olifants and the rest camp itself provide fine views of Kruger Park's most beautiful river.

Wildlife The hunter's 'big five' (lion, leopard, elephant, buffalo and rhino) all flourish in this country of knobthorn and marula, and the Olifants and Letaba river valleys provide fine opportunities for photographing both mammals and birds.

Special precautions Before entering the park, visitors should take a course of anti-malaria pills (obtainable at gates and rest camps, from family doctors and at any chemist without prescription).

South Africa's first official game warden. Briefed to make himself 'generally disagreeable', he set to work, armed with little more than this vague authority – and a good share of courage and determination. It was enough. Over the years, and with the help of a handful of dedicated men such as 'Gaza' Gray, Cecil de Laporte, Thomas Duke, Major A A Fraser and the redoubtable Harry Wolhuter, Stevenson-Hamilton gave shape to what we today know as the Kruger National Park.

Stevenson-Hamilton's African assistants, with good reason, nicknamed him 'Skukuza' (he who sweeps clean). Poachers were caught and convicted – including, on one occasion, a party of senior policemen. The depredations of some species of carnivore, especially lion and wild dog, were brought under control, and new rangers were taken on. The protected areas grew from strength to strength until, by 1903, the Sabie's northern boundary had been extended to the Olifants River.

Later, a brand-new reserve, Shingwedzi, was established between the Great Letaba and Limpopo rivers.

The game population increased steadily, though by today's standards it remained sparse: in 1912 Stevenson-Hamilton estimated that the two reserves had a combined population of 7 000 impala (now over 120 000), 250 buffalo (now 15 000) and just 25 elephant (now numbering 8 000).

In 1923 the South African Railways included the area in its 'round-in-nine' (days) tour of the Transvaal, and passengers travelled through the Sabie Game Reserve in an afternoon. The keener visitors were taken on a short wilderness trail by a ranger. The tours won many new friends for the sanctuary.

The success of the 'round-in-nine' venture convinced Stevenson-Hamilton that if the reserves were to prosper they would have to earn their keep, and that meant throwing them open to the public. He lobbied for the creation of a publicly owned 'national park' modelled on the highly successful parks established in the United States and Canada, and managed to drum up influential political support.

LOWVELD: KRUGER NATIONAL PARK

On 31 May 1926 Parliament passed the National Parks Act. Its first venture was the consolidation of the Sabie and Shingwedzi reserves, with the inclusion of the awkward wedge that separated them. This enormous slice of territory was formally proclaimed a national park and named, appropriately, in honour of Paul Kruger.

There are 26 camps – Pretoriuskop, Malelane, Skukuza, Lower Sabie, Berg-en-dal, Jakkalsbessie, Jock of the Bushveld, Crocodile Bridge and Biyamiti in the south; Satara, Nwanetsi, Talamati, Tamboti, Maroela, Orpen, Olifants, Balule, Letaba and Roodewal in the central region; Shingwedzi, Boulders, Punda Maria, Mopani, Shimuwini, Sirheni and Bateleur in the wilder north. The larger camps have family cottages, many air-conditioned and with kitchenettes, as well as rather less sophisticated accommodation, caravan and camping sites, outdoor facilities, fuel points and shops. There are restaurants at ten of the camps. Skukuza, Satara and Letaba, from which the Automobile Association operates full services, have motor-repair workshops.

The visitor to the Kruger Park has to observe a code of conduct. Ordinary common sense is the basis of regulation: the environment is precious, so do not throw lighted cigarettes into dry bush; drive within the speed limit because you will not see much unless you do and, more importantly, animals crossing the road could cause a nasty accident. On no account must you feed the animals. Nature, not man, dictates a creature's diet and baboons, especially, can become dangerously addicted to human hand-outs. Do not leave your car when in an unprotected area, even if there is no apparent danger, as appearances can be lethally deceptive. Do not drive on closed roads where nobody will find you in case of a breakdown. Explains a ranger, 'Never forget that the Kruger Park is part of Africa, and that Africa is wild and cruel.'

The Kruger Park is home to a growing body of scientists and researchers of various disciplines, but to the tourist it is the ranger's job that holds the most glamour. Only a small part of his work, though, brings him into contact with the general public.

Rangers spend most of their time in the field. 'I have very little routine work,' explains one. 'What it comes down to is that I have to look after a vast tract of land (40 000-60 000 ha) in every way. I'm like a farm manager, only I have to be more versatile. I manage the vegetation and the water supply, and I'm guardian to the animals in my area. My first loyalty is to the wildlife, from the lowliest snail and snake to the mighty elephant.'

One day a ranger may be involved in routine windmill maintenance (concrete reservoirs feed the drinking troughs), the next he

Below left: Trailists on the Wolhuter Trail in the southern Kruger National Park. **Left:** A census of the Kruger Park's elephant and buffalo is undertaken by helicopter in August each year. **Below:** A radio collar, used for monitoring the movement of an elephant family group, is fitted to a member of the herd.

might team up with rangers from neighbouring sections to burn off a block of veld or, conversely, to fight an unwanted fire sparked by lightning or poachers. Periodically, he helps the aerial survey teams.

Each year a research team from Skukuza 'capital' of the Kruger Park, surveys the park's vegetation and large game from fixed-wing aircraft and a helicopter, gathering information vital to the proper management of the area.

How many white rhino are there, and where are they? Is the number of sable increasing? Where are the kudu, and are the blue wildebeest maintaining their rate of recovery? Some species may be too numerous for their habitat, destroying it both for themselves and for other animals, so the surplus must be removed to restore the balance of nature.

Balule Rest Camp

More an enclosed caravan park than a camp (there are only six rondavels), Balule is on the Olifants River, in the central Kruger Park, a few kilometres south of Olifants Rest Camp, to which caravanners go for their shopping, or if they want a restaurant meal.

The Olifants River meanders across the width of the park, from just south of the Phalaborwa Gate to the Mozambique border in the east. Its banks are especially lush and rich in game in the Olifants/Balule area.

Balule, tiny and potentially vulnerable, has a high protective fence because animals can (and occasionally do) sneak into the rest

NORTHERN KRUGER PARK AT A GLANCE

When to go In earlier years the northern half of the park was closed in summer, but now it is open year round. The summer months bring lush vegetation and profuse birdlife, and large herds may be seen at waterholes during the dry winter months.

Reservations To book accommodation in a rest camp or apply for a place on the Nyalaland Wilderness Trail, write to National Parks Board, P O Box 787, Pretoria 0001, or telephone (012) 343-1991, or fax 343-0905; or National Parks Board, P O Box 7400, Roggebaai 8012, telephone (021) 22-2810, or fax 24-6211.

Getting there To reach Shingwedzi or Boulders from outside the park, enter at the Phalaborwa Gate, or enter by the Punda Maria Gate. To reach Punda Maria or Pafuri, enter by the Punda Maria Gate or Pafuri Gate. The nearest airport is at Phalaborwa and offers daily flights to and from Johannesburg. Mopani lies 45 km north of Letaba and some 74 km from the Phalaborwa Gate.

Accommodation Shingwedzi Rest Camp comprises two parts: an old section of rectangular wattle-and-daub huts, each with two or more beds and modernised interiors (shower and toilet), and a modern section in which each hut is equipped with two or more beds, a shower and toilet. A large swimming pool is also available. Punda Maria has wattle-and-daub huts with modernised interiors. Both camps have caravan and camping sites. Mopani Rest Camp offers a cottage for eight, as well as six- and four-bed cottages. Some accommodation at Shingwedzi and Mopani has been adapted for use by the physically disabled. Bateleur, Shimuwini and Sirheni bushveld camps offer self-catering cottages. The 12-bed Boulders private camp lies between Phalaborwa and Mopani, and has to be reserved as a unit. It has four two-bed units and one four-bed unit, each with bath, shower and toilet, and a verandah with superb views.

Eating and drinking Shingwedzi, Mopani and Punda Maria have licensed restaurants and snacks are available. Shops sell fresh meat, groceries, beer, wine and spirits. Shingwedzi and Punda Maria have field kitchens and braai places near their huts and camping sites. There are picnic places at Mooiplaas, between Shingwedzi and Letaba; at Babalala, between Shingwedzi and Punda Maria; and at Pafuri on the Luvuvhu River.

Getting around All main roads are tarred and secondary roads are gravelled. The speed limits vary from 40 to 50 km/hour. There are filling stations at Mopani, Shingwedzi and Punda Maria (with diesel fuel at Shingwedzi) and there is a garage at Letaba with a breakdown truck. Twice a week, parties of eight leave Punda Maria on the four-day Nyalaland Wilderness Trail. Hikers sleep in huts in a bush camp south of the Luvuvhu River. Bedding and food are provided but hikers must take their own drinks.

Wildlife The northern region is tusker country, famous for the Kruger Park elephants with abnormally large tusks. Antelope, including all the rare species such as eland, roan, tsessebe, sable and nyala, and predators, abound, and there are birds everywhere. The Pafuri area of the far north is one of the most picturesque in the park, featuring mammals, birds and insects found nowhere else.

Special precautions Before entering the park, you should take a course of anti-malaria pills (obtainable at entrance gates and rest camps, from family doctors and at any chemist without prescription). Keep to the roads and resist the temptation to explore firebreaks, where nobody will find you in the event of a breakdown.

LOWVELD: KRUGER NATIONAL PARK

camps, especially if they are accustomed to being fed by tourists.

If you feed an animal, you could be signing its death warrant. In 1978 a pair of spotted hyena took up residence in a storm culvert under the tarred road between Skukuza and Pretoriuskop. They produced cubs which quickly became used to traffic, basking by the roadside while their parents went scavenging. Motorists were thrilled to come across such tame creatures and fed them titbits to entice them even closer. Before long the cubs approached every car that arrived, and the area deteriorated into an eyesore of cans, bottles and litter.

'Animals like that become very dependent,' says Chief Ranger Bruce Bryden of Skukuza. 'Next thing they'll be raiding the camps.' On one occasion a hyena did enter a camp (Letaba), found a man sleeping on the ground beside his car, and tried to drag him away by the hand.

Hyena are not the only game misled by tourists. 'Not so long ago there was an elephant at Tshokwane that accepted biscuits,' recalls Bryden. 'One day two old ladies were feeding it, and when it snorted one of them got such a fright she fell down an embankment and broke her leg. It's stupid. One of these days that elephant will get really upset, and he'll trample someone.'

One of the rangers' biggest headaches is the baboon. 'Once he starts taking food he never stops,' says an information officer. 'He'll begin raiding huts in rest camps, and we've had them jumping into the backs of passing cars. Baboons like that will lead the rest of the troop into trouble, so we have to remove them from the population.'

Berg-en-dal Rest Camp

Situated to the west of the Malelane Gate, Berg-en-dal perches picturesquely on the banks of the Matjulu Spruit. Its name means 'mountain and valley' which aptly describes the scenery of the area – undulating hills and tree-lined, dry riverbeds.

The focus here is on the natural vegetation and tree-spotters will identify graceful acacias, red bushwillows, elegant jackalberries and the beautiful tree fuchsia. Game is plentiful and species commonly seen in the area include giraffe, zebra, rhino, kudu and other antelope species. Lion are spotted occasionally.

DEATH OF THE KING

Of all the impressive tuskers that have wandered over the vast mopane plains of the Kruger National Park, one in particular will always be remembered – Mafunyane, king of the elephants.

When he died in November 1983, Mafunyane had become the park's best-known elephant, remembered especially for his massive tusks – so huge that their pointed ends touched the ground.

Towards the end of his life, Mafunyane's wanderings through the bush were monitored by park officials, who feared poachers might try to lay claim to his tusks – priceless on the illicit ivory market.

Ultimately, though, the legendary tusker eluded everyone, and died as he had lived – mysteriously – in the privacy of the bush. His carcass was discovered in a dry riverbed, already torn apart by scavengers, the long bones scattered over a wide area. Only a small section of skin remained; even his radio collar had been partly eaten. From the evidence it appeared that he had died suddenly. His stomach contents revealed that he had been eating normally, and the area around him showed no signs of a struggle. Perhaps he suffered a heart attack, or maybe he simply died of old age. Either way, at 57, Mafunyane 'the irritable' died leaving a void in the mopane plains of northwestern Kruger Park.

It had always been thought that Mafunyane was a massive tusker, a bull similar to Kenya's Ahmed of Marsabit (declared a national monument when he was alive). However, when Mafunyane was darted and measured in 1978, his tusks were smaller than had been expected. Dr Anthony Hall-Martin recalls: 'Though his tusks rested on the ground, they were only 251 cm long and perfectly straight – and I had long estimated them to be about 3 m long.' Extraordinarily this huge amount of ivory was carried by a bull of relatively small size.

Hugo van Niekerk, a helicopter pilot at Kruger Park, refused to be swayed by what the tape measure revealed. 'Mafunyane was huge; he was a giant; he was magnificent. Even in elephant dimensions he was a king.'

The tusks are a fine matching pair, each weighing 51,1 kg, and rightly deserve their place in Skukuza's museum alongside the other great tuskers of the Kruger Park.

Top: A giant land snail. These snails, which are native to the hotter parts of Africa, may often be seen crawling across park roads after rains. **Above:** Gossamer-like seeds such as these are sometimes carried several kilometres by the wind.

LOWVELD: **KRUGER NATIONAL PARK**

Berg-en-dal is an attractive rest camp constructed largely and imaginatively of natural materials, and is sheltered by graceful trees interspersed with paths. A trail for the blind has been laid out in the rest camp. Accommodation comprises a variety of comfortable, fully equipped bungalows – some designed for use by the physically handicapped, a number of guest cottages and 70 stands for caravans. There is a shop, a restaurant and cafeteria, a swimming pool, filling station and conference facilities, with a large hall that can be divided into three smaller units.

Crocodile Bridge Rest Camp

Adjacent to one of the Kruger Park's two southernmost gates is Crocodile Bridge, with its 20 bungalows, small shop and caravan park set charmingly on the banks of the Crocodile River. This is acacia country, and the grass is good, attracting zebra, wildebeest, impala, kudu, waterbuck and large herds of buffalo.

The Crocodile is a perennial river, but now often shrinks to chains of pools during the dry months of winter and in times of drought – but it nevertheless supports an impressive variety of wildlife.

In fact, water is the key to survival, and it is along the banks of the streams and at the pools that visitors can best view the bigger game.

Above: The common joker butterfly (*Byblia ilithyia*), a nymphalid, is distributed throughout the Kruger Park.
Right: A scrum of hippo in the Luvuvhu River near the northern boundary of the park. Each adult consumes as much as 180 kg of food a day – mostly grass and the young shoots of reeds. Hippo spend most of their day in water because they cannot endure very high temperatures. In winter, however, they may often be seen sunning themselves on sandbanks. Hippo calves suckle underwater, but have to surface at regular intervals (less than a minute) to breathe. They also suckle on land. A hippo bull may attain a weight of 2 500 kg (about 1 500 kg for cows), and a healthy specimen can live 40 to 50 years.

Above: Yellow-billed storks (also known as wood ibis) wade in the shallows of the Luvuvhu River in apparent harmony with the crocodiles. The storks feed on frogs, small mammals, fish, crabs and aquatic insects, probing both deep and shallow water with their long bills. They nest on cliffs or in trees, producing a clutch of two or three white eggs.

KRUGER NATIONAL PARK REVEALS ITS PAST

A bone fossil belonging to the dinosaur genus *Euskelosaurus*, discovered in northern Kruger.

In March 1995, while trails ranger Adriaan Louw was leading a group of hikers in the Nyalaland Trail area of northern Kruger, one of the party bent down to pick up what he at first thought was a stone tool. On closer examination, and much to the excitement of the group, they concluded that the strange-looking stone was, in fact, a fossil. Louw visited the area with a second group and picked up a giant petrified vertebra. He then realised that he had stumbled upon a jumble of fossil bones scattered in a gully in the hot Lowveld sun. It was the first vertebrate fossil site to be discovered in the park.

After he had reported his discovery, National Parks Board officials contacted palaeontologist Dr Francois Durand, who hiked the substantial distance to the find. On reaching the gully he realised that the area – about the size of two rugby fields – was littered with fossil bones. Louw also discovered a second site, with black petrified wood, and a third, which revealed more fossil bones. It became evident that the fossils were being weathered from a layer of a nearby koppie and were rolling down its slope. Then they asked the question on everybody's mind – what animal had left these fossils?

The size of the bones indicated that the animal was larger than any other found previously in the area. After much research it was established that the remains belonged to *Euskelosaurus*, a genus of primitive, herbivorous dinosaurs that lived some 210 million years ago in the Triassic Period. A titan of its time, it is thought to have attained a length of up to 10 metres. At that time the region bore no resemblance to the mopane bushland present today. These dinosaurs lived in areas of seed fern and conifer forests, and vanished when the climate became drier and the region started to resemble the Karoo, interspersed with the occasional big river.

The site is currently still under excavation, a joint venture undertaken by the National Parks Board, the Council for Geoscience and the SA Society for Amateur Palaeontologists.

About 6 km from Crocodile Bridge camp is a splendid viewing point from where you can watch, among other things, hippo basking on a sandbank. Hippo and crocodile are probably the most spectacular inhabitants of the waterways. The two species (there are over 2 500 of each in the park) share their living space amicably enough for most of the time, each an integral part of nature's delicate balance. But the truce is sometimes broken – crocodile have a taste for baby hippo, and when a cow is about to give birth the big reptiles are chased from the vicinity.

Up to 2 500 kg in mass, with immense jaws and lethal teeth, the hippo is a fearsome enemy, and should be treated with the greatest respect. Peaceful enough in their riverine homes, hippo migrate across the open veld, sometimes over long distances, when water is scarce. They have acute senses of sight, smell and hearing, and they are unpredictable creatures, occasionally attacking without provocation when out of their natural element. Your car and the camp fence, however, are protection enough. Fights between adult males, for dominance of a herd and for territory, are impressive spectacles, almost unequalled among mammals in their intensity. Most of the habits of hippo, though, are rather more endearing, and some a little curious. For instance, they are easily contained. They never attempt to step over an obstruction: a mere metre-high, three-wired fence is enough to turn them away. But water is their element, and they cannot stay on dry land for too long. Their skin, thick (up to 50 mm at the shoulder and back) and tough though it may be, is sensitive to the sun and overexposure can cause injury.

A hippo can stay submerged for anything up to five or six minutes, although on average it surfaces for air every minute or so. While

Not so obvious are the smaller fauna supported by the park's placid rivers – otter, terrapin, leguan, colourful waterbirds and the myriad aquatic insects on which they feed. The park is also host to some 45 species of freshwater fish and four renegade marine varieties. In 1950 a 1,47 m Zambezi shark was found in the shallows near the confluence of the Luvuvhu and Limpopo rivers at Pafuri, nearly 400 km from the sea.

LOWVELD: **KRUGER NATIONAL PARK**

underwater it is often party to a curious symbiosis – shoals of a freshwater fish species, *Labeo rubropunctatus*, accompany hippos, feeding on the algae that grow on their hide.

The hippo is a vegetarian, daily consuming up to 180 kg of grass (trampling much more underfoot) and the young shoots of river reeds. Its companion the crocodile, however, is a somewhat indiscriminate carnivore. Iron-jawed, living an impressive 100 years and more, it is a dinosaurian oddity – the species has existed virtually unchanged for about 60 million years.

Crocodile are essentially fish-eating reptiles, but they supplement their diet by taking water tortoise, antelope and other game that come down to the water to drink – sometimes very big game. Their recorded victims include giraffe (two known cases in the Kruger Park), full-grown buffalo, and lion. The great 19th century hunter Frederick Courteney Selous once saw a crocodile seize, drown and devour a rhinoceros. In fact, it is nearly always by drowning that the crocodile kills its land-based prey, fastening onto muzzle or limb and pulling its victim beneath the surface.

In Africa, crocodile account for more human deaths than leopard, rhino, lion, elephant, buffalo and snakes put together. The visitor to the Kruger Park is quite safe, provided he or she takes elementary precautions, but the park has not been without incident. One such incident is memorable for the courage and tenacity displayed by the victims.

On a November day in 1976, patrolling rangers Tom Yssel and Louis Olivier, accompanied by Hans Kolver, an off-duty helicopter pilot, were crossing a side stream of the Sabie River when a large crocodile erupted from the shallows and seized Yssel by the thigh. It was the start of an epic struggle for survival.

When Yssel fell, the crocodile took a firm grip and began dragging the ranger towards deeper water. Yssel twisted his body and tried to jam his thumbs into the animal's vulnerable eyes, but succeeded only in infuriating it. 'He was shaking me like a rag doll,' he recalls. 'He'd let go, and then he'd bite me again, up my leg and across my belly. I was under the water. I didn't feel pain, but there was blood everywhere and I thought: "This is it. I'll never get out." '

Quickly grasping the situation, Olivier and Kolver plunged into the water and tackled the 680 kg crocodile. Kolver jumped on its back and lunged for the eyes; Olivier went for its thrashing tail. Kolver was hurled off, climbed back on again, and then found himself submerged as the crocodile turned over.

Olivier moved up to hold Tom Yssel's head above the surface. The crocodile released Yssel and fastened its jaws around Kolver's wrist. Although badly injured, Yssel had no

Above: A nyala ram. There are thought to be between 800 and 1 000 of these large, shaggy antelope in the park. The female is considerably smaller and lacks horns. Nyala are usually seen in small groups, though they have been known to gather in herds of up to 30 individuals. They seldom stray far from water. **Right above:** The striking colours of the carmine bee-eater make it one of the most beautiful birds in the Kruger Park. It is seen only between September and March, spending the rest of the year in the tropics. **Right below:** A tsessebe seeks shelter from the harsh midday sun in the Kruger Park. These medium-sized antelope (they may weigh between 135 kg and 160 kg) live in family groups or small herds which may swell to larger herds during the dry season.

compulsion to escape. Instead, he thought: 'Now there's going to be a real fight. I'm going to get him.' But Yssel could not stand up – his leg was broken. He lay helpless while the other two struggled on, Kolver freeing himself briefly only to find his right arm in the vice-like grip.

Finally, Louis Olivier closed in with his hunting knife, plunging its 14 cm blade into the creature's eye. It opened its jaws wide, releasing Kolver, and retreated in defeat to deep water. Olivier was unhurt; Kolver had only slight injuries.

Both men were decorated for bravery. Tom Yssel, though, was less fortunate: he was hospitalised for nine long months.

Letaba Rest Camp
The camp is strategically placed in the central region, nestling comfortably above a sweeping loop of the Great Letaba River. It is also the junction of three main roads: to the west is the Phalaborwa Gate; Shingwedzi is to the north; Olifants and Satara are to the south. Visitors enjoy a fine view across evergreen bushes, sycamore figs and the water (stream-linked pools and sandy flats in winter and during times of drought, wide and grand when in flood), which attract elephant and buffalo, zebra and waterbuck. There are also roan and sable, nyala, tsessebe and cheetah to be seen in the countryside around Letaba. Neat lawns, the sparkle of flowers and tall shade trees give the camp its character. Busy little vervet monkeys scramble along the fence – a constant source of amusement and interest.

Letaba is a middle-sized camp, with varied accommodation, a good restaurant, shop and Automobile Association garage. The adjoining Fish Eagle and Melville guest cottages can accommodate up to eight and nine people respectively. It is also home to the Goldfields Environmental Centre, which houses a striking exhibition of the original 'magnificent seven' elephants, together with the tusks that made them famous.

There are some excellent drives in the vicinity, the best probably being the one taking you (for most of the way) southeast along the Great Letaba River to Olifants Rest Camp. Two lookout points, Engelhard Dam to the east and Mingerhout Dam to the northwest, are within easy reach and well worth visiting.

To the north, about halfway along the tarred road to Shingwedzi, the Mooiplaas picnic and lookout spot is a refreshing place to stop. It has a large, thatched shelter above the Tsende River from which you can watch elephant and buffalo, and for those who wish to braai, gas braais are available.

When driving in the Letaba area, indeed when driving anywhere in the park, you might just see a kill, and that means scavengers – jackal, vulture, and hyena, with their lunatic cackle, something between a giggle and a laugh, that they make when angry or excited.

Of the two types of hyena found in the park, the spotted hyena is larger and much more common than its cousin, the brown hyena. Spotted hyena often hunt in packs but brown hyena tend to be solitary creatures and are generally nocturnal (they sleep heavily during the day). Spotted hyena gather to follow lion and wild dog on the hunt – then quarrel over the remains of a kill (though they are predators as well as scavengers). With their massive heads, jaws and forequarters, sloping backs and ungainly gait, they are not the most attractive of the park's inhabitants.

More graceful – but only in their natural element, the air – are the Kruger Park's vultures. They can be seen everywhere, soaring high over the veld, their sharp eyes missing nothing. Of the six southern African species, the white-backed vulture is the most common. Cape vultures (similar to but more scarce than the white-backed vulture) tend to nest on rocky ledges, while white-backed vultures prefer to nest in trees. Then there is the lappet-faced vulture, which is generally so aggressive that it keeps the other birds at bay while it eats its fill of a carcass. Lappet-faced vultures are less sociable, less gross in their eating habits, and fewer in number.

Lower Sabie Rest Camp
Lower Sabie, situated some 35 km from Crocodile Bridge in the south, is a medium-sized camp with pleasant bungalows overlooking the game-rich Sabie River, which affords visitors excellent 'sundowner' viewing. The camp's restaurant is particularly good. There are some rewarding drives in the area, especially one along the tarred road flanking the river's south bank.

If you want to view lion, you are likely to be luckier in the Lower Sabie area than in most others. The 1 500 or so lion of the Kruger Park

Left: A white-backed vulture. This species nests mainly in acacia, producing one egg which is incubated by both parents for 56 to 58 days. **Right above:** *Euphorbia*, a hardy and well-protected succulent, photographed in the Pafuri area of the Kruger Park. **Right below:** The large and powerful spotted hyena, although ungainly in appearance, is an efficient scavenger and equally good hunter, and quite capable of bringing down prey as large as a zebra. There are about 2 000 spotted hyena in the Kruger Park, and they are a familiar sight wherever there is a carcass. Their powerful jaws are able to crunch the bones with ease. **Below:** A nyala ewe.

go where their prey congregates. The Sabie River and the lushness of the countryside attract herds of wildebeest, zebra, kudu, buffalo, giraffe, waterbuck and impala – and predators follow.

Probably the best time to see lion in summer is during the early morning and late afternoon (they tend to rest in dense bush during the heat of the day). In winter they appear at the waterholes. When travelling through the Kruger Park in late autumn, winter and early spring, though, you should drive especially slowly and watch carefully: the lion's coat blends almost perfectly with the ochre grass.

Universally known as the 'King of the Beasts', this large cat certainly looks the part, but its lifestyle is often rather less than regal. Lion are prone to parasite-borne diseases and fatal injuries incurred during the hunt. Some are killed by buffalo or by the lethal kick of a giraffe, and a high proportion, particularly old lion, by the humble porcupine, whose needle-sharp quills pierce their throats and tongues and infect them. When the rains are abundant and game is dispersed, many young lion can die of starvation.

It was north of the Sabie River, close to the Lindanda flats, that Harry Wolhuter, armed only with a knife, fought and killed a full-grown lion. On that fateful night in August 1903, Wolhuter, on horseback and riding ahead of his assistants, stumbled upon two male lion in search of prey. His horse bolted and one of the lion sprang; Wolhuter fell and found his shoulder seized in the great feline jaws. The lion dragged him 50 m into the bush. The ranger's

BALLET DANCERS OF THE BUSHVELD

Rangers estimate that the Kruger Park accommodates over 120 000 impala. They are so common that most tourists simply take them for granted. Yet these graceful antelope deserve more than a mere passing glance.

Alert and agile, an impala can leap three metres into the air without any apparent effort – and this in spite of the fact that it is a fairly large animal by antelope standards, weighing up to 65 kilograms. To watch a whole herd move among the thornbushes, to see them, startled by some suddenly discovered danger, dash away in unison, is to witness a natural symphony of coordinated movements – a completely fluid motion made up of hundreds of single steps, the kind of action that a ballet troupe might take months to perfect, executed here in the wilderness sans choreographer.

The scientist finds an even greater fascination in the impala's behavioural mechanisms. For much of the year impala live in peaceful herds, showing no animosity and little competitiveness, but with the coming of autumn the rut begins and the impala lifestyle changes dramatically. The adult males now become passionately territorial.

Researchers have discovered that the production of male sex hormones increases, the testes grow larger and begin to produce a great amount of sperm cells and, as a result of these changes, the males become highly aggressive towards one another. Each discovers an urge to be a proud (and individual) 'landowner', the most assertive among them carving out territories within the most favoured feeding grounds.

Impala have diffuse glandular areas on the forehead, and territorial rams may rub these on bushes – leaving a scent. They also have a surprising ability to proclaim their ownership with loud barks and grunts – so fearsome that many a tourist visiting the park for the first time in autumn has imagined himself in the company of a leopard.

Herds of female impala, made up of mothers and daughters, sisters and aunts, wander through these territories that the males have established in the prime feeding grounds, and the females in heat are mounted by the proud males. The males also work hard at keeping their harems within their territory, which means herding them back whenever they wander too close to the boundaries.

face was pressed close into the animal's mane, and he heard in its throat that deep, terrifying sound that passes for a purr. Frantically, he searched for his sheath knife, found it and stabbed twice at the heart. The lion, roaring in pain, dropped him but stood its ground, straddling the ranger. Again Wolhuter lunged, drawing spurts of blood from an artery in the throat. The lion made off into the night. It was found later, dead from two knife wounds in the heart and a severed carotid artery.

Wolhuter dragged himself to a tree and managed to climb it. Faint from loss of blood, he tied himself to a branch with his belt. It was just as well he did, for the second lion returned some minutes later and reared up against the tree-trunk. It was eventually distracted by the barking of one of the ranger's dogs.

The following morning, the game guards found Wolhuter, cut him down and carried him to camp, where they dressed his terrible wounds. He was then taken to Barberton, and remained in hospital for many months.

Meanwhile, news of his exploit had made the headlines – and he found himself a celebrity. The lion's skin and the knife are on display at the Stevenson-Hamilton Memorial Library at Skukuza, and the stump of the tree he climbed can still be seen on the plains of Lindanda.

Malelane Rest Camp

Founded in 1925 as a culling post to control the menace posed to farmers by marauding prides of lion, it is now an attractive little rest camp, close to the park's southernmost Malelane Gate.

Malelane is a bushveld camp, administered from Berg-en-dal Rest Camp, with six rondavels and 15 caravan sites situated on the Crocodile River. If you travel north for a short distance along the gravel road to Skukuza and then turn right for the 53 km stretch to Crocodile Bridge, you are likely to see kudu, buffalo, impala and, perhaps, elephant.

Five well-planned circular drives are within easy reach of the camp. This area is a favourite haunt of one of the park's rarer and more fascinating inhabitants, the wild dog.

The wild dog is only distantly related to the dog we know. About the size of an Alsatian, it has a 'tortoise-shell' coat, a white tip to its bushy tail, and huge, bat-like ears. It plays an important part in controlling the numbers of its favourite prey – impala and reedbuck. Having eaten its fill, a wild dog rarely returns to the carcass, as it prefers fresh meat.

Observing a pack in the area between Malelane and Skukuza, scientist Allen Reich noted that the dog who had led the hunt had the smallest portion of the carcass. 'All were eating peacefully, save for the subordinate male,' Reich writes.

'He had made the kill; he had trotted back to the others; he had let them taste the blood on his mouth, and he had led them back to the kill. Now he waited for what, to our human minds, was rightfully his. He eventually managed a few scraps (although not much more). What a remarkable creature!'

This incident illuminates the intricate social order that governs a pack of wild dog. Each member knows its exact place in the group, whom it dominates and to whom it is subservient, with whom it may mate, and its position in the hunt. The order, though, changes from time to time as members pair off and pups are born, and as dominant individuals die, or when their authority is subtly and successfully challenged. The wild dog's yelp, uttered when disturbed, is more like that of a baboon than the domestic dog; and its rallying cry, which you can sometimes hear before sunrise or in the early evening, is a plaintive howl, repeated half a dozen or so times.

Mopani Rest Camp

A newish camp, Mopani, with its shaded bungalows and huts of stone, wood and thatch, is set into a rocky incline overlooking the Pioneer Dam some 45 km north of Letaba Rest Camp. Although the area is not particularly well populated with game, scenic drives along the Letaba River towards Letaba Camp and towards the Engelhard Dam are very likely to reveal elephant, buffalo, zebra, wildebeest and plentiful species of antelope.

The camp lies 74 km from the Phalaborwa Gate, and also offers conference facilities for groups of up to 30 delegates.

Nwanetsi Private Camp

Twenty-five kilometres to the east of Satara, along the central region's Nwanetsi River, is the small, private camp of that name. Accommodation is available only on a block-booking basis, and its four bungalows and two smaller huts can sleep up to 16 people (facilities for the disabled are available). Those enjoying this exclusive hideaway check in at Satara, and use Satara's shop and restaurant to stock up and eat out (though the guesthouse's kitchen is very well equipped). Close to the private rest camp is the attractively sited Nwanetsi picnic site, which offers excellent facilities for the tired tourist and a truly magnificent viewing spot perched atop a cliff and overlooking a waterhole in the Sweni River below.

The 50 km gravel road running south – it passes close to the Mozambique border – takes you to the Lindanda Memorial and, a little further on, to the Eileen Orpen Dam, where

Below left: Vervet monkeys are seen throughout the park, where they feed on insects, fruit and birds' eggs. **Below:** Wild dog pups in the Kruger Park. This is a relatively rare predator, and it is believed that competition with other species – lion in particular – could be a reason. Diseases such as distemper are another factor in the limiting of its numbers.

The camp itself is the Kruger Park's oldest and third largest, boasting one of only four swimming pools (the others being at Shingwedzi, Mopani and Berg-en-dal), accommodation (including sizeable family cottages) for over 400 people, a restaurant, shop, filling station and caravan park. The surrounding countryside is enchanting, studded with picturesque granite hills and, in the springtime, by blood-red coral trees, white wild pear trees and the ever- present white and yellow acacias.

Exploring this countryside is a joy. The 47 km drive to Skukuza is worthwhile for both its luxuriant beauty and the game you can see along the way. Better still are the views from the Hippo Pool and Doispane Road, from which you can look down over the Sabie and its riverine beauty. Southeastwards of Pretoriuskop runs the original transport riders' route, now known as the Voortrekker Road – Jock-of-the-Bushveld country. Beacons on the way commemorate the life and travels of that most lovable of all South Africa's animal characters. The two-day Wolhuter and Bushman hiking trails penetrate the richly vegetated countryside between Pretoriuskop and Malelane, giving walking enthusiasts the opportunity to see the varied bird and mammal life of the area.

The region's game is plentiful, especially sable, reedbuck, klipspringer and the lordly giraffe. It is also white rhino country.

Black rhino were once common in the Lowveld but by the 1890s hunters had slaughtered them to the brink of extinction (though spoor were spotted in the southern Kruger Park as late as 1936).

Their cousins, the white rhino, suffered even more badly: the region's last specimen was spotted in 1873.

But it was the white rhino that was the first to make a comeback. In 1961 the Natal Parks Board presented four of the species to the Kruger Park as a pilot project of its 'Operation Rhino'. The pioneering quartet were penned in a 280 ha camp at Pretoriuskop to form a breeding herd.

More of the animals were introduced as the years went by, and in 1971 the rhino population received a particularly healthy boost: Natal (now KwaZulu-Natal) had built up a large surplus of white rhino, and the Kruger Park agreed to take 200 of them. It was an enormous exercise in capture and translocation, but the undertaking was successful, and the newcomers were all released in the Kruger Park by early 1972. The 'immigrants' flourished in their new habitat, and today the white rhino population exceeds 2 000.

During 1971 the Natal Parks Board also presented the Kruger Park with 20 black rhino. Three were kept in a camp near Skukuza for research purposes, and the rest were released directly into the bush (those in the camp were

Above: An elephant fording a river. Elephant may sometimes be seen completely submerged apart from the trunk, which serves as a snorkel. This mighty mammal needs to spend most of the day eating or drinking to satisfy its daily requirements, which can be as much as 200 litres of water and 250 kg of leaves, grass and bush. Cows weigh some 3 000 kg, while a mature bull may reach 5 500 kilograms. **Right:** Sharpe's grysbok, a small antelope found mainly in the park's mopane woodlands. They live singly (except in the mating season) and feed on fruit, roots, leaves, young shoots and grass.

set free after five years). In the following year, 14 more rhino were introduced, 12 from Zimbabwe and two from Hluhluwe in KwaZulu-Natal. A second phase of introductions commenced in 1980, and since then another 30 animals have been received from KwaZulu-Natal and released in the southern and central districts of the park. The park now has a viable and successful breeding population of about 300 animals.

Punda Maria Rest Camp

A small, unpretentious camp of rectangular wattle-and-daub huts set attractively on the slope of a hill, Punda Maria started as a ranger post in 1919 to counter ivory poachers. The place was named by the camp's first ranger, Captain J J Coetser, in honour of his wife Maria, and the Swahili name for a zebra (*punda milia*). It is said that zebra were the first animals that Coetser saw on his arrival in the park. The camp grew in popularity and size as the road network improved, and it now supports a small shop, restaurant and filling station.

The region of deep valleys and grand hills north of Punda Maria and around the Luvuvhu River is magnificently wooded – syringa and ebony, ironwood and mahogany (a popular circular drive is the Mahogany Loop, which starts and finishes at the camp), sycamore fig and the ubiquitous bright green mopane.

Driving northeast on gravel, you pass Gumbandebvu Hill, home of the legendary rainmaker Khama, and then the turn-off to Klopperfontein, a waterhole well worth visiting. Gravel becomes tar after 17 km and the road takes you almost directly north, through baobab and mopane country, to the Luvuvhu River at Pafuri – altogether a 42 km drive from Punda Maria.

East of the road/river junction, towards the picnic spot and police border post of Pafuri, is a forest of ghostly yellow-green fever trees and a wealth of wildlife, with splendid views of

LOWVELD: KRUGER NATIONAL PARK

crocodile and hippo from small loops on the river bank. To the west of the junction is more splendid viewing at Hippo Pool. The rich riverine forest is the home of the stately and elusive nyala, bushpig, crested guinea fowl and many rare and beautiful species of tropical trees and birds.

The northernmost part of the park is at the crossroads of nine of Africa's major ecosystems. Here wetland meets the arid bush, forest the open plain, rock the deep sand. The countryside is full of contrasts: there are wide lava flats, high ridges, deep valleys, dramatic river gorges, swathes of woodland – and a prolific wildlife population.

Especially worth looking out for are the Lebombo ironwood and the primeval baobab forests of the Mashikiri plateau. The Hlamalala plains have been called 'South Africa's own Serengeti'. Several bird species (including the long-tailed starling and the yellow-bellied sunbird), Livingstone's suni, the shovel-footed squeaker (a frog), the long-tailed garter snake and many other species are confined to this particular part of the country.

Roodewal Private Rest Camp

Roodewal is a small, private camp on the banks of the Timbavati River, about 47 km from Satara Camp. Accommodation is available only on a block-booking basis: the tree-shaded family cottage and three huts can sleep a maximum of 19 people. Visitors check into the camp at Olifants, where they may do their last-minute shopping.

To reach Roodewal, drive north on the main tarred road from Satara towards Olifants. About 36 km from Satara (and 4 km short of the Olifants River) turn left onto the northern leg of the Timbavati Loop. The camp is situated about 11 km from the turn-off. The Timbavati is one of the most beautiful seasonal rivers in the park and offers outstanding gameviewing.

Satara Rest Camp

Satara, in the park's central region, is a large, modern camp (the second largest in the park) and popular with overseas visitors. The camp sprawls in the knobthorn veld, nestling in dappled shade and surrounded by imaginatively landscaped gardens. Birdlife is prolific – the luminous blue starlings are legion, but there are also yellow- and red-billed hornbills that strut rather pompously between the tables. Lunchtime at Satara – drinks outside and then an excellent restaurant meal – is an especially pleasant midday break.

The 47 km road leading west from the camp takes you to the Orpen Gate. But for good gameviewing you should turn right after 7 km (or, preferably, after 18 km) onto the gravel roads that lead to the Timbavati picnic spot. From there the route follows the course of the Timbavati River past the Roodewal turn-off until, after about 25 km, it branches off to join the main Olifants/Satara route.

Along the water pipeline between Satara and the Olifants River there are 13 strategically sited watering places; 20 km east of the camp is the well-populated Gudzani Dam. Huge herds of buffalo can be seen within easy driving distance of Satara. A gathering of 300 to 400 zebra around water is not an unusual sight.

The area has some of the best grazing land in the park, and is famed for giraffe and its predators: visitors staying at the camp stand a good chance of hearing lion roar in the night. On one occasion, guests lined the fence listening to a loud cacophony of lion grunts, jackal howls and the mad laugh of hyena. From the sound of it, scores of animals had gathered at a kill. Some of the tourists insisted they could see what was happening and provided a running commentary for their neighbours.

'That was quite amusing, because the whole thing was artificial,' says Ian Whyte of the Kruger Park's research staff. 'The calls were on tape and were coming from two loudspeakers on the roof of a caravan. I was inside, trying to attract a pride of lion to a carcass I'd chained to a tree. That's the way I sometimes carry out lion research. The lions would come to the carcass, some 20 m from the caravan. I then fired darts and drugged them. That way it's safe to measure or mark them or fit radio collars around their necks.'

The park's lion project was launched in response to a drastic decline in the blue wildebeest population. At first it was assumed that

A FLASH OF POWDER IN THE NIGHT

Paul Selby was an American mining engineer who managed a Johannesburg gold mine in the 1920s. In 1924 he and his family were introduced to the Sabie Game Reserve, and thereafter he made frequent trips to Pretoriuskop to photograph game. He set up his camera on the back of a truck and went to elaborate lengths to disguise the vehicle with branches. There he would sit, with a large camera fitted with a 500 mm lens (powerful even by today's standards), waiting patiently until giraffe and other animals came into view.

The results, from the beginning, were spectacular. Selby had special success with photographs taken at night. Flashbulbs were not yet on the market, so he had to rely on magnesium powder held aloft on a tray and ignited as he exposed a plate.

When Parliament debated the National Parks Bill in 1926, Selby was asked for prints so that members could see what the reserve was all about. The pictures were enthusiastically received, and played a significant part in helping the House to come to its decision.

Top: *Ipomoea* photographed near the Luvuvhu River in the Kruger Park. **Above:** The fever tree is found in low-lying, swampy areas, and grows in groups. Its characteristic yellow or yellow-green bark is best seen in spring, when the trees are bare of leaves. Because fever trees grow in swampy areas – ideal breeding grounds for mosquitoes – they were once regarded as a cause of malaria.

LOWVELD: **KRUGER NATIONAL PARK**

Above: White rhino in the Kruger Park. There are more than 2 000 white rhino in the park – most of them in the area between the Sabie and Crocodile rivers. This species differs from the black rhino in several respects. The white rhino is a grazer with a big, wide mouth, whereas the black rhino has a pointed mouth with a prehensile upper lip which it uses to strip leaves from branches; the white rhino keeps its head low, while the black rhino generally keeps its head in line with its back; the white rhino is heavier, less aggressive, and prefers open areas, while the black rhino likes thickets. Despite their names both species have the same colour. **Right above:** The marabou stork, a large and unlovely bird, is frequently seen with vultures at a carcass. The marabou stork nests in large trees and occasionally on cliff ledges, producing a clutch of two to four eggs. **Right below:** Bushbuck are generally found in thickets in the Kruger Park, and keep to watercourses. There are estimated to be over 1 500 bushbuck in the park.

lion were the only cause, and it was decided that they should be culled. But the move did not halt the wildebeest slump, so researchers wondered whether the lion had been unjustly accused. 'We began studying their habits,' Whyte explains. 'We looked at their pride structure, where the prides lived, what they ate, how they interacted with other prides.'

The study showed that the lion were only partly to blame. 'A contributory problem was the western boundary fence. Erected as a safeguard against the spread of foot-and-mouth disease, it blocked wildebeest migration to and from areas outside the park. When they came to the fence they couldn't understand what had gone wrong, so they remained in the area next to the fence – which made it easy for lion prides to prey on them. Now the wildebeest have accepted the fence. Another important factor was the tall grass conditions which prevailed throughout this favoured habitat during the 1970s. Once again, this led to above-normal mortality through lion and hyena predation. Their decline has now bottomed out, and the numbers are on the rise again – particularly since the drier habitat conditions and short grazing prevailing since the advent of the eighties favour the habitat preferences of this species.'

Shingwedzi Rest Camp
The 73 km road southeast from Punda Maria to the largest of the northern region's three rest camps takes you through flattish savannah country (though there are rocky outcrops) brightened by the perennial green of mopane bush. About halfway along the route is the Babalala resting spot (notable for its splendid fig tree), from which you can continue on tar or, for better gameviewing, turn right onto the 30 km gravel loop that follows the Shisha and Mphongolo streams.

Shingwedzi is a medium-sized, somewhat old-fashioned (though part of it is modern), friendly camp of lovely trees, spectacular pink-and-white impala lilies, rectangular bungalows with shady verandahs, a restaurant, shop and swimming pool. There are some very rewarding drives from this pleasant spot – southwest along the Shingwedzi River to the Tshange lookout point, from where you can survey the vastness of parkland, or southeast, following the same river to the Kanniedood Dam and Crocodile Pool near the Mozambique border. From there you carry on south for 47 km to rejoin the main Shingwedzi/Letaba road, crossing the Tropic of Capricorn and passing the Hlamvu and Nshawu dams on the way.

The riverine forest around and north of Shingwedzi is home to some of the Kruger Park's 900-plus leopard community. Beautiful, secretive, brave, unsociable, silent, these big cats are seldom seen, resting in trees or rocks

Far left: Usually seen in small parties, the speckled mousebird is a sociable species. It even sleeps with other mousebirds, forming a tightly packed group with heads together and bodies hanging downwards. It eats flowers, fruit and berries. **Left above:** A klipspringer in the northern sector of the Kruger Park. These small (15 kg) antelope live in rocky locations, and browse on a wide range of shrubs and plants. **Left below:** The crested francolin is easily distinguished from other (similar-looking) francolins by its habit of cocking its tail feathers.

in the hot hours of the day or stalking the thick riverine reed beds. The smaller antelope – reedbuck, impala, duiker – provide the bulk of their diet, but they are more or less indiscriminate hunters, capable of bringing down something as large as a kudu, but not averse to small fry such as cane rat, fish and porcupine. Monkey and baboon also feature on the menu, though older male baboon will often fight back, quite effectively, rather than run. Oddly enough, and quite unlike the domestic cat, the leopard takes easily to water. Females feeding cubs have been seen swimming to the islands of the Sabie River, sometimes carrying with them prey as large as impala.

Kruger Park has fewer of the leopard's cousin, the cheetah – possibly no more than two hundred. Smaller and longer-legged, these fine hunters are built for speed (one has been clocked at 110 km/hour) and thus prefer the open countryside to the dense bush that covers a large part of the park. They are most common on the plains around Satara, in the central region and in the Pretoriuskop section.

Skukuza Rest Camp
Although the old Selati railway line, completed in 1912, has long since been rerouted outside the park, there remains a short stretch over the cantilevered Sabie Bridge, only a stone's throw from Skukuza Rest Camp. When the Sabie floods its banks, staff from the camp man small rail trolleys to ferry passengers to and from the airport across the river. James Stevenson-Hamilton would feel at home: in the early days he rode such trolleys all the way to Komatipoort, and he must often have seen the Sabie in flood.

Skukuza itself, however, would surprise him: what he knew as a tiny, ramshackle camp has grown into quite a large settlement. Apart from the rest camp that caters for the ever-rolling tide of visitors, there is an attractive staff village with its own church, primary school, (unfenced) golf course, extensive maintenance workshops and even a sophisticated meat-processing factory.

For visitors, the heart of Skukuza is the large thatched complex, on the bank of the Sabie River, which houses a restaurant, shop and cafeteria. There is also a large reception area at the gate to the camp which has a bank, post office, and a car-hire office. Not far away is the Stevenson-Hamilton Memorial Library, which accommodates a well-stocked library and impressive exhibition hall. Close to the camp is a nursery where indigenous plants – palms, cycads, baobabs and so forth – are cultivated and sold to the public at very modest prices. Adjacent to the library is a small cemetery with headstones commemorating dogs that died or were killed in the line of duty.

There are guesthouses, family cottages, self-contained huts, furnished tents and camping sites – a total of over 600 beds.

During 1896 and 1897, the buffalo as a species was almost exterminated by the epidemic of rinderpest that devastated most of Africa south of the equator. But over the decades the herds recovered, and over 15 000 can now be seen throughout the Kruger Park.

Normally shy, retiring creatures, the buffalo can be savagely vengeful if wounded or molested: it is one of the most dangerous of the big game animals. Healthy adult buffalo do not often fall victim to lion or other predators: when threatened, they tend to form a defensive ring, reminiscent of a laager.

Rangers tell a charming story of an especially hospitable herd of buffalo. In 1971 five baby elephants were released near a dam to the southwest of Skukuza. There was an elephant herd nearby, and it was assumed that the five would join it.

Months later, however, a tourist reported spotting a young elephant in the middle of a group of buffalo. Park authorities thought this was the product of an overactive imagination until the aerial census crew came upon the group and took photographs: the elephant already stood half a metre taller than the buffalo. In the weeks that followed it was seen several more times.

The growing elephant stayed in close contact with the buffalo, though not necessarily with the same group (buffalo come together at waterholes, and it would have been easy for the elephant to arrive with one herd and leave with another). The late Dirk Swart, then a ranger at Skukuza, studied the elephant's behaviour, and was amused to see that it was adopting buffalo habits. When approached by

LOWVELD: **KRUGER NATIONAL PARK**

a vehicle, buffalo dash away for a short distance, then return to inspect the intruder. The elephant did the same, with his little trunk held high. Park biologists were confident that the elephant would soon forsake the buffalo and join up with its own species, but each year during the aerial census they found he had remained with his friends. Interestingly, he was moving north, and by 1980 he was in the Balule area south of the Olifants River. By that time he was ten years old and of formidable size.

One day a tourist watched amazed as the elephant and 20 or so buffalo teamed up to drive eight lion from a dam. The lion fled, two of them taking refuge up a tree. As the tourist described it afterwards, the buffalo bellowed and the elephant trumpeted, and the noise alone must have terrified the lion. The group encircled the treed cats, who tried to retaliate with loud roars. Eventually the elephant and buffalo lost interest and went back to the dam for a drink. The lion waited 15 minutes before venturing very cautiously from the safety of their tree.

Since 1980 this curious elephant has spent time in the Satara and Tshokwane areas. He is sexually mature, and should become involved with females of his own kind, but some believe that he is afraid of other elephants. Said one of the rangers, 'I've seen him drinking with the buffalo when a herd of elephant arrived. The buffalo made off, and so did he.' To ensure that his movements don't pass unnoticed, rangers have marked him in such a manner that they'll be able to recognise him wherever he goes.

A pleasant halfway resting place on the road north from Skukuza is Tshokwane, where there is a tearoom and picnic spot. The area features a large number of wildlife species and, for the birdlover, is an enchanting piece of veld.

There are some splendid gravel drives radiating from Tshokwane, especially the route eastwards to the Eileen Orpen Dam – a fine viewing place. But although this region has great scenic appeal, it is probably best known for its unusual lion.

Back in 1927, it is said, a ranger named Crous shot a white lion near Tshokwane. Ex-Chief Director Dr Tol Pienaar explained: 'In the early days there was a policy of carnivore control – in some areas lion and other predators were destroyed to keep their numbers down. Ranger Crous shot the white lion and kept the skin, but the old boy would never show it to anyone.'

Even so, many people knew about the unusual skin and supposed the lion to have been an albino. There had been reports of albino waterbuck and reedbuck in the park and James Stevenson-Hamilton had once spotted an albino ground hornbill.

Then, in 1959, two rangers patrolling near Tshokwane came upon a pair of white lion

HAIL TO THE KING!

A lioness with her giraffe kill in the Kruger Park. In one recorded case, 19 lion – some of them cubs – fed on a giraffe for over a week.

In storybooks he is portrayed as the King of the Beasts, a dignified ruler of mane and muscle that few of his subjects would dare to cross.

In reality, however, this large cat – the largest carnivore on the continent – is the sleepy-eyed sultan of the savannah, his reign a succession of lazy days spent eating, sleeping and playing with his offspring.

But Africa's largest and most powerful carnivore should not be dismissed as a mere pussycat. He can break a wildebeest's neck with one swipe of a massive paw and he is so powerful that he can carry twice his weight in those terrible jaws. At times he will do his duty by his lusty harem, signalling his intent with a ritual snarl, and copulating with a display of passion unmatched in the animal world.

Many myths surround these mammals, including the mistaken belief that they cannot climb trees, or are afraid of water. On the contrary, the lion is an accomplished climber. As for speed, it can cover 100 metres in four seconds when involved in a chase.

Another of its talents is the ability to see clearly in what we would regard as darkness. Caught in the glare of a torch or a car's headlights, its large eyes glow like two reflectors and, in fact, that is what they are. Like other members of the cat family, the lion's vision is aided by a special tissue, known as the *tapetum lucidum*, lining the retina of each eye. Any light that passes the rods of the retina is reflected back, thereby concentrating the incoming light. This remarkable structure enables the lion to see 50 per cent more light.

Despite the obvious differences in appearance, the lion is a close relative of the Asiatic tiger, and the two species can interbreed, producing baby 'ligers' or 'tigons'. The tiger has stripes which create the perfect camouflage as it stalks its prey through tall grass and jungle, while the lion has a tawny hide that blends into the dry grass of the African bushveld.

But while there are many similarities, there are distinct behavioural differences. While the tiger is strictly a loner, the lion is very much a social animal, living in loosely formed prides of ten or more members. In fact, it is not entirely accurate to look upon the lion as the overlord of the African carnivores: instead it is really the lion pride that ranks top of the hunting hierarchy.

One benefit of living in a pride is that it makes finding a meal far easier. A solitary lion does not have the speed or the stamina to run down a healthy antelope or zebra, and even the stalk-and-pounce technique is only occasionally successful. But a whole pride of hungry lion can, and does, resort to much surer methods. The male will approach a herd of antelope at a very leisurely pace, while the females circle the herd and conceal themselves on the far side. When they are in position, the male closes in and drives the herd towards the spot where the females lie in wait.

However, the males do play a part in defending the pride. Lionesses might be driven from a kill by a particularly bold band of hyena, but if a male lion suddenly appears on the scene the hyena promptly retreat. Males will also defend the pride's territory from encroachment by other lion.

Above: Hikers look out over the plains of the southern Kruger Park from the Wolhuter Trail, one of seven wilderness trails which are operated in the park (the others, from south to north, are Bushman, Napi, Metsimetsi, Sweni, Olifants and Nyalaland). The trails are led by experienced rangers who are always willing to share their extensive knowledge of the bush with trailists.

cubs. The pair were not seen again and probably perished, but these were not albinos – for there was colour in their eyes.

So far there had been only mild interest in the white lion phenomenon, but that changed dramatically in 1976 when a snow-white male was born at Tshokwane – and seemed set to survive. Shortly afterwards, three white lion were born in the Timbavati Private Nature Reserve across the Kruger Park's western fence. Two of the three were later translocated to the National Zoological Gardens in Pretoria (the third disappeared without trace), and in the meantime Tshokwane's white male was seen regularly. Clearly it was flourishing.

At least nine more white cubs have been born in the vicinity of Tshokwane and Timbavati. Biologists say that they are the product of a recessive gene, present in local prides, which determines a lack of melanin pigment in the hair of these animals. In every case the white cubs have had normal siblings, and as a rule other lions seem to accept them without question. Several of the white variety have reached maturity – but, to the frustration of tourists, their coats and particularly the manes of the males have gradually darkened to a light straw colour (or darker).

Walking in the wilderness

Overlooking the spectacular Luvuvhu Gorge is a ruined hilltop citadel built by an eccentric Venda chief, Makahane. When this cruel leader suspected undue interest in the royal wives by one of his warriors, he made the man, and the wives, strip naked and work together in the fields. If the warrior's interest then became obvious, he would be hurled to his death from the cliff.

That, anyway, is the story told by rangers on the Nyalaland Wilderness Trail, one of seven wilderness trails currently operating in the park. The ruined citadel is a regular stop on this, the northernmost trail, and as the ranger relates his tale, his charge of eight trailists take in the magnificent views of the gorge and its surroundings. Here, black eagles swoop and wheel in their quest for food and, far below, the cry of a crowned eagle, on its nest in a baobab, resounds through the valley.

Trails in Kruger operate twice a week throughout the year in the southern, central and northern districts of the park. In addition to the Nyalaland Trail are the Wolhuter, Napi and Bushman trails in the southwestern corner and the Olifants, Sweni and Metsimetsi trails in the central region. Bookings for the trails must be made in advance.

Accommodation on all trails consists of rustic huts, constructed of wood and thatch, in base camps which are a peaceful retreat from civilisation.

Prior to leaving for these camps, parties assemble at specific rest camps, and are then driven to the base camp. They arrive in time for a healthy evening meal and, early the following morning, set off on the first day's trail.

Groups are accompanied by two trained (and armed) rangers, whose task it is to interpret for the party the complexities of natural ecosystems, stopping often to discuss signs of the wild and the wonders of nature. The rangers know their territory and are glad to share their knowledge.

The pattern is repeated on the following two days, and on the fourth day the party returns to the rest camp. All food is provided, but trailists must supply their own drinks.

The emphasis is on relaxation and enjoying nature, and although game is often encountered, trails are not 'foot safaris to view animals', but rather a total experience of the bush, where all aspects of the wilderness – from the rocks and trees, to the birds, fish, reptiles and insects – can be discovered.

Kruger National Park offers approximately 2 000 000 ha of unspoilt bush. Wilderness trails are the ideal way to experience this raw, wild Africa, for the sights, sounds and smells of the bush are that much more intimate and impressive when you are on foot – far more so than when travelling by car.

SCALY DENIZEN OF AFRICA'S WATERWAYS

The only species of crocodile found in southern Africa, the Nile crocodile (*Crocodylus niloticus*) is a fearsome reptile, armoured with a thick scaly skin and a terrifying array of sharp teeth. It preys on large mammals and birds that come to the water's edge to drink. Lying submerged below the surface of the water, with only its eyes, nostrils and ear-openings protruding, the crocodile pounces on its prey, dragging it under the water until the hapless creature has struggled its last. Then, keeping a firm hold on its victim, the crocodile tears off its flesh by spinning its own body in the water.

Growing to a length of almost four metres (the largest specimen killed locally measured a monstrous 5,86 m, and weighed in at some 800 kg), the Nile crocodile is the world's largest reptile. It spends its nights in the water, emerging only at sunrise to bask lazily in the warmth.

Although it leads a rather lazy existence, and doesn't need to feed every day, this enormous reptile has a wide-ranging menu of favourite meals. Mammals ranging from small antelope to the huge buffalo are top of the list, followed by carrion, fish and nesting birds, which it catches with a single sweep of its hefty tail.

The male crocodile defends his territory and woos a female at breeding time. She deposits layers of 15 to 80 white eggs in a pit scraped in the sand of a river bank. Covering them well, she guards them carefully during the three-month incubation period. When they are ready to hatch, she uncovers her offspring and carries them in her mouth to a safe nursery area. Here she takes care of them for some three to six months before releasing them to fend for themselves.

Mopane country with a baobab king

Mopane trees dominate the northern half of the Kruger National Park and the rest of the Northern Province Lowveld that sweeps northwards to the Limpopo and South Africa's boundary with Zimbabwe. Occasional hills and mountains interrupt the spreading plains, but none comes close to matching the mighty Drakensberg and Soutpansberg ranges that buffer the northern Lowveld from the high country to the southwest. Dotting the mopane plains are awesome baobab 'elephant trees' that reach a great age.

The Northern Province Department of Environmental Affairs and Tourism has a number of sanctuaries in the northern Lowveld, including Hans Merensky and Langjan nature reserves, both of which are important for the rare species they shelter; Messina Nature Reserve, which accommodates an interesting concentration of baobabs; Tzaneen Dam Nature Reserve, with its fish-filled waters and myriad birds; and the tiny Lillie Flora Nature Reserve which is the preserve of a rare cycad.

A number of private reserves have also been established. Hopefontein reserve, to the north of Tzaneen, covers 500 ha of pristine grasslands; Kate's Hope Game Lodge embraces bushveld, baobab and a rich birdlife; and Ndzalama Wildlife Reserve, also near Tzaneen, is home to the largest herd of the endangered sable antelope outside the Kruger National Park.

Brackenridgea Nature Reserve
Situated in the mountain sourveld of the remote northeastern corner of the Northern Province, Brackenridgea Nature Reserve is currently being established to protect the rare *Brackenridgea zanguebarica*, a small tree endemic to this region. The reserve is 110 ha in size, and will also be a sanctuary for the steenbok, duiker, vervet monkey and baboon that make their home here.

Brackenridgea is not yet open to the public, but those who wish to visit the reserve should contact The Sub-Regional Head, Private Bag X2654, Sibasa 0970, telephone (0159) 2-1411, or fax 2-2713, to make arrangements.

Greater Kuduland
Peace and tranquillity are the order of the day in Greater Kuduland's two 10 000 ha privately owned game reserves. Both are situated in the Northern Province, one near Tshipise and the other near Alldays.

With a professional game ranger always on hand, visitors are free to set their own schedules, which might include birdwatching, hikes and game drives. Both areas are regarded as a paradise for bird- and gamewatchers. And the reason is simple: because of their varied vegetation, the reserves play host to more than 50 species of game and more than 200 different types of bird.

Alldays Lodge can accommodate four couples or eight people sharing. The rooms are

Below: A red-knobbed coot chick. Coots are distributed throughout southern Africa, and are common wherever there are rivers or expanses of water.

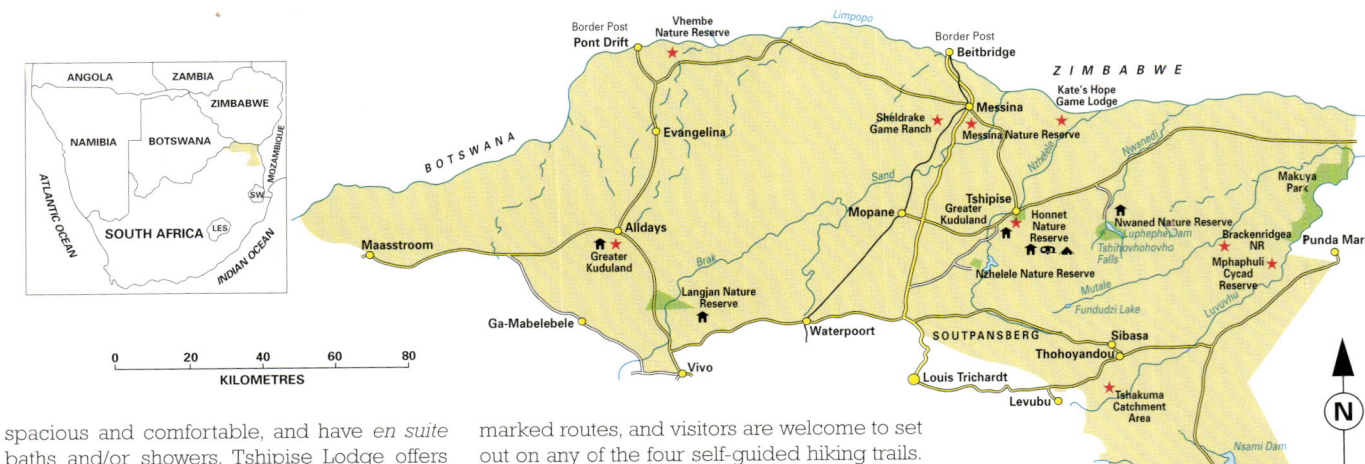

LOWVELD: THE FAR NORTH

spacious and comfortable, and have *en suite* baths and/or showers. Tshipise Lodge offers comfortable accommodation for five couples, or 13 people sharing, in thatched, air-conditioned bungalows, with baths and/or showers.

Greater Kuduland also operates a hunting lodge, aimed mainly at international clients. For further information, contact Greater Kuduland Safaris, P O Box 1385, Louis Trichardt 0920, telephone (015539) 720, or fax 808.

Hans Merensky Nature Reserve

About 70 km east of the Tzaneen Dam (and 50 km west of the Kruger National Park) is a large and complex provincial sanctuary – the Hans Merensky Nature Reserve, which includes the Aventura Eiland Resort, a popular mineral spa.

In 1950 the province acquired the farm, Eiland, for the sake of its hot springs, and soon afterwards began using it to breed species then scarce in most parts of the former Transvaal – notably giraffe and sable. The farm was proclaimed a nature reserve in 1954, and renamed to honour the well-known geologist and agriculturalist who had put the region on the map and donated a vital borehole.

Both giraffe and sable flourished in the new sanctuary, and in 1962 a number of young giraffe were captured and translocated to Mpumalanga's Loskop Dam Nature Reserve and the Langjan Nature Reserve (*see separate entry*) in the Northern Province. Since then, more than 200 giraffe have been moved to new homes all over the northeastern parts of South Africa. The sable are also bred for translocation to other reserves.

In 1964 the provincial authorities developed a prestigious spa resort, designed for fun-filled family holidays. Today, the spa provides accommodation for those visiting the nature reserve, while the reserve offers diversion for those staying at the spa. The Department of Environmental Affairs and Tourism offices are an easy stroll from the public resort, and 4x4 tours of the reserve can be arranged. Private cars may be used, providing they keep to the marked routes, and visitors are welcome to set out on any of the four self-guided hiking trails. Wildlife film shows are held regularly in the resort's auditorium.

The Giraffe Hiking Trail is a vigorous 33 km/three-day circular trail that winds through the southern section of the reserve, beginning and ending at the nature reserve offices. No more than 13 km are covered each day, which makes it perfect for beginners, leaving plenty of time to relax or to explore the surroundings. The trail's overnight camp, with its three thatched huts each equipped with four

Above: A tree frog perches above its foam nest on a branch overhanging the water. **Above right:** The Tzaneen Dam is one of the most beautiful spots in the Lowveld. **Right:** This newly moulted earwig can be recognised by the pair of pincers on its tail. Its name is something of a mystery: scientists say they are harmless, and there is no foundation in the belief that they crawl into peoples' ears.

32

home of a profusion of birds, as well as the much sought-after 'Big Five' – elephant, rhino, lion, buffalo and leopard. Giraffe, hippo, zebra and many antelope and bird species may also be seen, either from open safari vehicles or, for the more energetic, from the numerous guided walking trails on offer.

Gameviewing drives, led by experienced rangers, are conducted in the early mornings and in the evenings.

Visitors are accommodated luxuriously in the tented Buffalo Camp (sleeps 12 in six elevated tents), the Kapama Guest House (eight guests in four luxury bedrooms) or the semi-self-catering Lion Den. There are fine dining facilities and a lapa at Kapama Guest House and the Buffalo Camp, while a swimming pool at the former offers respite from the hot Lowveld days.

Visitors can choose to fly in by air charter, using the reserve's private airstrip. For further details, contact Kapama Game Reserve, P O Box 912031, Silverton 0127, telephone (012) 804-5890/9, or fax 804-3943.

Klaserie Private Nature Reserve

The absence of commercial game lodges makes Klaserie the least known of the larger private reserves. The reserve, which spreads across 62 000 ha, lies on either side of the Klaserie River, a tributary of the Olifants. The eastern border of the sanctuary adjoins Timbavati Reserve and Kruger Park to the northeast, and the fences between the three have been removed.

All the larger game species may be spotted here, including many giraffe, and the reserve is also an ornithologist's paradise.

Short of being invited as a guest of a landowner, the only way members of the public may visit Klaserie is by way of a five-day trail. Two operators run the trails in Klaserie, both of whom worked with Clive Walker, who initiated the reserve's trail system in the 1970s. The two camps are rustic but comfortable with hearty meals prepared over an open fire. The walks, led by experienced tour guides, are conducted from the camps, or are taken after a short 4x4 journey, and one or two nights are spent under the stars. Trailists (up to eight may undertake each outing) are fully catered for and, as a bonus, may be treated to sightings of elephant, buffalo, rhino, lion or leopard.

For further information or to make a booking, telephone Patrick's Trail Camp on (011) 462-7540, or (083) 261-4992, or contact Gary Freeman Safaris, P O Box 1885, Nigel 1490, telephone/fax (011) 814-2855.

Lowhills Private Game Reserve

Lowhills has a rich history dating back some 70 years, although its importance as a game reserve is relatively recent. Here visitors can experience the pristine thornveld, with its thick indigenous bush, as it was before the advent of civilisation. Lying to the southeast of Malelane, Lowhills offers accommodation in luxurious, fully catered and air-conditioned rondavels sleeping a maximum of 12 people, or in a rustic self-catering bush camp.

Visitors may indulge their love of nature by embarking on game walks, hiking trails, safari drives or horseback tours – all accompanied by an experienced ranger. Mammals to be seen include elephant, rhino, giraffe, hippo and an abundant selection of antelope. Afterwards, a plunge in the cool swimming pool will wash off the dust.

To reach Lowhills, follow the N4 east towards Komatipoort, and take the second turn-off to the right to Jeppe's Reef. Turn off to the left to Strijdomblok – the entrance to Lowhills lies 4 km further along on your right. The reserve is open all year round. A course of anti-malaria tablets is recommended. For details and to

---

NATURE'S AMAZING DO-IT-YOURSELF PROGRAMME

A lesser masked weaver constructs its nest at the end of a slender branch. The finished product is sturdy and secure from most predators.

For a species to survive, it must breed. But the newly born animal is especially vulnerable to predators, and surviving the first few days of life is the weakest link in almost every animal's life cycle. Birds have a particularly tough time: they are first locked away inside an egg, then must survive for a while longer as a nestling – unable to fly, and clearly ill-equipped for defence. A host of wild creatures dines on eggs and nestlings – the rat, cat, mongoose, snake and numerous others.

Even a nest built high in a tree is far from safe – many predators are able to climb trees. So the weaverbird's answer to the problem is a hanging nest tied securely to the end of a long, slender twig that would pose difficulties even for a snake. The kidney-shaped nest is so constructed that it can be entered only from the air, although certain snakes have mastered the acrobatic trick of entering from below by clinging to its supporting twig.

In addition to protecting the young from predators, a nest such as this offers shelter from rain and the merciless heat of the summer sun. But the greater marvel is invisible – the extent to which the entire programme for building such a nest has been encoded into the weaverbird's genetic blueprint.

The nest is mainly the work of the male bird. The energetic little home-builder first selects a suitable site, then begins to twist and knot pieces of grass and leaves around a supporting twig.

He flies back and forth with strands of grass in his bill, tucking each new piece into the existing structure, then flies around to the opposite side and pulls the loose end through the structure. Again and again he carries, tucks, twists and pulls, and in this way creates an amazingly sturdy construction of tightly knotted basketwork.

Once the main framework is in place, an inner lining of more delicate materials is moulded into a smooth-walled chamber. By the time the male has finished, a complete little home has been constructed, conforming exactly to the age-old design typical of each particular species.

make reservations, contact Lowhills Private Game Reserve, P O Box 152, Hectorspruit 1330, telephone (013) 790-4310 or (082) 455-2790, or fax (013) 755-1935.

Lowveld National Botanical Garden

In 1969 the Nelspruit Municipality and a local citrus producer (H L Hall and Sons) provided 154 ha of land on the banks of the Crocodile and Nels rivers for a Lowveld garden, a regional garden of the National Botanical Institute.

The Crocodile sweeps through the garden from west to east, on its way negotiating the churning Nelspruit Cascades, and is joined by the Nels River (from the north) by way of the Nels River Falls. The cascades are spectacular during the summer rainy season, when the rivers are in flood.

Much of the Lowveld garden remains pure wilderness. A granite koppie north of the Crocodile River has been left intact, and on the south bank the 1,5 km River Trail meanders along the steep cliff face and through the forest overhanging the Nelspruit Cascades. A plant survey commissioned when the garden opened has shown that at least 500 different species are indigenous to the Nelspruit area. Only 22 ha of the garden are in any way developed, and many of the local species of flora can be seen here, as well as other types drawn from all over southern Africa. Animals sheltering here include baboons, monkeys, buck, snakes and lizards, and a beautiful array of birds and butterflies.

About half of South Africa's indigenous tree species may be seen, including kiaat, paperbark thorn tree, yellow fever tree, baobab and wild pear. Flowers include the impala lily, Barberton daisy and Pride-of-De-Kaap, and these are at their best in the summer months, when the garden is open daily from 8 a.m. to 6 p.m. During winter the gardens are open from 8 a.m. to 5.15 p.m. To reach the sanctuary, follow the signs from the centre of Nelspruit. For further details, contact The Curator, Lowveld National Botanical Garden, P O Box 1024, Nelspruit 1200, telephone (013) 752-5531, or fax 752-6216.

Mahushe Shongwe Game Reserve

Spring and autumn are recognised as the best times to visit this beautiful 1 120 ha reserve, lying to the south of Malelane, near the Swaziland border. Although owned by the local Matsamo community, the reserve, which is home to a myriad bird species and mammals such as giraffe, nyala, waterbuck, kudu, steenbok and duiker, is managed by the Mpumalanga Parks Board.

Nestled beneath a grove of lofty jackalberry trees on the banks of the seasonal Mzinti River, the Mthomeni Bush Camp (self-catering) is an exclusive retreat for those seeking intimate contact with the bush. Accommodation is in four safari-style tents (with *en suite* bathrooms) on raised wooden platforms overlooking a riverine forest. The camp sleeps a total of eight, and has a central kitchen, dining area and bar. There is also a braai area and swimming pool. Guided game drives are offered, and visitors are free to walk through the bush (there are no predators). Visitors are advised to take precautions against malaria.

For details about the reserve, contact Mpumalanga Parks Board, Private Bag X11233, Nelspruit 1200, telephone (013) 753-3931 or 758-1035, fax 755-4796 or 755-4109.

Manyeleti Game Reserve

During the early 1960s the South African government began buying up white-owned farms adjoining the Kruger National Park for the purpose of resettling local families. One owner refused to sell his farm unless the government turned it into a nature reserve. The result is Manyeleti, which now forms a 23 000 ha section of the Sabi Sand Game Reserve.

The terrain and vegetation is much like that of the Kruger National Park, as is its population of larger mammals – among them herds of impala, blue wildebeest, zebra, giraffe and buffalo. Predators to be seen include cheetah, leopard and lion, but for most of Manyeleti's visitors these are eclipsed by the massive dignity of the occasional elephant and the lumbering rhino.

Manyeleti's staff present video and slide lectures to the schoolchildren who comprise some 60 per cent of Manyeleti's visitors (upwards of 22 000 people a year). The children are accommodated in an educational bush camp. The public rest camp offers both self-catering and ordinary rondavels, a restaurant, bar, shop, post office, filling station and bottle store.

Two additional privately owned camps at Manyeleti provide visitors with back-to-nature wildlife experiences – with the emphasis on walking trails in the company of armed, professional rangers. There are also game drives after dark in 4x4 vehicles.

Khoka Moya (capture the spirit) Game Lodge can accommodate up to 16 people (in eight *en suite* timber-and-thatch cabins). The lodge also has a splash pool and bar facilities. The rustic trails camp, known as Sky Beds, offers accommodation for eight people in a bush camp with a thatched deck overlooking a busy dam. Also within the Manyeleti Game

LOWVELD: WEST OF KRUGER

Box 462, Hazyview 1242, telephone (013) 735-5459, or fax 735-5432; or Central Reservations, P O Box 2617, Northcliff 2115, telephone (011) 888-3713, or fax 888-2181.

Sabi Sand: Djuma Bush Lodge

Lying in the northern section of Sabi Sand on a 9 000 ha tract of bushveld, Djuma offers the perfect opportunity to view the 'Big Five' as this reserve is unfenced from Mala Mala and Kruger to the east. Other animals to be seen include buffalo, spotted hyena, African wild cat, tsessebe (reintroduced to Kruger National Park, but fast making their home here at Djuma) and wildebeest. Guided game drives and walking trails are offered, one of which may lead past the Tsonga burial site, identified by the buffalo thorn trees traditionally used to mark these graves. Visitors are comfortably housed in ten thatched *en suite* chalets, serviced by a dining and recreation area, bar, swimming pool and patio overlooking a waterhole. Although the service is lavish, Djuma has managed to preserve its bushveld atmosphere. To make reservations, contact Djuma Bush Lodge, P O Box 338, Hluvukani 1363, telephone/fax (013) 735-5118; or telephone (011) 789-2722, fax 789-5160.

Sabi Sand: Inyati Game Lodge

Situated in northwestern Sabi Sand, Inyati is a small, exclusive camp, catering for a maximum of 20 people in luxury thatched chalets scattered among manicured lawns overlooking the Sand River.

For most people who visit private game reserves, the highlights are the gameviewing safaris in open 4x4 vehicles. Inyati is no exception. Accompanied by a tracker and an armed ranger you will have an excellent chance of spotting rhino, elephant, buffalo, lion and leopard, as well as abundant birdlife. And if that's not enough excitement for one day you can also arrange night safaris, guided walks and fishing trips (within earshot of harrumphing hippo, for which the lodge is named). You can also use the two-decked timber-and-thatch viewing platform erected beside the river.

Visitors enjoy fine meals served in an elegant dining room, or in a traditional boma under the starry sky. There is also a bar, as well as a swimming pool and gym to work off the effects of overindulgence. Inyati has its own airstrip. Motorists can reach it via a turn-off on the Hazyview/Skukuza road. For bookings and further information, write to Inyati Game Lodge, P O Box 38838, Booysens 2091, or telephone (011) 493-0755, fax 493-0837.

Sabi Sand: Londolozi Private Game Reserve

In the middle of Sabi Sand is Londolozi Game Reserve, the creation of brothers John and Dave Varty. Starting in the early 1970s with four primitive rondavels, they gradually extended and improved the camp as funds allowed until, before long, Londolozi became one of the most popular lodges in the Lowveld.

Londolozi is a Zulu word meaning 'protector of living things', and that has been the lodge's aim from the outset. The Vartys have involved themselves in a host of projects ranging from rescuing endangered cheetah (and releasing them in Sabi Sand) to introducing 34 elephant cows in a bid to start a breeding herd. They have publicised some of their projects by enlisting the help of show business celebrities, and Londolozi is as famous for beautiful people as it is for beautiful animals.

Main Camp at Londolozi accommodates up to 24 visitors in tree-shaded double chalets and its four original rondavels – greatly improved since the early days. The chalets and the lodge's dining room overlook lush riverine

Above: Buffalo in the Mala Mala Game Reserve. These large, powerful creatures are frequently a match for lion, which prefer to attack females and their young. Because they have a large daily liquid intake, buffalo seldom stray far from water.

47

LOWVELD: WEST OF KRUGER

vegetation in the bed of the Sand River. Separate from the main camp but only 1 km upstream is the luxury Bush Camp, with eight chalets, each with its own elevated balcony overlooking the riverine vegetation. Bush Camp has its own rangers and staff. For the last word in wildlife experiences for those who can afford it, Tree Camp offers accommodation for eight people who take their meals in a dining room suspended high above the ground in an ancient ebony tree.

To make reservations, write to Conservation Corporation Africa, Private Bag X27, Benmore 2010, or telephone them at (011) 784-6832, fax 784-7532.

Sabi Sand: Mala Mala Game Reserve

Only a few minutes' drive from Londolozi is Mala Mala, the largest privately owned reserve within Sabi Sand. Sited within an oxbow in the perennial Sand River, Mala Mala extends over some 18 000 ha of prime bushveld, and gameviewing in this wildlife paradise is exclusive to guests staying at one of the reserve's four camps. Guests are accompanied by highly qualified rangers, who lead expeditions from all of the camps, each of which have access to the entire reserve. Over 200 species of game are to be found, including the 'Big Five', which are regularly seen on these outings.

Mala Mala Main Camp is the reserve's flagship, and the oldest of its kind in the Lowveld. A maximum of 50 guests are accommodated in comfortable, thatched rooms, with air-conditioning, *en suite* bathrooms and spectacular views. Kirkman's Camp is smaller, accommodating up to 20 visitors in ten twin rooms. The camp, which is filled with interesting historical artefacts, is quaintly decorated in the colonial style with photographs of early pioneers. Some 300 m away is Kirkman's Cottage, housing eight people in four twin rooms. Harry's Camp, painted with geometric Ndebele designs, has seven twin rooms with air-conditioning and *en suite* bathrooms. All the camps have reed-enclosed bomas for dining under the stars, and swimming pools.

For further information, write to Mala Mala Game Reserve, P O Box 2575, Randburg 2125, or telephone (011) 789-2677, fax 886-4382. Precautions against malaria are advised.

Sabi Sand: Sabi Sabi Game Reserve

Visitors to the Sabi Sabi Game Reserve have a choice of three luxury lodges and a tented camp from which to explore this animal-filled paradise. Each claims to offer a unique wildlife experience.

River Lodge, with its 20 thatched chalets, two suites and executive Mandleve Suite, overlooks the Sabie River, home to hippo and crocodile. Bush Lodge lies 10 km to the north, offering accommodation in 22 chalets and five luxury suites in a typical Lowveld setting, and overlooking a waterhole much visited by animals in search of liquid refreshment. Selati Lodge, on the banks of the Msuthlu riverbed, has seven thatched chalets with a real colonial flavour. Each of the lodges has its own central dining, lounge and bar areas. One of the main attractions of these three lodges is the excellent gameviewing drives they offer. Taking place during the day and at night in open 4x4 vehicles, guests are accompanied by highly trained rangers and trackers.

Nkombe Tented Camp caters for up to seven guests, and uses the bush as a wilderness classroom for those wishing to further their knowledge of the environment. The reserve's prolific wildlife includes the 'Big Five', and all of Africa's game indigenous to the area, in their natural, unfenced environment. Over 350 bird species have been recorded. The fully licensed lodges also offer swimming pools, conference facilities and 'bundu' shops stocked with African curios. You will be pampered during your stay, and enjoy fine cuisine. Breakfasts and buffet lunches are served on the safari terrace, while venison and braai dinners are enjoyed in the open-air boma.

Sabi Sabi can be reached via a signposted turn-off approximately 10 km from Hazyview on the Hazyview/Skukuza road. Booking is essential, and precautions against malaria are advised. Contact Sabi Sabi Game Reserve, P O Box 52665, Saxonwold 2132, telephone (011) 483-3939, fax 483-3799 for more information.

Above left: A female waterbuck in the Mala Mala Game Reserve. The female lacks horns and is generally smaller and lighter than the male of the species. **Above right:** A male waterbuck. This antelope seldom moves far from its home territory. When hunted it may seek refuge in water, sometimes hiding in reeds with most of its body submerged. **Right:** A bloom of *Gardenia spatulifolia* in the Mala Mala Game Reserve. This shrub may grow up to 5 m in height. **Right below:** The brightly coloured shield bug (sometimes known as a 'stink bug' because it produces an unpleasant odour if roughly handled) is common throughout southern Africa. It can cause serious damage to fruit crops if unchecked.

Sabi Sand: Singita Private Game Reserve

In the tongue of the local Shangaan, Singita means 'the miracle', and the owners of this new 15 000 ha private reserve believe that their rescue of this beautiful land from the hands of overly zealous hunters has been nothing short of just that – a miracle. Very exclusive, Singita offers accommodation to a privileged few in eight lavishly appointed suites, each with its own *en suite* bathroom, outside shower, fireplace, leisure deck and living area.

Guests are taken on gameviewing drives – the 'Big Five' find sanctuary here and the birdlife is plentiful. Guided walks can also be arranged. Other facilities include a rock-hewn swimming pool set under trees whose branches ring with the chatter of monkeys, an open-air boma, and a timber deck overlooking the bushveld plains.

Open all year, Singita is a five-hour drive from Johannesburg via Nelspruit, White River and Hazyview. Follow the R40 from Nelspruit to Hazyview, then take the R536 towards the Paul Kruger Gate. After 36 km turn left onto a gravel road (a vehicle entrance fee will be charged here). Enter the Sabi Sand gate and follow the Singita signs for some 28 km to the camp. However, guests usually choose to fly in via Skukuza, from where a light aircraft transfers them to Singita's private airstrip. Precautions against malaria are advised.

For more detailed information and to make reservations, contact Conservation Corporation Africa, Private Bag X27, Benmore 2010, telephone (011) 784-6832, or fax 784-7532.

Sabi Sand: Ulusaba Game Reserve

Fine gameviewing and unobtrusive service are the selling points of this reserve lying in the northwestern section of Sabi Sand. Guests are housed extremely comfortably in two lodges. Rocklodge accommodates up to 22 guests in luxury chalets situated some 250 m above the surrounding reserve, or in the sumptuous Martial Eagle and Bateleur cottages. Safari Lodge sleeps a maximum of 12 in chalets set on a platform on the banks of the Mabrak watercourse.

Both lodges are fully catered, and have swimming pools and laundry facilities.

Gameviewing drives are rewarding – this is, after all, 'Big Five' country – and ranger-led walks are also popular.

The best time to visit is between May and October. Precautions against malaria are advised. To reach Ulusaba, follow the R536 leading to the Kruger National Park's Paul Kruger Gate, but turn off north towards Newington. Follow the Ulusaba signs.

For further details or to make a booking, contact Ulusaba Game Reserve, P O Box 239, Lonehill 2062, telephone (011) 465-4240 or 465-6646/7, or fax 465-6649.

> **NATIONAL PARKS**
>
> 'That paradise upon earth' wrote the great Swedish botanist, Linnaeus (Carl von Linné, 1707-78), of the Cape of Good Hope, which he knew only by specimens of its flora and fauna brought to Europe by early explorers. Pre-industrial indigenous man lived lightly on this southern land, but within a relatively short time of the establishment of a permanent European settlement in 1652, many species – especially of tree – had become scarce, and others, locally extinct. Interestingly, the first conservation edict, issued before the settlement was 10 years old, sought to preserve the trees of the Hout Bay valley.
>
> Overall, conservation proceeded tardily, and too often it was too late, as in the case of the bluebuck and the quagga. The National Parks Act was passed in 1926. Its emphasis, at first, was on the preservation of game, but later expanded to the conservation of regions of great beauty or of natural and geological interest. Inevitably, perhaps, national parks came to be seen by many as land set aside for the leisurely enjoyment of a privileged class. Nor was goodwill gained by the misguided removal or exclusion of rural communities. Wars, poaching and the demands of a burgeoning population added to the difficulties.
>
> In the past decade, however, emphases and policies underlying conservation have changed. Preservation, while still vital, has become part of a process of integrated conservation that counts man as a vital part of the ecology, and not merely a tourist or an onlooker. Communities adjoining national parks are shown that these reserves provide them with meaningful employment and business opportunities. Ideally, national parks will be self-funding rather than dependent on state subsidies.
>
> In addition to affirmative action and community support, the National Parks Board – no longer the highly centralised organisation it was – has turned its attention to the commercially orientated marketing of ecotourism, both nationally and abroad. Decentralisation of management of national parks actively involves people most closely affected by a park's existence, and ensures the survival of ecological integrity while sustaining tourism, cultural, inspirational, educational and research activities.

Sandringham Private Nature Reserve

Four delightful *en suite* stone-and-thatch huts provide the accommodation at this exclusive private reserve nestling on the banks of the Timbavati River.

Here the 'Big Five', as well as zebra, waterbuck, kudu, blue wildebeest, impala, bushbuck, giraffe, warthog and numerous smaller mammals, roam freely through the 5 000 ha of unspoilt bush. The game may be viewed from a safari vehicle or from one of the bush trails – under the watchful eye of an experienced game ranger. Tree houses at waterholes ensure undisturbed gamespotting during the day or at night.

The reserve lies on the northern side of the R531 between Klaserie and the Kruger Park's Orpen Gate. It has its own landing strip for light aircraft. Visitors are advised to take precautions against malaria. For details, contact Sandringham Private Nature Reserve at P O Box 1214, Hoedspruit 1380, telephone/fax (01528) 3-2449, or (015) 793-2449.

Thornybush Game Reserve

Located on a vast tract of Lowveld wilderness adjacent to the Kruger National Park, Thornybush (10 000 ha) is home to a large variety of mammals, including the ever-popular 'Big Five', and a proliferation of birds. The vegetation is as varied as the wildlife, with mixed woodland, acacia and marula veld, and grasslands ranging from waving blue buffalo to short rolling grass.

Guests are accommodated in five lodges. Thornybush Main Lodge has 16 *en suite* chalets, with a central lounge and dining area, a fully equipped conference centre, a swimming pool and a boma overlooking the Monwana riverbed. Serondella Lodge offers four separate chalets linked by wooden walkways to a central living area. N'Kaya Lodge has four luxury, air-conditioned chalets, each with its own private lounge and two bathrooms. Chapungu Lodge, known for its fine cuisine, comprises five bedrooms with a central boma and swimming pool, while Jackalberry Lodge, situated on the Klaserie River and offering dramatic views across to the Drakensberg mountains, is also a luxury camp sleeping ten.

Like other Lowveld lodges, Thornybush offers game drives in open 4x4 vehicles in the early mornings and late afternoons. Gameviewing from hides is popular, as is birdspotting – over 280 bird species have been recorded. Those keen on getting really close to nature can join a tracking team and learn how to identify animal spoor.

Motorists trying to find Thornybush should follow the R531 leading eastwards from Klaserie to the Kruger Park's Orpen Gate and turn left after some 13 km onto a secondary

49

LOWVELD: WEST OF KRUGER

Above left: Ignoring the interested bystanders, hippo take a leisurely bathe. **Top:** A broad-nosed weevil, common to the Mpumalanga bush. If threatened, a weevil will immediately sham death by falling on its side and extending its legs. This is an automatic reflex triggered by the insect's nervous system. Weevils make up the largest of the beetle families – indeed, the largest animal family – in the world. There are more than 2 500 species in southern Africa alone. The 'snout' or rostrum at the front of the head varies in shape and size among the different species – from short and squat to long and narrow. Weevils enjoy the unenviable reputation of being pests. They are perhaps most notorious for destroying stored grain.
Above: The lucky-bean creeper is a familiar sight throughout the Lowveld, and its seeds are very poisonous. This specimen was photographed in the Timbavati Private Nature Reserve.

road to the reserve. The entrance lies approximately 30 km along this road. Further information is available from Thornybush Game Reserve, P O Box 798, Northlands 2116, telephone (011) 883-7918, or fax 883-8201.

Timbavati Private Nature Reserve

The third of the Lowveld's great private sanctuaries dates from the mid-1950s, when a landowner named Peter Mostert urged his neighbours to help create a 'private Kruger Park' for their mutual benefit. (Today the reserve falls within the boundaries of the Kruger National Park.)

The various Timbavati farms, encompassing a massive 65 000 ha, are the property of more than 30 separate landowners, who have banned professional trophy-hunting on the reserve and pooled resources to reintroduce species such as white rhino and sable, and to give Timbavati's cheetah population a healthy boost.

Among Timbavati's claims to fame are white lion (also found in the Kruger Park), and what is said to be the densest giraffe population in the world (although there is another impressive giraffe population in the Klaserie reserve across the provincial road to the west). The reserve also has 13 000 impala, 4 500 blue wildebeest, 2 500 zebra, 1 000 buffalo, about 100 elephant (including a few breeding herds), a number of kudu and waterbuck, predators, small mammals, and a bird population that for many visitors is the greatest drawcard. Remember when visiting this area that precautions against malaria are recommended.

Timbavati: Kambaku Game Lodge

This small lodge, tucked into a corner of Timbavati's bushveld countryside, offers informal accommodation in seven thatched chalets, each with an *en suite* bathroom. There is a swimming pool for cooling off after an outing in the hot Lowveld sun, and evenings are spent enjoying a braai around a companionable campfire.

Game drives are offered, with spotting the 'Big Five' an ever-possible reality. Also on offer are ranger-led bush walks, and night drives in search of elusive nocturnal creatures. Rewarding hours can be spent in the lodge's hide.

To get to Kambaku, take the R40 leading south from Hoedspruit. After 7 km, turn left at the signpost to Timbavati. Continue for about 31 km to reach the Timbavati boundary, then turn right. Continue for a further 6 km, then turn left into the reserve. Kambaku lies 1,8 km further on to your left. Precautions against malaria are advised. For details, contact P O Box 26350, Arcadia 0007, telephone (012) 329-8220, fax 329-6441.

Timbavati: Kings Camp

The privately owned Kings Camp is home to the 'Big Five', which hobnob with numerous antelope species and hosts of birds, including lilac-breasted rollers, hornbills, cuckoos and raptors. The area forms the centre of a continuous bush-clearing programme created to re-establish the original grassland habitat. In fact, the camp has a lengthy history of nature conservation – it was here that Timbavati was founded in 1955.

Today Kings Camp has nine luxury, thatched bungalows, subtly decorated and fully air-conditioned, while nearby is the equally luxurious Waterbuck Lodge. Visitors take their meals on a wooden deck or in a reeded boma overlooking the waterhole, much frequented by warthogs, waterbuck and other game. Day and night drives can be arranged, as well as bush walks with experienced and

TALL AS THE TREES

Giraffe gather at a waterhole in the Timbavati Private Nature Reserve.

A fully grown bull giraffe is the tallest creature on earth, soaring to a full 6 m on its stilt-like legs. Weighing an impressive 1,5 tons, the *Giraffa camelopardalis* is also one of the four largest land animals.

Yet, despite its bulk, this gentle giant blends almost perfectly with its surroundings, its patchwork hide matching the sun-dappled thorn trees of the African savannah so perfectly that it is possible to walk past an entire herd of giraffe without noticing them.

The giraffe's long neck is a classic example of form being moulded by natural selection: the taller individuals could eat leaves and shoots that were beyond the reach of shorter giraffe, and therefore enjoyed a larger food supply.

Their ability to feed more easily, and their improved chances of survival in the lean seasons, enabled the taller giraffes to breed more successfully – thus concentrating in the ancestral gene pool those genes which have caused them to grow tall.

While the advantages of such a long neck are fairly obvious, the biological engineering problems which had to be overcome in its design are perhaps less apparent. Like any other mammal, including man, the giraffe has only seven vertebrae in its neck, but these have become enormously elongated, and are attached to one another with ball-and-socket joints that give the whole structure flexibility.

The giraffe also has a unique 'plumbing' system: to pump blood 2,5 m uphill to the brain, it has had to develop a large heart, with walls more than 7 cm thick.

To make matters more difficult, nature had to devise some way of controlling the flow of this blood, otherwise, every time the giraffe lowered its head to drink, the massive rush of blood to the brain would knock the animal unconscious. To solve this problem the giraffe maintains an aortic blood pressure twice that found in man.

The jugular vein (which returns blood from the brain to the heart) has a series of one-way valves that prevent the blood from flowing back to the brain when the head is lowered, and the huge carotid artery, which carries oxygenated blood from the heart to the brain, divides into a great network of lesser blood vessels before it actually reaches the brain.

This remarkable structure is known as a *rete mirabile* (wondrous net) and as it passes through a pool of cool venous blood which has drained from the nasal sinuses, it acts as a heat exchanger, thereby keeping the giraffe's brain cool.

---

knowledgeable rangers. 'Sleep-outs' under the stars are also a popular attraction.

To get to Kings Camp, follow the R540 from Belfast to Lydenburg, and then continue to Hoedspruit. Follow the signs to Timbavati where, in turn, signs will lead you to Kings Camp. Alternatively, visitors can fly to Phalaborwa, where a transfer will take them to Kings Camp. For more detailed information, contact Kings Camp, P O Box 1255, Hoedspruit 1380, telephone (01528) 3-1123 or (015) 793-1123. To make reservations, contact P O Box 2298, Northriding 2162, telephone (011) 465-9387, or fax 465-9309. Remember to take precautions against malaria.

Timbavati: Motswari-M'bali

Opened in 1977, Motswari Game Lodge and its sister camp, M'bali, offer visitors luxurious base camps from which to discover the 'Big Five' and all the wonderful bird species found at the world-renowned Timbavati Private Nature Reserve.

Motswari accommodates a maximum of 32 guests in tastefully furnished thatched rondavels, which overlook the Sohelbele River and surrounding bushveld. M'bali, reminiscent of Ernest Hemingway's hideaway in Africa, consists of nine *en suite* safari tents raised above the ground to ensure broad, uninterrupted views. Both camps have swimming pools and are well known for their excellent cuisine (three full meals are served daily).

Two game drives are conducted daily in open 4x4 vehicles under the guidance of professional game rangers who also arrange walks through the bush. Alternatively, you can relax in a hide beside a waterhole and wait for the game to come to you.

The M'bali Dam is home to a number of hippo, whose grunts and squeals are punctuated by the calls of the resident fish eagles. Most species of antelope are represented, as are cheetah and other predators.

For further information, contact Motswari Reservation Office, P O Box 67865, Bryanston 2021, or telephone (011) 463-1990, or fax 463-1992. Take precautions against malaria.

Timbavati: Ngala Private Game Reserve

Nearly all of the Lowveld's private reserves and lodges adopt a wildlife emblem to adorn their stationery, their vehicles and their staff members' epaulettes. Sabi Sabi's emblem is an elephant, Mala Mala has a sable, and Thornybush a leopard. A luxurious private game reserve and lodge that opened in the south of the Timbavati reserve in 1981 was named Ngala, the Shangaan word for lion, so the lodge chose as its emblem the lion's four-toed pug (footprint).

Many treats await visitors to Ngala, which has one of the densest populations of lion in southern Africa. And there is little that compares with that first close encounter with an elephant bull, or the heart-stopping thrill of spotting a lion less than 3 m away. Visitors explore in 4x4 vehicles, on day and night safaris, or on foot, accompanied by an armed ranger, to get an even closer feel of Africa. However, if you really want to take it easy, you can even watch game from the comfort of the lodge's lounge which overlooks a waterhole.

Ngala is regarded as a pioneer in the field of ecotourism – its owners (Conservation Corporation Africa) negotiated an unprecedented agreement with the National Parks Board Trust whereby the management would be allowed to concentrate on the accommodation and hospitality side of the enterprise, while the land and its wildlife would be cared for by Kruger National Park officials. The lodge offers fine air-conditioned accommodation in 20 twin-bed

LOWVELD: WEST OF KRUGER

Left: A rare white lion cub in the Timbavati Private Nature Reserve. In the background, its brother has conventional colouring.

chalets as well as the distinguished Safari Suite. It has a plant-fringed swimming pool from which water cascades over natural rock formations into a waterhole frequented by numerous animals, including herds of elephant. A verandah overlooks the waterhole, allowing visitors the opportunity to observe the game, as well as the reserve's plentiful birdlife. There is also a conference centre, which caters for up to 42 delegates.

To reach Ngala, enter Timbavati from a turn-off (signposted 'Argyle') 6,5 km from Hoedspruit on the Hoedspruit/Acornhoek road. After travelling 31 km along this road, follow signs to Ngala. Visitors may drive or fly to the lodge – it has its own airstrip and operates its own fly-in safaris.

For bookings and further information, write to Conservation Corporation Africa, Private Bag X27, Benmore 2010, or telephone (011) 784-6832, or fax 784-7532. Remember to take precautions against malaria.

Timbavati: Tanda Tula Game Lodge

Tanda Tula is a small and exclusive lodge whose rangers tailor programmes to their guests' individual requirements.

Its main camp is a complex of eight twin-bed tents (all with *en suite* bathrooms) set under acacia trees around a swimming pool. The game drives range over 7 000 ha of varied terrain in the heart of Timbavati. A speciality of this beautiful area is the rare and appealing pride of white lions which, incidentally, are not albino lions, but rather the product of a recessive gene. Animals range freely throughout the reserve – look out for lion, leopard, cheetah, wild dog, buffalo, white rhino, elephant (they breed here at Tanda Tula and are a little aggressive), giraffe and over 300 bird varieties. Walking tours through the dense bush can be arranged. There are also two waterhole hides.

To reach Tanda Tula, enter Timbavati by the main gate on the road to Shlaralumi and follow the signs. For further information, contact Tanda Tula Bush Camp, P O Box 32, Constantia 7800, telephone (021) 794-6500, or fax 794-7605. To contact the lodge itself, telephone (015) 283-2435. Precautions against malaria are advised.

Timbavati: Umlani Bush Camp

Comfortable two-bed (or double-bed), reed-and-thatch *en suite* rondavels, 10 000 ha of traversing area filled with some 40 mammal species and a myriad birds, all collaborate to create the unspoilt bushveld experience at Umlani Camp. Visitors are treated to an early-morning bush walk followed by an ample breakfast. Midday hours are spent relaxing in the camp next to the splash pool or in a tree house overlooking the busy waterhole, followed by a light lunch. Late afternoon brings a game drive (with a spotlight), stopping for sundowners in the bush, and then a night drive to look for nocturnal species. The day ends with a campfire dinner and comparisons of the day's sightings. Bar facilities are available.

Umlani is situated in central Timbavati and can be reached by road from Hoedspruit and Klaserie. For details and to make reservations, contact Umlani, P O Box 26350, Arcadia 0007, telephone (012) 329-3765, or fax 329-6441. Precautions against malaria are advised.

Tshukudu Game Lodge

Imagine a star-filled African sky, the sizzle of venison steaks on a boma braai, orphaned animals roaming freely about a camp, and mouth-watering 'African home cooking'. These are just some of the memories that visitors to Tshukudu Game Lodge, near Hoedspruit, have taken home with them.

No more than 30 visitors are allowed at any one time on the 5 000 ha reserve, ensuring complete privacy for its guests. The owners have also acquired traversing rights over a further 3 500 ha on the fertile, sycamore-forested banks of the Olifants and Blyde rivers.

Among the activities offered is a ride with an armed ranger in an open vehicle, through countryside known for its lion, leopard, cheetah, giraffe, kudu, zebra and white rhino. The more adventurous can hike along a trail so narrow 'that you can almost feel the animals' presence'. However, those who wish to laze around the camp all day are free to do so, too.

Accommodation is in a comfortable rondavel or chalet with private facilities. A bush camp for the adventurous, a cheaper alternative to the lodge, takes a minimum of four people.

For bookings and further information, contact The Director, Tshukudu Game Lodge, P O Box 289, Hoedspruit 1380, telephone (015) 793-2476, or fax 793-2078.

Umbabat Private Nature Reserve

Spanning some 15 300 ha of mopane-studded Lowveld north of Timbavati, Umbabat Private Nature Reserve is home to a wide variety of game, including the 'Big Five', cheetah and numerous other predators, as well as most antelope species.

The reserve is open only to its owners (the Umbabat Private Nature Reserve Executive Committee), and to guests staying at Motswari Game Lodge (*see separate entry*), which lies within its borders but is reached via Timbavati.

Kingdom of the wild

Swaziland's coat of arms consists of the Swazi royal shield supported by a lion on the left and an elephant on the right. The lion represents Swaziland's king, who traditionally looks after warfare, hunting and other manly pursuits, and is the symbol of Swazi nationhood. The elephant represents the queen mother, who by Swazi custom wields nearly as much authority as the king. She oversees an appeal court against unpopular judgments given by the king, governs internal relations and acts as custodian of the ritual rain-making equipment.

Both lion and elephant have been reintroduced to Swaziland after a 50-year absence. It is also home to other animal species, including leopard, cheetah, white rhino, buffalo, giraffe and a wide range of antelope. They can be seen to advantage in the kingdom's variety of game parks and nature reserves.

His Majesty, the late King Sobhuza II, recognised the importance of protecting the country's wildlife and some four per cent of the country is now protected, administered either privately or by the Swaziland government. Traditionally, ownership of all game still vests in the king.

The Mlilwane Wildlife Sanctuary, south of Mbabane, was established in 1960 and is a favourite of both local and foreign visitors. Hlane Royal National Park in the Lowveld to the east, belongs to the king, who holds it in trust for the nation (part of this land is the royal hunting preserve). Mlawula Nature Reserve lies northeast of Hlane on the Swaziland border, while Malolotja Nature Reserve, in the northwest, offers some of the finest scenery in southern Africa. Mkhaya and Phophonyane are two of the most recent additions to the country's excellent line-up of nature reserves.

Hlane Royal National Park

One of the highlights of Swaziland's social round is the annual *Butimba*, a week-long hunt in an area adjacent to the royal game reserve at Hlane. Hundreds of Swazis in traditional dress chant excitedly as the king leads them into action. The hunters may carry arms such as spears, knobkerries and guns, and the game they kill is presented to the king. Elsewhere, conservationists might view *Butimba* with dismay – but Swaziland's game rangers believe this is a valuable way of emphasising traditional values and a useful means of culling surplus game.

Hlane came into being during the 1940s when the king acquired a large private ranch on behalf of the Swazi nation. The ranch was ideal game country, so it was set aside as a royal hunting reserve. Unfortunately, the game soon attracted large numbers of poachers who set snares and other traps, almost denuding the area of its wildlife. In 1967 the king proclaimed the area a national sanctuary and, to this day, His Majesty King Mswati III holds the park in trust for the nation.

At the time, Hlane was a paradise of virgin bushveld. The grass was sweet and the bush had not encroached, but there was very little game to be seen – no more than 100 zebra, 200 blue wildebeest and perhaps 600 impala, with small numbers of greater kudu, bushbuck and other antelope. A team of rangers worked hard to drive out the poachers, and before long the game increased dramatically. Waterbuck found their own way in and many white rhino were translocated from the old Umfolozi Game Reserve in Natal (now KwaZulu-Natal). The population grew so handsomely that some of Hlane's animals, including impala, zebra and blue wildebeest, were used to restock Mlilwane Wildlife Sanctuary, which had been the victim of poaching.

Today the 35 000 ha Hlane Royal National Park offers a wealth of wildlife for the visitor. There are more than 10 000 animals, including elephant, hippo, warthog, lion, cheetah, leopard, waterbuck, kudu, grey duiker and steenbok, and large herds of zebra, wildebeest, and rhino (their horns removed as a safeguard against poachers, who destroyed about 80 per cent of these magnificent creatures in the late 1980s). The reserve is also home to the world's most southerly colony of marabou storks. Birdlife is of a splendid variety (over 400 species have been recorded), including lilac-breasted rollers, shrikes, glossy starlings and a large population of vultures.

The reserve is watered by the Black Mbuluzi River, which also forms part of the northwestern and western boundaries. The banks of this river attract hosts of animals during the dry winter months; during the wet summer months the game moves to the south. The vegetation includes fine knobthorn and ancient leadwood trees.

Left: Blue wildebeest drinking at a dam in the Hlane Royal National Park. There is usually a gathering of harem troops on the remaining pastures at the beginning of the dry season, after which these split up to join large herds. With the appearance of fresh grass after the first rains, the herds once again split up into troops dominated by old males, which establish and protect their territories against incursions by other males. On their massive migrations, the younger, non-territorial males are relegated to the perimeter of the herd, often relying on the timidity of accompanying zebra for an early warning if predators are about. Blue wildebeest are tough and, although normally timid, will fight ferociously when cornered. The young, born in early summer to take advantage of the summer rains, are able to follow the mother within five minutes of birth and are very playful.

LOWVELD: SWAZILAND

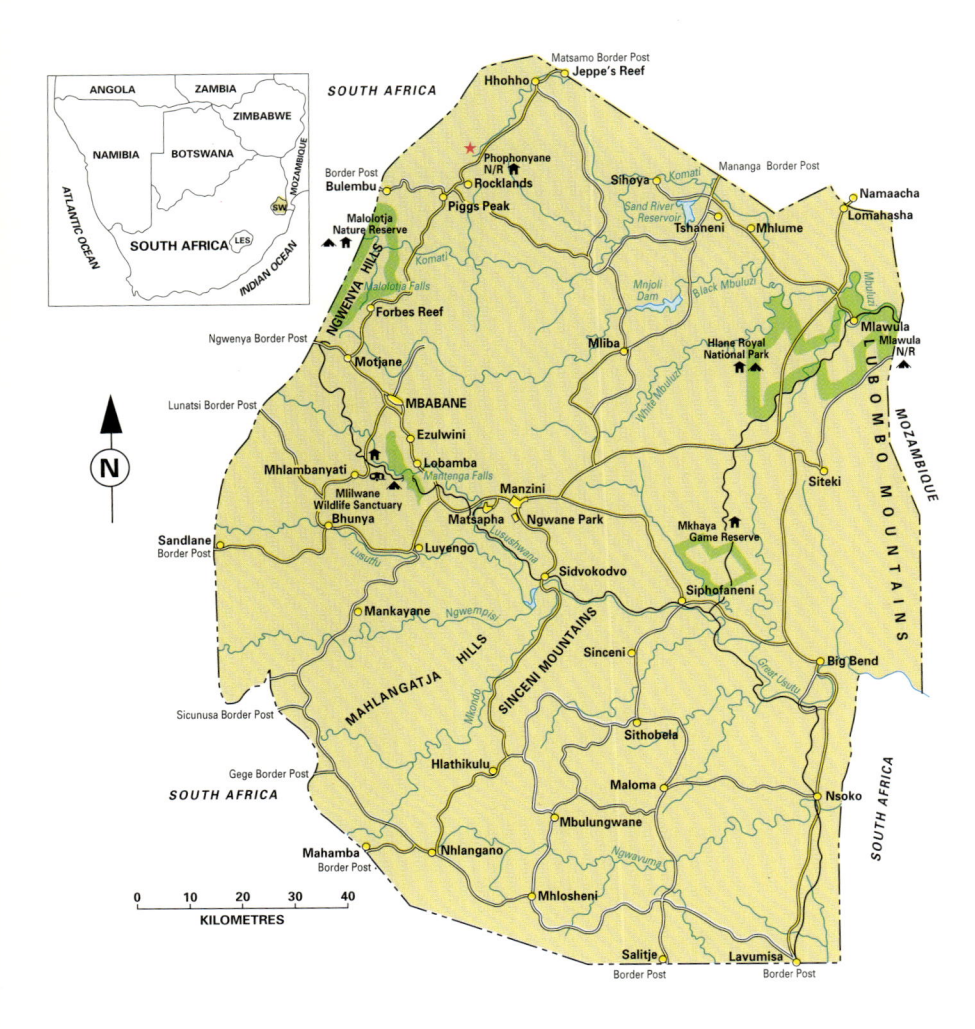

Above: Cattle egrets in the Mlilwane Wildlife Sanctuary. They provide an 'early warning' system for game, taking flight at the first sign of danger.

There are two camps within Hlane Royal National Park, each offering comfortable self-catering accommodation. Bhubesi Camp, overlooking the gentle, tree-lined Mbuluzana River, has luxurious two-bedroomed cottages, each supplied with a stove, refrigerator, cutlery, crockery and bedding. Ndlovu Camp has two fully equipped, thatched rondavels (more are being built) overlooking a waterhole. Day visitors may use the facilities at Ndlovu, which also offers a large camping and caravan site.

Self-guided game drives are popular, although in summer the luxuriant vegetation may obscure your view, and rainy weather makes the roads slippery and difficult to negotiate. Guided tours in your own transport or on foot may be arranged (especially exciting is a ranger-led excursion radio-tracking lion).

To reach the reserve, take the road between Manzini and the Lomahasha customs post and watch for the signposts. Precautions should be taken against malaria. For information and to make reservations, write to Big Game Parks Central Reservations Office, P O Box 234, Mbabane, telephone (09268) 4-4541, fax 4-0957; or Hlane Royal National Park, P O Box 33, Mbabane, telephone (09268) 6-1591/2/3.

Malolotja Nature Reserve

One of the methods used to reduce Hlane's game population has been to translocate species to the impressive Malolotja Nature Reserve in Swaziland's western highlands. Malolotja was founded in 1974 after Ian Grimwood, a conservationist working with the United Nations Food and Agriculture Organisation, was brought to the country to assist in the establishment of a system of national parks. This lovely sanctuary was the government's first nature reserve.

Some 18 000 ha in extent, Malolotja is named after the 90 m Malolotja Falls, the highest in Swaziland. Other attractions include superb mountain scenery and the Komati Gorge, with sides so steep that hikers wanting to explore it have to take to the river. Also worth seeing are the Mahulungwane Falls lying to the northwest of the Malolotja Falls, and the Mhlangamphepha Valley, with its tree-fern-cloaked slopes, in the southwestern corner. An attraction of a different sort is the old Ngwenya iron-ore mine, an immense pit with terraced sides and pools of water at the bottom. On the northwestern side of the pit is the Lion Cavern, a small mine from which red hematite pigment was removed (for colouring purposes) over 41 000 years ago. Middle Stone Age artefacts have been found on its northeastern rim.

Even without its game Malolotja's scenery is sufficiently impressive to qualify it as one of the leading nature reserves in southern Africa. The grassland is well watered, lush and in prime condition, and the wildlife it supports is thriving. Visitors will see indigenous oribi, bushbuck, mountain and common reedbuck, red hartebeest, grey rhebok, baboon, klipspringer, leopard, bushpig and warthog. This is primarily a walking reserve with trails suitable for almost all degrees of fitness. You are likely to spot many of the reserve's 280 bird species, which include blue crane and Stanley's bustard, as well as two resident colonies of bald ibis. Birdwatchers may also be lucky enough to catch a thrilling glimpse of the rare blue swallow. There are two small dams for trout-fishing (a permit is needed).

To reach Malolotja from Mbabane, follow the main road northwest to the Ngwenya border post. After 15 km, at Motshane (Motjane), take the road leading to Piggs Peak. The reserve lies on the left some 18 km from Motshane.

Left: *Adenium swazicum* (summer-flowering impala lily) in the Hlane Royal National Park. This lily produces its bright pink or reddish-purple flowers in January. **Right:** The distinctively crested African hoopoe at its nest hole. This bird is distributed all over southern Africa, where it is usually found in savannah veld (though it sometimes enters towns). It nests in hollow trees, beneath eaves, among stones and even in termite mounds, producing four to seven eggs which hatch after 17 days. The hoopoe's name is derived from its call in the breeding season – a repeated 'hoop, hoop' sound.

Accommodation is provided in five self-catering log cabins, each sleeping six. The main camp at the entrance has a small three-bed hut and a campsite. Bookings should be addressed to Malolotja Nature Reserve, P O Box 100, Lobamba, telephone (09268) 6-1151 or 6-1178/9, fax 6-1875; or The Senior Warden, Malolotja Nature Reserve, P O Box 1797, Mbabane, telephone (09268) 4-3060.

Mkhaya Game Reserve

'If you don't see black rhino at Mkhaya then chances are you never will,' claim the owners of what has become known as Swaziland's 'Rhino Reserve'. Although the small private reserve offers visitors one of the best opportunities for seeing these endangered animals in Africa, it was the reintroduction of elephant here in 1986 that really attracted the attention of the public. Mkhaya's small herd features the first elephant to live in the country for over 50 years despite their featuring in Swazi folklore and on the Swazi crest.

The association of Mkhaya with conservation dates back to 1976 when King Sobhuza II expressed concern at the fact that the Nguni – Swaziland's indigenous cattle – were being wiped out as a pure breed. Ted and Liz Reilly of Mlilwane responded by establishing Mkhaya and, since then, this colourful, resilient strain has been successfully preserved and bred here for export throughout southern Africa.

The 6 200 ha wilderness of broadleaf and acacia-dominated savannah, incorporating the once-famous Red Tiger Ranch, teems with game such as elephant, black rhino (some donated by President Lee Teng-Hui of the Republic of China to His Majesty King Mswati III), buffalo, white rhino, hippo, leopard, crocodile, tsessebe and kudu. A unique partnership exists between Mkhaya and Hlane Royal National Park whereby endangered species are established and propagated at the former for translocation to Hlane when numbers allow. Over 120 species of bird are found, including hawk, hornbill, francolin, and the Wahlberg's, booted and crowned eagle, as well as one of the reserve's most treasured residents, the bateleur. This rare, exuberantly coloured bird returned to Mkhaya after a 20-year absence and is one of the amazing success stories of this magnificent sanctuary for endangered animals. Also among its prized possessions are Swaziland's national bird, the purple-crested lourie, and the elusive Narina trogon.

Stone Camp has an attractive, two-bedroomed stone-and-thatch cottage and ten luxury safari tents secreted below shady trees in the southeastern corner of the reserve. There is a kitchen, an ablution block with solar-heated water, and even a honeymoon tent – equipped with a king-sized bed! Camp staff prepare meat dishes over an open fire.

Trips in 4x4 vehicles enable visitors to get close to the bigger game, or you can get even nearer to nature by walking (with a guide) through the bush. Precautions against malaria are advised.

White-water rafting on the Great Usutu River, which tumbles and boils on its way through the reserve's Bulungu Gorge, has become increasingly popular. Eight-man dinghies or two-man rafts, with professionals at the helm, carry visitors between 10 and 20 km down the river, stopping at tranquil spots to birdwatch, and lingering below a plummeting waterfall for a leisurely lunch. Book well in advance, and remember to take precautions against malaria.

Only overnight guests who have made reservations are permitted to visit the reserve. For further details, write to Mkhaya Game Reserve, P O Box 234, Mbabane, or telephone (09268) 4-4541, fax 4-0957.

Mlawula Nature Reserve

The Swaziland railway runs east of Hlane Royal National Park and divides it from the Mlawula Nature Reserve, another venture of Swaziland's National Trust Commission. Mlawula's 12 000 ha incorporate the Ndzindza Nature Reserve and cut through the Lubombo Mountains bordering Mozambique. The mountaintops offer spectacular panoramic views across the Lowveld and Middleveld beyond, with the even taller peaks of Swaziland's Highveld just visible in the west.

The reserve's surprises include a dark forest of ironwood and other species, including the cycad *Encephalartos umbeluziensis* which grows nowhere else in the world. Further afield are intriguing examples of termitarium bush clumps – bush-covered termite mounds that look like islands in the surrounding sea of thick grass. In the wide Siphiso Valley and woodland of the west there are some 50 km of game-viewing roads to explore.

MLILWANE AT A GLANCE

When to go Mlilwane is open throughout the year. Warm clothing is recommended for the cold winter nights. The reserve's main gate is open from sunrise to sunset. A 'night route' allows access to the sanctuary when the other routes are closed, enabling guests to visit restaurants or the casino. The rest camp is accessible at all times.

Reservations and information To book accommodation or obtain further information, contact The Mlilwane Wildlife Sanctuary, P O Box 234, Mbabane, telephone (09268) 4-4541 or 6-1591/2/3, fax 4-0957.

Getting there The reserve is in the Ezulwini Valley, about 15 km south of Mbabane. Follow the signs from a turn-off on the main highway between Mbabane and Manzini, 2 km north of Lobamba.

Accommodation The reserve's rustic, modest rest camp consists of thatched huts, traditional 'beehive' huts, a stone cottage, dormitories and a caravan and camping site. The ablution blocks have hot and cold water. There is also a newly established 40-bed youth hostel with laundry facilities.

Eating and drinking The lounge and 'Hippo Haunt' restaurant overlook a hippo pool where crocodile, hippo and catfish swim below a large viewing window. The camp shop sells groceries and there is a field kitchen next door (for which visitors supply their own food and cooking and eating utensils). Venison braais are a popular feature of the camp. The new 'Inkundla' is a venue able to accommodate functions for up to 300 people.

Getting around The road system takes visitors to some spectacular lookout points, and close to Mlilwane's wildlife. Petrol is on sale at the rest camp. Tours by open safari vehicle can be arranged on request. One of the best ways to explore Mlilwane is on horseback, and tours can be arranged on request. Self-guided mountain trails afford spectacular mountain scenery. Mountain bikes can be hired.

Special attractions Small museums in the rest camp illustrate Swaziland's wildlife heritage and the evils of poaching. The Gilbert Reynolds Memorial Garden has a fine aloe collection (at its best in winter) and a number of trees labelled according to South Africa's National Tree List. A large swimming pool provides an alternative to swimming in the river. Traditional Sibhaca dancing available for functions.

Wildlife White rhino, hippo and giraffe are among the species reintroduced to Mlilwane. Others include eland, buffalo, kudu, sable, blesbok, blue wildebeest, impala and warthog. The area is rich in birdlife and Mlilwane's dams and vleis are ideal nesting grounds for waterbirds.

You are likely to see white rhino, warthog, oribi, blue wildebeest, waterbuck, impala, kudu and, if you are lucky, leopard, nyala, spotted hyena, honey badger and ant bear. There are abundant crocodile in the Mbuluzi and Mlawula rivers.

Birdlife is prolific (over 350 species have been recorded), including African finfoot and the spectacular Narina trogon. Birdwatchers may also visit the 'vulture restaurant'. From the nearby Emangceni hide you will see up to five species of vulture, including the endangered Cape vulture, which are lured by carcasses left there by park officials.

Mlawula offers accommodation at Siphiso Camp in the south, with camping and caravanning facilities and, further to the west, a second site offering three two-bed, fully equipped overnight tents for hikers. There is an information centre at the entrance gate, and a guidebook outlines attractions and trails. Fishing and canoeing are available (permits needed), and safari vehicle tours can be booked. Take precautions against malaria.

The entrance to the reserve lies just off the Manzini/Lomahasha road, 10 km north of Simunye. For further details, contact Mlawula Nature Reserve, P O Box 100, Lobamba, telephone (09268) 6-1151 or 6-1178/9, fax 6-1875.

Mlilwane Wildlife Sanctuary

Sprawled across the escarpment that divides Swaziland's Lowveld from its Highveld is one of the country's top tourist attractions – the Mlilwane Wildlife Sanctuary. This beautiful reserve is watered by four rivers centred on the Ezulwini Valley. To the north the land climbs away to the famous 'Sheba's Breasts' – twin, sharp-peaked koppies that are said to have suggested the scenario for Rider Haggard's classic, *King Solomon's Mines*. These mountains are a natural backdrop to a varied population of animals ranging from small scavengers such as the jackal, through a wide variety of buck, to one of the park's major attractions – white rhino.

Being situated near the country's major tourist hotels, Mlilwane is an obvious destination for motorists. Nearly 100 km of good gravel roads lead to a number of observation points – including specially constructed hides for the photographer. Birdlovers are also well catered for, with hides overlooking several dams in the reserve.

Mlilwane is justly famous for its wide variety of birdlife. There are about 240 different species in the reserve, including such unusual specimens as the black eagle, plum-coloured starling and blue crane, as well as several species of duck, and the brightly flashing and ever-active sunbirds.

Visitors without cars can usually arrange tours at the rest camp (although advance booking is advisable). Bridle trails take pony trekkers through the heart of this magnificent park – providing the added thrill of gamespotting from horseback. Visitors are reassured to learn that the reserve's white rhino are non-aggressive (unlike their black cousins). Most of these huge beasts will cooperate quite trustingly while being photographed at close range, though you should, of course, still be cautious.

Most of the guided tours of Mlilwane begin at the rest camp, and this itself is worth lingering over. Tame animals and birds live at the camp, providing a special treat for children. And, after a bout of gameviewing, there is a sparkling natural river pool to refresh yourself before lunch.

This sanctuary, the first of its kind in the kingdom, owes its existence to the efforts of Ted Reilly, a local farmer who gained his early knowledge of the wild as a game ranger in KwaZulu-Natal, the old Transvaal, and Northern Rhodesia (Zambia). When his father died, he inherited the family farm, Mlilwane, south of Mbabane, and decided to turn it into a game sanctuary.

There was a lot to do. At the time, the only animals left on Mlilwane were a few grey duiker, steenbok and other small mammals. During 1960 and 1961, Reilly began capturing zebra, blue wildebeest and impala in other areas of Swaziland (where they were in danger of extermination by poachers) and moved them to Mlilwane. Later, he reintroduced several species from South Africa, among them white rhino, hippo and giraffe. The sanctuary was

LOWVELD: SWAZILAND

Above: A thick-tailed bushbaby at its hole in a tree in the Mlilwane Wildlife Sanctuary. It lives alone or in pairs, sleeping during the day and emerging at night to feed on small roosting birds, fruit and seeds. **Above right:** *Dicoma zeyheri* in the Malolotja Nature Reserve. This perennial plant belongs to the daisy family. **Far right:** The Mbuluzi River gorge in the Mlawula Nature Reserve is sanctuary to more than 350 different bird species. **Right:** 'Winnie', a female hippo imported as a calf into Mlilwane Wildlife Sanctuary from England's famous Whipsnade Zoo.

opened to the public in 1964 and aroused considerable interest – and enthusiastic support from King Sobhuza II, whose chief residence was close by. Since then Mlilwane, in the capable hands of Ted and his wife Liz, has grown to nearly ten times its original size, and now occupies an area of almost 5 000 hectares.

Years ago Mlilwane's mountain slopes were mined for tin, and were left deeply scarred and eroded. Today a dam hides the most visually offensive workings (at the same time providing a home for crocodile, hippo and waterfowl). There is also a series of vleis or shallows along one of the two perennial streams flowing through Mlilwane, leading to the deep pool beside the rest camp. The mining scars have been allowed to grass over and indigenous trees have been planted at strategic points throughout the sanctuary.

One of the most startling sights at the reserve's rest camp is a collection of more than 200 000 poachers' snares – crude wire hoops strung on a cable overhanging a walkway in the rest camp. The snares have been amassed since 1960 – over 6 500 a year – as the rangers wage a never-ending war on poachers.

Mlilwane was Swaziland's pioneer reserve, and its success spawned an awareness of conservation culminating in the formation of the Swaziland National Trust Commission in 1972. The reserve remains a frontrunner – among its visitors are parties of schoolchildren who attend lectures at the National Environmental Education Centre (some 30 000 schoolchildren attend annually).

Phophonyane Nature Reserve

Those who have already savoured Swaziland's imposing line-up of tourist attractions will know that a small stretch of paradise lies tucked away in a nature reserve, about 14 km north of the pretty mountain village of Piggs Peak. The reserve (and lodge) is called Phophonyane – and behind its gates you will find a world where river, mountain, forest, ravine and garden reverberate to a non-stop, combined chorus of songbirds and cascading waterfalls.

Although it is situated within walking distance of one of Swaziland's premier tourist routes, one of the hallmarks of Phophonyane is the privacy it is able to guarantee its visitors. Here, in delightful seclusion, guests can take part in activities that range from footslogging across rugged countryside to drives in luxury minibuses. Several walks and hikes – offering spectacular views of the surrounding countryside – are handy for energetic lovers of the outdoors. But worth considering, too, are the trips (in 4x4 vehicles) to places such as the Mlumati Valley cycad forests, the Nkomati Bushman (San) paintings and the spectacular viewsites along the Sondeza Mountain. Guided tours of sanctuaries such as Malolotja, Mlawula and Hlane are also offered. Luxury minibus tours of nearby Kruger National Park (some 70 km away) are also available.

Phophonyane's attractive accommodation is in the form of two separate self-catering camps. One has double-storeyed thatched cottages decorated in ethnic style, while the second offers a luxurious A-frame cottage. All units are self-contained and fully serviced, and are sited near an à la carte restaurant. Prior booking is essential.

For further information and to make reservations, write to Phophonyane Lodge and Nature Reserve, P O Box 199, Piggs Peak, or telephone (09268) 7-1319.

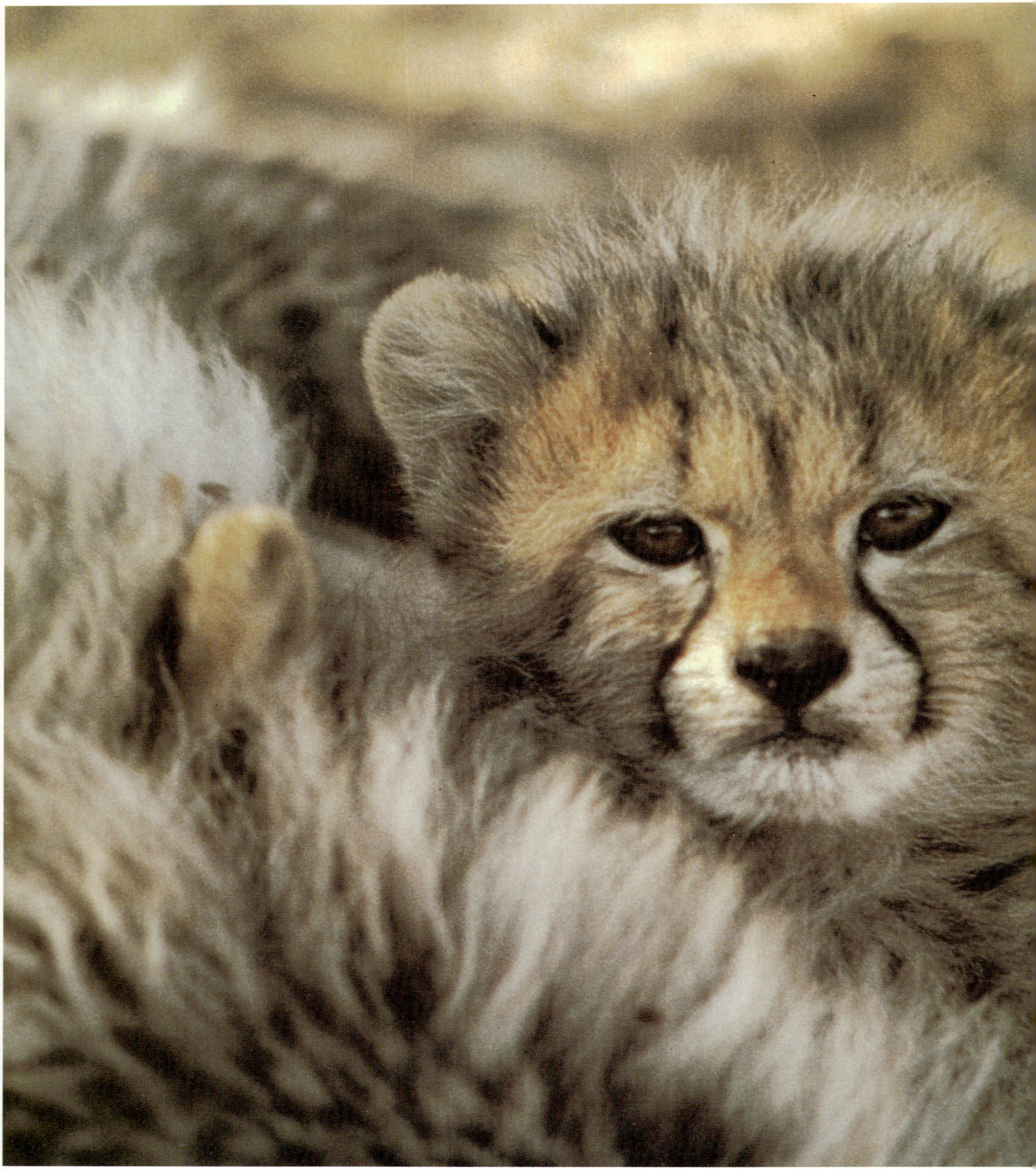

HIGHVELD

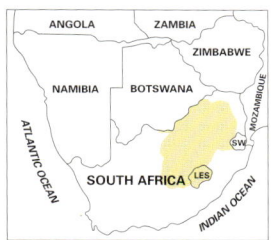

Like waves washing against a sea wall, the green hills of the low country roll westwards until they strike the stark escarpment fringing the plateau of the interior. The locals refer to the escarpment as the 'Edge of the Berg' – a reference to the imposing mountain range that the Voortrekkers dubbed the Drakensberg or 'Dragon's Mountains'. North of the Drakensberg is the east-to-west range known as the Soutpansberg, another impressive boundary between the low country and the interior. Both ranges are cloaked in indigenous and exotic forests.

The country to the west and southwest is often loosely described as Bushveld, a land of sweet and sour grazing and low scrub that merges gently with the windswept Highveld of Mpumalanga and the Free State. To the west are mountain ranges that offer a striking contrast to the spreading plains – the Waterberg and Magaliesberg, overlooking a stretch of Kalahari sand, and the Pilanesberg in the North-West Province.

The Highveld is peppered with a network of game and nature reserves, both provincial and private. Among these are the well-known Blyde River Canyon – popular with holiday-makers and hikers – and, in the far south, the Free State's Tussen die Riviere Nature Reserve. The National Parks Board offers the Golden Gate Highlands National Park, tucked beneath rust-coloured sandstone formations in the Free State. Lesotho's Sehlabathebe National Park is perched on an extension of the Drakensberg, on the eastern edge of this dramatic mountain kingdom.

A baby cheetah photographed at the De Wildt Cheetah Research Centre, west of Pretoria.

Crystal cascades and the river of joy

Seen from the Lowveld, the granite wall of the Drakensberg escarpment seems grey and forbidding. There is no hint of the natural wonderland at the top – verdant forests and myriad mountain streams that create a hundred crystal-clear cascades. The Sabie area features some of the prettiest waterfalls in the whole of southern Africa, and there are more in the Magoebaskloof area west of Tzaneen, and in the Soutpansberg range, running west and east of Louis Trichardt in the north.

Among the escarpment's streams are two named by Hendrik Potgieter's Voortrekkers in 1840. While some of the men descended to the Lowveld to seek a route to the coast, the others (mostly women and children) camped by a watercourse. Weeks went by and, when the men did not return, the women named the stream Treur (Mourning) River and began to return inland. All was well, however, and the scouting party overtook them at a second stream that they named Blyde (Joy) River.

The flow of the Treur and Blyde rivers to the edge of the escarpment is blocked by hard rock that forces them to change course. They meet at right angles with such force that the resulting turbulence has created the famous Bourke's Luck Potholes, later the scene of a frantic, scrabbling rush for gold after its discovery in the area in 1870.

Downstream of the potholes, the running water has worn away the softer rock to create the Blyde River Canyon – centrepiece of an exquisite provincial nature reserve. The Blyde River area, with its mist-shrouded forests and grassy mountain slopes, is a major attraction for hiking enthusiasts. Several trails are also found on the escarpment, including the Fanie Botha, Blyde River Canyon, Prospector's and Magoebaskloof hiking trails, and a number that wind through the Soutpansberg.

Ben Lavin Nature Reserve

One of the most restful hideaways in the Northern Province is a 2 500 ha sanctuary lying 12 km southeast of Louis Trichardt. The reserve was originally a farm owned by Ben Lavin and his wife Molly – both of whom were keen conservationists. When her husband died in the early 1970s, Molly Lavin asked the Wildlife Society of Southern Africa if it would be interested in taking over the farm and running it as a nature reserve. The society took up the offer, and within a few years the farm's

Left: Lichen on a rock in the Blyde River Canyon. **Above:** The awesome beauty of the Blyde River Canyon itself (the cylindrical formations are known as The Three Rondavels). The area is rich in natural treasures, and visitors delight in exploring the hundreds of kilometres of footpaths in and around the reserve. You may see the most northerly remnants of Cape flora, such as true yellowwood, protea and heath, as well as rainforest reminiscent of equatorial jungle, with orchids, ferns and tree moss. There are seven species each of erica and protea, 18 species of everlasting, and four of cycad. The Blyde River Canyon Nature Reserve is considered to be among southern Africa's most beautiful natural showpieces, occupying a large area of the escarpment between the Lowveld and Highveld.

HIGHVELD: **NORTHEASTERN ESCARPMENT**

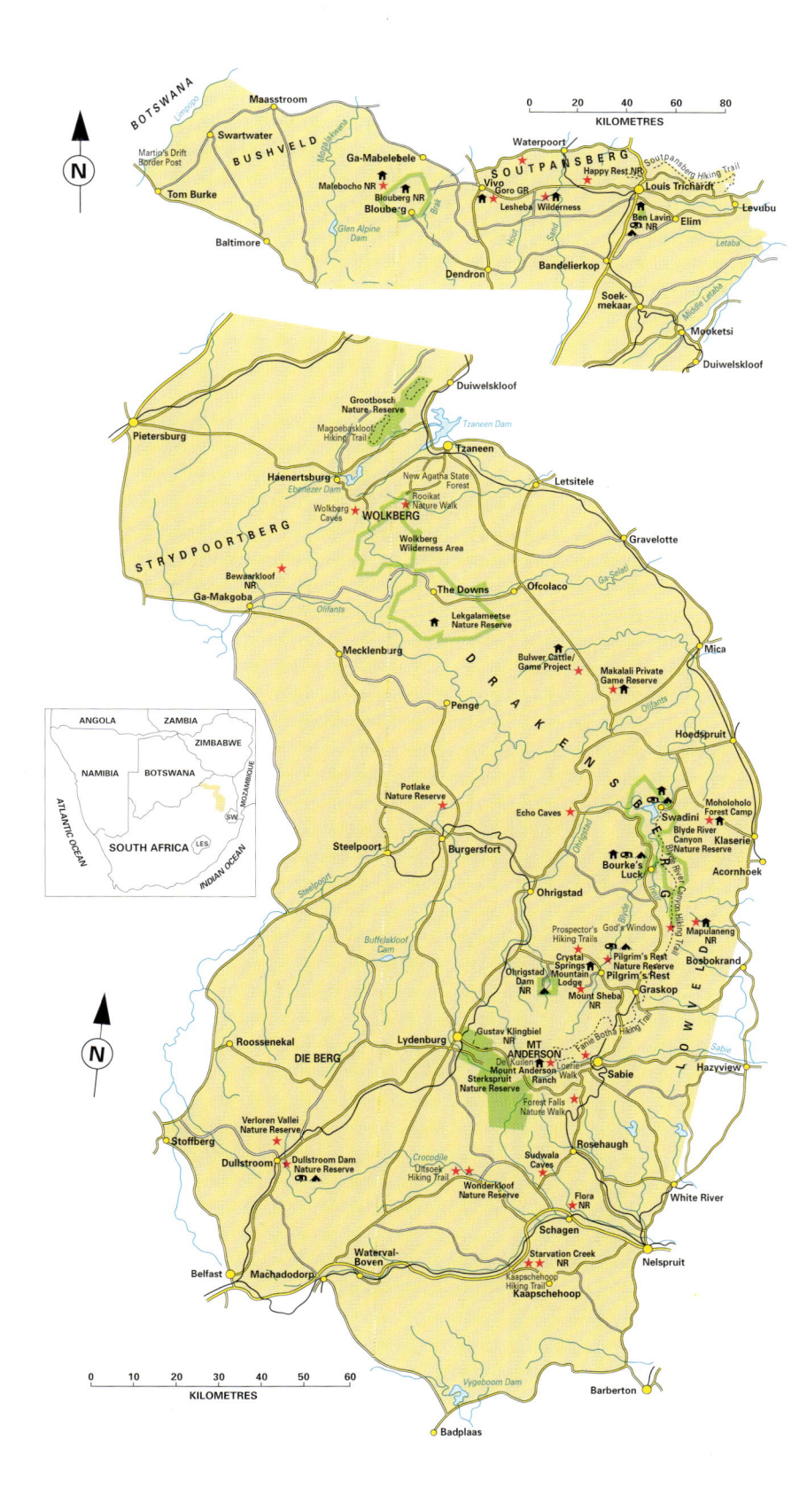

transformation was complete. Neighbouring farmers say that the Ben Lavin reserve has some of the sweetest veld in the province – and it shows. The gently rolling terrain features an unobtrusive, 40 km network of roads and various walking trails, but otherwise nature is in control. Giraffe peer over the tree-tops, impala shelter in the bushes, and blue wildebeest, black-backed jackal and zebra run free on the grassy plains. The reserve is also noted for its prolific birdlife (over 230 species have been recorded), ranging from the large Wahlberg's eagle to the tiny lesser double-collared sunbird. Rare game species, such as tsessebe and red hartebeest, have also been introduced.

Some visitors like to spend time in the three hides overlooking waterholes – one of them only a stone's throw from the shaded rest camp, with its charming two-bed to five-bed thatched cottages. These have electricity and are fully equipped. There are also tents for hire, although visitors may choose to sleep in their own caravans or tents. To reach the Ben Lavin reserve, take the road north from Pietersburg and turn right to Fort Edward, 8 km short of Louis Trichardt. The entrance is reached after 5 km along this road.

The reserve is open daily from 6 a.m. to 2 p.m. Prior arrangements can be made to keep the gate open for visitors arriving from far away. For more information, write to Ben Lavin Nature Reserve, P O Box 782, Louis Trichardt 0920, telephone/fax (015) 516-4534.

Bewaarkloof Nature Reserve

The Strydpoort mountain range is a rugged, steep wilderness area, home to reedbuck, kudu, klipspringer, duiker and the shy leopard. This is the location of the 21 008 ha Bewaarkloof Nature Reserve, falling under the auspices of the Northern Province's Department of Environmental Affairs and Tourism. The reserve is not yet open to the public and, in certain areas, the ore dumps left by discontinued asbestos-mining operations pose a health hazard (they are currently being cleared). However, should you wish to visit Bewaarkloof, the best time to do so would be between April and September, when the mountain sourveld is at its most attractive.

For further information, contact the Department of Environmental Affairs and Tourism, P O Box 217, Pietersburg 0700, telephone (0152) 295-9300, or fax 295-5819.

Blouberg Nature Reserve

Situated in the arid bushveld of the Northern Province, some 15 km from the small town of Vivo, is the 9 360 ha Blouberg Nature Reserve. Its varied topography, ranging from Kalahari sandveld in the north to fynbos-topped mountains, grassveld plains and riverine areas in the south, creates a variety of habitats frequented by diverse game and bird species. Tamboti cluster figs and baobab woods dominate the plains. Game found at Blouberg includes steenbok, grey duiker, impala, eland, kudu, gemsbok, mountain reedbuck, klipspringer, warthog, zebra, giraffe and buffalo. Predators include leopard, cheetah, brown and spotted hyena, and caracal. Over 230 bird species have been recorded, among them being two of the largest breeding colonies of Cape vulture, which occur on the southern side of the reserve. It is also home to 56 types of reptile.

Tamboti Bush Camp offers rustic accommodation for eight people, with beds, mattresses, blankets, chairs, tables, and cooking and eating utensils. Guests must take their own bedding and gas equipment. A second camp, Mashatu, is not yet open to the public.

Blouberg, which lies west of Vivo, is reached along a gravel road which may be corrugated and, although the roads within the reserve are graded regularly, 4x4 vehicles are recommended. Visitors should note that this is a low-risk malaria area.

For further information, contact Blouberg Nature Reserve, P O Box 69, Vivo 0924, telephone (015) 593-0702, or fax 593-0156.

Blyde River Canyon Hiking Trail
Near Graskop, God's Window, with its fine views across the Lowveld, is an important landmark on the northeastern Drakensberg escarpment, marking both the end of the Fanie Botha Trail and the beginning of the trail named after the Blyde River Canyon.

Some enthusiasts combine the two, walking from the Ceylon Forest northwards to Swadini in a nine-day marathon. However, most hikers tramp from God's Window to Swadini, a five-day/65 km trek. For much of its length the trail passes through the reserve that shares its name. Hikers spend most of the second and all of the third day of the hike outside the reserve's boundaries, and the fourth day's route is only just within its perimeter. All the trail's overnight huts are within the reserve and are maintained by its conservation officers.

Fann's Falls, New Chum Falls and Bourke's Luck Potholes are welcome landmarks along the trail route, but most hikers agree that the climax comes with the final leg between Blydepoort and Swadini. The route takes them through magnificent scenery dominated by The Three Rondavels (hillocks clearly visible from the resort), down to the Blyde River and across it by a dramatic suspension bridge (built by the reserve staff), then along the shore of the Blydepoort storage dam. Below the dam wall they rejoin the Blyde River for the final walk to the Aventura Swadini Resort.

The Blyde River Canyon overnight huts accommodate up to 30 hikers at a time, thus setting limits on the number that may tackle the walk. Bunks, mattresses, cooking utensils and firewood are supplied but hikers must provide everything else.

Those accepted for the trail are supplied with detailed maps of the route and helpful lists containing practical advice. To apply for places or request further information, write to Reservations, Blyde River Canyon Nature Reserve, Private Bag X431, Graskop 1270, telephone (01315) 8-1215 or (013) 768-1216, fax 8-1105 or 769-6005. They can also provide information on two other trails through the canyon: the 22 km/two-day Yellowwood Trail and the 40 km/four-day Protea Trail.

Blyde River Canyon Nature Reserve
Several of South Africa's provincial nature reserves fully deserve national park status, and a prime example is that of Mpumalanga's Blyde River Canyon. Few will forget their first glimpse of this breathtaking gorge, the third largest in the world and one of southern Africa's scenic wonders. Its scenery is unsurpassed, its vegetation both varied and lush,

---

BLYDE RIVER CANYON AT A GLANCE

Where to go The reserve and its two resorts are open throughout the year. The resorts tend to be rather crowded at weekends and in school holidays (there is ready access: their gates are manned 24 hours a day).

Reservations and information For information on the reserve as a whole, contact The Officer-in-Charge, Information Section, Blyde River Canyon Nature Reserve, Private Bag X431, Graskop 1270, telephone (01315) 8-1215 or (013) 768-1216, fax 8-1105 or 769-6005.

Addresses for the two resorts are: Aventura Blydepoort Resort, Private Bag X368, Ohrigstad 1122, telephone/fax (01323) 8-0155 or (013) 769-8005; and Aventura Swadini Resort, P O Box 281, Hoedspruit 1380, telephone (01528) 3-5141 or (015) 795-5141, fax (01528) 3-5113 or (015) 795-5113.

Getting there Bourke's Luck, the location of the famous potholes and headquarters of the reserve's nature conservation team, lies close to the public road running along the reserve's western boundary. The entrance to the Aventura Blydepoort Resort is 16 km to the north. As the crow flies, the Aventura Swadini Resort is only a few kilometres away, but the road trip involves a journey of 120 km around the head of the Drakensberg. However, there are alternative routes: visitors may approach from Hoedspruit or Bosbokrand (via Nelspruit) in the Lowveld.

Accommodation The Aventura Blydepoort Resort offers fully equipped chalets with up to five beds in two bedrooms, a sitting room, bathroom and kitchen, and also two-bed suites with sitting room and bathroom but no kitchen. There is a caravan and camping site. The Aventura Swadini Resort provides family chalets with five beds in two bedrooms, sitting-cum-dining room, bathroom, large kitchen and patio. Again, there are well-equipped caravan and camping sites.

Eating and drinking Both the Aventura Blydepoort and Aventura Swadini resorts have licensed restaurants, bottle stores, cafeterias and supermarkets selling, among other goods, fresh meat. There are braai facilities at the chalets and at the caravan and camping area.

Getting around Motoring in the reserve is severely restricted through lack of roads, though the various viewpoints are easy to reach. Lookout points like God's Window and Lowveld View are readily accessible from the public road – the Panorama Route – along the edge of the escarpment.

Hikers, however, can move more freely. There are a number of short nature walks around Aventura Blydepoort Resort and more around Aventura Swadini's visitors' centre; more ambitious hikes begin and end at Bourke's Luck visitors' centre. The reserve also contains sections of the Blyde River Canyon Hiking Trail.

Special attractions The Bourke's Luck and Swadini visitors' centres offer outstanding introductions to the reserve's vegetation and wildlife. The public resorts offer swimming pools, tennis and other entertainment (Aventura Blydepoort also offers horse rides, pony rides and mashie golf).

Wildlife The Blyde River Canyon is more famous for scenery than for its wildlife, but one of its distinctions is that it can claim to have representatives of all southern Africa's primates: chacma baboon (on the mountain slopes), vervet and samango monkey (in the wooded areas), thick-tailed bushbaby (in the montane and riverine forests), and lesser bushbaby (on the savannah grasslands). Other species indigenous to the area include bushbuck, bushpig, mountain reedbuck and the occasional leopard. Impala, waterbuck, kudu, zebra and blue wildebeest have been reintroduced to Swadini.

HIGHVELD: **NORTHEASTERN ESCARPMENT**

Left: The Pinnacle, near Graskop, is one of several features that overlook the great Drakensberg escarpment and the Lowveld. The Blyde River Canyon Nature Reserve, which lies within this majestic sweep of natural beauty, was established in recognition of its scenic appeal. A road known as the Panorama Route leads along the escarpment from Graskop to Quartzkop, taking visitors to viewpoints and picnic sites. From Quartzkop the route leads away from the escarpment and then alongside the canyon to Bourke's Luck Potholes. **Top:** *Protea rubropilosa*, one of the most beautiful species of protea. **Above:** *Athanasia acerosa*, a common sight along the Blyde River Canyon Hiking Trail.

JOCK OF THE DRAKENSBERG

Illustration of an incident described in *Jock of the Bushveld*, by Sir Percy FitzPatrick.

Sir Percy FitzPatrick's *Jock of the Bushveld* is a true and riveting account of the adventures of a young ox-wagon driver and his wonderful dog during the eastern Transvaal's (part of which is now Mpumalanga) gold-mining boom of the 1880s. Most of this moving tale is set in the low country that wagons had to cross on their way between the coast and mining settlements inland, but an entrancing section deals with the steep ascent of the escarpment and the beautiful plateau on its summit. It is in this setting that the dog hero earns the name, Jock of the Drakensberg.

Paradise Camp, south of the Blyde River Canyon, was where transport drivers spent their summers, away from the sweltering humidity of the low country and safe from the tsetse fly. There Jock was reunited with his mother Jess, who belonged to another transport driver.

On one occasion these fearless terriers, their masters and a servant set off to track a leopard. Later, after discovering its lair, they came upon a troop of baboons. As Fitz-Patrick describes, the baboons were responding to the anguished cries of a sentinel. The three men watched as the angry baboons formed an irregular semicircle and slowly advanced down a steep cliff face, throwing handfuls of stones and earth ahead of them.

At first the onlookers could not understand what was happening, but then they spotted the baboons' target – a leopard, sprawled on a rock ledge with its left paw pinning down a baboon.

'The voices from the mountain boomed louder and nearer,' wrote FitzPatrick, 'as, clattering and scrambling down the face, came more and more baboons; there must have been hundreds of them; the semicircle grew thicker and blacker, more and more threatening, foot by foot closer. The tiger [sic] raised himself a little more and took swift looks from side to side across the advancing front, and then his nerve went, and with one spring he shot from the rock into the bush.'

The baboons rushed forward and thronged onto the ledge to rescue their comrade. Two grabbed the injured baboon by the arms and helped him climb the hill. The men stared in fascination as the baboons regrouped, then realised the two dogs were missing: they were after the baboons. FitzPatrick and his companions ran down the cliff in hopes of heading them off, but came to a halt at a steep precipice above a stream. There they took their station, ready to fire on any baboon that might try to attack their dogs.

'With guns gripped and breath held hard, watching intently every bush and tree and rock, every spot of light and shade, we sat not daring to move. Then, over the edge of a big rock overlooking the two dogs, appeared something round; and smoothly yet swiftly and with a snake-like movement, the long spotted body followed the head and, flattened against the rock, crept stealthily forward until the leopard looked straight down upon Jess and Jock.

'Three rifles cracked like one, and with a howl of rage and pain the leopard shot out over the dogs' heads, raced along the stony bed, and suddenly plunging its nose into the ground, pitched over – dead!'

and the rich selection of birdlife includes a breeding colony of the rare bald ibis.

The canyon from which the reserve takes its name cuts nearly 20 km through the escarpment's granite, and in some places is 700 m deep. Just over halfway down, the swift-flowing Blyde River is joined by the Ohrigstad River from the west. Here engineers have built an unobtrusive dam wall in a bottleneck below the confluence. The result is the Blyde Dam.

The Blyde Dam is the heart of the reserve, but its nerve centre is the nature conservation team's headquarters at Bourke's Luck. Close by, a network of pathways and footbridges allows visitors to explore the potholes (some of which are 6 m deep) at the confluence of the Blyde and Treur rivers. Another attraction at Bourke's Luck is the visitors' centre, which has numerous interesting displays. A newly developed, 180 m circular trail, accessible to the physically disabled, starts at the visitors' centre and has as its main theme the lichens found in the area. Wildlife in the canyon area is as varied as the habitats. There are mountain reedbuck on the escarpment, dassies on the canyon walls, hippo and crocodile in the Blyde Dam, and impala, kudu, blue wildebeest, waterbuck and zebra on the Lowveld plain near the canyon's mouth.

To most visitors, the 24 984 ha reserve is a two-level attraction to be approached from either west or east. A public road runs along the long western boundary and there is easy access to beauty spots like The Pinnacle, God's Window with its kloof-framed view of the Lowveld, Bourke's Luck, and a lookout point fronting on The Three Rondavels – unusually shaped hillocks that are also visible from the Aventura Blydepoort Resort, a short distance to the north. Anyone wanting to explore the upper level more carefully should take to the trails from this resort.

The eastern approach, at Lowveld level, is via a road that enters the reserve on the flank of Mariepskop and follows the canyon bottom to the Aventura Resort at Swadini. This resort represents a good example of planning: the dam-builders lived in the houses that now function as chalets for visitors.

Beyond, the road continues to the nature conservation visitors' centre, built on high ground overlooking the Blyde Dam. In effect, the reserve's lower level is quite separate from the upper, and offers quite different experiences. The only direct link between them is the final leg of the relatively undemanding Blyde River Canyon Hiking Trail, and even that is strictly one-way (a cableway link is currently under consideration).

Bulwer Cattle/Game Project

Situated some 60 km south of Tzaneen off the R36 to Lydenburg is the 1 600 ha Bulwer Cattle/

HIGHVELD: **NORTHEASTERN ESCARPMENT**

Game Project, established for cattle research. Generally a hunting camp, the farm is opened between hunting seasons to visitors who wish to view the game. Impala, bushbuck, kudu, reedbuck and waterbuck can be seen, as well as many fine examples of arid Lowveld vegetation. Visitors are advised to use 4x4 vehicles, as the gravel roads are bad, especially after rain. Accommodation is available in a five-bed, thatched chalet with bathroom, kitchen, patio and braai facilities. There are no hiking trails, but guests are free to walk around the farm. For details and to make reservations, contact The Officer-in-Charge, Lekgalameetse Nature Reserve, Private Bag X408, Trichardtsdal 0890, telephone (0152302) and ask for 15.

Crystal Springs Mountain Lodge
Tucked in the wooded mountains some 10 km to the west of Pilgrim's Rest, is Crystal Springs Mountain Lodge, a tranquil haven for hikers and outdoor enthusiasts.

This 5 000 ha reserve, which offers accommodation in four-bed, six-bed and eight-bed chalets at the Crystal Springs Mountain Lodge, as well as in 28 comfortable suites, is popular for its clear mountain air, its wildlife and its trails, all of which are between 4 km and 6 km in length. These meander through the mountains, revealing dams, hides, a waterfall and splendid views around every turn. Wildlife includes caracal, zebra, bushpig, kudu, eland, waterbuck, klipspringer and other species of antelope, and, if you're lucky, you may catch a glimpse of the elusive leopard.

Visitors may use the restaurant, braai facilities, fully equipped kitchens, swimming pools and laundry. The reserve is open year round. For more information, contact Crystal Springs Mountain Lodge, P O Box 10, Pilgrim's Rest 1290, telephone/fax (013) 768-1153.

Dullstroom Dam Nature Reserve
Dullstroom lies tucked below the Steenkampsberg range some 33 km north of Belfast. Known to botanists because of its unique sub-Alpine climate and vegetation, Dullstroom is one of the coldest towns in South Africa.

On the outskirts of the village is the Dullstroom Dam, well known for its trout and the nature reserve that surrounds it. The reserve is the perfect spot from which to explore this lovely area, with its twinkling streams, dramatic kloofs and gulleys, rich birdlife and fascinating flora. There are caravan and camping sites within the reserve area itself and, in the vicinity, a number of lodges, hotels and private farms offer accommodation.

Various hiking trails traverse the area, including the Ratelspruit Trail, Misty Valley Hiking trails, Trout Royalty trails and Salpeterkrans Trail – all on privately owned land. For more detailed information, you should write to The Town Clerk, P O Box 1, Dullstroom 1110, or telephone/fax (01325) 4-0261.

Echo Caves
In 1923 a farmer bought land in the hills north of Ohrigstad, and an elder in the local community told him of an underground river that had created a network of caves in the dolomite. Years earlier, Bushmen (San), Swazis and others had periodically taken refuge in the caves with their cattle. The farmer was able to turn the caves to his advantage. First he excavated large quantities of bat guano – valuable as a fertiliser – then he used the caves to dry tobacco. Eventually he decided to develop them as a tourist attraction.

Above: Bourke's Luck Potholes, at the confluence of the Treur and Blyde rivers, where the grinding action of sand and pebbles has hollowed out formations in the soft rock. **Right:** A cuckoo wasp about to enter the mud nest of a mud-dauber wasp, where it will parasitise the larvae. The emerging parasitic larva feeds on the host larva (or on its food supply). When fully grown, the parasite spins a cocoon inside the cell, emerging as an adult the following season.

Cave explorers say that the complex stretches a considerable distance, but today only a small portion is open to the public. A tour guide taps dripstone stalactites with a rubber hammer and produces the ringing echoes for which the caves are named. According to legend, they are the tomb of a party of mysterious white-robed strangers. Local people distrusted them and led the newcomers to the caves, where they were immured in a side passage. Historians have speculated that the strangers were early Arab traders in search of gold.

The remains of skeletons have been found, but they are those of Bushmen (San) or Swazis. These are displayed at a small Museum of Man in a Bushman-painted shelter close to the caves' approach road. Because of their historic importance, the caves have been proclaimed a national monument. They are open throughout the year from 8 a.m. to 5 p.m. and are reached from a signposted turn-off west of the road between Ohrigstad and the Strijdom Tunnel, 23 km north of Ohrigstad. There is a motel at the caves. For information, write to The Manager, Echo Caves Motel, P O Box 34, Ohrigstad 1122, telephone (01323) 8-0015, fax 8-0301.

Fanie Botha Hiking Trail

The Fanie Botha Hiking Trail, opened in 1973, is one of the best-known of the country's nature trails, revealing the green splendour of the Highveld Drakensberg at close quarters. A five-day/79 km trek, the Fanie Botha trail is not for the faint-hearted. Hikers depart from the Ceylon Forest Station (close to Sabie), tramp through Tweefontein and Mac-Mac forests, and pass the town of Graskop to reach the trail's end at God's Window. Those with less time or energy may end or start the trail at Mac-Mac Forest Station, take shorter routes, or opt for any of a number of two- to four-day routes available. Another alternative route passes through Pilgrim's Rest to join the Prospector's Hiking Trail (see separate entry).

Hikers regard the Fanie Botha trail as one of the most strenuous of the trails in this area. The route passes Lone Creek Falls, crosses the eastern slopes of Mount Anderson (2 277 m) and, if hikers are not tempted to take a short cut, Mac-Mac Falls and the cool Mac-Mac Pools a few kilometres downstream, which are among several welcome swimming spots along the route. It was to this region that large numbers of foreigners flocked after the discovery of gold in 1873. When the president of the then Zuid-Afrikaansche Republiek (later the Transvaal), T F Burgers, visited the area, he named it Mac-Mac after the numerous Scotsmen he encountered.

The Pinnacle, a 30 m tower of rock that rises steeply from the bottom of a densely wooded gorge, is a landmark on the later stages of the walk. God's Window, which affords magnificent views over the patchwork of Lowveld plantations, marks the end of the route and the start of the Blyde River Canyon Hiking Trail (see separate entry). Overnight huts on the trail accommodate up to 30 people. Bunks with mattresses are provided, as are fireplaces, firewood, and toilets. Those who embark on the hike must have the necessary permits and must adhere to the arrangements they have made: in particular, they must sleep at their assigned hut, as the others may already be full.

Starting points for the Fanie Botha Trail at the Ceylon Forest Station are reached from Sabie (there is a signposted turn-off on the R532 to Graskop) and the President Burgers Hut near Mac-Mac Forest Station (on the R532 from Sabie to Graskop, 11 km from Graskop). The trail may be tackled year round but the most popular times are school holidays and weekends from spring to autumn.

For more information, or to apply for the necessary permits, write to SAFCOL, Private Bag X503, Sabie 1260, telephone (013) 764-1058, fax 764-2071.

Flora Nature Reserve

Situated between Nelspruit and Lydenburg in the striking Mpumalanga Drakensberg, this small (47 ha) reserve was created for the protection of one cycad species, *Encephalartos humilis*, which is unique to the area.

There is an exquisite little waterfall, part of a stream that (lower down) joins others to form the Houtbosloop River. The reserve is open during daylight hours, and a permit is required. Further information is available from SAFCOL, Private Bag X503, Sabie 1260, telephone (013) 764-1058, fax 764-2071.

Forest Falls Nature Walk

The neat picnic place sited near Mac-Mac Forest Station marks the start (and finish) of a short walk to the Forest Falls.

Walkers amble comfortably through a pine plantation and pockets of shady indigenous forest – a round trip of some 4 km – to reach these beautiful falls, which have been spared the ravages of overexposure to the public because they lie a little off the tourist route. Across the road from the picnic site are the graves of pioneering miners, and a swimming hole. Permits are not required, but those wishing to visit the falls may obtain a map from SAFCOL, Private Bag X503, Sabie 1260, telephone (013) 764-1058, or fax 764-2071.

Goro Game Reserve

This private reserve, proclaimed in 1995, covers 5 000 ha of bushveld wilderness east of Vivo and west of Louis Trichardt. Guests stay in rustic stone, reed and thatch cottages, either fully serviced or self-catering, from which they can explore the surrounding countryside. Wilderness walks, under the able guidance of professional rangers, and gameviewing drives by day or night are offered (over 50 mammal species, including leopard and Hartmann's zebra, find sanctuary here). More than 230 bird species have been recorded.

The lodge caters for a maximum of eight visitors. To get there, drive north from Pietersburg to Vivo along the R521. Drive north from Vivo for 6 km, then turn right onto the R523. The reserve entrance is 19 km further along on the right. Advance booking is essential. Contact Goro Game Reserve, P O Box 144, Vivo 0924, telephone/fax (01554) 645 for details.

Grootbosch Nature Reserve

Some of the finest of all South Africa's indigenous forests are in the Magoebaskloof area

Left: Mac-Mac Falls. The story goes that the falls (and the siding bearing the same name) refer to the Scottish diggers who worked the gold fields in the Pilgrim's Rest district. **Right above:** A vervet monkey with its young. This is an agile, intelligent monkey found in dense bush and thick forests. It lives in family groups of 6 to 20 (occasionally as many as 100), spending its day feeding (on fruit, insects, leaves, shoots, birds' eggs and sometimes crops), grooming, and producing the cacophony typical of its kind. Vervet monkeys may be recognised by their black- and yellow-flecked fur (with white patches on the cheeks, forehead, stomach and throat) and black-tipped tail (the male's scrotum is bright blue). Their major enemies are leopards and large birds of prey. **Far right:** Dense vegetation in one of the Magoebaskloof forests. In some areas the undergrowth is so thick as to be impenetrable, and visitors might be excused for thinking they were in a South American jungle. **Right below:** A spiny coreid bug (*Pephricus livingstonei*).

around Tzaneen. Large parts of this beautiful region, including well-known landmarks such as Debengeni Falls, are protected within the 4 625 ha Grootbosch Nature Reserve.

Typical evergreens found here include real yellowwood, broom, cluster fig, bastard stinkwood, wild peach and forest elder. These give shade and shelter to leopard, oribi, the rare samango monkey and red duiker. The densely wooded mountain slopes are often shrouded in soft mist; summers are humid and winters are dry and cold. About once every ten years, a snowfall delights locals and visitors alike.

Wild, beautiful and unspoilt – the area can be explored on the strenuous, three-day Grootbosch, and the slightly less arduous, also three-day, Dokolewa sections of the Magoebaskloof Trail (see separate entry). In addition, motorists can venture through the forest on the Forest Drive.

More information can be obtained from SAFCOL, Private Bag X503, Sabie 1260, telephone (013) 764-1058, or fax 764-2071.

Gustav Klingbiel Nature Reserve

During the 1950s the Lydenburg Town Council, at the instigation of one of its members, Gustav Klingbiel, began introducing game species on municipal land east of the town. Today blesbok, eland, kudu, Burchell's zebra, giraffe, blue wildebeest and smaller antelope can be seen on the reserve which bears the name of its champion. Four trails, one of which has an overnight hut, meander through the reserve, which also has a museum illustrating the town's history – this is open daily. Unfortunately, in August 1996 this sanctuary was badly damaged by fire.

Before visiting, obtain updated information from The Town Clerk, Lydenburg Municipality, P O Box 61, Lydenburg 1120, telephone (01323) 5-1108, or fax 2121.

Happy Rest Nature Reserve

The reserve, situated on the southern slopes of the Soutpansberg, lies 18 km west of Louis Trichardt and covers an area of 2 700 hectares. It extends from the green-swathed foothills of the mountains to the top of its high cliffs, embracing striking scenery, and including a group of rare cycads (*Encephalartos transvenosus*). There are also many indigenous trees such as Outeniqua yellowwood, lemonwood, marula, Bushman's tea, baobab and waterberry. Most of South Africa's snakes are found in the reserve, while mammals include kudu, impala, red duiker, bushbuck, leopard, bushpig, porcupine and jackal. Among the bird species are black eagle, breeding pairs of snake eagle, and both helmeted and crested guinea fowl.

Also at Happy Rest is one of the province's environmental education centres for high-school students, at which participants learn the ways of the wild.

The reserve, managed by the Directorate of Nature and Environmental Conservation, is open to those interested in hiking or using the environmental centre. For more information, contact The Principal, Schoemansdal Environmental Education Centre, P O Box 737, Louis Trichardt 0920, telephone (015) 516-4273, or fax 516-2586.

Kaapschehoop Hiking Trail

Two disused railway coaches (called 'Barretts') at the Berlin Forest Station are the somewhat unusual base camp for some magnificent mountain trails near Kaapschehoop. The trail system, consisting of two circular routes (each of which can be hiked separately), can be hiked over three to five days and covers a total of 60 kilometres.

The Coetzeestroom Circle winds through pine plantations from Barretts Coaches to the Coetzeestroom overnight hut for some 17 km, although a shorter route of 10 km is also available. On the second day, hikers return to Barretts via a selection of routes, all offering panoramic views across the indigenous forest of Coetzeestroom. The trail also passes Blouswawelvlakte, site of the breeding ground of the endangered blue swallow. The Wattles two-day route covers 24 to 28 km of fairly level ground and is more suitable for beginners and the less energetic. Several geological sites are a focal point of this route. Animals in the area include vervet monkey, baboon, oribi, bushbuck, mountain reedbuck and bushpig, as well as more than 200 bird species.

Kaapschehoop's mountain region is the site of one of the country's earliest (and least successful) gold rushes. A thousand dreams of riches must have died among the old stone buildings and mine shafts you will see dotted along the side of the mountain.

Accommodation for hikers is provided at Barretts Coaches, and at overnight huts which are equipped with bunks, mattresses, toilets, fireplaces and firewood. A maximum of 30 hikers is allowed. The trail starts 33 km west of Nelspruit. For more information, contact SAFCOL, Private Bag X503, Sabie 1260, telephone (013) 764-1058, or fax 764-2071.

Lekgalameetse Nature Reserve

South of the Wolkberg Wilderness Area (see separate entry) lies 18 750 ha of jagged mountains, caves, sinkholes, sparkling streams and deep forested gorges – a reserve ideal for hikers, birdwatchers and lovers of nature.

Seven luxury log cabins, nestled in a kloof, provide idyllic accommodation from which visitors are able to venture on short day trips to natural swimming holes in the crystal-clear mountain water of the Makhutswi River. Also an attraction are two trails – a two-day route and a three-day circular route.

At Lekgalameetse you will find a mosaic of grassland, woodland and forest. In the cool, high-lying valleys, moist carpets of epiphytic orchids are found near the giant yellowwood, Natal mahogany, protea and matumi. Botanists will be interested to note that more than 1 200 plant species have been recorded.

The reserve is renowned for its rare butterflies, many of which have still to be classified. Other animals which can be seen here are mountain reedbuck, eland, bushbuck, duiker, klipspringer, baboon, vervet monkey, samango monkey, black-backed jackal, honey badger, zebra and leopard. At night you will see the glinting eyes of bushbaby, lesser bushbaby, genet and civet.

Lekgalameetse lies some 60 km southwest of Tzaneen. Further information can be requested by writing to The Officer-in-Charge, Lekgalameetse Nature Reserve, Private Bag X408, Trichardtsdal 0890, telephone (0152302) ask for 15, or ask for 43 to send a fax.

Lesheba Wilderness

Some private game lodges in the northern Highveld are far bigger than Lesheba Wilderness. Others have camps that are more luxurious. But few can claim to match the feeling of old-time romance that permeates this 2 600 ha 'naturalist's retreat', situated between the towns of Vivo and Louis Trichardt.

The fact that Lesheba is stocked with an enormous diversity of wild animals, exotic birds, rare plants and giant trees can be attributed to just one thing: its location.

A subtropical setting atop the Soutpansberg means balmy temperatures and abundant rainfall; good rains mean succulent vegetation – which, in turn, means an influx of different species of bird and mammal. The rare Cape vulture, the black eagle and the purple-crested

Left: *Impatiens sylvicola*, a small perennial plant which grows on the edges of forests in the Northern Province. This specimen was photographed at Magoebaskloof in October. **Right:** A hawk-moth caterpillar displays its highly effective defence – false eyes which it uses to scare off enemies. **Below:** Ohrigstad Dam Nature Reserve, near Lydenburg. Visitors to this attractive reserve are likely to see a variety of buck (summer is the best time to visit).

lourie are some of the birds that have found homes here. Among the mammals that can be seen are leopard, sable antelope, monkey and white rhino.

A bonus for nature lovers (as well as photographers) is the magnificent scenery provided by the jagged cliffs, deep gorges and giant, eroded rocks. Hiking enthusiasts may follow any of the 14 trails that wind and weave through Lesheba. Abseiling and mountain biking facilities are also available.

Accommodation is provided at the traditional Venda village camp, Rahledziva. Duluni Camp sleeps 12, while Hamasha and Venda camps each sleep eight. All camps are equipped with their own washbasin, flush toilet and convenient gas-heated shower. Kitchens are equipped with a hotplate, a refrigerator and a freezer. Braai areas have been set up outside. Visitors are requested to book in advance.

Lesheba is currently being developed as a health farm, where the city-worn can retreat for one to two weeks to regain their mental and physical composure. For further information, write to Lesheba Wilderness, P O Box 795, Louis Trichardt 0920, or telephone/fax (015) 593-0076.

Loerie Walk

The Bridal Veil Falls and the lesser Glynis and Elna falls to the northeast are prime attractions of the 1 km Loerie Walk, which begins and ends at the Ceylon Forest Station, some 6 km from Sabie, or alternatively at the Castle Rock Municipal Caravan Park on the outskirts of the town. The walk leads through grassveld, indigenous forest and plantations of pines and bluegums. For further information, write to SAFCOL, Private Bag X503, Sabie 1260, telephone (013) 764-1058, or fax 764-2071.

Magoebaskloof Hiking Trail

The Dokolewa and the Grootbosch hiking trails provide two walking adventures in a setting of great beauty. Hikers tramp through plantations of exotic pine trees and through Grootbosch, the largest indigenous evergreen forest in the Northern Province.

On the Dokolewa section, the easier of the two trails, hikers cover 36 km over three days. The route twists and turns through plantations and green mountain valleys – look out for the graceful forest tree ferns – to the foot of the escarpment, then ascends to a contour path from which there are breathtaking views over the Lowveld and Tzaneen. The path then leads to the top of the escarpment to reach the Helpmekaar Forest, before shadowing the northern slopes of Magoebaskloof to reach the starting point at Dokolewa. Groups of up to 30 hikers are permitted at a time, and are accommodated in huts along the way. The huts are equipped only with essentials, such as firewood, cooking pots, lamps, bunks, mattresses, toilets and water. Hikers must provide their own food and sleeping bags.

The 50 km/3-day Grootbosch section is to be attempted only by the very fit, and has overnight facilities on the first night only. For the remaining two nights, hikers sleep in simple overnight shelters, with no facilities. Hikers must provide their own food, kindling, first-aid equipment and sleeping bags. Groups may not exceed 12 people and, as the Grootbosch hut can accommodate only eight, it is advisable to carry a tent.

The trail, however, provides wonderful rewards for those intrepid enough to attempt it. It starts at the Dokolewa Hut, branching off after 10 km to follow an existing forest track,

---

PROTEAS OF THE NORTHEAST

Protea simplex, photographed in the Wolkberg area of the Northern Province.

The great Swedish botanist Carl Linnaeus named the genus *Protea* after a Greek god who was said to be able to change his shape at will. Africa south of the Sahara offers at least 114 species of protea, and 13 of them are found in summer-rainfall areas of Mpumalanga and the Northern Province.

One of the most attractive of the summer-rainfall proteas is the rosy pink *Protea caffra*, also known as the suikerbossie or sugar bush. Heidelberg's Suikerbosrand (or Sugar Bush Ridge) is named after the species, as is the nature reserve that has been established there. The sugar bush is also found in the Magaliesberg and on mountains to the east and south. It blooms in winter and is often confused with *Protea gaguedi*, which grows in the same areas and flowers during summer.

Protea rubropilosa is the prettiest of the proteas found in the northern parts of the country, and earns its name from the hairy red-brown covering on its bracts (petals). This shrub blooms in spring and is found in the Blyde River Canyon and Wolkberg areas. *Protea laetans* is a newly discovered species growing in the canyon.

Most of the proteas found in Mpumalanga and the Northern Province are tree varieties, and they include one of the rarest: the Barberton sugar bush or *Protea comptonii*, found only in the mountains around Barberton. The tree grows up to 6 m tall and in winter produces an array of white to pinkish flowers. As with all the species found in the area (except the *Protea roupelliae*) the bloom's petals are shorter than the flower head., which is 10 to 15 cm in diameter.

The protea is not peculiar to South Africa. Twenty-three species were grown in England's famous Kew Gardens in 1810, and they grow readily in the Scilly Isles, California and Australia.

Although these beautiful plants are usually associated with the southwestern Cape, the species found further north are a rich and colourful constituent of the province's floral heritage.

HIGHVELD: NORTHEASTERN ESCARPMENT

and crossing three mountain streams before nightfall. The route then climbs to the summit of a spur in the northern Drakensberg, winding through indigenous forest which clears every now and again to reveal spectacular Lowveld views. The third day brings a steep climb and crystal-clear waterfalls, before entering the Grootbosch plantation for the last leg of the journey.

Both trails start from the De Hoek Forest Station, in De Hoek Forest, about 22 km from Tzaneen. The hut is reached from the R71 between Tzaneen and Pietersburg (take the Debengeni Waterfall turn-off and follow the road to the forest station). Make reservations well in advance by writing to SAFCOL, Private Bag X503, Sabie 1260, or telephone (013) 764-1058, or fax 764-2071.

Makalali Private Game Reserve

This mighty reserve – 10 000 ha near Hoedspruit and Phalaborwa – lies on the banks of the Makhutswi River. The landscape here is a dusty combination of rugged bushveld, hills, mopane woodland and lushly vegetated riverine thickets, while, in the distance, visitors can see the rise of the mighty Drakensberg mountains. The 'Big Five' find sanctuary here, as do the rare sable antelope and numerous other buck species. Birdlife and reptiles are prolific.

Visitors are accommodated in three luxury 12-bed camps, within walking distance of one another. Each has its own swimming pool, boma and central living area, and is fully serviced. Every room has its own viewing platform. Guided game walks are offered, as are photographic and birding safaris, cultural tours and night-sky excursions. Guests may choose to visit Makalali by car or to take advantage of one of their fly-in packages. Precautions against malaria are advised.

For more detailed information, write to Conservation Corporation Africa, Private Bag X27, Benmore 2010, or telephone (011) 784-6832, fax 784-7532.

Malebocho Nature Reserve

The Soutpansberg is an area of dramatic contrast – ridges of quartz, sandstone and shale rise above a striking landscape and vegetation that ranges from thorny savannah to dense indigenous forests. This is the setting of the Malebocho Nature Reserve, near Blouberg Nature Reserve (see separate entry), further along the Blouberg mountain range.

Malebocho is home to a rich variety of bird species, and its game includes giraffe, ostrich, zebra, impala, gemsbok, blue wildebeest, waterbuck, kudu, eland, hartebeest and smaller antelope. The area is also known for its indigenous forests of true yellowwood and other trees. A selection of gameviewing drives is on offer (a 4x4 vehicle is recommended), and a picnic site has been laid out at the entrance gate. Accommodation is available in three 6-bed, thatched A-frame chalets with ablution facilities and a communal kitchen. There is a thatched lapa with braai facilities at the camp. Hunters are catered for during the season. Visitors should note that this is a low-risk malaria area.

The reserve, which covers 4 828 ha along the northwestern slopes of the Blouberg range, is administered by the Northern Province's Department of Environmental Affairs and Tourism. Note that the access roads to both Malebocho and Blouberg are gravel and may be corrugated. For information and to make reservations, contact The Officer-in-Charge, Blouberg Nature Reserve, P O Box 69, Vivo 0924, telephone (015) 593-0702, fax 593-0156.

Mapulaneng Nature Reserve

Hiking enthusiasts will be pleasantly surprised to discover this wonderland of forests, streams and mountains in Mapulaneng Nature Reserve – only a hop away from the Blyde River Canyon Hiking Trail.

A comfortable, fully equipped log cabin is the focal point of the reserve and from here hikers tackle either the Tambourine Trail which runs for some 17 km, or the shorter Trogon trails covering a distance of 11 kilometres.

Paths lead beneath the humid, dripping forest with its yellowwood, stinkwood and Cape chestnut trees, passing orchid, slippery moss and dripping liana vines. Through the trees you will catch fleeting glimpses of the spectacular Drakensberg and beautiful forest birds such as the Knysna and purple-crested lourie, and spectacular Narina trogon. There are also many butterflies and monkeys.

Accommodation is available in three chalets, two with six beds and the third with four beds. All are fully equipped.

The 6 600 ha nature reserve is reached by a turn-off 30 km north of Bosbokrand on the road to Hoedspruit. Bookings for accommodation should be made to Department of Environmental Affairs and Tourism, P O Box 217, Pietersburg 0700, telephone (0152) 295-3025, or fax 291-2654.

Moholoholo Forest Camp and Wildlife Rehabilitation Centre

Enveloped by tranquil Drakensberg rainforest and Lowveld acacia woodland, Moholoholo Forest Camp (some 900 ha) is tucked into the slopes of Moholoholo (also known as Mariepskop) Mountain. Visitors can take guided or self-led walks through the indigenous forest, or take advantage of the day and night drives offered, to see the game.

Giraffe, eland, sable, tsessebe, nyala, bushbuck, kudu, wildebeest, hyena, jackal, leopard, warthog and bushpig are among the many specimens that find sanctuary here. More than 300 species of bird have been recorded, including 34 raptors.

Up to 14 visitors can stay in thatched huts on stilts, each with en suite facilities. The reserve also offers training and educational courses for ranger guides, game-farm owners, and school and conservation groups. Tours of the reserve's wildlife rehabilitation centre, where the animals can be seen at close range, are available.

Moholoholo Forest Camp lies some 15 km west of Klaserie. To obtain further information, contact Moholoholo Forest Camp, P O Box

Above: *Moraea spathulata*. The flowers of this plant grow at the tips of long stems, and generally appear in autumn in Mpumalanga (in the eastern Cape it flowers in spring). The plant forms a large clump of long, green leaves (they grow to over a metre in length) with prominent midribs. **Top:** *Amanita muscaria* (or fly agaric) in its juvenile button form. This mushroom, photographed near Lydenburg, is hallucinogenic and highly poisonous.

HIGHVELD: **NORTHEASTERN ESCARPMENT**

Right: A newly hatched rainbow trout, with the yolk sac still attached to its body (fingerlings subsist initially on the yolk). The rainbow trout, recognised by the iridescent red-mauve stipe on its sides, was imported from America in 1897 and introduced to South African dams and rivers. Hatcheries throughout the country ensure a continuous supply of healthy stocks. The anatomical structure of the trout allows milt or ova to be expressed by hand without injuring the fish. Ova are expressed from the hen fish into a bowl, and the milt from a cock fish is added (together with water). The fertilised ova are washed and placed on trays in hatching troughs through which well-oxygenated water is circulated. When the ova reach the 'eyed' stage, some are packed in damp moss and taken to other hatcheries, while others are retained and hatched for use as breeding stock.

1476, Hoedspruit 1380, telephone/fax (01528) 3-5236 or (015)795-5236.

Mount Anderson Ranch
A newly established luxury reserve high in the Mpumalanga Drakensberg, Mount Anderson Ranch is a 7 000 ha conservancy owned by Michael Rattray, of Mala Mala and Mashatu fame. Previous overgrazing had left the area denuded, ravaged by soil erosion and open to invasion by exotic vegetation.

Wattle trees and other aliens were removed to make way for the regrowth of natural montane vegetation and, before long, several animal species – locally absent for many years – moved back to the region. These included baboon, African wild cat and black-backed jackal, while zebra, black wildebeest, oribi, kudu, blesbok, eland and other antelope species were reintroduced. The streams, partially dammed with weirs, were stocked with brown and rainbow trout.

Visitors to Mount Anderson are accommodated in three double rooms, all *en suite*, with lounges, a dining room, games room and verandah overlooking the trout ponds. Expert fly-fishermen and game guides cater for the visitors' needs – game may be viewed on foot, from a vehicle or on horseback.

Also to be seen are numerous relics of the gold-mining operation that was established in this area in the 1870s. For further information about Mount Anderson, write to Rattray Reserves, P O Box 2575, Randburg 2125, or telephone (011) 789-2677, or fax 886-4382.

Mount Sheba Nature Reserve
Mining and forestry ventures long ago put paid to most of the indigenous forest of the Pilgrim's Rest area, but an impressive remnant survives on a 400 ha private nature reserve that hugs the slopes of the towering Mount Sheba. The reserve, founded and established by Iain Crabtree in 1963, was proclaimed in 1967. It took on a fresh lease of life when new owners transformed the rest camp into a luxury hotel. Exquisite surroundings, dramatic architecture and the natural charm of the reserve make the hotel very appealing.

At least 1 000 plant species have been identified, among them 100 tree species, 60-odd ferns and some terrestrial and tree orchids. They can be seen to advantage in the course of forest walks – some strenuous and others less so. A drive to the top of Mount Sheba provides views over the whole area. To reach the reserve, drive west from Pilgrim's Rest and follow the signs to the Mount Sheba Hotel.

For reservations or further information, contact Mount Sheba Hotel, P O Box 100, Pilgrim's Rest 1290, telephone (013) 768-1241.

Mpumalanga Parks Board and Development Facility
Lydenburg's attractions include the 40 ha landscaped grounds of the province's largest research station, a centre renowned for its advanced work on fish. The institute has several laboratories, a large reference library, and is the home of the F C Braun Aquarium, named after a local jeweller who founded a 'trout protection society' in the 1920s. In 25 years the organisation introduced 600 000 trout fingerlings to streams in the Lydenburg district. The aquarium features examples of most of the species to be found in Mpumalanga waters, among them indigenous species including tilapia and yellowfish, and exotics such as trout, carp and black bass.

The aquarium is open daily from 8 a.m. to 4 p.m. To reach the complex, follow the signs from a turn-off on the road between Lydenburg and Sabie. For further information, telephone (01323) 2395 or (013) 235-2395, fax (01323) 2732 or (013) 235-2732.

Ohrigstad Dam Nature Reserve
The hilly country west of Mount Sheba features an important water-storage dam on the Ohrigstad River. The dam is the centrepiece of a 2 400 ha Mpumalanga Parks Board reserve that stretches both upstream and downstream and consists of grass-grown hills and ridges, and densely wooded ravines and kloofs. The reserve is situated about 40 km from Lydenburg. Ohrigstad's wide variety of flora includes several species of orchid and aloe, and also the intriguing 'resurrection plant' (*Myrothamnus flabellifolius*), so named because in the dry

Above: Autumn wreathes the landscape around Pilgrim's Rest with shades of russet, contrasting with its green-clad hills, which once echoed with the ring of the picks and shovels used by hopeful gold-prospectors.

season it appears dead and brittle. After a shower its branches are revitalised, becoming soft and supple.

Ohrigstad's birdlife includes some aquatic species, as well as the purple-crested lourie, Narina trogon and Piet-my-vrou (or red-chested cuckoo). Indigenous game includes eland, klipspringer, mountain reedbuck and duiker, while kudu and Burchell's zebra have been reintroduced. Anglers and boating enthusiasts use the dam (they can camp in the reserve overnight, but only beside the dam). Field toilets are the only facilities for visitors. The reserve is open from 6 a.m. to 6 p.m. throughout the year.

For further information, write to The Officer-in-Charge, Ohrigstad Dam Nature Reserve, P O Box 604, Lydenburg 1120, telephone (01323) 8-0302 or (013) 328-0302, or fax 2075.

Pilgrim's Rest Nature Reserve

About 30 km southwest of Bourke's Luck Potholes, the Blyde River passes the old gold-miners' village of Pilgrim's Rest, a national historical monument that falls under the control of the provincial authorities. Here the Blyde River is narrow but fast-flowing and clear, and provides excellent trout-fishing.

A 1 800 ha provincial nature reserve stretching 7 km downstream has been proclaimed over the river and its banks. The reserve is open for public fishing throughout the year. Anglers must possess current Mpumalanga trout-fishing licences, obtainable at the information centre opposite the Royal Hotel from 8.30 a.m. to 4.30 p.m. Near the office is a large caravan and camping site. Visitors may also stay in the old Royal Hotel or in one of several restored miners' cottages (there are also various restaurants). For details about the village, the reserve and accommodation, contact Pilgrim's Rest Information Centre, Private Bag X516, Pilgrim's Rest 1290, telephone (013) 768-1211.

Potlake Nature Reserve

The Northern Province's Department of Environmental Affairs and Tourism is introducing a wide range of species to its 2 786 ha Potlake (pronounced Pot-la-ki) reserve in the mixed bushveld 65 km north of Burgersfort. Giraffe, kudu, nyala, blue wildebeest, red hartebeest, Burchell's zebra, impala, gemsbok, ostrich and waterbuck have already been introduced to the reserve to boost the existing population of duiker, steenbok, baboon, vervet monkey, klipspringer and various bird species.

At the entrance to the reserve there is an information centre which has a curio shop and lecture hall. Refreshments are sold, and there are braai and picnic facilities nearby.

There are two interlinking circular trails of two to three hours, and six hours respectively. Trails and roads are to be built to facilitate gameviewing. For further information, write to The Officer-in-Charge, P O Box 108, Atok 0749, telephone (015) 619-6009.

Prospector's Hiking Trail

Starting from either Morgenzon Forest Camp, Morgenzon Hut, or from the Royal Stables in Pilgrim's Rest, hikers on the Prospector's Hiking Trail follow in the footsteps of early miners, through indigenous forests and exotic plantations, and passing an old mining area with shafts, tunnels and other gold-rush relics. Grassveld leads into pine plantation and, during spring and summer, the area is carpeted with orchids, lilies and irises in full bloom.

The 53 km/5-day trail is suitable for those who are relatively fit, while those less venturesome may opt for one of the shorter two-, three- or four-day hikes.

The trail's overnight huts each accommodate up to 30 people and provide basic essentials such as firewood, cooking pots, bunks, mattresses, water, toilets and rubbish containers. Prospective hikers must book well in advance by contacting SAFCOL, Private Bag X503, Sabie 1260, telephone (013) 764-1058, or fax 764-2071.

Rooikat Nature Walk

An 11 km forest walk named after the caracal or 'rooikat' follows a circular route in the New Agatha Forest, some 18 km from Tzaneen. For much of its length the walk follows the Bobs River, crossing and recrossing it several times. Attractions along the way include a picnic place at Die Akkers, 6 km from the starting point, the lovely riverine vegetation and grassland, and an impressive view from the top of the Letsitele Valley. Older visitors and those with less time or energy may take a short cut and reduce the journey (however, they will miss the view over the Letsitele Valley).

The walk begins and ends at the New Agatha Forest Station. Free entry permits may be obtained at the forester's office daily between 6 a.m. and 4 p.m. (but those wanting to walk at weekends or in school holidays should make arrangements in advance).

To reach the New Agatha Forest, take the road from Tzaneen (it is signposted 'Agatha'). Drive for 10 km, turn left at a T-junction, and follow the road for a further 3 kilometres – the New Agatha signpost is on the right.

For further information, write to SAFCOL, Private Bag X503, Sabie 1260, telephone (013) 764-1058, or fax 764-2071.

Soutpansberg Hiking Trail

The Hanglip section of the Soutpansberg Hiking Trail provides two separate routes on which you can explore South Africa's northernmost mountain range. This exquisite area provides hikers with a true wilderness experience, and you can walk all day without seeing another human being, accompanied only by haunting bird calls and the crunch of the undergrowth beneath your feet.

The first route is a one-day/14 km trail, marked with yellow footprints, that leads up the forest-clad, southern Soutpansberg slopes below the Hanglip cliff face. The circular two-day/18 km trail also passes through the Hanglip Forest, as well as plantations of exotic pine and gum.

The trail starts at Hanglip Forest plantation office, only 4 km north of Louis Trichardt (the route is well signposted).

Both trails have huts at the start, enabling you to start hiking fresh and early on the first day. The huts cater for parties of up to 30, and supply bunks, mattresses, cooking utensils and firewood. Hikers must supply the rest. To ensure accommodation in the huts, hikers should book places on the trail well in advance. A picnic area caters for day visitors.

For further information, write to SAFCOL, Private Bag X503, Sabie 1260, telephone (013) 764-1058, or fax 764-2071.

Starvation Creek Nature Reserve

Drained by the Elands River, which plunges into this forest reserve as a splendid waterfall, Starvation Creek is a 140 ha sanctuary lying approximately halfway between Nelspruit and Machadodorp on the escarpment of the Mpumalanga Drakensberg. The origin of the name is not known for certain, but at the turn of the century the area was a temporary home to

HIGHVELD: **NORTHEASTERN ESCARPMENT**

Left: Silvery mists rise above the floor of the Blyde River Canyon, a region of unsurpassed beauty and charm. **Above:** A nesting pair of bald ibis. Although this photograph was taken in Mpumalanga, most of these large birds are found in the KwaZulu-Natal Drakensberg, where they breed in small, isolated colonies. **Right:** Sudwala Caves, northwest of Nelspruit, are among Mpumalanga's top tourist attractions. A 12-m-high corridor leads from the cave entrance to a huge hall with a diameter of 66 metres.

gold prospectors. They found no gold – only hunger and loneliness. One of the main reasons for its existence – apart from the beauty of the countryside – is the protection of the endangered Kaapschehoop cycad species. In the wooded upper reaches of the valley there are forest bushwillow, real yellowwood and notsung; the lower-gallery forest has waterberry, and in the scrub thornveld of the dry northern slopes you can see mitserie trees (*Bridelia micrantha*).

The reserve is reached from a turn-off about 40 km from Nelspruit. It is not signposted as it is closed to the public (however, visitors may enter if in possession of a permit). The two-day/23 km Starvation Creek Trail, a section of the larger Kaapschehoop Hiking Trail (*see separate entry*), penetrates the reserve, revealing its shady forests, dramatic cliffs, cycads, waterfalls, striking views, and the old Bannisters gold workings. For more information, write to SAFCOL, Private Bag X503, Sabie 1260, telephone (013) 764-1058, or fax 764-2071.

Sterkspruit Nature Reserve

To preserve the purity of the Sterkspruit (strong stream), the provincial authorities of the former Transvaal bought the farms De Kuilen and Sterkspruit – a total area of about 1 600 hectares. These were proclaimed as the Sterkspruit Nature Reserve. The area was later expanded when neighbouring landowners suggested that their property be included within its bounds, and today it covers about 10 000 ha – consisting largely of grass-grown hills and valleys. Most of this area is private property; only 1 600 ha belong to the provincial authorities. The reserve is sanctuary to oribi, bushbuck, grey rhebok, mountain reedbuck and other mammals, and alien vegetation is being removed to restore the natural habitat. Sterkspruit is not yet open to the public.

Sudwala Caves

In the mid-19th century, Swazis occupied far more land than they do today, and one of their strongholds was a series of caverns in the mountains northwest of what is today Nelspruit. The dolomite caverns had been sculptured by an underground river (long since vanished), though its opening was high on a steep hillside. There was enough room inside for warriors, their families and their cattle, and a flow of fresh air protected the defenders from enemies who tried to smoke them out. The caverns were sufficiently important for the Swazis to post in the vicinity a guard party, which fell under the captainship of one Sudwala, who was to give his name to the caves.

But it was only in the 1960s that a road was built up the steep hillside, and the cavern opened to visitors. Today, the Sudwala Caves rank highly among the prime tourist attractions of Mpumalanga. The present owner (on whose farm the caves are located) has introduced lighting schemes.

Guides lead visitors on an hour-long tour every day. These are held regularly between 8.30 a.m. and 4.30 p.m. Included in the tour is a visit to a massive chamber with a 67 m dome that has near-perfect acoustics: it has even been used as a concert hall. The more comprehensive Crystal Tour (which explores the famous Crystal Chambers) takes six hours and is held only on the first Saturday of every month. (Large groups of 15 or more can make special arrangements to visit the Crystal Chambers on the remaining Saturdays.)

Adjoining the caves is a very different attraction – the world's most ambitious dinosaur park, where full-scale models of the giant reptiles are displayed in well-planned surroundings. The first of Sudwala's dinosaurs was commissioned to illustrate the age of the caves (upwards of 100 million years). Now there are 100 dinosaurs in the park, some representing species that once lived in southern Africa, others drawn from around the world, and all scattered among lovely indigenous trees and cycads on the Mankelekele Mountain. A mighty *Diplodocus* stands knee-deep in a large pond, while the small reptile *Ichthyostega* creeps shyly into the undergrowth.

The Dinosaur Park is open every day from 8.30 a.m. to 4.30 p.m. Visitors tour on their own, following the short circular path that winds between the huge sculptures and using the leaflet provided.

To reach Sudwala, follow the signs from the main road between Machadodorp and Nelspruit (there is a signposted turn-off 20 km from Nelspruit), or take the road heading south from Sabie. For further information on Sudwala, write to The Director, Sudwala Caves, P O Box 48, Schagen 1207, telephone (013) 733-4152, fax 733-4134.

Uitsoek Hiking Trail
In the depths of Uitsoek Forest, some 80 km from Nelspruit, a network of scenically spectacular one- and two-day walks has been carefully laid out by the Roodepoort Hiking Club. The area is liberally dotted with pools and cascading waterfalls, which provide cool relief if the going gets hot. There is also an invigorating rock slide.

Crossing the streams and rivers – the four-and-a-half-hour Beesteekraalspruit Route zigzags across the river 20 times in total – has been made easy by the construction of sturdy wooden footbridges. Trees have been numbered for easy identification, and include the massive Cape holly, false cabbage, white candlewood, white stinkwood and wild peach. The forest is dominated by a mass of sandstone mountains, topped by the 2 154 m Skurwerant Peak. Fauna includes red duiker, which tend to stay within the shelter of forests and dense bush, and oribi on the grasslands. About 100 bird species have been recorded, including white stork, and Narina trogon, and raptors such as rock kestrel, black-shouldered kite, and both the steppe and jackal buzzard. A comprehensive list of the birds, other animals and flora to be seen may be obtained from the SAFCOL offices.

The one-day/11 km Bakkrans Route passes through pine plantations and scrub-forested gorges, as well as the Bakkrans waterfall. The two-day Houtbosloop Route climbs the plateau to reach an overnight hut, then winds down again on the second day, passing the Bakkrans waterfall.

To make reservations and for further information, you can write to SAFCOL, Private Bag X503, Sabie 1260, telephone (013) 764-1058, or fax 764-2071.

Verloren Vallei Nature Reserve
Verloren Vallei (which is to be renamed Verloren Vallei Wetland Reserve) forms the nucleus of the wetland conservation area on the Steenkampsberg plateau, site of the highest mountain in Mpumalanga. Controlled by Mpumalanga Parks Board, the 5 850 ha reserve is a particularly rewarding area for botanists and birdwatchers. Some 50 flora species have been identified in the wetlands, including a hitherto undiscovered species of vygie. The endangered wattle crane is the focus of an ongoing project to isolate, rear and release the species back into the wild. There are currently five breeding pairs of this lovely bird. Also to be seen are the blue crane

---

THE BATS OF SUDWALA CAVES

An insectivorous bat (note how the claws of its 'thumbs' and feet grip the bark).

Sudwala Caves, in Mpumalanga, once accommodated many millions of bats, most of them belonging to species of the 'horseshoe' family, so named because of a horseshoe-shaped ridge on the nose. The bats remained until electric lighting was introduced for the benefit of visitors to the cave. Then, taking exception to this invasion of their sanctuary, they fled to a cave further up the hill and free of disturbance. Today no more than 200 bats remain in the main caves – tiny bundles hanging by their feet from the rock ceiling.

Five distinct species of horseshoe bat are found in this region – Hildebrandt's, Rüppell's, Geoffroy's, Darling's and Lander's.

Like their cousins in other genera, these primitive mammals bear live young and suckle them. Their most striking characteristic is their wings, made up of membranes of thin skin stretched between enormously long 'fingers' which can be spread like the ribs of an umbrella. The wing membranes stretch down the bat's sides and tail, and cover its hind legs up to the toes, which are relatively short and tipped with claws. The bat uses the claws as hooks when hanging upside down.

Because its knees point backwards and cannot be straightened, the bat is incapable of walking on all fours. Instead, it moves along the ground by hooking the claws of its 'thumbs' into a protrusion, and dragging itself along the surface. The bat also uses its claws to climb rock faces.

In flight the bat emits a series of high-pitched sounds which 'bounce' off objects and return to its ears, thus providing a natural 'radar' detection system which enables it to avoid obstacles in flight and detect prey. The sounds have a frequency far beyond the auditory range of the human ear.

HIGHVELD: NORTHEASTERN ESCARPMENT

Far left: *Tetraselago wilmsii*, with its delicate blue flowers, is found high up in the mountains of Mpumalanga.
Left: A common tree fern (*Alsophila dregei*) in the Sterkspruit Nature Reserve. This is the most widespread of the tree ferns, and occurs mainly in well-wooded ravines.

(*Anthropoides paradisea*), which is South Africa's national bird, and the grey crowned crane (*Balearica regulorum*).

A small office houses an information exhibition – the only concession to visitors. No accommodation is available. Because of the ecological sensitivity of the area, those wishing to visit Verloren Vallei must book in advance. Guided excursions are available for groups numbering no fewer than five and no more than twenty.

To get there, travel north from Dullstroom to Lydenburg and turn left after 6 km at the Die Berg sign. After 8 km on the gravel road, turn left again and look out for the Verloren Vallei sign. To make reservations, contact The Manager, Verloren Vallei Nature Reserve, P O Box 98, Dullstroom 1110, telephone (01325) 4-0522, or fax by calling 4-0151, and ask for the fax connection.

Wolkberg Caves

The impressive Wolkberg Caves in the mountains south of Magoebaskloof came to light only in the 1920s, when a hunter tracked his dog (and the wounded mountain reedbuck it was pursuing) to the lip of a deep hole concealed by a wild-fig tree. The hole proved to be a vertical shaft 20 m deep, at the bottom of which both animals lay dead. On exploration, the shaft opened into a chamber rich in stalactites and stalagmites.

Today the inner chambers remain unspoilt, but the outer chamber has suffered at the hands of visitors who broke off stalactites and stalagmites as souvenirs. Further damage was caused by diggers who removed bat guano (for use as fertiliser).

To protect the caves, they were placed in the care of the provincial authorities, and currently they are not open to visitors.

Wolkberg Wilderness Area

The Wolkberg's high mountains and deep valleys straddle both the northern Drakensberg and the Strydpoort range. The Department of Environmental Affairs and Tourism controls a 20 000 ha tract of the region, containing several noted peaks and a number of minor rivers as a wilderness area. Indigenous forests thrive in the valleys and on the southern and southeastern slopes of the mountains, while grassland is predominant in most other areas.

The vegetation consists mainly of mixed sour grassveld on the high plateaus and savannah-type bushveld on the drier slopes. Trees vary from marula (*Sclerocarya caffra*), kiaat and round-leaved kiaat (*Pterocarpus angolensis* and *Pterocarpus rotundifolius*) in the grassveld and bushveld, to patches of evergreen species in the montane forest. The Thabina Falls, several lesser falls and potholes on the Mohlapitse River are all worth a closer look. In the aptly named Cycad Valley, some 4 000 Modjadji cycads, the largest of the 17 cycad species found in South Africa, are found.

There is rich birdlife in the Wolkberg. In the savannah grasslands are lilac-breasted roller, long-tailed wagtail and clapper lark, and the riverine areas are home to Egyptian goose, yellow-billed duck and black crake. Also to be seen are black eagle, white-bellied stork, rock kestrel, lesser honeyguide, hamerkop and fork-tailed drongo. Game is relatively scarce (the result of an era when dagga-growers hid in the ravines and lived on buck). However, visitors may spot leopard, brown hyena, bushbuck, klipspringer, kudu, grey rhebok, mountain reedbuck, vervet monkey, samango monkey, lesser bushbaby and caracal.

Although no official trails have been laid out, the Department of Environmental Affairs and Tourism allows up to 30 day visitors into the area at a time (and up to 30 overnight visitors). Hikers can follow the jeep tracks and paths used by wilderness officials, and there are numerous spots perfect for swimming along the way. Permits are required and visitors must adhere to strict rules. An overnight party is limited to 10 members, and all visitors must enter the area on foot. The best time to visit the Wolkberg is between April and August.

Fishing and hunting are banned, and so is the making of fires (visitors may use portable stoves). Nobody may use soap or detergents in the streams (visitors are asked to do their washing in a light plastic bowl). Entrance is by way of Serala Forest Station, reached via a turn-off from the Pietersburg/Tzaneen road (R71). For more information, write to The Officer-in-Charge, Private Bag X102, Haenertsburg 0730, telephone (015272) and ask for 1303.

Wonderkloof Nature Reserve

The most striking feature of this reserve is its fine waterfall, delighting eye and ear as the Houtbosloop River tumbles over the northern Drakensberg escarpment between Nelspruit and Lydenburg (there are signposts 9 km from the Sudwala Caves). The reserve includes attractive indigenous trees such as wild quince, forest waterwood, candlewood, lemonwood, white stinkwood, forest lavender and false cabbage trees. Bird life is plentiful. The reserve is traversed by the Uitsoek Hiking Trail (*see separate entry*).

Of historical interest are the remains of Anglo-Boer War fortifications and the packed stone walls of Later Stone Age peoples. Entry is restricted to daylight hours, and prior permission is required.

A permit and more details may be obtained from SAFCOL, Private Bag X503, Sabie 1260, telephone (013) 764-1058, or fax 764-2071.

Craggy cliffs and a vast bushveld wilderness

Most South Africans can distinguish between the Lowveld and the Highveld, but they are not as familiar with the large stretch of country lying to the west of the Drakensberg and north of Johannesburg. This region is bounded by the Soutpansberg to the north, the Drakensberg to the east, the Witwatersrand and Magaliesberg to the south and the Kalahari sandveld to the west. It features a host of parks and reserves and several minor mountain ranges, among them the gaunt cliffs of the Waterberg.

The nature reserves at Doorndraai Dam, near Naboomspruit, and Loskop Dam, north of Middelburg, are the largest of several sanctuaries in this area. There is a scattering of conservation areas in and around Pretoria, including the South African National Zoological Gardens, and the city is also the headquarters of South Africa's National Parks Board. A number of conservancies have opened up in and around the Waterberg area while, to the south, is the Pilanesberg National Park, located in an area that used to be part of the old 'homeland', the Republic of Bophuthatswana, until 1994, when the area was incorporated into the new South African provinces.

Atherstone Nature Reserve

Sprawled across the far-reaching bushveld plains that reach to and beyond the Botswana border, is the Atherstone Nature Reserve, a commendable cooperative venture managed by the Northern Province's Department of Environmental Affairs and Tourism, and private landowners in the district. Hunters are catered for during the season, but the rest of the year is devoted to those who wish to enjoy the bushveld wilderness experience and view the game. Species found here include elephant, black and white rhino, giraffe, eland, hartebeest, impala, gemsbok, kudu, sable and roan antelope.

The reserve, which lies west of Thabazimbi, offers comfortable accommodation at the rustic Marula Camp, with its eight 2-bed tents, communal ablution and kitchen facilities, and braai fireplaces. Also available is the three-bedroomed house at Old Camp, with a large kitchen and bathroom, and a dining enclosure with braai facility. The best time to visit Atherstone is between April and October.

For further information, write to The Officer-in-Charge, Atherstone Nature Reserve, P O Box 21, Dwaalboom 0319, or telephone (014778) 802, or fax 935.

Austin Roberts Bird Sanctuary

New Muckleneuk in Pretoria features a fascinating bird sanctuary, extending for nearly four city blocks (11 ha), and named in honour of the great naturalist whose book on South African birds remains the standard work on the subject. Much of the sanctuary is hidden in dense vegetation and is closed to the public, but the four roads that form its perimeter provide an interesting walk. The willow-fringed dam in the northwestern corner of the sanctuary is overlooked by the Louis van Bergen hide, from which visitors can view the waterfowl at close

Left: Waterside willows camouflage a birdwatching hide at the popular Austin Roberts Bird Sanctuary in Pretoria. With the introduction of several small antelope, the sanctuary has extended its appeal to weekend visitors. **Above:** The European bee-eater, a summer migrant, is found throughout southern Africa. It has a beautiful, bubbling call, used to maintain contact between birds in flight.

HIGHVELD: BUSHVELD BASIN

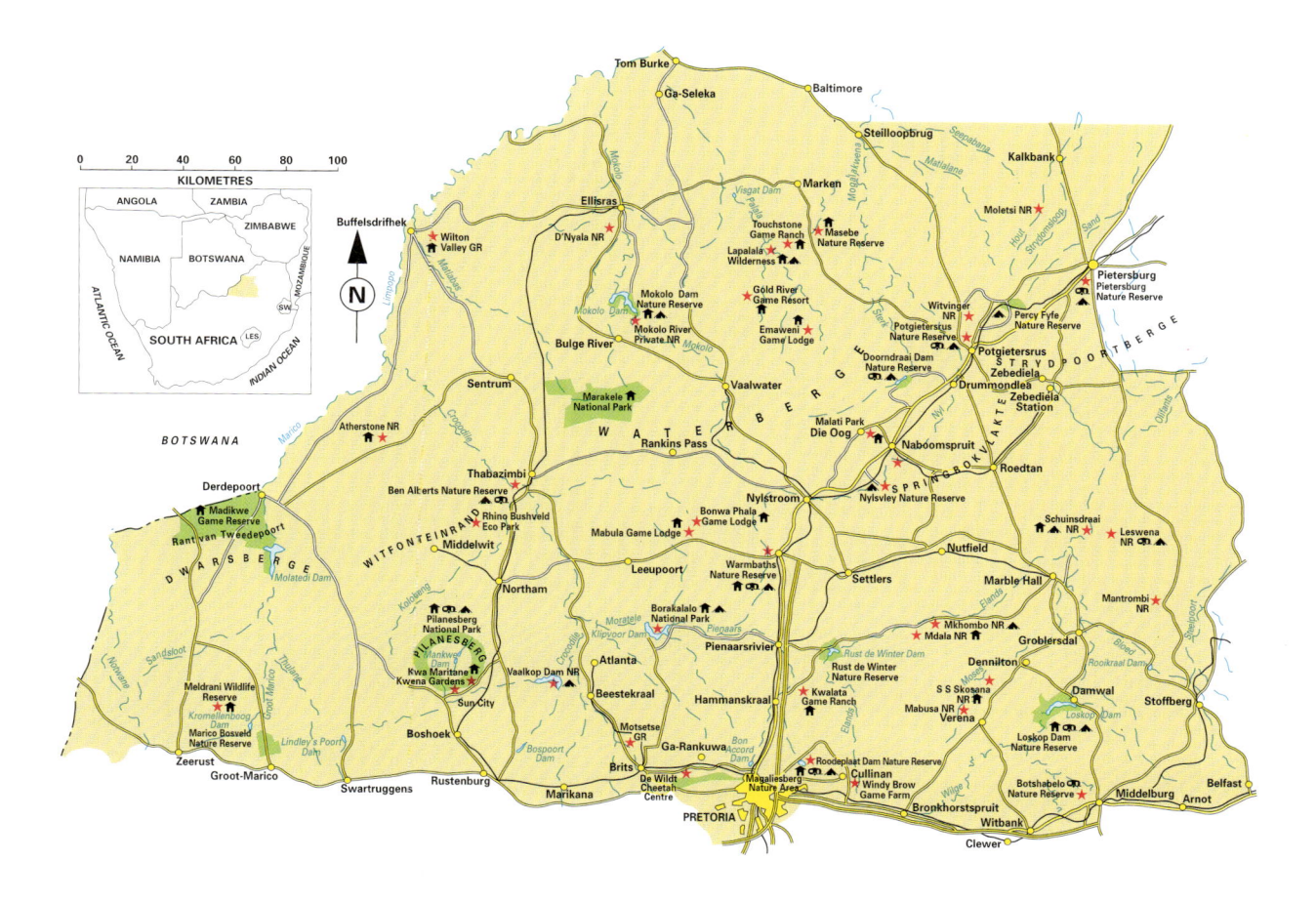

quarters. The Austin Roberts sanctuary attracts both city and country birds, among them aquatic species like duck, cormorant, weaver and heron. The most impressive aspect of the sanctuary is the large number of heron and egret that return to roost in the late afternoon. Birding enthusiasts should keep an eye open for the blue crane, South Africa's national bird, and the rare black swan. Several small antelope have been introduced to the sanctuary, and some are so tame that they approach visitors standing outside the fence.

The hide is open between 7 a.m. and 5 p.m. on weekends and public holidays. The entrance to the hide is in Boshoff Street, New Muckleneuk, which runs eastwards from Queen Wilhelmina Avenue.

For further information, write to The Parks and Recreation Department, P O Box 1454, Pretoria 0001, or telephone (012) 348-1266, or fax 313-0476.

Left: The Indian seringa is an invasive tree which competes with indigenous tree species by attracting Rameron pigeons, the natural seed dispersal agents of many South African forest trees.

77

Ben Alberts Nature Reserve

The Iron and Steel Corporation (ISCOR) has established a 2 156 ha game reserve near its iron-ore mine at Thabazimbi, in the western Northern Province. This spot, with its dun bushveld vegetation and rust-red soil, provides welcome relaxation for employees and their families, as well as for the public.

The reserve, named after a former manager of the mine, is set in the Crocodile River valley flanked by steep hillsides. Looming in the background is the Kransberg, the highest peak in the Waterberg range.

The Ben Alberts Nature Reserve, which forms part of Thabazimbi's recreation complex, offers fine scenery and an abundance of game – you should have no trouble seeing white rhino, giraffe, eland, kudu, waterbuck, zebra and warthog. Birdlife is prolific.

A comprehensive network of roads takes visitors to all parts of the reserve (a detailed map is printed on the reverse side of the entrance ticket). Some of the roads lead to various lookout points, one of them high on a koppie that commands views over the whole area.

There is a small rest camp with caravan and camping sites just outside the gates. The reserve is open daily throughout the year, from 7 a.m. to 6 p.m., and is at its best in the winter months (when the grass is not too long).

To reach the reserve, take the signposted turn-off from the R510 leading south from Thabazimbi to Northam. The turn-off to the reserve (also signposted) lies about 5 km further along on your right. For further information, write to The Warden, Ben Alberts Nature Reserve, P O Box 50, Thabazimbi 0380, telephone/fax (014773) 7-1670.

Bonwa Phala Game Lodge

Dusk at Bonwa Phala Game Lodge sees large herds of game slowly wending their path homeward across the wide open plains. With the lengthening of the shadows comes the night-time chorus – thousands of chirping crickets harmonising with the hoot of an owl and the far-off bark of a jackal.

Although these are the untamed sounds of old Africa, Bonwa Phala (look at the impala) can hardly be described as being off the beaten track. It lies near the R516, only a few kilometres west of the resort town of Warmbaths.

Bonwa Phala's main camp offers comfortably furnished thatched huts (with twin beds) with electricity and *en suite* bathrooms. Modern conveniences, including a fully stocked bar, have been laid on, but these do not detract from the rustic atmosphere of the camp.

Other attractions include a swimming pool, a selection of walking trails, sizzling campfire meals, and early-morning and late-night game drives in 4x4 vehicles (with an experienced ranger in attendance). Among the animals that can be seen are various antelope species, rhino, zebra and giraffe.

Only 12 people can be accommodated at the lodge, so booking is essential, although bush camps are also available. For further information, write to The Director, Bonwa Phala, P O Box 252, Warmbaths 0480, or telephone (014) 736-4101, fax 736-4767.

Borakalalo National Park

Open woodland, an interesting stretch of riverine bush along the Moratele River and the huge curve of the Klipvoor Dam attract a growing number of faithful holiday-makers to this lovely 14 000 ha reserve, which lies 60 km north of Brits and a mere 90-minute drive from Johannesburg.

The Klipvoor Dam, on the Moratele River, forms an integral part of Borakalalo (the Setswana word meaning 'the place where people relax'), where the plentiful fishing is just one of a host of attractions. Enthusiastic anglers of all ages flock to its shores in the fond hope of landing 'the big one', while those with other interests can indulge in hiking, birdwatching and gameviewing.

White rhino, sable, eland, giraffe, zebra and gemsbok are examples of some of the 30 large mammal species that can be seen from the 50 km network of good gravel roads to the west of the dam. The area to the east of the dam is maintained as a wilderness area with no man-made structures at all.

Self-guided walks along the well-wooded banks of the Moratele River offer birdwatchers the chance to see some of the reserve's 350 bird species. Notable among these is the distinctive African fish eagle.

Accommodation is offered in five secluded camps. Moratele Camp, on the banks of the river, has ten 3-bed safari tents with separate

---

ALL THE BIRDS OF SOUTHERN AFRICA

In spite of challenges from younger rivals, the book that birdlovers know simply as 'Roberts' remains the leading authority in its field. Austin Roberts was on the staff of Pretoria's Transvaal Museum when he produced his *Birds of South Africa* in 1940.

Despite its title, the book set out to describe birdlife all over the southern African subcontinent. Each species was given a 'Roberts number', but these have changed somewhat as new species were discovered and inserted, and when research revealed certain changes within the species.

Unfortunately for novices, southern African birdlife can be bewildering. Today 'Roberts' lists 920 species, and often the males, females and juveniles of a single species have quite different plumage patterns - making the identification of a bird in the wild a great problem. However, the Transvaal Museum provides a first-rate training ground where bird-lovers can hone their skills. Its 'Austin Roberts Bird Hall' displays specimens of most of the birds described in Roberts' book, from the ostrich (number 1) to the spur-winged plover (number 920) – including variations in plumage. This hall is unique, housing the only almost complete display of a country's avifauna.

The bird hall is on two levels. The systematic collection is on a mezzanine floor, arranged in continuous glass cases lining all four walls. The specimens are arranged in family groupings identified by backdrops in special colours. Each species is accompanied by a distribution map, an egg, and wherever possible, a nest. Downstairs are educational displays illustrating the origin of birds, their mode of flight, and their usefulness to man.

The museum is directly opposite the Pretoria City Hall and is open every day of the year except Christmas Day and Good Friday. On weekdays it opens from 9 a.m. to 5 p.m. and on Sundays and public holidays from 11 a.m. to 5 p.m. Telephone the museum at (012) 322-7632, or fax 322-7939.

HIGHVELD: **BUSHVELD BASIN**

Above: A king cheetah (right) shares the sun with a more conventional companion at the De Wildt Cheetah Research Centre. The king cheetah is distinguished from the normal cheetah by its long, broad stripes, and by the shape and length of its body. Cheetah may live in small parties of up to six, hunting together in the daylight hours by running down their prey. **Right:** The lunate ladybird (*Cheilomenes lunata*) lays her eggs in clusters of 20 or 30 on the undersides of leaves. In two weeks the eggs hatch into small, black larvae which feed on aphids - spearing them with their sharp, sickle-shaped jaws and sucking the juices from their bodies. The adult ladybird protects itself from predators by exuding a yellow, bitter-tasting fluid from between the joints of its legs.

ablution and cooking facilities; Pitjane Camp, on the northern shores of the dam, is primarily a fishing camp with secluded campsites and reed-walled ablutions; Phudufudu Camp has five fully catered, luxury tents, each sleeping three; Fish Eagle Camp, which must be booked in its entirety, has two self-catering tents with cooking facilities; and Bakgatla Camp, aimed at younger visitors, has 60 self-catering chalets. Picnic sites, washing-up facilities and ablutions provide for the day visitor. A shop sells basic supplies and firewood. Permits for angling are available at the entrance gate. Bookings and enquiries should be addressed to Central Reservations, Golden Leopard, P O Box 937, Lonehill 2062, or telephone (011) 465-5423, or fax 465-1228.

Botshabelo Nature Reserve and Museum
Botshabelo had its origins in January 1865, when two young missionaries bought a farm some 12 km north of Middelburg. Here they established a new mission station for the Berlin Mission Society. Today the historical buildings are preserved as a museum, together with a traditional South Ndebele open-air living museum highlighting the local culture and, on a hill, Fort Merensky, built in 1865 to protect the station.

The museum is situated within a 2 300 ha nature reserve, popular with hikers who enjoy exploring its three trails. The Botshabelo Trail is an easy 6 km walk on the escarpment, with broad views across the mission station, which has been declared a national monument, and its grounds. On the route you can see varied birdlife, as well as mammals such as baboon, vervet monkey, duiker, klipspringer, steenbok, grey rhebok and oribi.

On the 12 km Aasvoëlkrans and the 10 km Bobbejaanstert trails (both starting from Botshabelo village) you can explore the Klein Olifants River gorge and discover dense stands of cycads and a host of indigenous trees and shrubs. On the way you may also see game such as eland, zebra, hartebeest and black wildebeest. The routes are circular and are clearly marked with white footprints. Game drives can also be arranged.

Overnight accommodation, all self-catering, is available in a youth hostel, rooms for families and guesthouses. There is also a caravan park, a curio shop and a kiosk, from which basic supplies are available.

For further information, contact The Curator, Botshabelo Museum, P O Box 14, Middelburg 1050, telephone (013) 243-5020 or 243-1319, fax 243-1319.

Chamberlain Bird Sanctuary
Situated in the heart of Pretoria, a mere 4,5 km from the city centre, is a charming bird sanctuary created around a man-made wetland habitat. Numerous birds nest here, and it is particularly popular with aquatic species, including yellow-billed duck, brown ibis and kingfisher. There is also a hide.

To reach the Chamberlain Bird Sanctuary, travel east along Church Street and turn left into Beatrix Street. Turn left into Parker Street and, at the second traffic light, right into North Street. The sanctuary is on the corner of North and Keiser streets. The key to the hide may be obtained (on payment of a deposit) from Seniordal next to the sanctuary in Keiser Street. For further information, contact The Director, Department of Culture and Recreation, P O Box 1454, Pretoria 0001, telephone (012) 313-8820, or fax 308-8873.

De Wildt Cheetah Research Centre
This remarkable sanctuary, designed for the breeding of cheetah in captivity, was established in 1971 on 50 ha of land offered to the National Zoological Gardens of South Africa by Ann and Godfrey van Dyk. In the late 1960s it was thought that the cheetah would not breed in captivity, but Dr D J Brand, then Director of the National Zoological Gardens, was determined to accept the challenge.

The Van Dyks fenced off part of their farm at De Wildt and acted as honorary game rangers. Godfrey died in 1976, but Ann continued her work on the project. Assistance came from a veterinarian, Dr Woody Metzer, who, in a voluntary capacity, attended to the animals and started a research programme. In 16 years the breeding station has produced over 500 cubs,

HIGHVELD: BUSHVELD BASIN

Left: A wild dog (*Lycaon pictus*) suckles her pups. **Above left:** A tsessebe (*Damaliscus lunatus*) pauses to pick up a scent in the Northern Province savannah. It is believed to be one of the fastest of all African antelope. **Above right:** Ostriches, the largest living birds, can flee predators at speeds of up to 60 km/hour. Bred extensively for their feathers, hide, eggs and meat, they are capable of surviving in harsh environments.

of which roughly three-quarters have survived. Many of De Wildt's cubs have been distributed to various game parks, nature reserves and zoos throughout southern Africa and even further afield. Some of these have been released into the wild.

De Wildt's most prized inhabitants are the king (or striped) cheetah, which sport a variant colour pattern that years ago misled scientists into believing that this breed was a separate species. It was subsequently discovered that, like the white lion of Tshokwane and Timbavati, the distinctive markings of the king cheetah result from recessive genes in both parents. Those at De Wildt are the only king cheetah ever born in captivity.

In recent years the centre has embarked on a breeding programme involving other rare and endangered species, most of them elusive and seldom spotted in their natural habitat. Several litters of Cape hunting dog have been raised (36 pups were born in 1995, of which 29 survived), as have the young of brown hyena, suni, blue duiker, red duiker and Cape vulture. Two breeding pairs of Egyptian vulture are also protected here.

The centre lies to the north of Johannesburg. Visitors are welcome, provided that they make arrangements in advance. Adults, and children over the age of six years, are taken on a guided drive of the area while school parties may walk along a nature trail. Besides cheetah, they will see wild dog, serval, caracal and brown hyena.

For more information about the centre and its programme, write to De Wildt Cheetah Research Centre, P O Box 16, De Wildt 0251, or telephone/fax them at (012) 504-1921.

D'Nyala Nature Reserve

Sprawling across 8 281 ha of baobab-studded bushveld to the south of Ellisras, the ten-year-old D'Nyala Nature Reserve offers sanctuary to blue wildebeest, hartebeest, kudu, waterbuck, tsessebe, impala, mountain reedbuck, nyala, white rhino, giraffe and Burchell's zebra.

A 4 km informative trail meanders through the reserve, and two hides offer perfect spots from which to watch the mammals and the myriad bird species that nest in the area.

D'Nyala, which lies some 13 km south of Ellisras on the road to Vaalwater, offers accommodation for conference delegates only in a complex of seven 4-bed log chalets, four 5-bed brick chalets (all with bathrooms and kitchens), and two luxury rooms. There is also a fully equipped kitchen and a dining area with braai facilities. The conference centre caters for up to 45 delegates, and a swimming pool offers relief from the heat of the Highveld. Day visitors may use the picnic site. The best time to visit is between April and September. For more detailed information, write to The Officer-in-Charge, D'Nyala Nature Reserve, P O Box 66, Ellisras 0555, or telephone (014) 763-5148, or fax 763-3251.

Doorndraai Dam Nature Reserve

The escarpment of the Waterberg range provides a spectacular backdrop for the 442 ha Doorndraai irrigation dam on the Sterk River, roughly 50 km north of Naboomspruit. The dam is an angler's dream, containing blue kurper, red-breasted kurper, carp, yellowfish, large-mouth bass and several other species. Powerboats are allowed, but are restricted to the northern half of the dam.

The dam is the focal point of a 7 299 ha nature reserve that specialises in the protection of rare species – particularly the sable and tsessebe. Sour bushveld dominates the woody hills at Doorndraai (Transvaal silver-leaf, boeken hout, wild olive and wild seringa), and the tsessebe have thrived on it. In fact, many surplus animals have been distributed to other reserves. Kudu, reedbuck, mountain reedbuck, bushbuck, waterbuck, klipspringer, impala, giraffe and leopard also live here, and the more than 290 recorded bird species include fish eagle, Wahlberg's eagle, black eagle, martial eagle and a variety of hawks.

Gameviewing is allowed along the main road passing through the reserve, as well as between the dam's shore and the main road. A 30 km/two-day hiking trail, with overnight facilities, traverses the wilderness (make reservations in advance).

The Doorndraai reserve has two gates, one on the road approaching from Naboomspruit and another on the road from Potgietersrus. They are joined by a 14 km road that runs along the dam's eastern shore.

Doorndraai is open throughout the year (the gates are open between 6 a.m. and 6 p.m.), but the best time to visit it is in the cooler season between April and October.

There are three camping and caravan sites with simple ablution facilities, and a thatched building for groups. Two picnic and braai sites have been laid out for day visitors.

Permits for boating on the dam are available at the reserve. Visitors are warned that bilharzia has been confirmed in this dam. For more detailed information, write to The Officer-in-Charge, Doorndraai Dam Nature Reserve, P O Box 983, Potgietersrus 0600, or telephone (015403) 629.

Emaweni Game Lodge

Situated in a section of beautiful countryside some 100 km from Nylstroom, Emaweni, established in 1960, offers something worth savouring for everyone – including more than 40 species of mammal, hosts of beautiful birds and some fine examples of Bushman (San) rock art. Game drives, birdwatching, a leisure cruise on the lodge's lake, fishing and various sports are offered.

Accommodation comprises 26 thatched-roof chalets (with *en suite* bathrooms), and 25 two-bed cabanas situated on the slopes of the Waterberg, overlooking the lake. The luxurious accommodation is accompanied by restaurants offering fine cuisine, a pool deck, bar and conference venue. Two bush camps offer dormitory-style accommodation.

For further information, contact Emaweni Lodge, P O Box 5996, Pretoria 0001, telephone (012) 325-3601/2/3 or 45-2415, fax 325-4108.

Faerie Glen Nature Reserve

Surrounded by the suburbs of Faerie Glen, Lynnwood Park, Lynnwood Glen and Lynnwood Ridge, this 100 ha nature area has been described as one of the prettiest open spaces in Pretoria.

Several markedly different soil types occur at Faerie Glen, and this, coupled with varying micro-climates, has given rise to a fascinating variety of plant communities.

Due to Pretoria's position at the transition from Highveld to Middleveld, a large variety of birds is found in the city's natural areas, and this is especially true of Faerie Glen.

Gold River Game Resort

Huge herds of giraffe, hartebeest, gemsbok, kudu, zebra and impala have drawn many lovers of the wild to this private 4 000 ha game resort. It lies about 250 km north of Pretoria and is an ideal retreat for families or groups wishing to get away from it all.

You can swim, fish, canoe, or go on game drives from Main Camp, which consists of six 6-bed and ten 8-bed chalets, and youth-group facilities. Being near Pretoria, and in a malaria-free area, Gold River has become popular as a conference centre. There are also guided walks to enjoy, with highlights including a visit to Bushman (San) paintings and a lookout offering a panoramic view over the reserve.

In addition to Main Camp, Wooden Camp accommodates up to 20 hikers, and Fountain Camp has facilities for up to 35 hikers. For further information, contact The Manager, Gold River Game Resort, P O Box 9848, Pretoria 0001, telephone (012) 322-1160, fax 320-0919.

Groenkloof Nature Reserve

Groenkloof, at the source of the Apies River, and the southern gateway to Pretoria, is one of the most beautiful areas in the city. Much of its indigenous vegetation has survived the rapid encroachment of buildings, roads and railways, and blesbok, Burchell's zebra and other mammals have been given sanctuary within its leafy confines.

The two-day Groenkloof Trail winds through the reserve's bird-rich, white stinkwood woodland, and hikers overnight at a base camp with bunk beds, cooking utensils, and braai and

---

DIFFERENT STRIPES

No two zebra wear the same coat – just like human fingerprints, the pattern of their markings is unique to each animal and it also differs between species.

The zebra of the Highveld plains, Burchell's zebra (*Equus burchelli*), shows distinctive yellow-grey 'shadow stripes' between the black bars on its hindquarters, while the mountain zebra (*Equus zebra zebra*), shows no shadow stripes at all. The body stripes of a Burchell's zebra continue round the underside, but the mountain zebra has a white underside with a central, lengthwise black stripe.

In nature, their habitats do not overlap, the mountain zebra occurring only in parts of the Western and Eastern Cape and (as a subspecies) in Namibia. Sociable, noisy, restless and timid, Burchell's zebra prefer life on the open plain or on lightly wooded veld rarely more than about 10 km from water. Zebra herds are made up of family groups of about four animals each – a stallion, mares and foals – and bachelor groups of young stallions.

All zebra are primarily grazers, favouring grasses, but will occasionally browse on herbs and the leaves, twigs and pods of a few trees or shrubs. They are often seen grazing in the company of black wildebeest. Other antelope may also be present and, although zebra do not react to the behaviour of smaller species such as springbok and blesbok, they respond immediately to the flight or alarm signals of the wildebeest.

The zebra's defence, apart from flight, is by biting and by kicking – a mare has been seen to kill a spotted hyena with a single, well-placed kick with a front hoof.

Early settlers, noting that zebra were not affected by horse-sickness, attempted to use them as beasts of burden but found that, although they could be trained, they lacked the strength and stamina of the horse.

Burchell's zebra will mate readily with donkeys and the resulting hybrid, a zebdonk, shows typical zebra stripes on the front and outside of the legs and, sometimes, on the rump as well.

Left: The cup-shaped *Tritonia lineata* shows its six-petalled face to the sun in the Loskop Dam Nature Reserve. Each flower has delicate, faint stripes of dark brown. **Above left:** The Loskop Dam Nature Reserve is a favourite haunt of biologists, because its vegetation represents a change from the bushland in the south to the grasslands in the north. Numerous animals abound in the reserve, including white rhino, blue wildebeest, buffalo, giraffe, eland and kudu. There are regular guided tours of the 14 000 ha reserve. **Above right:** The reserve is a haven for myriad butterflies, one of the most prolific being the African monarch, also known as the African queen (*Danaus chrysippus*). The photograph shows an African monarch drinking from moist sand.

ablution facilities (cold water). There is also a mountain-bike trail.

Adjacent to this 500 ha reserve is the 60 ha Fountains Valley Recreation Resort, an area with picnic facilities, swimming pool, children's playground, a tearoom and a miniature train. Nearby is a municipal caravan and camping site – one of seven in the city.

Groenkloof is open throughout the year from 7 a.m. to 12 p.m. (except on Sundays and public holidays, when no entry is allowed after 6 p.m., or after 8 p.m. on Saturdays). It is reached via the entrance to the Fountains Valley resort. Drive to Fountains Circle in Pretoria's southern suburbs and take the turn-off leading to Johannesburg and Centurion. The entrance to Fountains Valley is on the left, about 1 km further on.

For details, telephone (012) 44-8316, or fax 345-3928. To make reservations for the trail and to book the overnight facility, telephone the Fountains Valley resort on (012) 44-7131, or fax 341-3960.

Kwalata Game Ranch

To the north of Pretoria, in a 900 ha wonderland of bushveld and riverine vegetation, is the private Kwalata Game Ranch. Established in 1990, the ranch is home to sable, kudu, red hartebeest, blesbok, impala, ostrich and zebra, as well as an impressive variety of bird species.

Accommodation is available in log cabins, stone chalets and a guesthouse (the ranch specialises in group functions, with 20 being the minimum number accepted). All are fully catered, and have access to a swimming pool, bar and conference facilities. Game drives through the bush are offered, as well as a number of guided walks ranging in length from one to five kilometres. For further information, write to Kwalata Game Ranch, P O Box 386, Hammanskraal 0400, telephone (0127) 21-0486/7, or fax 21-0245.

Kwena Gardens Crocodile Paradise

One of the many attractions at the hugely popular Sun City is Kwena Gardens, a park-like reserve of crocodile-filled pools linked by a network of walkways, and dotted with stands of indigenous trees and shrubs. The more than 700 crocodiles are fed at 4.30 p.m. daily, providing visitors with a close view of the immense strength and awesome jaws of this ancient reptile species. Included in their number is 'Footloose', the oldest captive Nile crocodile in the world, at over 100 years old and weighing a massive 600 kilograms. Kwena Gardens is open seven days a week from 10 a.m. to 6 p.m.

For further information, contact Kwena Gardens, P O Box 234, Sun City 0316, telephone (01465) 2-1262, or fax 2-1264.

Lapalala Wilderness

The Lephalala and Kgokong rivers are the scenic focal points of the 25 650 ha Lapalala Wilderness, a privately owned stretch of territory situated in the Waterberg range, northwest of Nylstroom.

Although you could encounter zebra, wildebeest, hippo, giraffe, tsessebe, kudu, gemsbok, roan and rhino, and any number of the 261 bird species recorded here at Lapalala, the prime objective of this unique wilderness is not simply for visitors to seek out the biggest game, but also to gain a broader and more intimate experience of nature, conservation and ecology. This philosophy has led to the establishment of the Lapalala Wilderness School, which offers comprehensive two- to five-day courses for schoolchildren. They are taken on hikes that introduce them to the concepts of ecology, the identification of flora and fauna, survival in the wilderness, animal behaviour, and the lost cultures that once thrived in these parts. Although the courses are, in the main, conservation-orientated, the children also have plenty of time for exciting pursuits such as walking, swimming, climbing, canoeing, or simply being alone with nature.

The main camp, Rapula House (72 beds) is a stone-and-thatch building, and there is additional accommodation at Mosetse Camp (22 beds) and Molope Camp (12 beds), situated beside the Lephalala River. Each camp is fully equipped (scholars have to bring their own sleeping bags).

In addition to the school, Lapalala offers accommodation at Kolobe Lodge, a 16- to 22-bed thatched camp, where you can bask in the tranquillity while enjoying all the creature comforts and fine food – at a price. Rhino Camp, on the banks of the Kgokong River, has safari-style tents with *en suite* facilities, and a boma, lounge and birdwatching platform. Other attractions include bush drives, adventurous guided and self-guided walks, visits to Bushman (San) rock paintings, a swimming pool, conference facilities and a discreetly located tennis court.

Less expensive, but still very comfortable accommodation is provided in six rustic, self-catering bush camps, sleeping two to eight guests. All are situated on river banks, but are some distance away from one another to ensure privacy. Each has its own walks, trails and fishing spots, and offers plenty of opportunity for birdwatching. Visitors to the bush camps have to bring their own provisions, but bedding, cooking equipment, firewood, crockery and cutlery are all provided. There are bomas for fireside meals.

There is a landing strip in the sanctuary, and those arriving by air will be met and driven to their camp. Visitors can also drive to the camp in their own transport.

To make bookings for the school, lodge or bush camp, you should contact The Booking Office, Lapalala Wilderness, P O Box 645, Bedfordview 2008, telephone (011) 453-7645/6/7, or fax 453-7649.

Leswena Nature Reserve

Fishermen trying their luck at the Lolamontes Dam will also delight in the sights and sounds of the surrounding 1 610 ha nature reserve. The mixed bushveld vegetation, filled with an array of *Combretum* species, *Sclerocarya caffra*, *Burkea africana* and *Dombeya rotundifolia*, is dotted with round-bouldered granite koppies and is home to impala, waterbuck, kudu, eland, tsessebe, bushbuck and klipspringer. Hundreds of bird species inhabit the thick trees. Leswena, which will be opened to the public at the end of 1996, is situated north of Marble Hall, near the Tompi Seleka Agricultural College. Visitors are accommodated in five 2-bed huts, which share ablution facilities with the camping/caravan site.

For more information you should write to The Department of Environmental Affairs and Tourism, P O Box 217, Pietersburg 0700, or telephone (0152) 295-3025, fax 291-2654.

Loskop Dam Nature Reserve

Loskop Dam Nature Reserve is one of the largest and most beautiful of Mpumalanga's sanctuaries. At its heart is the Loskop irrigation dam on the Olifants River, completed originally in 1938 but much enlarged in the late 1970s when the dam wall was raised. The dam covers a surface area of 2 300 ha (it stretches for 24 km), while the nature reserve as a whole covers 14 000 ha, most of it on the north shore. Visitors have a fine view of the dam and the bush-covered hills that surround it from the attractive public resort near the dam wall.

For biologists, Loskop's chief attraction is its remarkably varied bushveld vegetation, representing an intriguing transition from the lush trees and shrubs typical of the Lowveld to the grasses which tend to dominate the higher altitudes. For some visitors, however, there is more interest in the many animal species that have been reintroduced, among them white rhino, ostrich, giraffe, zebra, buffalo, eland, kudu, waterbuck, sable and blue wildebeest.

The bush throbs with bird calls – kingfisher, bee-eater, francolin, flycatcher and wood hoopoe, while, over the dam, you can watch the soaring African fish eagle.

The public resort at the dam is the second to provide visitors with a recreational facility, the first having to be rebuilt when the dam was enlarged. Today it offers comfortable log cabins and chalets situated well apart to ensure privacy. The cabins are fully equipped and sleep three or five people. There is also an extensive caravan and camping site. A restaurant complex, launching ramps, swimming and paddling pools, and tennis courts also provide holiday fun.

Across the road from the public resort is a 1,6 km nature trail which leads to a lookout point high above the dam. Game drives are also available, and more walking trails (one with an overnight stop) are planned. Those wanting a closer look may embark on the resort's 26-seater pleasure craft, which takes visitors on two-hour tours. Tickets are sold at a nearby hut, on a first-come, first-served basis.

There are several routes to Loskop Dam but the most popular approach is from Middelburg, which is 53 km to the south. The resort is sited between the road and the dam, and the turn-off is 1,5 km from the dam wall. Other routes approach from Groblersdal to the north and Bronkhorstspruit to the southwest. The

Below: The yellow-billed stork comes to South Africa as a migrant from the northern tropics of Africa and Madagascar. It nests on large trees or cliffs, and forages near or in dams, rivers, streams and estuaries. This bird is comparatively tame and, when not feeding, may rest on islands or protected sandbanks in the company of herons, spoonbills and other waders.

HIGHVELD: **BUSHVELD BASIN**

Right: The striking white markings on the head, rump and legs of these blesbok (at Malati Park) make them an easy target for camera-toting visitors to this lush, mixed bushveld area. Blesbok are grazers, inhabiting open grassland in herds ranging from six to 30 in number (though occasionally their ranks may swell to hundreds). When disturbed, a herd usually forms a single file and runs upwind.

resort operates year round (the gates are manned 24 hours a day). To make reservations for the resort, write to Aventura Resorts, Private Bag X1525, Middelburg 1050, or telephone (01202) 3064 or 3076, fax 5269.

Mabula Game Lodge
An African king named Mabula once reigned over this stretch of the Northern Province bushveld. Now his name is recalled by a luxury game lodge, a drawcard with visitors anxious to take guided 4x4 tours to see the 'Big Five' of the continent's animal kingdom. (Both day and night drives are offered, as well as walking and horse trails through the bush.) More than 12 000 ha in extent, Mabula Game Lodge stretches from just off the R516, outside Warmbaths, to the game-rich foothills of the Waterberg, where over 50 mammal species and 280 species of bird have been recorded. The reserve is particularly well known for white rhino, with one of the largest privately owned herds in South Africa.

Accommodation is offered in luxurious thatched chalets, all with private bathrooms. Besides excellent bar and restaurant facilities, the reserve also offers three fully equipped conference rooms.

The resort is served by a private airstrip and heliport. For further information and to make bookings, contact The Director, Mabula Game Lodge, Private Bag X1665, Warmbaths 0480, telephone (014734) 616 or 765; or Private Bag X15, Bryanston 2021, telephone (011) 463-4217, fax 463-4299.

Mabusa Nature Reserve
This 15 800 ha reserve, situated to the west of Loskop Dam and south of S S Skosana Nature Reserve (*see separate entry*), is a sanctuary for a variety of mammals, as well as numerous bird species. Black wildebeest, blesbok, impala, eland, kudu, hyena, zebra, baboon and monkey may be seen on the tree-lined slopes and open grasslands.

Accommodation is provided at the privately owned Zithabiseni Holiday Resort, with a bar, braai facilities, restaurant and swimming pool. Game drives are available, and hiking trails are under consideration. The reserve, which is open throughout the year, falls under the authority of Mpumalanga Parks Board, Private Bag X11233, Nelspruit 1200, telephone (013) 753-3931, fax 755-4796.

Madikwe Game Reserve
Covering an immense 75 000 ha of *Acacia*- and *Combretum*-punctuated Kalahari sandveld reaching to the Botswana border, Madikwe Game Reserve is home to the much sought-after 'Big Five', which were brought here by the largest translocation programme in South Africa – Operation Phoenix. Apart from these famous species, the reserve also offers sanctuary to wild dog, cheetah and brown hyena, as well as over 230 recorded bird species.

Visitors stay in the Madikwe River Lodge, comprising 16 thatched, luxuriously appointed chalets. Each has a wooden deck overlooking the tree-fringed Marico River. Facilities are generous, and guests can cross a wooden bridge leading from the lodge to a small island in the river, where a boma serves as an outdoor dining area.

Guided game drives and walks are offered. In a malaria-free area, Madikwe is best visited during July and August, although it is open throughout the year.

For details, contact Madikwe River Lodge, P O Box 17, Derdepoort 2876, telephone (014778) 891/2, or fax 893; or make reservations through Country Escape Lodges, P O Box 52702, Saxonwold 2132, telephone (011) 788-1258/9, or fax 788-0739.

Also within Madikwe is Tau Game Lodge, a luxurious resort offering gameviewing by day or night, and game walks. Visitors are accommodated in 30 thatched chalets overlooking a waterpan. For details and to make reservations, contact Sun Game Lodges, P O Box 782553, Sandton 2146, telephone (011) 780-0356, or fax 780-0033.

Malati Park Nature Reserve
The privately owned Malati Park safari, game ranch and conference centre covers roughly 1 200 ha of rolling terrain and mixed bushveld,

yellow-billed kite, maribou stork and migratory steppe eagle. Game to be seen includes impala, klipspringer and kudu.

An information centre, braai, picnic and ablution facilities are provided.

The 350 ha reserve lies about 35 km northwest of Pietersburg. More information and directions to Moletsi can be obtained by writing to The Department of Environmental Affairs and Tourism, P O Box 217, Pietersburg 0700, telephone (0152) 295-3025, or fax 291-2654.

Moreleta Spruit Nature Trail

Pretoria's Moreleta Spruit winds through a variety of natural landscapes in the city's eastern suburbs. At one point it enters a chain of vleis flanked by reeds; at another it crosses open, grassy plains; elsewhere it traverses secret, shady paths through areas of thick bush. The Pretoria city authorities have established a nature trail along the banks of the spruit, starting at a stone beacon in Menlyn Drive, Constantia Park (near the source of a minor tributary of the Moreleta Spruit), and continuing beyond the Witbank freeway to Hardekool Avenue in Val de Grace, a total distance of about 8 kilometres.

It passes through several urban sanctuaries, including the Meyerspark Bird Sanctuary, Struben Dam and the Faerie Glen Nature Reserve (see separate entry). A second section has also been opened between Watermeyer Street in Meyerspark and the Pioneer Open-air Museum in Pretoria Street, Silverton. In time the trail will be extended to the Magaliesberg and upstream to its source near the Van Riebeeck Nature Reserve.

The trail can be completed in a day; otherwise hikers may join it or leave at points along the route. There are no braai or toilet facilities along the route. Hikers are advised to take a water bottle. The municipality suggests that hikers use local bus services to reach their starting point, and for the return trip. That way they avoid the nuisance of having to return to the starting point to pick up their cars.

For further information, contact Tourist Rendezvous Travel Centre, P O Box 440, Pretoria 0001, telephone (012) 313-7694 or 313-7980, or fax 313-8460.

Motsetse Game Reserve

The Motsetse Game Reserve covers 1 000 ha of undulating grasslands and thornveld, and is home to a diversity of animals. Leopard, warthog, baboon, vervet monkey and brown hyena share the savannah with eland, kudu, gemsbok, red hartebeest, blue wildebeest, blesbok, impala, waterbuck, zebra and giraffe. The air rings with the calls of numerous grassland birds – guinea fowl, francolin, shrike, blue crane, martial and black eagle, and vulture. Visitors are housed comfortably in four twin-bed safari tents tucked beneath shady trees. Open-air toilet facilities complete the bushveld appeal. Guests cater for their own needs in a fully equipped kitchen.

Game drives are offered by day or night, as are guided walks to view the game. Guests can also look out for wildlife from specially constructed hides at a number of waterholes.

Motsetse lies close to Lanseria in the Kromdraai area, to the west of Pretoria. For details and to make reservations, contact Motsetse Game Reserve, P O Box 37, Lanseria 1748, telephone (011) 659-2615, or fax 659-1470.

National Zoological Gardens of South Africa

Southern Africa's oldest zoo covers roughly 80 ha in Pretoria's northern suburbs. The Apies River runs through its centre and a steep hillside marks the northern boundary, providing an impressive backdrop for the rest of the zoo. During the Depression of the 1930s, an army of unemployed men built massive stone terraces on the hillside, giving it the appearance of an Inca temple. The terraces are partly landscaped and provide unusual settings for the zoo's lion, tiger and Barbary sheep.

All told, the zoo features some 120 species of mammal and 200 bird species, some indigenous to southern Africa, but the majority from other parts of the world. The zoo is particularly proud of its collection of antelope and its exotic array of rare and endangered species, including Brazilian maned wolf, Indian gaur, red panda, Przewalski's horse from Mongolia and scimitar-horned Arabian oryx. The zoo has also built up a breeding herd of each of the antelope species, and is in a position to supply animals to other sanctuaries.

Although the zoo has long been one of Pretoria's premier attractions, the display of animals is not its sole function. Conservation and education are high on its list of priorities. Several staff members are full-time education officers, and while their chief task is to look after school parties, they also provide courses for interested adults; even the casual visitor can learn a great deal.

Adjoining the main part of the zoo is the impressive Aquarium and Reptile Park. Among the reptiles are several full-grown crocodiles and a selection of southern Africa's poisonous snakes. Especially popular with children is the farmyard where they can encounter the animals face to face.

Both sections of the zoo are open daily from 8 a.m. to 5.30 p.m. in winter and until 6 p.m. in summer. To reach them from central Pretoria, drive north on Paul Kruger Street and watch for the Aquarium and Reptile Park on the right. The entrance to the main part of the zoo is in Boom Street, which crosses Paul Kruger Street at right angles. Further information may be obtained from National Zoological Gardens, P O Box 754, Pretoria 0001, telephone (012) 328-3265 or 328-6020, fax 323-4540.

Above: Nyslvley Nature Reserve is considered one of southern Africa's principal wetland areas. Over 400 bird species have been recorded here, including 102 types of waterbird.

PILANESBERG AT A GLANCE

When to go Pilanesberg National Park is open daily throughout the year. Gameviewing is best in the winter months (April to September); birdlife is interesting in spring.

Reservations and information To book accommodation, write to Golden Leopard, P O Box 937, Lonehill 2062, or telephone (011) 465-5423, fax 465-1228.

Getting there Pilanesberg has four entrances for visitors. Bakubung Gate is situated close to Sun City – which in turn is well signposted from Rustenburg. The second gate is located at Kwa Maritane – a luxurious time-share and hotel complex near Pilanesberg Airport, while a third entrance is Manyane Gate at Mogwase, reached from the main road between Rustenburg and Thabazimbi. The fourth gate is Bakgatla Gate, reached from the road that approaches from Northam and Thabazimbi.

Accommodation Kwa Maritane (telephone (01465) 2-1820, fax 2-1268) is a hotel and time-share complex offering accommodation. Bakubung Lodge, near the southern Pilanesberg's Bakubung Gate, has comfortable accommodation in luxury rooms. The sumptuous Tshukudu Camp is located in the southwest of the park. Telephone (01465) 2-1862, fax 2-1621 for Bakubung and Tshukudu.

The more modest Mankwe Bush Camp lies near Mankwe Dam in the centre of the park. The camp consists of ten safari tents, each containing two beds, and ten wooden cabins sleeping a total of forty. Other tented accommodation is provided at Kololo Camp (four tents) and Metswedi Camp (seven tents). There is also accommodation at the luxurious Manyane Camp and Caravan Park, while Bosele has dormitory facilities.

Eating and drinking Kwa Maritane provides full board. The Tshukudu and Kololo camps provide catering on request, while Metswedi is fully catered. Those staying at Mankwe Bush Camp must provide their own cooking utensils, food and drink. Firewood, however, is provided. Manyane Camp has a restaurant. Sun City, with its many restaurants and bars, lies just beyond the Bakubung Gate.

Getting around A network of roads carries visitors to most parts of the reserve, and petrol is available outside its gates. Those wanting to hike through the reserve should ask for a game guide. Guests can arrange a 4x4 safari tour. These take place in the early mornings and late afternoons.

Wildlife Elephant, giraffe and both black rhino and white rhino are among the species reintroduced to Pilanesberg. Others include eland, kudu, red hartebeest, blue wildebeest, nyala and buffalo. The park is rich in birdlife, and a detailed checklist is available at Manyane Gate.

Nylsvley Nature Reserve

The largest natural vlei in the Northern Province lies on the sprawling floodplain of the Nyl River, some 20 km south of Naboomspruit. What used to be the farm Nylsvley is today a 4 000 ha wetland reserve (enclosed by a 16 000 ha floodplain) – one of the most important such areas in the country. Its chief attraction is its birds: more than 400 species have been sighted, including both aquatic birds drawn to the vlei and the river, and land birds attracted by the savannah woodland that flanks the water. The spring breeding season is probably the best time to watch the woodland birds, but most waterbirds can be seen later in the year (from December to April), depending on the extent of flooding in the Nyl River floodplain. In South Africa, the Nyl River supports the largest (and in some cases, the only) breeding colonies of great white egret, lesser moorhen, lesser gallinule, squacco heron, bittern and others.

Giraffe, leopard, kudu, impala and smaller antelope occur naturally at Nylsvley, and roan and tsessebe have been reintroduced. The terrain is relatively flat and it is easy to spot birds and mammals.

To reach the reserve, take the Boekenhout turn-off from the N1 between Naboomspruit and Nylsrivier, 13 km southwest of Naboomspruit. Cross the railway line and watch for the reserve's entrance on the left. The reserve may be explored by car or on foot. There is a small camping spot offering toilets, cold-water showers and communal fireplaces, and a self-catering camp, with electricity and cooking facilities, for a maximum of 30 guests. The reserve is open daily (including weekends) from 6 a.m. to 6 p.m.

For more detailed information, write to The Officer-in-Charge, Nylsvley Nature Reserve, P O Box 508, Naboomspruit 0560, or telephone/fax (014) 743-1074.

Percy Fyfe Nature Reserve

This Highveld sanctuary has been used to breed threatened antelope, especially roan and tsessebe, which have been bred here so successfully that their survival is now assured. The reserve is named after the farmer who donated it to the province. A road and a railway line divide the Percy Fyfe Nature Reserve's 3 032 ha into three sections, one large and two somewhat smaller. The large area is used for breeding roan from animals captured on farms in the Waterberg range, as well as Cape buffalo from Addo. The breeding programme has been very successful, and surplus animals have been moved to the other reserves. Tsessebe is bred at one of the smaller camps, while the other is maintained as a multispecies camp.

Ironically, Percy Fyfe's chief interest was in a species no longer found on his farm – the blesbok. In 1933 he bought a few head of blesbok in the then Orange Free State and, within 20 years, their numbers had grown to more than 600. In 1954 he gave his blesbok sanctuary to the authorities and, while he was alive, it was managed as such – even though blesbok were never naturally recorded off the Highveld, and were historically alien to the lower altitudes. After 'Oom Percy' died they were moved to more appropriate habitats, notably the Suikerbosrand Nature Reserve.

At Percy Fyfe's request, part of his farm was developed as a camping area for youth organisations. Groups provide their own tents, bedding and other equipment, and must be fully self-sufficient. Guests are welcome at a five-stand caravan site, but they are asked to make arrangements in advance. Day visitors are welcome – Roan Camp (1 600 ha with breeding roan antelope and Cape buffalo) is open for vehicles only, Tsessebe Camp (450 ha with breeding tsessebe) is open to hikers and bikers, while Sable Camp is currently closed. There is a one-day hiking trail within Tsessebe Camp. A circular mountain-bike trail, forming part of the Thabaphaswa Mountain Bike Trails, explores part of Percy Fyfe.

The Percy Fyfe reserve is about 35 km northeast of Potgietersrus. To reach it, drive north from Potgietersrus on the road to Pietersburg and take the signposted turn-off to the left. From there the route is well signposted as far as the reserve's main entrance at Lunsklip Station. To arrange a visit or for further information, write to The Officer-in-Charge, Percy Fyfe Nature Reserve, P O Box 824, Potgietersrus 0600, telephone (0154) 5678, or fax 5688. To make reservations for the mountain-bike trail, contact Jacana Country Homes and Trails, P O Box 95212, Waterkloof 0145, telephone (012) 346-3550/1/2, or fax 346-2499.

Pietersburg Game Reserve

A 3 000 ha area of the town commonage south of Pietersburg has been set aside as a game sanctuary – and is one of the largest municipal nature reserves in the Northern Province. The

HIGHVELD: **BUSHVELD BASIN**

Left: The white rhino, also known as the square-lipped rhino, uses its wide, flat mouth to crop short grasses almost to ground level. In common with other rhino species, the white rhino has a penchant for mud baths. This habit is not simply a cosmetic indulgence: the mud traps ticks, and when it dries and is rubbed off, or falls off, the parasites are shed at the same time. **Above:** The Pilanesberg, once the scene of volcanic activity, is now a sanctuary for a variety of game.

flat terrain is scattered with dense stands of acacia bush and occasional rocky outcrops, allowing fine gameviewing. There are some 21 species of game, including white rhino, eland, red hartebeest, blue wildebeest, zebra, impala, springbok, nyala and gemsbok, and more than 190 recorded bird species. The 18 km Rhino Trail leads through the reserve, providing a glimpse of the mammals and the wide variety of birds that are found. The trail may be completed in a day or, for those who like to make their bushveld experience last a little longer, a farmhouse provides overnight accommodation. There are no other overnight facilities within the reserve.

The Pietersburg reserve is open year round from 7 a.m. to 6 p.m. in summer and until 5 p.m. in winter. Just outside the entrance is the municipal caravan and camping site and Pietersburg's Union Park, which features a picnic area and rondavels. At Union Park you can book for the hiking trail and pay entrance fees to drive into the reserve. To reach the reserve, follow the signs from the centre of town.

For further information, contact Union Park, P O Box 111, Pietersburg 0700, telephone (0152) 295-2011 ext 1003, or fax 291-3106.

Pilanesberg National Park

The eroded crater of a long-extinct volcano is the setting of the largest sanctuary on the Middleveld, a 55 000 ha national park created in 1979 by the then Republic of Bophuthatswana (it now falls within the North-West Province). The heart of the crater is fringed by three concentric ridges or rings of koppies, and the whole formation rises from the surrounding plains like a bubble. Pilanesberg itself (pronounced Pilan-Es-berg) is the highest peak, and gives its name to the whole formation. It overlooks the Mankwe Dam, which is in the middle of the park.

Until the mid-1970s the Pilanesberg area accommodated a large population of farming families. Then the Bophuthatswana government decided to create a substantial game reserve (not the least of their intentions being to attract foreign tourists and their money: the Sun City hotel and casino complex is a close neighbour).

The resident farmers agreed to move to new farms, a game fence was erected, and the stage was set for 'Operation Genesis', one of the most ambitious game-stocking ventures ever carried out in southern Africa.

Much of the impetus of 'Operation Genesis' came from the Southern African Nature Foundation, an arm of the World Wildlife Fund. Eland were translocated from Namibia; waterbuck and Burchell's zebra from the then Transvaal; red hartebeest from Namibia and the Northern Cape; white rhino from KwaZulu-Natal; and elephant and buffalo from the Addo Elephant National Park in the Eastern Cape. The Natal Parks Board donated 17 black rhino, and today the park pulses with its wide variety of game species, including the popular 'Big Five'.

Pilanesberg's rangers were drawn from as far afield as the animals, though most came from Natal (now KwaZulu-Natal) and Zimbabwe. They planned Pilanesberg's priorities, deciding that utilisation and education were more important than recreation. Indeed, the park staff encourages local people to think of the park as an important economic asset. Surplus animals are culled and the meat is sold to the locals at low prices.

Visitors can take two- to three-hour safaris in open safari vehicles or in open buses. The safaris take place in the early morning and late afternoon – the best times for viewing game. Visitors staying in the park can also go on exciting night drives and book for some fascinating nature walks.

Within Pilanesberg is the luxurious Kwa Maritane (the place of the rock) Lodge, set among the koppie-dotted plains, and the equally luxurious Bakubung (people of the hippo) Lodge. Manyane Camp offers 60 self-catering chalets and a large caravan/camping site. Mankwe Camp is a rustic bush camp with ten tents and ten wooden chalets (braai facilities only). Kololo Safari Camp sleeps 12 on a koppie overlooking the park. Metswedi Safari Camp is a luxury, catered camp in the more secluded wilderness area of Pilanesberg, while Bosele Camp is a dormitory camp providing facilities for up to 180 people. There is also a conference centre, two large 'walk-in' aviaries and a waterfowl area at Manyane. Over 200 km of good gravel roads traverse the park, allowing visitors the opportunity to view the game, and balloon safaris are available for those with a penchant for the unusual.

For information and further details, contact Golden Leopard, P O Box 937, Lonehill 2062, telephone (011) 465-5423, or fax 465-1228.

Potgietersrus Nature Reserve and Game-Breeding Centre

South Africa's National Zoological Gardens has established two animal-breeding centres, one near Lichtenburg in the North-West Province and the second on the northern outskirts of Potgietersrus, in the Northern Province. The Potgietersrus Game-Breeding Centre covers some 800 ha of what used to be farmlands, and

HIGHVELD: BUSHVELD BASIN

Far left above: The Percy Fyfe Nature Reserve, situated some 35 km northeast of Potgietersrus in the Northern Province. Breeding of threatened antelope, such as roan and tsessebe, in this sanctuary has assured their survival in the province. **Above left:** *Triumfetta sonderi*, photographed in the well visited Pilanesberg National Park. **Above:** The pygmy hippopotamus (*Choeropsis liberiensis*) from West Africa is a rare and valued possession at the Pretoria Zoo. About the size of a wild boar, it has pig-like characteristics, with a relatively small head and a massive body. It lives in swampy forests and in thickets along creeks and streams.

consists partly of bush-covered koppies (one hillside features a large euphorbia forest), an extensive grassy plain, and a fair-sized dam surrounded by reeds. As might be expected, the breeding centre specialises in rare species from southern Africa, as well as a few from other parts of the world. Near the main gates visitors can see Madagascan lemur, hog deer from Asia and, from the Amazon, the capybara, which is the world's largest rodent.

A railway line divides the exotic from the indigenous African species – the latter having the run of the rest of the reserve. They include pygmy hippo from West Africa.

A variety of game may be seen at Potgietersrus, including herds of tsessebe (the original animals came from the Doorndraai reserve), sable, nyala, blue wildebeest and Burchell's zebra. Waterbuck, impala and black rhino frequent the bush areas. A 3 km trail winds through the reserve.

The Potgietersrus Centre is open year round from 8 a.m. to 4.15 p.m. during the week, and until 5.30 p.m. on weekends and public holidays. To reach it, take the Potgietersrus/Pietersburg road and watch for the signpost. Visitors drive through the reserve in their own cars, following a one-way route that takes two hours to complete. There is a picnic site at the entrance, and across the highway is a municipal caravan and camping site. Contact The Manager, P O Box 170, Potgietersrus 0600, telephone (0154) 491-4314, or fax 7510 for more information.

Pretoria National Botanical Garden

In 1990 the head offices of the National Botanic Gardens in Kirstenbosch and the Botanical Research Institute in Pretoria amalgamated to form the National Botanical Institute. The 76 ha Pretoria National Botanical Garden houses the research headquarters, the National Herbarium and the biggest botanical library in the southern hemisphere.

The garden's main objectives are research, conservation and education and, to this end, its extensive plant collection is partnered with a nursery containing rare and endangered plant species. A nursery at the gate is open all week, and a tea garden, open every day except Monday, provides refreshments for thirsty flora enthusiasts. The popular annual plant sale and wildflower show take place every October.

The Pretoria National Botanical Garden, which was declared a national monument in 1979, is open to visitors every day. A nominal entrance fee is charged (pensioners free on Tuesdays). Guided tours can be arranged. To reach the garden from central Pretoria, take the road towards Silverton and then follow the signs to the CSIR. The garden and the National Herbarium are on the left, and are well signposted. For further information, write to The Curator, Pretoria National Botanical Garden, Private Bag X101, Pretoria 0001, or telephone (012) 804-3200, fax 804-3211.

Rhino Bushveld Eco Park

Unspoilt African bushveld, home to 22 species of mammal, 150 bird and 140 tree species, and endowed with fascinating geological phenomena, is to be found on the 9 000 ha Rhino Bushveld Eco Park lying 14 km southwest of Thabazimbi.

Two hiking trails set out from Mokekhe base camp, a stone hut sleeping a total of 12 people in two bedrooms. Leopard Trail is a 16,5 km circular route named for the Tygerkloof (Leopard's Valley) it traverses. Hikers may be lucky enough to spot the rare sable antelope, while leopard still occur in the area. An alternative 12,5 km route, via a mountainous ridge, offers breathtaking views across the bushveld. Zebra Trail is a 12,5 km circular route (with an 8 km alternative) winding to the crest of the Witfontein Hills past Miracle Wall – an exceptional geological phenomenon featuring stalactite and stalagmite formations out in the open. Hikers may see impala, reedbuck, kudu, red hartebeest, zebra, giraffe and vultures.

Trailists should carry sufficient water (at least three litres each per day), and the longer Leopard Trail should be attempted only by the physically fit. For further details and reservations, contact Jacana Country Homes and Trails, P O Box 95212, Waterkloof 0145, or telephone (012) 346-3550/1/2, fax 346-2499.

Roodeplaat Dam Nature Reserve

The reserve at Roodeplaat Dam northeast of Pretoria is special for several reasons. One is its position (within 30 km of South Africa's administrative capital), a second is the dam's Olympic-standard rowing and canoeing course (six lanes wide, 2 000 m long, and supported by boat-houses and launching ramps), and a third is its Aventura Resort on the border of the reserve.

Set on the Pienaars River, the Roodeplaat Dam has a surface area of 395 ha (the total area of the reserve is 1 695 ha), and has been specially zoned to avoid conflicting interests among various rowing, canoeing, powerboating and shorefishing enthusiasts.

Because some activities disturb birds, the upper reaches of the dam have been cordoned off as a bird sanctuary. More than 275 species have been spotted on and around the water, among them African fish eagle, black eagle, various members of the kingfisher family, duck and egret.

Roodeplaat's shore area is also zoned. The western portion is largely recreational with shady picnic, caravan and camping sites. The eastern portion, scenically the most beautiful

Above: The scenic Elands River. **Right:** Visitors frolic in the warm, mineral-rich waters of the spa at Warmbaths. One of the best-known spa resorts in South Africa, Aventura Warmbaths, with its numerous family-orientated attractions, is host to more than a million people every year.

part of the reserve, boasts an Aventura Resort. The south has been left as a natural area and features game such as kudu, sable, waterbuck, Burchell's zebra, impala and smaller species. A camp here for 100 people provides accommodation for nature-orientated groups.

Roodeplaat Dam is open year round and the gates are open from 6 a.m. to 6 p.m. To reach it from Pretoria, take the Pietersburg highway and drive north through the Magaliesberg range (which overlooks the city), then turn off the highway at the Wonderboom and Cullinan sign. Take the right turn and continue until you reach a four-way stop, then turn left and follow the signs to Roodeplaat, which lies 10 km further along on the right.

For further information, write to The Officer-in-Charge, Roodeplaat Dam Nature Reserve, P O Box 15163, Lynn East 0039, or telephone (012) 808-0510, or fax 808-1164.

Rust de Winter Nature Reserve

Some 60 km north of Roodeplaat Dam is another nature reserve that has an irrigation dam as its focal point – this time on the Elands River, near Rust de Winter.

The dam has a surface area of 566 ha and the nature reserve as a whole covers some 1 200 hectares. As yet, the reserve is not open for gameviewing, but the dam has long been popular with anglers and a dedicated fraternity of watersport enthusiasts. Fish include bass, mudfish, kurper, barbel, carp and yellowfish. There are also crocodile in the dam, but this does not appear to deter sailing and skiing enthusiasts. Overnight camping is allowed in the reserve (booking is necessary), but there are no facilities, and visitors should bring everything they need.

To reach the Rust de Winter reserve, follow the Pretoria/Pietersburg highway and then turn off at the Pienaarsrivier/Rust de Winter intersection. For more information, contact The Officer-in-Charge, Rust de Winter Nature Reserve, P O Box 508, Naboomspruit 0560, telephone/fax (01474) 3-1074.

Schuinsdraai Nature Reserve

Fishing for bream at Arabie Dam is the main drawcard at Schuinsdraai Nature Reserve, but other attractions are the many open bushveld areas that are ideal for gameviewing. Animals include herds of impala and zebra, and eland, blue wildebeest, mountain reedbuck, klipspringer, bushbuck, kudu, steenbok, roan, giraffe and warthog. If you are lucky you may even hear the distant bark of a brown hyena or catch a fleeting glimpse of a prowling leopard. Over 160 bird species have been recorded.

Crocodile lurk in the depths of the 1 300 ha dam and, although they usually feed on the slow-moving barbel, they are opportunists, and fishermen should keep well back from the water's edge.

This 9 037 ha reserve, named after a sharp bend in the Olifants River, lies north of Marble Hall. Hunting will be allowed in the reserve when game numbers warrant culling.

The 28 km/two-day Bosveldkrokodil Trail, with two overnight huts, weaves through the mixed bushveld. Accommodation is provided in six 2-bed thatched rondavels with *en suite* bathroom and kitchen facilities. There is also a campsite at the dam, where a boat-launching ramp is provided. Shops and fuel are available at Marble Hall.

For more information, contact The Officer-in-Charge, P O Box 666, Marble Hall 0450, or telephone/fax (012020) 2607.

S S Skosana Nature Reserve

While S S Skosana Nature Reserve's conference facilities and informal open-air dining area provide an ideal business venue, its 1 800 ha of unspoilt bush also offer surroundings tailor-made for relaxing.

The thrill of gametracking and the patient art of birdwatching are some of the highlights on the Tjhetjhisa Trail, a 17 km/three-day foray into the mountain bushveld, passing the ruined kraal of an old chieftain, a small dam in which hikers can refresh themselves, and revealing spectacular scenery.

Game includes kudu, blue wildebeest, tsessebe, eland, grey duiker, klipspringer, steenbok, giraffe, Burchell's zebra and baboon, as well as large predators, such as leopard, caracal and brown hyena. A lion park within the reserve is home to a number of these elegant creatures.

Birdlife is abundant, with typical bushveld species such as mocking chat, rock bunting, freckled nightjar and spotted eagle owl among those most commonly seen.

The reserve offers comfortable self-catering accommodation in 16 two-bed rondavels at the C N Mahlangu Lodge, set beneath tall indigenous trees below a rocky outcrop.

Overnight huts are provided for trailists. The reserve is reached 95 km after turning off the N1 leading north from Pretoria. Booking is essential. For more detailed information, contact Mpumalanga Parks Board, Private Bag X11233, Nelspruit 1200, telephone (013) 753-3931, fax 755-4796. To make reservations, contact the offices at P O Box 1990, Nelspruit 1200, telephone (013) 758-1035, fax 755-3931.

Touchstone Game Ranch

Situated in the Waterberg region of the Northern Province, Touchstone Game Ranch is a private reserve encompassing 17 500 ha of bushveld wilderness.

The reserve is home to white rhino, elephant, buffalo, leopard, giraffe, black impala and other antelope. The rich birdlife includes raptors such as the black and martial eagle.

Visitors are accommodated in four luxuriously decorated lodges. Flagstone Lodge consists of five cottages with *en suite* facilities, bar, swimming pool and conference centre; Millstone Lodge has four fully equipped rooms overlooking a waterhole; Flintstone Lodge has three luxury safari tents, all with panoramic views; and Rock Lodge is a rock cabin with a plunge pool. Some of the lodges offer both self-catering or fully catered options.

Visitors are advised to take precautions against malaria. For further information and to make reservations, contact Touchstone Game Ranch, P O Box 57, Marken 0605, telephone (014) 765-0045 or 765-0230, fax 765-0108.

Vaalkop Dam Nature Reserve

While many visitors enjoy the fine fishing and boating opportunities at Vaalkop Dam, this 3 996 ha nature reserve (including 1 045 ha of water surface) is tailor-made for birdwatchers. Over 340 bird species, mainly waterfowl, have been recorded in the reserve and there is a checklist available that helps to keep track of your tally.

Some 800 ha of the dam has been set aside for watersports and recreation. Swimming, waterskiing, boating and canoeing attract enthusiasts, while fishing for carp and large-scale yellowfish is also a very popular pastime. An 800 ha section of the reserve, more than half of which comprises wetland, has been set aside as a bird sanctuary. This area is not open to the general public and those wishing to observe the birds must book in advance (they must also be members of registered bird clubs).

On the shores visitors can see kudu, impala, waterbuck, spotted hyena and ant bear. Picnics and camping are permitted.

The dam lies near Beestekraal, northeast of Rustenburg. For bookings and enquiries, write to The Officer-in-Charge, Vaalkop Dam Nature Reserve, P O Box 1846, Rustenburg 0300, telephone (0121177) 1676.

Warmbaths Nature Reserve

A 530 ha nature reserve adjoining the public resort at Warmbaths' hot springs is home to red hartebeest, impala, kudu, wildebeest, Burchell's zebra, giraffe and other (smaller) game. Visitors are taken on guided walks or game drives, and horse trails provide an unusual angle from which to view the game. Night drives can be booked.

The spa is the busiest in the province's network of public resorts, and is generally considered the best in the world after the spa at Baden-Baden. Besides the reserve, it offers fully equipped chalets, a caravan and camping site, and the complex of hot-water pools that makes Warmbaths famous. Other popular attractions include water slides, a wave pool and mini-golf.

The resort is close to the centre of the town. It is open year round and the gates are manned daily between 7 a.m. and 5 p.m.

For further information, write to Aventura Warmbaths, P O Box 75, Warmbaths 0480, or telephone (014) 736-2200, fax 736-4712.

Wilton Valley Game Reserve

For a truly bushveld wilderness experience, the 3 500 ha Wilton Valley Game Reserve offers rustic accommodation under starlit African skies, and wildlife that includes 20 mammal species (ranging from eland and giraffe to leopard and cheetah) and a rich variety of birds.

Visitors can stay in any of three camps: Wilton Valley Camp offers luxury thatched accommodation on the banks of the Matlabas

---

THE SOARING WORLD OF THE EAGLE

The distinctively marked black eagle (*Aquila verreauxii*) in flight.

The Latin word raptor means 'one who seizes and carries away', a name well suited to the members of this sharp-taloned, curved-beaked family. The world of birds includes two great groups of these powerful creatures – owls and falconiformes, embracing falcons, hawks, vultures and eagles – some 292 species worldwide.

Raptors occur in most habitats, ranging from Arctic tundra to arid desert, from open grasslands to equatorial forests. Those found in southern Africa include the kites, fish eagles, vultures, snake eagles, harriers, sparrowhawks, falcons and the graceful secretary bird.

The black eagle, (*Aquila verreauxii*), is one of the most familiar and commonly seen of the southern African eagles. Occurring throughout the mountainous and hilly regions of Nambia, eastern Botswana, Zimbabwe, Lesotho and most of South Africa, this magnificent bird, with its jet black plumage, (distinguished by a white V-shaped marking on its upper back and its vivid yellow feet and lower bill) may be spotted soaring and gliding on the thermals.

One of its favourite foods is the dassie (*Procavia capensis*), as well as small mammals and birds. The black eagle builds a twiggy nest on a rocky ledge, lining it with grass and leaves. The female lays two large white eggs, sometimes tinged wih red and mauve, which are incubated for some 45 days before hatching. The stronger chick usually kills the weaker so as to receive all the food, and leaves the nest after 13 to 19 weeks.

The martial eagle (*Polemaetus bellicosus*), also common in the bushveld, is a shy, solitary bird that may occasionally be seen perched on pylons or in the upper branches of trees. It is the largest of the true eagles found in southern Africa, and is easily recognised by its brown-spotted leg feathers, giving it an interesting 'trousered' look. The martial eagle lays one white or bluish egg with darker blotches in a huge twig nest constructed in the upper reaches of a tall tree or atop a power pylon, and up to two metres in diameter. The fledgling leaves the nest some 97 days after incubation, but retains its dependence on its parents for three to eight months.

HIGHVELD: BUSHVELD BASIN

Left: A view across Pilanesberg's golden savannah.
Above: Pretoria's wonderboom is a major tourist attraction. The smooth-barked wonderboom generally grows in the moist kloofs, open woodland or rocky areas of the Highveld. It seldom exceeds 9 m in height, and bears masses of yellowish fruits.

River; Ou Hoek Camp is slightly more rustic, and Twee Riviere Camp on the banks of the Limpopo River has a reed-enclosed communal braai area. All accommodation is self-catering. Provision is made for hunters as well as for those who wish simply to enjoy the game and the bushveld. Game drives can be arranged, and a 5 km walking trail is popular with those interested in the indigenous flora and birdlife. There is also a a hide overlooking a waterhole.

The reserve lies some 97 km west of Ellisras in the Northern Province. For further information, contact Wilton Valley Game Reserve, P O Box 13, Steenbokpan 0533, telephone (014) 766-0232/3, fax 766-0232.

Windy Brow Game Farm

This large farm, which once formed part of the larger farm, *Elandsfontein*, that was the site of the discovery of the Cullinan diamond, is now the setting for a number of fascinating hiking trails. Varying in length from three to 15 km, the trails highlight various aspects of the farm – its archaeological site, its geology, ecology and rich birdlife. Some 14 species of game can be seen, including giraffe and zebra, and antelope such as red hartebeest, kudu, gemsbok. More than 45 tree species have been marked for easy identification.

Hikers depart from a thatched base camp that offers two dormitories, each with six double bunks, toilet and cooking facilities. School groups are welcome during the week, when they make use of the environmental centre, which can sleep up to 100, although you may have to take your own mattress. For further details about Windy Brow, which is 27 km from Pretoria and a mere 4,5 km from Cullinan, contact Jacana Country Homes and Trails, P O Box 95212, Waterkloof 0145, or telephone (012) 346-3550/1/2, or fax 346-2499.

Witvinger Nature Reserve

Lying some 20 km to the north of Potgietersrus is a little-known 4 450 ha bushveld reserve – the Witvinger Nature Reserve. This is a particularly lovely mountainous region, its foothills and plains dotted with various *Acacia* species, *Faurea saligna* and the striking *Protea caffra*. Wildlife to be found includes bushbuck, kudu, mountain reedbuck, tsessebe, klipspringer, leopard and zebra, as well as species of bird.

No visitors are allowed as yet, but more information may be obtained from The Officer-in-Charge, Witvinger Nature Reserve, P O Box 1661, Potgietersrus 0600, telephone (0154) 5678, or fax 5688.

Wonderboom Nature Reserve

Pretoria's wonderboom or 'wonder-tree' is the sum of many parts. At its heart is the trunk of a wild fig (*Ficus salicifolia*) more than 1 000 years old and some 5,5 m in diameter. Branches from this trunk first spread out radially but gradually drooped towards the ground, where they sent out roots from which sprang a circle of new trunks. In time, two of the offspring produced a third generation.

Today the wonderboom has 13 distinct trunks with a 'canopy' spreading across 55 m (it reaches a height of 15 metres). The tree would be able to provide enough shade for more than 1 000 people.

In earlier times the wonderboom's 'umbilical cords' were clearly visible, but they have been broken over the years. In the 1920s there were rumours that the legendary 'Kruger millions' were buried among the roots of the wonderboom, and fortune hunters dug holes up to 3 m deep. Now the tree has been proclaimed a national monument, and the Pretoria city authorities have created a 450 ha nature reserve around it. There are many picnic and braai sites located among the trees, and a nature trail leads to the old Anglo-Boer War Wonderboom fort on top of a koppie.

To reach Wonderboom reserve from central Pretoria, drive north on Paul Kruger Street, pass through the Wonderboom Poort in the Magaliesberg Hills (which overlook the city) and follow the signs towards Warmbaths. The reserve is on the right, within 1 km of the turn-off beyond the entrance to the poort, on the northern side of the Magaliesberg.

Wonderboom is open daily throughout the year, from sunrise to sunset. For further information, contact the Tourist Rendezvous Travel Centre, P O Box 440, Pretoria 0001, telephone (012) 313-7694 or 313-7980, fax 313-8460.

Sandy plains and the mighty Magaliesberg

Flat, sandy grassveld and an overwhelmingly blue sky are the hallmarks of the area lying west of the bustling metropolis of Johannesburg. The region hints strongly of the great Kalahari thirstland to the northwest: the sand is white rather than red, but the clumps of thornbush scattered in the sweet and sour grassveld are plainly related to the vegetation of the plains of neighbouring Botswana.

The similarity extends to many bird and game species, though the black wildebeest – a creature of Mpumalanga and Free State Highveld – is a notable exception. Nature reserves near Lichtenburg, Klerksdorp, Bloemhof and Christiana illustrate the consistent flatness of Gauteng and the North-West Province – valued by those who live there, but unsettling for visitors used to more varied terrain. There is a different feeling at Krugersdorp, which lies at the threshold of the beautiful Magaliesberg range, and this feeling is even more pronounced at Hartbeespoort Dam and at the provincial nature reserve near Rustenburg, which includes the range's highest points.

Abe Bailey Nature Reserve

In the early 1900s, the mining magnate Sir Abe Bailey maintained a stud farm and hunting lodge on a stretch of land some 5 km north of where Carletonville stands today. Sir Abe was a member of the Transvaal Game Protection Association, forerunner of the Wildlife Society of Southern Africa. In 1977 the Society took a lease on his old property and began to create a nature reserve named in his honour.

The reserve was later enlarged to its present area of 4 200 ha, and the Society soon afterwards handed all but a small part of it to the province. It is now administered by the Gauteng provincial authorities.

The reserve's terrain comprises four ecozones: wetland, acacia bushveld, acacia woodland and grassland. These support Highveld species such as springbok, black wildebeest, red hartebeest, duiker, steenbok and Burchell's zebra. However, the reserve's special pride is its waterfowl.

Water pumped from local mines has created vleis with a total area of nearly 400 ha and many scores of species are regular visitors here, including flamingoes and fish eagles. Also to be seen are more than 220 resident species, especially ducks, geese, cormorants, cranes, storks and kingfishers.

The old hunting lodge, still controlled by the Wildlife Society, now serves as the project manager's house and an old milking shed is used as an education centre. Guided outings with an environmental theme are available to school and special-interest groups.

The reserve is still being developed, but day visitors may make arrangements through The Senior Education Officer, Abe Bailey Education Project, P O Box 6444, Oberholzer 2502, telephone (0149) 786-3431, fax 788-3015. To reach the reserve, leave Carletonville on the

Left: Red-knobbed coots settle for the night. They are aggressive birds, and have often been seen harassing other waterfowl. Nests are of the floating type, built of reeds and weeds. **Above:** Night herons at their daytime roost on the Highveld. At dusk these nocturnal birds move to rivers and streams, where they spend the night hunting for crabs, frogs and fish. **Right:** A termite soldier and pale worker feeding on white fungus nodules they have grown in their nest.

HIGHVELD: NORTHWESTERN HIGHVELD

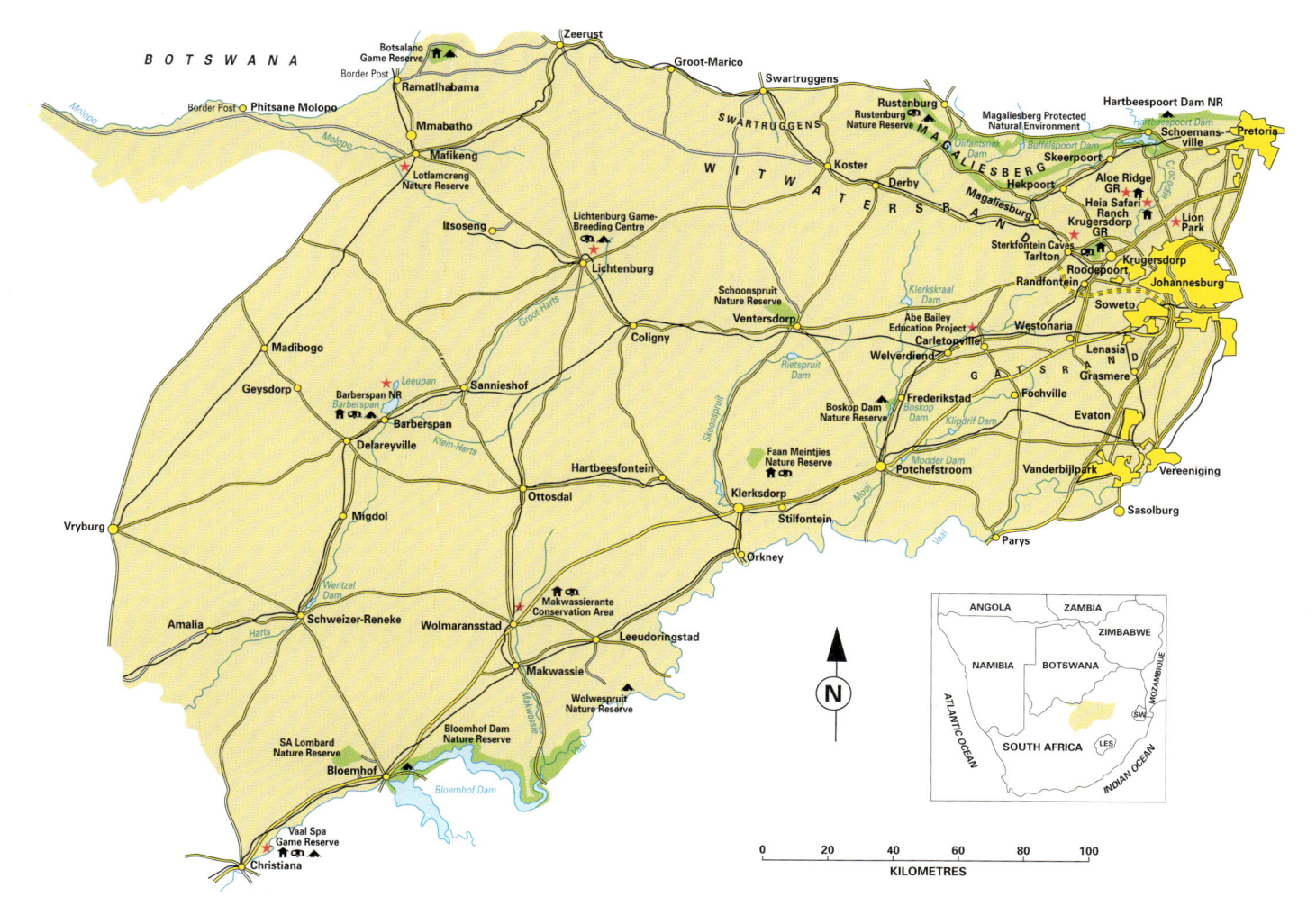

Pretoria road and, after about 5 km, turn left towards Welverdiend/Khutsong. The reserve is approximately 5 km from the turn-off.

Aloe Ridge Game Reserve
The game reserve, hotel and authentic Zulu village (called Phumangena Zulu Umuzi) are magnificently situated at the foot of the Swartkops Hills near Muldersdrift.

The 1 000 ha reserve offers gameviewing in open safari vehicles, hiking and excellent birdwatching (some 230 species have been recorded). Game to be seen includes white rhino, hippo, buffalo, eland, gemsbok, black wildebeest, nyala, waterbuck and zebra.

At the Zulu village and craft centre, visitors are treated to traditional meals and dances. Overnight accommodation is offered in traditional beehive-shaped huts.

The main accommodation is at Aloe Ridge Hotel, which has 72 bedrooms, four suites, a restaurant, indoor heated pool, outdoor pool, tennis and squash courts, and conference facilities. For further details or accommodation, write to Aloe Ridge Hotel, P O Box 3040, Honeydew 2040, or telephone the reserve at (011) 957-2070, fax 952-2017.

Barberspan Nature Reserve
One of the largest waterfowl sanctuaries in South Africa is Barberspan, a huge 2 000 ha body of water located some 16 km northeast of Delareyville.

The pan is the focal point of a 3 100 ha provincial nature reserve and is fed by the Harts River. Over the ages, herds of springbok and other species trampled the bottom of the waterhole, steadily enlarging the area already eroded by wind. The springbok have disappeared but birdwatchers have recorded more than 350 bird species.

Barberspan's terrain is flat and grassy and sometimes seems rather bleak, but its rich and varied birdlife makes it an ideal study area. Every year research station staff ring birds to monitor their migration patterns. The results can sometimes be startling — a ruff ringed at Barberspan was found in Siberia only two months later.

The pan's population varies greatly from month to month. For example, between November and January Barberspan's ducks leave the pan for breeding grounds in other areas. Waders, herons and egrets take their place, but in autumn the ducks return. Because it is a perennial pan, it provides sanctuary for birds when other pans are dry.

The southeastern part of the pan has been set aside for anglers, and there is a caravan park and campsite with toilets and braai sites. The remainder of the reserve has been preserved as a natural area, providing outstanding birdwatching and walking.

Self-catering accommodation is available for up to ten people. The reserve is open daily from 6 a.m. to 6 p.m. Barberspan is signposted from the N14 which links the small towns of Delareyville and Sannieshof.

For further information on Barberspan, write to The Officer-in-Charge, Barberspan Nature Reserve, P O Barberspan 2765, telephone (053) 948-1854 or fax 948-0101.

Bloemhof Dam Nature Reserve
Eland, red hartebeest, blesbok and springbok used to roam freely on the sandy grassveld of the area now known as the North-West Province, and all are represented in a 14 000 ha nature reserve situated on the northern shores of Bloemhof Dam. The U-shaped dam extends upstream as far as Kommandodrif, while its southern arm reaches Hoopstad in the Free State. Its impressive 5 km dam wall is one of the longest in the country. The nature reserve stretches 136 km east from Bloemhof and, between its two arms, embraces the Free State's Sandveld Nature Reserve.

Below left: A Cape fur seal, far from Cape waters but apparently content in the Hartbeespoort Snake and Animal Park. **Above:** A blesbok herd galloping across the grassland at Bloemhof Dam Nature Reserve.
Below right: A leafcutter bee lines its hole with a rolled-up leaf. The female uses oval sections of leaves or flower petals to line the nesting cells in which she later lays her eggs. There are about 24 species of leafcutter bee in southern Africa, some referred to – incorrectly – as bumblebees.

Black wildebeest, zebra, ostrich and white rhino add variety to the Bloemhof reserve's game population but, as yet, most of its visitors are anglers and their families, who spend most of their time on the shoreline.

The 22 802 ha dam is stocked with carp, yellowfish, mudfish, barbel and several other species. Many anglers set up their camps close to the reserve's main gate, only a stone's throw from the bridge that crosses the dam, on the road between Bloemhof and Hoopstad. The gate is open every day between the hours of 8 a.m. and 6 p.m.

The Hoopstad bridge provides fine views of both the Bloemhof reserve and the Sandveld Nature Reserve (see separate entry) on the other side. To the east is the dam, its flat shores stretching as far as the horizon.

To reach the reserve from Bloemfontein, travel northwest on the R64, then on the R59 to Hoopstad. Turn west onto the R34 to Bloemhof – the reserve flanks the road as you enter the town. Bloemhof is situated on the N12 between Kimberley and Klerksdorp.

For further information, write to The Officer-in-Charge, Bloemhof Dam Nature Reserve, P O Box 729, Bloemhof 2660, or telephone (01802) 3-1706 or (053) 433-1706, fax (01802) 3-1705 or (053) 433-1705.

Boskop Dam Nature Reserve
The 373 ha Boskop Dam, situated on the Mooi River about 20 km northeast of Potchefstroom, is the heart of a 3 000 ha nature reserve noted for outdoor recreation. Yachtsmen and canoeists ply the dam's surface while fishermen probe beneath it for bass, carp, barbel, yellowfish and mudfish.

The dam and its surroundings harbour a rich bird population, including duck, crake, avocet, Goliath heron and fish eagle. The reserve's wildlife also includes black wildebeest, eland, springbok, red hartebeest, zebra and blesbok.

Boskop Dam is one of the most visited reserves in the North-West Province, but few people spot one of its rarest species – *Lithops lesliei* – a succulent that resembles a stone.

However, the well-known Orange River lily (*Crinum bulbispermum*) and the beautiful coral bush (*Erythrina zeyheri*), with its characteristic scarlet flowers, are more readily visible.

MOUNTAIN REEDBUCK – SHY INHABITANT OF ROCKY SLOPES

Nervous and shy by nature, and always on the lookout for danger, the mountain reedbuck has an excellent alarm system. One or more of a herd's members, on sensing the approach of danger, will utter a shrill trill of warning, and the entire group will scuttle to safety, running, with tails erect, across the slopes with their unusual rocking horse motion.

Herds, ranging in number from three to about 30 individuals, inhabit the dry, stony slopes of hills and mountainsides, taking cover below the trees and bushes during the midday hours, and breaking cover in the early morning and late afternoon to feed on the soft, moist grasses. When resting, they nestle closely together. If stormy conditions prevail, they simply turn their backs to the bad weather, or take shelter on the slopes, standing or lying down until the rain has cleared.

The mountain reedbuck (*Redunca fulvorufula*) is a medium-sized antelope, with a shoulder height of 70 to 80 cm, and a weight of some 30 kg (the females are slightly smaller and lighter than their male counterparts). Its coat is a reddish grey or greyish fawn, with a yellowish head and neck, and snowy white under-parts. The bushy tail is also white underneath. The males bear short, ridged horns that curve forward, ending in blunt points.

The mountain reedbuck's natural range is mainly the area north of the Vaal (formerly known as the Transvaal province). It also occurs in the hilly, rocky regions of KwaZulu-Natal, Free State and Eastern Cape, and is found as far away as south-western Mozambique.

These attractive antelope breed throughout the year, the male winning the female of his choice by approaching her with his head lowered. She indicates her submission by bending her head to meet his. After a gestation period of some eight months, a single calf is born, and the bond between mother and offspring is broken only when she gives birth to another calf.

Overnight camping is allowed at the reserve, and the gate is open daily from 6 a.m. to 8 p.m. To reach Boskop Dam, take the road between Potchefstroom and Carletonville and follow the signposted turn-off.

For further information, contact The Officer-in-Charge, Boskop Dam Nature Reserve, P O Box 24, Boskop 2528, telephone (0148) 298-1330 or (0142) 3-1050, or fax (0142) 95-0950. (The second telephone number belongs to the Rustenburg Nature Reserve, which controls the Boskop Dam reserve.)

Botsalano Game Reserve

At Botsalano – the name of the reserve means 'friendship' in Tswana – visitors can expect not only to be well looked after but also to be treated to some first-class facilities for game-viewing, picnicking and camping.

Despite the fact that in the old days – until the start of the 20th century – a combination of rinderpest and hunters almost wiped out herds of indigenous game, numbers in the 5 800 ha reserve have started to swell once more.

You should be alert for white rhino (these have flourished here in one of the most successful breeding programmes on the subcontinent), giraffe, buffalo, hartebeest, springbok, eland, gemsbok, kudu, steenbok, duiker, impala, warthog and zebra.

These and other game species can be spotted from the reserve's well-marked game-watching routes, as well as at dams and waterholes. The 180 bird species recorded at Botsalano are mainly those that favour grasslands – for example, bustard and korhaan.

Game can also be seen from Mogobe Camp, which has four two-bed safari tents that are set beside a shady thicket on the banks of Mogobe Dam. Visitors may choose to stay at Botlhaba Camp – an A-frame chalet with four double beds and two single beds.

At the entrance to the reserve a boma caters for groups and there are also camping and picnic sites with water and toilets provided.

Botsalano is situated some 30 km north of Mmabatho, capital of North-West Province. For bookings, contact The Manager, Botsalano Game Reserve, Private Bag X2078, Mafikeng 8670, telephone (0140) 86-2433.

Faan Meintjies Nature Reserve

One of the loveliest municipal sanctuaries in the North-West Province is Klerksdorp's Faan Meintjies Nature Reserve – 1 300 ha of grassy plains and sandy ridges located some 14 km north of the town.

The sweet and sour grassveld supports buck such as eland, gemsbok, red hartebeest, black wildebeest, waterbuck, sable, blesbok and springbok, and visitors may also spot giraffe, zebra and white rhino. Some species are so well established that every year the municipality allows trophy-hunters (under strict control) to remove surplus animals. This ensures that numbers remain within the carrying capacity of the land.

The Faan Meintjies reserve, named after a local businessman, has become one of Klerksdorp's most valued tourist assets. Three guesthouses cater for overnight visitors, and there are ten caravan stands, while a picnic spot at the heart of the reserve is a favourite destination for day visitors, particularly over weekends and public holidays.

A drive along the 40 km road that winds through the reserve takes motorists two hours to complete, if they observe the speed limit. The reserve is open daily throughout the year from 10 a.m. to 6 p.m. in summer and until 5 p.m. in winter.

To reach Faan Meintjies, follow the signs from the middle of Klerksdorp or from the N12 between Klerksdorp and Potchefstroom. The reserve is also accessible from the R30 and the R53 between the N12 and Ventersdorp.

For more information, write to The Town Clerk, Klerksdorp Municipality, P O Box 99, Klerksdorp 2570, or telephone/fax (018) 462-5700 or 3635.

Hartbeespoort Dam Nature Reserve

The 2 000 ha Hartbeespoort Dam at the foot of the Magaliesberg is one of this region's favourite playgrounds – especially for tired city-dwellers from Gauteng. Yachtsmen, anglers, windsurfers and waterskiers are among

CORNWALLIS HARRIS

'Hunting the Ostrich' – a lithograph from a book by Cornwallis Harris.

Some 160 years ago much of the former Transvaal was home to an incredible variety of game, a paradise for sportsmen who came not just to hunt, but also to record for posterity the many and fascinating wild animals of southern Africa.

Such a man was Captain Sir William Cornwallis Harris, an Indian army officer who left behind a superb collection of illustrations of African game and an account of his travels in *Narrative of an Expedition into Southern Africa*, in a volume first published in Bombay in 1838.

Harris arrived in Algoa Bay in May 1836 and travelled to the frontier town of Graaff-Reinet where he kitted up for his expedition north. He crossed the Orange River below its junction with the Vaal and moved on to Kuruman and the home of the Ndebele king Mzilikazi – then at war with immigrant boers trekking north. Harris entered the Magaliesberg, where he reported seeing up to 300 elephant in one herd, 32 white rhino, large numbers of giraffe and antelope of all kinds.

It was in the Magaliesberg that Harris saw an antelope no European had ever reported. He managed to shoot one bull (he also tried for a cow), and took the complete skin back to India and the taxidermist. For many years this beautiful antelope was referred to widely as the 'Harris buck'. Later it was renamed sable, the name it bears today.

Harris also crossed the Witwatersrand and travelled down the Mooi, Vaal and Modder rivers before reaching the Orange River near Philippolis.

By January 1838 Harris was back in India, where he published the first account of his travels. He also painted many pictures of the animals he had seen on the expedition, 32 of which were later published as engravings in a single volume – today regarded as a rare collector's item.

Harris never returned to southern Africa, although he did lead an expedition to Ethiopia – then better known as Abyssinia – in 1841. He died of a 'lingering fever' near Poona, in India, in 1848.

---

the many thousands of regular visitors, and the shores are lined with holiday and retirement homes. The nature reserve comprises the dam itself and five sections of the shore. Together these five sections stretch for 40 kilometres.

Four of the five sections – Schoemansville in the north, Oberon to the west, Meerhof and Ifafi to the southeast – are little more than beaches. All are open to visitors daily throughout the year, and camping is allowed. Gates are open from 6 a.m. to 6 p.m.

Boating is permitted and anglers may fish from the shore for the dam's rich store of kurper, yellowfish and carp. Schoemansville is not clearly signposted, but Meerhof and Ifafi are easily reached from the road along the dam's eastern shore. This drive reveals lovely views across the water.

The fifth section is Kommandonek, which is located off the road to Kosmos. Some 200 ha in size, Kommandonek features an attractive recreation and camping area for visitors, as well as an enclosed game camp where zebra, kudu and bushbuck may be seen. Also at Kommandonek is a vulture restaurant, where the Magaliesberg's Cape vultures are fed with bone fragments to supplement their diet.

For more information, contact Hartbeespoort Transitional Local Council, P O Box 976, Hartbeespoort 0216, or telephone (01211) 30-0378 or 53-0505, fax 3-1949.

Hartbeespoort Snake and Animal Park

The steep shoreline rising from Hartbeespoort Dam's northern boundary is an entrancing setting for one of South Africa's smaller, yet extremely popular, zoos.

Visitors can see Kalahari lion, leopard, cheetah, tiger, jaguar, puma and panther, as well as chimpanzee and other primates, among a wide variety of animals. Many of them are movie stars, having appeared in a number of local and international productions.

The park also features a fine collection of reptiles. The zoo contains a seal pool surrounded by a large arena in which visitors are given regular snake-, seal- and animal-handling demonstrations, and is much visited by school groups.

From the park, visitors can embark on a scenic 20-minute cruise of the dam on a passenger launch, or ascend to the top of the Magaliesberg by means of a 1,1 km cableway. Nearby is the Hartbeespoort Aquarium, which houses both freshwater and saltwater fish species, crocodiles and performing seals. The aquarium is located beside the road that runs along the dam's eastern shore, while the zoo itself is on the main Hartbeespoort Dam/Johannesburg road.

Both the zoo and the aquarium are open daily throughout the year, from 8 a.m. to 5 p.m. in winter and from 9 a.m. to 6 p.m. in summer. For more information you should contact Hartbeespoort Dam Snake and Animal Park, P O Box 109, Hartbeespoort 0216, telephone (01211) 3-0162 or administration 53-0195/6, fax 53-0091.

Heia Safari Ranch

The Heia Safari Ranch in the Swartkops Hills near Muldersdrift caters for conferences and also welcomes private guests. The ranch consists of luxurious, thatched, two-bed bungalows and a licensed restaurant complex tucked between koppies on the bank of the Crocodile River.

Blesbok, zebra and impala wander through the grounds and guests spend their time fishing, riding and generally 'taking it easy'. There is a braai every Sunday, followed by traditional African dancing. To reserve accommodation, or to request further details, write to Heia Safari Ranch, P O Box 1387, Honeydew 2040, telephone (011) 659-0605, fax 659-0709.

Johannesburg Botanical Garden

Brick-paved pathways wind their way discreetly between stands of indigenous and exotic plants and trees within these lovely gardens set on the western shores of the Emmarentia Dam.

The gardens were established in 1968 and are home to over 30 000 trees, among them a fascinating array of exotics such as cork oaks, English oaks, Californian redwoods and silver birches. A huge, formal rose garden features some 4 500 of these scented treasures, and a herb garden includes samples of ancient medicinal herbs used by early travellers and traditional healers (*sangomas*).

The succulents section, which may be visited by appointment only, features more than 2 500 species.

HIGHVELD: **NORTHWESTERN HIGHVELD**

Indigenous vegetation includes reedbeds, Highveld grasses and an *Erythrina zeyheri,* known as the *ploegbreker* (plough breaker), because of its extensive root system. A prehistoric garden, with a collection of cycads and tree ferns, is currently being planned. Gardening demonstrations are held regularly, and visitors may picnic on the manicured lawns.

A number of ponds within the garden attract breeding waterfowl, and birding enthusiasts can expect to see – among others – moorhen, dabchick, crested grebe and Egyptian goose.

The gardens are open every day. Further information may be obtained from The Information Manager, Johannesburg Botanical Garden, P O Box 85481, Emmarentia 2029, telephone (011) 782-0517, fax 782-7082.

Johannesburg Lion Park

Among the more unusual game parks in the region is a 200 ha lion reserve that features more than 60 lion – and the population is growing. Visitors drive along a (one-way) winding road through the game area, where they may see black wildebeest, gemsbok, impala, blesbok, zebra and ostrich. Thereafter they travel through the lion area.

The lion park is open daily between 8 a.m. and 4.30 p.m. There is an entertainment area that offers a restaurant, a traditional old Ndebele village, swimming pool, picnic spots and other facilities. A special Pets' Corner is aimed at attracting young children. To reach the park from Johannesburg, drive to Four Ways, north of Bryanston, then follow the signs towards the Pretoria/Krugersdorp road and turn left.

For more information, write to Greater Johannesburg Publicity Association, P O Box 4580, Johannesburg 2000, or telephone (011) 337-6650, fax 333-7272; or contact Lion Park, P O Box 11346, Johannesburg 2000, telephone (011) 460-1814 or 37-6978, fax 337-8557.

Kloofendal Nature Reserve

Roodepoort's Kloofendal reserve is home to indigenous trees, proteas, orchids and other flora, and includes an attractive rocky koppie.

A stone amphitheatre on the western edge is used for open-air events, and two circular walking trails take visitors past the old Confidence Reef gold-mine shaft (now restored as a national monument), a small dam, and various sites of geological and botanical interest.

The air is filled with the songs of more than 120 recorded bird species. The 150 ha reserve is open daily from sunrise to sunset between the months of September and April (May to August are high fire-risk months).

To reach Kloofendal, drive along Ontdekkers Road from east to west, turn right into Christiaan de Wet Road, then turn left into Wilgerood Road, second left into Topaz Avenue and right into Galena Avenue, which leads to the entrance. For more information and a map, write to Parks, Sport and Recreation Division, Roodepoort City Council, Private Bag X30, Roodepoort 1725, or telephone (011) 470-3639, fax 672-7040.

Kromdraai Conservancy

Lying a mere 40 km from the centre of Johannesburg and 10 km north of Krugersdorp is the Kromdraai Conservancy, a recreational and conservation area that has served as home to mankind for more than a million years.

Deep underground, water at the source of the Crocodile River rises through layers of

Above: The Fiestaland recreational area on the Crocodile River, just below Hartbeespoort Dam.

dolomitic rock and, over the ages, has sculpted a world of caves and tunnels that became one of man's earliest homes. Here, man may have made his first fire and, in recent times, has dug for gold, limestone and for fossils.

This is the unique setting for the Kromdraai Conservancy Trails, a series of guided hikes through land belonging to some 30 farmers who have allowed trails to be laid out across their properties. Trails range in length from a half-day (5 km) circular route leading through the Rhino and Lion Nature Reserve (*see*

Left below: Cabbage trees (*Cussonia paniculata*) in the Rustenburg Nature Reserve, on a plateau in the Magaliesberg. **Left above:** *Frithia pulchra*, a species of dwarf vygie indigenous to the Magaliesberg. The flowers of most vygies generally open when the sun shines, but some open only at dusk, or after sunset. **Above:** A long-horned cricket eats aphids on a *Cotyledon* flower. This cricket, widespread in the region, is a nocturnal predator, spending the day in a shelter of rolled leaves secured by fine strands of silk.

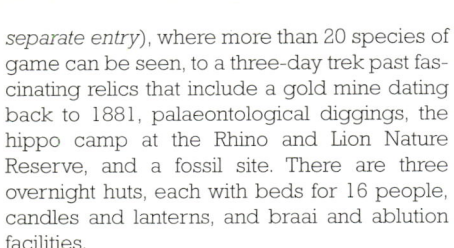

separate entry), where more than 20 species of game can be seen, to a three-day trek past fascinating relics that include a gold mine dating back to 1881, palaeontological diggings, the hippo camp at the Rhino and Lion Nature Reserve, and a fossil site. There are three overnight huts, each with beds for 16 people, candles and lanterns, and braai and ablution facilities.

Trailists must take their own sleeping bags, water (one litre each is usually enough), food, cutlery, matches and cooking utensils. At the Tobacco Kiln Camp (which has electricity), horses can be hired. Those who visit the Rhino and Lion Nature Reserve can participate in night-time game drives. The hikes are open to children under supervision, and to adults, and are strictly controlled. There is also a one-day trail for the disabled.

Apart from the Rhino and Lion Nature Reserve, attractions at Kromdraai include the Wonder Cave, a 125 m long chamber dating back 2 200 million years, and boasting a wealth of intricate, glittering formations that may be seen on guided tours involving no crawling or cramped, dark passageways. Within the cave are also rimstone pools and cave pearls, as well as striking stalactite and stalagmite forma-

tions. Light snacks are available, and there are braai facilities. There is also a curio shop, and an educational centre and museum are expected to open in the near future.

At the Rainbow Trout Farm, trout fishermen may use any tackle they choose, although there is a separate section for anglers who prefer the traditional fly. Disselboom Farm provides educational tours and fun for children in an old-fashioned farmyard.

For further information and to make reservations, contact the Kromdraai Conservancy, P O Box 393, Paardekraal 1752, telephone (011) 957-0241, or fax 957-0344.

Krugersdorp Game Reserve

Grassy hills and bush-filled ravines provide a widely varying habitat for some 30 mammal species in this 1 500 ha reserve on the outskirts of Krugersdorp.

Visitors may spot giraffe, white rhino, buffalo, eland, black wildebeest, kudu, sable, roan, blesbok, impala and tsessebe among them. A special attraction is a 100 ha lion camp at the heart of the reserve, while 150 bird species fascinate ornithologists. Nocturnal animals include brown hyena, black-backed jackal and genet, while an occasional bold leopard has

been known to venture down from some rocky lair in the nearby Magaliesberg.

The reserve is little more than 40 minutes' drive from the centre of Johannesburg, and is one of the most visited reserves in the province. A day-visitors' area near the entrance provides picnic and braai places, two swimming pools, and self-catering lapas can be hired.

For longer stays, visitors are accommodated in self-catering, thatched rondavels or family chalets, or in luxury units with up to four beds. The adjoining restaurant and bar are also open to day visitors. There are conference facilities, and a well-equipped caravan site has recently been opened.

Walking within the reserve is strictly prohibited, but visitors may accompany guided gamewatching drives in open vehicles by day and night. Visitors are also permitted to travel the reserve's roads in their own vehicles, on payment of a fee.

The reserve is open daily from 8 a.m. to 5 p.m. To reach it, drive west from Krugersdorp towards Rustenburg on the R24. Watch for signposts indicating the reserve on the right.

For more information and to make reservations, contact Krugersdorp Game Reserve,

P O Box 5237, Krugersdorp West 1742, telephone/fax (011) 665-4342 or 665-1735.

Lichtenburg Game-Breeding Centre

Pretoria's National Zoological Gardens of South Africa has a lively offspring on the flat grassveld of the Lichtenburg district.

This 6 000 ha game sanctuary, situated north of the town, is first and foremost a breeding station that concentrates on valued animal species (both indigenous and exotic). White rhino share the reserve with scimitar oryx from North Africa, while hippo from southern Africa live beside pygmy hippo (rapidly diminishing in number in the wild) from the Côte d'Ivoire, Liberia and adjacent areas of Sierra Leone.

Fences divide the Lichtenburg reserve into three main sections. The largest section covers 4 000 ha and features a comprehensive road network. This is where most of the animals are to be found. Near the entrance are 200 ha of shallow pans that are home to a large number of bird species. The second section covers 2 000 ha and is reserved for species that might interbreed with animals in the main enclosure. The third (and smallest) section is the 200 ha exotic camp.

The flat terrain and stunted vegetation make it easy to spot game in the Lichtenburg reserve, and visitors are advised to pack a pair of binoculars along with other essentials. The sanctuary is open daily throughout the year, from 8 a.m. to 4 p.m. on weekdays and until 6 p.m. at weekends and on public holidays.

To reach the reserve, drive out of Lichtenburg on the Koster road (R52) and turn left at the four-way stop. Then drive a further 2 km to reach the entrance gate, which also gives access to the adjoining municipal caravan park and camping site.

For more information, contact The Officer-in-Charge, Lichtenburg Game-Breeding Centre, P O Box 716, Lichtenburg 2740, telephone (01441) 2-2818, fax 4-1535.

Lotlamoreng Nature Reserve

About 5 km from Mafikeng, along the Vryburg road (R49), is the Lotlamoreng Dam and nature reserve, where the water surface and surrounding reed beds create an ideal environment for aquatic birds. The 200 ha reserve is controlled by the local Barolong Boo-Ratshidi clans under the overall management of the National Parks Board, and offers cool, green lawns with braai places, a refreshment kiosk and two swimming pools. There is also a centre for environmental education and it is hoped that a Rolong cultural village will be developed at the site.

For more information, write to The Officer-in-Charge, Lotlamoreng Nature Reserve, Private Bag X2078, Mmabatho 2735, or telephone (0140) 82-3411, fax 2-1468.

Magaliesberg Protected Natural Environment

A few hours from Johannesburg's skyscrapers, smog and traffic, there lies an unspoilt wilderness where you can still get away from it all and witness such stirring sights as the rare Cape vulture soaring on silent mountain updraughts.

This is the Magaliesberg – a 125 km ribbon of mountain rising to about 1 852 m above sea level – that stretches on an east/west axis from Pretoria to Rustenburg.

In 1977, to preserve this wilderness from the relentless spread of urban areas, farming and other developments, the 40 000 ha region was placed under the administration of the former Transvaal provincial government. It is now administered by the governments of two provinces – Gauteng and the North-West.

While much of the Magaliesberg remains in private land, you can still find many places in which to absorb the mountain atmosphere. The Rustenburg Nature Reserve (*see separate entry*) offers a two-day hiking trail and a two-hour ramble, and there are many other routes that give access to the streams and cliffs that are typical of the area.

Above: Cheerful cosmos blossoms transform drab fields into a riot of colour in autumn. Although regarded as a weed in South Africa, and not indigenous, cosmos is cultivated in many gardens.

Certain climbing areas, such as Castle Gorge, Tonquani and Cedarberg, are controlled by the Mountain Club of South Africa, which issues a limited number of permits every week.

Cape vultures nest on the south-facing slopes west of Olifantsnek, at Nooitgedacht and at Skeerpoort, while brown hyena, leopard and baboon are found among the nearly inaccessible ravines of the area. Duiker, steenbok, jackal and reedbuck are common.

For further information, write to the Directorate of Nature Conservation, Private Bag X209, Pretoria 0001, or telephone (012) 323-3403, fax 325-3869; or contact the Department of Tourism and Environmental Affairs, Private Bag X2078, Mmabatho 2735, telephone (0140) 89-5126, fax 2-0468.

Makwassierante Conservation Area

Giraffe and several species of large antelope feed on the tree canopies and sweet grass of

> ### WHERE VULTURES DINE
>
> The Magaliesberg range is one of the last strongholds of the Cape vulture, once a familiar sight all over southern Africa but today threatened by a variety of factors, including poisoning, shooting, electrocution (on power lines), a declining food supply – and a shortage of calcium in the diet.
>
> The problem lies with the extermination of the bone-crunching hyena in this region: adult vultures can no longer find the bone fragments so essential to their chicks' diet.
>
> Without this important source of calcium the chicks develop crippled limbs – and eventually perish. Adult birds find the calcium in the form of bones stripped from carcasses, but modern farming practices leave few such carcasses, and the vulture population has declined dramatically as a result.
>
> To help remedy the situation, the Vulture Study Group has encouraged local farmers and landowners in the Magaliesberg area to create a number of 'vulture restaurants' where carcasses of domestic animals can be provided for the birds. The 'restaurants' are open spaces where the carcasses of cattle, horses, pigs, and sometimes game are laid out. When the carcasses have been scraped clean, volunteer groups crush the bones, using mallets, to provide the birds with the much-needed bone fragments. Not everyone finds the vulture appealing, but its less attractive features have a purpose in nature. Its bald head and neck are thrust deep into a carcass, receiving a potentially harmful coating of bacteria – yet there is nowhere for the bacteria to breed, and they are killed off by sunshine. The same applies to the vulture's bare legs, which often come into contact with putrid flesh (in nature, vultures actually prefer fresh meat to decomposing carcasses). However, like other scavengers, they are highly resistant to bacterial contamination of their food, and experiments have shown them to be resistant to even anthrax and botulism. The massive beak is a highly effective implement, designed to rip easily through hide and flesh. Nature's feathered undertakers may not be pretty, but they are certainly efficient. To find out more about these powerful, vulnerable birds, write to the Vulture Study Group, P O Box 12334, Parkview 2122.

this 5 500 ha private reserve and resort some 6 km from Wolmaransstad. Two hiking trails are offered – one of 6 km and the other of 15 kilometres. Accommodation includes huts and rondavels, and there are ablution blocks and a fully equipped kitchen, as well as fully appointed stands for 25 caravans.

To reach Makwassierante, turn right onto the Leeudoringstad road (R504) at the northern end of Wolmaransstad. After approximately 1 km on the R504, turn right onto a signposted gravel road, reaching the gate to the reserve after a further 5 kilometres. For further information, contact The Manager, Makwassierante Conservation Area, P O Box 553, Wolmaransstad 2630, or telephone his office at (01811) 2-1019.

O P M Prozesky Bird Sanctuary

As in several other centres, the sewage treatment plant in Potchefstroom provides purified water for many bird species – especially waterbirds and waders – in an easily accessible environment of open grassveld, reed, eucalyptus and willow.

An area of 72 ha near the south end of town (turn from Mooi River Drive into Viljoen Street) is open at all times and, in addition to more than 200 bird species, is home to several species of small mammal, including mongoose, otter and small rodents.

The sanctuary area, which was opened in 1988, is well developed and well maintained, and offers an information kiosk, two hides, toilets, paths and park benches. In addition, there are two hikes – the Squacco Heron Route (4 km) and the Grey Heron Route (9 km). Bird-ringing is done on the first Sunday of every month, from very early in the morning to about noon. The sanctuary is always open and there is no entrance fee. A guard is on duty during working hours.

Further information can be obtained from Potchefstroom City Council, Information Bureau, P O Box 113, Potchefstroom 2520, telephone (0148) 299-5130, fax 297-6388.

Rhino and Lion Nature Reserve

Set in the peaceful Kromdraai Conservancy (*see separate entry*), a mere 30 minutes' drive northwest of Johannesburg, this reserve is a valuable refuge for both man and animal. From high points among its 1 000 ha of wind-ruffled grassland at the foot of the Swartkop Mountain, the city skyline is no more than a hazy smudge in the distance, making the reserve an ideal place for a weekend outing.

Apart from white rhino, large mammals include hippo, lion and buffalo, and antelope range from suni and steenbok to grysbok – altogether over 500 head of game. A vulture hide provides visitors with an opportunity to view and capture on film the rare Cape vulture (*Gyps coprotheres*).

Day visitors may drive in their own vehicles through the reserve (allow two to three hours) and, afterwards, picnic in an enclosed area where facilities include a swimming pool (and a separate crocodile pool), refreshment kiosk, curio shop, bar and braai places. Trout dams provide excellent fishing. Guided 4x4 tours of the more remote areas, and escorted walking trails may be arranged. Overnight accommodation is available in three, fully equipped chalets, each sleeping four people. All have a kitchen (with gas), dining room, lounge and *en suite* bathrooms. An old farm dam has been converted into a thatched lapa area for large private functions.

To reach the reserve, drive north from Randburg along D F Malan Drive (which becomes Muldersdrift Road) towards Honeydew. Cross over the R28 and continue for a further 2,8 km until you reach the Zwartkop/Tweefontein signpost. Turn left here and continue for 8 km until you see the reserve entrance on your right.

For further information, contact the Rhino and Lion Nature Reserve, P O Box 180, Krugersdorp 1740, telephone (011) 957-0109, fax 957-0344.

Rustenburg Nature Reserve

The Magaliesberg range rises 1 852 m above sea level, but only 400 m above the surrounding plains. It nevertheless offers breathtaking vistas of the town that bears its name, of the Pilanesberg and Waterberg to the north and of plains of rippling grass to the south and west. Against the northern slopes of this lovely range and rising to its summit is the 4 257 ha Rustenburg Nature Reserve.

This reserve is distinguished by its extensive valley basin, forming a valuable catchment area between the mountain ridges. Steep quartzite cliffs and enormous boulders tower over wooded ravines where young streams plunge over high precipices. The main watercourse that rises here flows east as the Waterkloof River and eventually joins the Hex River, having created a number of crystal-clear rock pools along the way.

Rustenburg Nature Reserve had its beginnings on the farm Rietvallei, originally the property of President Paul Kruger and subsequently donated by his descendants to the Rustenburg Town Council. The land, together with a number of adjoining properties, was then passed to the provincial authority and proclaimed a reserve area in 1961.

More than 230 bird species have been recorded here and the mammal population includes caracal, aardwolf, black-backed jackal, leopard and the shy brown hyena, as well as antelope species such as sable, waterbuck, kudu, red hartebeest, mountain reedbuck, springbok and eland.

One of the best ways to explore the reserve is to set out on the two-day/21 km Rustenburg Overnight Trail. Many hikers like to arrive at the sanctuary in the afternoon or evening and spend the first night in Kudu Hut, near the entrance. On the following day they walk 9 km to Red Hartebeest Hut on the plateau, and on the second day of the trail cover 12 km to return to their starting point. Each hut accommodates ten hikers, and each consists of two bedrooms and a cooking/dining area. A braai grid and firewood are provided.

The Peglarae Interpretive Trail offers day visitors a 5 km hike lasting about three hours and climbing fairly steep, rocky terrain, while the pleasant 2 km Vlei Ramble passes the vlei, the site of a viewing hut from which the reserve's mammals and birds may be observed at close range.

Those with less energy may choose to drive through the reserve or peruse the wildlife displays at the reserve's visitor centre which is situated in the middle of the sanctuary. Close by is a small caravan park and campsite (with ablution block), and a picnic area for day visitors, who are admitted to the reserve between 8 a.m. and 4 p.m. (the reserve's gates are locked at 6 p.m., and at 4.30 p.m. on Fridays).

Reservations for accommodation and for the trails must be made well in advance.

To reach the reserve, drive southwest along Wolmarans Street from the centre of town and follow the signs into Boekenhout Street at the four-way stop street. For more detailed information, you should write to The Officer-in-Charge, Rustenburg Nature Reserve, P O Box 20382, Protea Park 0305, or telephone (0142) 3-1050, fax 95-0950.

S A Lombard Nature Reserve

Named in honour of a former provincial secretary who did much to create an awareness of the need for conservation, this reserve lies northwest of the town of Bloemhof.

The sanctuary covers 3 660 ha of flat grassveld dotted with small clumps of thorn trees. After heavy rains a large pan in the sanctuary fills with water, attracting huge clouds of wheeling and screaming waterbirds.

More than 250 bird species have been recorded, among them the black korhaan,

Above: The mountain reedbuck may live in open grassland as well as on hills and mountains. It is fiercely territorial, marking and guarding its home ground against other adult males. Only males carry the short, forward-curving horns.

Left: Burchell's zebra are generally gregarious by nature and frequently associate with other animals, such as impala and wildebeest. Timid and restless, they tend to bolt from a waterhole after drinking.

white-browed sparrow-weaver, blue crane (South Africa's national bird), shaft-tailed whydah and ant-eating chat.

Since its inception, the reserve's priority has been the breeding of Highveld mammal species. Black wildebeest, or gnu, were introduced as early as 1949 (from the last remaining herd in the former Transvaal), and today the reserve has a large number of these animals, which have been joined by red hartebeest, springbok, impala and zebra.

Capturing the animals without injuring them is a difficult task, but it has been made simpler since the introduction of radio-controlled techniques in 1987. The animals are most often captured while drinking at a waterhole, and injuries are kept to the minimum.

Research into problem animals (once a function of the reserve) was concentrated on black-backed jackal and caracal, and at one time the reserve bred dogs that were used to hunt the jackal. The dogs were replaced by the more humane and efficient 'coyote-getter' imported from the United States. This research on the reserve was stopped in 1971 but, in January 1996, the Problem Animal Control Unit was re-established.

Day visitors are welcome, but arrangements must be made with the officer-in-charge. To reach the reserve, leave Bloemhof on the Schweizer-Reneke road and, after 5 km, turn left onto the Holfontein gravel road and drive another 12 kilometres.

For further information about the reserve, contact The Officer-in-Charge, S A Lombard Nature Reserve, P O Box 174, Bloemhof 2660, telephone (01802) 3-1953 or (053) 433-1953, fax (01802) 3-1917 or (053) 433-1917.

Sterkfontein Caves

The area north of Krugersdorp features a number of impressive cave formations formed by underground water slowly and relentlessly dissolving the dolomitic rock. With the sudden growth of mining and industry along the Witwatersrand, limestone – used in the manufacture of cement – was quarried here.

One day in 1896 a controlled explosion blasted open an unsuspected cave system below the ground, glittering with glorious stalactites, stalagmites and formations, both fragile and massive, that seemed to be made of the purest crystal. These were soon vandalised as 'souvenirs', but it was not long before a more thoughtful group visited the quarry.

Members of a religious order, the Marist Brothers, discovered fossilised bones, the first to be recovered from a site that has become one of the most important in the long prehistory of man and mammal in Africa.

Today this labyrinthine network of caves is world-famous as the discovery site of the fossil skull identified as belonging to a human-like primate, (*Australopithecus*), which existed on the African continent millions of years ago. Prompted by finds made earlier in the area, Dr Robert Broom of the Transvaal Museum in Pretoria began to explore the caves, and his work supports the theory, propounded earlier by anatomist Professor Raymond Dart, that southern Africa was the home of early man – the supposed 'missing link' between extinct ape-like forms and modern man. Until then it had been presumed – on no very good academic grounds – that man had originated in Europe.

When the owner of the land died in the late 1950s, his children presented a particularly handsome part of it to the University of the Witwatersrand, to be known as the Isaac Edwin Stegmann Nature Reserve.

Later the university bought a neighbouring farm (Swartkrans) that also contains a rich fossil cave deposit. Thus the university owns two sites in the area – Swartkrans Cave to the west and the main Sterkfontein complex, which is open to the public.

From 1966 to 1996 Professor Phillip Tobias led successive teams from the university, systematically excavating the cave-filling at Sterkfontein and recovering some 600 specimens of early human-like creatures, as well as tens of thousands of animal bones. Sterkfontein has yielded the world's richest store of early pre-human remains.

Limestone-mining and the natural processes of cave formation have hollowed out large chambers within Sterkfontein, but it is not difficult to imagine the caves as they used to be. In places there are remnants of the old fossil-laden deposits, the deepest of them over three million years old.

Also to be seen are the fossilised remains of extinct hominids, monkey, antelope, sabre-toothed cat, horse and other mammals that lived between one-and-a-half and three million years ago.

Some underground galleries are flooded by the clear water of a lake that extends far into unexplored chambers. Even here, life goes on, where many people believe that it started. In the water are shrimps – sightless in the dark – that grow to no more than 1 cm in length.

The Sterkfontein Caves are open to visitors every day (except Mondays), and on all public holidays. Tours are conducted every half-hour from 9 a.m. to 4 p.m. A guide leads visitors into the caves and recorded talks in several languages explain their history.

There is a tearoom near the entrance, and beside it is the Robert Broom Museum, which contains exhibits illustrating the process of fossilisation and the area's natural history. To reach the caves, leave Krugersdorp on the R47 leading northwest to Tarlton. Turn right onto the R563. The turn-off to the caves is about 10 km further along on the right.

For more information, contact Sterkfontein Caves, P O Box 481, Krugersdorp 1740, telephone (011) 956-6342, fax 660-5833.

Vaal Spa Game Reserve

In lush green seclusion on the banks of the Vaal River to the northeast of Christiana is a well-frequented resort. One of the reasons for its popularity is a well-stocked game reserve situated between the river and the main road to the north – 2 300 ha of flat, sandy grassveld that is typical of the area. Animals that find sanctuary here include eland, black wildebeest, red hartebeest, zebra, blesbok, gemsbok, springbok, white rhino and impala.

The river runs along the reserve's northern edge and for much of the year provides a natural boundary. In winter, however, it becomes so shallow that buck can easily walk across (in the past they fell easy victim to game-hungry hunters).

Today there is a fence along the river. Perhaps it is a blessing in disguise, because it provides a rhino-proof corridor along the bank. Visitors may travel through the reserve in their own cars, or by special bus. Vaal Spa is open every day from 7.30 a.m. to 4 p.m. and the road network takes visitors to all parts of the reserve – including the river bank, which is rich in riverine bush and is the favourite habitat of the rhino and impala.

The resort complex includes 100 fully equipped chalets, two-bed flats, restaurants, a supermarket, a fine auditorium and a caravan park and campsite.

There are two swimming pools and a mineral bath. The resort is especially busy during the Christmas and Easter school holidays, though its dry climate makes it popular throughout the year.

To reach the Vaal Spa (previously known as the Rob Ferreira) Game Reserve, drive about 4 km along the main road from Christiana to the northeast: the resort is on the right, well signposted from the road. For more information, and to apply for accommodation, contact Aventura Central Reservations, P O Box 720, Groenkloof 0027, telephone (012) 346-2277, fax 346-2293.

Witwatersrand National Botanical Garden

This scenic, 300 ha garden lies within easy reach of Roodepoort and Krugersdorp.

Surrounding the 70 m Witpoortjie Falls, the focal point of the garden, is dense riverine woodland filled with the calls – some raucous, some shrill and some sweet – of its rich birdlife. Over 180 species have been recorded, including the only pair of breeding black eagles on the Witwatersrand.

The garden also supports aloes, summer-rainfall protea species and other flora. An interpretive centre outlines its history and geography, and exhibits its fauna and flora.

The garden is open to the public daily between 8 a.m. and 5 p.m. A restaurant operates on weekdays from 9.30 a.m. to 4.30 p.m., and at weekends and public holidays from 9 a.m. to 5 p.m. Indigenous plants are on sale.

The gardens are in Malcolm Street in Roodepoort. For further information, write to the Witwatersrand National Botanical Garden, P O Box 2194, Wilropark 1731, or telephone (011) 958-1750, or fax 958-1752.

Wolwespruit Nature Reserve

Originally an isolated section of Bloemhof Dam Nature Reserve (see separate entry), Wolwespruit is now a sanctuary in its own right.

The reserve covers 2 333 ha along the north bank of the Vaal River upstream from the Bloemhof Dam, and is named after a tributary of the Vaal. Game found here includes kudu, duiker, steenbok, blesbok, red hartebeest, black wildebeest and zebra, as well as smaller species such as Cape fox and caracal. The vegetation, comprising Kalahari thornveld with thick bush along the river banks, is home to a variety of bird species, including many different members of the thrush, shrike, starling and whydah families.

At this stage, visitors are unable to drive or walk around the reserve, its main attraction being for anglers and ornithologists who stay at any of the 35 campsites picturesquely situated on the river banks. The campsites are equipped with braai sites and toilet facilities.

The reserve lies approximately 18 km south of Leeudoringstad. For further information, contact North-West Nature Conservation, P O Box 729, Bloemhof 2660, telephone (01802) 3-1706 or (053) 433-1706, fax (01802) 3-1705 or (053) 433-1705.

THE ENCHANTING CAPE WHITE-EYE

This amiable little garden bird, widespread in a variety of habitats throughout southern Africa, belongs to the genus *Zosterops*, one of the largest of all bird genera. Occurring in a region extending from the arid areas of Namibia southward to the Kalahari and the riverine bush and forests of the Indian Ocean coast, and northeast to the dry bushveld of the Northern Province, this little bird is often seen at garden birdbaths and is easily lured by food-filled feeding trays. Small groups appear, flitting from branch to branch, and perching precariously on the ends of twigs, all the while twisting and turning their bodies in the never-ending search for insects, berries and other tasty titbits.

Highly gregarious by nature, the group is left only for breeding, after which the pair return to the flock. Musical chirrups and tweets accompany their movements, keeping alive their network of communication. Their song is a high-pitched series of sweetly piping notes, punctuated with calls imitating those of other birds and interrupted, every now and again, with a shrill call of alarm. The Cape white-eye (*Zosterops pallidus*) can be identified by its greyish-green dorsal feathers, its grey undercarriage, its yellow throat and the distinctive white ring, composed of dense, pure white feathers, around each eye.

It builds a small, cup-shaped nest of fine material, such as grass, stems, roots or hair, in a fork of a shrub or tree, and lines it with plant down or a few feathers to create a comfortable shelter for two to three eggs. Pale blue, pale green or white eggs are incubated for up to 12 days, and chicks stay in the nest for just under two weeks.

Where the bird is king

From its roster of nature reserves, the northeastern Highveld (including southern Mpumalanga) appears to be a bird paradise. The region contains a number of sanctuaries devoted to the conservation of birds, among them Germiston's Rondebult and Nigel's Marievale, which are among the most important in South Africa. Birds are the prime attraction at several of the reserves created around water storage dams (among them Jericho Dam and Rietvlei nature reserves) and figure prominently at Johannesburg's Melville Koppies – the city's chief nature sanctuary.

Most of the bird reserves are relatively small and compact, and are easily overshadowed in size by the Suikerbosrand Nature Reserve near Heidelberg and the Songimvelo Nature Reserve southeast of Barberton.

These two reserves typify all that is best in the northeastern Highveld – rolling terrain, grassveld vegetation and a variety of game, including eland, duiker, impala, black wildebeest, red hartebeest, Burchell's zebra, blesbok and springbok.

Bronkhorstspruit Dam Nature Reserve

One of the newer reserves in the northeastern Highveld is set around the Bronkhorstspruit Dam, some 15 km south of Bronkhorstspruit on the road to Delmas. The 952 ha dam has long been popular with boating enthusiasts and fishermen, many of whom camp on its shores at weekends and during school holidays.

The 1 800 ha reserve has been fenced, but as yet the only game reintroduced to the area has been black wildebeest, steenbok and blesbok. There is an impressive variety of bird species – predominantly waterfowl – in the sanctuary, which is open every day from 6 a.m. to 8 p.m. Facilities for campers include braai places, toilets and drinking water. The future status of the Bronkhorstspruit Dam reserve is uncertain, and those who wish to make enquiries should contact the reserve manager at Roodeplaat Dam Nature Reserve (*see separate entry*) at P O Box 15163, Lynn East 0039, telephone (012) 808-0510, or fax 808-1164.

Elandskrans Hiking Trail

Waterval-Boven sits atop the Drakensberg escarpment, a good 200 m higher than its counterpart, Waterval-Onder. Each weekend the village council organises a novel hike through a private nature reserve on the slopes of the escarpment. Hikers assemble early on Saturday mornings at the Elandskrans Holiday Resort and walk throughout the day, exploring an area rich with lush vegetation and enchanting waterfalls. The trail is a drawcard for birding enthusiasts, with the chance of spotting

Left: A distant shower at sunset in the Suikerbosrand Nature Reserve.
Above: Looper caterpillars (measuring worms) have no feet with which to support the middle part of their bodies, and walk by arching the body to bring the hind legs close to the front legs. Like all caterpillars, their bodies comprise the head capsule, three thoracic segments and ten abdominal segments. The simple eyes (usually six) are on the head at the base of a pair of very short antennae. **Right:** The hardy monkey's tail (*Xerophyta retinervis*) manages to survive long periods of drought. Its bristly, stunted trunk sprouts wiry stalks which are tipped with attractive, sweetly scented blooms.

HIGHVELD: NORTHEASTERN HIGHVELD

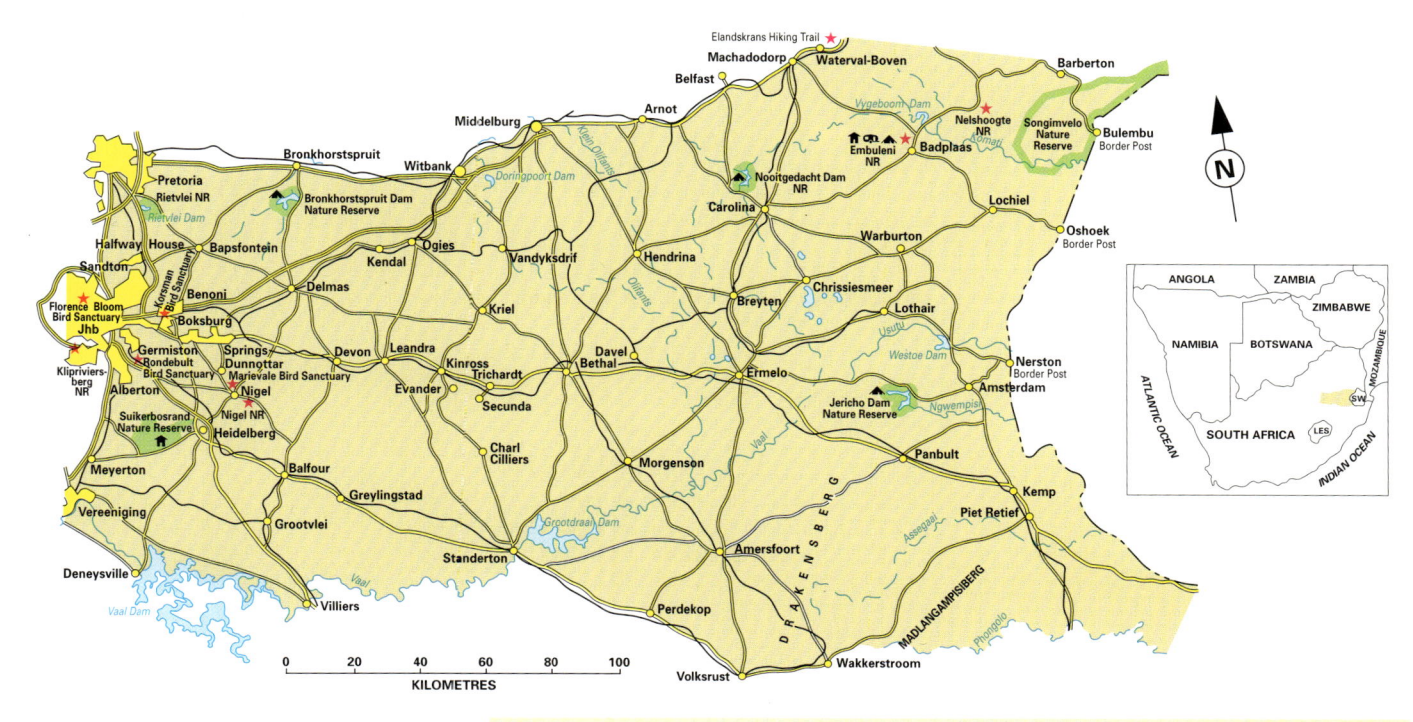

black eagle and the green Knysna lourie. Trailists then spend the night in six huts, each of which can accommodate a maximum of eight people. Firewood is provided. The hikers complete their walk at Waterval-Onder the following morning, before catching a train that transports them 12 km back up the escarpment to the station. From here it is a 2 km walk back to the resort. Trees along the route are identified and numbered.

To book places on the trail, write to the Village Council, Private Bag X05, Waterval-Boven 1195, telephone/fax (013262) and ask for 176.

Embuleni Nature Reserve

The blue-green Hlumuhlumu Mountains provide an attractive backdrop for the village of Badplaas, literally 'bath farm', the setting for one of the most popular of the province's hot-water mineral spas. The surrounding scenic slopes and foothills that adjoin the spa (administered by Aventura Resorts) form part of the 1 500 ha Embuleni Nature Reserve, providing plenty of room for the reserve's growing animal population as well as for its various hiking trails and horse riding – one of the Embuleni specialities.

The reserve's terrain is hilly and the vegetation is largely grassveld, which makes it easy to see game. Embuleni features species such as rhino, leopard, brown hyena, gemsbok, eland, black wildebeest and red hartebeest, springbok, zebra, steenbok, duiker, bushbuck, blesbok and impala. Vervet monkeys chatter in the trees and baboon can be seen on the rocky slopes. More than 120 bird species have been

A DAISY FROM THE DIGGINGS

The town of Barberton had its beginnings in a short-lived gold rush that occurred in the early 1880s. The boom attracted fortune-hunters from far and wide, among them a Durban jam manufacturer named Robert Jameson, a keen amateur botanist who served on the committee of the Durban Botanical Garden. Jameson spent only a short time on the diggings, but while there he grew to admire a 'dandelion' of brilliant scarlet that grew in profusion throughout the region. He presented samples to the curator of the Durban garden.

Jameson's dandelion (or *Gerbera*) is the well-known Barberton daisy, a favourite with gardeners all over the world. It became known internationaly in 1889, when the curator of the Durban Botanical Garden sent plants to Kew Gardens in London. One of the specimens survived and flowered.

At about the same time another amateur botanist on the Barberton fields sent seeds of the same species to a friend living in Cornwall. The friend raised seedlings and presented samples to Kew Gardens and to the Cambridge Botanical Garden. The curator of the Cambridge garden began cultivating the new daisy and, in the years that followed, steadily improved its quality, developing hybrids of other colours. Commercial growers followed suit, and the Chelsea Flower Show of 1912 featured Barberton daisies with colours ranging from the original scarlet to vivid orange, yellow, buff, salmon pink and rose.

The daisies became firm favourites in the Netherlands and in other European countries, and gained a strong foothold in North America and Australia. The Barberton daisy had become an international star.

recorded. There is a fine network of roads which gives visitors access to all parts of the reserve, and horses may be hired from the resort stable. The resort's accommodation includes rondavels, flatlets, a caravan site (with power points) and a campsite. There is also a restaurant, cafeteria, supermarket, butchery, bank, garage and a hotel with a bottle store. Recreational facilities include three outdoor swimming pools, two pools for toddlers, a spa with four swimming pools as well as private baths, tennis courts, a bowling green, miniature golf course and an entertainment hall.

Aventura Badplaas and Embuleni Nature Reserve are open year round, from 7 a.m. to 5 p.m., and can be reached along tarred and gravel roads from Carolina, Machadodorp and Barberton, and all routes are well signposted. For further information, you should write to Aventura Badplaas, P O Box 15, Badplaas 1190, telephone (017) 844-1020 or 844-1023/4, fax 844-1391. To book accommodation, contact Aventura Central Reservations, P O Box 720, Groenkloof 0027, telephone (012) 346-2277, or fax 346-2293.

Flora Reserves

The Barberton area has three 'special status' provincial nature reserves, each dedicated to conserving one or two rare species – in this case, aloes. None of the three is open to the public and their location is kept secret in an effort to frustrate would-be plant thieves. The 10 ha Tienie Louw Nature Reserve, named after a well-known economist, protects *Aloe albida* and *Aloe chortolirioides*. The Thorncroft Nature Reserve covers 16 ha of the mountains near Barberton and safeguards the rare *Aloe thorncroftii*, discovered there by G Thorncroft in 1914. The 8 ha Cythna Letty Nature Reserve, named after a well-known botanical artist, conserves the rare *Aloe vryheidensis*.

Florence Bloom Bird Sanctuary

This leafy 10 ha bird sanctuary is set around two small dams in Johannesburg's Delta Park. Visitors may not walk around the sanctuary, but may instead view the birds from hides overlooking the dams. Over the past few years over 190 species of bird have been sighted, including African black duck, Egyptian goose, blacksmith plover, hamerkop, owl and a number of kingfisher species. The hides are open to the public daily from sunrise to sunset.

Delta Park is home to an environmental centre which comprises exhibition halls, an auditorium, meditation room, aquarium and gift shop. The park and the Florence Bloom Bird Sanctuary are featured on the Braamfontein Spruit Trail (*see separate entry*, Johannesburg and Sandton's urban trails), which follows the stream after which it is named along the park's eastern edge. To reach Delta Park from the centre of Johannesburg, travel north along Barry Hertzog Avenue (which becomes Rustenburg Road), and turn right into Road No 3 in Victory Park.

For more information, contact Delta Environmental Centre, Private Bag X6, Parkview 2122, telephone (011) 888-4831, or fax 888-4106.

Fortuna Mine Hiking Trail

The charming town of Barberton, embraced by the green-clad foothills of the Makonjwa mountain range, is the setting for the 2 km Fortuna Mine Hiking Trail. Trailists pass through the Barberton Indigenous Tree Park (the approximately 100 tree species are labelled for easy reference), across hills and through shady gorges, introducing visitors to the heady atmosphere of Barberton's early days of gold-prospecting , as well as giving them an intimate glimpse of the area's lovely flora and fauna. The circular route, marked with yellow arrows, requires about one and a half to two hours to complete and affords marvellous views across the town of Barberton and the De Kaap valley, which is claimed to be the largest landlocked valley in the world.

The trail starts some 300 m from the parking area in Crown Street. One of its most interesting sections takes visitors through a 600 m tunnel cut through rock early this century to link the old Fortuna Mine to the mill (a torch is essential for this section but, take heart, it takes only seven minutes to complete). Some rocks found in this section date back 4 200 million years, and are considered to be among the oldest sedimentary rock formations found on earth. A second tunnel on the right-hand side of the bridge at the entrance to the Fortuna Tunnel was also used to transport the ore, but this one is not safe to enter. Hikers return through a creek bearing magnificent specimens of red ivory (*Berchemia zeyheri*) and climb past wild olive and bastard Cape iron trees which part to reveal the panoramic view across the town and the De Kaap valley.

The trail then passes under the aerial ropeway along which asbestos is transported from the Havelock Mine in Swaziland, and leads back to the parking area.

The Barberton Information Bureau has sketch-maps and information sheets. For more information, contact them at P O Box 33, Barberton 1300, telephone/fax (013) 712-2121.

Above: A gorilla at the Johannesburg Zoological Gardens. The gorilla occurs only in Africa, and the populations are believed to be declining. **Top:** A tree cricket. The male of this genus may often be found wedged in a pear-shaped hole he has gnawed in a leaf. When he stridulates, his wings are extended and pressed against the leaf to seal the hole – thus increasing the resonating surface of his 'sound baffle'.

THE OLDEST FOSSILS

Until relatively recently, the world's oldest sedimentary rocks – forming part of the Swaziland System, near Barberton – were believed to contain no trace of early life. Then, in 1966, two scientists named Barghoorn and Schopf, using an electron microscope, discovered fossil bacteria in wafer-thin slivers removed from the rocks known as the Pre-Cambrian Fig-Tree Series. The discovery of these minute fossil bacteria (*Eobacterium isolatum*) in rocks over 3 000 million years old, excited worldwide attention, and revolutionised the study of early life on earth. Microscopically small algae and fungi were found in the same rocks, and chemical analyses indicated that these ancient plants possessed the ability to photosynthesise: they were thus the earliest of the countless small green plants which released oxygen into the thin atmosphere, permitting the evolution of higher forms of plant- and animal life – including our own.

Above: The Florence Bloom Bird Sanctuary – a leafy refuge for a variety of waterfowl. The birds may be viewed from hides overlooking two dams.

Harvey Nature Reserve

Owned by the Greater Johannesburg Transitional Metropolitan Council, this 6 ha reserve – situated on Linksfield Ridge – offers visitors varied and interesting vegetation and occasional glimpses of small mammals. The Dassie Trail leads through the reserve.

Jericho Dam Nature Reserve

The 2 800 ha Jericho Dam Nature Reserve has fast become one of the Highveld's premier recreational areas. Visitors are enchanted by its prolific birdlife which includes waterfowl, wattled crane, blue and crowned crane, bald ibis, secretary bird, orange-breasted longclaw, long-tailed widow and kori bustard, while mammals to be spotted include the rare oribi, steenbok and duiker. Several large frog species, one of which is the imposing giant bullfrog, abound during summer. The dam's clear waters, impounding a section of the Mpama River, support exotic black bass – a favourite with anglers – and large-mouth bass. Camping is permitted on the shores, and drinking water is available.

To reach the dam, approach along the gravel road from Sheepmoor, Roodewal or Bankkop, or from the road between Ermelo and Amsterdam, or Ermelo and Piet Retief.

For further information about Jericho Dam reserve, contact Mpumalanga Parks Board, Private Bag X11233, Nelspruit 1200, telephone (013) 753-3931, fax 755-4796. To make reservations, contact the Parks Board offices at P O Box 1990, Nelspruit 1200, telephone (013) 758-1035, fax 755-3931.

Johannesburg and Sandton's urban trails

Witwatersrand means 'ridge of white waters', and the little streams – there are at least 14 of them – that gave birth to the name still flow through the region to the north and south of the ridge. Among these is the Braamfontein Spruit, which springs from the ground in northern Hillbrow and flows north to join the Sand Spruit and then the Jukskei River at Leeuwkop Prison in the northern areas.

Some years ago, the former city councils of Johannesburg, Randburg and Sandton (now known as Greater Johannesburg) joined forces to develop various trails along the ribbons of open spaces created by these rivers, so that picnickers, hikers, birdwatchers, mountain bikers and horse riders could enjoy the tranquillity of a green haven in the heart of Greater Johannesburg's urban sprawl.

The first and most successful of the urban trails is the Braamfontein Spruit Trail which follows rocky ridges and willow-draped streams, passing dams and waterfalls as it weaves its green path through the area. The 18,35 km trail is divided into various sections, each taking less than two hours to complete. One of these is the Jukskei Trail, a peaceful pathway that crisscrosses the metropolitan area in two separate sections. Bezuidenhout Park, at the end of the second leg of the trail, marks the start of the 12 km Sand Spruit Trail, taking in some of the city's prettiest parks, including Melrose Wild Bird Sanctuary (*see separate entry*), before the stream after which it is named converges with the Braamfontein Spruit at Paulshof.

The Parktown/Westcliff Urban Walk, comprising five circular walks, introduces participants to the stately mansions built in the 19th century by the city's 'randlords' who amassed their fortunes during the gold rush. This fascinating walk also passes Melville Koppies Nature Reserve (*see separate entry*), Emmarentia Dam and Delta Park (headquarters of the Delta Environmental Centre) until it ends at Lone Hill Tor, 100 m south of the Jukskei River. Here a large variety of plants and animals can be found. Three of the five walks wind through Parktown and two through Westcliff.

Despite being laid out within South Africa's largest metropolitan area, the trails pass through a wide variety of natural vegetation as well as important archaeological sites. Further information can be obtained by writing to the Greater Johannesburg Publicity Association, P O Box 4580, Johannesburg 2000, telephone

(011) 337-6650, fax 333-7272; or contact the Department of Urban Conservation and Health Management, Eastern Metropolitan Substructure, Greater Johannesburg Transitional Metropolitan Council, telephone (011) 803-9132/3, or fax 803-2066; or Braamfontein Spruit Trust, P O Box 44538, Linden 2104, telephone (011) 782-5473, fax 782-5169.

Johannesburg Zoological Gardens

Wildlife from all over the African continent can be seen at the Johannesburg's spacious 54 ha Zoological Gardens, where animals and visitors are separated by natural barriers (as opposed to bars). In all, the zoo accommodates some 400 mammal, bird and reptile species – a total of 3 500 animals. Of special interest – especially to children – are the elephant, gorilla, polar bear and the beautiful (and rare) white lion, as well as a popular farmyard where they can meet other animals at close quarters. The walk-through aviary is also a favourite with visitors who enjoy the chirping chorus of the hundreds of birds.

Rolling, manicured lawns, large shady trees and colourful beds of flowers make this an enchanting spot for a family picnic.

The zoo has existed since 1904, when the 200 ha Hermann Eckstein Park, of which it forms a part, was given to the municipality along with a collection of animals that was donated by the late Sir Percy FitzPatrick, author of *Jock of the Bushveld*.

Johannesburg Zoo is located east of Jan Smuts Avenue, opposite Zoo Lake, in the northern suburb of Parkview (parking is available in Upper Park Drive to the south). It is open daily throughout the year from 8.30 a.m. to 5.30 p.m. Refreshments are available at the restaurant and at numerous kiosks. For further information, contact Zooline on (011) 646-2000, or fax 486-0244. The zoo's postal address is Private Bag X13, Parkview 2122.

Klipriviersberg Nature Reserve

This nature reserve, the property of the Greater Johannesburg Transitional Metropolitan Council (formerly the Johannesburg City Council), features some remnants of old kraals that bear witness to the presence of groups of indigenous people who lived in the area long before it was officially settled.

Covering 550 ha to the south of Mondeor, Klipriviersberg comprises portions of three early Witwatersrand farms – Vierfontein, Rietvlei (of which the farmhouse and *waenhuis* still exist, though in a vandalised state) and Olifantsvlei.

An impressive array of 175 species of bird, and small mammals such as grey duiker, porcupine, hare and dassie may be seen.

Although certain species of alien vegetation such as the silver wattle, silver poplar and the prickly pear (all currently being eradicated) have invaded parts of Klipriviersberg, an impressive variety of indigenous vegetation may still be identified.

Guided tours of the reserve, which last about three hours, take place at 9 a.m. on the second Sunday of every month. The tours leave from Silent Pool which is situated at the cul-de-sac of Frandaph Avenue in Mondeor. At other times the public has free access to the reserve. No dogs are permitted. For further information, you can contact Klipriviersberg Nature Reserve Association, P O Box 968, Mondeor 2110, telephone (011) 483-1920.

Below: Southern Africa's most common duck is the yellow-billed duck (*Anas undulata*), easily identified by its bright, black-patched beak and black feet. Related to the exotic mallard (the two can interbreed if brought together), it finds much of its food on land, although it prefers to stay close to inland waters and estuaries. Unlike its northern hemisphere cousins, who fly long distances between breeding and wintering grounds, the yellowbill is not migratory, but a vagrant. It remains fairly sedentary during the day, staying close to the water's edge and making short foraging flights as dusk approaches.

Korsman Bird Sanctuary

Benoni's suburb of Westdene has a novel attraction in its 50 ha Korsman Bird Sanctuary (considered by some to be one of the best in South Africa), which centres on a shallow pan and is encircled by a road. The pan attracts large numbers of migratory waterfowl, including ibis and flamingo, and the surrounding shore is home to ostrich and game such as blesbok, springbok, steenbok and duiker.

The Witwatersrand Bird Club has a hide in the sanctuary and its members have a key to the gate, but casual visitors are not allowed. However, a fine view may be had from outside the fence.

The sanctuary is encircled by a road called The Drive, and is situated directly south of and adjacent to the Benoni Lake golf course.

Casual visits to the sanctuary may be arranged by contacting the Wildlife Society on (011) 880-9444 or 899-5222. For further information, contact City Council of Greater Benoni, Department of Parks and Recreation, Private Bag X014, Benoni 1500, telephone (011) 741-6000, fax 421-8019.

Marievale Bird Sanctuary

Marievale Bird Sanctuary is a 1 000 ha reserve located on a large vlei formed by the Blesbokspruit. Three well-organised hides have been built in this sanctuary, and more than 300 bird species have been spotted there – chiefly waterfowl, including greater and lesser flamingo, African spoonbill, virtually every indigenous species of duck and goose, and some of the rare wader migrants from the northern hemisphere.

Marievale, which is open daily from sunrise to sunset, can be reached from Nigel by following the signposts (on some maps marked 'Marieshaft'). At the mine complex, turn right and continue on the road through the reeds. There is a picnic spot near one of the hides.

For more information, contact The Reserve Manager, Gauteng Department of Agriculture, Conservation and the Environment, Private Bag H631, Heidelberg 2400, telephone (0151) 9-5060, or fax 9-5063.

Melrose Wild Bird Sanctuary

Like the Braamfontein Spruit, the Sand Spruit flows through Johannesburg's northern suburbs and, in the process, creates the vlei at the centre of Melrose Wild Bird Sanctuary – only a stone's throw from Johannesburg's M1 freeway. The 10 ha sanctuary contains reed beds and indigenous trees which provide ideal nesting sites for over 120 bird species.

Weavers and gregarious bishop birds – the black-and-scarlet plumage of the red bishop is particularly eye-catching – lurk among the reeds, while ducks, geese and moorhens paddle placidly on the still waters of the lake. There is a hide for birdwatchers. The sanctuary forms part of the James and Ethel Gray Park and is owned and controlled by the Greater Johannesburg Transitional Metropolitan Council. The Braamfontein Spruit Trail, part of the network of urban trails that weaves through Johannesburg and Sandton (*see separate entry*), passes through this leafy sanctuary.

Open daily from sunrise to sunset, it is best visited during the summer months. For details, contact Department of Culture and Recreation, Greater Johannesburg Transitional Metropolitan Council, P O Box 2824, Johannesburg 2000, telephone (011) 407-6824, fax 403-4495; or Greater Johannesburg Publicity Association, P O Box 4580, Johannesburg 2000, telephone (011) 337-6650, fax 333-7272.

Melville Koppies Nature Reserve

One of Johannesburg's showpiece sanctuaries is the 200 ha Melville Koppies Nature Reserve, which straddles D F Malan Drive in the city's northeastern suburbs. The highway divides a 60 ha closed section in the east from a 20 ha open section to the west. (To the east is also another 40 ha open section, the Louw Geldenhuys Viewsite.) The reserve's principal attraction is its flora, which includes 80 per cent of the species recorded on the Witwatersrand. There is also an arboretum with labelled trees including the silver oak, white stinkwood, Cape lilac and wild pear.

In addition, the reserve contains a valuable example of Witwatersrand geology, and an archaeological site occupied by man for an estimated 100 000 years, while stone tools bear witness to the presence of Stone Age hunter-gatherers. Also to be seen are a number of 500-year-old Iron Age furnaces, two of which have been excavated. There are also the remains of several kraals. Detailed records of excavations at Melville Koppies and research on Iron Age smelting can be found in the library of the University of the Witwatersrand's Department of Archaeology.

Of the area's many hundreds of plant species, more than 30 are edible, 112 are used medicinally, eight are potential poisons, two are

Above: *Clematopsis scabiosifolia*, an attractive wild shrub that graces much of the Highveld countryside. **Above right:** *Diospyros lycioides* (jakkalsbessie), a tropical tree that grows in woodland bush. The fruits are edible when ripe, and are eaten by a huge variety of birds and animals. **Right:** A brown lacewing larva of the insect family Hemerobiidae eating its favourite food – aphids (a dietary habit that endears it to farmers and gardeners). The adults are frequently attracted to lights, and are characterised by large golden eyes and green-brown, glass-like wings.

Left: The fan-shaped *Boophone disticha*, otherwise known as *gifbol* or red posy. The flowers form a large pink ball. **Above:** Eland graze in the well-stocked 3 200 ha Rietvlei Nature Reserve.

valued perfumes and 34 are used as ingredients in ritual magic. Witwatersrand University's Moss Herbarium has a section devoted to these fascinating plants.

Melville Koppies (it has been a provincial nature reserve since 1959 and a national monument since 1968) is also a magnet for the birdwatcher – ornithologists have recorded more than 180 species, including spotted eagle owl, crimson-breasted shrike, red-billed hoopoe, francolin, barbet, thrush, wagtail and red-throated wryneck.

Officially, the reserve is open to the public from 3 p.m. to 6 p.m. on the first and third Sundays (and between 9 a.m. and 12 noon on the second Sunday) of each month from September to April inclusive (when members of the Friends of Melville Koppies are on hand to lead conducted tours). Alternatively, visitors may follow a nature trail with the aid of the detailed Melville Koppies guidebook – obtainable at the Johannesburg Zoological Gardens (see separate entry).

At other times, those wishing to visit the reserve should telephone (011) 888-4831 during office hours, or fax 888-4106. Alternatively, write to Private Bag X6, Parkview 2122.

Nelshoogte Nature Reserve

The most prominent feature of this 211 ha nature reserve, situated within the Nelshoogte forest plantation, some 40 km from Barberton on the road to Badplaas (the turn-off is not signposted), is the 'Devil's Knuckles', a strikingly precipitous ridge of hills. Near the Nelshoogte Nature Reserve is the 25 ha Dr Hamilton Protea Reserve, established exclusively for the protection of the rare *Protea roupelliae* subspecies *hamiltonii*. Visitors may obtain further information and entry permits for both reserves from SAFCOL, Private Bag X608, Barberton 1300, telephone (013) 712-3114, or fax 712-5279.

Nigel Nature Reserve

On the outskirts of Nigel is an attractive 65 ha municipal nature reserve, stocked with ostrich, duiker, a small herd of springbok, and zebra (there are a number of ducks and geese on a small dam). The public may not enter the reserve, but there are good vantage points on a terrace situated just outside the fence.

The reserve is situated just southeast of Nigel, while the terrace is accessible from Bloekom Avenue, in the suburb of Ferryvale. For more detailed information, contact the Department of Parks and Recreation, P O Box 23, Nigel 1490, telephone (011) 360-6000, or fax 739-2972.

Nooitgedacht Dam Nature Reserve

This 3 420 ha provincial reserve, tucked around a dam about 10 km northwest of Carolina, has become a popular getaway for anglers and watersport enthusiasts. Large-mouth bass, small-mouth bass, barbel and carp entice fishermen to the dam's shores.

The rolling Highveld grasslands, devoid of trees because of harsh winter frosts and regular veld fires, conceal interesting flora species such as the scarlet-flowered ground coral bush. Game species to be found in the reserve include springbok, blesbok, grey rhebok, red hartebeest, black wildebeest, steenbok and grey duiker. Birdlife is plentiful. Camping is permitted along the shore. Further information can be obtained by writing to Mpumalanga Parks Board, Private Bag X11233, Nelspruit 1200, telephone (013) 753-3931, fax 755-4796. To make reservations, contact the offices at P O Box 1990, Nelspruit 1200, telephone (013) 758-1035, fax 755-3931.

Peacehaven Nature Reserve

Vereeniging's suburb of Peacehaven is home to a modest 30 ha nature reserve which, in turn, is home to some 15 fallow deer (the rest of the herd either swam to safety or were drowned during the disastrous floods of 1996), while the dam within its boundaries is home to various duck species, including yellowbill, redbill, white-faced whistling duck, and various other waterbirds. Plans are afoot to introduce ostrich. The public is not allowed inside, but there are good views from raised areas outside the fence. Birdwatchers, however, may arrange to collect the keys to Peacehaven by contacting the Parks and Recreation Department, P O Box 35, Vereeniging 1963, or telephone them at

Right: The elegant greater flamingo, which congregates and migrates in huge flocks, is a familiar sight in and around coastal lagoons and large stretches of water throughout southern Africa. It feeds on small aquatic invertebrates and microscopic algae.

(016) 50-3153, fax 50-3234. The reserve is bordered by General Hertzog Road, Dee Drive, Golf Road and Waterkant Street.

Rietvlei Nature Reserve

Rietvlei Dam, situated within the Pretoria municipal area and on the boundary of Centurion, is an important source of water for the city. It also lies at the centre of a 3 200 ha municipal nature reserve. Previously called the Van Riebeeck Nature Reserve, Rietvlei is open to anglers between 6 a.m. and 6 p.m. every day on presentation of a permit, which is obtainable at the entrance gate (on Sundays and public holidays), from Munitoria (on the corner of Vermeulen and Van der Walt streets), at the entrance gate to Fountains Valley, and from certain private businesses selling fishing tackle. Escorted bus tours may also be arranged.

A number of hiking trails, ranging in duration from one to two days, are available. Under the capable leadership of a trained nature conservation officer, hikers travel up to 21 km, encountering the reserve's rich game stock and passing several historical sites, one of which is an entrenchment of stones constructed by the British during the first occupation of Pretoria. Overnight huts with beds, mattresses, hot and cold water, cooking utensils and firewood, are provided. Day and overnight drives are available, as are horse rides. There is also an environment education centre.

Rietvlei lies some 1 470 m to 1 550 m above sea level (considerably higher than Pretoria) and it is the only proclaimed bankenveld nature reserve on a dolomite formation in South Africa. This veld type is valuable land for agriculture, so the chances are that this city reserve will remain the only one of its kind. Indigenous trees include species of acacia, rhus, white stinkwood (*Celtis africana*) and river bushwillow (*Combretum erythrophyllum*). It is home to blesbok, eland, black wildebeest, steenbok, grey duiker, waterbuck, springbok, mountain reedbuck, red hartebeest and Burchell's zebra, as well as several rare or threatened species of game such as oribi, white rhino and aardwolf. Numerous bird species, including the regal martial eagle, may be spotted wheeling across the blue skies. For more information, contact The Executive Director, Department of Culture and Recreation, P O Box 1454, Pretoria 0001, telephone (012) 345-2274, fax 345-3928.

Rondebult Bird Sanctuary

Gauteng's popular bird sanctuary is Rondebult, a 94 ha paradise of vlei and marshland

Above: Beautiful but deceptive – the wild flower *Striga elegans* (witchweed) is a member of the foxglove family. It is a root parasite, receiving water and food from its host. **Right:** Hikers survey the countryside from a viewpoint on one of Suikerbosrand's 66 km network of hiking trails.

that is sanctuary to over 150 species of bird. Although it is situated on the outskirts of Germiston in an area dominated by industrial activity, the sanctuary is a haven of tranquillity. Visitors may stroll around Rondebult or look out across the vlei from seven well-constructed observation hides which are roofed, carpeted, cushioned and equipped with colour photographs of many of the species that frequent the sanctuary. Three of southern Africa's four ibis species may be seen, and other attractions include spectacular individuals such as the purple gallinule, African snipe, black-winged stilt and avocet.

Most of the waterfowl species breeding in southern Africa have been spotted here. Keep an eye open for the avocet as it 'side-sweeps' the water with its bill upturned, and for the elegant greater flamingo as it wades through the water with its bill held upside down, filtering out delicate morsels of algae and aquatic invertebrates to eat. Rondebult's heronry has always been popular, and its population includes black-headed heron, cattle egret, grey heron, night heron and African spoonbill, all of which breed here. Studies of the bird and plant species are ongoing, and Rondebult also offers ideal opportunities for photographers.

The reserve is open every day from 8 a.m. to 5 p.m. For more information and to arrange a visit, contact The Head: Department of Parks, Sport and Recreation, Rondebult Bird Sanctuary, P O Box 374, Germiston 1400, telephone (011) 871-7355, or fax 871-7591. If you wish to visit at other times, contact the sanctuary directly on (011) 916-1948. To reach it, take the N3 freeway leading south from Germiston, then take the Wadeville off-ramp and follow the signs to the sanctuary, which is situated on Van Dyk Road.

Songimvelo Nature Reserve

Songimvelo (meaning 'the care of nature'), a vast 49 000 ha reserve situated 30 km southeast of Barberton, stretches from Swaziland's high peaks to the plains of the Lowveld. Besides grassland and savannah, representative species from the Cape floral kingdom and shrub forests, as well as three types of cycad, are found in this splendid wilderness area. Cool, misty highlands give way to warm, sheltered valleys and tree-filled ravines.

The river is home to otter, and its thickly wooded banks reverberate with the calls of many of the reserve's 300 bird species. Narina trogon, purple-crested and Knysna louries, and four species of nightjar are among those that shelter within the leafy canopy, while kingfishers and white-fronted bee-eaters flash across the green-cloaked banks. Ostrich and the elegant spotted eagle owl may be seen on the grassland.

Elephant, white rhino, giraffe, lion and herds of blue wildebeest, blesbok, impala, red hartebeest and Burchell's zebra roam the bushveld plains between the Komati and Lomati rivers, while black wildebeest, mountain reedbuck, grey rhebok, eland and leopard are found on the mountain slopes. A breeding herd of elephant, translocated from the Kruger National Park (*see separate entry*) is settling into their new home.

Ranger-escorted game drives are offered both day and night, as are walking trails and hunting expeditions. Of interest to those with geological leanings are the fascinating rock formations and, for those interested in archaeology, there is evidence of human habitation dating back many centuries. One school of thought is that the stone ruins on a hill overlooking Songimvelo resemble other Iron Age sites found all over the subcontinent, while another proposes that they were built by an Asiatic people some 2 400 years ago.

Hikers, picnickers and campers can discover mountains, forested ravines, waterfalls and pools, while kayakers can pit their wits against the white waters of the Komati River.

Songimvelo offers a four-day wilderness-awareness course, a bush-cuisine course, star identification weekends, as well as bush weekends for bridge players! Visitors can stay in the luxurious, safari-tented Komati River Lodge overlooking the Komati River. Each tent is built on a platform and offers *en suite* accommodation for two to four people. Guests eat in the main dining area, ingeniously constructed around a shady grove of cycads. Anyone wishing to visit the area should contact Mpumalanga Parks Board, Private Bag X11233, Nelspruit 1200, telephone (013) 753-3931, fax 755-4796.

To make reservations at Komati River Lodge, contact the Parks Board offices at P O Box 1990, Nelspruit 1200, telephone (013) 758-1035, fax 755-3931.

Suikerboschfontein Hiking Trail

A two-day circular hiking trail, situated on the escarpment some 20 km northeast of Carolina, has proved itself popular with weekend hikers keen to explore this rocky area. Laid out on the farm Suikerboschfontein, the trail traverses dramatic mountain scenery, passes interesting rock formations, penetrates deep gorges, follows mountain streams fringed with tree ferns and descends to forests of yellowwood and stands of rock aloe (beautiful when in flower during autumn). Magnificent views may be had, and numerous game and bird species can be seen. Trailists can cool off in rock pools.

Hikers stay overnight at two camps. Oom Japies Cottage, from which the trail starts, is a farmhouse sleeping 21 in several rooms, with bunks, mattresses, donkey-fired geyser, toilets and showers, as well as braai facilities and a kitchen equipped with cooking utensils. Rooikrans Camp has three huts sleeping six and one hut sleeping three, with showers, toilets, fireplaces and kitchen facilities.

For further information, contact Jacana Country Homes and Trails, P O Box 95212, Waterkloof 0145, or telephone (012) 346-3550/1/2, fax 346-2499.

Suikerbosrand Nature Reserve

Preserving as it does the rapidly disappearing bankenveld grassland, this vast sanctuary must surely be one of the northeastern Highveld's greatest natural assets.

Portions of 65 farms lie within the boundaries of the Suikerbosrand Nature Reserve near Heidelberg. It covers an expanse of more than 13 000 ha of ridges, dramatic kloofs, plateaus and open plains in the low Suikerbosrand range. Plantlife is as diverse as the animals it supports – ranging from proteas and acacia bushveld to vlei reed beds and grassland. Grey duiker, steenbok, mountain reedbuck and baboon are indigenous to the area, and they have been joined by zebra, oribi, eland, kudu, red hartebeest, black wildebeest and brown hyena. Birdlife is prolific, with some 200 species having found their way into Suikerbosrand's data banks.

A network of self-guided overnight trails – some 66 km in total – crisscrosses the reserve, revealing its bird-, plant- and mammal life. Scattered throughout the hiking trails are six overnight huts, each named after a game species found here. The huts consist of two bedrooms, each with five bunks and a central living area, with braai facilities and a stack of firewood. In planning a route, hikers must book places in a particular overnight hut and should avoid changes en route, as the huts are fully booked for most weekends.

One rather special option is the meditation hut, for those visitors who value solitude and quiet. Only four persons are allowed to use the hut at any one time.

Visitors should make their way to Diepkloof on the reserve's northern edge – headquarters

SUIKERBOSRAND AT A GLANCE

When to go The reserve is open year round, with the gates opening daily between 7 a.m. and 6 p.m. Although situated within the reserve, the Aventura Kareekloof resort does not form part of it, and is closed between 1 June and 31 August (although this situation is being reviewed). Winter nights can be cold in this region (warm clothing is essential), and hikers usually visit in spring, summer or autumn.

Reservations and information To reserve a camping site at Kareekloof, write to The Manager, Aventura Kareekloof, P O Box 372, Meyerton 1960, telephone (016) 365-5334, fax 365-5628. For further information about Diepkloof Visitors' Centre and the reserve, and to book places on the hiking trails (and accommodation in the overnight huts), contact The Officer-in-Charge, Suikerbosrand Nature Reserve, Private Bag H616, Heidelberg 2400, telephone (011) 904-3933 or 904-3937, fax 904-2965.

Getting there To reach the reserve's conservation headquarters at Diepkloof, take the tarred road branching west from the N3 between Heidelberg and Johannesburg, and follow the signs to Diepkloof. To reach the Aventura Kareekloof, take the signposted turn-off north of the main road between Heidelberg and Meyerton, 28 km from Heidelberg. This clearly signposted road leads to the resort.

Accommodation Aventura Kareekloof caters for caravanners and campers but has no huts or rondavels. Suikerbosrand's trail network has six overnight huts (advance booking is essential). There are three group camps near Diepkloof, but these are very much in demand, and it is advisable to book well in advance (at least ten months).

Eating and drinking Kareekloof has a licensed restaurant. Braai facilities have been supplied for day visitors and for those occupying the caravan and camping site. Bread, milk and other groceries are on sale in the resort shop.

Getting around A 60 km circular tarred road leads through the reserve. It may be undertaken daily from Diepkloof, or over weekends and public holidays from Kareekloof. No petrol is available in the reserve – the nearest sources are at Kliprivier and Heidelberg. Suikerbosrand features a network of hiking trails with a total length of 65 km – and hikers can choose to spend between one and six days exploring the trails. Hikers must book accommodation in the reserve's overnight huts well in advance. Visitors may choose to take the 4 km Cheetah Trail laid out in a loop northwest of Diepkloof's Visitors' Centre, or the longer Bokmakierie Trail.

Special attractions Diepkloof has an impressive visitors' centre with displays highlighting Suikerbosrand's habitats and species. Nearby is a Voortrekker farmhouse, dating from the 1850s, which has been restored and now functions as a farm museum. Aventura Kareekloof offers family activities such as putt-putt, trampolining, a supertube, horse riding, and also has a swimming pool and conference facilities.

Wildlife The acacia country in the southwest attracts eland; the grassveld elsewhere is the haunt of black wildebeest, blesbok and springbok, while red hartebeest, oribi, zebra, mountain reedbuck, grey rhebok, grey duiker, steenbok, kudu and brown hyena are found throughout the reserve. Suikerbosrand is famous for its cheetah, and the reserve is one of the best birdwatching venues on the Highveld.

THE AGILE AVOCET

The distinctively shaped bill of the avocet, with its upturned tip, is especially designed for feeding on the minute organisms that dwell below the surface of the water, and is even used for ferreting out the tiny creatures found in the muddy floor of shallow ponds, pans and estuaries. The bird may be spotted sweeping its bill from side to side through the water, then dropping its head to feed. At this point the bill's tip is in a horizontal position, perfect for feeding.

The avocet (*Recurvirostra avosetta*) can be recognised by its vivid black-and-white plumage, and its black-topped head and hindneck. Its long white legs enable it to wade into fairly deep water, briskly probing the depths for insects, crustaceans, molluscs, small fish and worms, as well as various seeds. It is found in both coastal and inland bodies of shallow water, usually brackish or saline.

Gregarious by nature, the avocet usually congregates in small flocks, which may be seen flying in close formation, their wings fluttering black and white against the sky.

Nests are a shallow scrape in damp ground, made cosy with twigs, grass and mud. Three to five greenish or yellowish, black-spotted eggs are laid. Both parents take turns to incubate their brood, which hatches after some three weeks, and the young take to the air four weeks later.

Above: Black wildebeest on the grasslands of the Suikerbosrand Nature Reserve. They are gregarious animals, once ranging the plains in their thousands. Over-exploitation and farming brought them almost to extinction, but today they are off the danger list.

of the conservation staff and home of an excellent visitors' centre. Pick up an informative map and identification brochure for two shorter trails, the 4 km Cheetah Trail that winds over the hillsides northwest of the centre, and the 10 or 17 km Bokmakierie Trail. Film and slide shows are also held, and there are a number of picnic spots. Also of much interest at the visitors' centre is a beautiful diorama, a three-dimensional picture painted by well-known American artist Timothy Prutzer, depicting a cheetah hunting scene.

The Aventura Kareekloof resort, situated in the middle of the reserve, is a popular weekend getaway and offers camp- and caravan sites, a restaurant, swimming pool and kiosk.

Transvaal Snake Park

Halfway House, situated between Johannesburg and Pretoria, is the home of the privately owned Transvaal Snake Park, where visitors may see up to 150 snake species, as well as other reptiles and amphibians from southern Africa and further afield.

Crocodile, alligator and terrapin float in special pools, while indigenous poisonous snakes laze in a snake-pit (staff herpetologists provide regular lecture demonstrations), and the more exotic species are kept in a climate-controlled terraquarium which replicates their natural environment.

The snake park was the brainchild of Bernie Keyter, who worked on venom extraction at the South African Institute for Medical Research in the 1950s. So many people asked to see the snakes that he decided to sink his savings into a permanent exhibition. The park opened in 1961 with 25 species on display. Today the exhibits number more than eighty. However, the emphasis is less on collecting specimens than on developing captive breeding programmes – especially those relating to endangered species.

To reach the park, follow the clearly signposted road to Halfway House (the park is about 1 km south of the town). It is open from 9 a.m. to 5.30 p.m. on Sundays and public holidays, and from 9 a.m. to 4.30 p.m. on weekdays and Saturdays. There are reptile demonstrations on weekdays at 11 a.m. and 3 p.m.; on Saturdays at 11 a.m., 2 p.m., 3 p.m. and 4 p.m.; on Sundays and public holidays at 11 a.m. and thereafter every hour until 4 p.m.

The park is open every day of the year except Christmas Day. For more detailed information, contact Transvaal Snake Park, P O Box 2378, Northcliff 2115, telephone (011) 805-3116, or fax 315-2966.

Vaal Dam

The Vaal Dam, stretching for an impressive, willow-lined 104 km and reaching a width of some 24 km in places, is one of the main water sources feeding the Vaal Barrage, which in turn supplies the households of Gauteng, the Highveld and the northern Free State with their daily water. Numerous recreational resorts dot its shores, and its waters attract watersport devotees and anglers keen to lure barbel, yellowfish and catfish onto their hooks. The dam once formed the nucleus of a 350 ha nature reserve. Today the sanctuary area is closed to the public, although the dam can still be reached via alternative routes.

The area is to be handed over to the province of Gauteng, and it is expected that it will be developed as a private resort area, rather than as a nature reserve.

The Wilds

A major attraction of the Empire Exhibition held in Johannesburg in 1936 was a display of South Africa's indigenous flora. Public response to the display was so overwhelming that it prompted the development of a park wholly devoted to the display of South African plants, shrubs and trees. The 20 ha area, which became known as The Wilds, was established on two koppies in Houghton.

The reserve is maintained but, sadly, it has deteriorated badly, due largely to the presence of vagrants, and the area is not considered safe for those venturing out on their own.

To reach The Wilds, turn into Houghton Drive from Louis Botha Avenue and proceed to the car park at the bottom of the hill. The park is open at all times. However, for their own safety, nature lovers are advised to visit in groups. There is a refreshment kiosk.

HIGHVELD: FREE STATE

Grassy plains and teeming game

Early in the 19th century the area now known as the Free State was a hunter's paradise. Its grassy plains were alive with game and it seemed that the supply could never end. Then settlers, both black and white, entered the region and the magnificent herds were rapidly reduced to a fraction of their former size. The plains were divided up, securely fenced and then turned over to agricultural production. Apart from a few token herds preserved by conservation-minded farmers, the Free State's game population simply faded away.

The 20th century saw the stirring of an awareness of the importance of conservation in the Free State and, indeed, elsewhere in southern Africa. Encouraged by the success of the handful of smaller reserves established in the 1920s and 1930s, the then Orange Free State Provincial Administration proclaimed the Willem Pretorius Game Reserve at Allemanskraal Dam. The South African National Parks Board's contribution was even more impressive – the proclamation of the Golden Gate Highlands National Park in the foothills of the Maloti Mountains. Later these two important sanctuaries were augmented by several new reserves and botanical gardens.

Today some of the most impressive game reserves in the Free State are Willem Pretorius, Tussen-die-Riviere Nature Reserve on the Orange River in the south and Sandveld Nature Reserve in the vicinity of the Bloemhof Dam in the northwest of the province. Soetdoring Nature Reserve near Bloemfontein is sanctuary to a large variety of game, as is the Golden Gate Highlands National Park, which is in all probability the most scenically attractive of the province's reserves.

The region's flora is conserved and cultivated at the Free State National Botanical Garden in Bloemfontein.

Bergdeel Private Nature Reserve
The Witteberg, Rooiberg and Maloti ranges – all snowclad in winter – form a dramatic backdrop for this small (563 ha) reserve midway between Bethlehem and Fouriesburg. Indigenous forest still clothes some of the high-lying areas reached by several well-marked walking trails of up to three hours. Game includes some 16 species of indigenous antelope and, among a few exotic species, fallow deer that look regally at home in their mountain setting. Visitors are accommodated in two-bedroomed, self-catering lodges.

For further information, write to Jacana Country Homes and Trails, P O Box 95212, Waterkloof 0145, or telephone their offices at (012) 346-3550/1/2 or fax 346-2499.

Bloemfontein Zoological Gardens
Those wanting a closer look at Free State game should start at the Bloemfontein Zoo, a 15 ha retreat of green lawns and shady trees lying close to the city's heart. The species on view include elephant, leopard, cheetah, white

Below left: This strange formation in the Rooiberg mountain range, known as Mushroom Rocks, forms part of the Golden Gate Highlands National Park – a region of sculpted mountains and green valleys.
Below right: *Dierama*, a member of the iris family. Some botanists believe there are only a few species in southern Africa (with many variations), but others recognise more than 20 species in South Africa alone.

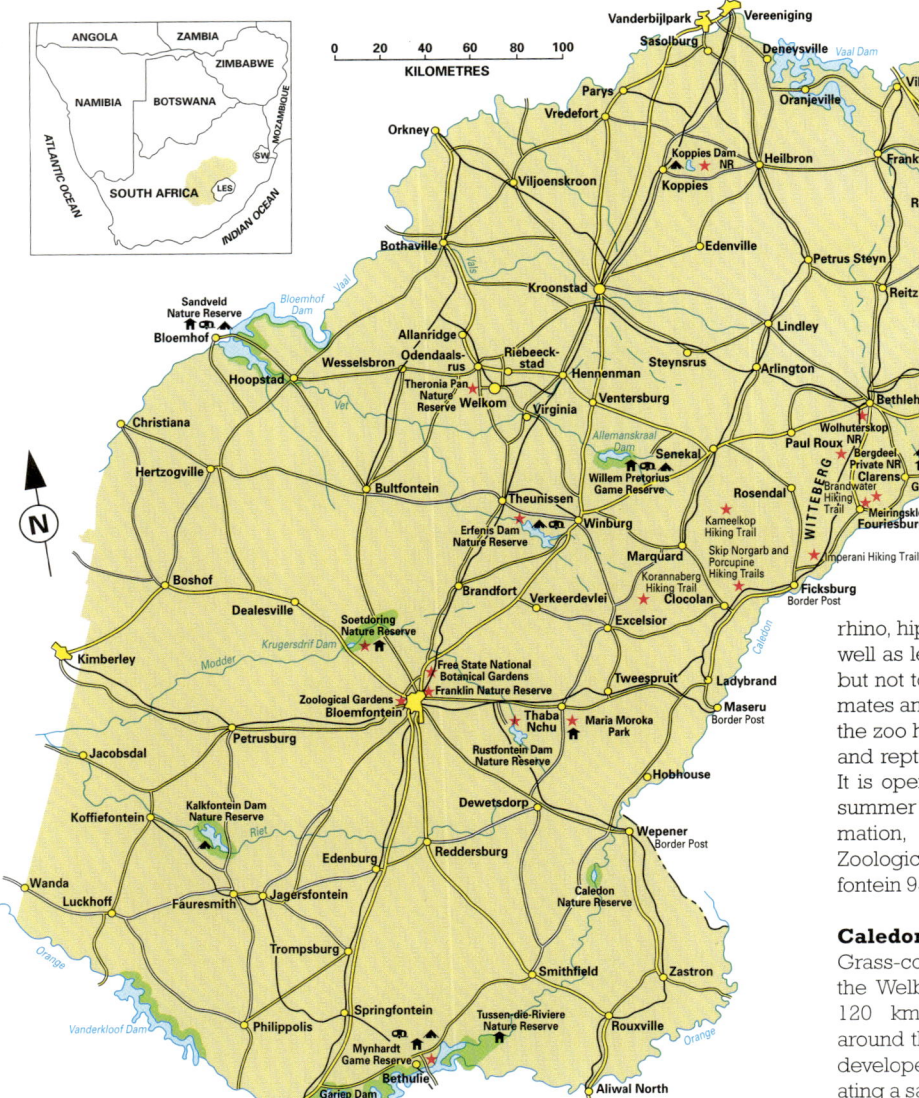

HIGHVELD: FREE STATE

Left: A cetoniid (fruit) beetle burrows in soil preparatory to laying its eggs. The adult beetle bores into ripe fruit to feed on the juice, while its larvae feed on decaying vegetable matter (they may often be found in compost heaps).

rhino, hippopotamus, buffalo and gemsbok, as well as lechwe (indigenous to southern Africa but not to the Free State), and a variety of primates and ungulates (hoofed animals). All told, the zoo has more than 100 species of mammal and reptile and more than 70 species of bird. It is open every day, from 8 a.m. to 6 p.m. in summer and to 5 p.m. in winter. For more information, contact The Curator, Bloemfontein Zoological Gardens, P O Box 3704, Bloemfontein 9300, telephone (051) 405-8483/4.

Caledon Nature Reserve

Grass-covered hills roll gently down to the Welbedacht Dam on the Caledon River, 120 km southeast of Bloemfontein. Land around the dam and along the river has been developed as a provincial nature reserve, creating a sanctuary of almost 5 000 hectares.

Apart from the black wildebeest, blesbok, springbok, zebra and other large mammals to which the reserve is home, it is also known for its varied vegetation that includes riverine bush, grasslands and the montane growths covering hill and cliff. Birds are plentiful (over 130 species have been recorded) and are reigned over by the black eagle and the strident fish eagle.

Two bush camps (one accessible by 4x4 vehicles only) float on the dam, offering unusual accommodation for hikers, mountain bikers and canoeists. The camps, each of which must be hired in its entirety, each sleep 16 and have braai and ablution facilities on the shore – visitors must bring their own food, cutlery and bedding.

Day visitors are allowed in the 1 600 ha game area where gamewatching (by motor vehicle, mountain bike or on foot) is a major attraction. Fishing is also popular, with barbel,

HIGHVELD: FREE STATE

Left: A tortoise beetle displays its striking colour and metallic sheen caused by the reflection of light on different layers of cuticle. The female lays her oval yellow eggs on leaves, each egg encased in a cocoon of transparent liquid that hardens rapidly. The larva appears after 10-12 days. It feeds on leaves, and carries its cast-off moults at the end of its body. The pupa anchors it to the leaf.

yellowfish, carp and mudfish being in plentiful supply. An easy two-and-a-half-hour trail starts and finishes at Kruidfontein bush camp. The reserve lies just east of the R701 between Smithfield and Wepener.

For more information, contact The Principal Nature Conservator, Caledon Nature Reserve, P O Box 84, Wepener 9944, telephone (051) 583-1920, fax 583-1921.

Erfenis Dam Nature Reserve

Boating, picnicking and fishing are the most popular activities at the 3 800 ha Erfenis Dam between Winburg and Theunissen in the central Free State. A 400 ha provincial game reserve adjoins the dam, and it is here that mammals such as black wildebeest, red hartebeest, mountain reedbuck and Burchell's zebra can be seen.

One of the reserve's charms is its waterfowl, particularly South African shelduck and Egyptian goose that gather here by the thousands in their moulting season, usually in November and December.

The reserve is open daily from 7 a.m. to 6 p.m., and there are excellent facilities for camping and caravanning. To reach the dam, follow the signs from the Winburg/Theunissen road (R708); the turn-off is 14 km from Theunissen. Further information is available from The Principal Nature Conservator, Erfenis Dam Nature Reserve, P O Box 131, Theunissen 9410, telephone (05772) and ask for 4211.

Franklin Nature Reserve

Naval Hill is one of the prime landmarks of Bloemfontein, so named because gunners of the British Naval Brigade were stationed here during the Anglo-Boer War. On the summit and slopes is the 253 ha Franklin Nature Reserve, established in the 1930s and controlled by the Bloemfontein Zoo.

A network of roads runs through the reserve and provides visitors with glimpses of game such as giraffe, eland, blesbok, red hartebeest, wildebeest and springbok. The Franklin reserve is open daily and can be reached from the west side of Naval Hill. Within the boundaries of the reserve are an impressive radio communications complex and Bloemfontein's old Lamont Hussey Observatory, today used as a theatre.

For further details, contact the Bloemfontein Publicity Association, P O Box 639, Bloemfontein 9300, telephone (051) 405-8489/90; or The Curator, Bloemfontein Zoo, P O Box 3704, Bloemfontein 9300, telephone (051) 405-8483, fax 405-8473.

Free State National Botanical Gardens

One of Bloemfontein's treasures is the 70 ha botanical garden on its northwestern fringe. Some 6 ha of the garden have been developed to display and preserve as much of the Free State flora as will grow there – with particular emphasis on species such as *Crinum*, klipdagga and witgousblom.

The naturally wooded dolerite koppies beyond the cultivated garden contain cabbage trees (*Cussonia paniculata*), white stinkwood (*Celtis africana*), false olive (*Buddleja saligna*) and wild olive (*Olea europaea* subsp. *africana*). The winding paved path is ideal for the elderly and the physically disabled, while the more agile can climb the koppies (a one-and-a-half-hour trip) to take in the scenery. The Botanical Society of South Africa arranges periodic talks and moonlight walks, and sunset concerts are held during summer.

The garden is at its best in spring, when most of its flowers are in vivid bloom, but there is something of interest at all times of the year – even in midwinter, when the *Aloe grandidentata* brightens the koppies with splashes of warm red, and the wild pomegranate (*Rhigozum obovatum*) produces its yellow trumpets.

The garden has a well-stocked nursery where surplus indigenous trees, shrubs, bulbs and succulents are sold, and there is also a herbarium where 5 000 species are kept – a reference source much used by students. The garden is open daily from 8 a.m. to 6 p.m. (the nursery between 8 a.m. and 1 p.m. and 2 p.m. to 4 p.m. Monday to Saturday) and can be reached by way of General Dan Pienaar Drive (the turn-off is clearly marked). Braai sites have been laid out for visitors, and a spacious lapa is available for group functions.

For more detailed information, contact The Curator, Free State National Botanical Garden, P O Box 29036, Danhof 9310, telephone (051) 31-3530, fax 31-4101.

Gariep Dam Nature Reserve

The Free State's largest nature reserve is a combination of the 36 487 ha Gariep Dam (which holds back a vast 6 000 million cubic litres of water) on the Orange River and an 11 237 ha game sanctuary on its northern shore. The dam was officially opened in 1972 and has long been popular with anglers and boating enthusiasts. The game reserve accommodates the largest population of springbok in any reserve in the country and also features Cape mountain zebra, klipspringer, black wildebeest, red hartebeest and ostrich.

The reserve itself has accommodation in three self-catering chalets, as well as in camping sites with a lapa and ablution block.

Adjoining the reserve and close to the Gariep Dam wall, is the privately owned Aventura Midwaters public resort, which offers a range of accommodation and recreational facilities. For more information about the reserve, contact The Principal Nature Conservator, Gariep Dam Nature Reserve, P O Box 18, Gariep Dam 9922, telephone/fax (052172) and ask for 26. You can contact Aventura Midwaters at Private Bag X10, Gariep Dam 9922, telephone (052172) and ask for 45.

GOLDEN GATE AT A GLANCE

When to go Golden Gate is open year round, and weekends and school holidays tend to be busy. A public road runs through the park, so there are no gates in the east or west. Winters are cold: temperatures can plummet to 12 degrees below zero and there is often snow on the mountains (sometimes in the valleys too). Summer nights can also be cool.

Reservations To apply for accommodation, write to the National Parks Board, P O Box 787, Pretoria 0001, or telephone (012) 343-1991, fax 343-0905; or to the National Parks Board, P O Box 7400, Roggebaai 8012, telephone (021) 22-2810, fax 24-6211. For further details about the park, contact Golden Gate Highlands National Park, Private Bag X3, Clarens 9707, telephone (058) 256-1471.

Getting there The park is located 58 km southeast of Bethlehem and southwest of Harrismith.

Accommodation Golden Gate has two rest camps. Glen Reenen features partially equipped huts (some with bathroom and kitchen facilities) and a large caravan park and campsite. About 1 km to the west is the Brandwag Lodge, with luxury double and single rooms in the main complex, and adjoining fully equipped family chalets. It also has a laundromat, a curio shop and an information centre.

Eating and drinking Brandwag has a licensed restaurant and a ladies' cocktail bar. Glen Reenen has a shop that stocks fresh meat, groceries, firewood and liquor. There are braai facilities among the huts, in the caravan park and campsite, and at an adjoining picnic site.

Getting around A loop in the east of the park takes motorists through the area where most of Golden Gate's game is concentrated. Night drives are offered. The park is also famous for its hiking trails. The two-day Rhebuck Trail starts and finishes at Glen Reenen. Shorter rambles (ranging from one to five hours in duration) start at Glen Reenen and lead to landmarks such as Wodehouse Kop, Mushroom Rocks, Boskloof, Echo Ravine and the top of Brandwag, which overlooks Brandwag Lodge. A trail leading to Holkrans starts at Brandwag Rest Camp. Ponies can be hired at stables near the western entrance of the park. A favourite ride leads up to the mountain hut on the Rhebuck Trail.

Special attractions Brandwag Rest Camp is flanked by tennis courts, a nine-hole golf course and a bowling green, and is a favourite venue for conferences. There is a natural swimming pool at Glen Reenen.

Wildlife Golden Gate is best known for its scenery, and gamewatching is a bonus. Even so, the park accommodates a population of eland, black wildebeest, mountain reedbuck, grey rhebok, blesbok and Burchell's zebra, as well as springbok and oribi. Birdlife includes the black eagle and an occasional lammergeyer.

Special precautions Be sure to take warm clothing: sudden chills can occur without warning.

Golden Gate Highlands National Park

Ages of erosion have carved magical formations in the sandstone sediments of the Maloti foothills and have created a deep valley that runs through the heart of the area. The feature called Golden Gate consists of two massive bluffs that face one another across the valley, each standing about 100 m high, with warm sandstone faces highlighted by tints of purple and gold. Deservedly, it is for its scenery that this approximately 12 000 ha park is most renowned.

The 'Gate' is spectacular, but an even more striking formation is the massive Brandwag (the name means 'sentinel'), a glowing sandstone rampart that juts from the valley wall like some impregnable fortress. Below the Brandwag is a luxury rest camp named after it, and around the corner is Glen Reenen, where there are huts and campsites. From Glen Reenen, visitors can hike to the crest of the Brandwag for a panoramic view of much of the park, or set out on the circuitous Rhebok Hiking Trail, a two-day/31 km hike that fords mountain streams and traverses rugged kloofs to reach the highest peaks. Hikers rest overnight at the Rhebok Hut in the Oudehoutskloof and, the following day, ascend Generaalskop, which at 2 837 m is the highest point in the Free State. There are several shorter trails, and another way to see Golden Gate is from the saddle – horses and ponies may be hired.

A high average annual rainfall of 806 mm ensures a rich flora in the area. From spring to autumn the valleys and surrounding mountains appear fresh and green and there is a dazzling variety of wild flowers – watsonias, fire lilies, red-hot pokers, arum lilies and many more. In such glorious surroundings wildlife tends to take a back seat, but hikers and those who drive through the park's eastern hills may come upon eland, black wildebeest, blesbok, grey rhebok and the timid oribi. Birdlife is magnificent, including the orange-throated longclaw and ground woodpecker, as well as raptors such as the jackal buzzard, the rare lammergeyer (bearded vulture) and the equally uncommon bald ibis.

Golden Gate has put considerable effort into environmental education: there is a large youth hostel and schoolchildren from all over the country attend courses that last from one to five days. In the mornings they are taught various aspects of conservation; in the afternoons there are physical activities such as canoeing, riding, swimming or hiking; in the evenings there are discussions and slide shows.

Fences that formerly separated Golden Gate Highlands National Park from the adjoining Qwa-Qwa Park have been removed and, although it is fairly certain that the two parks will be amalgamated, they are currently administered as separate units.

For further information, write to The Park Warden, Private Bag X3, Clarens 9707, or telephone (058) 256-1471.

Kalkfontein Dam Nature Reserve

The 4 500 ha Kalkfontein Dam, 35 km north of Fauresmith in the southwestern Free State, is one of the few angling areas in the province where yellowfish are relatively abundant. Not surprisingly, anglers are frequent visitors to the complex.

The dam and its adjoining area of 162 ha have been proclaimed a provincial nature reserve, but the land area is too small to support significant quantities of game. Instead, the reserve is maintained chiefly as a recreational area catering for anglers, campers, picnickers and boating enthusiasts. The reserve is open daily from 7 a.m. to 6 p.m. and visitors are allowed to camp overnight. For details, contact The Principal Nature Conservator, Kalkfontein Dam Nature Reserve, P O Box 78, Fauresmith 9978, telephone (051722) 1422.

Koppies Dam Nature Reserve

This 4 300 ha nature reserve northeast of Kroonstad has at its centre a dam that teems with yellowfish, barbel, carp and mudfish,

HIGHVELD: FREE STATE

Left: A fairytale stream meanders through the Golden Gate Highlands National Park. **Top:** Mating ladybird beetles. Most ladybirds (both adults and larvae) feed on soft-bodied insects such as mealybugs and aphids, but there are also species of vegetarian ladybirds in southern Africa. These are identified by their orange-and-black colouring. Predacious ladybirds have a shiny carapace coloured red and black. The females lay clusters of eggs on the underside of leaves or in other spots infested by aphids. When the eggs hatch two weeks later, the larvae feed on the aphids, penetrating their soft bodies with sharp, sickle-shaped jaws and drawing out the body juices. **Above:** A honeycombed sandstone formation on the floor of a cave in the Rooiberg mountains.

HIGHVELD: FREE STATE

drawing anglers from near and far. Along its shores the mixed grassveld, dotted with dense thickets of sweet thorn and shady glades of willows along the banks of the Renoster River, is sanctuary to large mammals, including white rhino and buffalo. There is also a rich birdlife of some 250 recorded species, including many waterfowl.

The reserve is situated east of the small town of Koppies and some 64 km from Kroonstad on the R82. Visitors may use the rustic camp of four three-bed tents and a lapa, while reed-and-thatch shelters with braai places (intended for fishermen) line the shores of the dam. There are shady picnic sites along the river. For further details, contact The Principal Nature Conservator, Koppies Dam Nature Reserve, P O Box 151, Koppies 9540, telephone/fax (05672) ask for 2521.

Maria Moroka Park

This is the area affectionately known to many as 'Big Sky Country', where undulating grassy plains, ringed with wooded hills and overlooked by the historic mountain landmark of Thaba 'Nchu, surround the silent Montloatse Setlogelo Dam.

The 5 800 ha Maria Moroka Park, which takes its name from the late Maria Moipone Moroka – a prominent regent to the chieftainship of the local Morolong community – is a haven for Highveld wildlife, including springbok, eland, blesbok, steenbok, black wildebeest, red hartebeest, gemsbok and zebra. Among more than 200 bird species recorded are black korhaan, blue korhaan, ostrich and large flocks of blue crane. The park is also home to Cape hyrax, clawless otter, yellow mongoose, water mongoose and ground squirrel.

For fitter visitors there are two hiking trails. The Eland Trail (four to five hours) weaves through densely vegetated kloofs echoing with bird calls, before emerging above the trees to reveal an enchanting view across the plains. The Ostrich Hiking Trail is a two-hour ramble for the less energetic.

Thaba Lodge, situated within the park, is a safari camp rented to hunters. There are picnic facilities and an ablution block for day visitors. The park lies 20 km from the town of Thaba 'Nchu and adjoins the Thaba 'Nchu Sun Hotel, which arranges guided day and night drives to view the game.

For more information, write to The Head, Maria Moroka Park, P O Box 246, Thaba 'Nchu 9780, or telephone (051871) 2466.

Meiringskloof Nature Park

The Meiringskloof stream cuts its way through the yielding sandstone of the Rooiberg mountains, an outlier of the Maloti Mountains along the rugged border of Lesotho. Caves have

Below left: Grey rhebok are generally found in hilly or mountainous areas.
Right: The African honeybee is well adapted to the harsh conditions of its natural environment. Although the long periods of drought, numerous predators and irregular supplies of nectar take a heavy toll on colonies, this species compensates by its ability to migrate to areas where food is more plentiful, by rapid reproduction and by the accelerated development period of queens, drones and workers.
Below right: The elegant eland: these large browsers feed on bushes and fruits.

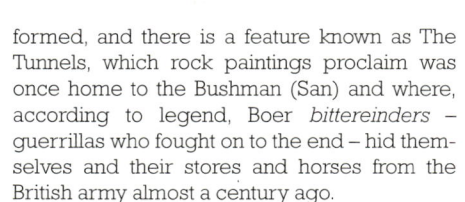

formed, and there is a feature known as The Tunnels, which rock paintings proclaim was once home to the Bushman (San) and where, according to legend, Boer *bittereinders* – guerrillas who fought on to the end – hid themselves and their stores and horses from the British army almost a century ago.

Meiringskloof Nature Park, of some 42 ha, is situated in these stirring surroundings 2 km northeast of Fouriesburg. Birdlife is rich in the large areas of indigenous bush, and trees along the several walks have been labelled for easy identification. The most visible mammals include blesbok and smaller antelope species. A two-day trail may be arranged with the park manager, and accommodation consists of fully equipped self-catering chalets and stands for some 30 caravans.

For more information, telephone the park manager at (058) 223-0067.

Mount Everest Game Reserve

Four easy but exhilarating trails thread through the plains and indigenous forests around the mountains of Everest, Mooihoek and Glen Paul some 20 km northeast of Harrismith, off the N3.

Ranging in duration from two to six hours, the trails offer an opportunity to enjoy magnificent scenery and to view an impressive selection of animals, including white rhino, some 15 species of indigenous antelope, several exotic large mammals and a claimed 290 bird species. Black eagle are known to breed in the mountains here, and a vulture restaurant has been established in an attempt to conserve the local population of Cape vulture.

Accommodation includes log chalets, rondavels and three caravan parks, while among the activities offered are game drives, horse riding, and fishing for bass and trout in several dams. For more information, write to Mount Everest Game Reserve, P O Box 471, Harrismith 9880, or telephone (05861) 2-1816.

Mynhardt Game Reserve

The attractive old-world town of Bethulie (the name means 'chosen by God'), in the Free State's deep south, is sandwiched between two major provincial reserves: the Gariep Dam to the west and the Tussen-die-Riviere Nature Reserve to the east. Even closer to home is Bethulie's 160 ha municipal nature reserve at the town dam. Named after a former mayor of the town, the Mynhardt reserve was established in 1937 – which makes it one of the oldest in the province. Its game population includes black wildebeest, blesbok, zebra, gemsbok, impala and springbok.

Signs at the entrances to Bethulie direct visitors to the reserve, which features a small holiday resort (open day and night) of chalets, rondavels and a caravan park and campsite. Visitors wanting to stay in the chalets and rondavels must provide their own bedding, cutlery, crockery and cooking equipment. There are ablution facilities with hot and cold water.

For further information, write to The Town Clerk, P O Box 7, Bethulie 9992, or telephone (051762) and ask for 2.

Platberg Nature Reserve
The slopes of Platberg – that unmistakeable flat-topped landmark overlooking Harrismith on the main route between Gauteng and the KwaZulu-Natal coast – are home to both a nature reserve and a wildflower garden. Natural springs of fresh water called for man-made dams which, in turn, required an enduring fort to guard them. Mellowed now, all these are part of the restful scene.

Well over 1 000 head of game include black wildebeest, blue wildebeest, red hartebeest, springbok, mountain reedbuck, waterbuck, blesbok, zebra and duiker. The reserve, which spreads over some 7 000 ha, is also home to more than 130 species of bird, among them breeding pairs of black sparrowhawk and long-crested eagle.

The two-day/27 km Platberg Hiking Trail leads to the top of the mountain which, at close range, belies its name. It does, though, offer wide views. Spring is a good time to do this trail, as summers can be unrelentingly hot and snowfalls are not uncommon in winter.

For more information, contact the Harrismith Municipality, P O Box 43, Harrismith 9880, telephone (05861) 2-1061, fax 3-0923.

Platberg Wildflower Gardens
The Drakensberg range extends from the Northern Province to the Eastern Cape, and its midpoint could well be Platberg, the aptly named tabletop mountain that overlooks the town of Harrismith.

Today, Platberg's chief attraction is the 114 ha garden, situated in the foothills about 2 km from the Platberg summit. Its purpose is the cultivation, display and conservation of the flora in the Drakensberg's three main altitudinal zones: montane (the zone which, at 1 200 to 1 800 m above sea level, includes most of the garden's cultivated area); subalpine (1 800 to 2 800 m) and alpine (2 800 to 3 300 m).

The Platberg Wildflower Garden is administered by the Harrismith Municipality, part of it

THE GROUND SQUIRREL

This speedy and resourceful little animal, known also as the Cape ground squirrel, uses its tail as a sunshade while feeding, holding it in a bent position over its back. The squirrel also uses its tail as an alarm signal, moving it up and down in the face of danger. This little creature confines its activities to the ground (it is a poor climber) and to the daytime. Colonies numbering up to 30 live in a complicated network of interconnecting burrows, often betrayed by a low mound of soil raised by excavations from the warren. Quite often the warren is shared with suricates and yellow mongooses – for the most part amicably, although mongooses have the nasty habit of killing and eating, more vulnerable ground squirrels.

Ground squirrels sunbathe with their bellies to the ground and all four legs stretched out. They 'dustbathe' in the same position, every now and then scratching the sand all over their bodies and then shaking it off.

Their social organisation is a feminist's fantasy: groups consist of a number of females and their offspring, the dominant female defending the territory.

being developed and the remainder left as 'wilderness'. The developed area centres on two dams built by British forces in the Anglo-Boer War. A stone blockhouse was also erected, to protect the town's new water supply. On the slopes behind the dams a 3 km bush trail winds through a dense thicket and past massive rock formations.

The hillsides are dotted with berg lilies (*Galtonia candicans*), red hot-pokers (*Kniphofia*), harebells (*Dierama*), orange gazanias and the blue flowers of the bloulelie (*Agapanthus*); while the gnarled, crooked branches of the ouhout (*Leucosidea sericea*) form dense clusters on the slopes. The garden is open daily from sunrise to sunset and is well signposted from the middle of Harrismith, about 5 km away.

For more detailed information, contact the Harrismith Tourist Information Office, telephone (05861) 2-3525; or the Harrismith Municipality, telephone (05861) 2-1061. Both organisations share the following address and fax number – P O Box 43, Harrismith 9880, fax (05861) 3-0923.

Qwa-Qwa Park
This 22 000 ha park is a natural wonderland of soaring sandstone formations, well-watered vleis, lush kloofs, and caves adorned with ancient artwork. In winter, much of it gleams white and silent under snow and, in spring, hills and valleys are ablaze with watsonias, gladioli, arum lilies and dozens of vivid, indigenous flora species. The trees (white stinkwood, karee, wild olive and yellowwood) and undulating grasslands harbour mammal species that include eland, red hartebeest, springbok, zebra and black wildebeest. Among the bird species are the secretary bird, ostrich, numerous waterbirds, and raptors including bearded vulture and Cape vulture, black eagle and martial eagle.

The park, which stretches from the borders of Golden Gate east to Phuthaditjhaba, has a two-day/22 km hiking trail that traverses mountain scenery of great beauty where both waterbirds and raptors are frequently seen. A 40 km trail for 4x4 vehicles is open during winter, and includes an overnight hut. Centrally situated in the eastern section is the Basotho Cultural Village which highlights the historical and cultural heritage of the South Sotho people.

Qwa-Qwa Park is about 60 km from Harrismith on the road to Golden Gate. For more information, contact Free State Eco-Tourism, Private Bag X826, Witsieshoek 9870, telephone (058) 713-4415/6/7 or fax 713-0691/4342.

Rustfontein Dam Nature Reserve
Lying 50 km east of Bloemfontein off the Thaba 'Nchu road (N8), Rustfontein Dam is a popular playground for both anglers and watersport devotees. Its grassed and gently

HIGHVELD: FREE STATE

DOWN CAME A BLACK BIRD

There are three species of crow in southern Africa, ungainly birds that have relatively few admirers because their habits can be messy and annoying. Some clutter telegraph poles with their nests (and have been known to short-circuit the wires); others dig newly planted crops from the fields; yet others are said to attack sick and weak sheep. Around settlements they raid rubbish tips, on farms they peck their way into grain bags, and on roads they scavenge carcasses run over by vehicles.

The most common of the three species is the pied crow, black all over except for its snow-white breast and shoulders. It is found throughout the subcontinent. The black crow has a similar distribution, but is absent from Tongaland and Mozambique. The third species is the white-necked or Cape raven (pictured above), also black but with a broad white band behind its neck. It occurs from the southwest Cape to Namaqualand, then eastwards to Zimbabwe and beyond.

The raven has a large hooked beak quite different from the comparatively slender bills of the other species, but otherwise the three crows have much in common. They may gather in quite large parties, but generally prefer to attach themselves to a mate and remain constant for life. Each pair builds an untidy platform nest of twigs and other materials – the white-necked raven on a cliff ledge and the pied and black crow in a tree or up a telegraph pole.

---

rolling shoreline, dotted with tree-studded koppies, attracts a wide variety of birds.

Contact The Principal Conservator, Rustfontein Dam Nature Reserve, P O Box 529, Bloemfontein 9300, telephone (051) 526-2970 for more details.

Sandveld Nature Reserve

The Bloemhof Dam, at the confluence of the Vaal and Vet rivers in the northwestern Free State, has created a large, stubby peninsula north of Hoopstad. The Sandveld Nature Reserve encompasses the northwest portion of the peninsula and a small area across the dam to the west – its total size is 37 700 hectares.

Sandveld ranks as one of the three main provincial reserves in the Free State, along with the Willem Pretorius and Tussen-die-Riviere reserves. Among game in the area are giraffe, eland, blue wildebeest, gemsbok, red hartebeest, springbok, roan and sable antelope, rhino and buffalo. Smaller game abounds, including aardwolf, ant bear, springhare, porcupine, duiker and steenbok. Among large numbers of waterbirds, egrets, cormorants, ducks, geese and flamingoes gather in the shallows, while raptors include white-backed vulture, pygmy falcon, martial eagle and fish eagle. The savannah veld and thorny vegetation have much in common with the sandy Kalahari to the northwest.

Along the shores of the dam – popular with anglers and boating enthusiasts – certain areas have been set aside for caravanning, camping and picnicking. Toilets and electricity are provided. Air-conditioned holiday chalets also offer accommodation and there is a large conference hall, a lapa and a small shop.

To reach the dam, follow the signs along the R34 from Hoopstad – the reserve is some 30 km from the town. For further information, contact The Tourist Officer, Sandveld Nature Reserve, P O Box 414, Bloemhof 2660, telephone (01802) 3-1701/2, fax 3-1090.

Seekoeivlei Nature Reserve

Rising on the western slopes of the Drakensberg near the town of Memel, the winding Klip River creates a unique wetland with no fewer than 220 meanders – a key habitat for 26 per cent of the Free State's endangered bird species. Birdlife is abundant and mammal species are being cautiously reintroduced. The last free-roaming hippo in the old republican Orange Free State, for instance, was shot in the marshes here in 1894 – a wanton act for which ample atonement is now being made.

According to legend, 48 British soldiers were trapped and drowned in the peat fields that now form part of the reserve. (Peat, rare in South Africa, consists of vegetable material that has decomposed at the bottom of a swamp, gradually converting to humus, an early stage in the formation of coal.)

The 6 500 ha reserve was formerly 'closed', but is now being developed for visitors and it offers limited facilities for overnight stays. There are picnic and braai sites for day visitors and three well-sited observation hides.

For further information, write to The Principal Nature Conservator, Seekoeivlei Nature Reserve, P O Box 236, Memel 2970, or telephone/fax (0174) 4-0183.

Skip Norgarb and Porcupine Hiking Trails

About midway between Ficksburg and Clocolan the 22km/two-day Skip Norgarb Trail passes from river gorge to high plateau, revealing panoramic views across farmlands to the hazy Maloti Mountains of Lesotho. The route includes old kraals, rock paintings, fascinating rock formations, and wildlife such as springbok, blesbok and a myriad bird species.

Overnight accommodation is provided in a stone farmhouse with bunk beds, and a kitchen with a large coal stove to cheer cold winter evenings. Both days on the trail follow circular routes that start and end at the farmhouse.

Nearby is the Porcupine Hiking Trail, another two-day/22 km trail, starting and ending at the sandstone Vierfontein farmhouse. The figure-eight route circles two mountains, passing fine indigenous flora (trees are labelled), rich birdlife and ancient rock paintings.

For details and to book the Skip Norgarb Trail (maximum of 26 people), contact the Skip Norgarb Hiking Trail, P O Box 261, Ficksburg 9730, telephone (05192) 3959. Information about the Porcupine Hiking Trail may be obtained from the same postal address, or telephone/fax (05192) 4542.

Soetdoring Nature Reserve

The Modder River snakes through the 7 500 ha Soetdoring Nature Reserve, entering on its eastern boundary and exiting through the Krugersdrif Dam to the west. The dam holds many attractions for anglers, boating enthusiasts and waterskiers, but the real drawcard for nature lovers is the vast number of game species that roam the reserve's open plains.

HIGHVELD: FREE STATE

Left above: *Wahlenbergia* (also known as bell flower and wild bluebell) is a large genus (over 140 species in South Africa). **Left below:** Spur-winged and Egyptian geese. Despite their names and their similarity to geese, these birds are regarded as ducks.

beneath shady thorn trees. To reach Soetdoring, take the Bultfontein road (R700) from Bloemfontein and follow the signs. Contact Soetdoring Nature Reserve, P O Box 529, Bloemfontein 9300, telephone (051) 33-1011 for further information.

Sterkfontein Dam Nature Reserve
The water in the Sterkfontein Dam is pumped uphill over the great Drakensberg escarpment from the Tugela River basin. Some 23 km southwest of Harrismith, on the Bergville road (R74), the dam was constructed to ensure that the water continues to flow uphill and on to Gauteng. The dam itself, focal point of the reserve, is 6 km wide and 19 km long, and its waters cover nearly 7 000 ha when it is full.

The reserve is an 18 000 ha sanctuary encompassing steep and shady cliffs, grassy mountain slopes, moist kloofs and crystal-clear waters. Vegetation is lush, with yellowwood, wild peach and bush guarri flourishing in the sheltered kloofs, and ferns and mosses enjoying the shade of the dense, leafy canopy. Tree fern is found on the mountain slopes.

The reserve is home to a wide variety of birdlife, including many aquatic birds and raptors such as martial eagle and black eagle, bearded vulture and Cape vulture. Oribi, reedbuck, mountain reedbuck and grey rhebok are to be seen in the mountain areas.

Watersport enthusiasts are drawn to Sterkfontein by its excellent facilities and anglers hope to hook trout or yellowfish. The two-day/28 km hiking trail is named for the *sterretjies* or tiny golden flowers (*Hypoxis* species) that cover the ground in summer. The impressive scenery ranges from dazzling sandstone cliffs and an enormous cave to cool, indigenous forests and the plains that slope to the dam's shore.

Accommodation includes fully equipped chalets overlooking the dam and the mountains, and a caravan park and campsite along the water's edge. For more information, contact The Tourist Officer, Sterkfontein Dam Nature Reserve, P O Box 24, Harrismith 9880, telephone (05861) 2-3520, fax 2-1772.

Theronia Pan Nature Reserve
Saline water pumped from the Free State's gold mines has created a number of large, shallow pans around Welkom and Odendaalsrus, in the northwest of the province. These pans attract thousands of waterfowl, especially large numbers of greater and lesser flamingo and, curiously enough, even seagull – though

White rhino, gemsbok, eland, red hartebeest, black wildebeest, zebra and wild dog may be seen on the grasslands, while the shy steenbok, duiker and mountain reedbuck tend to keep to the riverine bush. Smaller mammals include small-spotted genet, African wild cat, otter and water mongoose, and over 250 bird species have been recorded. There is a lion park within the reserve.

Easy one-day hiking trails crisscross the reserve and night drives allow a close look at the habits of nocturnal creatures. Boating and angling are popular pastimes.

There are braai facilities along the river, and a conference centre near the eastern gate may be hired for special occasions. Also available is an unusual camp which accommodates visitors in modified train coaches arranged

125

the sea is nearly 650 km away. Birdwatchers converge on the pans from far afield, the most accessible being Theronia Pan, lying within Welkom's city limits.

Tussen-die-Riviere Nature Reserve
It was originally planned to build the Gariep Dam at the confluence of the Orange and Caledon rivers, east of Bethulie. In the area that was expected to be flooded, a number of farms were purchased by the state and evacuated. Then the plans were changed; the dam wall arose far to the west and the farms were no longer in danger from flooding. Instead of being returned to the agricultural sector, however, the farms were transferred to the Free State Provincial Administration for use in nature conservation. The result is the 23 000 ha Tussen-die-Riviere Nature Reserve.

At the reserve's western point, where the two rivers converge, there is a floodplain, but throughout the rest of Tussen-die-Riviere the rivers are separated by high rocky ridges, occasional plateaus and lower-lying grassy plains. The area was proclaimed a nature reserve in 1972, when it held only a few mountain reedbuck, duiker and steenbok. Before long a massive restocking programme was introduced, with the result that today Tussen-die-Riviere has vast herds of blesbok and springbok, as well as eland, blue wildebeest, impala, gemsbok, mountain reedbuck, red hartebeest, kudu and zebra.

After scientific assessment by conservation staff and ecologists, surplus game is offered annually to the public for hunting, and hunters are accompanied by experienced guides. This aspect of game management has become enormously popular.

Tussen-die-Riviere offers much to see, with plentiful indigenous vegetation, prolific birdlife and, near the eastern border of the reserve, Aasvoëlkop, a prominent koppie on which ancient rock paintings proclaim the early presence of Bushman (San) people. A network of more than 120 km of roads offers superb gameviewing. There are three self-guided hiking trails, and 1996 saw the opening of two additional trails. One of these is the self-guided route for 4x4 vehicles, and the other, also self-guided, includes cycling, canoeing and walking. Accommodation consists of six two-bed chalets overlooking the Orange River, and five unequipped shelters for hunters, each shelter capable of accommodating five adults.

To reach Tussen-die-Riviere reserve, take the signposted turn from the road between Bethulie and Smithfield (R701), about 15 km from Bethulie. The reserve is closed between May and September, which is the season for controlled hunting.

For more information, contact The Principal Nature Conservator, Tussen-die-Riviere Nature Reserve, P O Box 16, Bethulie 9992, telephone (051762) and ask for 2803.

Willem Pretorius Game Reserve
At the heart of the reserve is the Allemanskraal Dam, fed by the Sand River that traces a line of demarcation between the contrasting habitats of the northern and southern sections.

The south consists of grassy flats, ideal for large herds of plains game such as springbok, blesbok and black wildebeest. In the north is an area of plains, koppies and ridges of the Doringberg and Bakkersberg, inhabited by baboon, mountain reedbuck, red hartebeest, kudu and duiker. This well-bushed area (some trees have been numbered for easy identification) is favoured by white rhino, buffalo, giraffe, gemsbok and impala – the last three not indigenous to the region but introduced to provide variety for visitors. Although 12 000 ha in area, the reserve is too small to support large predators, the largest being caracal and black-backed jackal. The dam – which covers 2 500 ha when full – attracts great numbers of aquatic birds. The bird checklist for the reserve totals some 220 species.

In the northern section are ruins of stone buildings that date to prehistoric Sotho occupation, and one such settlement, on the Bakkersberg, has been restored and proclaimed a national monument.

Activities include boating and fishing, and gamewatching on an extensive network of roads, and there are tennis courts, an education centre, a swimming pool and a restaurant. Accommodation is in fully equipped chalets on the shore of the dam, and there are caravan and camping sites. A bush camp is even closer to nature. For further information, contact The Principal Nature Conservator, Willem Pretorius

---

FREE STATE TO THE RESCUE

An illustration from the book A Breath From the Veldt *by the artist and naturalist John Guille Millais.*

The blue wildebeest is a creature of the lowlands but its cousin, the black wildebeest, prefers the high country of the Free State grasslands and the Highveld. (The black wildebeest, with its dark-tipped mane and long-fringed chest, is actually dark brown and is often referred to as the white-tailed gnu.) Early in the 19th century the species was one of the most numerous in the region, but farming settlers soon changed that: the meat of the black wildebeest fed their workers, and its hide made fine harness straps and even grain bags.

In the 1870s, professional hunters hastened the wildebeest's decline by shooting it for its hide, which was shipped to Europe for paltry sums. By the end of the century the only black wildebeest left were on two private farms in the Free State.

The great hunter Frederick Selous believed that the species would have become extinct had it not been for the farmers concerned. In the 20th century, other Free State farmers followed their example. In 1936 the Free State Provincial Administration was persuaded to buy a few black wildebeest from one of the farmers and place them in its Somerville Game Reserve, close to Bultfontein. More animals were added, and by 1945 they numbered 52.

Early in the 1960s the Somerville reserve was closed and its resident game was moved to the new Willem Pretorius Game Reserve around Allemanskraal Dam. By 1966 there were 370 black wildebeest in the reserve and, as their numbers were still growing, the Administration began relocating the surplus.

Today there are about 450 black wildebeest in the Willem Pretorius reserve and lesser numbers in several other Free State reserves. Many private farmers have built up their herds of black wildebeest, and the species is no longer endangered. Indeed, it is now so numerous that it is once more being hunted.

HIGHVELD: **FREE STATE**

Above: Tranquillity radiates from the countryside between Fouriesburg and Clarens. Over the centuries erosion has sculpted a remarkable variety of forms from the sandstone sediments in the area. Some of the most dramatic are in the Golden Gate Highlands National Park.

Game Reserve, Private Bag X07, Ventersburg 9450, or telephone (05777) 4003/4, fax 4005.

Wolhuterskop Nature Reserve

Hundreds of kilometres from the sea a passable imitation of a Union Castle steamship serves as a restaurant at Loch Athlone, just south of Bethlehem. Loch Athlone, together with Gerrands Dam in the adjacent Wolhuterskop Nature Reserve, forms a wonderful focus for birdlife, and both dams are passed on the Wolhuterskop Hiking Trail.

The two-day/18 km trail starts and finishes at Loch Athlone, and leads through varied landscapes of field, hillside and forest plantation, brightened by the seasonal colours of proteas and wild flowers. Views from Wolhuterskop itself are especially attractive. In addition to some of the 100 or so recorded bird species, hikers often see game that includes springbok, waterbuck, red hartebeest, zebra, reedbuck and duiker. The trail is popular, so make reservations well in advance. There are picnic and braai sites near the reserve entrance, and many facilities are available next door, at the Loch Athlone resort. The resort and the reserve lie just west of the Fouriesburg road (R26), a few kilometres out of Bethlehem. For details, contact Jacana Country Homes and Trails, P O Box 95212, Waterkloof 0145, telephone (012) 346-3550/1/2, fax 346-2499.

WILLEM PRETORIUS AT A GLANCE

When to go The reserve and the adjoining public resort are open throughout the year. The resort, at the western end of the reserve, is open at all hours, but the reserve hours are from 6 a.m. to 7 p.m. (summer) and 8 a.m. to 6 p.m. (winter). The resort tends to be full at weekends and during school holidays.

Reservations Applications for accommodation should be addressed to Willem Pretorius Game Reserve, Private Bag X07, Ventersburg 9450, or telephone (05777) 4003/4, fax 4005.

Getting there The reserve may be approached from west or east. From the west, watch for the signposted turn-off on the N1 between Winburg and Ventersburg, 18 km from Ventersburg. From the east, take the signposted turn-off on the road between Senekal and Ventersburg (R70), 20 km from Senekal.

Accommodation Several grades of accommodation are available at the resort near the entrance to the reserve. Within the reserve there are fully equipped chalets at the water's edge, a caravan park and campsite, and a bush camp sleeping sixteen.

Eating and drinking The resort has a licensed restaurant and a supermarket selling groceries and fresh meat. There are braai facilities among the rondavels, in the caravan park and campsite, in the adjoining picnic area and at the bush camp.

Getting around The northern half of the Willem Pretorius reserve has an extensive network of good roads. Visitors must remain in their cars. There are speed limits of 50 km/h in the reserve and 25 km/h in the resort. Petrol and oil are available from a filling station at the entrance to the resort.

Special attractions The public resort organises launch trips on the dam, and other facilities include tennis courts, a bowling green, nine-hole golf course, swimming pool and entertainment complex offering badminton, billiards, snooker and table tennis. There is also a fully equipped environmental and conference centre.

Wildlife Giraffe, white rhino and buffalo are among the larger species to be seen. Visitors are also likely to spot eland, kudu, black wildebeest, red hartebeest, blesbok, springbok and impala.

More than 200 bird species have been recorded in the area – many of them close to the dam.

Fishing There are plentiful numbers of carp, bass and yellowfish in the dam, but anglers must hold a Free State angling licence (obtainable from the resort office). Fishing is allowed only within the area demarcated by red floats.

127

Where the sky is the only limit

Lesotho is southern Africa's kingdom in the sky, a geologist's wonderland of towering peaks, table-top plateaus and verdant kloofs – in this tiny country, only the sky is the limit. Even the lowest point in Lesotho is more than 1 250 m above sea level. Lesotho also has the highest peak in southern Africa: Thabana-Ntlenyana, 3 482 m above sea level and the pride of the Maloti range.

Roughly 85 per cent of Lesotho's more than 3 000 000 ha are a tumble of dark mountains, stretching to the horizon and offering spectacular scenery to delight hikers and pony trekkers. Among the finest attractions are the Maletsunyane Falls, one of the highest in Africa, the Ha Baroana rock paintings (with a nature reserve around them), fossilised footprints like those at Moyeni, a selection of fine tourist lodges such as the New Oxbow Lodge (a cluster of comfortable chalets used as a base by riders and climbers), the various pony-trekking organisations in the foothills (with courses for all age groups), and the spectacular Sehlabathebe National Park in the east.

Late in the 18th century, a Griqua hunter passed through Lesotho on horseback. Local tribesmen had never seen a horse before, and supposed it was an ox without horns. But before long, traders introduced Javanese horses and these became the progenitors of the famous Basotho pony, known for its sweet temper and sure-footedness.

Today's Basotho still travel long distances on horseback, as do visitors who want to take advantage of Lesotho's tourist attractions. Many of the country's hotels and lodges have ponies for hire and supply guides, and there are two main centres from which pony treks begin.

More ambitious (and experienced) riders may embark on a seven-day cross-country pony safari to Marakabei and the Maletsunyane Falls, beginning either at the Molimo Nthuse Lodge on the 'Mountain Road' or at Qaba, east of Mafeteng (the latter route takes in other falls along the way). Ideally, a party includes between six and ten riders who assemble in Maseru and are driven to the starting point by bus. A guide and grooms accompany them, and each day they ride up to 20 km, spending five or six hours in the saddle.

The going is rough, and even seasoned riders become saddle-sore. At night the party camps in huts. Food is supplied by the tour company but riders must provide their own sleeping bags and warm clothes. At the journey's end the party returns to Maseru by air. Although the trip is physically demanding, it offers an opportunity to view spectacular scenery and is an adventure you will never forget. The safaris are organised only when there is a demand for them, so prospective riders must book well in advance.

For further information and details on how to book for the trail, contact the Lesotho Tourist Board, P O Box 1378, Maseru, telephone (09266) 31-2896, or fax 32-3638.

Fossil footprints

Several sites in western Lesotho feature remarkable collections of fossil footprints left by reptiles that stalked the region some 200 million years ago. In most cases the footprints

Left: Bright clusters of everlastings (*Helichrysum ecklonis*) brighten the veld in Lesotho's Sehlabathebe National Park. The dried blooms are often used in flower pictures and wreaths, and were once used to stuff mattresses. These hardy plants are widely distributed in southern Africa.
Above: Water tumbles over the Maletsunyane (or Le Bihan) Falls near the village of Semonkong, southeast of Maseru.

were left in mud, covered by drifting sand and possibly lava, compressed in a layer of sandstone, and finally re-exposed through the forces of erosion. The most famous of the sites is Moyeni in the Quthing district of the far south, where palaeontologists have identified more than 500 sets of prints – most of them left by three-toed creatures that are believed to have been dinosaurs.

Another rich site is the mountainside at Morija, between Maseru and Mafeteng, on which may be seen large numbers of fossil footprints, and petrified wood that protrudes from the rock. Geological specimens, fossil bones and Stone-Age tools are displayed in a small museum at Morija. At Tsikoane, near Leribe, there are caves with 'relief' or 'negative' footprints in the roof. In fact, as many as nine different types of fossil footprint have been found in the Leribe district alone. Qalo (near Butha-Buthe in the north), Kolo (west of Morija) and Maphutseng (near Mohale's Hoek in the south) all have interesting fossil collections. Subeng, 4 km from Leribe on the way to Butha-Buthe, has a gallery of footprints in a riverbed – these appear to have been made by a five-toed animal.

Lesotho attracts palaeontologists from around the world. In some cases the scientists can link the footprints to fossil bones found in Lesotho or elsewhere; in others the footprint may be the only relic of the passing of a species.

Ha Baroana cave

To the visitor, Lesotho contains relatively little evidence of abundant wildlife, but centuries ago this mountainous region teemed with game. Lion, leopard, eland, red hartebeest and smaller antelope, as well as birds, are recorded in rock paintings which were left by artists whose existence can be traced back some 5 000 years. The finest collection is at Ha Baroana (also known as Ha Khotso), a rock shelter accessible from the 'Mountain Road' branching north from the highway between Maseru and Roma. The shelter lies within a small nature reserve in a pretty river gorge, and is open daily from 9 a.m. to 5 p.m.

Some of Ha Baroana's paintings are certainly over 1 000 years old. They represent the work of the Bushmen (San) who lived in the region until they were absorbed by tribes who came here from the north and west.

This shelter has, sadly, been badly vandalised. Restoration is currently under proposal, but visitors should not be deterred – there is still a lot to see.

For details about the cave, which is a National Heritage Site and falls under the auspices of the Protection and Preservation Commission of the Government of Lesotho, you should contact the Lesotho Tourist Board,

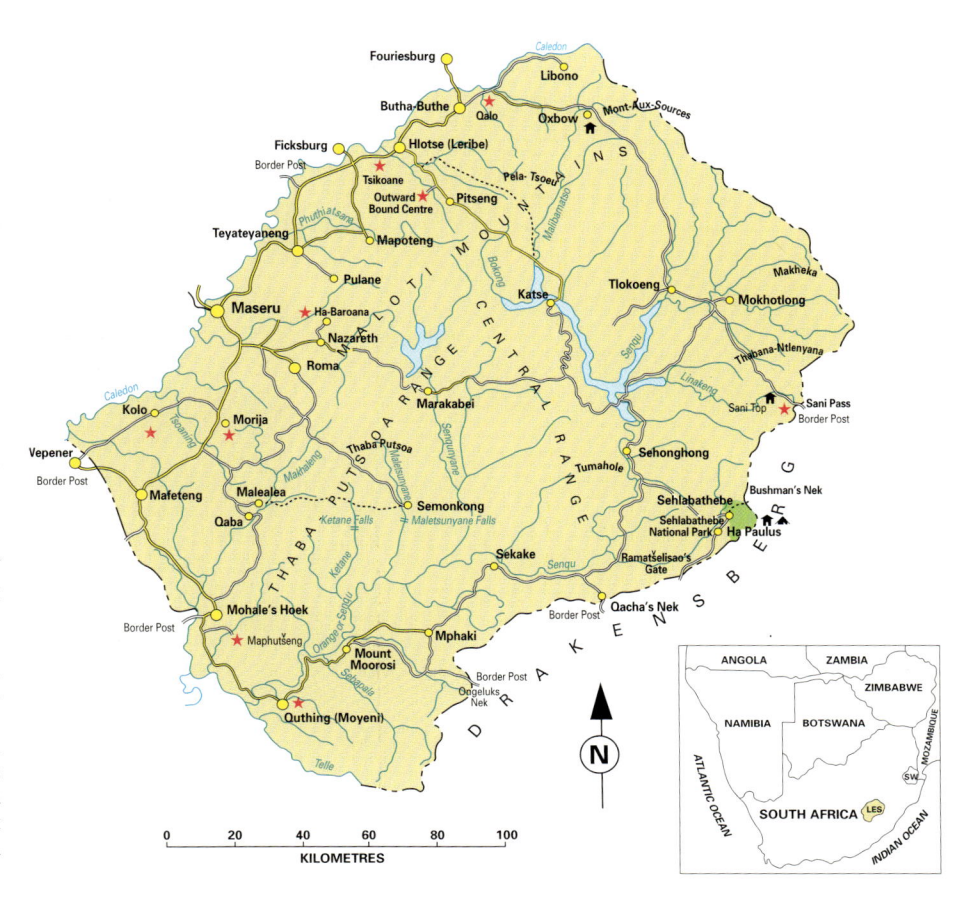

ROLLING HOME THE DINNER

To the ancient Egyptians it was an object of reverence, a symbol of renewed life. Its likeness has been found inscribed on monuments, tombs and ornaments.

In southern Africa the familiar scarab beetle is better known as the dung beetle, from its amusing habit of rolling balls of dung with its back legs. It is a natural scavenger of the veld, carving out for itself a generous portion of dung which it pats into a rough sphere. This is rolled away (the beetle using its back legs), gathering dirt and dust en route. Finally, a suitably soft spot is chosen and the ball is buried a few centimetres underground. It is then eaten.

The female beetle has a further use for the dung ball. She chooses soft and nutritious pieces of dung which are buried in a chamber about the size of a man's fist. She pats these into smooth spheres, leaving an egg on top of each.

These eggs eventually hatch into white grubs that live off the dung until they metamorphose into adult beetles.

Competition for good dung is keen – and two or more beetles can often be seen fighting over a particularly appealing ball of droppings. Predatory birds also pose a threat – swooping down on the beetles as they roll their precious cargo.

P O Box 1378, Maseru, or telephone (09266) 31-2896, or fax 32-3638.

Maletsunyane Falls

Lesotho's many waterfalls include one of the highest in Africa, variously known as Le Bihan Falls (after Father Le Bihan, a French missionary, who stumbled upon them in 1881), Semonkong ('the place of smoke', referring to the spray), and Maletsunyane (after the river that plunges 192 m over a rim of basalt).

Below the falls the river has excavated a deep gorge which can be descended by a steep path (but visitors should beware of stinging nettles near the bottom, and remember the arduous return journey – you should be reasonably fit). Lesotho's rare spiral aloe also grows on the surrounding hillsides, providing a splash of colour in November.

The falls can be reached by foot or on horseback from Semonkong, a small village about 4 km away. Ponies may be hired at the self-catering Semonkong Lodge, which is attached to the local trading post. The lodge makes a good base for exploring the surrounding countryside: bedding, cutlery, crockery and cooking equipment are provided and food is obtainable at the store. Catering is also provided for those who wish to take advantage of it. To reach Semonkong, visitors may either fly from Maseru, drive from Roma (though not in a vehicle with a low chassis), or join a pony safari from Qaba/Malealea.

The pony safari from Qaba/Malealea passes two other notable waterfalls: Ribaneng on the Ribaneng River and Ketane on the Ketane River (which requires a special diversion). Guests at Semonkong Lodge may organise an all-day pony expedition to Ketane and back.

To reserve accommodation at Semonkong Lodge, contact The Manager, Semonkong Lodge, P O Box 243, Ficksburg 9730, telephone (05192) 2730, or fax 3313. For information about pony trekking, contact the Basotho Pony Trekking Centre, P O Box 1027, Maseru, telephone (09266) 31-4165, or fax 31-1500, or the Matelile Pony Owners' Association, c/o Lesotho Tourist Board, P O Box 1378, Maseru, telephone (09266) 31-2896, or fax 32-3638.

New Oxbow Lodge

Many tourist brochures describe Lesotho as 'the Switzerland of Africa' – referring to its winter resorts. One of the most popular is the New Oxbow Lodge, a cluster of 26 *en suite* chalets located on a steep-sided loop in the Malibamatso River in the Butha-Buthe district of the north. The altitude (2 700 m) and the chilly Alpine conditions guarantee sufficient snow for the skiing enthusiast. A 2 km ski slope, serviced by a manually operated ski lift, lies 11 km from the lodge. (A more sophisticated ski lift is currently under discussion.)

In summer (and in those winters when there is no snow) the lodge makes a useful base for hikes and rides in the surrounding mountains, and there is good trout fishing in the area. To reach Oxbow, follow the road between Butha-Buthe and Letseng-la-Terae diamond mine (the tar ends at Oxbow and, further east, the route is best suited to 4x4 vehicles). Near Oxbow, where the Malibamatso River converges with the Tsehlanyane River, is the location of the mammoth Lesotho Highlands Water Project which is designed to be completed in 2019. For further information on the lodge or on ski conditions, write to New Oxbow Lodge, P O Box 60, Ficksburg 9730, or telephone (05192) 2247, fax 6093.

Outward Bound Centre

Canoeing, rock climbing and map reading are only a few of the activities at Lesotho's Outward Bound Centre, a wilderness adventure school that sets out to encourage initiative, responsibility, comradeship and concern for the needs of others. The Outward Bound concept originated in Wales during the Second World War, when young merchant seamen were sent on a course to learn how to survive shipwreck by enemy action. After the war the course was successfully adapted to civilian needs, and today there are more than 40 Outward Bound Centres around the world.

The adventure school was established in 1974. Its most popular course lasts two weeks and is designed for young men between 17 and 30 years old. The participants are divided into groups of ten or 12 and led by professional instructors, who introduce them to something fresh every day – like sailing, orienteering (a kind of cross-country race using map and compass), abseiling (a roped descent of a sheer cliff) and raft-building. As a fitting finale to the course, each student has to spend two days alone in the wild.

The centre organises a similar course for girls, a less arduous 'senior course' for the older generation, and a 'junior course' for youngsters. No previous experience of the wilds is required, for one of Outward Bound's chief aims is to show people that they are more resourceful than they imagine, and can make major advances within a short period. The most popular courses focus on team building, and the development of management and leadership skills. The centre is reached from a

---

A HEAVYWEIGHT IN EFFORTLESS FLIGHT

More than 240 bird species have been spotted in Lesotho, but easily the most impressive is the large and powerful lammergeyer, or bearded vulture (*Gypaetus barbartus*). Lammergeyers feed on carrion – often dead sheep and goats – but otherwise they resemble eagles more than vultures. Their heads and necks are feathered (a vulture's are bare); they live in pairs rather than in colonies; and unlike the vulture they can carry prey in their claws. Their 'beards' consist of long bristles under the beak. In earlier times the lammergeyer had an extended habitat, but today it is rarely seen further afield than the Drakensberg and Maluti ranges. The species generally nests on a precipice and the eggs are laid on a jumble of sticks surmounted by softer materials – often wool. The male and female take turns to incubate two eggs while the other goes hunting. When the eggs hatch, the senior offspring kills the junior: a phenomenon common among birds of prey. From an early stage, the survivor is fed meat and fragments of bone.

Lammergeyers sometimes fly up with a bone, then drop it onto a rock to smash it, exposing the marrow. The species is noted for its outstanding speed, strength, courage and eyesight – qualities that so appealed to the 19th-century Basotho that they expected the same of their military leaders. Praise poems of the time regularly compared the chiefs with their aerial counterparts.

HIGHVELD: LESOTHO

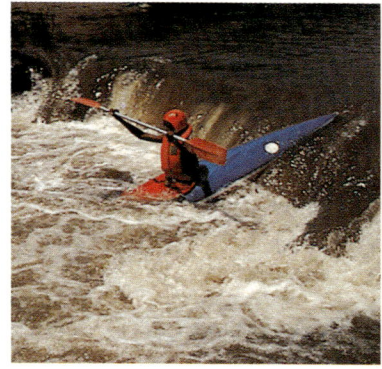

Left: From Sani Top, the pass bearing its name twists across the mountains, revealing breathtaking views over tumbled hills and peaks to a misty blue horizon. **Above:** A student at Lesotho's Outward Bound Centre negotiates rapids in the Tsoinyane River as part of his training as a canoeist. The course may sometimes be arduous and nerve-wracking, but the adventure is unforgettable.

signposted turn-off on the road from Leribe to Pitseng. For further information, contact The Director, Outward Bound, P O Box 367, Leribe, telephone (09266) 40-0543; or P O Box 346, Ficksburg 9730.

Sani Top

The most dramatic route into Lesotho climbs from KwaZulu-Natal by way of the Sani Pass, 2 860 m above sea level. Beyond the South African border post is Sani Top, with an arch of welcome and a mountaineers' chalet containing six twin bedrooms and three four-bed rooms. Bedding, cutlery, crockery and cooking equipment are provided but visitors must supply their own food. (Catering is available on request.) Most types of liquor are available at the bar. The chalet is used by those hiking, climbing, fishing and cycling in the surrounding mountains, one of which is the 3 482 m Thabana-Ntlenyana (pretty little mountain) – the highest point south of Mount Kilimanjaro.

Winter snowfalls attract optimistic skiers to Sani Top, but the snow does not last for long. Only 4x4 vehicles may attempt to negotiate the pass, which, though difficult in summer, is treacherous in winter. However, there is a daily safari-vehicle service to Sani Top. For information, contact Travel Underberg, P O Box 69, Himeville 3256, telephone/fax (033) 701-1466.

Sehlabathebe National Park

The 6 500 ha Sehlabathebe National Park, tucked into the rugged southeastern corner of Lesotho, is characterised by bristling mountain peaks and grassveld punctuated with stark outcrops of sandstone and intersected by the twisting Tsoelike River. To most visitors, Sehlabathebe's chief attractions are its magnificent scenery and its soul-cleansing solitude. Merely getting there is an adventure. The most comfortable way is to fly from Maseru to the Ha Paulus landing strip, 12 km from the entrance to the park (guests ride the rest of the way to the park's lodge by 4x4 vehicle, or on horseback). More enterprising visitors may drive to the park by way of the trans-Lesotho 'Mountain Road' (which in its eastern stages is suitable only for 4x4 vehicles) or by the southern road that approaches from Qacha's Nek and Ramatselisao's Gate.

Yet another method is to arrive through the 'back door', walking into the park by way of the South African border post at Bushman's Nek. In this case, visitors leave their cars at Bushman's Nek Hotel, 2 km short of the border. Once inside the park, they either walk to the lodge or cover the 10 km on horseback (provided they have arranged to be met with ponies). Sehlabathebe has little game apart from a resident population of mountain reedbuck, and occasional eland and oribi that find their way in from KwaZulu-Natal and then leave again when snow arrives. The park also accommodates baboon, black-backed jackal, wild cat, otter, fish and a host of mountain birds (including rock kestrel, black eagle and jackal buzzard). Four dams close to the park lodge are stocked with trout and other species, and there is said to be even better fishing in the south, downstream from a 20 m waterfall that is a favourite destination for hikers and riders. The Tsoelike and Leqooa rivers, which run through the park, harbour the little-known fish *Oreodaimon quathlambae*, a species which was once thought to be extinct.

Most of Sehlabathebe's visitors sleep in the park lodge, which has rooms with two or four beds and provides everything except food. The adjoining six-bunk hostel has water and cooking facilities. Hardier visitors may camp out anywhere in the park but must be self-sufficient. All visitors should take enough food to last the duration of their visit. Situated some 9 km from the lodge is a shelter containing a gallery of about 130 Bushman (San) paintings.

To reserve accommodation or request further information on Sehlabathebe, write to Lesotho National Parks, Ministry of Agriculture, P O Box 92, Maseru, or telephone (09266) 32-3600 or 32-2876, fax 31-0190.

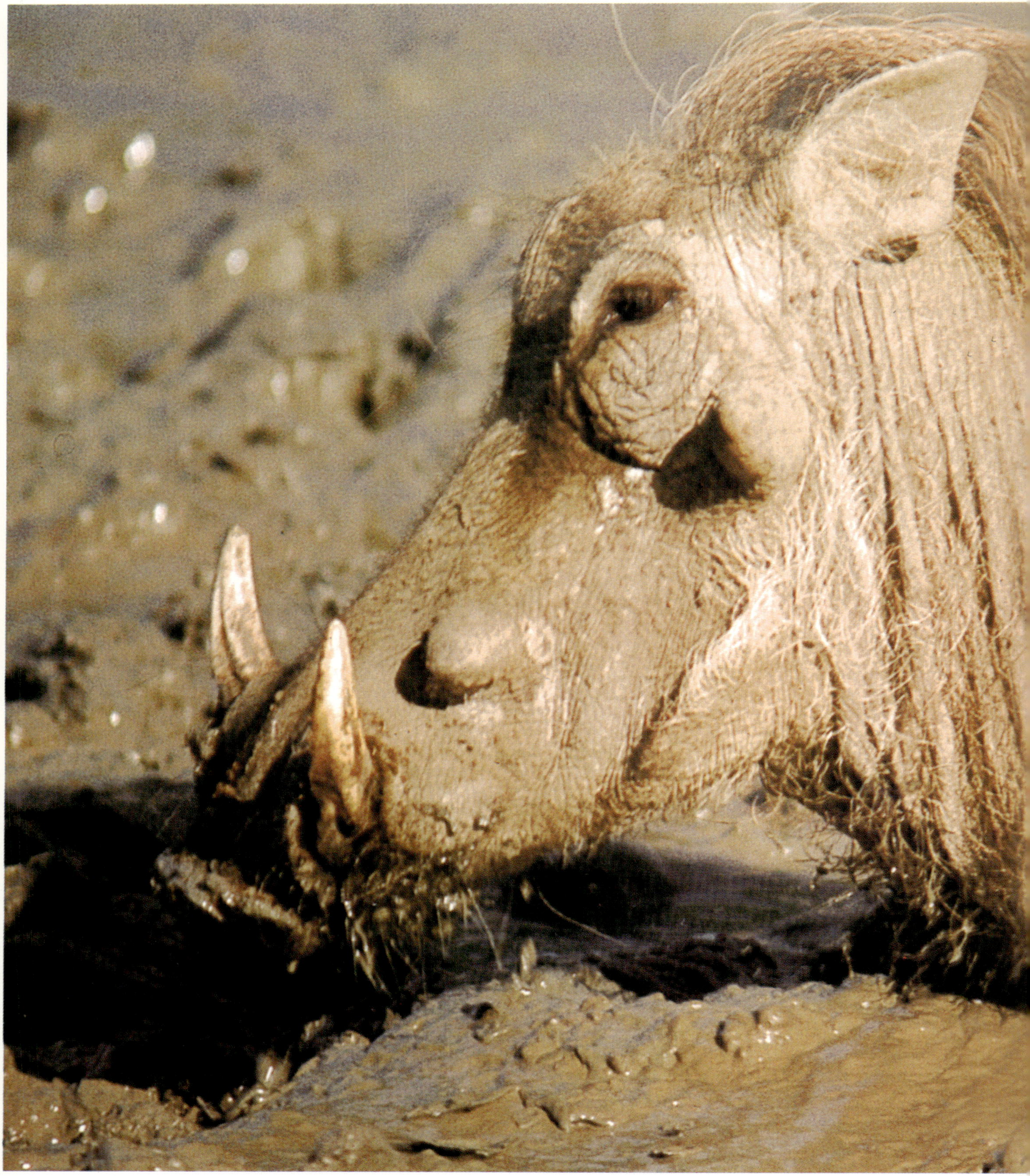

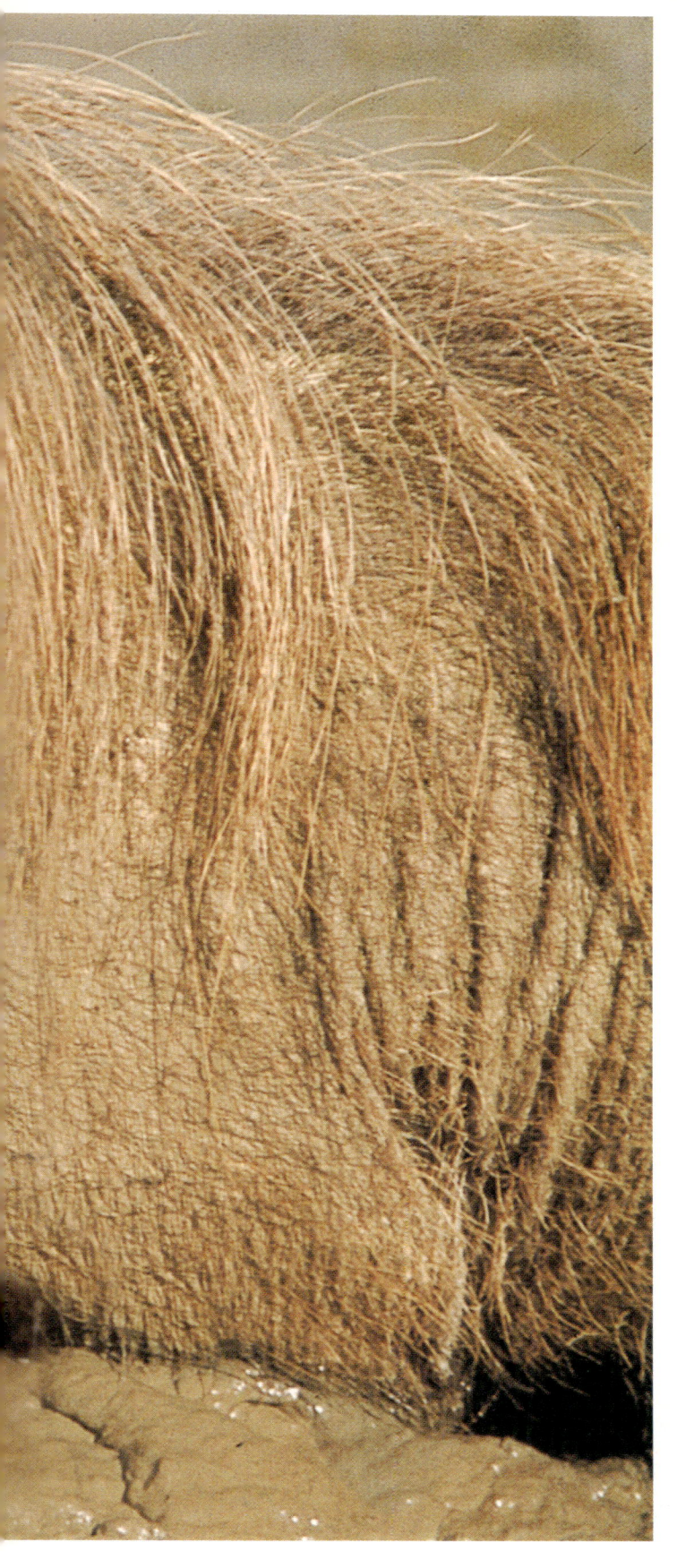

KWAZULU-NATAL

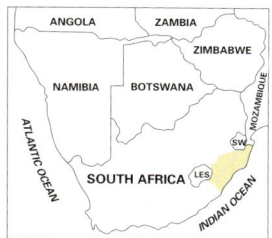

This verdant and beautiful region, bordering the east coast of southern Africa from Port Edward northwards to the Mozambique boundary, is regarded as South Africa's 'garden province'. KwaZulu-Natal's subtropical coastline, its sweeping savannah grasslands in the east and the magnificent Drakensberg range in the west, provide a naturally opulent backdrop for its rich wildlife heritage. The lammergeyer soars majestically over its mountain kingdom and the buffalo ranges the plains of the Mfolozi reserves, while stately palms grace the playgrounds of Durban and Margate.

The province's vast complex of game parks, nature reserves and wilderness trails is controlled by a number of authorities, ranging from the strictly private to the Natal Parks Board, a semi-autonomous body which controls 64 sanctuaries stretching from Sodwana Bay in the north to Umtamvuna Nature Reserve in the south, and from the Drakensberg parks in the west to the eastern seaboard. The Board's conservation activities are aimed at promoting the wise use of natural resources in perpetuity and to prevent degradation of the environment. To this end it conducts a wide range of educational programmes, keeping in constant touch with the media.

KwaZulu-Natal's parks and reserves offer visitors an opportunity to see wildlife in habitats varying from scrubland to dense forest, from green hills to spray-lashed seashore, ranging in size from the vast Hluhluwe-Umfolozi Park to the modest Doreen Clark Nature Reserve. Also worth seeing are the magnificent sanctuaries to the north, including those at Kosi Bay, Lake Sibayi, Mkuzi, Ndumo, and Tembe – forested home of the province's last free-ranging elephant herds.

A pensive warthog wallows in muddy bliss. This uncompromisingly ugly animal lives mostly in family parties. It feeds on herbs and short grasses, which it plucks with its incisors, but may also root for bulbs and tubers – much like a pig.

The Dragon's Fangs

The KwaZulu-Natal Drakensberg, moss green in summer and icy white to grey in winter, is one of the world's loveliest mountain ranges. Dividing the province from the roof of Africa in Lesotho, the mountains span some 200 km along KwaZulu-Natal's western boundary, reaching heights of up to 3 400 metres. Home first to the eland and the Bushmen (San) who hunted them, they are today the winter playground of South Africa. The area has been proclaimed the Natal Drakensberg Park – a vast conservancy encompassing some 16 reserve areas and stretching southwards from Cathedral Peak to Bushman's Nek. Controlled by the Natal Parks Board, the park comprises a wide variety of natural, and dramatic, attractions.

It is to this ancient wilderness of flower-decked foothills, trout streams and fearsome lava peaks that visitors are constantly drawn. They delight in the rugged splendour of Giant's Castle – more than 34 000 ha of grassy plateaus and deep valleys ranged by a large variety of wildlife. Those visitors who are more intrepid may even choose to sleep in a cave or mountain hut.

Rivers, waterfalls and a huge backdrop of majestic mountains characterise the Royal Natal National Park, with its dramatic 5 km rock wall known as the Amphitheatre. Visitors to the area can spend the days exploring the many trails on foot or on horseback, and the nights in comfortable bungalows and cottages.

Hiking trails abound in the protected areas of the Drakensberg, and detailed pamphlets outlining the various routes and the attractions to be seen are available from the reserves themselves, or may be obtained by writing to The Reservations Officer, Natal Parks Board, P O Box 1750, Pietermaritzburg 3200, or telephone (0331) 47-1981, fax 47-1980.

Coleford Nature Reserve

Lying in the southern Drakensberg area some 50 km southwest of Bulwer, Coleford is set slightly apart from the towering mountains of the Natal Drakensberg Park. Wildlife found in the reserve includes black wildebeest and blesbok, which occur predominantly on the reserve's open foothills, as well as oribi and reedbuck. The varied birdlife includes wetland species such as wattled crane.

Excellent trout-fishing is available in the series of four man-made and natural reservoirs created by the Ngwangwane and Ndawana rivers (a licence and permit, both available from the camp office, are necessary), and trout-fishing clinics are held occasionally.

Above: *Wurmbea krausii*, at an altitude of 3 000 metres, photographed in October. **Top:** *Delosperma herbeum* (a vygie) among dolerite rocks in the Kamberg area. **Right:** The eastern buttress of Devil's Tooth, one of the best-known rock formations in the Drakensberg range. These mountains draw many hundreds of hikers and climbers every year, and the experience is frequently put to good use on expeditions abroad.

NATAL PARKS 'PASSPORTS'

Golden Rhino Passports may be purchased from most reserves and resorts, or from the Natal Parks Board, P O Box 1750, Pietermaritzburg 3200, telephone (0331) 47-1981, or fax 47-1980. Each passport admits a driver, car and passengers, trailer, caravan or boat free of charge to any reserve or resort controlled by the Natal Parks Board, and it is valid for one year (from 1 February to 31 January). The permit is available at half price after 31 July.

To make reservations for hutted accommodation and wilderness trails, contact the Natal Parks Board at the address above. General queries about parks may also be addressed to the board.

For campsite bookings, consult each reserve individually.

This is an excellent area for walking, and the reserve also offers facilities such as riding, tennis and a library.

Accommodation is offered in a number of six-bed, five-bed and three-bed chalets, as well as in six three-bed rustic cabins. The chalets have their own cooking facilities and bathrooms, while the cabins share a communal kitchen and ablution block. Bedding, cutlery and crockery are provided, but visitors should take their own food.

Also available is Sunnyside Cottage, which houses seven in rustic accommodation some 5 km from the main hutted camp. It has a gas stove, refrigerator and lights, but no linen, and visitors must also provide their own food.

Reservations for the hutted camp and Sunnyside Cottage can be made by contacting the Natal Parks Board, P O Box 1750, Pietermaritzburg 3200, telephone (0331) 47-1981, or fax 47-1980. The reserve is open daily in summer from 5 a.m. to 8 p.m., and in winter from 6.30 a.m. to 7 p.m. Office hours are from 8 a.m. to noon, and from 2 p.m. to 4 p.m. Braai and picnic sites in the camp may be used by day visitors. Visitors may also picnic anywhere along the river (fires are prohibited).

Himeville Nature Reserve

A 105 ha sanctuary next to the Drakensberg foothills village of Himeville, this is a popular spot for trout-fishermen and for those who enjoy the tranquillity of its bluegum-sheltered camping and caravan site. The campsite overlooks two small dams, both of which are frequented by several species of waterfowl, as well as by the occasional antelope.

To get there, take the Underberg road from Pietermaritzburg. The reserve, which is open from sunrise to sunset, is signposted from Himeville village. Bookings for the ten campsites (with ablution facilities) are made by contacting The Officer-in-Charge, Himeville Nature Reserve, P O Box 115, Himeville 3256, telephone (033) 702-1036. Provincial fishing licences and daily angling permits are available from the reserve office. Rowing boats are also available for hire.

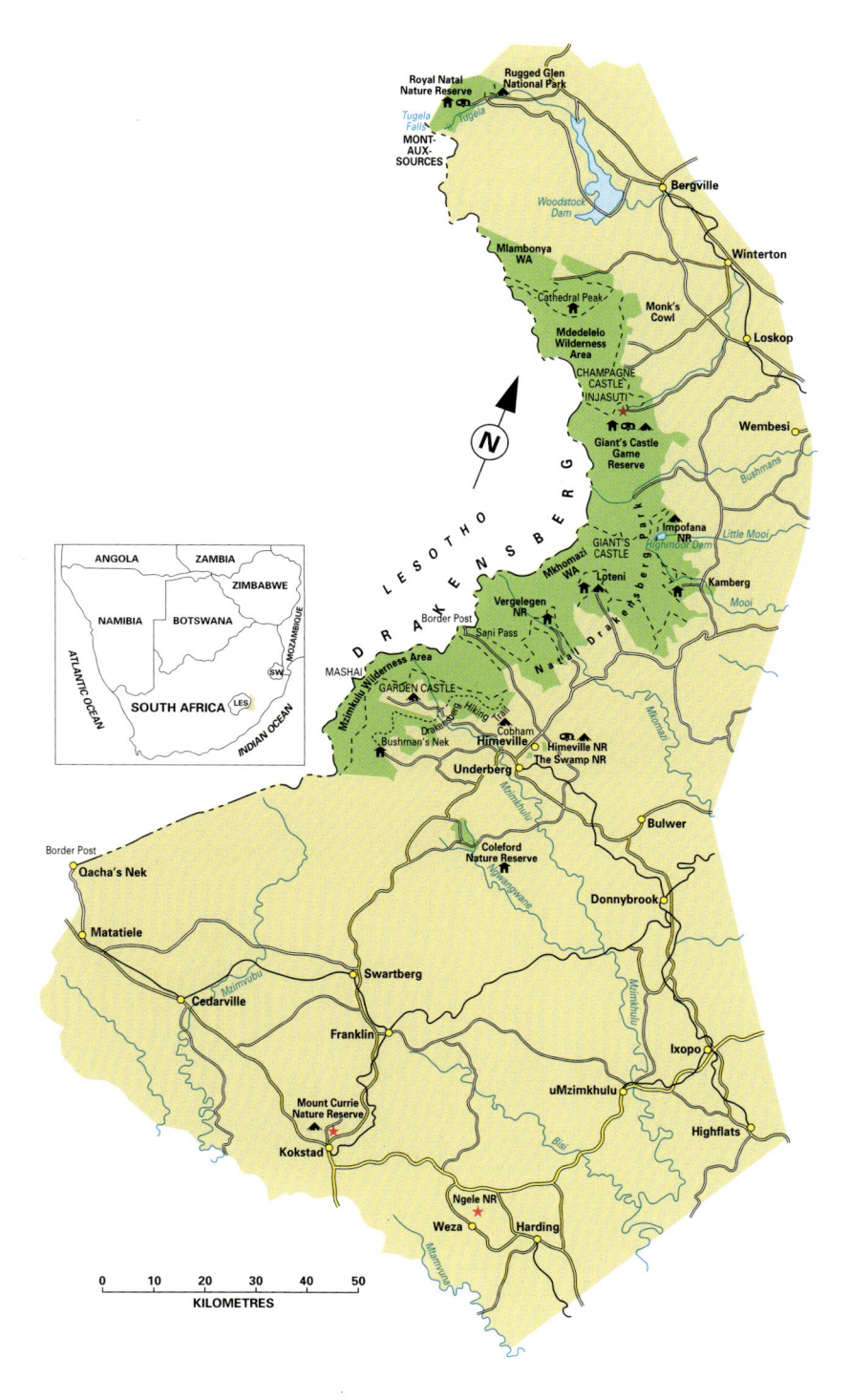

Mount Currie Nature Reserve

A monument in the Mount Currie reserve commemorates the laager site and grave of Adam Kok III, the harassed Griqua leader who sold his land to the Free State government in 1863, and led his 2 000 people, their wagons and 20 000 head of stock in an epic trek over the Lesotho mountains to their new home,

Above: Giant's Castle from above the Bushman's River. The peak's name was originally applied to a castle-shaped mountain near Underberg, but was later transferred. The reserve abounds in peaks, valleys and tumbling streams.
Right: An eland – the largest of the African antelope – in the Giant's Castle Game Reserve.

No Man's Land – the capital of which later became Kokstad. The reserve is about 5 km northeast of Kokstad, off the Franklin/Swartberg road. The access road is gravel.

In spring, the proteas on this 1 777 ha Natal Parks Board reserve (on the slopes of Mount Currie) are particularly lovely. Visitors may spot mountain reedbuck, grey rhebok, oribi, bushbuck, grey duiker, blesbok and springbok roaming this wild and beautiful area, which overlooks the well-stocked waters of Crystal Dam (large-mouth bass and bluegill). Permits for fishing are available, and watersports are popular in summer.

There are many charming walks and climbs. Old cattle tracks and paths can be used by hikers, who may also choose to follow the Crystal Dam self-guided trail.

The birdlife at Mount Currie includes blue crane (South Africa's national bird), rock kestrel, bearded vulture, jackal buzzard and eagle, while flufftail are common at the vlei. Altogether, over 220 species have been recorded, and bird lists are available from the reserve office. Picnic areas and campsites (with hot- and cold-water ablutions) have been provided for visitors. The reserve is open all year, from sunrise to sunset.

For further information, and to reserve campsites, write to The Officer-in-Charge, Mount Currie Nature Reserve, P O Box 378, Kokstad 4700, or telephone (037) 727-3844.

Natal Drakensberg Park: Bushman's Nek

The southernmost section of the KwaZulu-Natal Drakensberg, Bushman's Nek also marks the end of the Giant's Cup Hiking Trail, a 68 km path that passes through indigenous forest and mountain grassland, climbing steep slopes and revealing views to the crests of the mountains. Wildlife commonly seen in the area is varied, and includes eland, reedbuck, grey rhebok, oribi and klipspringer, as well as dassie and porcupine. Jackal buzzard and black eagle may be seen soaring above the slopes. The streams are stocked with trout.

Bushman's Nek also provides access to Sehlabathebe National Park in Lesotho (see separate entry), and to the wilderness areas popular with hikers and overnight campers. There is a border post just inside the park for those intending to enter Lesotho.

No overnight facilities exist within Bushman's Nek, but there are hotels and campsites nearby. The area is privately owned.

To reach Bushman's Nek, take the R626 from Underberg. Pass the turn-off to Garden Castle and turn onto the second gravel road. The route is clearly signposted. For more detailed information, contact Natal Parks Board, P O Box 662, Pietermaritzburg 3200, telephone (0331) 47-1961, or fax 47-1037.

Natal Drakensberg Park: Cathedral Peak

Some 32 000 ha in extent, Cathedral Peak, like so much of the Drakensberg, is a haven for hikers, with a selection of trails winding through mountain scenery, stands of indigenous trees, gurgling streams and trout pools. With its jagged peaks thrusting their blue-grey pinnacles above the Little Berg in the northern Drakensberg range, Cathedral Peak is also a favourite haunt of mountaineers.

Animals commonly spotted ranging through the montane vegetation include grey rhebok, reedbuck, bushbuck, grey duiker, caracal, jackal, chacma baboon and dassie. Birdlife abounds, from the high-soaring lammergeyer to brilliantly plumaged sunbirds hovering above the spring flowers. Snakes – rinkhals, berg adder and puff adder – also occur, but they are wary of hikers and are rarely seen.

Accommodation is available at a campground with 12 sites and communal ablution facilities. The campground is open from 6 a.m. to 6 p.m. and, on Fridays, until 9 p.m. Also within the area are approximately 15 caves in which hikers may spend the night – caves and campsites should be booked at least one month in advance.

Nearby is the Cathedral Peak Hotel (telephone/fax (036) 488-1888 or P O Winterton 3340), which offers excellent accommodation. From the hotel, a number of trails reach into the mountains, many of them penetrating the

Miambonya Wilderness Area, which forms part of Cathedral Peak. People not staying at the privately owned hotel should start the trails at the campsite, which lies at the foot of Mike's Pass, some 4 km south of the hotel. Look out for bearded and Cape vulture, martial eagle and both black and white stork. Altogether, some 200 bird species have been recorded, as have more than 300 indigenous types of flora.

Striking galleries of rock art, a legacy of the Stone Age hunter-gatherers, decorate rock shelters and caves. Hikers are requested not to stray from the designated paths, so as to reduce the rate of erosion.

To reach Cathedral Peak from Pietermaritzburg, travel northwest on the N3 and take the Winterton/Colenso turn-off. Continue into Winterton and turn left over the railway line. Follow the Cathedral Peak signs. From Harrismith or Ladysmith, follow the signs to Bergville and 1 km after the town, follow the Cathedral Peak signs. Mike's Pass reception office is 3 km beyond the Mhlwazini Store. The office, and the reserve's curio shop, are open between 8 a.m. and 4.30 p.m.

For further information, contact Natal Parks Board, P O Box 662, Pietermaritzburg 3200, telephone (0331) 47-1961, fax 47-1037. To make campsite and overnight cave bookings, contact The Officer-in-Charge, Cathedral Peak, Private Bag X1, Winterton 3340, telephone/fax (036) 488-1880.

Natal Drakensberg Park: Cobham

About 150 km west of Pietermaritzburg, Cobham was established in 1959 by the forestry department, but has been administered by the Natal Parks Board since 1988.

Within the Cobham area are the reserve areas of Vergelegen, iNzinga, KwaMehlenyati and Mkhomazi, which together are managed as a single, huge (52 000 ha) section of the southern Drakensberg.

Cobham is also a haven for hikers, being the setting (with Garden Castle Reserve, see separate entry) for the main portion – Giant's Cup section – of the Drakensberg Hiking Trail. Weaving a scenically splendid path through the foothills of the Drakensberg, the trail takes hikers through a rich variety of indigenous flora (mainly forest and grassland), passing through one of the most beautiful parts of southern Africa. Breathtaking views extend far across the mountain peaks and crests. The full distance of some 60 km takes five days and nights, starting near the Sani Pass Hotel (on the pass of the same name) and ending at Bushman's Nek. Shorter options are available.

The main route is indicated by white footprints. Yellow footprints indicate connecting or alternative routes, and blue footprints indicate the route to drinking water or a swimming spot. Overnight accommodation, usually a converted farmhouse, is provided for up to 30 people, with beds and mattresses. Hikers must bring their own bedding, cooking equipment (including portable stoves, if required) and food. There are flush toilets.

The Cobham area is rich in animal life, although the birdlife at this high altitude is less prolific. Look out for eland, dassie, porcupine, blue crane, black eagle and jackal buzzard. Bushman (San) paintings decorate the cave walls – notably those at Bathplug Cave, named for the hole in the cave floor, through which surface water drains.

Within Cobham, the Mkhomazi Wilderness Area is named for the Mkomazi River, which flows eastwards to reach the Indian Ocean on KwaZulu-Natal's south coast. A permit is needed before setting out to explore this rugged

GIANT'S CASTLE AT A GLANCE

When to go The reserve is open throughout the year, from sunrise to sunset. It is busiest during the Christmas and Easter school holidays.

Reservations Bookings for Giant's Camp, Injasuti Hutted Camp, Hillside mountain huts, the caves and mounted trails are made by contacting The Reservations Officer, Natal Parks Board, P O Box 1750, Pietermaritzburg 3200, telephone (0331) 47-1981, or fax 47-1980.

Bookings for the Hillside camping and caravan sites are made through The Officer-in-Charge, Hillside, P O Box 288, Estcourt 3310, telephone (0363) 2-4435 between 9 a.m. and 12 noon daily. Bookings for the Injasuti campsite are made via The Camp Manager, Injasuti Camp, Private Bag X7010, Estcourt 3310, telephone (036) 488-1050. Bookings for the Lammergeyer Hide can be made by contacting The Officer-in-Charge, Giant's Castle, Private Bag X7055, Estcourt 3310, telephone (0363) 2-4718.

Getting there The reserve is reached from the main highway (N3) between Durban and Johannesburg. It is situated some 69 km west of Mooi River and 64 km southwest of Estcourt and is well signposted. To reach Injasuti, turn off the N3 at the Loskop/Central Berg Resorts sign, follow the tarred road for some 27 km, and turn left at the Injasuti sign. The camp is 30 km along this road.

To reach Giant's Castle main camp from the north, turn off the N3 at the Loskop/Central Berg Resorts interchange, drive into Estcourt and follow the Ntabamhlope road out of the town. At White Mountain Lodge, turn left and follow the signs to Giant's Castle (some 65 kilometres). From the south, follow the N3 and take the toll plaza into Mooi River. Follow the signs to Giant's Castle (about 64 km along a gravel road).

Accommodation Giant's Castle main camp offers Giant's Lodge which sleeps seven, and Giant's Castle hutted camp, which has beds for 68 people in two-, three-, five- and six-bed cottages and bungalows. Hillside has a camping/caravan ground that accommodates 150 visitors. The Hillside rustic hut is a fully equipped eight-bed unit (visitors must bring their own bedding and towels). Injasuti Camp has 17 fully equipped six-bed cabins, and two eight-bed cabins. Camping facilities are available at Injasuti for 80 visitors. There are two caves and three mountain huts that may be reserved by hikers.

Eating and drinking Visitors should supply their own food and drink, as the nearest main source is at Estcourt.

Getting around Daily horse trails of varying duration are arranged at Hillside, and there are also mountain rides lasting two and four days. Petrol is available only at the Giant's Castle main gate. An extensive network of hiking trails allows visitors to explore large areas of the reserve.

Following the massive rescue of more than 100 people after heavy snowfalls in 1996, the Natal Parks Board decided that the park would be closed to overnight hikers if severe weather was forecast. Those already hiking are advised to abandon their trail should the weather become unfavourable. Registers must be completed by hikers both before starting out and on their return.

Special attractions The reserve offers a panoramic feast of mountains, grasslands, streams, waterfalls and beautiful wild flowers. Caves close to Giant's Castle Camp contain a Bushman Site Museum and hundreds of Bushman (San) paintings. The two museum sites are Main Caves, near Giant's Castle Camp, and Battle Cave in the Injasuti Valley. Swimming in the river is permitted. The Lammergeyer Hide, open weekends only, offers an excellent opportunity for bird-watching. It must be booked in advance.

Wildlife The reserve is noted for the lammergeyer, or bearded vulture, and numerous antelope species. Over 140 bird species have been recorded.

Fishing Brown trout are found in the Bushman's River and its tributaries. Permits and licences are obtainable from the camp superintendent.

wilderness area, which stretches north to Giant's Castle, and south to the Sani Pass.

For further information, contact Natal Parks Board, P O Box 662, Pietermaritzburg 3200, telephone (0331) 47-1961, or fax 47-1037.

Cobham has a rustic campsite with just four toilets and cold-water ablutions. To make campsite reservations, contact The Officer-in-Charge, Cobham, P O Box 168, Himeville 3256, telephone/fax (033) 702-0831. Trout Bek Cottage offers comfortable accommodation for nine people. Anyone wishing to book the cottage or a place on the Giant's Cup Hiking Trail should write to The Reservations Officer, Natal Parks Board, P O Box 1750, Pietermaritzburg 3200, telephone (0331) 47-1981, fax 47-1980.

Natal Drakensberg Park: Garden Castle
The Natal Drakensberg Park reaches southwards to Garden Castle, a 35 300 ha wonderland of dramatic peaks, rolling green slopes and trout-filled streams. Many of the caves and rocky overhangs are decorated with Bushman (San) paintings, and the area has enormous appeal for the hiker. Three of the five overnight huts that shelter those undertaking the Giant's Cup Hiking Trail (*see separate entries* for Bushman's Nek, Cobham), are within Garden Castle. Each of these sleeps up to 30 people, and is equipped with beds and mattresses. Hikers must, however, supply their own sleeping bags, food, lighting and cooking equipment. The huts may be reserved by both casual walkers and those on the longer trail, but preference is given to the latter. Trailists may also sleep in the caves, but no fires are allowed.

Animals roaming these slopes include various antelope species such as grey rhebok, common and mountain reedbuck, eland, grey duiker, oribi and klipspringer. Birds to look out for are black eagle and lammergeyer. Trout-fishing is popular, especially with those eager to pit their angling skills against the 'wild' mountain-stream rainbow trout (a permit is needed).

Within the Garden Castle section of the Drakensberg is the Mzimkulu Wilderness Area, a 28 140 ha expanse named after the 'great home of all rivers' that reaches the sea at Port Shepstone. The wilderness area features stately yellowwood forests, evergreen and seasonal grassland, montane heath scrub and a few other vegetation types. Several antelope species occur here, as do the black eagle, martial eagle, bald ibis and Cape vulture.

To book a place in one of Garden Castle's overnight huts, contact Natal Parks Board, P O Box 1750, Pietermaritzburg 3200, telephone (0331) 47-1981, or fax 47-1980.

For information about camping and fishing, contact The Officer-in-Charge, Garden Castle, P O Box 378, Underberg 3257, or telephone (033) 701-1823, fax 701-1822.

Natal Drakensberg Park: Giant's Castle
In the 19th century, as each new migrating human wave – Zulu, Voortrekker, Briton – swept over the former Natal, the 25 km long mountain ridge and its adjacent 3 000 m peak, now known as Giant's Castle, acquired a variety of colourful names. Its English name dates back to 1865.

For hundreds of years before that, the mountain was home to the Bushmen (San), or 'people of the eland', as they were called. Unlike their successors, these hunter-artists who followed the herds of eland were not warriors, and were themselves hunted and harried until they vanished from the region. They have, however, left monuments to their long occupation, in more than 700 paintings in the open-air museum at Main Caves in the reserve. Also worth visiting is Battle Cave in the Injasuti Valley, the site of a splendid artistic rendering of a battle scene between rival Bushman (San) groups. Forty per cent of all known rock art in South Africa is found in the twilight overhangs of the KwaZulu-Natal Drakensberg, and guided tours of Main Caves and Battle Cave are available. There is also an excavated hearth, and tools, weapons and clothing are on display.

There are 800 species of flowering plant in the Drakensberg, of which 63 are ground orchids. Game in the reserve is particularly plentiful, and includes eland, mountain and common reedbuck, grey rhebok, oribi, red hartebeest, bushbuck, blesbok and grey duiker. Black-backed jackal, baboon, serval and caracal are also found, and there are trout in the Bushmans and Injasuti rivers.

A hide from which visitors may watch the rare lammergeyer and other birds of prey may be reserved, and birding enthusiasts will enjoy looking out for the more than 140 species that have been recorded.

This area offers excellent hiking, and guided wilderness trails and horseback trails are on offer, with nights spent in caves. Numerous shorter, self-guided walks may also be taken.

Giant's Castle Game Reserve dates back to 1903, and was expanded in 1980 to include Injasuti Camp (once known as Solitude Mountain Resort) to the north, creating a total area of more than 34 000 hectares. Injasuti is named after the triple eNjesuthi peaks that form part of the 3 000 m northern buttress of the adjacent Giant's Castle, on its border with the Mdedelelo Wilderness Area. At their base, the Injasuti River flows through an exceptionally beautiful valley of forests and sandstone cliffs – a tranquil, silent haven with a charming hutted camp. The reserve is dominated in winter by a looming wall of ice and snow – the 3 202 m Greater Injasuti buttress.

Giant's Castle offers a variety of accommodation, including cottages, bungalows, caravan parks, caves and mountain huts. There are 17 six-bed cabins and two eight-bed group cabins at Injasuti, each with a lounge/dining room, bathroom, toilet and kitchenette with

Left below: The call of the cicada (Christmas beetle) is probably the most familiar of all sounds in the wilds of southern Africa. It is only the male that produces the shrill cry; the sound-producing organ consists of a cavity on either side of its abdomen in which the timbals (or miniature drums) and folded membranes are lodged. The cicada makes these timbals vibrate, and the membranes amplify the noise. The sound is believed to act as an assembly call and may also be part of a mating ritual. **Left above:** *Helichrysum squamosum*. **Right:** *Aster perfoliatus* at an altitude of 2 500 metres.

stove and refrigerator. Linen is provided. There is also a campsite for up to 150 visitors.

Applications and enquiries should be addressed to The Reservations Officer, Natal Parks Board, P O Box 1750, Pietermaritzburg 3200, telephone (0331) 47-1981, fax 47-1980. For cave and campsite bookings, write to The Camp Manager, Private Bag X7010, Estcourt 3310, or telephone (036) 488-1050.

Natal Drakensberg Park: Highmoor
'Impofana' is the Zulu name for the eland, largest of African antelope and resident in the Drakensberg. The gracefully undulating hills of Impofana Nature Reserve, which is embraced by the Highmoor section of the Natal Drakensberg Park, provide a home for these and many other animals, including grey rhebok, mountain reedbuck and oribi. The only nesting site of wattled crane in the KwaZulu-Natal Drakensberg occurs here, and the area also contains the largest breeding colony of the threatened bald ibis in any protected area of KwaZulu-Natal. Also found are Cape vulture, lammergeyer, black harrier and jackal buzzard.

Bordering the Mkhomazi Wilderness Area, Highmoor is one of its entry points. Apart from Mike's Pass at Cathedral Peak, it is also one of the few areas in the Drakensberg where vehicular access to the top of the Clarens sandstone is permitted. Anyone bold enough to walk to one of the many vantage points on the High Berg will be rewarded with panoramic views of both the Little Berg and the main Drakensberg escarpment. A small, rustic campsite is available for 20 people and, for those embarking on an overnight trail, caves may be booked.

Three dams in the area are stocked with trout, which provide trophy fishing for anglers, and there is a wide variety of waterbirds, including white-backed duck.

MOTHERHOOD – THE EASY WAY

A striped cuckoo's greenish-blue egg (far left) is an almost perfect match to the eggs of an arrow-marked babbler. In this species, the chick does not attempt to evict the eggs or young of the host bird.

One of the mysteries of evolution is the phenomenon of the brood parasites – birds that lay their eggs in the nests of other species and leave the upbringing of their chicks to an unknown mother. The best-known of these is the cuckoo, which breeds in summer after migrating south from the African tropics. The female looks for a suitable host nest before laying a single egg among the foreign clutch. Up to 15 eggs are laid by the cuckoo in different nests – and usually the cuckoo eats one of the host eggs while laying her own.

Hatching takes about two weeks – after which the battle for survival starts in earnest. Although blind and frail-looking, the young cuckoo has powerful feet, a flat back and strong wing stubs. By lying on its back and using the wing stubs to manoeuvre, the baby bird pushes the remaining eggs or nestlings out over the edge of the nest. This eviction impulse lasts about five days. If any host chicks survive, they and the cuckoo grow up together. The foreign mother then raises the young cuckoo as her own.

Certain honeyguides, whydahs and finches are also brood parasites. A newly hatched honeyguide uses a remarkable hook at the end of each mandible to kill the other occupants of the nest. This bill-hook disappears during the nesting period. The cuckoo finch does not evict its nesting mates, but being smaller and weaker, the host chicks usually die off. Whydahs also leave the host brood alone and several may be raised alongside the host chicks.

A fascinating aspect of this evolutionary con-trick is that the eggs of the parasitic birds have come to resemble those of the host bird – nature's way of ensuring that the host mother cannot recognise the menace among her own eggs until it is too late. Nature has come up with yet another marvel: some parasitic birds use more than one species of host, and apparently produce a suitable egg for each one.

To reach Highmoor take the Nottingham Road/Rosetta turn-off from the N3. At Rosetta, take the road signposted Kamberg/Giant's Castle for 31 km, where a sign indicates Highmoor on your left. From the north, turn off at Mooi River and follow the road to Rosetta. Access to Impofana Nature Reserve is by permit only. For more detailed information, contact Natal Parks Board, P O Box 662, Pietermaritzburg 3200, telephone (0331) 47-1961, or fax 47-1037. To book a campsite, contact The Officer-in-Charge, P O Box 51, Rosetta 3301, telephone (0333) 3-7240.

Natal Drakensberg Park: Kamberg
The great white shields carried by warriors of the Zulu royal regiments came from the hides of royal cattle that Shaka, founder and fighting king of the Zulu nation, kept in the Kamberg area of the Drakensberg.

Today, this impressive 2 232 ha reserve, set in the undulating foothills in the vicinity of the Loteni and Giant's Castle sanctuaries, caters for the tranquil pursuit of trout-fishing in dam and river. The trout hatchery supplies trout for all Natal Parks Board areas in the Drakensberg, and is open to the public.

As in any part of the Little Berg region, there are numerous scenic walks among the hills and along the well-named Mooi River. One of the walks is routed to include the yellowwoods, tree ferns (*Cyathea*) and proteas of the area, and a recent innovation is a nature trail devised for visitors in wheelchairs.

Wildlife in the reserve includes black wildebeest (the emblem of KwaZulu-Natal), reedbuck, grey rhebok, eland, duiker, red hartebeest and oribi.

Kamberg lies in rolling hills some 42 km from Rosetta, which is itself 11 km south of Mooi River. Another route is via the village of Nottingham Road.

The reserve offers a delightful hutted camp comprising five rest huts (each sleeping three), with a communal lounge, kitchen and ablution facilities. There is also a five-bed, self-contained cottage. All cooking and cleaning is done by camp staff. There is also a five-bed, self-catering chalet where visitors do their own cooking. Visitors provide their own food and drink. Some 8 km from the main camp is Stillerust, an old, self-contained farmhouse with accommodation for ten. Guests do their own cooking and must supply their own food, drink and linen.

Accommodation may be booked through The Reservations Officer, Natal Parks Board, P O Box 1750, Pietermaritzburg 3200, telephone (0331) 47-1981, or fax 47-1980.

Natal Drakensberg Park: Loteni

Loteni is wild and lonely, a ravine hideaway in the shadow of the high peaks. Its name means 'in the ashes', from the burnt appearance of the shale found in this river valley in the magnificent southern Drakensberg.

In the early 19th century the Loteni Valley formed part of a Bushman (San) hunting route. Later, part of it became a sheep farm run by William and Catherine Root. Today their renovated homestead houses the Loteni Settlers Homestead Museum, with exhibits including farm implements, furniture and household utensils.

Brown trout in the Loteni River are a major attraction. The green flanks of the valley provide refuge for common and mountain reedbuck, eland, grey rhebok, oribi and grey duiker, and the birdlife includes black eagle, bearded vulture, Cape vulture, lanner falcon, black stork and giant kingfisher. Swimming in the Loteni River is allowed (although chilly), and there is an especially good spot about 1 km below the camp.

The reserve has a hutted camp of 12 self-contained bungalows, each with its own refrigerator, gas stove, bathroom and toilet, as well as bedding, crockery and cutlery, and two self-contained cottages. Visitors bring their own food and do their own cooking (the nearest shop is at Loteni, some 14 km away).

The campground, lying 2 km from the hutted camp, has 12 sites with an ablution block with hot and cold water. Simes Rustic Cottage, equipped with gas, lies on the shore of a small, trout-stocked dam, which is reserved for use by the occupants of the cottage. Visitors must bring their own food and linen. The campsites may be booked through The Camp Manager, Loteni Nature Reserve, P O Box 14, Himeville 3256, telephone (033) 702-0540. To book hutted accommodation, write to The Reservations Officer, Natal Parks Board, P O Box 1750, Pietermaritzburg 3200, telephone (0331) 47-1981, fax 47-1980.

Loteni lies 72 km west of the village of Nottingham Road, on the road to Himeville (turn right at the Loteni Store and you'll reach the entrance to the reserve after ten kilometres). The gates are open between 5 a.m. and 7 p.m. from 1 October to 31 March, and from 6 a.m. to 6 p.m. between 1 April and 30 September. Fishing licences and permits may be obtained

---

ROYAL NATAL AT A GLANCE

When to go The Christmas and Easter seasons are the favourite holiday times in the mountains, when accommodation is most in demand. The Tendele Camp and Royal Natal National Park campsite gates are open between sunrise and sunset. Entrance to the Royal Natal National Park Hotel is not restricted.

Reservations and information The 28 Tendele bungalows, chalets and cottages must be booked well in advance. Tendele Lodge provides luxury accommodation for six people in three *en suite* bedrooms. For reservations, write to Natal Parks Board, P O Box 1750, Pietermaritzburg 3200, or telephone (0331) 47-1981, or fax 47-1980. The 40 campsites at Mahai may be booked through The Officer-in-Charge, Royal Natal National Park, Private Bag X1669, Bergville 3350, telephone (036) 438-6303, fax 438-6310. Nearby Rugged Glen's campsites may be booked at the same address. There is a visitors' information centre in the park, and a comprehensive brochure is available.

Getting there The park lies 48 km west of Bergville along a tarred road, or 72 km from Harrismith via the Sterkfontein Dam and Oliviershoek Pass.

Accommodation Apart from Tendele, and the campsites at Mahai, accommodation is also available at the privately run Royal Natal National Park Hotel, Private Bag 4, Mont-aux-Sources 3350, telephone (036) 438-6200, fax 438-6101. Rugged Glen, a 4 km/five minute drive from the Royal Natal gates, has a campsite that caters for up to 45 visitors.

Eating and drinking Limited food supplies may be purchased at the hotel shop.

Getting around The speed limit is 40 km/h and visitors are asked to exercise caution. The horse-riding service is excellent. Hiking and climbing are the main activities.

Special attractions There is a small museum in the visitors' centre with exhibits covering the vegetation, history, archaeology, fauna and geology of the park. There are many proteas and other wild flowers, none of which may be picked. Yellowwood, stinkwood, wild chestnut, assegai-wood and dog-plum grow in the forests.

Wildlife The checklist of birds recorded in the park covers 184 species, including the lammergeyer, Cape vulture and black eagle. Mammals include hare, the agile klipspringer (in the higher reaches), bushbuck, grey rhebok, mountain reedbuck, black-backed jackal, porcupine, baboon and, in the savannah, grey duiker.

Fishing There is a large dam for fishermen. Angling licences are available from the visitors' centre.

Special precautions Visitors intending to climb or walk to the summit of the Drakensberg should always obtain prior permission from the reserve warden. Rescues are organised from the warden's office (fatal accidents unfortunately continue to occur). There are two basic rules: never walk or climb alone, and if mist comes up, do not move away until it clears. Following the massive rescue of more than 100 people after heavy snowfalls in 1996, the Natal Parks Board decided that the park would be closed to overnight hikers if severe weather was forecast. Those already hiking are advised to abandon their trail should the weather become unfavourable. Registers must be completed by hikers both before starting out and on their return.

Above: A Bushman (San) cave museum in the Giant's Castle Game Reserve illustrates the centuries of occupation from the late Stone Age. This reconstruction portrays a group of these hunter-gatherers in their cave home. **Above right:** Bushman (San) cave paintings in the Drakensberg. Many of these paintings have been destroyed by thoughtless visitors over the years: people scribbled on them, lit fires in the caves, and even splashed water and other liquids on the paint in attempts to enhance the colours. **Right:** *Hesperantha schelpeana* high on the slopes of Sentinel Peak in the Drakensberg.

from the camp manager. Picnickers are welcome, but should note that fires are prohibited.

Natal Drakensberg Park: Monk's Cowl

Proclaimed specifically to act as a buffer zone, this reserve divides official wilderness areas from private properties. The aim is to screen the effects of man and his activities, and as far as possible to keep the wilderness zones in their largely unspoilt state. Monk's Cowl, which is controlled by the officer-in-charge of Cathedral Peak, lies to the east of the vast wilderness area known as Mdedelelo (literally 'make way for him' – the term given to a bully).

One of the remoter areas of the Drakensberg, Mdedelelo is wild and untamed, with black basalt peaks clawing at the bright blue skies, and shady, natural overhangs concealing galleries of striking rock art. Ndedema Gorge, a secluded, steep-sided valley dotted with chilly pools, tinkling cascades and verdant vegetation, is the site of some 17 sandstone rock shelters and caves in which there are 4 000 individual paintings dating back to the Stone Age. They are protected, and visitors may not sleep or make fires in the caves and rock overhangs.

The scenery here is outstanding, and the Monk's Cowl itself, with its soaring, craggy pinnacle (which has claimed the lives of a number of mountaineers), provides a truly magnificent backdrop. The gorge also provides access to the Mlambonya Wilderness Area, where hiking and overnight camping are permitted. The Monk's Cowl campground has 15 sites accommodating up to 90 visitors. There is an ablution block, with hot and cold water.

To reach the reserve, follow the Berg Resorts signboards from Winterton, until you get to Monk's Cowl Forest Station. Permits to enter the wilderness area are available at the station. For further information, and to book a campsite or obtain permits, write to The Officer-in-Charge, Monk's Cowl Forestry Station, Private Bag X2, Winterton 3340, or telephone (036) 468-1103.

The sanctuary's gates are open between 5 a.m. and 7 p.m. from 1 October to 31 March, and between 6 a.m. and 6 p.m. from 1 April to 30 September.

Natal Drakensberg Park: Royal Natal National Park

This park is a majestic oval, bounded by green-clad mountains that rise vertically towards the sky like the walls of an Olympian amphitheatre. It is the foremost of the parks in the Drakensberg, extending for 8 094 ha and boasting some of the most spectacular scenery in the country. Because of its size and terrain the park is probably best explored on horseback. There are several bridle paths, and horses are for hire. Hiking is another option, and 31 walks and climbs have been mapped out, ranging from the 3 km Otto's Walk (for beginners) to the more adventurous 45 km Mont-aux-Sources, named after the highest peak of the plateau. A popular hike is the 7 km trail that leads up the Tugela Gorge, passing grasslands bedecked with proteas and striking stands of yellowwoods. You can also try trout-fishing, or swim in crystal-clear (but icy) streams, picnic in fairy-tale glens, watch birds, paint or just absorb the beauty of this lovely wilderness.

The Mont-aux-Sources area of the park is the backstage plateau of the towering Amphitheatre, a 5 km wall of solid rock that cups the Tendele Valley far below, an impressive panorama of mountain beauty and one of the grandest sights in all of southern Africa. The Mont-aux-Sources peak itself is a large but rather unprepossessing hump on the Drakensberg rim, above the plain between Lesotho and KwaZulu-Natal.

KwaZulu-Natal's largest river and highest waterfall, the Tugela, and eight other rivers, including tributaries of the westward-flowing Orange River, with its 2 000 km course, are born at Mont-aux-Sources. The Elands River rises here, flowing into the Vaal River, which itself becomes part of the Orange. Two French missionaries, trekking along the escarpment in the 1830s and impressed by the number of streams they encountered, named the peak 'mountain of sources'.

Visitors can drive along the rim of the 'Berg' for 8 km – almost as far as the Sentinel, the northernmost wing of the Amphitheatre. The Sentinel is situated 150 km from the Royal Natal park via Oliviershoek Pass.

The 18 hour/45 km circular walk to the Sentinel from the visitors' centre in the park via Tendele Camp and Mahai Falls finally ascends the Amphitheatre by means of two chain ladders of 100 rungs. Climbers should exercise particular care in winter, when the rungs ice up and become extremely slippery.

Weather at the top of the Drakensberg can be treacherously unpredictable throughout the year, and is particularly so during summer.

Tendele Camp, with its dramatic views across to the Amphitheatre, can accommodate up to 114 people in 2-bed, 4-bed and 6-bed chalets, 2-bed and 4-bed bungalows and cottages. There is a central lounge adjacent to the reception office. Tendele Lodge offers luxurious, fully equipped accommodation for six, with a kitchen, large living area with a fireplace and outdoor braai site. Cooks prepare meals for those staying in the cottages, bungalows and lodge, but the chalets are self-catering. Mahai campsite, beneath shady trees, caters for up to 400 campers and caravanners, and has ablution blocks with hot and cold water. There are curio shops at the visitors' centre and at Tendele.

Also within the park is the privately leased Royal Natal National Park Hotel. A shop at the

KWAZULU-NATAL: DRAKENSBERG

Above left: The green mamba is rarely found outside forest or thick bush. This snake is often confused with the similarly coloured boomslang, but the boomslang has larger eyes and a blunt snout. **Above centre:** The elegant markings and large size of the wattled crane make it highly visible and easy to distinguish from other cranes. Wattled cranes are found in the Drakensberg foothills and other damp parts of southern Africa, usually occurring in pairs or small groups. **Above right:** The Tugela Gorge, a dramatic cleft in the Drakensberg sweeping through the majestic Royal Natal National Park. This 8 094 ha wonderland, foremost of the Drakensberg reserves, offers enchanting walks such as Fairy Glen, a short distance from the warden's office, with its *Begonia* and *Streptocarpus*; Gudu Falls (a three-hour walk); Surprise Ridge and Cannibal Caves (five hours); and Buttress Grotto, which is characterised by a profusion of cycads.

NATURE'S LIVING LIGHT BULBS

The female glow-worm (really a beetle), shown here, emits a steady light. The firefly is the male winged beetle.

Glow-worms and fireflies, closely related to each other, are misnamed. They are, in fact, neither worms nor flies, but species of beetle belonging to the family Lampyridae. These remarkable creatures are distinguished by their ability to create light.

The light-producing organ, situated at the lower end of the abdomen, is a highly efficient mechanism that controls the chemical reaction between a substance called luciferin and the enzyme luciferase. The interaction produces rays that are confined to the visible part of the spectrum (that is to say, almost no heat is generated), which is the kind of pure light source that scientific man was able to perfect only after decades of experiment.

The beetles' lights are essential to courtship and mating, serving as recognition signals between male and female of the same species. The male firefly's light, stronger than that of the largely sedentary female, flashes as he flies about at night. Among glow-worms, however, it is the wingless female that shines brighter – she emits a steady light (compared with the flickering of the male firefly) from her static position on the ground.

Entomologists, curious to find out how an adult male *Luciola* can distinguish a female in the dead of night, have established that the male recognises the flash-frequency of his own species. Despite the fact that the interval between each flash may be altered with a change in the air temperature, the male seems to be able to compensate for this phenomenon, as no cross-breeding seems to occur between species. There are about 30 species of firefly distributed throughout southern Africa, the larvae of most of them fairly closely resembling the female glow-worm.

hotel sells basic supplies. Reservations can be made by contacting Royal Natal National Park Hotel, Private Bag 4, Mont-aux-Sources 3350, telephone (036) 438-6200, fax 438-6101.

For more information about the reserve, contact Natal Parks Board, P O Box 662, Pietermaritzburg 3200, telephone (0331) 47-1961, fax 47-1037. To book campsites, write to The Officer-in-Charge, Royal Natal National Park, Private Bag X1669, Bergville 3350, or telephone (036) 438-6303, fax 438-6310.

Natal Drakensberg Park: Rugged Glen

Adjacent to Royal Natal and 4 km from its gate, is the 762 ha Rugged Glen reserve. There are nature trails and trout-fishing, and horse rides set out from the Rugged Glen stables. The game and birdlife are similar to those found in the Royal Natal National Park, and the sanctuaries share access roads from Harrismith and Bergville. The Rugged Glen campsite, dominated by the 1 890 m Camel's Hump, caters for 45 visitors and has ablution blocks with hot and cold water.

For further information about the reserve, contact Natal Parks Board, P O Box 662, Pietermaritzburg 3200, telephone (0331) 47-1961,

Above: A species of *Hesperantha,* or evening flower. It belongs to the Iris family and includes 33 species, most of which are found in South Africa. **Top:** A beautiful everlasting daisy, *Helichrysum adenocarpum,* found in the Drakensberg during spring.

fax 47-1037. To book campsites, write to The Officer-in-Charge, Royal Natal National Park, Private Bag X1669, Bergville 3350, or telephone (036) 438-6303, fax 438-6310.

Natal Drakensberg Park: Vergelegen Nature Reserve

Pine-covered Vergelegen, in the Umkomaas or Mkhomazi (Mkomazi) Valley, is a beautiful reserve. It lies 19 km up the Mohlesi Pass road towards Lesotho (there is no through road). Access to the reserve is via Nottingham Road on gravel, or 50 km further on tar via the small towns of Bulwer, Underberg and Himeville. At an altitude of 1 500 m, Vergelegen's tract of mountain sourveld, sliced by deep valleys, is particularly secluded.

You should obtain day permits and provincial fishing licences (there are brown trout) in advance. The reserve is open from sunrise to sunset, and overnight hiking is allowed. For more information, contact Natal Parks Board, P O Box 662, Pietermaritzburg 3200, or telephone (0331) 47-1961, fax 47-1037.

Ngele Nature Reserve

West of Port Shepstone, on the N2 to Harding and Kokstad, is the 7 000 ha Ngele Nature Reserve, controlled by the Department of Water Affairs and Forestry. Four hiking trails, ranging from 2 km to 20 km, cut through the indigenous forest and grassland, although visitors may prefer the options of exploring on horseback or by mountain bike.

Among the animals that may be seen are baboon, monkey, porcupine, caracal, jackal, bushbuck and duiker, and there are also many bird species.

Nearby, Ingeli Forest Lodge offers comfortable accommodation in 33 rooms and chalets, with facilities for horse riding, mountain biking, tennis and swimming. Conference facilities are also available, and the lodge is the perfect base from which to explore the reserve. For further information, contact Ingeli Forest Lodge, Private Bag X502, Kokstad 4700, telephone (039) 433-1175.

NATAL PARKS BOARD ACCOMMODATION GLOSSARY

Bungalow: A bungalow is a fully equipped one- or two-bedroom house with lounge/dining room, bathroom and toilet. Crockery, cutlery, a refrigerator and linen are provided. Food is prepared by a cook in a central kitchen.

Bush Camp: Bush camps provide rustic accommodation and are fully equipped with cutlery, linen, crockery and cooking utensils. A small gas refrigerator and stove are provided, although cooking is usually done over an open fire. Visitors may have to do their own cooking.

Cabin: (Injasuti) A cabin is a fully equipped, self-contained, serviced dwelling with two bedrooms, a lounge/dining room, bathroom, toilet and kitchenette. Linen is provided. Visitors do their own cooking.

Chalet: A chalet is a self-contained, serviced dwelling with one or more bedrooms, lounge/dining room, bathroom, toilet and kitchenette (equipped with cutlery, crockery, stove and refrigerator). Linen is provided. Visitors staying in chalets do their own cooking.

Cottage: A cottage is really a two- or three-bedroomed house with a lounge/dining room, bathroom, toilet, kitchen (equipped with cutlery, crockery, stove and refrigerator). Linen is provided and there is a cook in attendance.

Lodge: A lodge has the same facilities as a cottage (see **cottage** category) but on a more luxurious scale. Reservations for lodges are accepted only two calendar months in advance.

Log Cabin: (Umlalazi, Cape Vidal, Sodwana Bay and Mapelane) A log cabin is a serviced two- or three-bedroomed building with beds for five to eight people. It has a bathroom, toilet and kitchen (equipped with cutlery, crockery, stove and refrigerator). Linen is provided. Visitors do their own cooking and washing up.

Rest Hut: A rest hut is a fully equipped two- to four-bed rondavel or squaredavel, provided with cutlery, crockery, refrigerator and linen. Communal bathrooms are used. Food is prepared by cooks in a central kitchen.

Rondavel: (Albert Falls only) A rondavel comprises two beds, bathroom, toilet and kitchenette (equipped with cutlery, crockery, linen, stove and refrigerator). Visitors do their own cooking and washing up. The rondavels are serviced.

Rustic Cabin: A rustic cabin is a fully equipped four-bed hut with cutlery, crockery, hotplate and refrigerator. The units are served by a communal ablution block. Linen is provided. Visitors do their own cooking and washing up. The rustic cabins are serviced by camp staff.

Rustic Cottage: These cottages have several bedrooms and are provided with crockery, cutlery, cooking utensils, refrigerator and stove. Visitors do their own cooking and must provide pillow slips, sheets and towels.

Rustic Hut: Rustic hut accommodation is provided with crockery, cutlery and cooking utensils, but contains no refrigerator or stove. Meals are prepared by visitors over outside open-hearth fires. No linen or towels are provided.

Trail/Mountain Huts: One large room with a divider. Four double-bunk beds and mattresses (two at Meander Hut), a two-plate gas cooker, cold water and toilet only are provided. If booking is heavy, visitors may have to share the accommodation with other hikers.

The Swamp Nature Reserve

The focal point of the 220 ha reserve is some 60 ha of wetland that attracts a wide range of waterfowl, including the rare wattled crane, largest of the indigenous crane species, and the crowned crane. Southern reedbuck are found in the vlei areas. The best time of year to visit the reserve is summer, as the wetland is often frozen over in winter. The reserve is reached by travelling 14 km eastwards from Himeville on the road to Pevensey. There are no facilities. For more detailed information, write to The Officer-in-Charge, Himeville Nature Reserve, P O Box 115, Himeville 3256, or telephone (033) 702-1036.

'Twixt berg and beach

There is a little of the gentle English countryside and much of Africa in the Midlands of KwaZulu-Natal, a fascinating mixture of undulating farmlands studded with charming towns that lie between the snow-topped Drakensberg and the holiday beaches of the coast. This was where Boer fought Briton almost a century ago, and many a simple cross stands as lonely tribute to their valour.

Great herds of game once wintered here – these are all gone now, but remnants have been preserved or reintroduced in parks that still perpetuate the original habitat.

Albert Falls Resources Reserve

This is one of the most inviting spots in the KwaZulu-Natal Midlands and lies a mere 24 km from the centre of Pietermaritzburg. Sloping grassy banks – ideal for picnicking and birdwatching – surround the 2 274 ha Albert Falls Dam and its adjacent 816 ha resort.

There is plenty of scope for horseback riding, sailing and canoeing (races are held regularly below the falls), while fishing and walking are also very popular. Each September, the Albert Falls Bass Masters Tournament draws hosts of hopeful anglers to the dam, while the National Bass Tournament is held here once every four years.

The reserve also houses several antelope species, including oribi and waterbuck, and giraffe. Among waterfowl are ducks, cranes, cormorants and herons, while fish eagles nest in tall trees nearby. The game park captures a delightful bushveld air, and visitors may drive or walk through the area. Day visitors are catered for, with a number of pretty picnic spots scattered throughout the reserve.

Notuli Hutted Camp offers accommodation in rondavels and chalets, equipped with stove, fridge, linen, pots and cutlery: visitors must supply only their food and drink. There are also 60 campsites situated on the water's edge, equipped with hot and cold water.

To make reservations at Notuli, you should contact The Camp Manager, Albert Falls Resources Reserve, P O Box 31, Cramond 3220, telephone (033) 569-1202/3, or fax 569-1371. To reach Albert Falls reserve, take the Church Street exit from Pietermaritzburg for Greytown (R33) and drive for 22 km before turning left at the Albert Falls turn-off. Visitors are admitted year round, and a game guard is on duty at the gate from first light to 10 p.m.

Baynesfield Estate

Undulating hills covered with grasslands and forests of indigenous yellowwood, Cape chestnut and black stinkwood dip to reveal a secluded and beautiful valley within the confines of the lovely Baynesfield Estate.

Once the property of farmer Joseph Baynes, son of an early settler, Baynesfield was left to the state for the fostering of scientific agricultural research, to create agricultural colleges, and to train students in the scientific methods of laying out public parks. One- and two-day trails meander through the estate, passing wetlands and forests, and climbing a series of natural terraces to reach an old quarry from which stone was excavated for the original buildings. Hikers spend a night in Baynes Cottage, which is equipped with ten beds, water, toilet and cooking facilities – take your own food, crockery and sleeping bags.

Left: The famous plunge of the Howick Falls. **Above:** Egyptian geese (the bird at the far left is a knob-billed duck) occur throughout southern Africa, having adapted remarkably well to the incursion of man into their territory. It is the only species of duck (in spite of its name, it is really a form of shelduck) that breeds both north and south of the Sahara Desert.

Some 115 bird species have been recorded (including the rare blue swallow), and the trees and grasslands provide shelter for large numbers of antelope, Cape clawless otter, caracal, genet, vervet monkey and samango monkey.

A museum exhibits mementoes of Baynes's life and times – his farming diary and a collection of books, as well as trophies and medals.

For more information, contact Baynesfield Estate, P O Baynesfield 3770, telephone (0332) 51-0043, or fax 51-0045.

Biggarsberg Conservancy

Encompassing grassy plains and treed plateaus of the Biggarsberg range in northern KwaZulu-Natal, the conservancy comprises a number of privately owned farms.

This lush area is home to more than 270 bird species, as well as several antelope species. Nocturnal animals include Cape fox, serval black-backed jackal, African wild cat and genet. Watercourses shelter water mongoose, Cape clawless and spotted-necked otter.

Although the Bushman (San) paintings in the area reveal the existence of eland and leopard, and archaeological digs have unearthed the remains of giraffe, rhino and hippo, these animals have long been absent from the Biggarsberg. Mountain flora includes proteas, red-hot pokers, aloes and crocuses, and a list of the indigenous trees and shrubs is available.

There are two hiking trails. Oribi Hiking Trail is a 29 km/two-day circular route that passes stone kraals, crosses a dam wall, scales steep cliffs and explores shady kloofs. Hikers begin and end this scenic trail at the converted stone-walled barn on the farm Gartmore. The overnight stop is an early 20th-century farmhouse on the farm Inkruip, equipped with 12 beds and mattresses, hot- and cold-water ablutions and firewood (no electricity).

Monks Hiking Trail is a 23 km/two-day trail traversing flower-bedecked plateaus, a pretty waterfall, and the Maria Ratschitz Mission, a partly used Trappist mission station established in 1886 by two monks from the Mariannhill Mission outside Durban. The trail starts and ends on Gartmore, and trailists spend a night at the mission. Bunk beds and mattresses are provided for up to 16 hikers, and there is cold water (no electricity).

To reach the Biggarsberg Conservancy, follow the N11 from Ladysmith to Newcastle for some 40 km, turn off to Dundee/Wasbank and follow the signs. For further information, contact Jacana Country Homes and Trails, P O Box 95212, Waterkloof 0145, or telephone (012) 346-3550/1/2, fax 346-2499.

Bisley Nature Reserve

Situated in Pietermaritzburg (with its main entrance on the corner of Murray Road and Alexandra Road extension) is a 250 ha reserve,

KWAZULU-NATAL: MIDLANDS

Below: Sailing on Midmar Dam. Powerboating and waterskiing are also permitted, but are restricted to the top end of the dam. **Left:** The jumping spider is common to most parts of southern Africa. These small, strongly built spiders circle their prey and capture it with an impressive leap. Their enormous eyes, situated at the front of their heads like headlamps, make them the most long-sighted of all spiders.
Right: *Sandersonia aurantiaca* (Christmas bells) in a sheltered glade beside a stream. This beautiful plant – a climbing member of the lily family – is endangered in many parts of KwaZulu-Natal because of indiscriminate picking. It flowers in the final months of the year, and remains dormant during the winter.

established in 1985 and home to 160 bird species, as well as numerous mammals that include impala, common duiker, zebra, giraffe, vervet monkey and bushbaby. Two short trails penetrate the reserve's acacia savannah and grassland, and there is also a conference centre and a bird hide.

Further information may be obtained from the Parks and Recreation Division, Pietermaritzburg Transitional Local Council, P O Box 31, Pietermaritzburg 3200, or telephone their offfices at (0331) 42-2970, fax 42-7107.

Blinkwater Nature Reserve

Rippling grasslands and a tumble of hills, their slopes covered with stands of indigenous and cultivated trees, combine with tranquil vleis and dams and tinkling streams to make Blinkwater a paradise for hikers.

The Umvoti Centre (the KwaZulu-Natal branch of the Wildlife Society of Southern Africa), together with private companies and the Natal Parks Board, has developed some 100 km of trails through this 6 000 ha wilderness. All trails are circular, and are interlinked at two access points, enabling hikers to plan routes from two to six days. Four huts, each equipped for up to 12 people, with bunk beds, toilets, showers, fireplaces, water and firewood, provide overnight accommodation.

The trails have been designed to incorporate as many as possible of the area's best features – one section passes an old railway line, used at the turn of the century to transport timber from the southern slopes of the Blinkwater, while another reveals traces of old Bushman (San) pit-traps at the forest fringe.

The forests themselves, home to yellowwoods and other mist-belt species, shelter an abundance of birds. The shy, crested guinea fowl may be glimpsed in the undergrowth, while the canopy echoes with the calls of louries, chats, robins and doves. This is one of the few remaining breeding areas in southern Africa of the rare and endangered blue swallow, and the grasslands provide sanctuary for oribi and reedbuck.

For further information about the trails, you should contact Umvoti Centre, P O Box 47, Sevenoaks 3495, telephone (033) 507-0047, or fax 507-0048. To make reservations for the trail and for more information about Blinkwater Nature Reserve, contact the KwaZulu-Natal Branch of the Wildlife Society of Southern Africa, 100 Brand Road, Durban 4001, or telephone (031) 21-3126, fax 21-9525.

Chelmsford Nature Reserve

Leeukop Mountain dominates the 6 015 ha Chelmsford Public Resort, whose waters are favoured by Egyptian and spur-winged goose, spoonbill, yellow-billed duck, darter and dabchick.

Powerboats ply the waters, too, and fishermen take carp, mudfish and bass. The gamepark section has been stocked with springbok, black wildebeest, zebra, red hartebeest, rhino and blesbok. There are eight five-bed chalets, and camping and caravan sites are available for hire. The resort lies south of Newcastle, on the N11 to Ladysmith. It is open all year, 24 hours a day. To reserve camping and caravan sites, contact The Officer-in-Charge, Chelmsford Nature Reserve, P O Box 3, Ballengeich 2942, telephone/fax (03431) 7-7205.

Chalets may be booked by contacting the Natal Parks Board, P O Box 1750, Pietermaritzburg 3200, telephone (0331) 47-1981, or fax their offices at 47-1980.

Darvill Bird Sanctuary

Embracing four dams and vegetation ranging from woodland and plantation to grassland and scrub, Darvill is regarded as one of the best inland water habitats in KwaZulu-Natal and, in

1988, was awarded national recognition by the South African Ornithological Society.

Over 200 bird species have been recorded, including dabchick, Egyptian goose, grey and black-headed heron, southern boubou and various species of kingfisher. Summer visitors include African marsh, great reed and European sedge warblers, as well as the distinctive European swallow.

The reserve lies alongside Pietermaritzburg on the N3. Take the New England turn-off, turn right over the freeway and continue for some two kilometres. The entrance is on the left. Further information may be obtained by contacting Msinsi Holdings (Pty) Ltd, P O Box 53301, Yellowwood Park 4011, or telephone/fax (031) 42-8375.

Doreen Clark Nature Reserve

Only 5 ha in extent (the smallest of the Natal Parks Board reserves), Doreen Clark is an 'island' of indigenous evergreen forest situated within the Winterskloof area some 12 km from Pietermaritzburg, off the N3 to Johannesburg. Birdlife is plentiful, and a pleasant walk has been laid out through the forest. There is also a small picnic site. The reserve is open throughout the year.

Game Valley Estates

Huge sandstone cliffs tower above this attractive reserve, set beside the Mkomazi River at Hella-Hella. The 1 504 ha sanctuary has been declared a Natural Heritage Site and supports oribi, nyala, wildebeest, zebra and warthog. It is home to some 370 recorded bird species.

The estate offers hiking, gameviewing and photographic safaris, and also caters for casual visitors. A camping area and lodge offer year-round accommodation.

The main entrance to the estate is 25 km from Richmond, reached 2 km from the bridge over the Mkomazi River. For more information, contact Game Valley Estates, P O Box 70, Richmond 3780, telephone (03322) 3171.

Game Valley Lodge

This ten-year-old, 960 ha Natural Heritage Site encircles the only remaining rainforest in KwaZulu-Natal, and boasts an impressive tally of 400 identified bird species.

The sanctuary is home to buffalo, white rhino, giraffe, sable and roan, wildebeest, eland, hartebeest, bushbuck and impala. Guided and self-guided trails include the 6 km Buffalo Trail, which leads to the Karkloof Falls.

Accommodation is provided in fully serviced lodge rooms and cottages, and there is also a tennis court and a swimming pool. This is a malaria-free area, and visitors are welcome all year round.

To reach Game Valley Lodge from Pietermaritzburg, take the turn-off to Greytown from the N3, and turn left at the Woodlands/Claridge off-ramp. Follow this road for some 20 km, looking out for the lodge signs. For further information, contact Game Valley Lodge, P O Box 13010, Cascades 3202, telephone (033) 569-0011, fax 569-0012.

Geelhout Trail

Situated on the farm Glendale, in the foothills of the Drakensberg some 50 km southwest of Newcastle, the Geelhout Trail is a self-guided 23 km/two-day hike across tree-covered mountain slopes.

The farm itself is 2 500 ha in extent and is conserved as a private wilderness area. Richly grown with Natal bottlebrush, cabbage trees, Outeniqua yellowwood and sugar bush, it is home to oribi, wildebeest, mountain reedbuck, duiker, bushbuck, blesbok, monkey, baboon, serval and bushpig. In the kloofs and valleys the birdlife includes secretary bird, and eagle and stork species.

The first section of the trail is a fairly strenuous climb to the top of a forested plateau, to reach an overnight hut (with beds, showers, toilets, refrigerator and braai facilities for ten people) at the Normandien Pass. The second section of the route meanders through forests with streams punctuated with tinkling waterfalls before returning to the base camp. Magnificent views may be had along the way.

Hikers should take adequate water in case the streams are dry, as well as a gas stove and extra gas (open fires are not permitted).

Reservations can be made by contacting Glendale Farm, P O Box 1901, Newcastle 2940, telephone (03431) 8-6560.

Green Belt Trails

A 20 km network of trails, known collectively as the Green Belt Trails, crisscrosses the 1 067 m escarpment close to Pietermaritzburg. Passing through vegetation ranging from lush temperate forest to thornveld and grassland, the trail

A COLOURFUL SPEEDSTER

The beautiful dragonfly does not possess a sting, and is harmless to humans.

Is it a bird? Is it a plane? No, it's the speedster of the insect world ... the dragonfly. This remarkable creature is deserving of many superlatives – it is one of the largest insects on earth and, at speeds in excess of 60 km/h, is probably the fastest.

Dragonflies (there are about 120 species in southern Africa) generally live near water, and a fisherman is the most likely person to see the flash of colour and hear the whirr of wings that signals the approach of a male insect patrolling his territory.

The male stakes out a territory for hunting and for mating, and will vigorously defend this area against invaders – midair battles can result in mutilated wings and legs. After mating, the female dragonfly lays her eggs in, or close to, water – usually depositing them on underwater plants or forcing them into moist sand at a river's edge. Occasionally the female skims the water, her eggs dropping just under the surface from the tip of her abdomen. The eggs then drift to the bottom.

They hatch into gill-breathing nymphs hidden in the mud or among aquatic plants, and they live on other insect larvae, tadpoles and small fish until ready to transform into adults. They then crawl above the water surface and cling to a support – such as a plant – while shedding their nymphal skins for the last time. The life cycle from egg to adult dragonfly may take up to three years, depending on the species.

The dragonfly remains a predator at all stages of its life. The flying dragonfly captures insects in midair by forming its six legs into a 'basket' that scoops up the victim. This has earned it the sobriquet 'mosquito hawk'.

KWAZULU-NATAL: MIDLANDS

Left: Aloe marlothii grows in almost any terrain in KwaZulu-Natal. This is among the most attractive of the aloes, producing orange-yellow flowers through most of the winter. The dried leaves are used by some of the local people to make snuff. *Right:* Fire lilies are so named because some species appear in profusion after veld fires. This species, *Cyrtanthus contractus*, was photographed among dolerite boulders in the grassland of KwaZulu-Natal. *Below:* An oribi doe in the foothills of the Drakensberg near Estcourt. These rare antelope are usually found in short grass near water.

area is home to a rich variety of birds, small mammals and colourful flowers.

The Ferncliffe Trail system explores a 250 ha indigenous forest some 12 km northwest of Pietermaritzburg, revealing flowering Cape chestnut, bush lily, ferns and mosses. Lemonwood Trail, the main route in the Ferncliffe system, embraces six walks that radiate from its central path, exploring, among other delights, Bats' Cave, Sunset Rock and The Everglades.

The 2 km Dorpspruit Trail starts in the city and follows the river, after which it is named, before linking up with the start of the trail to World's View. World's View Trail starts at Voortrekker Road in the city and pierces bird-haunted pine and wattle plantations, following an old Voortrekker route to a superb lookout point 1 000 m above sea level.

The Upper and the Lower Linwood trails both start at Celtis Road (a trail map mounted on a plinth indicates the route). The former follows an old railway line (built in 1916 but long since abandoned), and the latter winds through gum plantations.

For more information and for maps of the Green Belt Trails, contact the Parks and Recreation Division, Pietermaritzburg Transitional Local Council, P O Box 31, Pietermaritzburg 3200, telephone (0331) 42-2970, fax 42-7107.

Holkrans Hiking Trail

This private trail has been developed in the Drakensberg foothills near Newcastle, on the farm Buffelshoek, of some 1 200 hectares.

The trail offers a 17,5 km/two-day stroll through indigenous forest and grassland where bushbuck, grey duiker, mountain reedbuck and common reedbuck may be seen at close quarters, as well as shy forest birds. Trees are numbered for identification, and, from certain points, hikers are afforded distant views across to the Free State and Mpumalanga. One of the highlights of Holkrans (Hole-in-the-rock) Trail is its tunnel, through which hikers can walk upright for several metres. Three mountain-bike trails have also been developed.

Accommodation is offered at the base camp and at 'Pioneers' Camp', complete with traditional dung floor and reed ceiling. Overnight huts can accommodate up to 60 people.

Bookings may be made by writing to The Manager, P O Box 2734, Newcastle 2940, telephone/fax (03435) 600 or (034) 351-1600.

Howick Falls

Named after Viscount Howick (later Earl Grey), Secretary of State for the Colonies from 1846 to 1852, the picturesque borough of Howick and its famous waterfall lie 22 km from Pietermaritzburg, off the N3 to Johannesburg. From the viewing platform, the Mgeni (uMgeni) River can be seen as it hurtles a dizzy 95 m into a deep pool, to continue through a twisting, forested ravine on its way to the Indian Ocean. A one-hour trail follows the ravine to the base of the Howick Falls.

Many people have lost their lives in the cauldron that boils and churns in the gorge below. In 1940 a young student, Charles Booker, accepted a dare and dived into the chasm, with tragic consequences. Over the years, a number of people have committed suicide by hurling themselves over the edge.

The falls are only a minute's drive from the centre of town. A small caravan park provides accommodation nearby, and there are also a number of comfortable hotels, guesthouses and tearooms in the vicinity.

Further information may be obtained from Howick Publicity Association, P O Box 881, Howick 3290, telephone (0332) 30-5305.

Isibindi Eco-Reserve

Rafting on the Buffalo River, gameviewing, birdwatching and just enjoying the wild outdoors are the main attractions of this new 1 100 ha reserve southeast of Dundee.

Established in 1990, Isibindi reserve, with its bushveld vegetation (*acacia* and *combretum*

KWAZULU-NATAL: **MIDLANDS**

Left: The scenic Valley of a Thousand Hills is believed to have taken its present form during the Pleistocene geological period, when the ocean receded to about 100 m below the present sea level. During this period rivers such as the Mgeni (uMgeni), which meanders through the valley for over 60 km, gouged channels deep into the earth.

3150, telephone (0388) 7-5239, or fax 7-5303. For general information, contact Natal Parks Board, P O Box 662, Pietermaritzburg 3200, telephone (0331) 47-1961, fax 47-1037. For reservations, you should contact the Natal Parks Board, P O Box 1750, Pietermaritzburg 3200, telephone (0331) 47-1981, fax 47-1980.

Entrance to the reserve, which is open to day visitors between sunrise and sunset all year, is through Louwsburg. Anti-malaria precautions are recommended in this area.

species predominate), is home to a number of mammals, including giraffe, zebra and some 12 species of antelope. Birdlife is abundant.

Rafting – on a 55 km section of the Buffalo River – is much requested by intrepid visitors, whose care and well-being are in the secure hands of trained and experienced guides Rafters overnight at the KwaNtula Camp, which offers thatched four-bed bungalows, open-air showers (with hot and cold water) and a charming thatched lounge and bar area.

Those wishing merely to visit the reserve can stay at the comfortable Isibindi Lodge, which offers accommodation in thatched *en suite* bungalows serviced by a restaurant. Guided walks are available, as are tours of the nearby battlefields, scenes of significant action during the numerous Boer-Zulu, Anglo-Zulu and Anglo-Boer struggles.

The reserve is privately owned and, although open all year, offers rafting only from mid-November to the Easter weekend.

For further information, contact Isibindi Eco-Reserve, P O Box 124, Dundee 3000, telephone/fax (03425) 620.

Itala Game Reserve

One of the few signs of civilisation in the rugged 30 000 ha Itala Game Reserve, near Louwsburg in northern KwaZulu-Natal, is a row of telephone poles – and these are regularly flattened by rhino using them as rubbing posts to relieve irritating itches.

Part of the old Pongola Game Reserve, the first to be proclaimed in Africa, this green, knuckle-ridged wilderness through which six rivers flow to join the Phongolo River, is home to the province's only herds of tsessebe. It also contains KwaZulu-Natal's largest concentration of klipspringer, crocodile, leopard, cheetah, blue wildebeest, red hartebeest, giraffe, white and black rhino, warthog and a variety of raptors in the jagged dolerite cliffs.

Among 320 bird species recorded, birds of prey include martial, black, Wahlberg's and fish eagle, as well as both black-breasted and the rare southern banded snake eagle. There is also a breeding colony of the threatened bald ibis or *umXwagele*, as it is known locally.

The reserve is laced with a network of gravel gameviewing roads leading to viewpoints and picnic sites. Guided day walks are offered, as are three-day trails through the wilderness, conducted between March and October. An added attraction for ecotourists, especially those with a leaning towards geology, is the interesting rock formations that date back 3 000 million years.

Ntshondwe Camp accommodates 220 people in fully equipped, self-catering, one-, two- and three-bedroomed units tucked below weatherworn cliffs. It also offers a conference centre, restaurant, takeaway food outlet, swimming pool and viewing deck overlooking a marsh that is home to hundreds of Cape weavers. Ntshondwe Lodge has three serviced *en suite* bedrooms and a swimming pool. If you prefer a less tame environment, then opt for the smaller, self-catering Mbizo and Thalu bush camps in the west, or Mhlangeni Bush Camp, situated on a rocky outcrop overlooking a stream.

The Natal Parks Board organises day and weekend wilderness trails in Itala Game Reserve. There are two picnic sites and a rustic campsite. Visitors should direct their enquiries regarding campsites to The Officer-in-Charge, Itala Game Reserve, P O Box 42, Louwsburg

Karkloof Nature Reserve

Twenty kilometres from Howick are the Karkloof Falls, falling an impressive 115 m into a deep, wooded gorge, and considered by some to be even more beautiful than the Howick Falls. The 936 ha Karkloof Nature Reserve provides sanctuary for duiker, bushbuck, leopard, bushpig, and a large variety of birds that may readily be seen moving through the sheltering branches of the great yellowwood and stinkwood canopy. Both crowned eagle and martial eagle breed in the forest.

Although the reserve itself is not open to the general public, visits may be arranged by contacting Natal Parks Board, P O Box 662, Pietermaritzburg 3200, or telephone (0331) 47-1961, fax 47-1037. There are picnic and braai sites for visitors at the falls.

Malandeni

This vlei, lying some 2 km west of Ladysmith, is a Wildlife Society sanctuary that serves as home to more than 200 recorded bird species, including a number not often recorded in the province, such as lesser gallinule and Baillon's crake. The shallow lake and surrounding flooded areas along the Klip River are unusual in that they border on a municipal sewage farm, and their waters are recycled effluent, which promotes algal and insect growth, thus providing an ideal source of food for birdlife.

The area is kept locked, and permission and keys must be obtained from the office, about 500 m from the gate. For information about after-hours access, contact Mr K Gordon, telephone (0361) 31-1854 or 2-6819; or Ladysmith Publicity Association, P O Box 29, Ladysmith 3370, telephone/fax (0361) 2-2992.

Mhlopeni Private Nature Reserve

The 1 325 ha Mhlopeni Private Nature Reserve, lying between Greytown and Muden, sustains a rich variety of mammals, including impala,

149

blesbok, bushbuck, reedbuck and zebra, the endangered blue duiker, oribi, aardwolf, leopard and four-toed elephant shrew.

Declared a Natural Heritage Site, Mhlopeni is also home to some 220 recorded bird species. Accommodation (for groups of up to 12 people) consists of a hutted bush camp tucked beneath beautiful indigenous trees.

For further information, write to Mhlopeni Private Nature Reserve, P O Box 386, Greytown 3250, telephone (03346) 722.

Midmar Public Resort Nature Reserve

The 2 844 ha Midmar Public Resort lies 24 km west of Pietermaritzburg off the N3, and is surrounded by the emerald Inhluzana hills. In keeping with the elegant setting, the terraced lawns are manicured, while yachts bob and weave in the waters of the Midmar Dam.

Situated along the upper reaches of the dam is an 820 ha game park – the Midmar Nature Reserve. From Natal Parks Board vehicles or boats, wildlife enthusiasts can view several antelope species as well as a rich birdlife (especially waterfowl). The reserve also has a network of gameviewing trails and comfortable chalet accommodation.

The recreational resort has much for sporting visitors, including tennis, bowls and squash. There is a swimming pool, a children's playground, and camping and caravan facilities. Fishermen try for bass, bluegill and carp in the Mgeni (uMgeni) River – permits are available at the Parks Board office.

Adjacent to the resort is Midmar Historical Village, with its re-creation of a country village as it was at the turn of the century. Among the authentic displays are a blacksmith shop, a traditional Zulu homestead with beehive huts, a Siva temple, two steam locomotives, a fire engine and numerous agricultural implements. One of the highlights of the village is the original York Public Library which was dismantled and meticulously rebuilt here, brick by brick. The Village Hall has also been created in keeping with tradition, but its interior is equipped for film shows and lectures.

Accommodation at the resort is offered in 31 fully equipped chalets, including a six-bed chalet adapted for the physically handicapped. Also available are 16 rustic cabins with stoves, fridges and communal ablution facilities, as well as three campsites, all situated at the water's edge.

For further information, contact the Natal Parks Board, P O Box 662, Pietermaritzburg 3200, telephone (0331) 47-1961, fax 47-1037; or The Officer-in-Charge, Midmar Nature Reserve, Private Bag X6, Howick 3290, telephone (0332) 30-2067/8, or fax 30-5868. To make reservations, contact the Natal Parks Board, P O Box 1750, Pietermaritzburg 3200, telephone (0331) 47-1981, or fax 47-1980.

Montello Safari Lodge

This private lodge, situated on 2 200 ha of grassland and thornveld near Greytown, combines the wonders of the wild with the comfort of a luxury bush camp.

Regular gamespotting outings are arranged – either in vehicles or on horseback, and visitors are encouraged to walk the trails through the lodge's bush, gorges and ridges. Game to be seen includes several large antelope species, giraffe, zebra, warthog, leopard and lynx. Ostrich are numerous, and birdwatchers will be enchanted by many other species.

Visitors may stay in a number of lodges and rondavels, all set beneath camelthorn trees. Mgamazi is a luxury lodge for eight to 12, with *en suite* bathrooms and a private sitting room. Mvelase Lodge sleeps six to eight, while the Ondini rondavel (also *en suite*) has facilities for two to four guests. A bush camp of five rondavels accommodates up to 20 people. There are conference facilities (both formal and in the bush), and a swimming pool. Two dams are stocked with Florida bass, and a nearby forest-fringed lake attracts trout-fishermen.

To reach Montello, follow the R33 from Pietermaritzburg to Greytown, turn left at the first traffic light and, after 10 km, turn right at the Montello signpost. The lodge is open all year. For details and to make reservations, contact Montello Safari Lodge, P O Box 267, Greytown 3250, telephone (0334) 3-3334 or 3-1465, fax 3-3334 or 3-3033.

Moor Park Nature Reserve

Moor Park is named after the family who originally donated the land to the province – Sir Frederick Moor was KwaZulu-Natal's last prime minister. The reserve's high, forested bluffs overlook the waters of the Bushmans River and Wagendrift Dam while, on its boundary, Greystones, once the home of Sir Frederick, now houses an educational and recreational centre with campsites, fully catered and self-catering accommodation.

The wildlife at Moor Park includes black wildebeest, mountain reedbuck, grey duiker, bushbuck, blesbok, impala and zebra. Over 110 bird species have been recorded.

The self-guided 'Old Furrow Trail', which lies within the reserve, follows the course of an old irrigation furrow. Interpretive displays are placed along the route.

To reach Moor Park, take the Ntabamhlope route from Estcourt and follow the signposted road. For more information about the reserve and Greystones, contact Estcourt Municipality, P O Box 15, Estcourt 3310, telephone (0363) 2-3000 or 2-3007, fax 33-5829.

Nagle Resources Reserve

Encircling the horseshoe-shaped Nagle Dam is a 3 500 ha reserve – established in 1994 – that is home to ostrich, zebra, blesbok, grey duiker and impala, as well as a varied birdlife. Visitors are also drawn by the well-stocked dam and the pleasant picnic spot on its shores.

An exclusive lodge sleeps six, and a conference centre caters for 18 delegates.

To reach the reserve, follow the N3 between Durban and Pietermaritzburg, and take the Mpumalanga/Hammarsdale/Inchanga turn-off. Turn right over the bridge and right again at the Nagle Dam sign, continue for 16 km and cross the Duzi bridge, then a second bridge. Turn left up the hill, follow the tar road and you will see the picnic site on the right-hand side.

For further information, contact Nagle Resources Reserve, P O Box 40, Cato Ridge 3680, or telephone (082) 454-5344; or The Officer-in-Charge on (082) 446-7809. Information may also be obtained from the reserve's controlling authority, Msinsi Holdings (Pty) Ltd, P O Box 53301, Yellowwood Park 4011, telephone/fax (031) 42-8375.

Natal Lion and Game Park

This privately owned park, 18 km east of Pietermaritzburg off the Durban freeway, was established in 1966 on 240 ha of forested hills in the upper reaches of the Valley of a Thousand Hills. A relaxed hour-long drive through the park is a sure way to see lion, giraffe, zebra, impala, nyala and elephant (including the park's prized Asian elephant, believed to be the only such specimens in Africa). Among over 120 recorded species of bird are the stately sacred ibis and black-billed kites. The

KWAZULU-NATAL: MIDLANDS

Left: Morning glory (an exotic) is represented by many species in southern Africa, and in some areas exotic species have become troublesome weeds, choking existing vegetation and blocking off sunlight. One genus, *Cuscuta*, is parasitic (because it cannot create chlorophyll, it is totally dependent on its host). **Above:** A fruit beetle. **Right:** A lithograph by the artist William Cornwallis Harris, showing a somewhat corpulent eland, from his book *Portraits of the Game and Wild Animals of Southern Africa*.

park is 72 km from Durban and is open from 8 a.m. to sunset. Opposite the Lion Park are the Natal Zoological Gardens, home to Bengal tiger, black and spotted leopard, water buffalo and a bright (and noisy) collection of parrots.

Details may be obtained from the Natal Lion and Game Park, P O Box 36, Umlaas Road 3730, telephone/fax (0325) 5-1411. Natal Zoological Gardens may be contacted at the same postal address, telephone (0325) 5-1423, or fax 5-1411.

Natal National Botanical Garden

The 120-year-old Natal National Botanical Garden, off Mayor's Walk in Pietermaritzburg, consists of two sections – an exotic garden, and a garden featuring flowers and plants indigenous to KwaZulu-Natal. The 49 ha garden, established in 1874, offers a network of shady paths, lily ponds, show gardens, a 200 m avenue of plane trees, a duck pond, a demonstration garden, a fever-tree vlei, and about 138 recorded bird species.

The garden is open daily from 8 a.m. to 6 p.m. between October and April, and closes at 5.30 p.m. during the cooler months between May and September. There is a restaurant, also open year round.

Group tours can be arranged, and visitors may follow the Turraea Trail to explore the various habitats and the birdlife of each. Further information can be obtained from The Curator, Natal National Botanical Garden, P O Box 21667, Mayor's Walk 3208, telephone (0331) 44-3585, fax 44-1284.

New Formosa Nature Reserve

A variety of buck and small game may be seen in this 250 ha reserve, situated about 2 km from Estcourt. The 8 km New Formosa Nature Trail leads to a vulture restaurant, and offers sightings of the reserve's wildlife.

Open all day throughout the year, the reserve has no camping facilities, and vehicles are prohibited, but there is a caravan park about 1 km away. Permission to enter the reserve should be obtained from Mr G Goode, Fort Durnford Museum, P O Box 15, Estcourt 3310, telephone (0363) 2-3000, or fax 33-5829.

Pietermaritzburg Bird Sanctuary

The 105-year-old Pietermaritzburg Bird Sanctuary is situated opposite the brickworks off Chatterton Road, near the Hyslop intersection. Snow-white cattle egrets, with their yellow bills and harsh 'kraak-kraak' call are there by the thousand in the trees around the lake. (Although many of the original trees have died, replacements have been planted.) Visitors are also likely to see a variety of smaller birds. The sanctuary's lake was formed from the clay pit excavated in 1860 to make the bricks needed to rebuild Pietermaritzburg's town hall, which had been destroyed in a fire. The sanctuary is open all year, from sunrise to sunset.

Pongola Bush Nature Reserve

The largest dam in KwaZulu-Natal is the Jozini Dam on the Phongolo River. Three game and nature reserves are found on the banks of this river: Ndumo, Itala (*see separate entries*) and Pongola Bush. The last, 858 ha in extent, includes a stretch of indigenous evergreen forest that is home to bushbuck, duiker, baboon and samango monkey. Pongola Bush is situated between Vryheid and Piet Retief, about 30 km northwest of Paulpietersburg.

You should contact The Officer-in-Charge, Pongola Bush Nature Reserve, telephone/fax (035) 573-1059, before arrival. Further information may also be obtained from the Natal Parks Board, P O Box 662, Pietermaritzburg 3200, telephone (0331) 47-1961, fax 47-1037.

Queen Elizabeth Park Nature Reserve

Headquarters of the Natal Parks Board and home of the Douglas Mitchell Centre with its theatre and library, and facilities for research and education, this scenic reserve is situated 8 km west of Pietermaritzburg. A major task performed at the centre is processing the thousands of requests for accommodation in the Natal Parks Board's many reserves.

On the 93 ha of wooded slopes around the centre, there are zebra, impala, blesbok and grey duiker to be seen, while forest footpaths lead to pleasant picnic sites and river cascades. The circular, self-guided iDube Trail attracts casual strollers. There is a curio shop.

The reserve is constantly being improved by the planting of indigenous vegetation, and there are hundreds of species of aloe, cycad and protea. A question-and-answer worksheet has been prepared for schoolchildren.

To reach the reserve, take the Montrose exit from the N3 to Johannesburg, or the Howick road from town. If approaching from Durban, drive through the centre of Pietermaritzburg. The park is open daily, from sunrise to sunset.

151

MUTUAL COOPERATION IN THE WILD

A honeyguide chick emerges from its foster parents' nest.

One of southern Africa's most remarkable birds is the honeyguide, a small, rather drab creature that employs an unorthodox method of obtaining its favourite foods – beeswax, bee grubs and honey. When a honeyguide finds a nest of wild bees, it quickly seeks out a honey badger or even a human to help. This it accomplishes by 'displaying' and making a chattering noise to attract attention – once this has been achieved, it leads the way to the nest.

The honeyguide perches nearby while the nest is torn open and robbed of its honey – and then it takes its turn. The honey badger is interested only in the honey, but the honeyguide seeks out the honey comb and grubs. A special enzyme in its digestive tract enables it to break down the wax into substances of nutritional value – something no other bird is able to do. Men and honey badgers are not the only helpers exploited by this bird. Like the cuckoo, it lays its eggs in another bird's nest, delegating the upbringing of its young to foster parents. Failure to reward the honeyguide with its portion of comb is said to bring bad luck.

Details may be obtained from The Officer-in-Charge, Queen Elizabeth Park, P O Box 662, Pietermaritzburg 3200, or telephone (0331) 47-1961, fax 47-1037.

Soada Forest Nature Reserve

This 498 ha forest slopes down to the deep Mkomazi River valley, just beyond the Hella-Hella bridge and about 24 km from Richmond on the Eastwolds road. It is rich in giant yellow-woods and cycads, and visitors may see bushbuck, vervet monkey and duiker. Also in the reserve is an impressive two-stage waterfall, with a drop of 90 metres. Although Soada Forest is controlled by the Natal Parks Board, the only access is through a privately owned farm – and this may account for the fact that there are few visitors. For further information, write to The Director, Natal Parks Board, P O Box 662, Pietermaritzburg 3200, or telephone (0331) 47-1961, or fax 47-1037.

Spioenkop Public Resort Nature Reserve

All day long on Wednesday, 24 January 1900, the noise of battle rolled across the bare summit of Spioenkop, the rugged mountain that dominates the KwaZulu-Natal Midlands. Boer and Briton fought for control of the high ground just north of the Tugela, and for access to the long-besieged town of Ladysmith.

Standing on the summit today, visitors look across a grand sweep of Drakensberg peaks, sun-bleached sky and lush green plain – a vista unequalled anywhere in southern Africa. The Tugela has now been dammed, and its muddy waters attract yachtsmen, weekend fishermen and waterskiing enthusiasts. The 5 979 ha resort, 14 km from Winterton and 35 km from Ladysmith, offers accommodation in Iphika Tented Camp (spacious two-bed tents, lounge, kitchen, ablution block), and Ntenjwa Rustic Camp (thatched A-frame structures, hot- and cold-water ablutions, equipped kitchen, no electricity), as well as camping and caravan sites. Iphika is situated on the slopes of Spioenkop and offers excellent opportunities for walking, while Ntenjwa, accessible only by water, nestles in thickly wooded vegetation on the slopes descending to the dam. Spioenkop is treasured by birdwatchers, who enjoy searching for its 270 bird species.

The resort offers tennis courts, a swimming pool, open-air chess, a badminton hall, table tennis, children's playground, curio shop, wildlife film shows, horseback riding, boat rides, guided tours of the battlefields, self-guided trails and walks in the adjacent 400 ha game park (stocked with white rhino, wildebeest, eland, kudu, and mountain reedbuck). A highlight is the Anglo-Boer War Museum. Bookings for Iphika, Ntenjwa and the camping and caravan sites may be made through The Officer-in-Charge, Spioenkop Public Resort Nature Reserve, P O Box 140, Winterton 3340, telephone (036) 488-1578, or fax 488-1065.

Umgeni Valley Nature Reserve

Winding 10 km along the Mgeni (uMgeni) Valley below the famed Howick Falls, this lush 759 ha nature reserve, with its sheer sandstone cliffs and gentle grasslands, supports an abundance of animals, including zebra, giraffe, nyala, impala and wildebeest. Over 210 bird species have been recorded, ranging from the tiniest of warblers to the eagles seen swooping dramatically above the cliffs.

Owned and managed by the Wildlife and Environment Society of South Africa, the reserve specialises in environmental education: about 15 000 to 20 000 schoolchildren and adults attend its courses every year. These begin at the resources centre (which has lecture facilities and impressive wildlife exhibits), and then progress to the bush camps in the Mgeni Valley. From the camps – home to the youngsters for most of their stay – the Society's staff guide their charges on field trips geared to a prepared syllabus. The facilities are open to the general public when they are not being used for educational purposes, and fully equipped, self-catering cottages, each sleeping two to six people, are available for hire.

Footpaths crisscross the reserve, as well as a number of short trails – take care, as these are often steep and demand more energy than you might anticipate. There are picnic sites at the head of the valley, and visitors may drive the 5 km to the viewsite area.

The entrance to the reserve is about 1 km from Howick on the Karkloof road. For further information, write to Umgeni Valley Nature Reserve, P O Box 394, Howick 3290, telephone (0332) 30-3931 or 30-5721, or fax 30-4576.

Umvoti Vlei Conservancy

Vleis are vital to many types of wildlife – especially waterfowl. But these reed-fringed pans take many years to develop and, once destroyed, are almost irreplaceable. The Umvoti conservancy's 600 ha of vlei in the catchment area of the Mvoti River lie on a turn-off 11 km south of Greytown, on the Pietermaritzburg road. This mist-belt area of reed swamp and open water is an important wildfowl sanctuary, and the Umvoti Vlei Bird Trail, and a hide, have been created for the convenience of birdlovers.

Those wishing to visit the conservancy should contact The Chairman, Umvoti Vlei

Conservancy, P O Box 47, Sevenoaks 3495, telephone (033) 507-0042, or fax 507-0048.

Valley of a Thousand Hills
The most spectacular view of this 50 km panorama known as the Valley of a Thousand Hills is from *emKhambathini* – KwaZulu-Natal's Table Mountain. But most of the viewsites overlooking this rumble-tumble of misty hills lie between Botha's Hill and Drummond, off the old main road between Durban and Pietermaritzburg. Take the Hillcrest exit 29 km from Durban or 52 km from Pietermaritzburg. Within the valley are hotels, restaurants and a good selection of curio shops.

Vryheid Hill Nature Reserve
Vryheid is one of northern KwaZulu-Natal's coal towns, situated in the lee of the wooded Lancaster Hill, named after the regiment that occupied it for some 18 months during the Anglo-Boer War. Part of the area has been converted into an attractive little game reserve containing, among other species, blesbok, impala, oribi, common and mountain reedbuck, and bushbuck. About 190 species of bird have been recorded.

The reserve, which lies about 1 km from town (follow the signposts), offers an environmental centre, and a rustic, 60-bed camp for groups. There are also three picnic/braai spots. Three hiking trails, including a self-guided historical trail, wind through the trees. For more detailed information, contact the Natal Parks Board, P O Box 224, Vryheid 3100, telephone (0381) 81-2133, fax 80-9637.

Wagendrift Nature Reserve
The Ntabamhlope road heads west from Estcourt towards Giant's Castle. An 8 km drive brings you to the Natal Parks Board's 500 ha Wagendrift Dam Resort on the Bushmans River, surrounded by hills.

Fishing, sailing and boating are popular on the dam, and picnic sites have been laid out. A self-guided trail for birdwatchers penetrates Wagendrift, as well as the adjoining Moor Park Nature Reserve (*see separate entry*).

The reserve has one fully equipped, four-bed chalet, as well as camping and caravan sites with hot- and cold-water ablution facilities. There is also a youth centre, with dormitories and a dining hall.

The resort is open from 6 a.m. to 6 p.m. between 1 April and 30 September, and from 5 a.m. to 7 p.m. between 1 October and 31 March. For bookings, contact the Booking Office, Wagendrift Nature Reserve, P O Box 316, Estcourt 3310, telephone (0363) 33-5520.

Weenen Nature Reserve
Weenen Nature Reserve lies at the heart of the Thukela Biosphere – a 60 000 ha wilderness in which boundary fences have been removed to allow reintroduced game to roam freely.

This 5 000 ha Natal Parks Board reserve lies just off the road to Weenen, about 28 km northeast of Estcourt. It supports some 20 large mammal species, including aardwolf, Cape clawless otter, black-backed jackal, white and black rhino, red hartebeest, mountain reedbuck, kudu, eland and giraffe (reintroduced) – all of which are particularly easy to spot in the summer months when water is plentiful. Over 250 bird species have been recorded, and a new hide has been constructed. Vultures may be seen coming to feed at their own 'restaurant' where carcasses are made available.

There are three self-guided trails: the 2 km iMpofu Trail leads through savannah thornveld and passes a dam to a viewsite overlooking the reserve; the 2 km Reclamation Trail illustrates erosion-control techniques used in the reserve, and the 3 km Beacon View Trail winds up to a beacon point which offers magnificent views of the reserve and the Weenen valley. Guided trails are also available. These are led by experienced rangers, and hikers are given the opportunity to see Cape buffalo and black rhino at close quarters.

There are 12 campsites with ablution facilities, as well as a tented bush camp and one 5-bed, self-contained cottage. Facilities for caravanners and a curio shop are located near the entrance gate, and picnic sites, with braai facilities, are available. The reserve is open all year from sunrise to sunset. To reserve camping and caravan sites, write to The Officer-in-Charge, Weenen Nature Reserve, P O Box 122, Weenen 3325, or telephone/fax (0363) 4-1809.

World's View
Taking in the view from the 305 m mountain above Pietermaritzburg is a grand experience. Access is via the Commercial Road/old Howick road exit or via the freeway west of the city, at the Hilton village turn-off. Ask for directions at the first garage, and follow the national monument signs. Originally called Boesmansrand, the old Howick road down to Pietermaritzburg from World's View was the wagon route of the 1837 Voortrekkers. Walking and (unofficial) pony trails link at World's View.

Right: A western Natal green snake (*Philothamnus natalensis occidentalis*) glides effortlessly over a moss-covered rock in the foothills of the KwaZulu-Natal Drakensberg. These snakes are distinguished by their large eyes and slender body.

Palms, pelicans and dunes of gold

A land of lakes and sunshine, of golden dunes and mysterious swamps. This is Maputaland, that northern slice of KwaZulu-Natal named after the lower reaches of the Usutu, or Maputo, River, which reaches the Indian Ocean near the Mozambique capital once called Lourenço Marques. Bounded by the rugged gorges and ravines of the Lubombo Mountains in the west, Mozambique to the north and the Indian Ocean, this 900 000 ha wilderness has had many names. Seeing fires on the mainland as he sailed past, Portuguese explorer Manuel de Mesquita Perestrello called it *Terra dos Fumos*. Waxing even more poetic, he referred to the northern coast, from Kosi Bay to Ouro Point (today's Mozambique border lighthouse), as *Rio de la Medaos do Ouro* – 'river of the dunes of gold'.

This fragile land of contrasts, of palms, pelicans and hippos, is really one enormous nature reserve. It is the transition zone between the tropics and subtropical KwaZulu-Natal and has 21 different ecosystems, including three huge lakes (St Lucia is the best known), the last of the province's elephants found in the wild at Tembe Elephant Park, Fomothini Pan, swamps, two magnificent game reserves at Ndumo and Mkuzi, the wide Pongola floodplain, dotted with one waterfowl-crowded pan after another, turtles – those large and curiously dignified denizens of the great coral reefs – and the beautiful St Lucia complex. Evenings vibrate with the mating calls of countless reed frogs.

Maputaland deserves to be classed with the biggest of southern Africa's wild areas: Kruger, Zimbabwe's Hwange and Botswana's Okavango and Central Kalahari reserves.

Bonamanzi Game Park

At this striking private reserve in northern KwaZulu-Natal, you can sleep in splendid leafy isolation some 5 m above the ground – in tree houses. Situated near the village of Hluhluwe, Bonamanzi (meaning 'see the water') offers wonderful views of Lake St Lucia and is close to the great northern game reserves of Mkuzi, Hluhluwe and Umfolozi.

The park offers accommodation in the tree houses (two double bedrooms, kitchenette, ablution and braai facilities) and in a six-bed luxury Tree Lodge. If you prefer sleeping nearer the ground, you can stay in a cluster of 10 thatched twin-bed cottages at Lalapanzi Camp, set among shady trees and waving ilala palms. There is a swimming pool and a network of trails to explore. Guests are also free to explore the 800 ha area around the camp, where they may drive or walk where they wish.

Dinizulu Camp, perched on the edge of a picturesque stretch of water, can be reached only with a 4x4 vehicle, and is especially attractive for wildlife photography. However, guests are warned that there are crocodiles in the river, and an intimate encounter with a white rhino or leopard is not impossible. Guided game drives and walks are available.

Over 300 species of bird have been recorded at 4 200 ha Bonamanzi (a SA Natural Heritage site), and there are elephant, nyala, red duiker, impala and reedbuck to be seen. Also found here is the rare and shy suni. Bookings should be directed to Bonamanzi Game Park, P O Box 48, Hluhluwe 3960, telephone (035) 562-0181 or 562-0516, fax 562-0143.

Bushlands Game Lodge

Bushlands Game Lodge is an unusual and enchanting camp. Not only are its lodges built on stilts, but even the dining room and lounge hover above the ground in leafy seclusion. Meals, however, are served in a traditional boma, and guests have the use of a swimming pool and bar. The lodge accommodates up to 40 guests, and booking is essential.

Animals to be seen within Bushlands' 300 ha expanse include warthog, numerous antelope species, and zebra so tame they drink from the swimming pool, while, among the bird species, visitors may catch a glimpse of the Narina trogon.

For more information, contact Bushlands Game Lodge, P O Box 79, Hluhluwe 3960, telephone (035) 562-0144, or fax 562-0205.

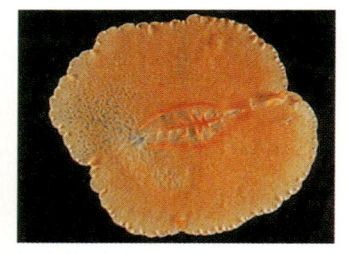

Left: Tropical vegetation at Lake St Lucia. **Above:** A marine flatworm on the KwaZulu-Natal north coast. Scientists have performed a remarkable experiment in which flatworms were taught a specific response to a stimulus, and then cut up and fed to a group of 'naive' flatworms: the second group inherited the memory. The flatworm's digestive processes are equally fascinating – it has a branched gut that distributes food throughout the body. If starved for too long, however, it begins to digest its own tissue, and may be reduced to a fraction of its former size. **Right:** An impala ram in the Mkuzi Game Reserve.

KWAZULU-NATAL: THE LAKES

Greater St Lucia Wetland Park

This scenic stretch of country on the northern KwaZulu-Natal coast includes a wilderness of reed-fringed lake, swamps, palm veld, grasslands, savannah, sand dunes bordering the breakers of the Indian Ocean, and a long strip of the ocean itself, with coral reefs and a rainbow assortment of marine life.

Because the area straddles both subtropical and tropical climatic zones, the vegetation (and the wildlife it supports) is extremely diverse. Here five ecosystems coexist, each distinct but interconnected: the marine ecosystem, with its coral reefs and beaches; Mfabeni, forested dunes separating the land from the sea; Mkuze swamps, formed by sediments washing down from the Mkuze catchment area into the northern reaches of the lake; the lake itself, with its bird-rich islands; and the western shores, with their fossil marine life and sand forests.

Each of the park's different sections is a separately proclaimed conservation area. Linked with Mkuzi Game Reserve to the west, the Greater St Lucia Wetland Park covers an expanse of some 260 000 hectares. The profuse wildlife found here includes an abundance of Nile crocodile, as well as hippo, black and white rhino, elephant, buffalo, giraffe and numerous antelope species. There are many thousands of waterbirds, and species include pelican, stork, heron and flamingo.

Lake St Lucia, along with the 'turtle beaches' and the coral reefs further to the north, has been listed by the Ramsar Convention on Wetlands of International Importance as having international conservation value, and it is hoped that the area will soon be awarded World Heritage Site status.

The Greater St Lucia Wetland Park is a favourite haunt of fishermen and campers, with its huge complex of shallow lakes, dunes and beautiful beaches stretching from Sodwana Bay and the lower Mkuze Road in the north to a point south of Mapelane, and from the seaward edge of the marine reserves in the east to the lake's western shores. Grunter may be caught at the estuary in October, while the best time for prawns and game fish is between March and May.

Campers and visitors staying in the fully equipped huts and log cabins should bring their own food and drink, although some provisions are available from the curio shops. The St Lucia village resort has a variety of shops where food can be purchased.

Remember that anti-malaria precautions should be taken before entering the area. Because of the presence of crocodile, no bathing or paddling is allowed in the lake (the hippo may also be dangerous, and boats should not venture too close). Walking trails, along with the rest of the tourist facilities, have been concentrated in a relatively small section of the complex, leaving the greater portion of the reserve to nature and conservation.

To reserve accommodation in the St Lucia Complex, write to Natal Parks Board, P O Box 1750, Pietermaritzburg 3200, or telephone (0331) 47-1981, fax 47-1980.

For camping and caravan accommodation, write to the relevant reserve, resort or park. The Public Relations Officer of the Natal Parks Board, P O Box 662, Pietermaritzburg 3200, telephone (0331) 47-1961, fax 47-3137 will assist with further information.

Greater St Lucia Wetland Park: Cape Vidal

On the coast and forming part of the Tewate Wilderness Area (*see separate entry: Mfabeni*) is Cape Vidal, which lies 35 km north of St Lucia Estuary (turn left at the T-junction at the entrance to St Lucia village, and follow the road past the Crocodile Centre to Cape Vidal).

The game fishing here is superb – South Ledges and Bishops Rock promise fine surf angling – bring your own ski-boat if you intend to go deep-sea fishing. Scuba diving is allowed and there is a safe (but unprotected) bathing area sheltered from the sea by a reef,

A number of hiking trails traverse the area. Mziki Trail (three days) consists of three circular routes through indigenous dune forests and pine plantations. Hikers spend the night at Mount Tabor, a Second World War radar station where you are asked to bear in mind that 'the litterbug is an unprotected species', and where there are bunks, mattresses, gas cooker, cooking and eating utensils. Groups are limited to eight, who must leave their transport at Mission Rocks (14 km from St Lucia village).

Emoyeni self-guided trail is a five-day/ 65 km hike that starts and ends at the Natal Parks Board's Mission Rocks outpost. Trailists wind along the lake shore and the forested coastal dunes, overnighting in simple campsites (hikers must supply their own tents).

Animals likely to be seen on the trails include kudu, reedbuck, waterbuck, duiker, vervet and samango monkey, hippo, crocodile, buffalo and bushpig, as well as hosts of birds. Humpback whales may be watched from a tower near the chalets – some 1 000 of these

Above: The Chinese lantern or sickle bush (*Dichrostachys cinerea*) is characterised by these bicoloured flower spikes. This specimen was photographed in the Ingwavuma region of KwaZulu-Natal. **Right:** A bluebottle fly is attracted by the smell emanating from the newly hatched egg of a Nile crocodile. The mortality rate among hatchlings is very high, and few of any particular brood will attain their fearsome adulthood.

giants are estimated to pass Cape Vidal between mid-June and the end of August.

Visitors are encouraged to walk through the forest, traversed by the self-guided Mvubu Trail which emerges to follow the shores of Lake Bhangazi. Also self-guided, the 3 km Imboma Trail picks its way through the wetlands lying south of the lake.

On the left-hand side of the road to Cape Vidal, some 1,5 km north of Mission Rocks, a small car park marks the start of a short trail leading through thick forest to the Mfazana Pans. Here, two hides provide a perfect site from which to view waterfowl, hippo and crocodile. A secluded 50-site camping area, with hot- and cold-water ablution facilities, nestles below a canopy of thick dune forest. Also available are 18 five-bed and 11 eight-bed Swiss-style log cabins. These have either two or three bedrooms, a bathroom, a fully equipped kitchen and a small dining/lounge area. The cabins are serviced by camp staff. In addition, there are five fully equipped cabins, primarily used by fishermen, on the shores of Lake Bhangazi. Bhangazi Bush Camp, on the western shores of the lake, sleeps eight people in four two-bed, self-contained and serviced units. Take precautions against malaria.

To reserve Cape Vidal campsites, write to The Officer-in-Charge, Cape Vidal, Private Bag X04, St Lucia Estuary 3936, or telephone (035) 590-1404, fax 590-1300.

Visitors arriving to occupy camping or caravan sites must report to the Natal Parks Board office, which is open between 8 a.m. and 12.30 p.m., and from 2 p.m. to 4.30 p.m. Fuel and firewood are available. Those wishing to book a log cabin, bush camp or fishing cabin, should contact Natal Parks Board, P O Box 1750, Pietermaritzburg 3200, telephone (0331) 47-1981, or fax 47-1980.

Greater St Lucia Wetland Park: Crocodile Centre

Crocodiles have long played a pivotal role in the life of the northern KwaZulu-Natal region. The Crocodile Centre, lying to the north of St Lucia village, is an interpretation centre stressing this reptile's importance, as well as displaying its life cycle. Large ponds house numbers of Nile crocodile, as well as long-snouted and dwarf species. Visitors may see them being fed on Saturday afternoons at 3 p.m., and may attend an informative talk.

A curio shop sells a variety of souvenirs, and both the centre and the shop are open daily. To reach the Crocodile Centre, cross the St Lucia Estuary bridge and drive 2 km along the Cape Vidal road.

Greater St Lucia Wetland Park: False Bay Park

False Bay Park is a pristine wilderness sanctuary forming the northwestern edge of the battleaxe-shaped Lake St Lucia.

The park's 3 200 ha is a wonderland for birdwatchers, with huge flocks of migrating flamingoes (a figure as high as 20 000 birds has been estimated at one time) having been seen on the lake when the salt levels are high. Other species include pelican, paradise flycatcher, golden-tailed woodpecker and the purple-crested lourie, while the woodland echoes with the calls of crested francolin, brown-hooded kingfisher and puffback shrike.

The coastal bush of False Bay Park is particularly rich in game, including nyala, waterbuck, suni, reedbuck, bushpig, warthog, duiker, porcupine and vervet monkey.

The reserve has no permanent accommodation apart from the rustic Dugandlovu Camp (four 4-bed huts, bucket showers and paraffin-powered lighting), but there are 38 shady caravan/camping sites overlooking the lake. Visitors who have booked sites should report to the Officer-in-Charge on arrival (the office is open during normal business hours). The gates are open daily from 8 a.m. to 12.30 p.m. and from 2 p.m. to 4.30 pm. There are also numerous delightful picnic spots, and there is a small curio shop.

Activities for visitors include fishing, boating (boating enthusiasts must keep to designated sections of the lake), photography, gameviewing, birdwatching and hiking. The 8 km/five to six hour, open-ended Dugandlovu (lost elephant) Trail meanders through the southern section of the park. Winding along the shoreline, the path leads through bush to the Dugandlovu Camp before returning to the starting point. Some variations on its route may be followed. Mpophomeni (waterfall) Trail is a circular, self-guided, 10 km/three hour hike (with a shorter option) passing through woodland, thicket and sand forest. The brochure for the walk describes the various tree and bird species encountered. This is home to the suni, the country's rarest antelope.

To reach the park, follow the N2 north from Mtubatuba for some 55 km, then turn off right to Hluhluwe village (the nearest source of petrol). Follow the road through the village and beyond – False Bay Park is well signposted.

For further information and to make bookings, write to The Camp Manager, False Bay Park, P O Box 222, Hluhluwe 3960, or telephone/fax (035) 562-0425.

Greater St Lucia Wetland Park: Mapelane

On the south bank of the Mfolozi River mouth is Mapelane, a wonderland of coastal dune forest, white-sand beaches, abundant birdlife (some 220 species have been recorded), and good fishing waters.

The tangled primeval forest is home to red milkwood, wild fig, black mangrove and liana. The beaches, with promising names such as Crayfish Point and Mussel Drop, provide visitors with many hours of enjoyment, and are also the site of both loggerhead and leatherback turtle nesting grounds. But there is titanium in the dunes and tiny (900 ha) Mapelane, with its 9 km length of unique forest, has fought a long and arduous battle to prevent mining consortia from enveloping the area.

Visitors are accommodated in ten five-bed, self-catering log cabins, tucked within the dune forest, or at the 45-stand campsite. Activities include excellent fishing, from the beach and from ski-boats, and those who enjoy walking may follow the short trail that leads to the top of the highest dune, from where there is a panoramic view. Swimming is not permitted at the river estuary, and the beach itself is unprotected, but paddling in the inlet in front of the cabins is considered safe.

For more detailed information or to reserve a cabin, contact the Natal Parks Board, P O Box 1750, Pietermaritzburg 3200, telephone (0331) 47-1981, fax 47-1980. For campsite reservations, contact The Camp Manager, Mapelane, Private Bag, St Lucia Estuary 3936, telephone /fax (035) 590-1407.

Greater St Lucia Wetland Park: Mfabeni and Tewate

These two areas, previously known as Eastern Shores Nature Reserve and Cape Vidal State Forest, are now administered as a single unit by the Natal Parks Board.

Mfabeni, a narrow, 15 000 ha strip of land between Lake St Lucia and the Indian Ocean, consists of rare dune forest and coastal grassland that supports an enormous population of reedbuck – there are some 6 000 within the entire Mfabeni/Tewate region. An interesting fact about these pretty antelope is that, when faced with danger, they run away with a characteristic rocking-horse motion, emitting a shrill alarm whistle and often a 'plop' sound like a cork being removed from a wine bottle.

The Tewate Wilderness Area is an 11 000 ha area of dune forest (some of the sand dunes here reach a height of 180 m above sea level) and marshy grasslands. The trees on the western side of the dunes (where they are protected from the salt spray) grow to an enormous size, and give sanctuary to red duiker, bushbuck, bushpig, vervet and samango monkey, and a wonderful array of birds.

Wilderness trails are conducted within Tewate between April and September. The trails, lasting five days and four nights, start on a Friday afternoon when trailists are met at Cape Vidal and escorted to the base camp at Bhangazi, where they spend the first and last nights. Accommodation includes tents, bedding, showers, toilets and lounges. Meals are provided, and personal supplies are packed onto a team of donkeys. A number of other trails are also available.

Greater St Lucia Wetland Park: Sodwana Bay National Park

Sodwana means 'little one on its own', a plaintive cry unheard by the 4 000 caravanners who invade the 413 ha forested dunes of this Indian Ocean resort during school holidays.

But, although droves of holiday-makers flock to Sodwana Bay, they tend to stay near the campsite, and much of the rest of the park, with its dune and swamp forests and small, pretty lakes, remains tranquil and undisturbed. In days of yore a base for gun-runners and ivory

---

TURTLES SAVED FROM THE SOUP

Newly hatched loggerhead turtles head for the sea on KwaZulu-Natal's north coast. Very few of the young reach maturity.

For many centuries, southern Africa's great sea turtles – the 2 m leatherbacks and smaller loggerheads – braved the seas to reach favoured breeding sites on KwaZulu-Natal's Tongaland coast.

But they had to contend with more than their natural enemies. The depredations of man reduced their number almost to extinction. Prized for their meat, oil, bones and eggs; in demand as talismans; slow-moving, clumsy and utterly helpless during the nesting season, turtles are easy prey to a variety of poachers.

In 1963 the Natal Parks Board launched an intensive rescue operation, mounting shore patrols and seeking to obtain (with gratifying results) the understanding and cooperation of the Tonga villagers.

During the ensuing years, the board's staff, helped by the KwaZulu Department of Nature Conservation, released more than 120 000 tagged hatchlings.

The results were dramatic: in the 1966-7 breeding season only five female leatherbacks were sighted, and ten years later this figure had climbed to 65 sightings. Over 5 000 hatchlings were tagged with satellite transmitters and returned to the sea in the 1981-2 season. Over the years, scientists found that 30-50 per cent of the tagged adults came back to nest at least once (some as many as six times), and the overall turtle population has climbed sharply.

The turtles' migration patterns have also been monitored. In collaboration with the University of Pisa, six loggerheads and one leatherback were tagged. Two of the transmitters failed, but the others showed that the loggerheads migrated to Madagascar, while the leatherbacks travelled much further – south to Cape Town and beyond. In 1995/6 more than 500 turtles were tagged and, in all, 255 613 hatchlings have been marked and released since 1971.

The Natal Parks Board is optimistic that the two still-rare species will survive and flourish to a point where they can once more (though on a controlled basis) become a valuable source of food, especially in Tongaland.

hunters, the protected hinterland forest hides suni, steenbok, reedbuck, aardwolf, banded mongoose, thick-tailed bushbaby and bushpig. Among the snake population are the East African egg-eater and the highly venomous Gaboon adder. In the swamp forest, birds find shelter in huge fig trees. During summer, loggerhead and leatherback turtles nest on the beaches at night, and turtle tours, arranged at the park, are held in December and January.

Protected by a reef and the jutting Jesser Point, Sodwana Bay is the outlet for the pretty lakelets of Ngoboseleni and Shazibe.

The park attracts angling enthusiasts, whose ski-boats roar through the gap in the reef with their catches of kingfish, tuna, king mackerel, dorado, wahoo, blue marlin, black marlin and the most beautiful of them all, the majestic sailfish. Game fish competitions are held here regularly and the catches are almost always magnificent. No fishing is allowed in the sanctuary areas. Beachcombing is also a favourite pastime, and hiking devotees can follow the 5 km Ngoboseleni Trail that leads to one of KwaZulu-Natal's few coastal lakes. Environmental Awareness Officers lead walks over most weekends and during peak season.

There are hundreds of campsites of varying sizes (describe your camping equipment when booking), and 33 large, deluxe campsites set apart from the main camp. The latter sites each have a water and power point, as well as braai facilities. Twenty log cabins, some of which sleep five and others eight, are also available. These are fully equipped and are self-catering. A community centre may be hired for approved functions. There is a supermarket, and petrol is on sale. Bait, firewood and ice are available, and there are 196 freezer drawers for storing your catch. The gate is open daily from sunrise to sunset.

To reach Sodwana Bay, turn off the N2 to the north of Hluhluwe or at Jozini. Follow the signs for some 70 km to Mbazwana, then turn south on the signposted route for some 15 km. For information and to reserve the cabins, contact Natal Parks Board, P O Box 1750, Pietermaritzburg 3200, telephone (0331) 47-1981, fax 47-1980. To make campsite reservations (early booking is essential), contact The Camp Manager-in-Charge, Sodwana Bay National Park, Private Bag 310, Mbazwana 3974, telephone (035) 571-0051/2/3, or fax 571-0115.

Greater St Lucia Wetland Park: St Lucia Estuary

This area, the gateway to the eastern shores of Lake St Lucia, has the highest vegetated dunes in the world, as well as extensive wetland and grassland systems. Here you'll also see large stands of *ncema* grass, used by the Zulu people to weave their intricate sleeping and sitting mats. Birdlife in the area is prolific, and the grasslands support the world's largest concentration of common reedbuck, as well as grey duiker, red duiker, bushbuck, kudu, buffalo, bushpig, hippo and crocodile.

There are three campsites (Sugarloaf, Iphiva and Eden Park) at St Lucia village. One (which has a swimming pool) faces the St Lucia Estuary, while the other two are near the Crocodile Centre (*see separate entry*). The showers and baths in the ablution blocks have hot and cold water. St Lucia Estuary provides access to Cape Vidal and the Mount Tabor 'Mziki' Trail, and is a good starting point for the Umfolozi, Hluhluwe and Mkuzi game reserves. The short Gwalagwala Trail winds through the coastal forest on the edge of the estuary, a haunt of many birds and small animals. There is also a network of trails in the game park near the Crocodile Centre.

Launch tours on the *Santa Lucia*, lasting up to 90 minutes, leave three times a day and are an ideal way to explore the lake shore and see its hippo, crocodile and many birds. The launch seats 80, and has a viewing deck, a bar and a toilet. Other activities include surf bathing (there are life guards on duty) and fishing.

There are hotels and comfortable guesthouses in this attractive holiday village, and fuel is available. Campsites and launch tours are booked through The Officer-in-Charge, St Lucia Resort, Private Bag, St Lucia Estuary 3936, telephone (035) 590-1340, fax 590-1343.

To make reservations at the campsites, contact The Officer-in-Charge, St Lucia Resort, Private Bag, St Lucia Estuary 3936, telephone (035) 590-1340, or fax 590-1343.

Greater St Lucia Wetland Park: St Lucia Game Reserve

St Lucia Game Reserve, the oldest of all the reserve areas within the Greater St Lucia Wetland Park, was established in 1895 and consists of the large lake, its islands and the coastal area of Mapelane (*see separate entry*). St Lucia Lake is connected to the sea by a narrow channel (21 km long) that is rich in hippo, crocodile, Goliath heron and numerous fish-hunting birds. The lake is reed-covered and marshy in the east and, where the Natal Parks Board hutted camps of Fanies Island and Charters Creek (*see St Lucia Park entry*) are sited in the west, it is steep-banked and well-treed.

Four rivers feed Lake St Lucia, including the Mkuze and Hluhluwe, maintaining the delicate balance against the inflow of sea water and evaporation.

This area is home to white pelican and flamingo, which cluster in hundreds and sometimes thousands in the shallows. Pelican, swooping through the air like flights of bombers, cruise over the water, then 'herd' the fish in an ever-tightening circle before dipping their beaks for the kill. Hippo (700 in all) are most numerous in the south and crocodile are everywhere, the former grunting and blowing, the latter sliding stealthily off the banks. Hippo wander at night in search of sweet grazing, and notices in the hutted camps advise you to be careful. Penaeid prawns, spawned at sea, mature in the lake, making the St Lucia lake system the most important prawn habitat in South Africa. The lake's waters also shelter a myriad fish, from freshwater barbel to saltwater milkshark, spotted grunter, river and yellowfin bream and kob.

The Nile crocodile (*Crocodylus niloticus*) can grow to over 4 m in length. Playing an important part as a consumer in maintaining the ecological balance, crocodile used to be found as far south as Plettenberg Bay; now their southernmost limit is the Tugela River. This ancient reptile is probably better looked after

Left: The blue-raft shell is kept afloat by a frothy 'raft' of bubbles (this specimen was photographed on KwaZulu-Natal's north coast). Sea creatures have produced an ingenious array of buoyancy-regulating methods – bluebottles are suspended by their distinctively coloured, gas-filled floats; the nudibranch *Glaucus atlanticus* actually gulps air and fishes employ swim bladders, which are small 'balloons' located in the gut cavity, behind the backbone. The bladder's gas content is so regulated that the fish has neutral buoyancy, remaining suspended at a certain depth. The secretion of lactic acid into the blood supplying the bladder results in the reduction of solubility of oxygen in the blood. Gas bubbles form, and these are pumped into the bladder. When the acid additive is removed, the oxygen is re-dissolved, and the fish's buoyancy decreases.

KWAZULU-NATAL: **THE LAKES**

border is known as Maputaland Marine Reserve. This is an underwater wonderland containing some of the southernmost coral reefs in the world.

The reserve is also a breeding ground for many of the fish that currents distribute along the southern African coast, and the natural habitat of turtles, two of which (the loggerhead and leatherback) breed on the beaches.

Rod and line angling, ski-boat fishing, and spearing for game fish are permitted, but bottom fishing is strictly forbidden, as is the collection of bait and any marine specimens. Part of the reserve – the 25 km between Leven Point and Rooiwal – is a sanctuary area in which no fishing, or even swimming, is allowed. Camping is also taboo along this beach.

Greater St Lucia Wetland Park: St Lucia Park

The park, proclaimed in 1939, consists of land around the estuary and a strip of approximately 1 km around most of the lake shore. Within this area of 12 545 ha are the hutted camp at Charters Creek, the hutted camp and campsites at Fanies Island and the St Lucia Resort.

At Charters Creek, 15 huts perched on the high bank overlook Lake St Lucia and the distant eastern shore. There are 14 three-bed huts, another with two beds, a seven-bed cottage, a community lounge, two centrally situated kitchen blocks and an ablution block. A small fridge has been installed in each unit and the deep-freezers in the kitchen may be used on request. The shoreline in front of the camp is a grand place to stroll and is an excellent base for birdwatchers.

There are two self-guided walking trails. The two-hour/7 km Isikhova Trail penetrates the coastal forest, and the 5 km Umkhumbe Trail wanders through the forest and along the lake shore. Trail booklets are available. Cycling is also permitted. You may see a variety of mammals such as vervet monkey, nyala, duiker, reedbuck, bushpig and porcupine.

Bait can be bought and boats (without outboard motors) hired. Fuel is available and there is a curio shop and a swimming pool. The turn-off to the camp is 20 km north of Mtubatuba or 30 km south of Hluhluwe village on the main N2 highway. The entrance gates are 13 km further on this road (the route is well signposted). In winter, the gates open at sunrise and close at 7 p.m. (they close at 8 p.m. in summer). Visitors arriving to take up accommodation should report to the office by 4.30 p.m. To make reservations at Charters Creek, contact Natal Parks Board, P O Box 1750, Pietermaritzburg 3200, telephone (0331) 47-1981, fax 47-1980; or fax the camp on (035) 550-048.

Despite its name, Fanies Island Camp is not on an island, but is instead a rather secluded

Above left: A plate entitled 'New and remarkable species of lepidoptera from Natal and the Zulu country', from a book by the 19th century artist, zoologist and traveller George French Angas. Like other early travel volumes with colour plates, Angas's book is much prized by collectors of Africana.
Above right: A female bushbuck at Charters Creek, in St Lucia Park. Bushbuck vary greatly in size and colouration: one form (there are thought to be over 40) is dark brown with virtually no other markings, while another is coloured bright chestnut, with conspicuous spots and white stripes. **Right:** A painted reed frog in the St Lucia Estuary. At night these frogs may be heard calling in great numbers, their piercing whistles intensified by the resonant balloon-like vocal sac.

in KwaZulu-Natal than anywhere else in the world. The Natal Parks Board's Crocodile Centre (see separate entry) at St Lucia Estuary village is well worth a visit (the centre is regarded as the best of its kind internationally).

Visitors can stay at the Fanies Island and Charters Creek camps or at Mapelane, which offers 45 campsites and ten 5-bed, self-catering log cabins situated within the dune forest. Beaches here are unprotected, although the small bay in front of the cabins is considered to be safe for dipping at low tide. Local birdlife numbers 220 species and visitors are welcome to walk through the dune forests. An added attraction is the 80-seat *Santa Lucia* pleasure craft, which takes visitors around the estuary. To make reservations, contact the Natal Parks Board, P O Box 1750, Pietermaritzburg 3200, telephone (0331) 47-1981, or fax 47-1980.

Greater St Lucia Wetland Park: St Lucia Marine Reserve

Coral, cowries and colourful tropical fish predominate in the St Lucia Marine Reserve, stretching from 1 km south of Cape Vidal to a point 11 km north of Sodwana Bay, and 3 km out to sea. The protected marine area stretching north of this point to the Mozambique

AN AIRBORNE DESALINISATION PLANT

The giant petrel takes anything up to three months to make the 7 000 km journey from the harsh Antarctic wastes to southern Africa's pleasant shores. It is open sea all the way – a vast expanse of ocean unrelieved by islands or any other source of fresh water. Yet, even though these seabirds have the same body fluids as any other animal and cannot cope with an excess of salt, they manage to survive their epic flight.

This ability puzzled zoologists for decades, until the secret was revealed during a casual study of the albatross. These huge birds, clothed in seafaring superstition and legend, were much in demand by zoos and other institutions – but until fairly recently, none lived for long in captivity. They were given plenty of water, but died after a few weeks for no apparent reason.

Then an observer noticed a small, steady drip of clear liquid oozing from the beak of one specimen which, on examination, proved to be pure brine. The albatross diet was changed to include salt, and it recovered its health, and was soon thriving.

It was concluded that seabirds have evolved a special mechanism to extract the salt from seawater, a process essential to the proper function of their bodies and one that cannot be bypassed by the simple ingestion of fresh water. It is a process that man has yet to reproduce and exploit economically. The seabird is, in effect, a highly efficient airborne desalinisation plant.

---

compound on the western shore of Lake St Lucia, 20 km north of Mtubatuba and 11 km north of Charters Creek. To get there, take the road to Charters Creek and turn left after 12 km; the camp is 14 km further on. Here, the self-guided Umkhiwane Trail introduces visitors to the many species of bird and the smaller mammals of the shoreline. A pair of binoculars will enhance your enjoyment.

Accommodation at Fanies Island consists of one seven-bed cottage, 12 two-bed huts (with small fridges), two centrally situated kitchens and an ablution block. There is also a camping and caravan area with 20 shaded sites close to the water, served by two ablution blocks (hot and cold water).

Overnight visitors should report at the park office by 4.30 p.m.

Bait may be purchased, boats may be hired (bring your own motor), and petrol is available. To reserve a campsite, write to the Camp Superintendent, who will also provide further information. The address is P O Box 201, Mtubatuba 3935, or you may telephone (035) 550-1631, fax 550-1457.

Kosi Bay Coastal Forest Reserve

Kosi Bay is a misnomer. British Royal Navy Captain, W F W Owen, surveying the coast of Maputaland in 1822-3, mistook the 30 km necklace of four shore-hugging and inter-linked freshwater lakes for the estuary of the Mkuze River, which he spelt Kosi – and so it has been ever since.

The nature reserve consists of a series of four lakes: Makhawuleni, Mpungwini, Nhlange and Amanzimnyama, of which the largest is the 8 km long Nhlange (place of reeds). The lakes, with their unusual temperature variations, have long fascinated scientists – the water has a minimum temperature of 18°C but can reach 30°C in the shallows, and it is often warmer at the bottom of the lakes than it is at the top. The lakes near the estuary to the north (Makhawuleni is the northernmost) are exceptionally clear, becoming brown further south, due to the peaty water of the Sihadla River. Apart from Lake Amanzimnyama, all have a touch of salt water, especially after cyclones, which roar in from the ocean, leaving in their wake raised levels of both water and salt.

The Kosi Bay area was first proclaimed a reserve in 1950, and over the years has been extended and adjusted until, in the late 1980s, Kosi Bay Nature Reserve was incorporated into the Coastal Forest Reserve, with a combined area of almost 22 000 ha. Today the entire reserve has been resurveyed and renamed by the KwaZulu Government as the Kosi Bay Coastal Forest Reserve. More recently, in 1993, the surface area of Lake Sibayi (see separate entry) was incorporated into the sanctuary as Lake Sibayi Freshwater Reserve.

Fishing is very popular at Kosi Bay. Among the resident estuarine and freshwater species to be caught are queenfish, river snapper, kingfish, grunter and two species of pike that occasionally enter the lakes from the sea. Visitors to the northern reaches, where Lake Makhawuleni drains into the sea, may see local Tembe fishermen using fish traps, fashioned of timber and twine, to snare their catch – a method that has been used for over 700 years.

Swimming in the lakes is not recommended because bilharzia, crocodile and hippo are present. At Kosi Bay Estuary a small, colourfully populated coral reef provides visitors with excellent snorkelling opportunities. But take care, besides sharks and toxic creatures such as scorpionfish and stonefish, which are an ever-present danger, there is also a treacherous backwash. The area can be reached by 4x4 vehicles only and no more than five permits are issued each day.

The three-day Sihadla Hiking Trail takes in the mangroves, marshes, swamp forests and raffia palms that surround the Kosi lakes. There are also waterlilies and reeds and, to the west, undulating grasslands dotted with wild date and ilala palms. Also for the hiking enthusiast is the four-day Kosi Trail, which circumnavigates almost the entire lake system, exploring the beach and the swamp forest (trails must be booked well in advance). Shorter walks to Lake Amanzimnyama and Kosi Bay Estuary can be arranged. It is well worth bringing binoculars as flufftail, palm-nut vulture, fish eagle, white-backed night heron, kingfisher and crab plover are among 300 species of birds found in the area. Hikers should note that February brings unbearably hot weather, while conditions are at their most accommodating between April and August.

The narrowest part of the coast separating the lakes from the Indian Ocean is at Bhanga Nek. A ferry-ride from the camp and a hop over the dunes brings you to this magnificent stretch of unspoilt coastline from which a turtle survey team operates. Leatherback and loggerhead turtles, formerly endangered, crawl up the beaches here at night to lay their eggs, while numbered poles, dotted at regular 400 m intervals, record their arrival. Six loggerhead turtles were caught in 1996 and fitted with satellite transmitters to monitor their movements. Two of the devices ceased to function, but the others showed that the loggerhead turtles moved northwards along the coast of Mozambique after laying their eggs, and then travelled to Madagascar. A giant leatherback turtle, fitted with a transmitter in January 1996 after laying her eggs at Bhanga Nek, was recorded as having travelled 570 km out to sea off Cape Infanta by mid-March, then later moved south to Cape Town and Antarctica. The turtles' movements are still being monitored.

Three lodges and 15 campsites on the banks of Lake Nhlange provide accommodation for visitors. Mabibi Coastal Camp, lying in the coastal dune forest between Lake Sibayi, Sodwana Bay and Manzengwenya, was designed to blend into the depths of the lush coastal forest and offers 10 campsites with communal ablutions and braai facilities. (Visitors are requested to bring their own charcoal and not to purchase the bundled hardwood sold by roadside vendors, who are depleting the forests by chopping down the trees.)

No vehicles are allowed on the beach – and there are sturdy poles at Mabibi designed to keep it that way. A 4x4 vehicle is needed to reach the camp, which is reached from Jozini by following the road to Manzengwenya and then the signs to Mabibi. The camp lies some 148 km from the N2, and the last 45 km are on sand and gravel roads. Near Black Rock is Rocktail Bay Lodge (see separate entry), situated in the coastal forest just metres from the Indian Ocean breakers.

To reach Kosi Bay, you must turn off the N2 towards Jozini and follow the signposts to Mbazwana. Parts of the road are sandy, and a 4x4 vehicle is recommended. Reservations and enquiries should be addressed to the Department of Nature Conservation, Private Bag X9024, Pietermaritzburg 3200, or telephone (0331) 94-6696/7/8, fax 42-1948.

Petrol is available at Kwangwanase, and there are country trading stores en route. Bring your own food and drinks. Remember to take precautions against malaria before entering the area.

Lake Sibayi

Lake Sibayi, with an area of 7 700 ha, is the largest freshwater lake in South Africa – its average depth is 13 m, with depths of as much as 40 m having been recorded in places. It is clear, blue and beautiful.

One of the first references to this lake was made in the year 1554, when the Portuguese ship *Sao Bento* was wrecked south of Port Edward, and the survivors walked 800 km along the beach in a bid to reach the Portuguese settlement at Delagoa Bay (Maputo). Then, with only 150 km to go, they were killed by local inhabitants, apparently because they had resorted to cannibalism.

Some 5 000 years ago Sibayi (also known as Sibaya) used to be linked to the sea, possibly by the Pongola River which is thought to have followed a different course. Today the lake is cut off from the ocean by a massive rampart of forest-clad dunes, and is fed by rainwater and a small underground stream. Nevertheless, some 10 species of marine fish remain in its depths, having adapted over the aeons to freshwater conditions. The lake forms part of the enormous Kosi Bay Coastal Forest Reserve (see separate entry).

Baya Camp is a magnificent wilderness hideaway, with reed-and-thatch bungalows linked to a communal boma and sundeck by a network of interconnecting boardwalks. The seven bungalows sleep a total of 20 people, and there is a swimming pool. The camp is situated 150 m from the shore to accommodate the estimated 50-year high-water mark. Private launches are not permitted but boats can be hired for fishing (licences are available at the reception office) and sightseeing trips.

A multitude of fish may be caught, including catfish and the Mozambique tilapia, which is a small creature weighing in at less than 1,5 kg due to a low nutrient content in the water. There are approximately 120 hippo and plentiful Nile crocodile. Bilharzia is present so swimming is limited to the pool at the camp.

Two birdwatching hides overlooking small pans near the camp provide excellent bird-viewing – some 280 species have been recorded, including heron, cormorant and a number of kingfisher species. Look out for the African fish eagle, with its showy hunting drill and its ringing, plaintive cry.

White-tailed mongoose, side-striped jackal and reedbuck may be seen (if you are lucky!) during a 3 km guided trail that meanders through the forest and passes the hides before returning to the camp.

The sea is only a short distance from Sibayi, and permits for picnics at 'Nine Mile Beach' (which is not safe for swimming) are available to camp residents.

Sibayi lies (as the crow flies) 20 km north of Sodwana Bay, in an area covered with coastal forest and grassland. Access is via Mbazwana, 60 km north of the Mhlosinga turn-off on the N2, or via Mseleni on the Jozini/Tshongwe/Kosi

Right: White pelicans at Lake St Lucia. These huge birds have a three-metre wingspan. **Below:** A Gaboon adder – deadly inhabitant of northern KwaZulu-Natal's forest.

MKUZI AT A GLANCE

When to go The reserve is open daily throughout the year. Visitors should report to the Camp Superintendent's office on arrival (open daily from 8 a.m. to 12.30 p.m. and 2 p.m. to 4.30 p.m.; and from 8 a.m. to 12 noon and 2 p.m. to 4 p.m on Sundays and public holidays).

Reservations and information Camping and caravan site bookings should be made through The Camp Superintendent, Mkuzi Game Reserve, Private Bag X550, Mkuze 3965, telephone (035) 573-0003, or fax 573-0080. Reservations for Mantuma Camp, the tented camp and bush camps should be addressed to The Reservations Officer, Natal Parks Board, P O Box 1750, Pietermaritzburg 3200, telephone (0331) 47-1981, fax 47-1980. Reservations for trails and requests for further information should be directed to the same address. Remember to make enquiries well in advance.

Getting there Visitors arriving from the south should take the signposted turn-off to the reserve along the main north coast road (about 35 km north of Hluhluwe village). Follow the gravel road for 15 km and take the signposted turn-off through the Lebombo mountains: the hutted camp is 15 km from this point. Visitors from the north should travel to Mkuze village, which is 18 km from the reserve's entrance gate and 28 km from Mantuma Camp. The road is clearly signposted.

Accommodation Nhlonhlela Bush Lodge consists of four rustic chalets sleeping a total of eight. All have *en suite* facilities and are connected by boardwalks to the communal lounge, kitchen and viewing platform. Umkumbi Bush Camp is situated in the controlled hunting area in Nxwala, and is used as a general bush camp between November and March. Here, four large safari tents, each with two beds and *en suite* ablution facilities, are situated near a thatched lounge, dining room and bar beside a natural pan. The safari camp lying some 13 km east of the entrance, consists of ten tents (two beds and *en suite* ablutions). Mantuma Hutted Camp has six huts, each with three beds, five 5-bed bungalows, four 3-bed bungalows and two self-contained cottages. A camping and caravan area for 60 visitors, situated at the reserve entrance, has a communal ablution block.

Eating and drinking In the main camp, meals are prepared by cooks in the communal kitchens and served in the huts. In the safari camp, visitors do their own cooking (cooking utensils and cutlery are supplied). In the main hutted camp, everything is supplied for visitors except food and drink. A shop within the reserve sells basic provisions, and there is a supermarket at Mkuze village.

Getting around Fuel is sold at the entrance gate. An 80 km network of roads leads through a variety of bushveld country, offering excellent gameviewing. Interesting and informative day walks are conducted by a game guard (make arrangements a day in advance with the Camp Superintendent). More adventurous visitors may choose to walk the three-day Mkuzi Bushveld Trail with comfortable overnight accommodation provided. This trail operates from the beginning of March to the end of November. There is also an auto trail.

Wildlife The reserve has a large herd of impala, and other mammals include black rhino, white rhino, giraffe, nyala, blue wildebeest, warthog, kudu and smaller antelope. Lucky visitors may spot cheetah, hyena and leopard, as well as elephant. The elephant have only recently been reintroduced to this area in which they were once so plentiful. There is also an extensive bird population, including a huge variety of waterfowl at the Nsumo Pan.

Special attractions A number of hides have been erected, each overlooking a man-made waterhole, from which animals may be photographed as they come down to drink. There are picnic spots for day visitors at Nsumo Pan, Nxwala, Ediza and alongside the reception area at the main camp. Some of these very pleasantly combine a picnic with a spell of nature-watching.

Special precautions It is essential to take precautions against malaria, starting before your arrival at Mkuzi. Torches are a necessity and anything effective to shade yourself from the sun (such as hats and sun-block cream) should also be considered as essential.

Bay road. Access is via gravel roads and, because of seasonal variation in road conditions, 4x4 vehicles are recommended. If you are coming from Durban, follow the N2 through Hluhluwe village and turn off at the signpost.

Enquiries should be directed to the Department of Nature Conservation, Private Bag X9024, Pietermaritzburg 3200, telephone (0331) 94-6696/7/8, fax 42-1948.

Mkuzi Game Reserve

Sheltered by the formerly volcanic Lubombo Mountains, whose foothills form the western part of the reserve, Mkuzi differs from other reserves in the northern KwaZulu-Natal region in that its terrain is mainly flat, consisting of ancient coastal plains with savannah grasslands, fossil pans, wetlands, riverine fig forests and sand dunes.

Here the tropical and temperate climates merge, creating a transitional zone of widely differing habitats and supporting vast numbers of animals.

Established as long ago as 1912, Mkuzi (with an area of 40 000 ha) lies between the Mkuze and Msunduzi rivers, and is now open to the Greater St Lucia Wetland Park, lying to the east.

Over 80 km of tourist roads traverse the reserve (the speed limit is 40 km/h, although lower speeds are recommended for successful gameviewing). One of these roads passes the Bube and Msinga hides to reach a picnic site overlooking Nsumo Pan, a king-sized bird-bath, 5 km long, at the confluence of the Mkuze and Msunduzi rivers.

More than 400 bird species have been recorded at Mkuzi, including the lesser black-winged plover, honeyguide, bee-eater, African broadbill, plum-coloured starling, wild geese, duck and white-backed vulture. Many of the birds are permanent residents, but visitors may also see a fine range of breeding migrants, winter migrants and vagrants. At KwaMalibala, near the reserve's entrance, a vulture restaurant caters for the dietary calcium needs of these impressive birds.

Gameviewing hides are strategically placed at man-made waterholes. Game, which is best viewed in the dry season between June and October, may also be spotted on drives and walking trails. The best gameviewing areas are the Loop Road, around the airstrip and at Nsumo Pan. Black and white rhino, hippo, giraffe, zebra, warthog, blue wildebeest, kudu, bushbuck, klipspringer, eland, impala, leopard, black-backed jackal and a few cheetah find sanctuary here.

A family unit of 12 elephant was introduced from the Kruger National Park in 1996. These will join the existing group of 11 elephant, introduced in 1994, and will be the first of these gentle giants to have been resident in the

Mkuze area since the late 1800s, when the last survivors of the ancient local herds were shot.

South of Nsumo Pan, and stretching as far as the Msunduzi River, is Nxwala, a controlled hunting area that forms a natural extension of Mkuzi and is administered as part of the reserve.

The exciting three-day Mkuzi Bushveld Trail may be undertaken between the beginning of March and the end of November.

Mkuzi's vegetation varies from dense thicket to sand forest and savannah, but the most impressive features are its massive sycamore fig trees. A self-guided stroll through the fig forest is unforgettable. One of the last remaining unspoilt fig forests in Africa, it is characterised by the distinctive smell of the wild figs, the barking of baboon as they tussle over the delicacy and the heart-wrenching call of the resident bleating warbler.

Visitors may stay in comfortable rest huts, safari camps, bungalows, cottages, or they may choose the camping and caravan facilities.

Ndumo Game Reserve

Ndumo, the pocket-sized Okavango, is a wetland paradise. Situated in northern KwaZulu-Natal on the Mozambique border, 470 km from Durban, Ndumo's 10 000 ha floodplain comprises a delicate latticework of lakes that is home to hosts of fish, birds (over 60 per cent of South Africa's bird species have been recorded here), insects and other animals.

This is a fairytale wonderland of water and forest, where the gigantic twisted roots of sycamore figs form bizarre shapes and the fever trees are reflected in the silent, yellow-green waters of the pans.

Nyamithi Pan is some 4 km long, fringed with yellow-barked fever trees and vivid green grass that is kept closely cropped by the resident hippo population.

To the north, Banzi Pan, with its colourful waterlilies, is 6 km long and, together with Nyamithi, is a breeding ground for a tremendous variety of aquatic birds, including the brilliantly coloured and mercurial kingfisher, heron, stork, duck and sandpiper, as well as the rare Pel's fishing owl and the sooty falcon – a summer migrant. In all, 419 species have been recorded – a real treasury for the patient ornithologist.

The extreme northeastern areas of Ndumo suport the growth of dense forests of sycamore figs. Wild and undisturbed, this region is ecologically sensitive, so access is limited and may not be granted after heavy rains. The largest vegetation zone is the Mahemane area, densely treed and almost impenetrable, but home, nevertheless, to nyala.

It was here to Ndumo that the Victcrian hunter, Frederick Courtenay Selous, came to collect nyala for the London Zoo. Luckier inhabitants include bushpig, hippo, black and white rhino, giraffe, suni, nyala, bushbuck, impala and the ubiquitous crocodile, while buffalo may be spotted in the swampy floodplain areas (bring a pair of binoculars). The impressive Lubombo Mountains are on the left as you drive to Ndumo. Caution is advised as parts of Ndumo are flooded during the rains. The area is also rich in fossil deposits, which may be seen on the banks of Nyamithi Pan.

Guided 4x4 tours can be arranged, and visitors may drive through sections of the reserve in their own vehicles. Arrangements are made at the reception offfice. Guided day walks are also available – apply one day in advance.

NDUMO AT A GLANCE

When to go The reserve is open year round. The hottest month is February, the coolest July. The bird population is greatest during summer. Ndumo's moderately dry subtropical climate brings it 30 per cent less rain than falls at the coast. All visitors must report to the reception office on arrival (before 4.00 pm). The entrance gate is locked from sunset to sunrise.

Reservations Write to the Department of Nature Conservation, Private Bag X9024, Pietermaritzburg 3200, or telephone (0331) 94-6696/7/8, or fax 42-1948. Reservations for Ndumo Wilderness Camp can be made at P O Box 651171, Benmore 2010, telephone (011) 884-1458, fax 883-6255.

Getting there From Durban or Johannesburg: Ndumo lies 470 km north of Durban on the Mozambique border. Turn off the N2 to Jozini and proceed 21 km to the Jozini Dam and village. The road to Ndumo, which crosses the dam wall, is clearly signposted. It is tarred until the last 20 km. There is petrol at a store that lies some 2 km from the entrance to the reserve, and at Jozini and Ingwavuma.

Accommodation No camping or caravanning is allowed within the reserve. Ndumo has one rest camp with seven self-contained three-bed huts situated on a hill in the southeastern corner. Each has a gas-powered refrigerator and is equipped with bedding, cutlery and crockery. The camp is served by a communal ablution block. Ndumo Wilderness Camp, overlooking Banzi Pan, is built on raised wooden decks linked by walkways. Eight twin-bed tents offer luxury *en suite* accommodation. There is also a curio shop.

Eating and dining There are communal kitchen, dining and braai facilities. Meals at Ndumo Wilderness Camp are served in a raised dining room adjacent to a lounge, bar and swimming pool. At the rest camp, meals are cooked, and usually served in your hut, by the attendants. Visitors should bring their own food and drink.

Getting around Depending on demand, morning and afternoon tours are conducted around the pans (make arrangements at the reception office). Other areas are open to motoring by visitors, while several ranger-led day walks cater for the more energetic (once again, you should make arrangements at the reception area). Ndumo Wilderness Camp offers nature walks, gameviewing in open 4x4 vehicles, and outings to look at the birds.

Wildlife Many tropical East African birds can be seen at Ndumo – the reserve appears to be the southern limit of their range. Altogether 419 bird species have been recorded, almost as many as in Kruger Park, which is 190 times larger. The game includes hippo, crocodile, impala, nyala, kudu, reedbuck, bushbuck, red and grey duiker, white rhino, black rhino, buffalo, zebra and giraffe.

Special precautions Anti-malaria precautions are advisable. Bring hats and torches.

Ndumo is administered by the KwaZulu Department of Nature Conservation, but had its origins in 1924 when it was established by the Natal Parks Board to protect hippo. The population of these large mammals has now reached approximately 300, which is considered capacity for this reserve.

Ndumo is possibly one of the most attractive of all the KwaZulu-Natal reserves. It may at some time be expanded to include the area of the Tembe Elephant Park (*see separate entry*), home of the province's only remaining wild elephant population.

There is a rest camp set beneath giant marula trees on a hill in the southeastern

Above: A warthog and its offspring enjoy a mud bath in the Mkuzi Game Reserve. Although mainly grazers, warthogs also live on berries and wild fruits, and dig for roots and tubers with their tusks and cartilaginous snouts. Their hearing and sense of smell are acute.

corner of the reserve, comprising seven self-contained, three-bed huts. Ndumo Wilderness Camp, overlooking Banzi Pan, has eight luxury twin-bed tents built on raised wooden decks linked by walkways. There is an attractive site for campers and caravanners just outside the reserve's gates.

Phinda Resource Reserve

Owned and managed by a private organisation 'committed to demonstrating the sustainability and prosperity' of the African wilderness, Phinda is a 17 000 ha private sanctuary wedged between Mkuzi Game Reserve and the Greater St Lucia Wetland Park.

Seven distinct ecosystems, ranging from sand forest (increasingly rare), open savannah, montane bushveld and palm belt to wetlands and river valleys are found here. Each system, in turn, supports a fascinating collection of indigenous game, including elephant, rhino, giraffe, wildebeest, nyala, cheetah and lion. And ornithologists are sure to be content with the rich birdlife.

The reserve, officially opened in 1991, has been declared a Natural Heritage Site, complying with the five essential criteria. These are the recognition of stands of special plant communities, good aquatic habitats, sensitive catchment areas, plentiful habitats for threatened species and excellent natural features.

Guests are housed at Mountain Lodge in the south or Forest Lodge in the north. Mountain Lodge has four rock chalets and 16 luxury bush suites, each of the latter with its own private balcony. Forest Lodge has glass-walled suites raised on stilts, so that guests can view the birdlife in the forest canopy at close quarters. Dinners at both lodges are served in a boma, and the lodges have swimming pools and all modern conveniences. Guests are offered guided game and aerial safaris, black rhino tracking on foot, bush walks, canoe safaris, river cruises, snorkelling and deep-sea diving at nearby Sodwana Bay.

To reach Phinda from Johannesburg, take the N2 to Ermelo, Piet Retief, Pongola and Golela, and continue towards Mkuze/Empangeni. Some 35 km past the turn-off to Mkuze, turn left to Mhlosinga. After 2 km cross the railway line, turn right at the T-junction and then turn left at the next signpost to Sodwana Bay/Southern Maputaland. Proceed to Phinda Nyala Gate (8 km) or Phinda Forest Gate (21 km). If travelling from Durban, take the N2 towards Hluhluwe. Some 10 km past the turn-off to Hluhluwe, turn at the Southern Maputaland/Sodwana Bay signpost. Travel right over the N2, turn left at the T-junction, proceed about 4 km to the railway line and turn right at the Southern Maputaland sign. Proceed to the gates as described previously. Guests may also fly to Hluhluwe, and transfers to the reserve can be arranged.

For further information and to make reservations, contact Central Reservations, Private Bag X27, Benmore 2010, telephone (011) 784-6832, fax 784 7667.

Pongolapoort Biosphere Reserve

On 13 June 1894, President Kruger proclaimed a game reserve of nearly 20 000 ha in the Pongola district, a narrow corridor of land that runs between Swaziland and KwaZulu-Natal, forming part of the old Transvaal.

The corridor followed the course of the Pongola River through countryside thick with trees and blessed with plentiful game, rising steeply to the top of a 600 m cliff that forms part of the spectacular Lubombo Escarpment. The sanctuary, the first to be proclaimed in Africa, paved the way for the Sabie Game Reserve (later expanded into the Kruger National Park). In the early 1900s, however, the region fell prey to neglect and was subsequently deproclaimed and divided up as farmland. Then, in the 1970s, South Africa's Department of Water Affairs constructed the Jozini Dam (originally known as the J G Strijdom and, still later, as the Pongolapoort Dam) in this fertile valley below the Lubombo Mountains.

In 1995, nine private landowners, with the assistance of the Natal Parks Board, pooled their lands to create a 31 000 ha reserve around the dam.

This region is particularly rich in game and bird species, including rhino, giraffe, bushpig, warthog, zebra, waterbuck, impala, reedbuck, bushbuck, kudu and blue wildebeest. Buffalo are to be introduced, and the reintroduction of elephant is to follow.

Visitors may view the plentiful wildlife on guided vehicle or boat trips, while game walks, night drives and canoeing are also to be introduced. With an ecotourism plan being developed by the Centre for Eco-Tourism at the University of Pretoria, this reserve seems set to become one of the major ecotourism developments in the country.

Accommodation ranges from fully catered to self-catering facilities. Six different camps or lodges provide beds for 92 people. All rooms have air-conditioning (summers are frequently blisteringly hot), while all of the camps have swimming pools.

To reach Pongolapoort, drive along the N2 from Durban northwards to Mkuze. Some 24 km after Mkuze, take the turn-off east to Leeuwspoor/Pongolwane and follow the signs. If coming from Johannesburg, turn left at the Leeuwspoor/Pongolwane sign some 9 km after crossing the Pongola (Phongolo) River.

Further information may be obtained by contacting Pongolapoort Biosphere Reserve, P O Box 767, Pongola 3170, telephone (03843) 5-1123, or fax 5-1104.

Pumalanga Nature Reserve

African bushveld, ringing with a symphony of birdcalls and the trumpeting of elephant, is the site of the Pumalanga Nature Reserve.

Covering 3000 ha of land to the south of Mkuzi Game Reserve, Pumalanga, which has been owned by one family for three generations, is a wilderness of open grassland, thornveld and dense riverine forests. Guests can take game drives – elephant, white rhino, buffalo, hippo, giraffe, zebra, blue wildebest,

Above: Dense beds of reeds in the St Lucia Estuary section of the wetland park are a favourite habitat for an immense range of birds, but may just as easily conceal crocodile or hippopotamus. **Right:** A fading sun lights the water in one of the pans in Ndumo Game Reserve. The main pans here are Banzi and Nyamithi, and the combined bird list totals 419 species.

nyala, kudu and many other species find sanctuary here – or they may walk around at their leisure. Night drives are offered, as are visits to the nearby Sodwana, Lake St Lucia, Mkuzi and Hluhluwe-Umfolozi reserves. The scenery is superb and the birdlife is abundant. Facilities are also available for hunting, diving and freshwater fishing.

This private reserve offers accommodation in the rustic, self-catering Mfula Lodge (ten beds) equipped with all the essentials. There is a swimming pool for cooling off after a strenuous outing, and a tennis court for the indomitable! Only one party is booked at a time to ensure complete privacy.

To reach Pumalanga, which lies some three hours north of Durban, follow the N2 and turn right at the Southern Maputaland/Sodwana turn-off. The turn-off to the reserve lies some 16 km further along on your left.

For further information, contact Pumalanga Nature Reserve, P O Box 169, Hluhluwe 3960, telephone/fax (035) 562-0049.

Rocktail Bay Lodge

To the south of Kosi Bay, and situated within Maputaland's coastal forest reserve area, is Rocktail Bay Lodge, a secluded getaway tucked into the coastal forest just metres from the warm breakers of the Indian Ocean. From the lodge, consisting of 'tree house' chalets raised on stilts and blending with the forest canopy, a boardwalk winds and twists through the trees down to the beach.

Visitors can stroll along the shore, swim, snorkel and fish in the warm waters, trek through the coastal forest, take 4x4 drives to neighbouring beaches or simply return to the lodge to enjoy the tranquillity of life in the wild. Outings can be arranged to view the turtle-nesting site between November and February. The presence of some of the rare endemic bird species will cheer any ornithologists – green coucal, pink-throated longclaw, grey waxbill, wattle-eyed flycatcher, Livingstone's lourie and Woodward's batis nest in the coastal forest.

Accommodation consists of ten rustic chalets, each with two or three beds, and private toilet and bath/shower facilities. Guests dine in a thatched boma or on a deck constructed below the branches of a shady Natal mahogany tree. A plunge pool beckons those who want to rinse off the salt water.

For details, contact Wilderness Safaris, P O Box 651171, Benmore 2010, telephone (011) 884-1458 or 884-4633, fax 883-6255.

Sungulwane Game Lodge

Tucked away in the foothills of the Lubombo Mountains is Sungulwane Game Lodge, a 1 000 ha retreat in the undisturbed bush of western KwaZulu-Natal. Here nyala, impala, kudu, reedbuck, suni, duiker and zebra find sanctuary in the bushveld, and the air is alive with birdsong. Guests stay in catered or self-catering accommodation – and all rooms have *en suite* showers.

Guided walks are conducted in the early morning, which is the best time for birdwatching, and night drives are offered to those interested in the silent creatures of the moonlight. Hunting facilities are also available. Sungulwane lies east of the N2 approximately halfway between Hluhluwe and Mkuze.

For details, contact Sungulwane Game Lodge, P O Box Bayala 3966, telephone/fax (035) 562-0498.

Tembe Elephant Park

This 29 878 ha wilderness of dense, undisturbed sand forest and pans was proclaimed as a reserve in 1983 in an effort to save KwaZulu-Natal's last free-ranging elephant herds. In the past the traditional migration route of these elephant took them through Mozambique, where they were frequently poached for their tusks and meat. Scarred old bulls and others lucky enough to survive this hazard are now protected behind the new electric fence surrounding the entire reserve. There are presently a mere 100 resident elephant, but numbers are growing steadily.

The reserve is stocked with suni (it has one of the highest populations in southern Africa), nyala, kudu, blue wildebeest, impala, reedbuck, red and grey duiker, waterbuck, bushbuck, leopard, white rhino, black rhino, zebra, giraffe, warthog, bushpig, side-striped jackal and hyena.

Apart from those staying at the camp, only three groups of day visitors are permitted entry in 4x4 vehicles daily. Visitors may stop at two hides situated on the tourist route, one of which overlooks a pan in the Uzi Swamp. A walking trail has been established, with two alternative routes.

Between Tembe and Kosi Bay is the 54 000 ha palm veld area of Mfihlwini corridor, heavily populated with livestock. It is planned that this area will be co-opted into the parks, and controlled as a biosphere reserve, incorporating the inhabitants and their enterprises into the environment.

Guests stay in a rustic camp with four two-bed, furnished safari tents, and kitchen, dining room and common ablution facilities. One party books the entire camp at a time, and a camp cook eases the mealtime load (guests must, however, provide their own food). A 4x4 vehicle is necessary as roads are very sandy (this used to be part of the ocean floor).

To reach the reserve, take the N2 turn-off to Jozini and travel north for 72 km (the road is tarred to the entrance gates).

Information and accommodation enquiries should be addressed to Central Reservations, Department of Nature Conservation, Private Bag X9024, Pietermaritzburg 3200, or telephone (0331) 94-6696/7/8, fax 42-1948.

The kings' legacy

The pride of KwaZulu-Natal is the splendid wilderness of the Hluhluwe-Umfolozi Park, 270 km north of Durban, where careful conservation rescued the white rhino from the brink of extinction. Formerly the separate game parks of Hluhluwe and Umfolozi, the combined reserve, with its wealth of wildlife set in pristine surroundings, worthily crowns the longstanding efforts at conservation made throughout the province.

Despite the encroachment of the cane fields, the Zulu kingdom has much to offer. Its deep green forest sanctuaries, misty mountain peaks, coastal lagoons, private game ranches and the refreshing upland reserves around Eshowe offer quietness, beauty and peace in a land that, all too recently, has been torn by political violence. But there is an aura, still, of the natural majesty of old Zululand.

Amatikulu Nature Reserve

This coastal reserve lies just off the North Coast Road (N2) and extends for some 20 km from the north bank of the Tugela to the estuary of the Amatikulu (Matigulu) River, where it borders on the Umlalazi Nature Reserve. The reserve is made up of the separate conservation areas of Amatikulu and Red Hill nature reserves and Talmage Pan, a total of 2 100 ha, and its diverse habitats include seashore, coastal and riverine forest, wetland and grassland. Birdlife is rich and varied, and larger animals include zebra, kudu, nyala, impala, blue duiker, bushbuck, reedbuck and waterbuck.

In addition, there is the rare spectacle of giraffe browsing on the dune forests overlooking the ocean.

Popular activities include self-guided trails, beach-walks, canoeing on the Amatikulu and Nyoni rivers (bring your own canoe), fishing and birdwatching. Modest powerboating is allowed, but engine output must not exceed 15 horsepower. Because of the presence of crocodiles, swimming is not recommended.

Accommodation at Zangozolo Bush Camp is in tents on wooden platforms that overlook both the Amatikulu River and the Indian Ocean. The communal kitchen area is fully equipped and chefs are available. Precautions must be taken against malaria and bilharzia. The park gates are open from sunrise to sunset throughout the year. For further information, you should contact the KwaZulu-Natal Department of Nature Conservation, Private Bag X9024, Pietermaritzburg 3200, telephone (0331) 94-6696/7/8, fax 42-1948.

Dlinza Forest Nature Reserve

A 'place of tomb-like meditation' is the meaning of Dlinza (or Hlinza), the 205 ha forest reserve in Eshowe, off Kangela Street. Tracks through the forest were originally cut by British troops stationed in the town after the 1879 Anglo-Zulu war, and a natural amphitheatre known as the Bishop's Seat is the venue for Nativity plays held every three years. Open from 7.30 a.m. to 5 p.m., the reserve has bushbuck, blue duiker and red duiker, bushpig and vervet monkey, while butterflies and birdlife abound. There are picnic spots, several pleasant strolls and a 2 km self-guided trail.

This is one of South Africa's prime birding spots, where rarities such as spotted thrush and olive bush-shrike are relatively common. An eight-bed rustic camp is planned.

Dukuduku Forest Nature Reserve

Dukuduku – the 'place of hiding' – is so called because it was a sanctuary for both people and cattle during the Zulu succession struggle following Cetshwayo's death. A picnic spot is signposted at the 15 km marker on the road between Mtubatuba and St Lucia.

This nature reserve preserves a characteristic stand of subtropical coastal forest, of which very little survives in KwaZulu-Natal. Wildlife includes a variety of endangered waterfowl, forest birds and several endangered raptors (birds of prey). There are many rare butterflies in the reserve, and the extremely venomous Gaboon adder (very rare in South Africa) also occurs here. Self-guided hiking trails, of one and three hours respectively, start at the picnic site and are well signposted.

Entry is allowed during daylight hours only, and visitors explore the area on foot.

For further information and permission to explore the Dukuduku forests, you should write to The Nyalazi District Conservation Officer, Natal Parks Board, P O Box 111, St Lucia

Right: Long legs distinguish the grey duiker (*Sylvicapra grimmia*) from other duikers. This is a widespread species, occurring in dense savannah, high mountains, and even on the fringes of a desert. It is mainly nocturnal, feeding in the early morning and in the evening.

KWAZULU-NATAL: MFOLOZI VALLEY

3936, or telephone the office at (035) 550-0190, or fax 590-1343.

Enseleni Nature Reserve

The Nkonikini Trail leads for 7 km/three hours through grassland, forest and riverine woodland along the Nseleni River, a haven for aquatic birds and monitor lizards. Starting with giant umdoni or water myrtle trees (*Syzygium cordatum*) at the picnic site, the trail passes through ilala palms (*Hyphaene natalensis*), 10 m high freshwater mangrove trees and wild figs. The forest canopy is so dense that little light reaches the ground. There is also a 30-minute trail. Guided walks are available – telephone (0351) 92-3732.

There is a 294 ha game park in the reserve, with blue wildebeest, waterbuck, nyala, bushbuck, zebra and reedbuck. The reserve is open throughout the year on Saturday, Sunday and public holidays from 7 a.m. to 6 p.m. Antimalaria precautions should be taken.

This sanctuary, alongside the N2 some 190 km northwest of Durban and 16 km north of the timber-and-cane town of Empangeni, offers a foretaste of the great nature reserves of Zululand.

Entumeni Nature Reserve

Fields of sugar cane dominate the undulating hills of Natal's north coast, banishing most indigenous vegetation. But here and there the birds have found a sanctuary. The 700 ha mistbelt reserve of Entumeni, 16 km from Eshowe on the Nkandla road, is one of these. Only birds and butterflies seem to move in the gloom of this deceptively still, indigenous evergreen forest, but high in the bastard umzimbeet (*Millettia sutherlandii*), among the ferns and orchids, and on the damp compost of the forest floor, small mammals and a multitude of insects lead their own busy lives. The impressive bird list includes African broadbill, spotted thrush and yellow-throated warbler.

The reserve can be explored only on foot – there are two self-guided trails of up to four hours duration, and there is a picnic site. For more information, telephone The Officer-in-Charge at (0354) 4-2473.

Hlomo Hlomo Game Reserve

The spreading wild fig tree that shades the luxury tented camp and boma is one of about 90 tree species on this 800 ha reserve. Wildlife includes leopard, serval, black-backed jackal, giraffe, bushpig and warthog, zebra and some 16 antelope species, from the lordly kudu to the dainty klipspringer. Activities revolve around gamewatching, hikes and trails, a 40-km trail for 4x4 vehicles, and birdwatching.

To reach Hlomo Hlomo, turn right from the R69 onto the R618 about 25 km east of Vryheid, drive for about 60 km further and follow the

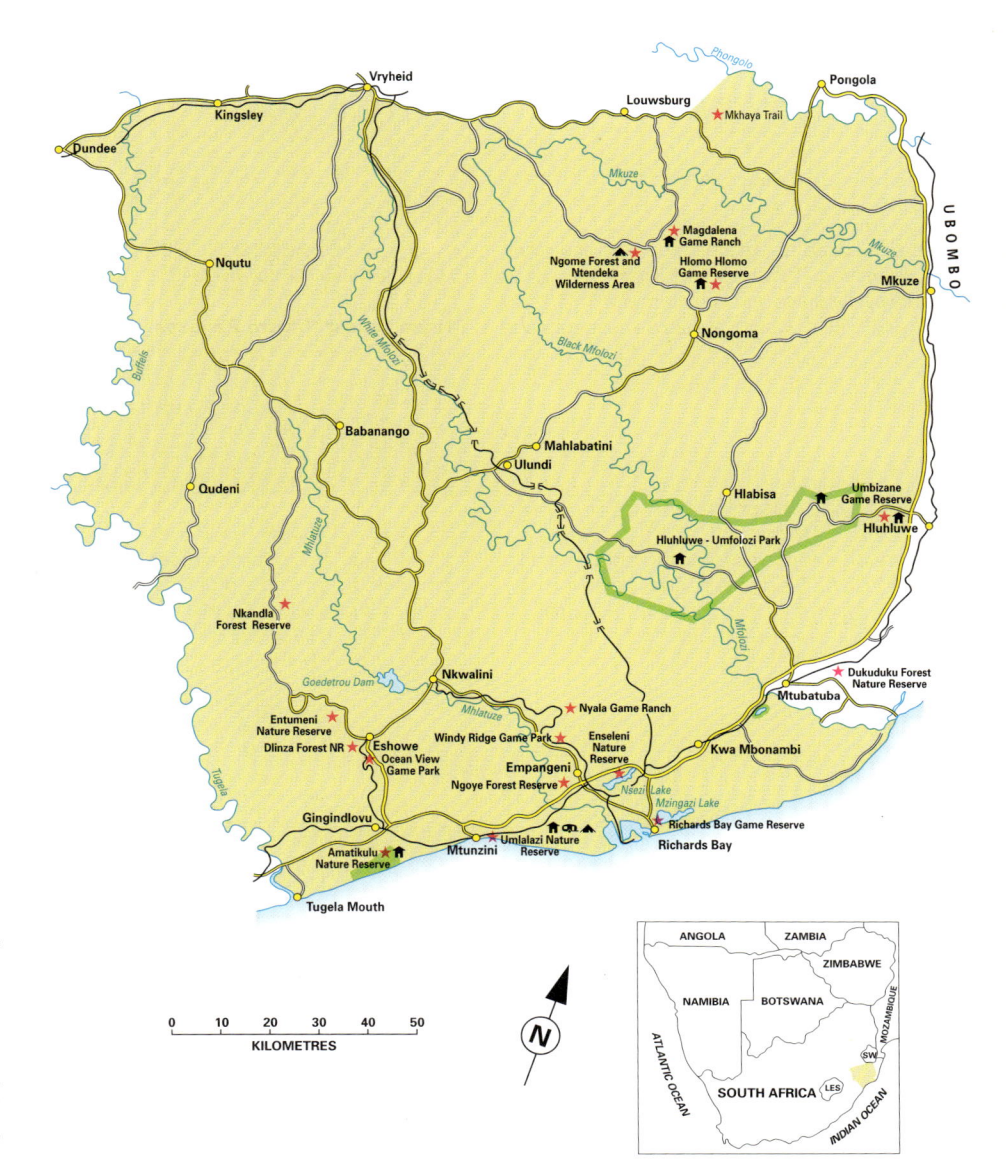

Right: The Dlinza Forest Nature Reserve at Eshowe. Although some visitors come only for braais and picnics, many prefer to spend their day exploring the complex of nature trails leading through the forest. The indigenous vegetation includes trees such as yellowwood, stinkwood, fig and forest umdoni.

Hluhluwe-Umfolozi Park

signs past Ngome. For further information, write to Hlomo Hlomo Game Reserve, P O Box 95192, Grant Park 2051, or telephone (011) 786-4764, fax 786-4770.

Hluhluwe-Umfolozi Park

Hluhluwe has been a game sanctuary since 1895 and before that it was a hunting preserve of the Zulu kings. Saved by the presence of tsetse fly and the malarial mosquito, which kept farmers and commercial hunters at bay, it is named after *umhluhluwe*, the thorny monkey rope (*Dalbergia armata*) that flourishes along the banks of the Hluhluwe River. Umfolozi Game Reserve took its name from the zigzag Mfolozi *mnyama* (black) and Mfolozi *mhlope* (white) rivers that meander and marry in its untouched wilderness. In 1989, with the incorporation of a 21 000 ha corridor between the two reserves, a single, magnificent conservation unit of 96 453 ha was created as the Hluhluwe-Umfolozi Park.

The Hluhluwe section has a landscape of green, rolling hills, while Umfolozi presents a scene of relatively dry, open bushveld. The park is the home of the Natal Parks Board's well-known Rhino Capture Unit. Rhino, appropriately, while poached to the edge of extinction in other parts of Africa, make up the park's proud 'big six', rather than big five – white rhino, black rhino, elephant, buffalo, lion and leopard. The park probably holds the world's greatest concentration of rhino – some 1 600 white rhino and approximately 350 black. In addition there are giraffe, hippo, wild dog, cheetah, crocodile and many antelope species. More than 300 species of birds have been recorded, including bateleur eagle, the ground hornbill (somewhat resembling a large black turkey) and the insatiable white-backed vulture that thrusts its whole head into the belly of a carcass.

The park boasts 214 km of roads for visitors, of which 15 km are tarred, the remainder having a well-maintained gravel surface. There are three self-guided auto-trails for those who prefer to drive, and four self-guided walks: the 30-minute Mbhombe Forest Trail from Hluhluwe's Hilltop Camp and three others – the Emoyeni, Mpila and Masinda – in Umfolozi. Guided walks are offered twice daily from Hilltop and Mpila camps, and night drives are also undertaken. The very popular, guided wilderness trails of up to five days must be booked well in advance through the reservations office in Pietermaritzburg.

Each section of the park has several picnic sites, and those at Umbondwe, Mpila and on the Sontuli Loop in Umfolozi have braai places and toilets. Another picnic site is conveniently close to the Thiyeni hide in Hluhluwe. The most rewarding gameviewing position is probably Mphafa hide in Umfolozi, the best times being

Above: A steenbok in the Hluhluwe-Umfolozi Park.
Top: *Euphorbia grandicornis*. This plant's sap can cause skin irritation while the vapour from a 'bleeding' plant can create a burning sensation in the throat.

from 9 a.m. to noon during the winter months from June to October.

The park entrance gates are open from 5 a.m. to 7 p.m. in summer (1 October to 31 March) and from 6 a.m. to 6 p.m. in winter (1 April to 30 September). Office hours at Hilltop (the park headquarters), are from 7 a.m. to 7 p.m., and, at Mpila, from 8 a.m. to 12.30 p.m. and from 2 p.m. to 4.30 p.m. Petrol is available at Hilltop and Mpila from 7 a.m. to noon and from 2 p.m. to 5 p.m. Basic provisions are available at Hilltop only, and visitors staying at other camps must bring all food supplies.

A curio stall featuring a wide selection of traditional arts and crafts is managed and run by the communities of eziMambeni as a Parks Board neighbour relations project.

There is a range of accommodation, including hutted camps at Hilltop, Masinda and Mpila, each unit sleeping up to four people in huts, cottages or chalets, either catered or self-catering (Hilltop camp also has a licensed

---

HLUHLUWE-UMFOLOZI AT A GLANCE

When to go The reserve is open all year, the gates usually opening at sunrise and closing at sunset (the times vary according to the time of year). The best time to visit is during the winter months.

Reservations To book wilderness trails and accommodation, write to The Reservations Officer, Natal Parks Board, P O Box 1750, Pietermaritzburg 3200, or telephone (0331) 47-1981, fax 47-1980.

Getting there The turn-off to the reserve is off the North Coast Road (N2) onto the Nongoma road, 3,4 km north of the Mtubatuba turn-off. The Umfolozi turn-off is 27 km further along this road.

Accommodation There are hutted camps at Hilltop (where there is a licensed restaurant), Masinda and Mpila. These have fully equipped and serviced rest huts with separate kitchens and ablution blocks. Other huts have their own bathroom and kitchen, as do the cottages. On a bank of the Black Mfolozi River lie the Sontuli and Nselweni bush camps, while Mndindini bush camp is set in the remote Umfolozi Wilderness Area. Among other lodges and bush camps are four that have a cook/caretaker and game guard in attendance.

Eating and drinking Bring your own food and drink; attendants will prepare your meals at some camps. There is a restaurant at Hilltop, and the nearest store is at Mtubatuba, 50 km away. A fridge, crockery, cutlery and cooking utensils are supplied at the bush camps.

Getting around Three-day wilderness trails, on which you hike and camp in the reserve's more remote areas, are the ideal way of seeing Umfolozi. A ranger accompanies each party (of no more than six people). Travel by private car, however, is the more usual method.

Wildlife Practically every species of big game is represented. Visitors may spot black and white rhino, elephant, zebra, buffalo, lion, leopard and cheetah. A wide variety of birds occurs within the reserve.

Special precautions Precautions against malaria and bilharzia should be taken. The water in the hutted camps is chlorinated but elsewhere it must be boiled or chlorinated as there have been instances of cholera in Zululand. Visitors should stay in their cars except at the designated viewpoints and game hides.

KWAZULU-NATAL: MFOLOZI VALLEY

Left below: A green reed frog (*Hyperolius tuberlinguis*). This small amphibian can change its colour to different shades of green and even yellow. It deposits its eggs in a mass attached to a leaf, reed or stem of grass a few centimetres above the surface of the water. **Left above:** A hiker pauses for a rest along a footpath in the Ntendeka Wilderness Area – part of the Ngome Forest. **Right:** Charming hutted accommodation in the verdant Hluhluwe-Umfolozi Park.

restaurant). In addition there are two lodges, while the two bush lodges and two of the bush camps each have a game guard and a cook/caretaker in attendance. Anti-malaria precautions must be taken. Reservations should be made by contacting The Reservations Officer, Natal Parks Board, P O Box 1750, Pietermaritzburg 3200, or telephone (0331) 47-1981, fax 47-1980.

Magdalena Game Ranch

Game drives, outrides and guided trails in a scenic area of high-lying grassland, thornveld and riverine forest are among the attractions of this private reserve near Vryheid. (From the R69 about 25 km east of Vryheid, turn onto the R618 for Nongoma. Turn left after a further 29 km and follow the signposts to Magdalena Game Ranch for 7 km.) Serviced accommodation is in a luxury lodge overlooking the Msihlengeni Falls, a bush camp by a river or in a cosy, timber-and-thatch cottage. Guests must provide their own food and drink. For more information, write to Magdalena Game Ranch, P O Box 476, Vryheid 3100, or telephone (0386) 7-1865.

Mkhaya Trail

Situated on a private farm, rather than on a proclaimed nature reserve, the Mkhaya Trail nevertheless provides an abundance of the natural elements – flora and fauna – of northern Zululand. The farm, Paradys, lies just south of the Phongolo River, and the splendidly scenic trail takes two or three days to complete. Among bushveld trees is a gigantic specimen of the paperbark thorn (*Acacia sieberana*) and there are many of the flat-crowned *Albizia adianthifolia* with their poisonous bark from which, interestingly, a traditional Zulu love potion is made. There are traces of ancient Zulu occupation, and King Dingane slept here on his flight to Swaziland. A variety of buck is to be seen, as well as prolific birdlife.

The trail is open from September to April, December and January being fairly hot. Ticks can be a problem, but not if precautions are taken. Take the R66 from the village of Pongola and, after 22 km, turn right onto the R69, and right again – after a further 21 km – at the Mkhaya sign. For more information, telephone (03841) 4-1076.

Ngome Forest and Ntendeka Wilderness Area

Some 25 km east of Vryheid on the road to Louwsburg is a side road (R618) to the village of Nongoma, the 'place of the diviner'. On the way, it twists around the hills for 47 km to pass the indigenous mountain forest of Ngome. In the 1820s this subtropical forest once hid Umbeje Khumalo, first cousin and ally of Mzilikazi, founder of Zimbabwe's Ndebele nation, and 50 years later provided a refuge to Cetshwayo after his capital, Ulundi, was put to the torch by an invading British army. In July 1996 a monument to Umbeje, presented by the Khumalo clan, was unveiled in the forest.

The list of trees and plants in this majestic expanse of land includes 19 of South Africa's 42 species of epiphyte, or tree orchid, and ferns of which at least one species (*Alsophila capensis*) reaches a height of eight metres along the streams. Other rarities include the olive woodpecker, the red bush squirrel and the Ngome lily (*Crinum moorei*). Wildlife abounds in the forest: there are leopard, baboon, duiker, caracal, samango monkey, a variety of snakes and innumerable birds, butterflies and moths. Birds include bald ibis and long-crested eagle (both threatened species), as well as the purple-crested lourie, Narina trogon and black-headed oriole.

Within the forest is the Ntendeka Wilderness Area, a 5 200 ha stretch of grassland and evergreen forest in which visitors may see traces of early Zulu occupation, a historic rock shelter, the Ntendeka cliffs and a host of fascinating trees and plants. There are several trails, the shortest of which takes three-and-a-half hours to complete, and the longest a day.

There are picnic spots and campsites at the edge of the wilderness area. Visitors may obtain permits from The Forester, Ngome Forest, Private Bag X9306, Vryheid 3100, telephone (0386) 7-1883.

Ngoye Forest Reserve

There are more than 100 indigenous forests in the old Zulu kingdom. Much of the flora and fauna of the 3 904 ha Ngoye reserve, southwest of Empangeni and 10 km from the University of

Above: Mole crickets use their powerful front legs as digging implements, burying themselves in a remarkably short time. These crickets are familiar throughout KwaZulu-Natal. **Top:** A white rhino in the Hluhluwe-Umfolozi Park. This is the second largest land mammal (after the elephant), the male weighing 3,5 tons. In spite of their intimidating size, these rhino are not aggressive: although they may charge when alarmed, they rarely follow it through with an actual attack.
Right: Nyala in the Hluhluwe-Umfolozi Park.

KwaZulu, is unique to the area. One of the world's rarest plants, *Encephalartos woodii*, a cycad named for an early curator of the Durban Botanic Gardens, is endemic to Ngoye.

In 1916, a clump of half a dozen male plants of the species were the only ones still surviving. These were removed: one was sent to Pretoria, one to Kew Gardens in London and four were planted in Durban's Botanic Gardens, where they still flourish. No female plants have ever been found. Overall, there is a wonderful diversity of plants in this reserve, with its attractive rock formations and scenic views of the coastal region.

The red bush squirrel, the forest green butterfly, the green barbet, Delegorgue's (bronze-naped) pigeon and the Ngoye centipede are all common here but extremely rare elsewhere in southern Africa.

Write to The Chief Director, Directorate of Nature Conservation, Private Bag X98, Ulundi 3838, or telephone (0358) 70-0552, fax 70-0580, for further information, directions and permission to explore the forest.

Nkandla Forest Reserve
Nkandla is magnificent – a huge indigenous mountain forest, beautiful and unspoilt.

Its 2 217 ha lie astride a mountain pass, 50 km northwest of Eshowe on a good gravel road that, another 50 km further on, joins the main Melmoth route. The moisture of perpetually drifting mists maintains the tree ferns, yellow-flowered creepers, cycads, orchids and lianas on the flanks of these brooding mountains. There is a waterfall in the Mome Gorge, the refuge and final stand of Bambatha – rebel or patriot – who, in 1906, challenged by force of arms the injustice of colonial conquest. Once at the heart of the forest, the site is now on the outskirts, an index of how the natural cover of the area has retreated.

A signposted turn-off some distance before Nkandla leads for 25 rigorous km around to the forest's western fringe, high over the valley of the Tugela River. Here, at journey's end, in a quiet grove of trees, is the grave of Cetshwayo, who died on 23 April 1884. A tombstone of black marble erected by a descendant recalls proudly the part Cetshwayo played in the turbulent history of the Zulu kingdom, and the grave is a revered site.

Leopard, duiker, bushbuck, vervet monkey and baboon inhabit the almost impenetrable forest. The leopard, perhaps, is more spirit than substance, but while forest officials have not seen it, local people swear to its presence. Further details and permission to enter the reserve are available from The Chief Director, Directorate of Nature Conservation, Private Bag X98, Ulundi 3838, telephone (0358) 70-0552, fax 70-0580.

Ocean View Game Park
Away from the hot, humid coast, the cool 'sighing winds' of Eshowe 30 km inland and 500 m above sea level are a welcome change. Eshowe has a 25 ha municipal game reserve (leased by the Natal Parks Board) called Ocean View Game Park at the southern entrance to the town.

Visiting hours are between 8 a.m. and 5 p.m. A game guard accompanies visitors around its

Left: A female Marico sunbird feeds on *Schotia brachypetala* (or weeping boer-bean) in the Hluhluwe-Umfolozi Park. This sunbird is found mainly in dry (acacia thorn) savannah, and lives on spiders, insects, butterfly larvae and the nectar of certain flowers. The female builds the nest of down and feathers (bark and seeds may be added to the outside of the nest), and suspends it from the branches of acacias and other trees.

Umlalazi Nature Reserve

The fish eagle is the symbol of the 1 028 ha Natal Parks Board reserve of Umlalazi ('the place of the grinding stone'), 1,5 km from Mtunzini. Forested coastal dunes, mangroves, several small lakes and the Umlalazi River Lagoon, adjacent to the shimmering waters of the Indian Ocean, are the dominant features of this appealing sanctuary.

Silent crocodile still occasionally frighten fishermen, but the main fauna to be found here – apart from the prolific birdlife – are bushpig, bushbuck, duiker, zebra and reedbuck. On the other side of the dunes, in the sea, huge skates and sandsharks move inshore to breed during the summer months.

Three self-guided trails through the mangroves and the dune forests have been prepared by Natal Parks Board staff. The shortest (one hour) and least strenuous is the Mangrove Trail. Trees in the reserve include both red and white milkwood, strangler fig and gwarri.

There are log cabins and a campsite and caravan park in the reserve. Water is available and showers are provided. Umlalazi is open year round, and the gates are open daily from 5 a.m. to 10 p.m.. There is a well-stocked curio shop, and the neighbouring town of Mtunzini stocks all requirements. The reserve is situated 128 km from Durban along the main North Coast Road (N2).

The log cabins may be reserved by contacting The Reservations Officer, P O Box 662, Pietermaritzburg 3200, or telephone (0331) 47-1981, fax 47-1980. To reserve campsites, write to The Officer-in-Charge, Umlalazi Nature Reserve, P O Box 234, Mtunzini 3867, telephone (0353) 40-1836.

Windy Ridge Game Park

Some 28 km from Empangeni (off the R34), this reserve of 1 500 ha has some 4 000 head of plains game, including giraffe, leopard, warthog, wildebeest, steenbok, red duiker, bushbuck and numerous other antelope species in a landscape of bushveld, savannah and riverine bush. Some 230 bird species have been recorded.

A large camp caters for up to 70 in youth groups and the smaller camp – self-catering or catered by request – accommodates up to 12 people. For more detailed information and to make reservations, telephone (0351) 92-8319, or fax 92-8317.

---

easy slopes, where zebra, impala, bushpig, blesbok, blue duiker and blue wildebeest have been reintroduced. There is also a wealth of birdlife.

For details, contact The Publicity Officer, at telephone (0354) 4-1141, fax 7-4733. Eshowe is the home of the Zululand Historical Museum, housed in picturesque Fort Nongqayi.

Richards Bay Game Reserve

Proclaimed in 1935, de-proclaimed decades later, when harbour development began, then reproclaimed in 1976, this reserve of 1 200 ha is really a marine sanctuary, lying some 18 km east of Empangeni and 2,5 km south of Richards Bay.

A limited number of people and vehicles are admitted from the Esikhawini side daily, according to a permit system. Fishing is permitted only in the New Mouth area, and the reserve is intended principally for the use of canoeists and birdwatchers. It is administered by the Natal Parks Board, assisted by Portnet. For information, telephone (0351) 3-2330.

Ubizane Game Reserve

Gameviewing safaris on foot and in 4x4 vehicles are offered to guests at Ubizane, a private game reserve 8 km from Hluhluwe village on the road to the Hluhluwe-Umfolozi Park.

The 4x4 drives provide an excellent opportunity to see white rhino (bred on the ranch), giraffe, nyala, impala, blue wildebeest, kudu, blesbok, reedbuck and waterbuck, while night safaris allow views of nocturnal animals such as aardvark, hyena, white-tailed mongoose and jackal. More than 400 species of birds have been recorded.

Visitors may stay in a luxury camp overlooking a forest of yellow fever trees (*Acacia xanthophloea*) and there's a reeded boma where the evening braais are held. There is also a self-catering bush camp and a swimming pool. The reserve is open to day visitors. Anti-malaria precautions should be taken.

For more detailed information and to make reservations, write to Ubizane Game Reserve, P O Box 102, Hluhluwe 3960, or telephone/fax (035) 562-0237.

Forest, gorge and bountiful sea

Contrary to the expectations of many visitors, the KwaZulu-Natal coast is distinguished not only by its bikinis and long stretches of white beach. For nature lovers, it has a great deal more to offer: each of its (mainly forested gorge) reserves is well worth visiting. The finest of these are probably Vernon Crookes, Krantzkloof, Oribi Gorge and, not far from the centre of Durban itself, the popular Kenneth Stainbank Nature Reserve.

Throughout this coastal region the birdlife is prolific and fascinating, the innumerable creatures of its shores even more so. There are no elephant left, but most of the reserves have reintroduced antelope and other game.

There is a luxurious tropical ambience about the countryside around Durban: forests and flowers, ilala palms, monkeys and wild bananas are everywhere. But the focus of attention is without doubt along the ever-changing Indian Ocean shore – its lagoons, estuaries and tidal pools.

Alfred Park

Set in Durban's western suburb of New Germany is a 3,25 ha reserve of pristine swamp forest. Over 100 bird species have been identified and, in 1995, a pair of woolly-necked storks bred and successfully raised a brood of three chicks within its secure boundaries.

Friends of Alfred Park, a group affiliated to the Wildlife Society, organises guided walks for schools and environmental groups. For further information, contact the Wildlife Society, 100 Brand Road, Durban 4001, telephone (031) 21-3126, or fax 21-9525.

Amanzimtoti Bird Sanctuary

A haven for exotic and indigenous birds lies some 27 km south of Durban, in Amanzimtoti. The focus of the sanctuary is its lake-like stretch of calm water framed by ilala palms.

An enchanting 30-minute trail winds through the forest, and longer hikes (and two well-positioned bird hides) introduce visitors to many of the sanctuary's 150 bird species. There are many park benches dotted strategically throughout the sanctuary, where you can relax among strutting peacock and enjoy the pleasant surroundings. A tea garden (open on weekends and public holidays) overlooks the lake, where inquisitive waterbirds are likely to take the food out of your hand.

The sanctuary lies in Umdoni Road and is open daily from 6 a.m. to 6 p.m. For more information, telephone (031) 903-2544.

Beachwood Mangroves Nature Reserve

The Mgeni, 'river of the acacia trees', is probably better known for its waterfalls. But on the north bank, and reached via the Durban North turn-off into Fairview Road (and thereafter sharp right), is the 76 ha Beachwood Mangroves Nature Reserve.

Mangroves – dense thickets of tropical evergreen trees and shrubs – throw out a profusion of prop roots that trap silt, plants and debris in a thick mesh that makes them natural land builders. They are also host to nesting birds, mudskippers (amphibious fish) and fiddler crabs. A trail penetrates the forest, offering an opportunity to explore the plant- and animal life. A rustic bird hide on the trail offers sheltered viewing, and a bird list is available.

The southern end of the reserve, near the Mgeni estuary, has an activities centre and a thatched gazebo, both are available for hire to educational groups. Access to the beach is via the Rocket Hut entrance in the north, and visitors can enjoy fishing and an interesting sandy shore. There is a picnic area at the gate. To explore the Beachwood Mangroves you need to get permission from The Officer-in-Charge, P O Box 930, Umhlanga Rocks 4320, telephone (031) 25-1721, or fax 25-1547.

Left: A spoonbill at its nest in the Bluff Nature Reserve. The spatulate tip of this bird's bill is adapted to its unique method of feeding: it wades into the shallows with its slightly opened bill sweeping from side to side, feeling for and catching waterborne organisms (including small fish) with the sensitive inner surface. It also feeds by probing in the mud. **Above:** Detail of mangrove branches, showing their seeds. These mangroves, photographed in the Beachwood Mangroves Nature Reserve, produce strangely shaped roots that protrude from the water and are used for breathing. Such roots have evolved in response to the low oxygen content of the soil in which these trees grow. **Above right:** A fiddler crab beside its hole in the Beachwood Mangroves Nature Reserve. This crab feeds by scooping up mud with its larger nipper, rolling it into balls, and extracting what food it can before discarding them.

KWAZULU-NATAL: SOUTH COAST

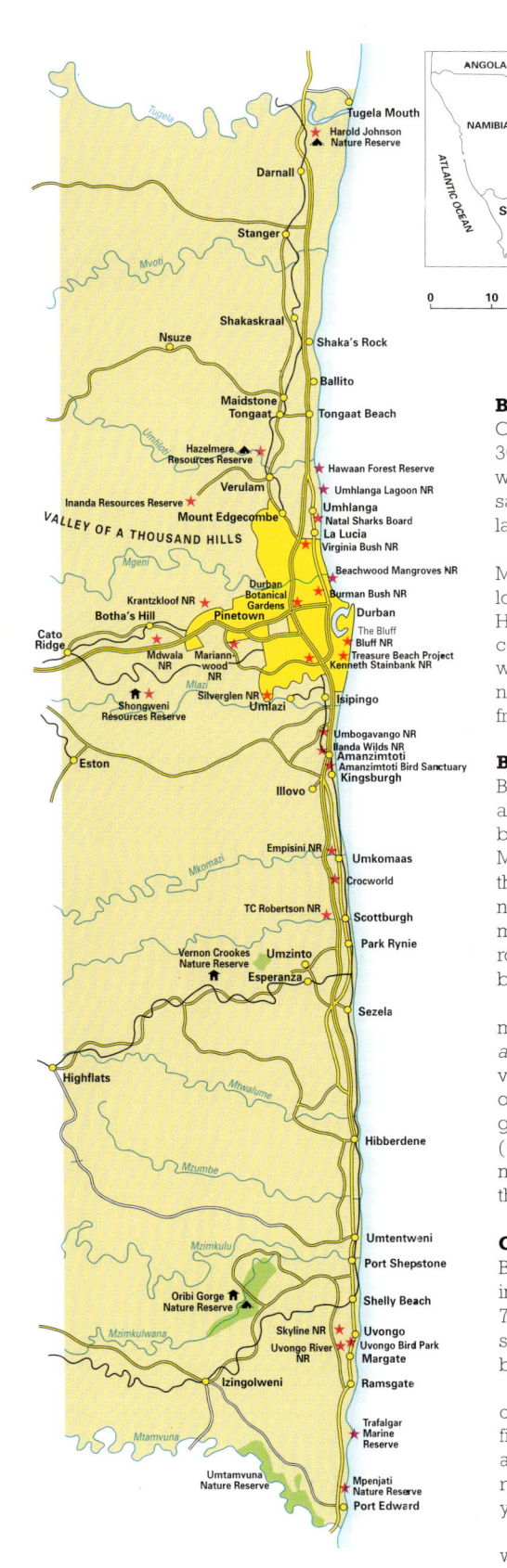

Bluff Nature Reserve

One of six Natal Parks Board reserves within 30 km of Durban, Bluff is a reed-fringed freshwater pan in the saddle between the two great sand dunes that are among Durban's familiar landmarks.

To reach the reserve, take the Jacobs/Mobeni exit off the southern freeway, and follow Quality Street to the corner of Tara Road. Hemmed in by suburbs, this 45 ha reserve of coastal forest and grassland, with its bird-watching hide, is an important centre for nature-conservation education. It is open daily from sunrise to sunset.

Burman Bush Nature Reserve

Burman Bush, one of 30 Durban city parks, lies along both sides of Burman Drive and Salisbury Road, off Umgeni Road, in the suburb of Morningside. It has picnic sites and toilets, and there are nature walks through 55 ha of indigenous bush. This area is rich in plant- and animal life, readily visible once you leave the main road and wander along the trails that have been cleared through the bush.

The animal most often associated with Burman Bush is the vervet monkey (*Cercopithecus aethiops*). There are about 200 in the area, and visitors are requested not to feed them. Birds often seen are the hadeda and the African goshawk. Large trees, including forest olive (*Olea woodiana*) and the bronze paper commiphora (*Commiphora harveyi*) grow along the trails. The reserve is open at all hours.

Crocworld

Basking on the grassy banks or lying log-like in the muddy waters, crocodiles – there are 7 000 of them here – are fearsome even when seen in the distance, from the walkways and bridges in this 27 ha park.

The park's aquarium claims to be the only one for crocodiles in Africa, and also contains fish and water monitors, alligators, terrapins and snakes. There is also a small natural history museum, a rabbit enclosure, and a farmyard, popular with children.

The park attracts birds such as hamerkop, weaver and plover, as well as small antelope and vervet monkeys that can be seen on the 3 km trail through the bush. Guided tours are also offered, and a skywalk above the forest is in the planning stage.

A restaurant has crocodile on the menu, as well as teas, and a curio shop sells a range of crocodile-based products.

Crocworld is signposted from the N2 between Umkomaas and Scottburgh. It is open from 8.30 a.m. to 4.30 p.m. Feeding takes place at 11 a.m. and 3 p.m. For further information, you should contact Crocworld, Old South Coast Road, Scottburgh 4181, telephone (0323) 2-1103, or fax 2-1423/2-1894.

Durban Botanical Gardens

Durban's 14,5 ha Botanical Gardens, established in 1849 on the eastern slope of the Berea Ridge as a site for growing experimental tropical crops, is a proud example of 19th-century enterprise and enthusiasm.

The gardens are world famous for the original specimens of *Encephalartos woodii*, a cycad that is still acknowledged as probably the rarest plant in the world, as well as for its comprehensive collection of other southern African cycad species.

The orchid house is named after Ernest Thorp, who built it up to its position of world fame as the first 'naturalistic' display house. It is at its best during the spring months and is open daily from 9.30 a.m. to 5 p.m.

The car park is in Sydenham Road, and the gardens are easily accessible from the centre of town (a Mynah bus leaves from the Pine Street). The charity tea garden offers teas and light refreshments from 9.30 a.m. to 4.15 p.m. There is also an information centre.

The Durban Botanical Gardens are open daily from 7.30 a.m. to 5.15 p.m. (16 April – 15 September) and from 7.30 a.m. to 5.45 p.m. (16 September – 15 April). Guided tours are offered every month and must be booked in advance – telephone (031) 21-1303, or fax 21-7382. There is also a herb garden and a garden for the blind.

The Botanical Research Unit, incorporating the Natal Herbarium, is at the corner of St Thomas Road and Botanic Gardens Road. The major aims of the unit are the provision of an information service regarding identification of the indigenous flora of KwaZulu-Natal, and continuing research into the flora of South Africa, with the aim of compiling an authoritative study of its findings.

The Natal Herbarium contains an impressive collection of more than 100 000 specimens of dried, pressed and catalogued plants – most of which originate in KwaZulu-Natal.

Empisini Nature Reserve

Empisini (place of the hyena) was initiated in 1973 by the Umkomaas Centre of the Wildlife

Left: A colourful example of the rich and diverse flora for which the Durban Botanical Gardens have become world renowned. **Above:** A family of dwarf mongoose reclines on a perch in the warm sun. These gregarious little animals live in colonies that may number up to 30 members. The dwarf mongoose includes snakes in its diet, the snake being attacked and killed in a communal effort.

Society, and comprises a 120 ha reserve of pristine coastal forest and old cane fields that are being converted into grasslands. Alongside the reserve's entrance is an expanse of marshland, while its grassy southern slopes are dotted with acacia, cheesewood, pigeonwood and red beech trees. Riverine forest occurs along the stream and at the reserve's pretty waterfall.

Four short trails provide an opportunity to see some of the 160 recorded bird species, while animals likely to be seen include monkey, mongoose, bushbuck, blue duiker, bushpig, otter and several bat species. The longer (14 km) Lighthouse Trail leads from Scottburgh to Empisini. Horse riding on the beach can be arranged, as can diving on the Aliwal Shoal.

Rustic accommodation is available in two overnight cabins, each sleeping four, with an ablution block (no hot water). A tree house sleeps up to 20 people, with its own shower and toilet, and 'downstairs' braai area. There are also rustic toilet facilities, a picnic area and a resource centre.

To reach Empisini, travel south from Durban on the N2 and take the Umkomaas/Widenham turn-off. Turn left at the stop sign, continue down a steep hill, then turn left at the Empisini sign. Follow the track to the picnic and parking area. For further details and to reserve accommodation, you should contact the Wildlife Society, P O Box 201, Umkomaas 4170, telephone (0323) 3-1321/3-0093, or fax 3-8135.

Fitzsimons Snake Park

Frederick Fitzsimons, who wrote the classic *Snakes of South Africa* in 1938, was the mastermind behind the Port Elizabeth Snake Park. His son Vivian wrote the modern successor to the book, called *Snakes of Southern Africa* (1962), while a second son, Desmond, established the Fitzsimons Snake Park in 1939.

More than 300 indigenous and exotic reptile species are represented here, and there are five snake demonstrations every day. At weekends, visitors may watch the snakes being fed after each show – the crocodiles are fed at 2 p.m. daily in summer. Lectures about snakes and their habits are given in English, Afrikaans and Zulu. There is also a curio shop.

The park is on the No 1 Marine Parade bus route, diagonally opposite the Holiday Inn Garden Court. It is open from 9 a.m. to 4.30 p.m. on weekdays, 9 a.m. to 5 p.m. at weekends and on public holidays. For more information, contact Fitzsimons Snake Park, P O Box 10457, Marine Parade 4056, telephone (031) 37-6456, or fax 37-3125.

Harold Johnson Nature Reserve

The Tugela, or Thukela, River (something that startles) drops from the Mont-aux-Sources area of the Drakensberg as a 2 000 m waterfall (the highest in South Africa) and snakes its way down through the Midlands, reaching the sea 24 km north of Stanger. On a grassy hill overlooking the estuary and the Indian Ocean is the Harold Johnson Nature Reserve.

This 104 ha reserve of coastal forest and thorny bushveld is one of a chain that protects some of KwaZulu-Natal's unique floral habitats. Beautiful tree orchids proliferate, and bushpig, bushbuck and blue, red and grey duiker are indigenous to the area. The reserve is also known for its butterflies (some 115 species). Among the interesting self-guided trails are the 7 km Bushbuck Trail, and the 2 km Remedies and Rituals Trail, which passes plants and trees prized for their medicinal properties. Labels describe the uses of the plants. The reserve boasts two historical monuments that date from the Anglo-Zulu War, fought in 1879.

Limited camping facilities are available (there are ablution blocks with toilets and hot and cold showers), and there is a picnic and braai area. For campsite reservations and for information, write to The Officer-in-Charge, Harold Johnson Nature Reserve, P O Box 148, Darnall 4480, telephone (032) 486-1574.

The reserve is open from sunrise to sunset, throughout the year. To reach it, take the turn-off some 5 km south of the John Ross Bridge over the Tugela River.

Hawaan Forest Reserve

On the south bank of the Umhlanga River, this 118 ha forest contains a variety of rare tree species, some interesting forest birds and a modest population of small mammals, including duiker, bushbuck and mongoose. Next to the forest is the Umhlanga River floodplain, a protected wetland of 77 hectares.

The reserve is privately owned and not open to casual visitors, but guided trails are available on request. Hawaan lies 1 km north of Umhlanga Rocks on the M4. To arrange a visit, write to the Umhlanga Centre of the Wildlife Society, P O Box 2985, Durban 4000, telephone (031) 561-1101, or 52-6218 after hours. The fax number is 561-1417.

Hazelmere Resources Reserve

The Natal Parks Board has managed to utilise this 304 ha area to cater for almost everyone's taste in watersports. And it's possible to find a quiet corner of the dam to sail, swim or fish for the various freshwater species that have been introduced, such as bass, tilapia and scalies. Fishing permits may be obtained from the office. There are 22 campsites (16 of which

KWAZULU-NATAL: SOUTH COAST

Far left: A view of the scenically spectacular gorge forming part of the Krantzkloof Nature Reserve, near Durban. **Left:** The cycad *Encephalartos ferox*, photographed in the Durban Botanical Gardens. The seed cones of these trees may weigh as much as 34 kilograms. The kernels in most species of Encephalartos (and sometimes the fleshy outer parts) contain a substance that is poisonous to humans.

have electrical plug points). A 1,7 km forest trail has been laid out, and visitors should report at the office before setting out.

To reach Hazelmere Dam, turn left from the N2, 14 km north of Durban, towards Mount Edgecombe/Umhlanga. Follow this road to the Hazelmere Dam signpost, on your left after passing under a large, arched bridge. The dam is 10 km from here.

Enquiries should be addressed to The Officer-in-Charge, Hazelmere Resources Reserve, P O Box 1013, Verulam 4340, or telephone (0322) 33-2315.

Ilanda Wilds Nature Reserve

Ilanda is a lovely forested nature reserve in Amanzimtoti, situated on the banks of the Manzimtoti River on the corner of Riverside and Old Main roads.

Three self-guided trails (Loerie, Mpiti and Mongoose) have been marked out through the 18 ha preserved river-bank area. They pass through successive riverine forest and thornveld, skirting steep cliffs echoing with the calls of many bird species.

Further information about Ilanda Wilds can be obtained from Amanzimtoti Publicity Association, 95 Beach Road, Amanzimtoti 4125, telephone (031) 903-7498, or fax 903-7493.

Inanda Resources Reserve

The chief attraction at Inanda reserve is watersports, including powerboating, angling, sailing and canoeing. Close to Durban and including the entire 30 km long Inanda Dam and its shoreline, only that portion of the reserve known as Mahlabatini Park is currently open to the public.

Among the many fish species in the dam are bass, tilapia, barbel, carp and scaly (*Barbus natalensis*). Angling permits are obtainable at the gate. Periodic sightings of crocodile have been reported, and swimming is prohibited. Wildlife ashore includes several species of small antelope and zebra, and other, smaller mammals, as well as a rich variety of waterfowl, all of which may be seen from the 2 km Tamboti Trail. The reserve is open to day visitors only, between 8 a.m. and 4 p.m. daily.

To reach Inanda, take the Inanda/Hillcrest road and, about 4 km from Hillcrest, turn left onto the M302 (signposted 'Inanda 6') and follow this road to the gates. For more information, telephone (031) 42-8375.

Kenneth Stainbank Nature Reserve

Situated at a place once known as Ndabenkulu, the Kenneth Stainbank Reserve was a gift to KwaZulu-Natal from a member of a long-established local family. The 214 ha sanctuary is sited along the gorge of the Little Mhlatuzana River, 9,5 km from Durban city centre, in Yellowwood Park (off Coedmore Road).

A unique feature of the Kenneth Stainbank is the Special Trail, designed to let handicapped people experience the joys of a nature reserve. Included on the trail (for which a booklet is available) is a herb garden where you can enjoy a variety of aromas, and a 'touch box' filled with a carpet of leaves and plants.

The reserve contains Durban's largest remaining coastal forest and is the only sanctuary in the city area with a viable population of the threatened red duiker. Blue duiker and bushbuck are also to be seen, and species of larger animals such as impala and zebra have been introduced.

Trees and shrubs include Outeniqua yellowwood, flatcrown tree and the wild date palm (*Phoenix reclinata*). Birds recorded include purple-crested lourie, hadeda, sacred ibis, fish eagle, African jacana, spotted eagle-owl, giant kingfisher and cardinal woodpecker – 160 species in all. There are picnic sites, well-marked nature trails and a dam.

The reserve is the headquarters of the Wilderness Leadership School, whose address is P O Box 53058, Yellowwood Park 4011, telephone/fax (031) 469-2807. The school runs conservation-education courses for anyone over the age of 15 years. These include field trips to Pilanesberg National Park in North-West Province, the Hluhluwe Umfolozi Park and the Lake St Lucia region of KwaZulu-Natal.

The gates are opened at 6 a.m. and closed at 6 p.m. To get there, follow the N2 South and take the Edwin Swales off-ramp. Turn left at the Cato Manor/Bellair intersection. Take the left fork into Cliffview Road and turn left onto Sarnia Road. At the second set of traffic lights, turn right into Coedmore Avenue.

Krantzkloof Nature Reserve

Six kilometres of forest gorge along the eMolweni (greetings) River, and the two-drop (90 m high) Kloof Falls, comprise the exceptionally pretty 535 ha Krantzkloof Nature Reserve, 26 km from Durban. To get there, turn off the N3 at Kloof and follow the Kloof Falls road, overlooking the Indian Ocean.

Visitors may eat sandwiches above the Kloof Falls, watch a film in the interpretive centre, visit the education centre, pause at two view-sites offering dramatic views of the gorge, gaze at a high-soaring crowned eagle on the cliffs, or choose to meander along one of the several nature trails through the dense 'jungle'. There you may see water leguan, grey duiker, bushbuck, otter, vervet monkey, baboon, bushpig and banded mongoose. There are also rare KwaZulu-Natal trees, cycads and more than 200 species of bird. The reserve is open between sunrise and sunset throughout the year, for day visitors only.

Further information may be obtained from The Officer-in-Charge, Krantzkloof Nature Reserve, P O Box 288, Kloof, or telephone (031) 764-3515, or fax 25-1547.

Mariannwood Nature Reserve

Some 20 ha of grassland, coastal forest and bush harbour indigenous antelope and other small mammals, as well as a variety of birds. There is a bird enclosure, and a display centre

KWAZULU-NATAL: SOUTH COAST

Left: A yellow-billed hornbill eyes a potential meal. In the dry season it likes to eat ants and termites. Its fare also includes centipedes and scorpions. **Above:** A Mauritian sambar deer (stag) and its young, photographed in a small wildlife sanctuary that forms part of Durban's Mitchell Park Aviary.

exhibits a varied selection of material of educational and conservation interest.

To reach the reserve, travel south from Pinetown on Richmond Road, or the M1, and turn left into Mariannhill Park. Turn left again into Holzner Road, right into James Herbert Road and continue past Brown's School to the entrance.

Mariannwood Nature Reserve – telephone (031) 72-3443, fax 709-1074 – is open daily from 7 a.m. to 5 p.m. Facilities include a picnic- and braai-site and toilets.

Mdwala Nature Reserve

This small (7 ha) reserve offers a close look at indigenous trees and a large bird population. It includes the source of the Mhlatuzana River, so the area is generally swampy.

In the north of the reserve, beside a sparkling stream, is a picnic site and the start of a short trail along the river, passing a weir, a waterfall and the large granite knuckles, or 'mdwala', from which the reserve takes its traditional Zulu name.

About 30 km from Durban on the N3, take the Assegay turn-off and, after a further 5 km, turn left at the junction with Old Main Road. Drive through Botha's Hill to Heidi's Farm Stall (a local landmark) and turn left into Clement Stott Road. After 1 km, just before you reach a stream, you will see the picnic spot on the left.

The Mdwala Nature Reserve is unfenced and may be visited at any time. For further details, contact the Assagay Local Authority, P O Box 196, Hillcrest 3650, telephone/fax (031) 75-2997 (weekday mornings only).

Mitchell Park Aviary

Home to a colourful population of indigenous and exotic birds and other creatures, the aviary is situated in one of Durban's oldest parks, and adjoins the Robert Jameson Rose Park in Morningside.

Among the animals here are parrot, crocodile, lemur, monkey and giant Seychelles tortoise that are always a delight for children.

To reach the aviary, which is open between 8 a.m. and 5 p.m., take a Berea Beach bus (number 22 or 22A) or a Mynah bus from Musgrave Road or the Pine Street terminus. To drive there, take the western freeway out of town, bear left at Berea, and turn right into Musgrave Road (follow this road to Mitchell Park). For further details, telephone the aviary at (031) 700-5902, or fax 23-7772.

Mpenjati Nature Reserve

This small (66 ha) resort at Mpenjati River Mouth, near Port Edward, comprises interlinking wetlands, grasslands and dune forests, and caters essentially for the day visitor.

Picnic sites and ablution facilities have been laid out, and there is a children's playground on the shady north bank. Plans are afoot to build a 90-bed camp.

Tern and spotted thrush are found along the tranquil lagoon mouth where recreational activities include fishing and windsurfing.

The 1,2 km Ipithi Trail on the south bank introduces visitors to *ipithi* (blue duiker), grey duiker and bushbuck, while the slightly longer Yengele Trail winds through one of the largest dune forests found along this stretch of coast.

Enquiries should be addressed to The Officer-in-Charge, P O Box 388, Port Edward 4295, telephone/fax (03931) 3-0447.

Natal Sharks Board

The headquarters of the Natal Sharks Board is situated on a slope at Umhlanga. Overlooking the bright waters of the Indian Ocean, the Board's main aim is to educate the public as well as to prevent attacks by sharks. Audiovisual presentations are held (including a popular shark dissection), while numerous displays highlight shark biology, their sensitivity to electrical impulses and their phenomenal sense of smell. A curio shop sells a variety of shark-related gifts and souvenirs. Shows and dissections are held on Tuesdays, Wednesdays and Thursdays, and on the first Sunday of every month. For further information, contact Natal Sharks Board, Private Bag 2, Umhlanga 4320, telephone (031) 561-1017, or fax 561-3691.

New Germany Nature Reserve

The New Germany Nature Reserve is a 40 ha area of forests, bush and coastal grassland situated in the hills near Pinetown. Opened in 1986, it forms part of the early 'commonage' set aside in 1893.

Today the reserve is known for its vivid spring flowers, its prolific birdlife and its trees. Two trails, which may be walked in sequence or separately, traverse New Germany. Imbali Trail takes some 60 to 90 minutes, passing two dams and offering sightings of most of the animals, including vervet monkey, mongoose, genet, zebra, bushbuck and impala. Ngqobeni Trail (for the more energetic) penetrates an impressive stand of proteas and bird-filled coastal forest. A walk-in aviary, housing some 70 bird species, may also be explored along a 30-minute trail. Brochures are available from the interpretation centre. The reserve is open to the public from Wednesday to Sunday every week, and picnic- and braai-sites are available.

For further information, write to the Borough of New Germany, P O Box 2, New Germany 3620, or contact the ranger by telephoning (031) 705-4360.

North Park Nature Reserve

This 52 ha reserve in the Durban suburb of Northdene is an attractive refuge. It lies 20 km from the city centre, at the end of Anderson Road, off Sarnia Road, and consists of a slice of coastal lowland forest as yet unclaimed by sugar cane or concrete. The area is rich in birdlife, and shelters a large population of blue duiker. Paths have been laid out, and picnic sites and braai facilities are available. It is open during daylight hours throughout the year. For further information, contact Natal Parks Board, P O Box 662, Pietermaritzburg 3200, telephone (0331) 47-1961, fax 47-3137.

Oribi Gorge Nature Reserve

From the Tugela north of Durban down to Port Edward, 250 km to the south, the coast is sliced through by 20 major watercourses and many lesser streams that have cut rugged gorges through cliff and crag in their rush to the sea. The most spectacular of these is Oribi Gorge, 24 km long, 5 km wide and 400 m deep.

The turn-off to the Oribi Gorge Hotel, 12 km from Port Shepstone, is the start of a 29 km scenic drive that offers dramatic views of the converging Mzimkulu and Mzimkulwana gorges. Visitors may try a variety of pleasant walks, climbs and self-guided trails, but must first inform the camp manager. Mziki Walk (9 km) climbs the escarpment, affording wonderful views over the valley; Hoopoe Falls Walk (7 km) follows the banks of the Mzimkulwana River to a waterfall; and Nkonka Walk (5 km) winds from the picnic site to a weir. The forests and sandstone cliffs hide bushbuck, vervet and samango monkey, duiker, common reedbuck, leopard, water leguan and innumerable birds. The 1 837 ha reserve is also known for its striking rock formations.

Palmiet Nature Reserve

This 90 ha municipal nature reserve is situated in the rugged Palmiet River valley. Its wooded cliffs, riverine forest and open grassland feature more than 140 indigenous trees and about 100 bird species. The name Palmiet refers to the river plant *Prionium serratum*, which, because of human disturbance, is now rare in this valley. Mammal life is not well represented, but visitors are occasionally rewarded with glimpses of vervet monkey, duiker and water mongoose.

Some 7 km of trails crisscross the reserve, and a three-hour nature trail is conducted on the first Sunday of the month, starting at 7.30 a.m. In winter, the popular Sunset Trails include a braai at the Cascade Indaba site on the Palmiet River, and a return walk in the dark.

Palmiet reserve is open daily between sunrise and sunset. To reach it, take the N3 to the Westville interchange. Follow St James Avenue for 1 km, turn right into Jan Hofmeyr Road, and turn left into Old New Germany Road. The reserve, which is managed by the environmental department of the Borough of Westville, is signposted at the end of this road.

Paradise Valley Nature Reserve

A coastal evergreen valley, this reserve offers forest walks, abundant birdlife and a waterfall on the Mbilo River. Wildlife includes small buck, vervet monkey and dassie.

Of historical interest is an old waterworks that used to supply Durban. There is also an information centre and a hall. The reserve is open from 7.30 a.m. to 5 p.m. throughout the year. One of Durban's many pleasant picnic spots, the 28 ha Paradise Valley reserve is at the New Germany turn-off, 18 km from the city on the N3 highway.

Pigeon Valley Park

A small reserve next to the Durban campus of Natal University, Pigeon Valley preserves one of the last local stretches of indigenous coastal forest (Stella bush vegetation). Of 75 species of tree here, the most valuable are the Natal elm (*Celtis mildbraedii*) and the fluted milkwood (*Chrysophyllum viridifolium*). Wildlife includes vervet monkey, slender mongoose and a vast and colourful array of birds.

There are picnic sites. The reserve is open on weekdays only from 7.30 a.m. to 4 p.m. To get there from Durban, take the western freeway and then turn left along South Ridge Road for about 2,5 kilometres.

Sea World, Durban

The aquarium and dolphinarium, situated at the point where West Street meets the 'Golden Mile' of the beachfront, offers close encounters with thousands of intriguing and exquisite creatures. Twice a day (11 a.m. and 3.30 p.m.) a scuba-diver handfeeds the fish, turtles and stingrays in the 800 000 litre reef tank. The shark tank houses one of the world's finest displays of large sharks and, in the dolphinarium, a spectacular dolphin, seal and penguin show is presented several times a day. Behind the scenes, stranded and injured mammals are treated and rehabilitated.

Entrance fees pay for research into sharks, angling fish, prawns, crayfish, mussels and other vital resources. Open daily from 9 a.m. to 9 p.m. (shark-feeding on Tuesdays, Thursdays and Sundays at 12.30 p.m.), Sea World may be contacted at P O Box 10712, Marine Parade 4056, telephone (031) 37-3536, fax 37-2132.

Shongweni Resources Reserve

Midway between Durban and Pietermaritzburg, Shongweni's 1 700 ha spread across the slopes of Mkangoma Hill, overlooking the Mlazi wetland and Ntshongweni cliffs. This is the meeting place of several habitats, including

---

ORIBI GORGE AT A GLANCE

When to go Oribi is worth a visit all year round, and is open between 5 a.m. and 7 p.m. from October to March, and 6 a.m. to 6 p.m. between April and September. To take up reserved accommodation, you should arrive before 4.30 p.m.

Reservations Contact Natal Parks Board, P O Box 1750, Pietermaritzburg 3200, telephone (0331) 47-1981, or fax 47-1980.

Getting there Follow the route marked 'Nature Reserve'. It is 21 km along the Harding road (N2) from Port Shepstone, which is 128 km south of Durban.

Accommodation The Natal Parks Board hutted camp consists of six three-bed, serviced huts, a six-bed cottage, and a kitchen and ablution block. Camping facilities are also available.

Eating and drinking Bring your own food and drink to the hutted camp; park attendants will prepare it for you. There is a braai site at the camp for those who wish to cook their own food and a picnic site with ablution and braai facilities has been established in the gorge.

Getting around You can drive right down into the Oribi Gorge and up again – a distance of some 8 km from the huts. The 29 km circular drive through and around the gorge is worthwhile. Nature walks have been mapped out, and you can stop along the way for numerous excellent views of the Oribi Heads, Horseshoe Bend and the Overhanging Rock.

Wildlife There are forest creatures such as bushbuck, blue duiker and grey duiker (occasionally leopard). The nearly 200 species of bird include seven eagle and five kingfisher species.

Special precautions There is bilharzia in the river and visitors picnicking on the river bank are advised not to swim or paddle in the water. Fire in a forest gorge like Oribi is devastating; be careful with cigarettes.

valley bushveld, grassland and cliffs, so the area attracts a wide range of animal life. It is especially rich in birds, with more than 200 species – and a mere 30 km from Durban.

Accommodation is in a luxury eight-bed bush camp, consisting of four *en suite* units, with a resident cook – visitors supply their own food. A game guard is available for walks or drives. Shongweni is open to day visitors from 6 a.m. to 6 p.m., and attractions include picnic sites, a nature trail and horse rides.

For more information, contact Shongweni Resources Reserve, P O Box 2444, Hillcrest 3650 or telephone (031) 769-1203.

Silverglen Nature Reserve
Two trails wind through this 220 ha reserve. One crosses a stream and cuts through riverine bush dotted with tree fuchsia and silver oak; the other runs through marsh and ascends to grassy heights. The plantlife attracts some 145 species of bird and many small mammals.

A medicinal plant nursery sells plants five days a week, between 7.30 a.m. and 3 p.m. To reach Silverglen, turn west from the N2 on the Chatsworth/Higginson Highway. Turn right onto Higginson Highway and, after some 2 km, turn left into Havenside Drive. Take the left turn into Klaarwater Road and then left again into Lakeview Drive, which leads to the gates. The reserve is open at all times.

Skyline Nature Reserve
The emphasis here is on botanical species (although blue and grey duiker and bushbuck do occur), and many of the almost 800 tree species are labelled. There are about 76 indigenous coastal species, 300 other indigenous and 400 exotic species. A series of short trails provides easy access to the trees.

Skyline is open daily between sunrise and sunset. To reach it, travel south from Port Shepstone on the old main road to Uvongo. When you reach the traffic light in Uvongo, turn right and then left into Pioneer Drive. Cross over the new highway and turn right onto the gravel road parallel to the highway. The reserve is signposted. For information, contact Natal Parks Board, P O Box 662, Pietermaritzburg 3200, telephone (0331) 47-1961, fax 47-3137.

Springside Nature Reserve
A variety of small mammals (including vervet monkey and duiker) and more than 100 bird species may be seen in this 21 ha reserve, owned by the Hillcrest Western Substructure. The vegetation is a blend of coastal bush, temperate forest and an important wetland area.

Springside has a resource centre, toilet, braai facilities and picnic sites, and visitors may enter at any time. To reach the reserve, drive west along the N3 from Durban towards Hillcrest. At the Hillcrest turn-off, take the road to Winston Park, then turn right at the first traffic light. Follow the signs to Springside.

T C Robertson Nature Reserve
Among the newest of KwaZulu-Natal's nature reserves, the 60 ha T C Robertson reserve is situated on the Mpambanyoni River, just a short walk from the beach. A 10 km trail system offers opportunities to view some 260 bird species, as well as 15 species of mammal, including black-backed jackal, mongoose and large-spotted genet, bushbuck and duiker. Over 100 tree species have been identified.

A midden, dating from AD 1000, shows that people who occupied the area were ironworkers who also made and used pottery, practised agriculture and may have herded cattle.

The reserve is situated 50 km south of Durban on the Old Post Office Road, which leads off the N2 in Scottburgh. For more information, contact The Officer-in-Charge, T C Robertson Nature Reserve, P O Box 91, Scottburgh 4180, telephone (0323) 8-3213.

Trafalgar Marine Reserve
The 51 km of banana-fringed beach stretching along the lower South Coast offers a string of 19 holiday resorts. Trafalgar, from the southern boundary of Mpenjati Nature Reserve (*see separate entry*), to the south side of Centre Rocks at Marina Beach and stretching 500 m out to sea, is a marine reserve. Swimming and angling are permitted, but bait-collecting is prohibited and the shellfish may not be touched. Licences are not required.

For further information, contact Natal Parks Board, P O Box 662, Pietermaritzburg 3200, telephone (0331) 47-1961, or fax 47-3137.

Treasure Beach Project
This Wildlife Society project lies at the southern end of Durban's Bluff, amid 16 ha of protected coastal grassland and rocky shore. Almost surrounded by urban development, the project nevertheless has access to a rocky shore, a coastal dune forest, a small wetland and the Beachwood mangrove swamps. Rock pools teem with life, and dune forest forms a cloak that shelters birds and small mammals.

Although industry and housing have made severe inroads on natural vegetation elsewhere along the coast, Treasure Beach is unspoilt. It is part of a proposed reserve, to be called Southern Coastal Park, which will include the Happy Valley Bird Sanctuary and Reunion Rocks area; a thin strip of coastal forest will connect it to the mangroves at Isipingo Estuary. This new conservation area will adjoin the Bluff Nature Reserve.

Visitors may wander through the grassland (at its best in August and September), but visits to the centre must be arranged in advance. Environmental education is offered, and conducted tours may be arranged. Education groups may spend a night in dormitory facilities that can accommodate a total of 45 people.

Details may be obtained from the Treasure Beach Project, 835 Marine Drive, Bluff 4052, telephone (031) 47-8507/8, or fax 47-8288.

Umbogavango Nature Reserve
Located some 15 km south of Durban, within the bounds of the AECI factory site at Umbogintwini, is the 15 ha Umbogavango Nature Reserve. The sanctuary is based on two stormwater holding dams which act as a trap for contaminated stormwater and prevent it from flowing into the Amanzimtoti River.

Umbogavango (light-heartedly nicknamed for its supposed similarity to the Okavango Swamps of Botswana) consists largely of wetlands and indigenous coastal bush, and was recognised in 1991 by the Natal Parks Board as a significant site.

To date, over 190 bird species and more than 100 tree types have been identified.

Umgeni River Bird Park
Cliffs 30 m high form a spectacular backdrop to this 4 ha site, once a disused quarry. The park boasts 400 species of bird in four walk-through aviaries and individual aviaries, amid waterfalls, tropical plants and numerous ponds.

Guided tours are offered, and visitors may watch the interesting process of training birds,

Above: Camel Rock makes a fine vantage point over the Oribi Gorge Nature Reserve, west of Port Shepstone. **Right:** Brightly coloured anemones and coralline form a lustrous underwater garden on the lower South Coast of KwaZulu-Natal. Flora such as this is to be seen in the marine reserve at Trafalgar.

including vulture and fish eagle, to respond to whistled signals while in free flight. The park is also a breeding centre, especially for macaws, cranes and flamingoes. Refreshments are served and an educational video and a self-guided tour pamphlet are available.

The park, on Riverside Road in Durban North, is open daily from 9 a.m. to 5 p.m. For more information contact Umgeni River Bird Park, P O Box 35205, Northway, Durban 4065, telephone (031) 579-4600, or fax 579-4574.

Umhlanga Lagoon Nature Reserve

Umhlanga Lagoon is one of KwaZulu-Natal's estuaries that has escaped 'development', and an attractive 26 ha nature reserve embraces the lagoon area to the east of the national road (N2) about 17 km north of Durban.

An important shell midden lies within this area and can be seen along a 1,5 km walk to the lagoon and river mouth. The Umhlanga Lagoon Nature Trail, which takes about 90 minutes, starts at the Breakers Hotel and leads across a footbridge and through coastal forest containing white stinkwood and many other indigenous trees. Blue and grey duiker, vervet monkey and water mongoose may be seen along the trail, as well as various weavers, bulbul and fish eagle. The reserve is open from sunrise to sunset.

One of the best places along the KwaZulu-Natal coast for birdwatching is the Umhlanga Ponds – the Municipal Sewage Disposal Works. Pink pelican, darter, hamerkop and sacred ibis may be seen, as well as leguan and water mongoose. The ponds are reached along Herrwood Drive in Umhlanga. Contact the Umhlanga Centre of the Wildlife Society for further details; telephone (031) 561-1101.

Umtamvuna Nature Reserve

There is a nesting colony of up to 75 Cape vulture in the precipices of this reserve on the KwaZulu-Natal/Eastern Cape border, a gaunt habitat for the large carrion birds whose droppings streak the cliffs.

This 3 257 ha Natal Parks Board reserve is home to numerous small mammal species, leopard and 250 species of bird. It also offers several walking trails in a kaleidoscope of wild flowers, ferns and lichens. To reach the reserve, turn inland at the Port Edward intersection and follow the signs to one of the entrances at the Old Pont or Beacon Hill. From 1 April to 31 August, the gates open at 7 a.m. and close at 5 p.m. During the rest of the year, they open at 6 a.m. and close at 6 p.m.

Uvongo Bird Park

Lying 1 km north of Margate off the R620 is the Uvongo Bird Park with its giant aviary containing macaws, toucans, king hornbills, cardinals, jays and many other birds. A farmyard – with a resident bushpig – is a delight for children, and other facilities include a shady braai area, a playground, a tea garden and toilets.

The park is open daily from 9 a.m. to 5 p.m. For further information, contact Margate Today, P O Box 1253, Margate 4275, telephone (03931) 2-2322, or fax 2-1886, due to change to telephone (039) 377-6886, or fax 377-7322.

Uvongo River Nature Reserve

KwaZulu-Natal rivers tend to be muddy, but the Uvongo runs through cleansing sandstone, fresh and pure, and actually reaches the ocean as a 23 m high waterfall that plunges straight into a beachside lagoon.

Jagged cliffs flank part of the 1 km section of the river that forms this community-sponsored reserve, 12 km south of Port Shepstone. Birdsong accompanies visitors along the cool, river bank forest track, and wild flowers such as the fire lily (*Cyrtanthus* species) and September bells (*Rothmannia globosa*) delight the eye. There are also pleasant picnic sites.

The two entrances are on Edward Avenue and on Marine Drive. The reserve is open from sunrise to sunset. For further information, contact Margate Today, P O Box 1253, Margate 4275, telephone (03931) 2-2322, or fax 2-1886, due to change to telephone (039) 377-6886, or fax 377-7322.

Vernon Crookes Nature Reserve

The plentiful game in this 2 189 ha reserve of upland grassland and forest includes blue wildebeest, eland, nyala, impala, bushbuck, zebra, four species of mongoose, porcupine and black-backed jackal.

The birdlife – with some 310 species – is a delight. And in September and October, the reserve's blaze of wild flowers almost rivals the displays in Namaqualand.

The Nyengelezi rustic camp sleeps up to 40 people in a forest setting. There are several drives and picnic sites, and conducted walking tours may be arranged (well in advance) with The Officer-in-Charge, Vernon Crookes Nature Reserve, P O Box 10624, Umzinto Station 4201, telephone (0323) 4-2222 between 8 a.m. and 4.30 p.m. The reserve, which is open from sunrise to sunset, lies off the Ixopo road. Turn off 3 km past Umzinto, and follow the signs.

Virginia Bush Nature Reserve

Some 38 ha of coastal forest and grassland, inhabited by vast numbers of birds, attracts enthusiasts from afar. Apart from two circular trails, there are no facilities, although visitors are allowed to picnic. To get to Virginia Bush, leave Durban on the M4 and take Exit 5 to Virginia Airport. At the end of the off-ramp, turn left and travel for some 200 m before turning left into Margaret Maytom Avenue. Turn right at the next traffic circle into Kensington Drive. Virginia Bush is on the left.

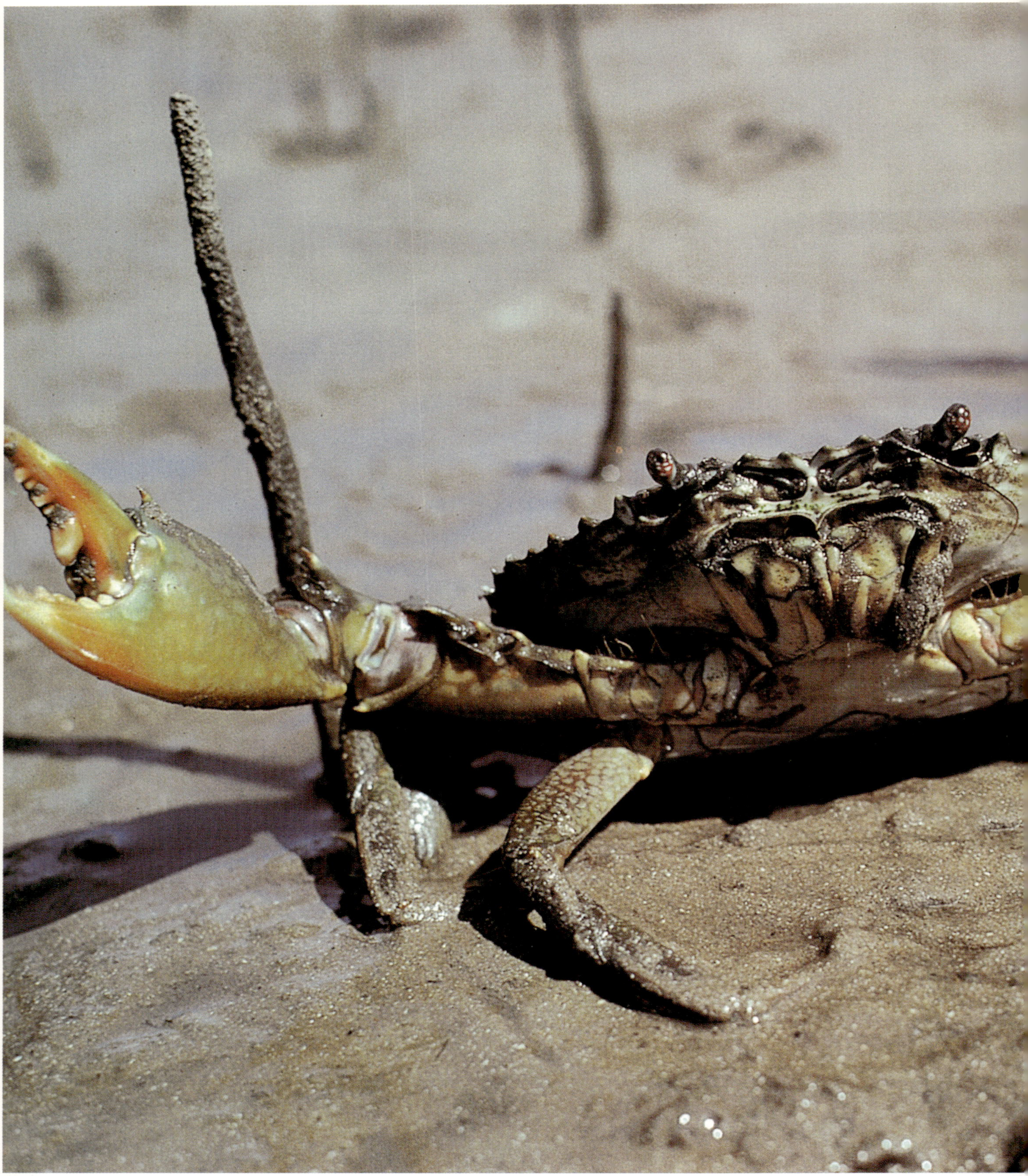

EASTERN CAPE

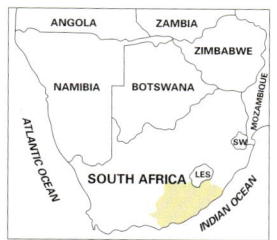

A land of rolling hills, summer thunderstorms on the mountains, far-reaching sweeps of grassland, rocky coves and bleached sea sand – the Eastern Cape encompasses all this and more. Like many parts of southern Africa, it is a place of contrasts: the once-threatened mountain zebra grazes among stunted Karoo shrubs; samango monkeys leap and chatter in the extensive forests; seabirds wheel over the 250 km stretch of high cliffs, long beaches and pounding seas of the Wild Coast.

There is much for the visitor here in the land of the Xhosa people. In the Auckland Nature Reserve, part of the Hogsback Forest, you may spot a crowned eagle or jackal buzzard. You can learn about reptiles at the Port Elizabeth Snake Park, and marvel at the antics of dolphins in the city's famous oceanarium. A visit to the Addo Elephant National Park will give you a glimpse of black rhinoceros, red hartebeest, eland and, of course, the magnificent elephant.

The Eastern Cape has scores of game parks, nature reserves and modest but well-run sanctuaries spread over a wide area. For those who prefer to explore with backpacks, a number of hiking trails lead through spectacularly beautiful countryside (hikers are advised to be security-conscious). For those seeking creature comforts on safari, there is a choice of accommodation in huts, bungalows and chalets. Variety is the essence of this region – the Eastern Cape has something of everything.

A giant mud crab (Scylla serrata) waves its nippers, adopting a threatening posture among the aerial roots of a mangrove on the Eastern Cape's rugged and beautiful Wild Coast.

Dramatic cliffs and a thunder of surf

Wedged between the fortress of the Drakensberg and the pounding waves of the Indian Ocean are the rolling plains of the far Eastern Cape. Previously known as the Transkei, this region is traversed by the N2 highway, which runs roughly parallel to the coast at a distance of 60 km to 100 km from the sea. Most of the conservation areas and scenic attractions are to be found only after venturing down some of the many secondary roads (usually gravel and mostly ill-maintained) which link the N2 to the beautiful Wild Coast.

Nature reserves are controlled by the Nature Conservation Directorate of the Department of Economic Affairs, Environment and Tourism, and reservations should be made at least 12 months in advance. Visitors should remember to be security-conscious and to treat the local people with respect.

Dwesa-Cwebe Reserve: Cwebe sector

A coastline of cliffs, rocky points and white-sand bays, fringed with forests of yellowwood, ebony and white stinkwood, typify the Cwebe sector of the Dwesa-Cwebe Reserve, lying between the Mbashe and Suku river mouths. With its sister reserve, Dwesa, Cwebe was established as a forest sanctuary in 1903 although, in fact, the two regions have been protected since as long ago as 1890. Today, the use of its forest produce is being allowed to assist neighbouring communities.

Some 2 150 ha in extent, Cwebe also boasts a lagoon, home to Cape clawless otter and swooped upon by the African fish eagle, and an enchanting waterfall on the Mbanyana River. Mangrove swamps, supporting their own peculiar and fragile ecosystem, add variety to the Mbashe estuary.

Paths crisscross the sanctuary, and visitors may see eland, bushbuck and duiker. Cwebe has no accommodation, but The Haven Hotel offers comfortable accommodation in thatched bungalows with en suite bathrooms, as well as a swimming pool, tennis courts and golf course. Fishing is excellent.

To reach Cwebe, travel south from Umtata on the N2 towards Idutywa. At the Elliotdale signpost, turn east, following the signs for The Haven.

Further information can be obtained from the Directorate of Nature Conservation: Eastern Region, Department of Economic Affairs, Environment and Tourism, Private Bag X5002, Umtata 5100, telephone (0471) 31-2712, or fax 2-4322. To make reservations at The Haven Hotel, write to Private Bag X5028, Umtata 5100, telephone/fax (0474) 62-0247.

Dwesa-Cwebe Reserve: Dwesa sector

This sector of the reserve lies on one of the most beautiful and unspoilt stretches of coastline in Africa, with its rest camp blending so well into the forest that you could pass close by and not see it.

Dwesa, some 3 900 ha in extent, lies to the south of its sister reserve, Cwebe, being separated only by the Mbashe River. The reserve is reached from Idutywa by a 90 km gravel road.

Dwesa offers accommodation in four- and five-bed chalets near the beach. They are equipped with refrigerators and gas stoves, as well as hot and cold water. There are magnificent views from all of the bungalows, some of which are on stilts, with verandahs jutting out to within reach of the forest canopy. The terrain includes beaches, open grassland and indigenous forests of yellowwood, Cape ebony and white stinkwood, all garlanded by creepers. Camping and caravanning facilities are also available. (Take care not to leave your valuables unattended, as theft from parked vehicles, caravans and tents is common.)

Fishing is allowed, both from the beach and the rocks, and aquatic life also flourishes in the many rivulets that rise in the forests and form beautiful estuaries. Spearfishing is prohibited, and you are not permitted to collect bait or

Left: A lonely stretch of surf-pounded beach on the Wild Coast. Clusters of wild banana trees (*Strelitzia nicolai*) can be seen in the background. **Above:** Hole in the Wall, known by the Xhosa as *esiKhaleni* (the place of sound), is one of nature's real wonders.
Right: A tricolour Cape tiger moth (*Dionychopus amasis*). It starts life as a hairy caterpillar, its tufts of brown hair interspersed with stiff black bristles.

EASTERN CAPE: **ACROSS THE KEI**

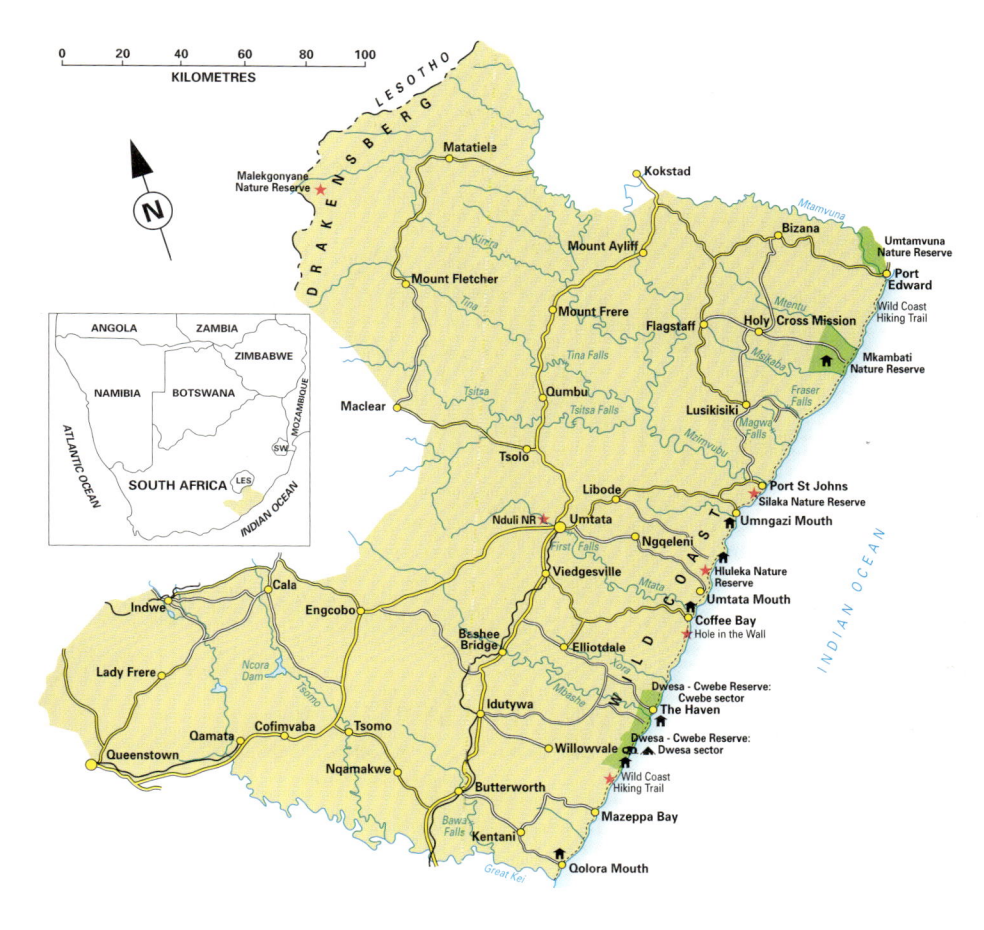

crayfish in the reserve. The shoreline, with its pristine, rugged beauty and windswept golden beaches, is a favourite haunt of collectors of seashells.

There are no roads though the reserve, but numerous paths lead through the forest from the camp. Game may be seen even on the beach, and includes blesbok, eland, buffalo, bushbuck, duiker and warthog, and a small number of crocodile. The Narina trogon and rare mangrove kingfisher are among the many bird species. There is no shop in the reserve, and supplies should be obtained in advance. The reserve is open from sunrise to sunset.

To make a reservation, you should contact the Directorate of Nature Conservation: Eastern Region, Department of Economic Affairs, Environment and Tourism, Private Bag X5002, Umtata 5100, telephone (0471) 31-2712, or fax them on 2-4322.

Hluleka Nature Reserve

Like Dwesa, Hluleka Nature Reserve includes stretches of unspoilt beach in its spread of some 772 hectares. It is 90 km from Umtata, and is reached by taking the tarred road east for some 28 km to Libode. The remainder of the route is along dirt roads. The reserve has 12 comfortable wooden chalets which can accommodate up to six people each. The chalets are fully furnished and equipped, but the nearest shop lies outside the reserve and can supply only bread, milk and a limited range of non-perishable foods. The chalets blend well into the picturesque surroundings and are only about 200 m from the beach.

Firewood is available from the nature conservation officer and cooking fires may be made only in allocated places. Fishing is allowed in the reserve. (This entire section of the Eastern Cape coastline is renowned for its angling, providing enthusiasts with good sport as well as good eating.) Note however that you are not permitted to collect your own bait or crayfish.

Footpaths lead through most parts of this picturesque reserve, and among the animals to be seen are blue wildebeest, eland, impala, red hartebeest, blesbok, bushpig and Burchell's zebra. During spring and summer the air is bright with butterflies, and birdlife is prolific throughout the year, featuring African fish eagle, Cape parrot, osprey, ground hornbill, Knysna lourie, as well as the rarer green coucal and African finfoot.

The reserve is open throughout the year from sunrise to sunset. Day visitors need not book in advance. Further information can be obtained from the Directorate of Nature Conservation: Eastern Region, Department of Economic Affairs, Environment and Tourism, Private Bag X5002, Umtata 5100, telephone (0471) 31-2712, fax 2-4322.

EASTERN CAPE: ACROSS THE KEI

HLULEKA AT A GLANCE

When to go You can visit the reserve throughout the year from 6 a.m. to 6 p.m. Day visitors need not book in advance.

Reservations and information For enquiries and bookings write to the Directorate of Nature Conservation: Eastern Region, Department of Economic Affairs, Environment and Tourism, Private Bag X5002, Umtata 5100, telephone (0471) 31-2712, fax 2-4322.

Getting there Hluleka is located 90 km from Umtata, and is reached by taking the tarred road east for some 28 km to Libode. The remainder of the route is along dirt roads.

Accommodation The reserve has 12 comfortable wooden chalets, lying 200 m from the beach, each of which can accommodate up to six people. The chalets are fully furnished and equipped.

Eating and drinking There are no restaurant facilities. The nearest shop lies outside the reserve and can supply only the most basic necessities. Visitors are advised to take their own provisions.

Getting around Hluleka is a hiker's paradise. Neat paths lead through most of the reserve.

Wildlife Blue wildebeest, eland, impala and zebra can be seen, and the birdlife is plentiful.

Fishing Kob, grunter, elf and various shark species can be caught in these waters.

Left above: The tree hibiscus (*Hibiscus tiliaceus*), which bears these large yellow flowers (deepening to orange as they mature), is found at river mouths along the Eastern Cape coast (and in KwaZulu-Natal).
Left top: Waterfall Bluff on the Wild Coast, where a river tumbles into the Indian Ocean from a high cliff.
Right above: The Natal black snake is usually confined to damp localities in the Eastern Cape. Although its bite can produce unpleasant reactions, fatalities have not been recorded. In his informative and often amusing book, *The Reptiles and Amphibians of Southern Africa*, Dr Walter Rose explains the snake's remarkable flexibility: 'The extreme litheness of a snake is due to the structure of the vertebral column, which consists of a great number, from 150 to 500, of small bones beautifully fitted together on the ball [and] socket principle, so as to give a maximum of flexibility and strength.'

Malekgonyane (Ongeluksnek) Nature Reserve

In the southern Drakensberg, on Lesotho's southern border, lies the 11 750 ha Malekgonyane Nature Reserve (also called Ongeluksnek), a wonder of montane grassland, streams and imposing cliffs. In spring the slopes of this mountain reserve are transformed from their golden brown winter hues into a luxurious carpet of green covered by gladiolus, pelargonium, red-hot poker and the flame-red fire lily.

Birdlife is spectacular and black eagle, jackal buzzard, lanner falcon, Cape vulture, and bearded vulture (or lammergeyer) glide overhead. Wherever bearded vulture are found, look for 'bone-breaking sites' or ossuaries. These vultures fly to a great height and drop the bones, with considerable accuracy, onto the rocks until the bone fragments are small enough to swallow. Unfortunately, as with many raptors, bearded vultures have suffered over the years, as the lack of carcasses inevitably drove them to prey on the remains of domestic animals. Many farmers reacted – thinking the birds were a threat to their livestock – by poisoning the carcasses. This severe recourse destroyed large numbers of Cape and bearded vulture, both of which are now, however, protected.

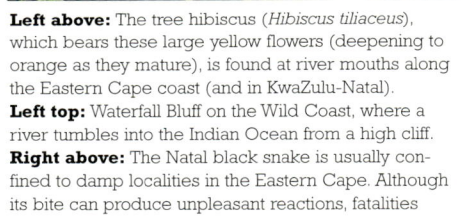

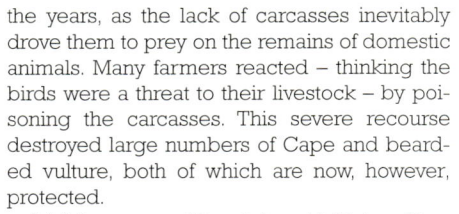

Malekgonyane (Ongeluksnek) Nature Reserve will be opened to the public when developments are completed. A rest camp is planned, which will give access to mountain walks, clear streams, quiet pools and tumbling waterfalls. Grey rhebok, klipspringer and baboon are common. Further information can be obtained from the Directorate of Nature Conservation: Eastern Region, Department of Economic Affairs, Environment and Tourism, Private Bag X5002, Umtata 5100, telephone (0471) 31-2712, or fax 2-4322.

Mkambati Nature Reserve

The highlights of Mkambati reserve are isolated beaches, gurgling waterfalls, wide river mouths and deeply incised, forested ravines. The 6 000 ha reserve's rocky coastline extends 10 km between the Msikaba and Mtentu rivers, including parts of the province's most scenic and secret coast. Its unique swamp forest, open grassland and ravines hide a variety of fascinating life forms, including the Mkambati palm (*Jubaeopsis caffra*) which grows only beside the valleys of these two great rivers.

The narrow, wooded Msikaba River reaches depths of 33 m in places, making it by far the deepest river in South Africa. Its sandy mouth, frequented by the ever-active tern, is ideal for walking, looking for shells or simply being alone and collecting your thoughts. Adventurous visitors may also canoe upstream for two kilometres. Along the way you will be able to see the feathery-leaved Mkambati palms, growing close to the waterline of the shady south bank. In spring, there are also various species of erica, protea, watsonia, gladiolus, ground orchid, and vivid displays of daisies.

The forest canopy and steep-sided cliffs of this beautiful river conceal a number of birds of prey, including the African fish eagle and crowned eagle, and a breeding colony of Cape vulture (*Gyps coprotheres*).

Other animals at Mkambati include gemsbok, red hartebeest, wildebeest, blesbok, eland and zebra. There is a variety of walks, including one along the Mkambati River to the dramatic Horseshoe Falls, where clear, fresh water rolls and tumbles over spectacular rapids before cascading into the sea below.

Open from sunrise to sunset, Mkambati offers accommodation in six- and eight-bed cottages and three-bed rondavels, as well as in a serviced lodge, with five double rooms and a lounge for guests.

To reach the reserve, travel north along the N2 from Umtata to Brooks Nek (about 162 kilometres). Turn east towards Bizana and, after 36 km, turn right at Magusheni onto the R61 leading to Flagstaff. After some 30 km turn left towards the Holy Cross Mission and follow the signs to Mkambati.

Further information can be obtained from the Directorate of Nature Conservation: Eastern Region, Department of Economic Affairs, Environment and Tourism, Private Bag X5002, Umtata 5100, telephone (0471) 31-2712, fax 2-4322; or Keval Travel, P O Box 388, Kokstad 4700, telephone (037) 727-3124, fax 727-3939.

Nduli Nature Reserve

This 180 ha reserve lies a mere 3 km from the centre of Umtata, on its western outskirts.

Nduli is the nucleus for the region's reserve game animals, which are kept here before being distributed to other areas. A circular drive (with a speed limit of 20 km/hour) enables visitors to see most of the animals, which usually include Burchell's zebra, black wildebeest, blue wildebeest, eland, red hartebeest, impala and mountain reedbuck. Birdlife is rich, and this is a nesting area of the crowned crane, which may often be seen 'dancing' with wings outspread, appearing to bounce as though on springs. Its Xhosa name, *Mahem*, is derived from its soft, trumpeting call. The reserve is open daily from 7 a.m. to 5 p.m. for day visits only. Camping and the lighting of fires are not permitted, but there are picnic sites laid out in attractive garden areas where drinking water is available.

For further details, contact the Directorate of Nature Conservation: Eastern Region, Department of Economic Affairs, Environment and Tourism, Private Bag X5002, Umtata 5100, telephone (0471) 31-2712, fax 2-4322.

Silaka Nature Reserve

Just to the south of Port St Johns, between Second Beach and the prominent rock formation known as Sugarloaf Rock, lies the small, but beautiful, Silaka Nature Reserve amid evergreen forest, grassland and rocky shore.

Set between the dense forest and the fine, sandy beach at Gxwaleni River Mouth are 14 thatched cottages and a picnic site, providing a base from which visitors can venture into the forest or along the pebbled beaches of this rocky coastline. The rock pools are fascinating, providing a microcosm of marine life, while offshore a colony of white-breasted cormorant and other seabirds inhabit Bird Island. The island is really a rocky outcrop and can be reached at low tide. Cape clawless otter are occasionally seen on the beach.

Exploring the forest is also exciting. Giant trees and water lilies line the fertile banks of the Gxwaleni River where exotic forest birds include cinnamon dove, grey cuckoo shrike and Knysna lourie. You are also likely to see kingfisher along fast-flowing sections of the river. In the forest fringes and on the grassy slopes of Silaka reserve are Burchell's zebra, blue wildebeest and blesbok, which have been introduced to complement indigenous duiker and bushbuck. For further details and to make bookings, contact the Directorate of Nature Conservation: Eastern Region, Department of Economic Affairs, Environment and Tourism, Private Bag X5002, Umtata 5100, telephone (0471) 31-2712, fax 2-4322.

Umtamvuna Nature Reserve

The Mtamvuna River – the natural boundary between KwaZulu-Natal and the Eastern Cape – is an area rich in indigenous flora and fauna. Separate reserves, both sharing the same name, have been established on opposite banks of the river's steep-sided ravine. The fertile gorge is a treasure-chest of plants, and includes numerous previously unclassified species, as well as the more common Natal strelitzia (*Strelitzia nicolai*). Umdoni (*Syzygium*) and Eastern Cape cycad (*Encephalartos altensteinii*) also occur.

Animals found are bushbuck, grey duiker, blue duiker, common reedbuck, oribi, chacma

---

MKAMBATI AT A GLANCE

When to go The reserve may be visited any time of the year. It is hot and often rains during summer. The gates are open between sunrise and sunset (but late arrivals will be allowed to enter).

Reservations and information To make enquiries and bookings, write to the Directorate of Nature Conservation: Eastern Region, Department of Economic Affairs, Environment and Tourism, Private Bag X5002, Umtata 5100, telephone (0471) 31-2712, fax 2-4322; or Mkambati Nature Reserve, P O Box 574, Kokstad 4700, telephone (037) 727-3101; or Keval Travel, P O Box 388, Kokstad 4700, telephone (037) 727-3124. A brochure with prices and facilities is available.

Getting there To reach the reserve, travel north for some 162 km along the N2 from Umtata to Brooks Nek (about 13 km south of Kokstad). Turn east towards Bizana and, after 36 km, turn right at Magusheni onto the R61 leading to Flagstaff.

After some 30 km turn left towards the Holy Cross Mission and follow the signs to Mkambati. From Flagstaff the gravel road is very pot-holed and bumpy. Caution is required, particularly on blind corners and after rains.

Accommodation Mkambati offers accommodation in six- and eight-bed cottages and three-bed rondavels, as well as in a comfortable lodge overlooking the Msikaba River, with five double rooms and a lounge for guests. Camping is not permitted.

Eating and drinking The cottages and rondavels are self-catering, and the lodge is serviced. Gas stoves and electric lights are provided. A store at reception sells some fresh and preserved foods, medicines and toiletries, bait and firewood, and curios – but at times various items are not available.

Getting around The reserve is ideally suited to walking – whether you are looking for a short ramble or a long hike. One walk includes a section of the long, but attractive, coastal hike between the Mtamvuna River in the north and Port St Johns in the south, taking in Waterfall Bluff and Cathedral Rock. Canoes are available for hire.

Wildlife Eland, red hartebeest, blue wildebeest, blesbok and gemsbok may be seen. There are also bushbuck, bushpig and baboon to be found. Among the many bird species are red-shouldered widow, long-tailed widow, yellow-throated longclaw, croaking cisticola and several species of sunbird. Endangered Cape vulture, fish eagle and crowned eagle may also be seen.

Fishing Angling at the Msikaba and Mtentu river mouths is excellent and usually yields a good harvest of fighting fish. Although large grunter, kob, bream, rock cod, galjoen and shad can be caught in this area, catches are always influenced by the vagaries of tides, water temperature, currents and climatic conditions along the coast. Bait can be bought from the shop. The removal of any invertebrate marine organism from the intertidal area is forbidden.

Left: The strikingly plumaged crowned crane (*Balearica regulorum*) forages in marshland and damp grassveld for lizards, insects, frogs and seeds of grain. It lives in flocks of 30 to 150 birds.

baboon and porcupine, while rare Cape vulture inhabit the cliffs on both sides of the river.

Unlike its counterpart across the river in KwaZulu-Natal, which is open to visitors, the steep ravines and misty grassland which make up the Eastern Cape reserve are undeveloped. There are plans to open the reserve in the future.

For further details, contact the Directorate of Nature Conservation: Eastern Region, Department of Economic Affairs, Environment and Tourism, Private Bag X5002, Umtata 5100, telephone (0471) 31-2712, fax 2-4322; or Natal Parks Board, P O Box 662, Pietermaritzburg 3200, telephone (0331) 47-1961, fax 47-1037.

Wild Coast

From the mouth of the Kei River to the Mtamvuna – a distance of some 250 km – stretches the rugged and unspoilt grandeur of the Eastern Cape's Wild Coast, a green belt of thick indigenous forest, hilly grassland, numerous mangrove communities, and sheer cliffs that fall to white, unspoilt beaches.

The N2 lies about 60 km from the coast in the south to 100 km in the north, and is connected to a series of seaside resorts by secondary roads. The condition of these gravel roads varies greatly and they are generally not suitable for caravans, so choose your routes carefully. Camping is allowed at 12 spots along the Wild Coast and, in all cases, a permit must be obtained from the Directorate of Nature Conservation. There are no facilities at most campsites, although Msikaba (Lusikisiki) and Coffee Bay (Mqanduli) have ablution facilities.

The first resort in the south is Qolora Mouth, close to the Kei River, which you reach by turning off to the coast at Butterworth. There are two attractive hotels at Qolora.

At Nxaxo Mouth, reached via Cebe, hundreds of crowned cranes sometimes roost on an island in the river mouth, and their calls can be heard throughout the night. Superstition has protected them, as they are believed to bring rain. There are no facilities at Nxaxo Mouth, but there is a licensed hotel at the Wavecrest resort.

The turn-off to the Mbashe river mouth is some 17 km past the spot where the N2 road crosses the river at Bashee Bridge. The Mbashe has cut an impressive and convoluted course to the sea, and at one point returns to within 1 km of its own course, 67 km upstream. Near the viewpoint known as Collywobbles is a breeding site of the Cape vulture. Close to the Mbashe river mouth is a hotel known as The Haven, but there are no camping facilities.

EASTERN CAPE: **NORTHEASTERN CAPE**

Left below: An aquatint by the artist and traveller Samuel Daniell, entitled 'Cascade on Sneuwberg' (from *African Scenery and Animals*). **Left above:** The scrub hare is generally found on bush-clad, stony hills. It is similar to the Cape hare, with long ears and a relatively long tail, and its fur may vary in colour according to the climate. **Above:** The Cape clawless otter (*Aonyx capensis*), a large species that lacks webs on its feet, is found near water in a variety of habitats south of the Sahara. It lives on fish, crabs, frogs, reptiles, waterfowl and even crocodiles' eggs. It is partly diurnal, and may be seen sunning itself on rocks or sand bars.

Ecowa Trail

Starting from below Gatberg – a sandstone peak with a hole seemingly bored through its centre – the Ecowa Trail leads beneath other spectacular summits and across the rolling, green foothills of the Cape Drakensberg to Barkly Pass, a distance of some 40 kilometres.

Many of the sculptured pinnacles, buttresses and peaks of this southern region are reminiscent of the KwaZulu-Natal Drakensberg, and one prominent feature even has the name of a similar formation there – 'Giant's Castle'.

The mountain landscape is rugged, and there is a timeless charm in its mountain streams, crashing waterfalls and cone-roofed Xhosa huts. The trail takes its name from the mushrooms (*ecowa*) that mingle with a myriad wild flowers after spring thunderstorms.

Because the trail crosses private land, groups must nominate a leader to ensure that no-one picks flowers, lights fires or defaces Bushman (San) paintings. No more than ten hikers are allowed on the trail at a time.

Although it is usually a three-day trail, one- and two-day routes are also available. Enquiries should be addressed to The Town Clerk, P O Box 21, Elliot 5460, telephone (045) 313-1011, fax 313-1361.

Fort Fordyce Nature Reserve

Once known as The Horseshoe, after the crescent-shaped edge of the plateau, the area of Fort Fordyce saw much conflict in the 19th-century frontier wars, or wars of dispossession. (The map of the Eastern Cape is liberally sprinkled with forts, most of them built between the 1830s and the 1850s. Garrisoned by red-coated British soldiers, few of the forts saw action, although many vigorous and bloody encounters took place in the near-impenetrable bush.)

Colonel Fordyce, the hard-bitten officer who commanded the 74th Highlanders, lost his life in a vain attack on The Horseshoe, then the stronghold of the legendary Xhosa leader, Maqoma. So the colonel's name lives on, although the grassveld of the escarpment and the indigenous forests of the valleys and kloofs brood today over a scene of peace.

Within the 2 146 ha reserve are black wildebeest, red hartebeest, bushbuck, Burchell's zebra, mountain reedbuck, blue duiker, baboon and tree dassie. Included on the extensive bird checklist are Knysna lourie, barbet, Cape parrot, sunbird, and the magnificent crowned eagle and black eagle.

Picnic and braai sites are placed alongside a dam (handy for bass fishermen) and in the shade of an old, spreading oak. Accommodation is available at Harris Hut (eight people), overlooking a stream in indigenous forest; Lourie's Rest (12 people), situated near the reserve's office and with a view of the Hogsback mountains; and Phakamisa House (eight people) on a spur of mountain overlooking the Katberg. All are fully equipped but only Lourie's Rest has electricity.

There are four circular trails that can be completed within one day, and there is also a two-day trail of some 25 km, on which the overnight hut accommodates a maximum of eight hikers. Horse rides are another treat for visitors, but it is recommended that horses be booked well before the date of the visit.

The reserve is situated off the Post Retief road between Adelaide (50 km) and Fort Beaufort (25 kilometres).

For more information, write to The Officer-in-Charge, Fort Fordyce Nature Reserve, Private Bag X232, Fort Beaufort 5720, or telephone/fax (046) 684-0729.

Karnmelkspruit Vulture Reserve

This 70 ha reserve lies in the Witteberg, approximately 12 km from Lady Grey on the Barkly East road, and consists mainly of sheer cliffs rising from the Karnmelks River.

The birds are protected largely by the isolation of their breeding sites – although they sometimes pick up meat from poisoned carcasses, as they range as far as 160 km in their search for food. The Cape vultures that live and breed here will, in future, be fed in the reserve.

Permission to visit Karnmelkspruit may be obtained from the owner, Mr I Cloete, on telephone/fax (05552) 1930.

Left: The Cape fox is widely distributed in southern Africa. It digs or 'adopts' a hole in the ground, from where it ventures forth at night in search of prey. It feeds on small mammals, lizards, ground-nesting birds, fruit and berries. **Above:** A longhorn beetle in the Mountain Zebra National Park. The larvae of this species are cannibalistic: on hatching, they immediately begin to eat each other and the carnage ends only when they are too widely scattered to continue the fight.

Koos Ras Nature Reserve

To reach this 271 ha reserve from Sterkstroom, take the Dordrecht road and turn right just before you get to the railway line. The gate is 3 km down a good gravel road and is open daily from 8 a.m. to 5.30 p.m.

Drinking water is available at the rest camp, which has chalets and rooms with electric lighting and stoves, and sites for 20 caravans and 20 tents. Visitors should bring their own firewood. Pets are allowed in the rest camp, but not in the game area. Smoking is not permitted in the game area.

A speed limit of 30 km/h operates on all roads in the reserve. Visitors may spot eland, springbok, blesbok, zebra, impala, gemsbok, kudu, hartebeest, wildebeest, rhebok and ostrich. Easy walking trails have been laid out. To make a reservation, write to The Town Clerk, P O Box 25, Sterkstroom 5425, telephone (04592) 8.

Lammergeier Nature Reserve

Set in the Witteberg range between Lady Grey and Barkly East, the reserve is named for the endangered bearded vulture (lammergeier) which, with Cape vulture, black eagle and jackal buzzard, is among some 282 bird species recorded here. Game includes several species of small antelope, lynx, jackal and wild cat, and the red hare is also seen.

Activities include hiking trails (up to four days in duration), courses for school groups, and taking to the various trails with mountain bikes, quad bikes and scramblers.

Among more restful pursuits are birdwatching, trout-fishing and day walks. Accommodation is in self-catering cottages. Summers are mild to hot, while winters are cold, with the possibility of snowfalls.

For more information, contact Dick and Margot Isted, P O Box 123, Lady Grey 5540, telephone (05552) 1902/2002, fax 2002.

Lawrence de Lange and Longhill nature reserves

Acacia and savannah veld, with aloes, cycads and bushy tamboekie thorn (*Erythrina acanthocarpa*), dominate the 1 600 ha of these reserves on the slopes of Madeira Mountain, overlooking Queenstown.

There are three hiking trails within the reserve, and parties may be accompanied by the ranger, if prior arrangements have been made with the conservation officer. More information may also be obtained from The Conservation Officer, Queenstown Municipality, Private Bag X7111, Queenstown 5320, or telephone (0451) 8-2687. There are no shops in the reserves, so take everything you need. No overnight camping is allowed, but chalets are being planned.

There is a speed limit of 30 km/h on the 20 km road network built for gamewatching, and visitors – other than those officially on trails – may get out of their cars only at the demarcated picnic spots.

With the exception of the shy kudu, visitors are likely to see most resident species, including white rhino, giraffe, grey duiker, springbok, blesbok, mountain reedbuck, red hartebeest, black wildebeest, impala, gemsbok, steenbok, eland, lechwe and Burchell's zebra.

Among the 166 species of bird recorded are Cape vulture, black eagle, martial eagle, buff-streaked chat, red-throated wryneck, southern tchagra and ground woodpecker.

The reserve's gates are in an extension of Hangklip Road, and open daily from 8 a.m. to 5 p.m. Motorcycles and pets are not admitted.

Mountain Zebra National Park

One of the world's rarest large mammals is the Cape mountain zebra, a subspecies that nearly didn't survive at all.

Back in 1937, when the farm Babylons Toren was bought as the nucleus of the reserve, there were few of the rare *Equus zebra zebra* left alive. A poorly informed cabinet minister of the day mockingly described them as 'a lot of donkeys in football jerseys'.

Today some 200 of them roam the 6 536 ha of the Mountain Zebra National Park on the northern slopes of the Bankberg, about 27 km west of Cradock. To ensure their survival, a number of Cape mountain zebra have been moved to other reserves throughout the Cape Midlands to recolonise their former range.

This is high Karoo country – the highest point in the park is a peak known as Spitskop (1 957 m above sea level), while the average altitude of the park is some 300 m higher than that of the surrounding country, with regular winter snowfalls on the higher ridges. In summer the weather ranges from mild to very hot.

About 37 km of good gravel roads traverse a combination of arid succulent veld of the Great Karoo type and the wetter eastern grassland.

Gameviewing is rewarding throughout the year, particularly on the Rooiplaat plateau, which attracts a large number of summer grazers. In addition to mountain zebra, there are eland, springbok, black wildebeest, red hartebeest, blesbok, mountain reedbuck, klipspringer, duiker and steenbok. The largest carnivore in the area is the caracal, rarely seen as it prowls the wooded kloofs. Among some 205 bird species recorded in the park is the rare booted eagle.

There are four species of mongoose; one of them, the shy and nocturnal water mongoose, is seldom seen. The Cape grey mongoose is a solitary thicket-dweller, active by day as it searches for its meals of small rodents, insects, birds and fruit. (Appearing dark grey from a distance, it is actually pale grey when seen close up.) The red mongoose is often seen in open areas, where it lives in large colonies, usually in old spring-hare burrows, although it is itself an efficient burrower. Hunting in pairs – mainly for insects – they are sometimes seen in the company of guinea fowl. The fourth species is the suricate, often confused with the ground squirrel, as both are gregarious and stand upright to survey their surroundings.

The Mountain Zebra Hiking Trail starts and finishes at the office at the rest camp, from where a number of shorter, half-day trails may also be followed. The trail covers 31 km with two overnight stops in huts at Olienhut and Kareehut. The first day's hike of 11 km takes five to six hours, with climbs and descents through gorges formed by the Fonteinkloof and Grootkloof streams.

The second day begins with a backtrack to the summit of the Bankberg, with views of the distant Kompasberg (compass mountain) and reaches the second hut after 12 km or seven to eight hours.

The third day is an easy 8 km walk, covered in two or three hours. Much of the trail is criss-crossed with game tracks. The overnight huts, for the use of hikers on the Mountain Zebra Hiking Trail, are provided with hot and cold water, beds and fuel.

Mpofu Game Reserve

Between the Katberg range and the Kat River is an area of dense yellowwood forest, rolling grassland and bush-covered ravines.

This is Mpofu, where visitors can walk the slopes and peaks of the Katberg, test their angling skills or watch an entrancing selection of game or birds. Larger animals include rhino, giraffe, kudu, eland, wildebeest, blesbok, lechwe, waterbuck and zebra, while hornbill and crowned eagle are among rarer birds that are often seen here.

Accommodation is in two colonial-style lodges which are self-contained and include the services of a chef. The reserve lies west of the main Fort Beaufort/Queenstown road (R67), about 17 km north of Fort Beaufort.

Enquiries should be directed to the Eastern Cape Tourism Board, P O Box 186, Bisho 5608, telephone (0401) 95-2115, fax 9-2756.

Oviston Nature Reserve

This reserve, which lies on the Eastern Cape side of the Gariep Dam, was used for many years for the breeding of animals for other conservation areas. Because of the high costs involved in game capture, however, other means are now used to regulate numbers.

The reserve supports large numbers of springbok, black wildebeest, mountain reedbuck, grey rhebok, red hartebeest, blesbok, steenbok, Burchell's zebra, kudu, gemsbok, eland and ostrich.

Oviston Nature Reserve is open during winter (May to August) from 8 a.m. to 4.30 p.m. and, during summer, from 7 a.m. to 7 p.m. The entrance is on the old Venterstad/Norval's Pont road, about midway between Venterstad and Oviston.

Overnight accommodation in the reserve consists of the fully equipped, self-catering Komweer Lodge, which can sleep up to 12 people. A braai lapa is also available.

MOUNTAIN ZEBRA NATIONAL PARK AT A GLANCE

When to go Visitors are admitted from 7 a.m. to 7 p.m. between 1 October and 30 April, and from 7 a.m. to 6 p.m. between 1 May and 30 September.

Reservations and information Applications to reserve accommodation and places on the Mountain Zebra Hiking Trail should be addressed to the National Parks Board, P O Box 787, Pretoria 0001, telephone (012) 343-1991, fax 343-0905; or the National Parks Board, P O Box 7400, Roggebaai 8012, telephone (021) 22-2810, or fax 24-6211. If accommodation is required within five days of an intended visit, telephone the tourist officer at the park on (0481) 2427, or fax 3943.

Getting there Take the Cradock/Middelburg road (N10) and turn west onto the Graaff-Reinet road (R61) about 6 km from Cradock. Drive for about 5 km, then turn left (towards the mountains) and follow the national park signs.

Accommodation The rest camp has 20 fully equipped chalets, each featuring two bedrooms, double insulation and double glazing, fireplaces and electricity. Historic Doornhoek farmhouse (it is a national monument) has three bedrooms, each of which has its own bathroom, a fully equipped kitchen and Victorian living room. There are 20 caravan stands and campsites, with ablution blocks and laundry facilities.

Eating and drinking Meals are available from the restaurant, and a shop supplies milk, bread, fresh meat, liquor, film, firewood and basic non-perishable foodstuffs.

Getting around The park is served by approximately 37 km of gravel road in good condition, and petrol and diesel are available at the rest camp during normal business hours. There is a speed limit of 40 km/h and some roads are signposted for one-way traffic only. Visitors may go on several nature trails, lasting from about one hour to a full day, or join a party on the more ambitious 31 km Mountain Zebra Hiking Trail, which starts at the rest camp.

Wildlife Among the park's antelope species are the rare Cape mountain zebra, eland, black wildebeest, red hartebeest, springbok, kudu, blesbok, reedbuck, duiker and steenbok. Among smaller creatures are suricate and caracal, and there are more than 200 bird species.

The adjacent construction town of Oviston has been converted into a holiday and residential resort. There is a caravan park, and facilities include hot and cold water, a laundry and connections for lights and appliances. There are tennis and badminton courts, a thatched recreation area and a swimming pool. Enquiries concerning the holiday resort, which is administered separately from the nature reserve, should be addressed to The Town Clerk, P O Box 24, Venterstad 9798, telephone (051) 654-0224/5.

The gameviewing area within the reserve has 25 km of fair gravel road, as well as a stretch of tarred road. Pets are not allowed in

Right: Blue tulp (*Moraea polystachya*). This large family of plants includes some with edible bulbs, others with poisonous foliage, and also the attractive 'peacock flower'.

the reserve, and fires may be made only at designated sites. No firewood may be gathered in the reserve. An entry permit may be obtained at the main gate.

Fishing is allowed in demarcated areas along the shore, but anglers require an Eastern Cape freshwater angling licence.

If you intend to fish from a boat, make sure that the boat is registered with the Free State Provincial Administration at Gariepdam (Hendrik Verwoerddam). You should also possess a valid Free State freshwater angling licence.

Boating in this vast inland lake is a major and fairly novel attraction, but sudden winds can make the surface of the dam extremely rough and treacherous, and it is essential to take full safety precautions. People unfamiliar with the area should ask the advice of more experienced boatmen before setting off. The water area, which falls outside the reserve, attracts more than 100 species of bird.

For more information, to make a booking or to request a brochure or animal checklist, write to The Reserve Manager, P O Box 7, Venterstad 9798, telephone (051) 655-0000, fax 655-0190.

Van Riebeeck Karoo Gardens

The hardy indigenous succulents of the Van Riebeeck Karoo Gardens at Cradock, flourishing even when the surrounding countryside withers in the grip of drought, are one of the wonders of the Karoo. The gardens, established in the early 1930s, also feature a number of exotic plant species.

Woodcliffe Cave Trails

Maclear, near the south end of the soaring Naudes Nek and Pot River passes, lies in a scenically beautiful area that has been little explored.

Seeking to remedy this is a series of trails – ranging from one-day outings to a strenuous four days – based on the farm Woodcliffe, situated west of the high road to Rhodes and 22 km from Maclear. Some of the overnight stops are in large caves and overhangs in which huts have been built, and there are also several stone cottages. A number of mountain tracks are suited to exploration in 4x4 vehicles. The scenery is mountainous, with indigenous forest along the courses of rivers, many of which are stocked with trout; and there are waterfalls, rock paintings and even dinosaur footprints. Summers are mild and winters cold, with frequent snowfalls.

For more information, write to Phyll Sephton, P O Box 65, Maclear 5480, or telephone (045) 323-1550.

A FINAL TUMBLE

Under an overhang of shale at the northern end of the Commando Drift Dam are some fading rock paintings. In black and ochre, they show men carrying sticks, as well as cattle and an animal that – just possibly – may represent a hyena.

Now that the Bushman (San) artists have gone, and visitors rarely arrive to disturb the soft, powdery soil, antlions have populated this sheltered spot with their neat, funnel-shaped lairs.

The adult antlion (Family Myrmeleontidae) resembles a dragonfly, but can be distinguished by much longer, clubbed feelers, like those of a butterfly. Unlike the dragonfly, the antlion is not active during the day, unless disturbed, and it has yellowish wings with brown or black markings.

The antlion's conical pit – about 2,3 cm in diameter and depth – is excavated by the insect moving about under the surface in ever-decreasing circles, throwing the sand out with a jerk of its head. It waits for unwary ants and other small insects to tumble in. Once over the edge, they slip even further down the steep, crumbling sides (the antlion flicks sand at its prey to ensure that it does not climb out) until they are within reach of the sharp, curving jaws. The antlion larva has no mouth, and narrow channels run through each jaw, so that the victims are not eaten, but sucked dry, the empty skins being discarded. If the site of its trap proves to be a poor hunting ground, the antlion simply moves off – usually at night – and digs another pit.

Eastern Cape wonderland

A region of tall coastal dunes, tumbling rivers, dense scrub, forests and abundant wildlife – this is the Eastern Cape between the Kei River mouth in the north and Algoa Bay in the south. It is an area of beautiful contradictions, offering a host of nature reserves, forests, hiking trails and resorts in widely varying terrain.

For those who are prepared to spend a little effort in their appreciation of nature, there are many walking trails – some signposted and others mere tracks in the soil – leading through some of the most attractive countryside in southern Africa.

Amalinda Fisheries Station and Nature Reserve

With its main entrance in Etheridge Road, this 134 ha reserve, centred on the old Amalinda reservoir, is entirely surrounded by the industrial area of East London. The fisheries station, being in a frost-free area, was established for the propagation of warmwater pond or dam fish and now breeds fish for stocking the province's many public dams.

The various habitats within the small reserve, ranging from open water to swampy, papyrus areas, attract a rich variety of birdlife – particularly waterfowl (in addition to the main reservoir, there are some 73 ponds).

The reserve area around the dam is open to the public every day throughout the year from sunrise to sunset. Toilets, picnic sites and fireplaces are provided, and boating (no powerboats) and angling are permitted. Anglers must have a valid freshwater angling licence and a permit issued by the officer-in-charge at Amalinda. The dam is well stocked and fish include large-mouth bass, barbel, kurper, carp, mullet and eel. Among several antelope species is the only viable breeding herd of southern reedbuck in the province.

Anyone wishing to visit the research and breeding section of the station should write to The Reserve Manager, Amalinda Fisheries Station, Private Bag X3, Amalinda 5252, telephone (0431) 41-2212, fax 41-3266.

Amatola Hiking Trail

The tumble of mountains and forests spanning the Eastern Cape between King William's Town and Hogsback is linked by the 100 km/six-day Amatola Hiking Trail. Not least of the route's charms – in addition to forests, pools and waterfalls – are the overnight huts, from the large-windowed Gwiligwili hut with its superb views, a rugged wooden cabin at Dontsa, and traditional Xhosa huts at Cata, to the luxury of Zingcuka, with solar-powered lighting, hot showers and a magnificent forest setting.

The trail, which starts at Maden Dam in the Pirie Forest and ends near the picturesque village of Hogsback, is fairly difficult and should not be attempted by unfit or inexperienced hikers. However, numerous shorter trails allow visitors to experience selected parts of this scenically magnificent route. These include the two-day Evelyn, Dontsa, Cata and Zingcuka Loop trails, and there are a few other points of exit and entry on the main trail.

Snowfalls may be expected during winter, and the best time to tackle the full trail is between October and March – despite occasional blisteringly hot days.

For more information, write to KEN Agency, 9 Chamberlain Street, King William's Town 5600, telephone/fax (0433) 2-2571.

Auckland Nature Reserve

The 218 ha Auckland Nature Reserve (its trees include some especially fine yellowwood specimens) lies on the southern slopes of the Amatole Mountains at Hogsback, and adjoins extensive forest plantations. It is a high-rainfall area (summer months are the wettest) and, though summers are cool and refreshing, probably the best time to visit the reserve is between June and September. Winter snowfalls are frequent.

Among the more common animals in the reserve are bushbuck, duiker, bushpig, porcupine, vervet monkey and samango monkey. Visitors may also spot the rare tree dassie, or even a genet. Auckland is noted for its rich bird

Left: *Pachypodium succulentum.* These plants have very large tubers that enable them to store quantities of food and water (for this reason they were much prized by the Khoikhoi).
Above: A tinted lithograph by artist T W Bowler from his book, published in 1865, describing the wars involving the British settlers in South Africa. It is entitled 'Keiskamma near Fort Cox, Amatola in the Distance'.

EASTERN CAPE: AMATOLA

population, which includes raptors, songsters and a variety of gloriously coloured species such as the African golden oriole, the red-billed hornbill, Knysna lourie and the rare Knysna parrot.

The Madonna and Child, the Kettlespout and several other scenic waterfalls are among a variety of tourist attractions. The final section of the Amatola Hiking Trail passes through the nature reserve, but there are many local walks in the Hogsback area with routes marked out by stones bearing the painted emblem of a hog. A detailed guide to these walks is obtainable from any of the hotels and lodging houses at Hogsback and should be regarded as essential equipment.

Visitors may enter the reserve at any time during daylight hours if they have a permit. Numerous well-signposted day trails have been established through the reserve and surrounding forests. For more information, contact The Manager, Amatola Forest, Private Bag X32, Stutterheim 4930, telephone (0436) 962-0155, or fax 3-1126.

Blaauwkrantz Nature Reserve

Local schools often visit this 200 ha reserve on the banks of the Blaauwkrantz River. Here the children are taught about conservation, the reserve's birds, animals, indigenous vegetation and about the wealth of small aquatic life forms in the little river and its pools. If you are lucky you will see a rare fish species, the East Cape Rocky (*Sandelia bainsii*), which is protected in the reserve.

Blaauwkrantz boasts several low cliffs, on which mountain enthusiasts practise their rock-climbing. Visitors must obtain permission to visit the reserve, which straddles the Grahamstown/Bathurst road. For more detailed information, contact the Environmental Conservation Branch, Western Region District Council, P O Box 318, Port Elizabeth 6000, or telephone them at (041) 56-1000.

Blanco Guest Farm

This 1 060 ha reserve of transitional Karoo grassveld is located at the foot of the Winterberg range, about 14 km from Tarkastad on the Adelaide road. Accommodation consists of cottages, while a central dining room serves three meals daily. A vehicle travels to Tarkastad on most days, and goods can be bought there on behalf of guests. There are on-site facilities for several sports, including horse riding.

No vehicles are allowed in the game-reserve area, which features springbok, blesbok, black wildebeest, grey rhebok, mountain

Left: Springbok in the Sam Knott Nature Reserve, which features a variety of buck and bigger game, and, with Double Drift Game Reserve, forms the extensive Great Fish River Reserve.

reedbuck, waterbuck, impala, red hartebeest, eland and zebra. Visitors may view game on foot or on horseback. Birdlife, too (190 species recorded), is prolific, especially in the vicinity of the reserve's three dams where large numbers of waterfowl may be seen.

Day visitors are also catered for, and the reserve is open all year, with the exception of the last two weeks in January. For more information, write to Blanco Guest Farm, P O Box 50, Tarkastad 5370, or telephone (04582) and ask for 263.

Bosbokstrand Private Nature Reserve

The 205 ha Bosbokstrand reserve overlooks the sea just east of Haga-Haga. At Mooiplaas, which lies about 40 km from East London on the main road (N2) to Umtata, turn onto the tarred R349 and follow the signs towards Haga-Haga. The road surface changes to gravel, but the route is well signposted.

Accommodation consists of fully equipped A-frame chalets, each accommodating six people, as well as a large caravan park and campsites with toilets, hot and cold water, electricity supply points and laundry facilities. Picnic sites are available for day visitors and a shop in the reserve sells general supplies. Fishing from the beach and rocks is excellent, and bait may be collected, or bought locally. Walking trails through the game area are clearly marked, and visitors may spot eland, blesbok, zebra, bushbuck and impala. A section of the 93 km Strandloper Trail passes through the Bosbokstrand reserve.

For more information and reservations, write to The Manager, Bosbokstrand Private Nature Reserve, P O Box 19545, Tecoma 5214, telephone (043) 841-1644, or contact the owner directly by writing to Bosbokstrand Private Nature Reserve, P O Box 302, Randfontein 1760, telephone (011) 696-1442, fax 696-1627.

Bridle Drift Dam Nature Reserve

The dam, in a nature reserve of 580 ha, lies on the Buffalo River some 25 km from East London. Sections of the dam have been allocated by the East London Municipality to the Border Aquatic Club, which controls fishing and boating activities here.

The reserve's gate is attended from 7 a.m. to 5 p.m. in winter and from 7 a.m. to 6 p.m. in summer, and facilities include picnic sites with fireplaces, toilets and fresh water. No overnight facilities are available. The wildlife consists mainly of bushbuck and the shy duiker, while birdlife in the dam area is prolific. A herd of donkeys can often be seen peacefully grazing in the open areas.

To reach the reserve from East London, take the Mount Coke road (R346) towards King William's Town and follow the signs from the Buffalo Pass road.

For more information, write to The Director, Community Services, P O Box 984, East London 5200, telephone (0431) 34-2364.

Cape Henderson Nature Reserve

Wild banana, milkwood and candlewood trees flourish in patches of forest alternating with steep cliffs broken up by rocky inlets along the coastal fringe of this 255 ha area some 60 km northeast of East London.

Because the climate here is essentially subtropical, the reserve offers an unusual variety of plantlife. The trees, especially, are representative of the subtropical flora further north: the Natal wild banana (*Strelitzia nicolai*) is typical, and visitors will also find sweet thorn (*Acacia karroo*), candlewood (*Pterocelastrus tricuspidatus*), milkwood (*Sideroxylon inerme*), coastal milkwood (*Mimusops caffra*) and coastal silverleaf (*Brachylaena discolor*).

Wildlife in the reserve includes bushbuck, blue duiker, bushpig, caracal, vervet monkey and smaller mammals; birds include Knysna lourie, black-headed oriole, emerald-spotted wood dove and many seabirds.

To reach the reserve, drive east from East London on the N2 for some 40 km and then turn right onto the R349 for Kei Mouth, Morgan's Bay and Haga-Haga. A footpath (extending for 5 km) is used by anglers to reach fishing spots along the coast. Access, for which a day fee is charged, is also available through Bosbokstrand Private Nature Reserve.

For information and entry permits, write to The Reserve Manager, East London Coast Nature Reserve, P O Box 5185, Greenfields 5208, telephone (0431) 41-2212, fax 41-3266.

Above: The common river frog (*Rana angolensis*) is found throughout South Africa – usually near dams and other permanent bodies of water. The males' oft-repeated 'krik-krik' is heard near almost any body of water by day or night.

Cycad Nature Reserve

Cycads are one of the world's oldest existing forms of plantlife, superficially resembling strange, palm-like trees and belonging to a very ancient species. The 208 ha area of fynbos and valley bushveld on the south bank of the Kariega River, south of Grahamstown, includes the largest known colony of the endangered cycad *Encephalartos caffer*. The reserve is not officially open to the public.

Double Drift Game Reserve

One of several frontiers arbitrarily imposed on the 19th-century Eastern Cape, the sinuous Great Fish River now forms the western boundary of this 23 000 ha reserve of typical valley bushveld along the road between Peddie and Alice. To the east lies the Keiskamma River, and the wildlife – most of it reintroduced to the area – includes kudu, eland, red hartebeest, impala, giraffe, zebra, elephant, hippopotamus, waterbuck and white rhino.

A public road – the main route between Peddie and Alice – passes through the reserve, which is open from sunrise to sunset throughout the year. Double Drift, named after the British fort located beside the Great Fish River, offers guided hikes with the distinct prospect of seeing animals in natural conditions in an area rich in historic relics, such as the remains of two other British forts, Willshire and Montgomery Williams. Examples of Bushman (San) rock art are to be seen, along with relics of Stone Age occupation. Accommodation includes thatched lodges (fully serviced with optional catering) and chalets.

Attractions, apart from walks and hikes, include excellent opportunities for game-watching, birdwatching, fishing for carp, barbel and eel (a local delicacy) and, in winter, limited trophy-hunting.

Bookings and enquiries may be made by contacting the Eastern Cape Tourism Board, P O Box 186, Bisho 5608, or telephone (0401) 95-2115, fax 9-2756.

East London Aquarium
Indoor tanks at the East London Aquarium provide a close-up look at a wide variety of marine life, including the pineapple fish, found only at great depth and therefore rarely captured. Also in the collection are invertebrates, and prized angling fish such as leervis, kob, white steenbras and musselcracker. The aquarium is famed for its seahorses, coral fish and penguins.

A visit to the aquarium is never complete without seeing the trained seals going through their paces. Shows are held twice daily, at 11.30 a.m. and 3.30 p.m.

The aquarium is sited on the beachfront esplanade, and is open from 9 a.m. to 5 p.m. The telephone number is (0431) 34-2209.

Ecca Nature Reserve
You can follow a well-marked nature trail through the 127 ha Ecca Nature Reserve to discover more about its fascinating plants, geology and history.

The entrance to the reserve is 15 km from Grahamstown on the Grahamstown/Fort Beaufort road – once known as the Queen's Road – at Ecca Pass.

A plaque commemorates Andrew Geddes Bain, who constructed this historic wagon route that now runs along the reserve's western boundary. Built in the 1840s, it was one of the first major engineered roads in the Eastern Cape and predates Bain's Kloof in the Western Cape by almost ten years.

Largely self-taught, Bain was not only an engineer, he was also one of our pioneer geologists. During construction he collected many fossils and rocks from which he made important palaeontological deductions about the prehistory of the area. Among the finds was the 56-toothed skull of a world-famous dinosaur – *Dicynodon bainii* – a discovery that Bain himself first referred to as the 'bidental' or, jokingly, as the 'Blinkwater Monster'.

The Ecca reserve was established by the Algoa Regional Services Council and developed jointly by the Wildlife Society of Grahamstown as an environmental project. The vegetation is mainly Fish River scrub, with euphorbia, aloe and spekboom. Kudu and smaller antelope occur in the reserve, although the species most likely to be seen is the sun-loving rock dassie. There is no entrance fee and no permit is required.

For more information about the reserve, contact the Western Region District Council, P O Box 318, Port Elizabeth 6000, telephone (0461) 31-2386.

1820 Settlers Wild Flower Garden
In Victorian times, military bands played here on Saturday afternoons and colonial citizens in their finery found the avenues of flowers a cool and pleasant haven.

The garden covers 61 ha of Gunfire Hill around Grahamstown's 1820 Settlers Memorial and displays the indigenous flora of the areas in which the immigrants settled. It came into being as the first botanical garden to be established by the British in the Cape Colony. Although development was hampered by periodic wars, the garden gradually took shape until it became the town's most popular public gathering place.

When it was decided to create a living monument to the 1820 Settlers and their descendants, work began on clearing exotic plants and weeds from the steep terrain. Countless Port Jackson trees were removed, and workers fought long and hard to dig out the vast root systems of huge gum trees. Their efforts eventually bore fruit, and the Gunfire Hill area has been transformed.

The Botanical Garden section has a fascinating collection of exotic plants, while the large protea collection includes the giant protea (*Protea cynaroides*), and makes a colourful display throughout the year. Other indigenous plants include the Cape tree fern, cycads and aloes. There is a restaurant in the 1820 Settlers Memorial building.

There are two entrances: in Grey Street off the main Grahamstown/Port Elizabeth road, and, in Lucas Avenue, the entrance is close to the old Provost building. The garden is open at all times.

Fort Pato Nature Reserve
Fort Pato is a 691 ha forest nature reserve some 25 km from East London along the old King William's Town road (R346). It was created – like nearby Umtiza Nature Reserve (*see separate entry*) – for the conservation of a number of indigenous tree species and the endangered blue duiker.

PLANTS FROM THE PAST

The fascinating white-haired cycad (*Encephalartos friderici-guilielmi*) is found only in a small area of the Eastern Cape.

Cycads – which the famous naturalist Charles Darwin called 'living fossils' – are the most primitive of all the world's seed-bearing plants. Most of the great cycad forests of the aeons-ago Carboniferous Period have long since turned to coal, and only a few small patches survive in remote areas and, most prominently, in South Africa's Eastern Cape Province.

Carl Thunberg, the Swedish botanist, was the first to describe the Cape cycads – though he mistakenly classed them as a species of palm.

For centuries, traditional healers have used the cycad in their mixtures; Khoikhoi made a type of bread from its pith (hence the term 'bread tree'); and one clump in the Soutpansberg is said to have helped the legendary Rain Queen Modjadji and her successors in their predictions.

It was only when they detected subtle changes in the foliage, and other small cycad signs, that they would order the traditional rainmaking ceremonies to begin. The Modjadji cycads flourish in a hillside reserve near Tzaneen to this day.

EASTERN CAPE: AMATOLA

Above: The crane flower (*Strelitzia reginae*) grows wild in the Eastern Cape, and is common in the area of Port Elizabeth. Its orange sepals and brilliant blue petals create a beautiful display. **Right:** The ruff is named after the ornate head and neck plumes seen on the males in their Palaearctic breeding grounds.

The woolly-coated, rare tree dassie (*Dendrohyrax arboreus*) takes advantage of protection, too, and may sometimes be seen during the course of an 8 km day hike that leads through the shady woodland.

Fort Pato is open to the public only during daylight hours. Permits and more information are available from The Reserve Manager, East London Coast Nature Reserve, P O Box 5185, Greenfields 5208, telephone (0431) 41-2212, fax 41-3266.

Ghio Wetland Reserve

About halfway between Alexandria and Kenton on Sea a road turns east off the R72 and leads for some 6 km to the Bushmans River and the Ghio Wetland Reserve.

The greatest attractions at these ephemeral pans are waders and migrants, including the black stork, and the busiest time is in summer, after the rains. Apart from a viewing hide, there are no facilities in this 70 ha reserve, which is open daily from sunrise to sunset.

For more information, contact the manager at Kap River Nature Reserve (*see separate entry*), telephone (0464) 25-0631.

Gonubie Nature Reserve

The seaside town of Gonubie, some 19 km northeast of East London, lies at the mouth of the Gonubie (Gqunube) River, and has a small (8 ha) nature reserve incorporating two vleis rich in birdlife.

The reserve is open to the public on Monday, Wednesday and Thursday (7.30 a.m. to 1 p.m. and 2 p.m. to 4.30 p.m.) and on Sunday (10.30 a.m. to 1 p.m. and 2 p.m. to 4.30 p.m.). At other times the key is available from the municipal office in Gonubie, telephone (0431) 40-4000, or fax 40-2358.

Observation stands and hides overlook the vleis, making ideal bases for birdwatching and for photography. Waterfowl are the major attraction of Gonubie, and a bird checklist, as well as useful information on trees and plants, is available in the information centre at the entrance to the reserve. Among the birds – some 130 species have been recorded – are crowned crane, which return annually to breed and raise their chicks.

The reserve has a representative collection of plants that are indigenous to the area, including *Protea simplex*.

Gulu Nature Reserve

Shifting coastal dunes separated by wide valleys make up the greater part of this 250 ha reserve about 20 km southwest of East London, between the Gulu and Igoda rivers.

The highest dune in the reserve soars to some 270 m above sea level. Visitors may observe several transitional stages in the growth of dune plants, ranging from indigenous coastal scrub and grass to coastal forest. The climate is subtropical, with a (mainly summer) rainfall of more than 800 mm per annum.

Among the flora are such species as sweet thorn (*Acacia karroo*), milkwood (*Sideroxylon inerme*), thorn pear (*Scolopia zeyheri*), septee (*Cordia caffra*), bush-tick berry (*Chrysanthemoides monilifera*) and bastard taaibos (*Allophylus decipiens*).

Mammals in the reserve include vervet monkey, caracal, tree dassie and bushbuck. Among the rich variety of birds are Knysna lourie, emerald-spotted wood dove and many species of seabird.

The reserve may be reached only on foot, and visitors leave from the parking spots at the Gulu and Igoda river mouths. There are picnic sites at the river mouth. Permits may be obtained during office hours from The Reserve Manager, East London Coast Nature Reserve, P O Box 5185, Greenfields 5208, telephone (0431) 46-3532, fax 41-3266.

Hogsback

The village and holiday resort are magnificently sited on the slopes of the Amatole Mountains, overlooking the rivers and fertile plains of the Tyume Valley, in a region dominated by three ridges said to resemble the bristles on a hog's back.

Among the early settlers was Thomas Summerton, a market gardener from Oxford, and his attempts to re-create the English countryside can still be seen in apple orchards, avenues lined with hazelnut, berry fruits and the flowering plants that have spread throughout the area.

There are also large tracts of indigenous forest, where the rich variety of birdlife includes parrot and lourie. Rivers tumble prettily to the plain, creating a number of small but spectacular waterfalls such as Madonna and Child, Swallowtail and Kettlespout – where the water flows through a natural spout in the rocks and, in windy conditions, arches up in a feathery plume some 9 m high.

There are hotels, caravan parks and campsites, at which facilities are provided for tennis, swimming and bowls. Horses may be hired. The area is also noted for its angling – some of the rivers are stocked with trout. Walks and trails range from 3 km to 20 km and some of the routes – which include places of historic and natural interest – are marked with painted hogs. The locally produced guidebook is an essential investment for visitors, especially those interested in exploring this lovely area on foot. Hogsback is 30 km from Alice, which in turn is 22 km from Fort Beaufort.

For more information, contact The Manager, Information Centre, P O Box 49, Hogsback 5721, telephone (045) 962-1050.

Joan Muirhead Nature Reserve

Serenely situated beside the seaside town of Kenton on Sea, the 20 ha Joan Muirhead Nature Reserve extends along the coastline in a narrow strip proclaimed to stabilise the massive dunes that line the shore.

It is well worth walking along the 1 km stretch of coast from the Kariega River mouth to the Bushmans River mouth. Here among high dunes, pristine coastal forest, calcrete cliffs and rocky coves there is much to explore. Three parking lots and a boat-launching site are provided for visitors. Additional facilities are to be found at Kenton on Sea.

For further information, write to The Town Clerk, P O Box 5, Kenton on Sea 6191, or telephone (0464) 8-1304/5, fax 8-2118.

Kap River Nature Reserve

It's easy to become captivated by this delightful little river banked by large trees, colourful flowers, and berry-sprinkled shrubs. From the dense foliage comes a chorus of birds, insects and small forest creatures. Wildlife includes bushbuck, southern reedbuck, Burchell's zebra, red hartebeest and impala, and there are close to 300 bird species such as African finfoot, heron, martial eagle, hornbill, crowned eagle, oriole and fish eagle, as well as numerous small mammals.

When developers proposed damming the Kap River, thereby threatening to flood these fertile banks, all this life was nearly lost. Fortunately, the Algoa Regional Services Council stepped in and its successor now owns a 670 ha reserve that has secured the survival of this charming valley.

Kap River includes the former Great Fish River Wetland Reserve at the mouth of the Great Fish River, where low tide exposes extensive mudflats stalked by innumerable long-legged wading birds in search of the varied invertebrate organisms that make up their food. Fishing – along the beach and the river bank – is a popular pastime, and bird-watching offers rich rewards.

If you obtain a permit you are welcome to explore the reserve. A self-contained, five-roomed guest lodge sleeps ten people, there are secluded campsites under huge wild fig trees and there is also a small fisherman's cottage. Trails for walking and for canoeing are other attractive amenities. Address enquiries to the Western Region District Council, P O Box 318, Port Elizabeth 6000, or contact the manager at Kap River Nature Reserve, telephone (0464) 25-0631.

Kariega Park Game Reserve

No fewer than 11 hiking trails – with duration ranging from a modest 35 minutes to all of five hours – explore the riverine forest, grassland and bushveld of this 660 ha reserve above the tranquil valley of the Kariega River. Cycling and gamewatching are other activities, while pools in the river make ideal swimming holes.

In addition to almost 200 bird species, there are some 35 species of large mammal, including giraffe, nyala, zebra, eland, blesbok, oribi and wildebeest.

Accommodation is in log-built lodges, each with three or four *en suite* bathrooms. Visitors usually bring their own food and drinks, but meals can be provided by prior arrangement.

Kariega Park is some 14 km north of Kenton on Sea, on the tarred R343 to Salem and Grahamstown. For further information or to make bookings, write to The Manager, Kariega Park Game Reserve, P O Box 35, Kenton on Sea 6191, or telephone (0461) 31-1049, fax 2-3040.

Katberg

Clear rivers and soft, green valleys, waterfalls and forested ravines, sweeping plantations and exposed, grassy summits make up the Katberg. Really a section of the Winterberg, this is a region of scenic splendour that, for many years, has been a favourite holiday destination.

Before that, it was long a scene of a bitter struggle for its possession, between colonists, supported by the British and colonial armed

Left: An endangered cycad, *Encephalartos caffer*, growing in the Cycad Nature Reserve south of Grahamstown (indigenous peoples made a crude bread from *Encephalartos*). Cycads are protected in South Africa and Zimbabwe. **Above:** The leervis, or garrick, (*Lichia amia*) is one of southern Africa's best-known game fishes. This fish (the specimen above is a juvenile) may weigh 30 kilograms when mature.

forces on one side, and Xhosa pastoralists-turned-soldiers on the other. A government-sponsored Khoikhoi settlement along the Kat River ended in tragedy in the 1850s, following yet another war.

There are several day walks lasting one to four hours in the vicinity of the forest station and the Katberg Hotel, and there are also the two-day Katberg Loop Trail and the two- to three-day Katberg Hiking Trail.

Among the pine plantations are to be seen some scattered and unusual exotic trees, such as Himalayan cedar and North American redwood, among other long-lived relics of 19th-century afforestation experiments.

Baboon, vervet and samango monkey, bushbuck and other small antelope may be seen, and the busy birdlife includes Knysna lourie, Cape parrot, crowned hornbill, double-collared sunbird and jackal buzzard.

The Katberg region is reached via the gravel-surfaced R351, which branches off the R67 between Fort Beaufort (30 km) and Queenstown (100 kilometres). The Katberg Pass, on which work under A G Bain commenced in 1860, provides a panoramic (but as yet untarred) route over the mountain.

For more information, write to KEN Agency, 9 Chamberlain Street, King William's Town 5600, or telephone/fax (0433) 2-2571.

Kologha Forest

The occasional troop of baboons may be spotted in open stretches of forest or where tall yellowwoods mingle with white stinkwoods and clusters of wild fig trees. There are caracal, bushpig, samango monkeys and small antelope, and numerous bird species share the high branches with bats.

Kologha Forest clothes the northeastern end of the Amatole Mountains near the town of Stutterheim, the centre of an area rich in indigenous flora. The forest lies to the north of the road (with a good but untarred surface) between Stutterheim and Keiskammahoek, via the Dontsa Pass. The forest is a favourite weekend haven.

Highlights include a picnic site at Kologha, with short walks, and a caravan park and picnic site beside the Gubu Dam.

Entry permits can be obtained from The Forester, Kubusi Forest, Private Bag X31, Stutterheim 4930, telephone (0436) 3-1546.

Kowie Nature Reserve

A riverside walk of 8 km through valley bushveld, with tree euphorbias and cycads along the way, is one of the attractions of this 174 ha reserve along the Kowie River.

Two picnic areas and braai sites are the only facilities, and are more readily accessible by river than by road, although vehicles with a high ground clearance should get through.

It is a scenically beautiful and peaceful place for boating, birding, fishing or just relaxing. Mammals include bushbuck, bushpig, duiker, otter (clawless and spotted-necked), vervet monkey, tree dassie and rock dassie, and birdlife is busy and readily visible.

To reach the reserve, turn off the Bathurst road about 6 km from Port Alfred onto the 43 Air School road.

For further information, write to the Eastern Cape Department of Nature Conservation, P O Box 13, Port Alfred 6170, or telephone (0464) 4-1140, fax 4-2669.

Kwelegha Nature Reserve

Most of the reserve, which lies between the mouths of the Kwelegha and Gonubie rivers, consists of ranks of dunes parallel to the coast, with wide valleys in between.

The highest dune is about 253 m above sea level. Wildlife includes bushbuck, blue duiker, caracal, vervet monkey and smaller mammals, while among the birds are emerald-spotted wood dove and Knysna lourie. Indigenous trees include sweet thorn, cherrywood, white milkwood, septee and wild silver oak.

The reserve offers opportunities for recreational activities such as surfing, fishing and swimming, and a small area has been set aside for picnicking. From East London, take the N2 East and turn off at the 'East Coast Resorts' sign about 10 km from the city.

For more information, write to The Reserve Manager, East London Coast Nature Reserve, P O Box 5185, Greenfields 5208, telephone (0431) 46-3532, fax 41-3266.

Above: Poplars (exotic trees) in winter in the Hogsback region. The Hogsback is a region of great natural beauty, with cool and bracing days in summer and sunny, though chilly, days in winter, sometimes with snowfalls. The rainfall is 1 000 mm a year.

Ntabathemba Tribal Reserve

Several ecosystems meet on this 3 000 ha reserve, which adjoins the Tsolwana Game Park (*see separate entry*) and is controlled by the people of the Amaqwati clan. Revenue from the reserve is invested in community projects. Accommodation – either self-catering or fully catered – is in colonial-style lodges.

The various veld types support herds of blesbok, mountain reedbuck, springbok, impala and some 40 Hartmann's mountain zebra. Exotic species are also well represented and a rare attraction is a breeding colony of Cape vultures. Activities include hiking an 8 km trail, gamewatching, climbing, and hunting in season. (The trail, fairly steep in parts, starts and ends at Lily Fountain.) There are periodic exhibitions of traditional dancing.

To reach Ntabathemba, take the Bedford road from Tarkastad, turn left at the end of the tar and follow the Upper Black Kei road. For more information, write to the Eastern Cape Tourism Board, P O Box 186, Bisho 5608, telephone (0401) 95-2115, fax 956-4019.

Pirie Forest

The best way to see these indigenous evergreen forests is on the circular Pirie Walk, a delightful one-day circular path of 9 km that starts at the southern end of Maden Dam. The trail winds gently past a disused sawmill and

EASTERN CAPE: AMATOLA

Left below: The dwarf tree (*Oldenburgia arbuscula*), a member of the daisy family, growing in a quartzite outcrop in the Thomas Baines Nature Reserve, near Grahamstown. **Left above:** The Pirie Trout Hatchery, near King William's Town. **Right:** The Cape centipede-eater (*Aparallactus capensis*) is a small, slender snake (it averages 25 cm to 30 cm in length) which is found mostly in open savannah, where it lives beneath shrubs, among grass roots and sometimes in termite mounds – where it eats termite eggs and larvae. Its favourite prey is centipedes, which it swallows head first. There may be a long struggle when it encounters large centipedes (which can attain half the length of the snake), but the snake is usually successful. It appears immune to the centipede's poison, which may be as powerful as bee venom. The Cape centipede-eater (also known as the black-headed snake) is found north of the Vaal to Zimbabwe, in the Free State, KwaZulu-Natal and the Eastern Cape as far west as East London.

logging railway – both dating from about 1910 – into the upper reaches of two streams, and turns north before swinging back to the southeast to follow the course of the Evelyn Stream back to the Maden Dam. Most of the area is forested, with tall yellowwood (*Podocarpus falcatus* and *Podocarpus latifolius*) dominating white stinkwood and white ironwood.

A second trail, the Sandile Walk, is a day-long out-and-return route that leads to a cave used by Paramount Chief Sandile shortly before his death in 1878. This route is pleasurable, but leave the cave to experienced cavers who are properly equipped. (The grave of Paramount Chief Sandile, a national monument and a place of veneration, lies on the edge of the forest.)

Birdwatchers will find plenty to see, from the soaring African goshawk to the small chorister robin and the red-billed hoopoe. Aquatic birds include grey heron, dabchick and reed cormorant, while mammals consist mainly of rodents and the occasional monkey.

A turn-off from the main King William's Town/Stutterheim road, about 12 km north of King William's Town, leads to the Pirie Forest.

For more information, write to KEN Agency, 9 Chamberlain Street, King William's Town 5600, telephone/fax (0433) 2-2571.

Pirie Trout Hatchery

Established in 1890 by the King William's Town Naturalist Society to acclimatise trout to the Eastern Cape, this hatchery, the oldest in southern Africa, continues to thrive. It is situated off the King William's Town/Stutterheim road and is open to the public from 8 a.m. to 4.30 p.m. on weekdays. Arrangements to visit should be made in advance through The Officer-in-Charge, Private Bag X0054, Bisho 5608, telephone (0433) 2-1001.

Pirie is the principal trout production station in the Eastern Cape and provides rainbow trout fingerlings for stocking rivers and dams in the province. The hatchery is on the edge of the Pirie Forest, near the source of the Buffalo River in the Amatole Mountains.

Potter's Pass Wildflower Reserve

This 10 ha reserve of unspoilt natural vegetation is located in the built-up area of East London, where some 70 species of flowering plants may be seen. The reserve is always open, but be careful of vagrants in the area.

This reserve, and much of historical East London, may be visited by walking on one of four routes offered on The Urban Trail, for which a brochure is available. Write to The Town Clerk, P O Box 984, East London 5200, telephone (0431) 34-9111.

Queen's Park and Zoo

This compact and well laid-out zoo, with its entrance from East London's Beaconsfield Street, is situated in a 34 ha garden of indigenous trees and shrubs on gently sloping ground between the city centre and the Buffalo River.

The zoo provides sanctuary for 49 mammal species, 41 species of bird and 9 species of reptile. The park and zoo are open to visitors daily between 9 a.m. and 5 p.m. all year round.

Roundhill Oribi Reserve

When alarmed, the little oribi whistles loudly and gallops from danger at great speed. As it runs it gives an occasional 'stot' – a delightful, stiff-legged jump – which allows it a view from above the long grass. At first sight it seems as though nature has provided perfect preservation mechanisms for the oribi, but not quite: the little antelope's inquisitive nature usually takes over after about 100 m, prompting it to stop and, sometimes, even to walk back to the source of danger. Many hunters have taken advantage of the habits of these springbok-sized antelope, and today their numbers are very low.

There are now 40 oribi on the 'Roundhill' (proclaimed in 1985) at Trappes' Valley between Bathurst and Kleinmond, while a further 600 animals have been recorded on farms in the district. The purpose of the 325 ha reserve is to monitor and breed the endangered oribi.

Other species include grey duiker, bushbuck, grysbok, springbok, Burchell's zebra and bontebok. Visitors may stay overnight in a three-roomed cottage that sleeps six people – for bookings, contact the manager, Kap River Nature Reserve, telephone (0464) 25-0631.

For more detailed information, contact the Western Region District Council, P O Box 318, Port Elizabeth 6000, telephone (041) 56-1000.

Sam Knott Nature Reserve

The landscape is rugged but dramatic. Among numerous steep-sided valleys are the 58 km gorge of the winding Great Fish River and that

EASTERN CAPE: **AMATOLA**

Above left: White rhino in the Thomas Baines Nature Reserve. **Above right:** A grey rhebok. This buck favours hills, plateaus and grassy valleys, and is sometimes found among low bush and scattered trees on mountainsides. In the breeding season, males frequently thrill visitors at game parks by staging fierce mock battles, pursuing each other and uttering sharp clicking noises. These contests usually end without harm to the combatants. **Right:** The rufous-naped lark is a familiar sight in southern Africa, and may often be seen perched on termite mounds or fence posts. Its nest, on the ground, often incorporates living grass woven into the structure.

of the Kat River (16 km), while vegetation consists of valley bushveld with some forest remnants. Incorporating the former Andries Vosloo Kudu Reserve, this conservation area of some 23 000 ha lies just across the Great Fish River from Double Drift Game Reserve (*see separate entry*). Including Double Drift, the total reserve area – known as the Great Fish River Reserve – is some 45 000 hectares.

Launched as a refuge for kudu in the Eastern Cape, the Sam Knott reserve also supports herds of buffalo, eland, red hartebeest and springbok. Warthog, grey duiker, ostrich, black-backed jackal, bushbuck, hyena and leopard are also present. Black rhino and the African rock python have both been successfully reintroduced. More than 230 bird species have been recorded.

There are no formal hiking trails in the reserve, although interested parties may make arrangements with the reserve manager. There is a campsite on the river at Double Drift and there are two picnic sites with basic facilities. Four self-catering cabins, each to accommodate four people, have been built in the northern section at Botha's Post on the Kat River. A network of roads permits gamewatching by car, and there is a hide suitable for watching both game and birds. Holders of valid permits are allowed to fish in the river at the campsite and at the picnic sites.

The entrance gate to the reserve can be reached via the Grahamstown/Fort Beaufort road (R67). The necessary entry permits are available at the gate. For more detailed information, write to The Reserve Manager, Sam Knott Nature Reserve, Private Bag X1006, Grahamstown 6140, or telephone (0461) 2-7909, fax 2-8472.

Shamwari Game Reserve
Among the ecosystems represented on the 12 000 ha that surround an 1820 Settler homestead (enlarged and upgraded to luxury hotel) are fynbos, eastern grassland, Karoo, savannah and temperate coastal forest. The wildlife, too, is abundant and varied, and includes elephant, lion, white rhino and black rhino, hippopotamus, giraffe, buffalo and 18 antelope species. Historically, all of these (and others) belong here, in the heart of the Eastern Cape. The area is also rich in human history and prehistory.

Guided game walks and drives are conducted, and there are sports and other facilities. Accommodation is also provided in self-catering lodges, and meals are taken in dining rooms or in riverside lapas. Some guests arrive from Gauteng via a museum-piece railway carriage attached to the *Algoa Express*. Road access to Shamwari is from the N2 about halfway between Port Elizabeth and Grahamstown. The reserve lies close to the village of Sidbury.

For more information, write to Shamwari Game Reserve, P O Box 91, Paterson 6055, telephone (042) 851-1196, fax 851-1224.

Shipwreck Trail and Strandloper Trail
Whether you choose to explore the east coast as a daring shipwrecked sailor, or as a resourceful *strandloper* (beach walker), your reward will be warm water, unspoilt beaches and only the crashing of waves and the cry of tern, gull and cormorant to intrude on your isolation. You will also have the chance for rock and surf angling, snorkelling, spearfishing and the inevitable in beach hiking – river crossing.

Crossing a river mouth is fun, but it can also be dangerous. There are rules to remember. Never cross on an outgoing tide (carry a tidetable) and beware of sharks in murky water. If you're in any doubt, walk upstream until you find a safer crossing point.

On the Shipwreck Trail you can experience some 64 km of beautiful coast over four days, or spend just one night on any isolated stretch of coast you choose. If camping on the beach doesn't suit you, there are also hotels on the way. Fresh water is available at organised camping spots only. Bookings for the Shipwreck Trail may be made through the Eastern Cape Tourism Board, P O Box 186, Bisho 5608, telephone (0401) 95-2115. A brochure is available and is an excellent practical guide; it also gives the often poignant history of this stretch of coast.

The complete 93 km/four-day Strandloper Trail lies between the Cape Morgan Nature Reserve and the Gonubie River, and is walked from east to west. There is abundant birdlife and there is also much to explore in the many pools that form in the rocky outcrops that are a feature of the route. A brochure, available from Tourism East London, gives details of all places passed, and of shipwrecks dating back to the early 16th century. Evidence of early occupation – consolidated piles of shells – may be seen at many places. Hikers stay in campsites, holiday resorts or hotels along the way and may not camp on the beach. Guided trails are also available.

Strandlopers – the Khoikhoi living in the area – were described by early settlers as families

203

EASTERN CAPE: **AMATOLA**

Left: A female oribi in Eastern Cape grassland. There are more than 400 oribi on farms in the Bathurst/Kleinmond area. The oribi is a solitary creature, preferring to roam alone or in small groups. It feeds on grasses, and is particularly partial to the new green shoots that sprout after veld fires. **Above:** This leaf beetle is just one of 30 000 different beetle species represented in southern Africa.

living on the sea shore, catching fish in stone tidal traps, and gathering shellfish. It seems that this was a mode of life periodically resorted to by groups of people who, through unwise trading or other misfortune, had lost their sheep and cattle. For information and bookings, write to Tourism East London, P O Box 533, East London 5200, telephone (0431) 2-6015, fax 43-5091.

Thomas Baines Nature Reserve
Situated off the Port Elizabeth road (N2) some 15 km from Grahamstown, this pleasant provincial reserve is open daily from 7 a.m. to 7 p.m. You reach the gates by turning from the N2 onto the R343 for Salem.

There are 15 km of road within the 1 005 ha reserve (the speed limit is 50 km/hour). The vegetation consists mainly of valley bushveld with fynbos, and typical species include wild olive, euphorbia and white ironwood. Specimens of the tall *Aloe bainesii* may also be seen.

Among the larger mammals found here are eland, mountain reedbuck, buffalo, red hartebeest, kudu, bushbuck, impala and white rhino. Prominent among the reserve's bird species (some 171 have been recorded) are a variety of kingfishers and red-billed hoopoe.

There are picnic and braai sites, and toilets in the recreation area at Settlers Dam, and there is hostel accommodation for organised educational groups only. An environmental education centre can accommodate up to 40 pupils – to book, telephone/fax (0461) 2-7043. A circular two-day trail between Grahamstown and the reserve is being developed.

For more information, contact the Department of Parks and Forests, Grahamstown TLC, P O Box 176, Grahamstown 6140, telephone (0461) 2-9488, fax 30-6072.

Tsolwana Game Park
This 7 000 ha reserve of semi-arid plain, grassland and scrub-covered slopes is popular with hikers, sightseers, gamewatchers and hunters. Among fascinating exotic animals introduced here are Barbary sheep, Corsican mouflon (a short-haired wild sheep), Himalayan tahr, Indian black buck and fallow deer. Animals indigenous to the area include giraffe, white rhino, eland, Cape mountain zebra, black wildebeest, red hartebeest, springbok, blesbok, steenbok and klipspringer.

Limited winter hunting (mainly of the exotic species) is permitted under supervision. More than 120 bird species have been recorded within Tsolwana.

Accommodation is in four luxury lodges (with eight, ten, 12 or 14 beds) and in two trail camps. All lodges are fully equipped and staffed (visitors must provide food and drink). Day and night trails have been laid out, and guests are accompanied by a game ranger. There are also tours in a 4x4 vehicle, and horse rides and hikes may be arranged. For day visitors, there are picnic sites near the entrance.

EASTERN CAPE: **AMATOLA**

Right below: A giant kingfisher on the lookout for a meal. This bird's bill equips it well to deal with its favourite food of crabs, which it catches by diving into the water. **Right above:** Terrapins move between land and fresh water at will. They are strong swimmers, fond of eating frogs, tadpoles, crabs and fish. **Far right below:** A vervet monkey on the ground. Found in rural parts of the Eastern Cape, these small creatures are regarded as pests by many citrus farmers.

Tsolwana applies the principle of allowing the local population to benefit from its operations – through the purchase of relatively inexpensive meat and the creation of employment, for instance.

The reserve may be reached from Queenstown via the R61 to Tarkastad, or via the R67 to Whittlesea and Fort Beaufort.

The park is open throughout the year – day visitors enter and leave between 8 a.m. and 6 p.m. Reservations and enquiries may be made through the Eastern Cape Tourism Board, P O Box 186, Bisho 5608, telephone (0401) 95-2115, fax 9-2756.

Umtiza Nature Reserve
Set in the gentle hills of the Eastern Cape coastal zone about 13 km from East London on the Buffalo Pass road, Umtiza's 560 ha of valley bushveld vegetation include rare specimens of cycad, Cape box and the spiky umtiza tree (*Umtiza listerana*), found nowhere in the world except here and along a section of the Buffalo River. Animals include tree dassie, bushbuck, blue duiker and samango monkey.

There are numerous pleasant day walks through the reserve. Entry is confined to daylight hours and is by permit, issued at the gate or obtainable from The Resort Manager, East London Coast Nature Reserve, P O Box 5185, Greenfields 5208, telephone (0431) 46-3532.

Waters Meeting Nature Reserve
A horseshoe canyon through which the Kowie River flows is a notable feature of this quaintly named reserve, an extensive (4 247 ha) sanctuary near Bathurst.

Various short nature trails wind through the area and there are several pleasant picnic spots. Fish eagle, blue duiker and tree hyrax – all endangered species – are among its wildlife population, though Waters Meeting is primarily a forest reserve, with dense, indigenous woodland along the river banks.

The Kowie River forms most of the Kowie combined hiking and canoe trail. There is a basic overnight camp for canoeists, from which they may undertake a circular walk before setting off downstream again.

Entry is during daylight hours only, and a permit is required. This may be obtained by contacting the Eastern Cape Department of Nature Conservation, P O Box 116, Bathurst 6166, telephone (0464) 25-0876, fax 25-0958. Permits for the Kowie canoe trail may be obtained from Riverside Caravan Park in Port Alfred, telephone (0464) 4-2230.

Woody Cape Nature Reserve
Formerly known as the Alexandria State Forest, the uniquely varied habitats include vast dunefields, part of the Alexandria Forest and the offshore island group of St Croix and Bird Island.

Birdlife is prolific and varied – Bird Island, home to 9 000 penguins, is also the world's most populous gannetry, with 140 000 voracious Cape gannets (*Morus capensis*) roosting there. Flora species number 208, mammals 27 and reptiles 45.

The reserve of 23 800 ha stretches along some 80 km of coastline between two relatively large rivers – the Bushmans and the Sundays – and is the setting for the two-day/36 km circular Alexandria Hiking Trail, which incorporates dunefield, forest and farmland, and proximity to the warm Indian Ocean.

There are overnight huts on the trail (12-person limit), and there are also attractive picnic sites and braai places for day visitors, for whom there is an easy 7 km walk. Advance booking is essential.

Mammals to be seen include bushpig, blue duiker, lynx and jackal – and, in the other direction – whales, including the humpback.

For more information and for trail reservations, write to The Officer-in-Charge, Eastern Cape Department of Nature Conservation, P O Box 50, Alexandria 6185, or telephone (046) 653-0601, fax 653-0302.

The last of the Cape herds

Port Elizabeth, the vibrant Eastern Cape port and fifth largest city in South Africa, is a convenient base for exploring the region's many and varied reserves, as well as the stretches of shimmering coastline, the river gorges thickly blanketed with indigenous trees, and the rolling bush country which is home to the Addo elephant. Two of the major attractions of the area – the Snake Park and the Oceanarium – are actually within the city, and Port Elizabeth's public parks and gardens are themselves colourful havens of nature in the midst of the commercial bustle.

Addo Elephant National Park
'If ever there was a hunter's hell here it was – a hundred square miles or so of all you would think bad in Central Africa, lifted up as by some Titan and planked [sic] down in the Cape Province.' Thus wrote Major P J Pretorius in his book *Jungle Man*. This was the Addo Bush, where, in 1919, he was employed to eliminate the elephant and to resolve, for all time, the contest between agriculturalists and game animals. Pretorius, last of the legendary great hunters, killed 120 elephant before the survivors – about 11 animals – fled to the impregnable region of valley bushveld.

The 'hunter's hell', between the Zuurberg and the Sundays River, is now a 54 000 ha refuge, of which some 12 126 ha are available to the elephant at present – an area which, proportionately, supports four times the number of elephant found in any other part of Africa. At present, there are over 200 elephant in the park. Other animals which have been reintroduced to their ancestral homeland are the black rhino, eland, buffalo, warthog and red hartebeest. The largely nocturnal animals (visitors will probably see only their spoor) include porcupine, jackal, bushpig, aardvark, polecat and caracal.

Also to be seen is the flightless dung beetle, which is found almost exclusively in Addo. In fact, the park must be the only place in the world where signs have been erected exhorting visitors to yield to these little creatures, which are often crushed under the wheels of motorists more intent on searching for elephant. Visitors are also asked not to drive over dungheaps, which might well have the dung beetles on them.

Approximately 185 bird species make their home in the sanctuary's valley-bushveld vegetation where the usual forest canopy grows to a height of 3,6 m, with taller trees on the slopes and in the ravines. The spekboom (*Portulacaria afra*) predominates in the area and is a favourite food of the elephant.

Among other plant species are the tree fuchsia, sneezewood, guarri, succulents and many types of shrub. There is no naturally occurring surface water within the park, and the authorities have had to sink boreholes, which supply earth dams.

The Addo Elephant National Park (proclaimed in 1931) lies some 75 km north of Port Elizabeth and is open throughout the year. Tourist accommodation consists of two luxury six-bed family cottages, 24 chalets sleeping four and six two-bed huts, all self-catering. There is a caravan and camping area with an ablution block, as well as communal cooking facilities and power points. Day visitors may use the picnic area with its ablution and braai facilities. The four-hour Spekboom Trail, designed for nature lovers and botanists, lies inside a fenced-off botanical reserve.

Left: A bull elephant takes a mud bath in the park. The 200 elephant at Addo are the last remnants of the great herds that roamed this region over 100 years ago. **Above:** The num-num shrub (*Carissa bispinosa*) in the Addo National Park carries succulent edible berries. The shrub is easily recognised by its stout green, forked spines. Certain other species of the num-num family are poisonous. **Right:** A canopy of green shelters about 185 bird species in the park. Spekboom – the elephant's favourite food – covers a large area of the park.

EASTERN CAPE: PORT ELIZABETH

An early problem in the park was the effort involved in keeping the elephant within their boundaries and away from the property of vengeful farmers. Having been hunted almost to extinction, the Addo elephant had the reputation of being the most dangerous in the world. An electrified fence failed to contain them. Farmers and others living near the outskirts of the park suffered damage and claimed large sums in compensation. There were fatal encounters, too, and among the victims were farmers, hunters, a ranger and a woman who blundered into a herd of elephant while making her way home at night.

There is also the story of a farmer who was riding a wagonload of oats into Port Elizabeth when he found that he was being followed by a herd of elephant. Becoming desperate as they gained on him, he threw a bale of oats onto the roadway. This delayed them only a short while, and soon they were on his trail again. Another bale tumbled onto the road. There was little of the farmer's crop left when he emerged from the elephant territory, but the bales had bought him his life.

The park's first warden, Harold Trollope, started putting out hay, pumpkins, pineapples and oranges in an attempt to keep the elephant within the park's boundary. The plan worked, and soon the elephant learnt to expect a regular evening feed. With the completion of an elephant-proof fence in 1954, they were safe from the farmers' guns, but by this time the feeding ritual had become so popular that the practice was continued. Each day a truckful of oranges was driven to a point close to a viewing ramp. The driver steered in tight circles, pursued by elephant as oranges rolled off in all directions.

The intention was good but the outcome of this feeding ritual was almost disastrous: the elephant became addicted to the citrus, and, during the winter feeding season, they dared not move away from the rest-camp area in case they missed the next feed. The result: a very small area of vegetation had to support some 75 per cent of the herd. Plant densities were drastically reduced by overgrazing, and the behaviour of the elephant was affected. Signs of stress and aggression increased as they competed for the oranges, which, in 1976, were being fed to them at the rate of about 30 tons every month.

Animals were being injured, and at least one calf was killed in the scramble for food, so the show was stopped in 1978. Today visitors may not bring any citrus fruits into the park, whether or not for their own consumption.

The Addo herd is not a separate subspecies, as was once believed. The Knysna elephant, too, are of the same general type, although each group differs in some ways from the herds found in the Kruger National Park and further north. Of the Addo elephant, only

EASTERN CAPE: PORT ELIZABETH

ADDO AT A GLANCE

When to go The park is open throughout the year from 7 a.m. to 7 p.m. On entry into the park, visitors who have booked accommodation must produce proof that their reservations have been confirmed. December and January are the busiest months. You are more likely to see the elephant during the mornings of warm days than at any other time.

Reservations and information Accommodation may be reserved up to 12 months in advance by writing to the National Parks Board, P O Box 787, Pretoria 0001, telephone (012) 343-1991, fax 343-0905; or to P O Box 7400, Roggebaai 8012, telephone (021) 22-2810, fax 24-6211. Submit requests for information to The Warden, Addo Elephant National Park, P O Box 52, Addo 6105, telephone (0426) 40-0556, or fax 40-0196.

Getting there When travelling from Port Elizabeth to Grahamstown, take a left turn to Addo some 10 km outside Port Elizabeth. The right-hand turn into the park is some 15 km beyond Addo, just past Coerney Station, and is well signposted. When travelling from East London, take the Grahamstown/Port Elizabeth road as far as the junction with the Ncanara/Cookhouse road. Turn right and drive as far as Paterson, then turn left to the Addo/Ann's Villa junction and left again at Coerney. After about 3 km turn left again to the park. Visitors from the north should pass through Cookhouse to Paterson and then follow the directions given.

Accommodation Addo has two six-bed family cottages, two-bed huts and chalets sleeping four. All are self-contained and include electricity and refrigerators, and some have been adapted for use by the physically disabled. (A communal kitchen, with crockery and cutlery, provides cooking facilities for the huts.) There are shady caravan and camping sites with ablution and braai facilities, and communal kitchens. The campsites have power points. For day visitors, there are pleasant picnic sites, with ablutions and braai sites.

Eating and drinking The camp restaurant serves à la carte meals. Bread and milk, as well as beer and wines, can be bought at the camp. Cooking is done out of doors over open fires, and bundles of firewood are sold at the camp shop.

Getting around Visitors are provided with a map showing the park's 43 km of roads and the numbered orientation points. No motorcycles, caravans or open cars are allowed in the park. Petrol is available during the normal selling hours, but not diesel fuel or bottled gas. Day and night drives are available. The Spekboom Trail weaves through the bush (three to four hours).

Wildlife Elephant are the main attraction of the Addo Park, but there are also buffalo, black rhinoceros, warthog, eland, kudu, red hartebeest and smaller antelope, and carnivores such as jackal, caracal and mongoose. Some 185 bird species have been recorded in the park. There is a hide for birdwatchers at a dam near the restaurant, and a lookout point in the game area provides access to a hide overlooking a waterhole.

Special precautions No citrus fruits of any kind may be taken into the park. Firearms must be sealed at the office, and no pets are allowed in the park.

Above: The male Cape rock thrush is recognised by its slate-grey head, neck, chin and throat, and tawny plumage (the female is spotted and barred, with mottled brown head and neck). **Top:** A female Cape rock thrush. This species (*Monticola rupestris*) is one of the more common of 37 species of thrush and chat in southern Africa, and its song is heard throughout the Addo National Park.

An elephant's great ears are not only used to display mood or as acute sensory organs – they also act as fans. As the temperature increases, the ears are flapped more frequently. This directs air currents over the body, and also exposes the inner side of the ear, where large numbers of blood vessels pass close to the surface. It is estimated that blood flowing through an elephant's ear is cooled by as much as 6°C.

Elephant are highly social animals, and the remarkable way they look after their own kind has always evoked a sense of wonder. Hunters found that a herd was often reluctant to desert a wounded companion, and would sometimes range themselves on either side to support it on its feet.

A cow has been seen endangering her own life by rescuing her calf from a flooded river, while another was seen carrying her dead calf on her tusks (she eventually buried it). Elephants often bury dead animals, even those of other species. However, the reasons for this, and for their apparent selflessness, remain something of a mystery.

For further information about the Addo Elephant National Park, contact the National Parks Board at P O Box 787, Pretoria 0001, telephone (012) 343-1991, or fax 343-0905; or at P O Box 7400, Roggebaai 8012, telephone (021) 22-2810, fax 24-6211.

the bulls have tusks, and these are usually fairly short. Extremely well nourished and secure in the bush, the Addo elephant has a thicker layer of fat than any other elephant in Africa.

One of the Addo elephant is an elderly cow known affectionately as Afslurpie – 'cut-off trunk'. She has successfully overcome the loss of that extremely sensitive organ, the tip of her trunk. The trunk, an extension of the elephant's nose and upper lip, is manipulated by about 40 000 to 60 000 muscles, and is the elephant's single most important organ used for day-to-day survival. With its trunk it feeds and drinks (the average daily intake is up to 200 kg of vegetation and 90 litres of water), dusts itself, trumpets, touches and smells things – and uses it as a shower. The water-holding capacity of the trunk is about 17 litres.

The low ratio between an elephant's body surface area and body mass means that it has no difficulty in keeping warm – but, by the same token, it may have trouble keeping cool. Where water is readily available, they wallow, bathe and spray themselves.

EASTERN CAPE: PORT ELIZABETH

Above: *Schotia* trees in the Addo National Park. These trees, also known as 'boerboon' or 'farmer's bean', have shiny foliage and small, brilliant-red flowers. In bloom, these nectar-rich flowers are a great attraction for birds and insects.

Addo Elephant National Park: Zuurberg section

Lying to the northwest of Addo is the strikingly beautiful mountainous region of the Zuurberg, three areas of which have been combined to create an enormous 34 000 ha reserve controlled by the National Parks Board.

Known as the Zuurberg section of the Addo Elephant National Park, this is an extremely lovely expanse of undulating hills and deep ravines where many attractive and fascinating plants are to be found. Some of them, such as the Zuurberg cushion bush (*Oldenburgia arbuscula*) and the rare Zuurberg cycad (*Encephalartos longifolius*), are not found outside this area.

In this hilly landscape – over 600 m separate the highest peaks from the deepest ravines – there are three quite different veld types: false fynbos, spekboomveld and evergreen forest. The most common of these is false fynbos, or macchia, which includes low-lying shrubs such as sugar bush, heath, 'tolbos', mountain cedars and buchu. In the deeply shaded ravines, ironwood, yellowwood, assegai and white stinkwood trees flourish, providing leafy shelter for a host of forest birds, including the Knysna lourie, black saw-wing swallow and black and crowned eagles.

Large game which used to occur in the area is being reintroduced by the National Parks Board, and there is already a large resident population of grey rhebok, mountain reedbuck, bushbuck, grey duiker, bushpig, baboon, caracal and jackal. The reserve, which was previously known as the Zuurberg National Park, is also a sanctuary for the endangered blue duiker. Kudu sometimes migrate in and out of the area.

There are no tourist facilities at present, but day visitors are permitted in the park, and accommodation is provided in a nearby hotel.

Bushbuck Walk

This walk follows an easy 16 km trail through indigenous forest once inhabited by elephant, buffalo and other large mammal species, and now the home of vervet monkey, bushpig and small antelope (including the rare blue duiker), as well as over 120 bird species.

Trailists pass through The Island State Forest (495 ha), some 25 km from Port Elizabeth, from which are revealed some fine views of the sweep of St Francis Bay and Jeffrey's Bay. Among the 40 tree species encountered, ranging from Outeniqua yellowwood to the sweet thorn (*Acacia karroo*), is the curiously named 'perdepis' (*Clausena anisata*), which translates into English as horse urine. The name derives from the unpleasant smell given off when the leaves are crushed, but an infusion of these leaves was once regarded as an effective medicine, particularly during the great influenza epidemic of 1918.

At the starting point is a picnic clearing with fireplaces (this is the only part of the area in which fires are allowed). Firewood is sold on site. Groups wishing to undertake the trail must number no more than 20 people.

To reach The Island State Forest from Port Elizabeth, take the Sea View turn-off from the Humansdorp road, some 35 km outside the city. The turn-off to the forest is well signposted. Permits should be obtained from The Manager, The Island, P O Box 50634, Colleen Glen, Port Elizabeth 6018, telephone (041) 74-1634, or fax 74-1607.

Cape Recife Nature Reserve

This 366 ha municipal reserve, established in 1973 around the Cape Recife lighthouse, is the perfect place for birding, fossicking along the beach and nature walks. The scenic 9 km of the Roseate Tern Trail winds along a bed of reeds to the beach, passing a bird hide from which enthusiasts may spot ducks and waders, as well as shy black crake, purple gallinule and little bittern peeping between the reeds.

The trail leads along the beach and past the lighthouse, near which there is a large roosting colony of terns sometimes visited by the rare roseate tern which once bred here. Also near the lighthouse is a sanctuary for African black-footed (jackass) penguins (no visitors allowed). The trail then turns inland and curves through scrub-covered sand dunes, home to grysbok and dikkop.

Vehicles may park outside the reserve, signposted from Marine Drive south of Summerstrand, but those desiring to take their cars into the reserve must obtain a permit from the adjacent Pine Lodge Resort or at the Beach Manager's office. Walkers do not need to obtain a permit.

For further information, contact the city's Department of Parks and Recreation, P O Box 12435, Centrahil, Port Elizabeth 6006, telephone (041) 55-9711, or fax 55-2907.

Gamtoos Coastal Nature Reserve

A rich lagoon wetland in the wide sweep of St Francis Bay is the focus of the 3 000 ha Gamtoos Coastal Nature Reserve.

Besides being a well-established fishing spot (popular for white steenbras and kabeljou), you will find a huge variety of waterfowl, including red-billed teal, yellow-billed duck, purple heron, red-knobbed coot and plenty of white egret and osprey.

The osprey, a migratory fish eagle, is usually seen near the water's edge or soaring over the estuary. It is recognised by its distinctive white-and-brown plumage.

A picnic site and caravan park are situated here and a second caravan park is located further upstream. The reserve lies about 55 km west of central Port Elizabeth, some 10 km off the N2. For bookings and to make enquiries, contact The Environmental Conservation Department, Western Region District Council, P O Box 318, Port Elizabeth 6000, telephone (041) 56-1000, fax 55-5213.

Groendal Wilderness Area

The whole of this large (29 074 ha) tract of proclaimed wilderness lies at the eastern extreme of the fynbos biome, in a setting of rolling mountains, deep river ravines and stretches of dense valley bushveld. It is situated on the Great Winterhoek mountain range, about 10 km west of Uitenhage, and is drained by the Swartkops River. The Groendal Dam is also within its boundaries.

There is a large variety of flora (60 tree species have been noted) and wildlife includes bushbuck, duiker, grey rhebok, mountain reedbuck, grysbok, bushpig, vervet monkey, chacma baboon and leopard. Visitors may also see many forest birds as well as francolin and pheasant. Trails have been laid out in the sanctuary, and visitors are warned that it is both difficult and dangerous to hike on routes other than the prepared ones. A maximum of 12 people and a minimum of three are allowed on the trails at any one time. Permits for hiking and overnight camping are available at the Groendal office, at the entrance to the wilderness area. To get there, drive along Caledon Road (in a northerly direction), turn left into Gibson Road and right into Groendal Road.

For further information about Groendal, write to The Manager, Groendal Wilderness Area, P O Box 445, Uitenhage 6230, or telephone (041) 992-5418, or fax 922-7570.

Loerie Dam Nature Reserve

You can sample some of the magic of the Baviaanskloof Mountains by exploring Loerie Dam Nature Reserve and its spectacular

Above: The Cape clawless otter (this one was photographed at the Port Elizabeth Oceanarium) spends less time in water than the spotted-necked otter, and passes most of its time sunbathing on rocks or sand bars. **Right:** An African black-footed (jackass) penguin stands sentinel on St Croix Island in Algoa Bay.

slopes, valleys and streams. It lies north of the town of Loerie, terminus of the famous Apple Express railway. This old steam train puffs and sighs through apple orchards in the fertile Longkloof region on one of the last remaining narrow-gauge railways in South Africa. There cannot be a more exciting way to visit the area if you are coming from Port Elizabeth.

The 636 ha reserve is used mainly for conservation and environmental education and provides accommodation for groups of up to 40 in a dormitory. There is also an 18-bed timber hut, which is ideal for smaller groups as well as hikers. Spectacular hiking opportunities are provided by the 7 km Wild Goose Trail, which leads through deep, forested valleys offering a chance to discover a diverse range of fynbos, birds and animals.

For more information, write to the Environmental Conservation Department, Western Region District Council, P O Box 318, Port Elizabeth 6000, or telephone (041) 56-1000, fax 55-5213. For more information on the Apple Express, write to the Apple Express Society, P O Box 21847, Port Elizabeth 6000, telephone (041) 507-2333, fax 507-3233; or to the Port Elizabeth Publicity Association, P O Box 357, Port Elizabeth 6000, telephone (041) 52-1315, fax 55-2564.

Maitland Nature Reserve

The main feature of the secluded 127 ha Maitland Nature Reserve, some 30 km from Port Elizabeth at the mouth of the Maitland River, is the large area of indigenous forest which clothes the steep slope of the river terrace. The reserve is named after Sir Peregrine Maitland, Governor of the Cape Colony between 1844 and 1847.

The area has been left undisturbed for many years, and as a result the forested slopes echo with the calls of hundreds of birds. They are sustained by the abundant food supply – during a single month (October) as many as 35 plant species bear flowers or fruit.

No fires may be lit in the reserve, and no accommodation is available (however, the reserve adjoins the camping area at Maitland River Mouth). Three short hiking trails have been laid out. To reach the sanctuary, follow any of the roads leading from Port Elizabeth to Sea View, and take the coastal road to Maitland River Mouth. No permits are required to enter the reserve which is open to visitors at all times. For further information about Maitland, contact the Environmental Conservation Department, Western Region District Council, P O Box 318, Port Elizabeth 6000, telephone (041) 56-1000, fax 55-5213.

Port Elizabeth Oceanarium

Streams of visitors flock to Port Elizabeth's Oceanarium every year, attracted by the nimble bottlenose dolphins, whose acrobatic antics have drawn gasps of admiration from decades of enthusiastic spectators.

Other exhibits at the Oceanarium, which forms part of the museum complex at Humewood, include Cape fur seals and jackass penguins – named for their call, which is remarkably similar to that of a braying donkey. There is also a large fish tank (under cover) containing local fish species, sharks and turtles, and a smaller invertebrate tank which houses a colourful collection of corals, sponges, anemones and other sea creatures.

The Oceanarium is open throughout the year, from 9 a.m. to 1 p.m., and 2 p.m. to 5 p.m. Performances are held daily at 11 a.m. and 3 p.m., and the dolphins can be viewed through the windows of an underwater observatory as they swim in their 6-million-litre pool.

The Oceanarium is situated on the beachfront, south of the city centre, and is distinguished by a dolphin mounted on the top of the building. For more detailed information, contact Port Elizabeth Publicity Association, P O Box 357, Port Elizabeth 6000, telephone (041) 52-1315, or fax 55-2564.

Port Elizabeth Snake Park

The original snake park consisted of a large outdoor enclosure built in the spacious grounds of the Bird Street Museum. When the museum was moved to its present locality in Humewood, a new snake park was built and opened its doors in 1959.

The park maintains the traditional open pit for exhibiting local snakes. Other snakes may be seen in glass-fronted cases, and indigenous and exotic members of the family can be seen in the Python House. Other reptiles – including lizards, alligators, leguans and crocodiles – are housed in large open pits, and their feeding makes for a spectacular show.

In the fascinating Tropical House, which adjoins the snake park, visitors can walk along a path leading through dense and luxuriant vegetation, past waterfalls and around an artificial mountain where large numbers of birds and waterfowl can be seen. The 'Night House' features nocturnal animals which, in conditions of simulated moonlight, are active during visiting times.

The snake park and Tropical House are open from 9 a.m. to 1 p.m., and 2 p.m. to 5 p.m. Videos covering the various aspects of snakes

EASTERN CAPE: **PORT ELIZABETH**

are held daily. For further information, contact Port Elizabeth Publicity Association, P O Box 357, Port Elizabeth 6000, telephone (041) 52-1315, fax 55-2564.

St Croix Island Nature Reserve

The three rocky islands that make up this 14 ha reserve – St Croix, Brenton and Jahleel – are situated just off the mouth of the Coega River in Algoa Bay. The reserve, which may not be visited by the public, was established as a breeding sanctuary for the endangered jackass penguin. When disturbed, this bird tends to leave its nest, and so exposes its chicks or eggs to attacks by gulls. Jahleel Island is home to some 4 000 Cape fur seals.

Sardinia Bay and Sylvic nature reserves

These reserves cover a stretch of coastline between Schoenmakerskop and Sea View, and are in effect two reserves combined to form one. The 'Sardinia Bay Marine Reserve' was established first (by the Dias Divisional Council). When it was found impractical to administer an area from the high-water mark to a point 1 km out to sea, the adjacent land was proclaimed the Sylvic Nature Reserve.

The marine reserve is not only a sanctuary for sea organisms, but also serves as a reference area which is used to assess the impact of civilisation elsewhere on the coast. An area of dune and sandflats, it is easily subject to human-induced deterioration, a situation which threatened the very existence of Port Elizabeth a century ago.

The balance between dune stabilisation by vegetation, and dune instability resulting from the action of wind and sea, is very delicate. Too much human activity on the dunes kills vegetation and causes instability of the dunes, so all developments that might lead to high human densities – car parks, toilets and launching ramps, for example – are carefully controlled. No vehicles are allowed in the Sylvic Nature Reserve or Sardinia Bay.

The 8 km Sacramento Trail traverses the Sardinia Bay Nature Reserve, starting at the western end of Schoenmakerskop and following the coast to Sardinia Bay. At Schoenmakerskop a bronze cannon points towards the wreckage site of the Portuguese galleon *Sacramento*, which foundered in these waters in June 1647. The 72 survivors who landed on the beach decided to return to Mozambique – a journey of some 1 300 kilometres. Only nine survived the journey, which lasted almost eight months. Local divers salvaged 40 bronze cannon from the wreckage in 1977.

Both Sardinia Bay and Sylvic reserves are open throughout the year. Fishing is prohibited, and nothing may be removed from the area. The reserves can be reached along the Schoenmakerskop, Lovemore Park and

WILLIAM BURCHELL: BOTANIST SUPREME

With a specially equipped wagon, two spans of oxen and six Khoikhoi attendants, a young Englishman, William Burchell, left Cape Town in June 1811 on an expedition that was to last nearly four years. Returning to England, he spent another ten years writing up the results of his observations: his *Catalogus Geographicus Plantarum* records 8 700 South African plants in 14 volumes of neat manuscript which may still be seen in the library at Kew, London. It was a remarkable feat of systematic scientific exploration, and of patient endurance.

Burchell is probably the most renowned of southern Africa's pioneer naturalists.

His explorations near Prieska enabled him to describe, for the first time, the 'stone plant' or lithops – almost a century was to pass before botanists noted any of the other 50-odd species of lithops. He also discovered the world's second largest land mammal – the white rhinoceros. As a painstaking and meticulous scientist, William Burchell did not believe in taking short cuts. He was not satisfied until he had accumulated data from ten animals.

Some of his reports were received with scepticism in Europe ('There can be no such animal,' it was once declared of Burchell's zebra), but Burchell was almost always proved correct. The name of this thorough and adventurous naturalist survives in the scientific names of many South African species, as well as in the plant genus *Burchellia*, of the gardenia family.

Above and right: Pencil and watercolour illustrations by William Burchell, painted from specimens collected at Kosi Fountain, Pintado Fountain and Jabiru Fountain in 1812. The seasonal springs of Pintado and Jabiru were in the arid Kuruman district of the Northern Cape.

Above: St Croix Island Reserve, near the mouth of the Coega River, is a breeding sanctuary for the endangered jackass penguin.

Sardinia Bay roads. The control point at Sardinia Bay lies some 20 km from the Port Elizabeth City Hall.

For more information about Sardinia Bay, write to The Department of Parks and Recreation, P O Box 12435, Centrahil, Port Elizabeth 6006, or telephone (041) 55-9711, fax 55-2907. For information about Sylvic Nature Reserve, contact The Environmental Conservation Department, Western Region District Council, P O Box 318, Port Elizabeth 6000, or telephone (041) 56-1000, fax 55-5213.

Sea View Game Park

The Sea View Game Park is situated some 24 km west of Port Elizabeth. Turn off the N2 national road at the sign 'Sea View/Greenbushes' and after about 8,5 km turn left onto a road marked 'Lion Park'. The entrance to the park is reached after 0,7 kilometres.

Game is readily visible from your car, and includes giraffe, lion, zebra, nyala, impala, wildebeest, kudu, blesbok and baboon. More than 50 bird species have been identified.

If you enjoy walking through the bush the Nyala Trail takes about 45 minutes.

A tearoom serves light meals and refreshments from 11 a.m. There are also braai facilities at the campsite which caters for tents and caravans. There are toilet facilities and cold showers. Campers must bring their own firewood and provisions.

The park is open daily throughout the year from 8 a.m. until 5 p.m. For further information, write to Sea View Game Park, P O Box 27173, Greenacres 6057, or telephone (041) 74-1702.

Settlers' Park Nature Reserve

The four floral regions which converge in the vicinity of Port Elizabeth are represented in this 54 ha reserve, close to the city's bustling central business district. The Baakens River, which flows through the reserve, has sculpted cliffs and ravines, and pools and running water sparkle amid wide lawns and a colourful variety of trees and flowers.

Plants characteristic of the Western Cape fynbos, such as ericas, proteas, leucospermums and leucadendrons, as well as daisies (belonging to the family Compositae) and Cape thatching reed (Restionaceae), flourish here.

The temperate to subtropical coastal flora is represented by both deciduous and evergreen trees, including yellowwood and coral tree (*Erythrina*), with climbing plants, forest lilies, ferns and water plants. Grassland flora includes many grass types, herbs and bulbous plants, while Karoo flora and valley bushveld provide spekboom, *Euphorbia*, *Aloe*, *Mesembryanthemum* and other succulents.

Grysbok, dassie and small grey mongoose may often be seen during the daylight hours. Among resident waterfowl are Egyptian goose, yellow-billed duck and moorhen. Other birds include Knysna lourie, paradise flycatcher, greater and lesser double-collared sunbird, white-browed coucal, dove, thrush, robin, canary and weaver.

There are paths and roads across the reserve between the car parks, and stepping stones with handrails enable visitors to cross the river at seven places. The 7,5 km Guinea Fowl Trail winds through the bird-rich Baakens River Valley, while the Jan Smuts Walk crosses the river, passes below a kloof over which water plunges after heavy rains, crosses the wall of the Holland Dam and traverses cool, wooded slopes.

Climbing on the cliffs is dangerous. Dogs are not allowed in the reserve, which is open during daylight hours. The main parking area is reached from Park Drive/How Avenue or Hallack Road. There are also entrances off Targetkloof, Fordyce Road in Walmer, and from Brickmakerskloof. For more information, contact The Department of Parks and Recreation, P O Box 12435, Centrahil, Port Elizabeth 6006, telephone (041) 55-9711, or fax 55-2907.

Tyler's Park Nature Reserve

Proclaimed in 1956, this small reserve combines both indigenous fynbos vegetation with natural park-like surrounds to create a restful haven from the hustle and bustle of the city. Small buck and other mammals leave traces of their presence in the reserve but are rarely seen by day. Birdlife is prolific, and visitors may be lucky enough to spot the lovely spur-winged goose. The reserve is controlled by the Port Elizabeth Municipality.

Uitenhage Nature Reserve

Established around the Uitenhage Springs Holiday Resort, the 1 053 ha sanctuary contains a network of easy paths that lead through typical valley bushveld to several outstanding viewing points. To reach it, take the signposted turn-off from the Graaff-Reinet road, about 8 km north of Uitenhage.

The reserve is open from 7 a.m. to 7 p.m. from October to March, and from 8 a.m. to 5.30 p.m. during the rest of the year. Permits must be obtained in advance from the supervisor of the Springs Resort.

Among the area's 300 plant types are many species of aloe. A network of paths crisscrosses the reserve, with the picturesque Kleinkop Walk being the shortest. It takes about 30 minutes to complete and leads up a koppie where the valley bushveld thins and is replaced by fynbos. An hour can be added to the walking time by taking the path northwards from Kleinkop to Grootkop.

A route branching to the left before the summit of Grootkop leads to Bayview, so named for its fine views of Algoa Bay. There is a lookout tower which visitors may use at their own risk. On top of the elevation known as 'The Tongue', reached after a short climb, is a variety of flowering plants, including *Crassula*, *Pelargonium*, *Mesembryanthemum*, *Haworthia* and *Aloe*.

The reserve has plenty of birdlife, and among the mammals are porcupine, duiker, bushbuck, grysbok, steenbok, vervet monkey, bushpig, mongoose and meerkat.

Facilities at the resort include single chalets, double chalets, double rondavels and six-bed huts. Visitors must provide their own linen, crockery and cutlery. There are also caravan sites, and a swimming pool, tennis courts, playground and trampoline. Horse rides through the reserve can be arranged on weekends and public holidays. To make a reservation, write to The Manager, Springs Holiday Resort, P O Box 45, Uitenhage 6230, telephone (041) 966-1161.

University of Port Elizabeth Nature Reserve

Besides being one of South Africa's leading academic institutions, the University of Port Elizabeth has an added distinction – the whole campus has been proclaimed a nature reserve. Students on their way to lectures pass grysbok, springbok and, occasionally, duiker and bushbuck. A total of 22 medium and large animal species has been recorded in the reserve, including the endangered honey badger and blue duiker. Over 130 bird species have been identified.

The vegetation in the 830 ha reserve is primarily dune fynbos, with patches of dune thicket, resulting in a diversity of plant species. Unfortunately, a large part has been invaded by Australian species of acacia, including Port Jackson and rooikrans, but attempts are being made to eradicate these invaders in order to maintain the indigenous flora and to provide fuel resources for disadvantaged communities.

Facilities in the reserve include the Grysbok Environmental Education Trail, a day hike, a picnic area and two water features at which waterfowl may be observed. The Grysbok Trail has three loops of differing length, varying from 400 m to 4,8 kilometres. Trail guides are available for educational groups, while a booklet is available for those who wish to explore by themselves.

This is a private nature reserve and it is essential to make reservations in order to follow the trail. If you require further information or wish to make reservations, contact the Zoology Department, University of Port Elizabeth, P O Box 1600, Port Elizabeth 6000, telephone (041) 504-2308, or fax 504-2317.

Van Stadens Wild Flower Reserve and Bird Sanctuary

Situated in Eastern Cape fynbos, with indigenous Alexandria forest in the south, the reserve lies some 40 km from the centre of Port Elizabeth, to the east of Van Stadens Pass.

The reserve is especially renowned for its wealth of proteas, as well as for the beauty of its tree and ground orchids. The crane flower, *Strelitzia reginae*, is native to these easterly parts of the 'Cape Floral Kingdom'. An important endemic plant is the fire lily (*Cyrtanthus stadensis*), and rare tree species include the Cape star-chestnut (*Sterculia alexandri*), 'bugmy-nie' (*Smelophyllum capense*) and the Cape wing-nut (*Atalaya capensis*). The dominant trees of the forest are the real, or 'true', ironwood and bastard saffron-wood (*Cassine peragua*), while the wild pomegranate (*Burchellia bubalina*), named after the naturalist William Burchell, is fairly common.

The air is rich with the calls and whirrs of a busy birdlife, and some visitors may be lucky enough to see the shy and elusive blue duiker.

The reserve is open throughout the year. There are picnic sites with braai spots at the old bridge over the Van Stadens River, but no other facilities. Walking is encouraged in the reserve and a hiking trail leads down to the Van Stadens River (there are few restricted areas).

Permits are required only in the case of groups of 20 or more people, and should be requested from the Environmental Conservation Department, Western Region District Council, P O Box 318, Port Elizabeth 6000, telephone (041) 56-1000, fax 55-5213.

Yellowwoods Nature Reserve

You can picnic beside a small river in the shade of ancient, spreading yellowwoods in this 20 ha municipal reserve outside Hankey.

At this tranquil spot you can also swim in the stream, run on the grass, or head for the adjacent golf course. Even if you don't get a 'birdie' during your nine holes you can expect to see kingfisher, francolin and sunbird in this beautiful little reserve. For the energetic there is nothing to beat a walk up Dassieskraal Mountain – the summit of which provides panoramic views of the whole town and the nature reserve, as well as the carefully mown fairways stretching up and down the golf course.

The reserve and golf course are signposted on the road leading to Kleinrivier. There is a camping and caravan site with toilets, showers and electricity in the reserve. For more information and to make bookings, write to The Town Clerk, Hankey Municipality, P O Box 3, Hankey 6350, telephone (04236) 4-0302.

Zwartkops Valley Nature Reserve

The lovely Zwartkops Valley Nature Reserve, which is located on the northern outskirts of Port Elizabeth, was proclaimed in 1993 to

Above: A bushbuck in the Sea View Game Park. This chestnut-coloured, nocturnal feeder enjoys browsing on leaves and young shoots, but will also eat tender roots. Bushbuck are rarely seen in the wild.

ensure the protection of the prime valley bushveld that grows along the banks of the Zwartkops River.

The reserve stretches for 6 km along the escarpment, and also encompasses a saltpan that serves as a breeding ground for hosts of seabirds, including gulls, cormorants and terns. Also here are flamingoes, of which up to 1 000 have been recorded at one time.

The 9 km Flamingo Hiking Trail passes up the side of a stormwater canal, revealing succulent-rich vegetation (this area receives much less rain than the city does) and, in winter, the path is lined with tall aloes. The trail then winds down a kloof to the saltpan, the first of a series of commercially operated evaporation pans in the valley. Grysbok and blue duiker may be spotted, if you're lucky.

Another treat for jaded city dwellers is the 22 km mountain-bike trail, a circular route that follows the river along the base of the escarpment, climbs a kloof and traverses the valley bushveld on the plateau. Next is a steep descent – take care here – and then another taxing climb back up to the plateau. The route follows the reserve boundary, before descending once more to the valley floor and returning to the starting point. Note that the clay soils become impassable after rain. Take all the necessary safety precautions and some first-aid items, including a puncture kit. It is advisable to travel in groups.

For further information, contact the Department of Parks and Recreation, P O Box 12435, Centrahil, Port Elizabeth 6006, telephone (041) 55-9711, fax 55-2907.

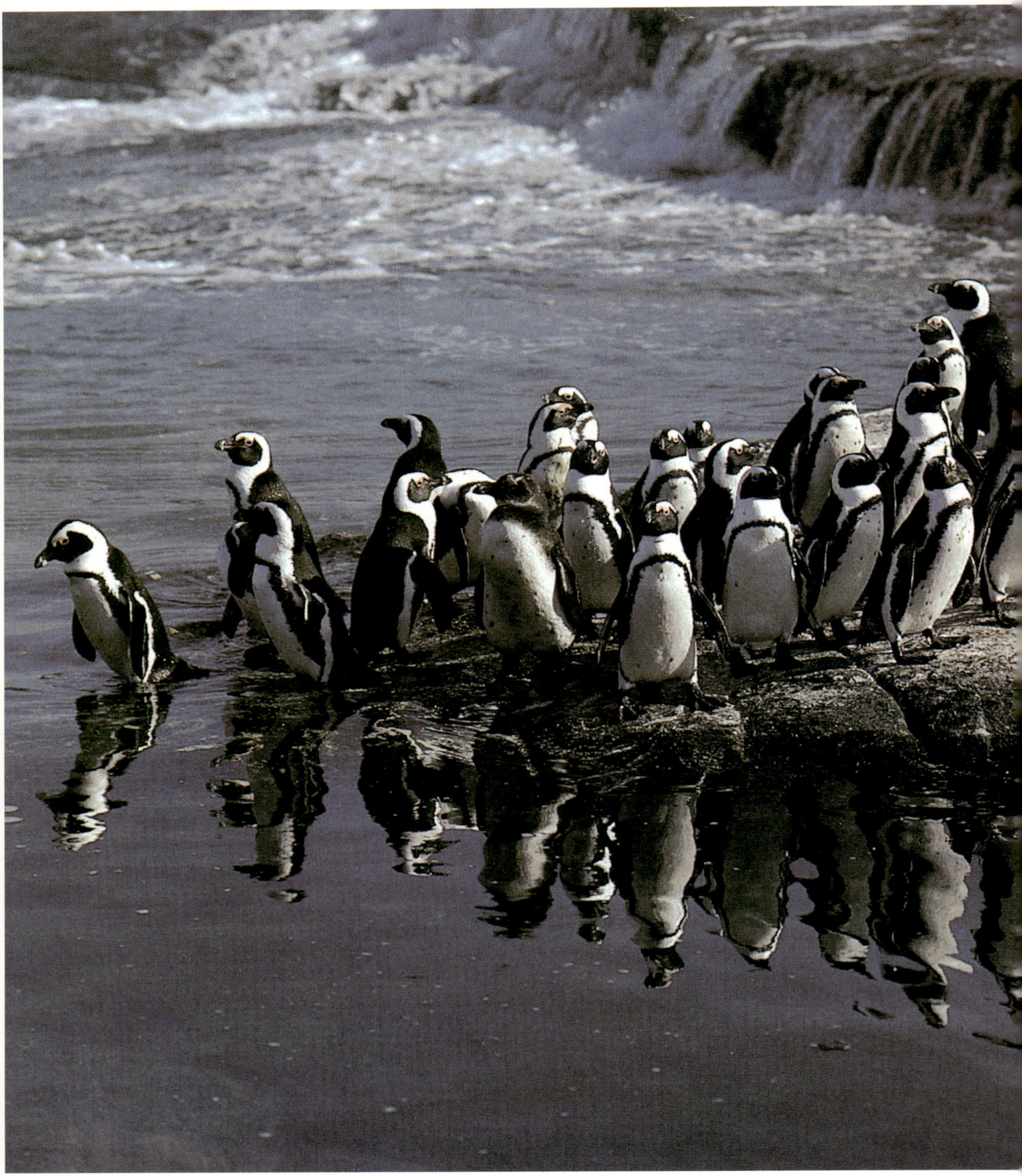

SOUTHWESTERN CAPE

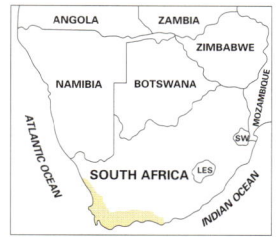

The southernmost edge of the African continent is a glorious patchwork of blue mountains, still forests, fynbos, tumbling rivers and sweeping coastline that more than justifies its accolade as the fairest Cape.

This is the home of Kirstenbosch – one of the world's most famous reservoirs of indigenous flora – and of Table Mountain, that much-loved, ever-familiar sentinel looming over South Africa's oldest city.

The cheeky chacma baboon wanders through the Cape of Good Hope Nature Reserve, sharing its territory with buck, zebra, porcupine, ostrich and a host of other creatures. Bushpig and caracal roam the Tsitsikamma Forest, while vultures wheel over the Potberg.

Much of this lovely region is accessible to the public. Hiking trails meander through ancient forests and across mountains, taking adventurers into landscapes of unforgettable beauty; and large numbers of individuals and organisations are dedicated to the recognition, appreciation and protection of the region's natural wealth.

In spite of crises in nature conservation management, few will deny the importance of the natural heritage of the southern tip of the country, displayed in the number of sanctuaries created for the preservation of indigenous flora and fauna. Private nature reserves abound, and wildflower gardens seem to display their floral treasures around every corner.

Like a party of dignified gentlemen in evening suits, African black-footed (previously known as jackass) penguins bask in the warmth of the sun on the southwestern coast of South Africa.

A stretch of earthly paradise

Entranced by the profusion of flowers near the Great Brak River, the 18th-century French naturalist Francois le Vaillant wrote lyrically of 'enamelled meads, and the most beautiful pastures' as two of 'the charms of this terrestrial paradise'.

Now aptly named the Garden Route, this region protects its rich bounty within numerous sanctuaries, mainly forest and coastal. Among these is the Bontebok National Park, home to several species of antelope and a large and varied population of birds. The ruggedly beautiful Tsitsikamma and Knysna forests, erratically crisscrossed by a number of trails and walks ranging in degrees of difficulty, encourage hikers to explore these unspoilt wildernesses of moody forests and tree-cloaked mountains.

Highly recommended to visitors driving through the area is the Lakes Road, which twists and curves scenically through green-swathed countryside between the Wilderness National Park and the Knysna National Lake Area, offering tantalising glimpses of the azure waters of the Indian Ocean. Whether you explore the area on foot or by car, a visit to the Garden Route is an unforgettable experience.

Bontebok National Park
The traditional home of the bontebok was originally the 56 km wide coastal plain of the southwestern Cape, between Bot River in the west and Mossel Bay in the east. Large herds of silver-coated bluebuck once grazed here, but, sadly, by 1800 they had been hunted to extinction, and within 30 years the numbers of bontebok, too, had dwindled to just a few dozen. Remembering the lost bluebuck perhaps, a few farmers from the Bredasdorp district banded together to ensure the survival of the bontebok.

In 1931 the first Bontebok National Park was proclaimed on an area of strandveld and coastal fynbos south of Bredasdorp, with a breeding nucleus of just 17 animals. However, poor grazing which resulted in the formation of internal parasites eventually prompted the move to the present site near Swellendam, where the second Bontebok National Park of 2 786 ha was opened in 1961 in the foothills of the Langeberg. Since then the herd has grown from 60 to more than 300 animals, with more than 1 000 found throughout South Africa. A favourite spot for viewing bontebok is at Lang Elsieskraal, site of the camp of an 18th-century Khoikhoi chieftainess. Bontebok are born during September, October and November.

Among other animals the visitor may see are grey rhebok, Cape grysbok, hartebeest, steenbok, grey duiker and Cape mountain zebra. Birdlife is prolific and includes the stately secretary bird, Stanley's bustard, several species of sunbird, fish eagle, Cape whydah, guinea fowl, hamerkop, francolin and even a few spur-winged geese which remain in the park throughout the year. Jackal and fox prowl the renosterveld that dominates the low shrub and grassland vegetation of this transitional fynbos region. More than 470 plant species, including 52 species of grass, have been identified in the park. The spring months are the best time to view them.

The Breede River, which flows through portion of the park, has been stocked with carp and large-mouth bass for fishing – large 10 kg carp may be caught there. Among other fish is the prettily named Kaapse nooientjie (Cape girl) or Cape moonfish (*Monodactylus falciformis*). Remember to obtain a provincial freshwater angling licence (available from any magistrate's office in the Cape) as well as permission from the park warden. Swimming is

Left: A large bontebok ram keeps watch over young lambs in the Bontebok National Park near Swellendam. The conspicuous white patch from the base of the bontebok's horns to its nose makes it easy to spot in its favourite habitat – open grassland. It is a grazer and roams in herds numbering between six and thirty.
Near right: An orange-red fungus (*Pycnoporus sanguineus*) grows on a fallen tree in the southern Cape's Tsitsikamma Forest. **Far right:** These chincherinchees (*Ornithogalum*), from the Prince Alfred's Pass, grow abundantly in the southern Cape. They are also known as stars of Bethlehem, or chinks, a name said to imitate the sound made by the shiny flower stalks rubbing together. This elegant species, a member of the lily family, is a favourite export flower and is shipped abroad in dry packages, remaining fresh for weeks.

THE CAPE: THE GARDEN ROUTE

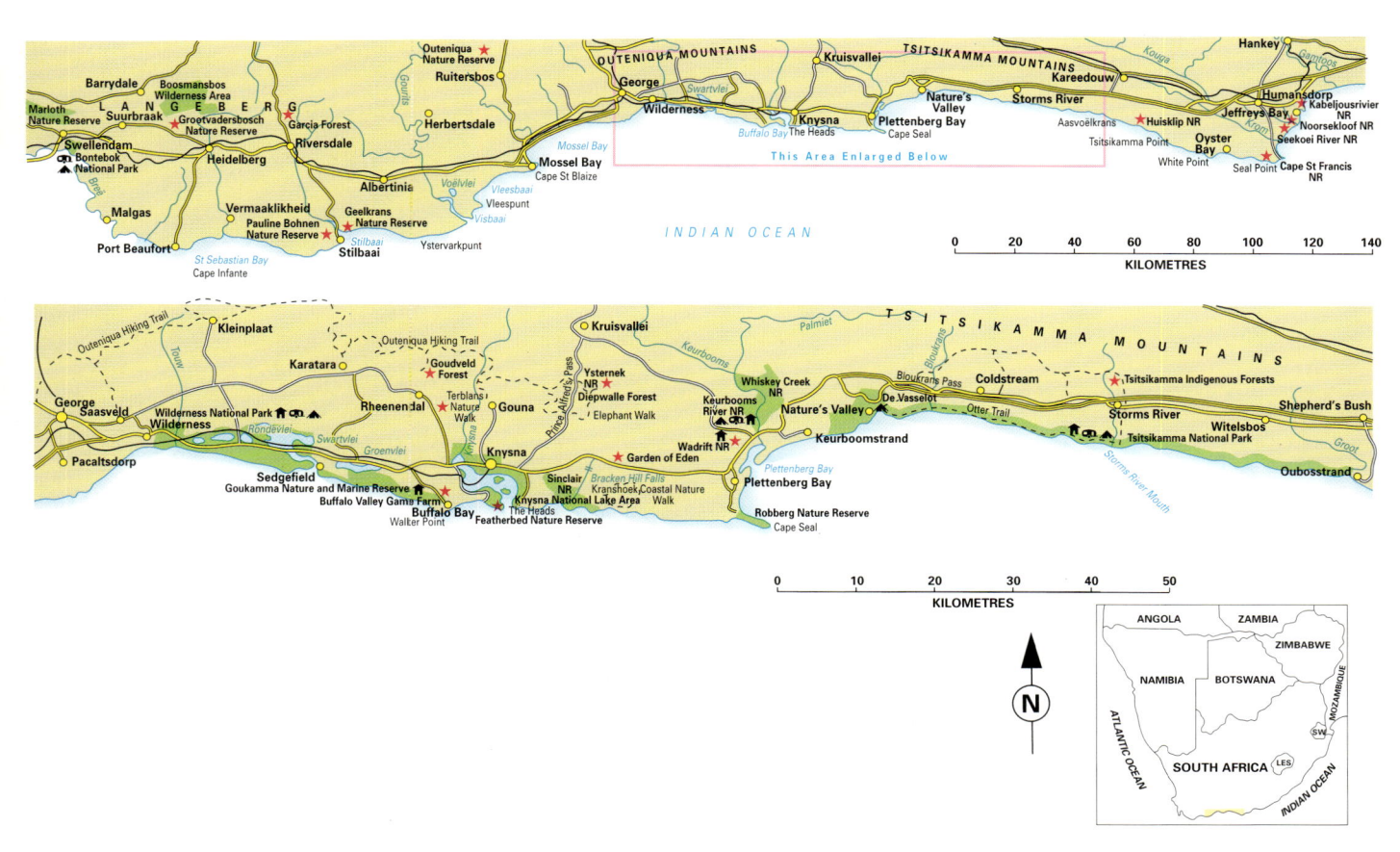

217

THE CAPE: THE GARDEN ROUTE

BONTEBOK NATIONAL PARK AT A GLANCE

When to go The park is open throughout the year. Visiting hours are between 8 a.m. and 7 p.m. from 1 October to 30 April, and from 8 a.m. to 6 p.m. from 1 May to 30 September. Rainfall is heavier in winter than in summer.

Reservations Camping and caravan sites are booked through the National Parks Board, P O Box 787, Pretoria 0001, telephone (012) 343-1991, or fax 343-0905; or the National Parks Board, P O Box 7400, Roggebaai 8012, telephone (021) 22-2810, fax 24-6211.

Getting there The park is 6 km southeast of Swellendam off the N2 to Cape Town.

Accommodation Overnight visitors stay in a camping and caravan park, which has ablution areas and braai sites (without grilles). Also available are 'chalavans' – permanently pitched caravans with six beds, wooden anterooms and a refrigerator.

Eating and drinking Essential groceries and meat may be bought at the park's shop. Visitors are advised to bring their own fresh food. The nearest grocery shops are in Swellendam. For day visitors there are several pleasant picnic spots with braai sites (without grilles).

Getting around There are 15 km of gravel road for gameviewing within the park. The speed limit is 25 km/hour. You may not leave your vehicle except at the campsite or to walk along the three trails that start and finish there (no reservations are necessary). The Riverside Walk takes approximately 45 minutes to complete and the Acacia and Aloe Hill walks take about 30 minutes each.

Wildlife Apart from bontebok, visitors to the park may spot a variety of animals, including grey rhebok, steenbok, red hartebeest, grysbok, grey duiker, Cape mountain zebra and small carnivores like otter, aardwolf, mongoose and jackal. About 170 species of bird have been recorded. There are also many species of reptile, amphibian and fish to be found.

Special attractions Erica, gladiolus, protea and mesembryanthemum are among the more than 470 species of plant flourishing within the park.
Along the Breede River are some beautiful indigenous tree species, including sweet thorn, Breede River yellowwood, boekenhout, wild olive and milkwood. An information centre at the campsite contains an assortment of interesting photographs and diagrams.

Fishing The Breede River has a high rating among anglers. Licences are available from any magistrates' office in the Cape, and are valid for one year.

Above: Grey rhebok in the Bontebok National Park. Sociable by nature, the rhebok (*Pelea capreolus*) lives in groups of up to 12 animals, usually under the leadership of a dominant male.

Buffalo Valley Game Farm

Set in the beautiful coastal forest near Buffalo Bay, the 175 ha Buffalo Valley Game Farm was established by the well-known conservationist, Hjalmar Thesen, in 1983.

Day visitors can enjoy a gentle 3 km circular drive, in their own vehicles, through the farm's grasslands and fynbos. Picnic sites have been set out in a coastal forest, and those with stamina can follow the bush walk to a lookout hide with panoramic views of the surrounding mountains and ocean. Birdlife is prolific, including the Knysna warbler and Cape francolin.

A comfortable lodge on an adjacent portion of the farm, bordering on the Goukamma River, has extensive wooden decking, a large indoor hearth and separate sleeping quarters with *en suite* facilities. The lodge overlooks a busy bird vlei.

Booking is essential and can be made by contacting Guy Thesen at P O Box 576, Knysna 6570, telephone/fax (0445) 2-2481.

Cape St Francis Nature Reserve

The promontory of Cape St Francis juts into the Indian Ocean some 30 km south of Humansdorp, and the 36 ha provincial nature reserve protects a coastal habitat of sand dune and fynbos rich in birdlife. To get there, drive to the village of Cape St Francis and proceed on foot, or drive to Sea Vista and walk from there to the reserve (the road from Sea Vista to The Point has been washed away, and only 4x4 vehicles can negotiate this route). The reserve is open at all times.

Diepwalle Forest

The last survivor of the great southern Cape elephant herds, along with two companions (all are cows) introduced from the Kruger National Park (*see separate entry*) in 1994, may occasionally be seen in the forests surrounding

allowed in the river below the rest camp, but boating is prohibited. The park is reached from the N2 along a signposted, good gravel road some 6 km long.

Boosmansbos Wilderness Area

Rushing rivers tumble through precipitous gorges in this rugged 14 200 ha wilderness region on the southern slopes of the Langeberg Mountains, between Heidelberg and Swellendam. A combination of pristine indigenous forest (stinkwood, yellowwood and red alder are prominent) high in the mountains, and fynbos, makes this wilderness an especially attractive area for hikes. Wildlife includes klipspringer, grysbok, grey rhebok, leopard, honey badger and a splendid variety of birds.

Boosmansbos constitutes the major part of the Grootvadersbosch Nature Reserve (*see separate entry*), and wilderness enthusiasts are encouraged to experience the natural character of this undeveloped area. A maximum of 12 visitors per day is allowed into the wilderness area. There are 64 km of self-guided hiking trails, with the most popular being a 27 km/two-day route that zigzags beneath a dark, magical canopy of trees. The overnight accommodation is rustic, and visitors are advised to bring their own tents or plan to sleep in the open. Take sufficient food and a camp stove, as open fires are forbidden. The spring-autumn period (September to April) is considered the best time to visit.

Boosmansbos is open throughout the year (the forest station is open from sunrise to sunset), and entry is by permit only (bookings have to be made at least two weeks in advance during the holiday season).

For further information (and to obtain a permit), write to The Reserve Manager, Grootvadersbosch Nature Reserve, P O Box 109, Heidelberg 6665, telephone (02934) 2-2412, or fax 2-2838.

Bracken Hill Falls

A turn-off from the main Knysna/Port Elizabeth road, about 11 km from Knysna, leads through a forest of gum and pine trees to the Bracken Hill Falls, a tumble of three cascades with a total drop of some 100 m, in the Noetzie River ravine. A number of pleasant picnic sites have been laid out beneath the trees.

THE CAPE: THE GARDEN ROUTE

Left: The base of a giant Outeniqua yellowwood tree (*Podocarpus falcatus*) in the Tsitsikamma Forest. Some of the yellowwoods in the park are about 800 years old, and reach heights of 60 metres. The crown of the tree is often festooned with 'old man's beard' – a species of lichen. **Above:** The rapid decline of the great elephant herds that roamed the southern Cape in the nineteenth century was due largely to the actions of elephant hunters, who treasured the heads, tusks and tails of these great pachyderms as trophies. Today only one of these magnificent specimens, the sole remnant of the famous 'Knysna' elephants, remains.

Diepwalle Forest Station. The station itself marks the start and finishing point of the 18,2 km Elephant Walk. No fewer than eight 'Big Trees' – Outeniqua yellowwood – can be seen along this easy trail through the indigenous forest; the largest is generally known as the 'King Edward VII Tree'.

The route, marked by elephant silhouettes, is open between 6 a.m. and 6 p.m and takes some eight hours to complete. Less energetic hikers may choose to follow any of the trail's three shorter loops, which range from 7 km to 9 km each. Drinking water is available at several places on the trail. No pets are allowed. Permits, available only from the Diepwalle Forest Station (telephone (0445) 82-6066), are required for the Elephant Walk and its subsidiary routes. Maps are also available at the forest station.

From Knysna, follow the N2 east for 6 km, take the Uniondale turn-off to the left and drive another 16 km to Diepwalle, which forms part of the 60 500 ha Knysna Indigenous Forests complex (*see separate entry*).

Featherbed Nature Reserve

The twin headlands guarding the entrance to the Knysna Lagoon are among the most popular attractions in Knysna, but few people realise that the westernmost headland is also a privately owned nature reserve that can be reached by scheduled ferry trips across the lagoon.

On Featherbed Bay Beach, The Tavern offers sumptuous food, such as oysters, champagne and fish braais, providing plenty of energy for an easy-going, hour-long guided walk along the 2,2 km Bushbuck Trail. The path cuts through bush that teems with 100 bird species and other small animals. Should you require it, a 4x4 will whisk you to a viewing platform high up on the headland overlooking the town, lagoon and sea. Featherbed is a Natural Heritage Site and is also renowned for being a sanctuary for South Africa's largest breeding herd of the endangered blue duiker (now numbering some 60 individuals).

For more information, contact Featherbed Nature Reserve, P O Box 753, Knysna 6570, telephone (0445) 2-1693, or fax 2-2373.

Garcia Forest

This 16 230 ha conservation area, stretching from Gysmanshoek Pass to Kuilsrivier in the high Langeberg range near Riversdale, is a wonderland of indigenous trees and rich fynbos species flourishing in settings varying from moist mountain slopes to drier areas reminiscent of the Karoo.

A number of trails traverse this beautiful region, ranging from the two-day Kristalkloof Trail to the pool-dotted Rooiwaterspruit Trail, which has two-, three-, four- and five-day alternatives. Overnight shelters, controlled by the Riversdale Municipality, sleep between six and eight hikers.

To obtain the necessary permits, write to The Manager, Tourist Camp, Nature Reserve, P O Box 29, Riversdale 6770, or telephone (02933) 3-2420.

Garden of Eden

To the north of the N2, about halfway between Knysna and Plettenberg Bay, lies an unspoilt area of indigenous forest that forms part of the larger Knysna Indigenous Forests complex (*see separate entry*). It is well signposted, and has a lay-by near the main entrance where cars may be parked. The area is unfenced and open at all times (no permits are required). Pets are not allowed. A trail, a little more than 1 km long, snakes over level country and rustic bridges while, for the physically handicapped, there is an 800 m 'Wheelchair Route'. There are also picnic sites and toilet facilities.

The forest mammals usually remain hidden, but their tracks can be spotted and may include those of elephant, bushbuck, blue duiker, honey badger, porcupine, caracal, two species of genet, mongoose, bushpig, baboon and vervet monkey. There are some 40 species of typical forest birds – most of which have loud and penetrating calls (in bird communication and defence of territory, sound is often more important than sight).

For more information, contact the Department of Water Affairs and Forestry, Private Bag X12, Knysna 6570, telephone (0445) 82-5466, or fax 82-5461.

Geelkrans Nature Reserve

Reclaimed driftsand on the coast to the east of Stilbaai lies at the base of this 165 ha sanctuary, noted for its interesting collection of dune fynbos, south-coast strandveld and coastal renosterveld. Trees found here include white milkwood, candlewood, coastal olive and kamferbos. Wildlife is typical of the coastal regions, and includes specimens such as shrews and members of the cat family, with the southern right whale breeding offshore. The reserve, which originally formed part of the Stilbaai Forest, was proclaimed in 1977 and gets its name from the fossilised sand cliffs on its eastern boundary. Evidence, in the form of middens, has been found – indicating the presence of Strandlopers some 12 000 years ago.

Geelkrans is open to hikers all year round from sunrise to sunset, and is at its best between October and March. It is situated about 4 km from Stilbaai East. Permits are available from Stilbaai Publicity Office, P O Box 245, Stilbaai 6674, telephone (02934) 4-2602, or fax 4-2549.

Goudveld Forest

Stretching along the upper plateau and across the foothills of the Outeniqua range, the Goudveld Forest – part of the Knysna Indigenous Forests (*see separate entry*) – covers some 8 500 ha, of which 4 418 ha are indigenous forest. There are extensive pine and eucalyptus plantations, as well as areas of natural fynbos.

Goudveld's name derives from the historic Millwood goldfields, the site of a minor gold rush in the 1880s. Today Millwood is being developed as a tourist attraction, with an information centre housed in the old mining town's last remaining building. A walk takes you through the mining area and to the processing plant of the Bendigo mine (currently being restored). There are also a number of picnic sites and attractively laid-out walks in the indigenous forest. At Jubilee Creek a 3 km walk passes some of the old alluvial diggings at Millwood, as well as a number of tunnels. Krisjan-se-Nek is the start of both the 9 km Woodcutter Trail and the 19 km Homtini Cycle Route for mountain bikers. Animals likely to be seen include lynx, bushpig, vervet monkey, honey badger, bushbuck and blue duiker, while the trees are home to numerous birds, notably the Knysna lourie, wood owl and Narina trogon.

Permits are required for cyclists only and can be bought at the entrance to the forest, where all visitors must register in the visitors' book. Entrance is permitted between 6 a.m. and 6 p.m. Information is available from the Department of Water Affairs and Forestry, Private Bag X12, Knysna 6570, telephone (0445) 82-5466, or fax 82-5461.

To reach Goudveld from Knysna, cross the N2 bridge over the Knysna River, drive 3 km towards George and then turn right onto the Rheenendal road, which joins the historic 'Passes Road' between George and Knysna. The forest reserve lies some 25 km from Knysna and is well signposted.

Goukamma Nature and Marine Reserve

South of the N2, between Sedgefield and the coastal resort of Buffalo Bay, lies the rich coastal and marine sanctuary of Goukamma. Its 2 230 ha of coastal reserve include the Goukamma River estuary, 14 km of coastline with extensive dunes that support a forest of milkwood, yellowwood and candlewood thickets, and Groenvlei, the Garden Route's only freshwater lake. Its marine reserve extends seawards for 1,8 km and covers 2 500 ha of the Indian Ocean and its floor.

Among the 220 recorded bird species are African fish eagle, spoonbill, jackal buzzard, marsh harrier, three species of kingfisher and the rare African black oystercatcher. Grysbok, blue duiker, bushbuck and bushpig inhabit the fynbos and dune-forest areas, while southern right whales can be seen offshore from August to December.

The reserve has four walking trails. There are two picnic sites and two accommodation

THE MASTER WEAVER AT WORK

The distinctive nest of a ground spider in the Tsitsikamma Forest. The ground spider can be distinguished from other spiders by its large jaws.

Southern Africa's many spider species are immensely varied in form, colouring and behavioural pattern – and in the ways they spin and use their silken threads.

Gossamer – those fine strands of silk you see floating free in the breeze – is one of the better-known types of thread, and it has a unique function: it serves as the baby spider's transport to survival.

When the spiderlings leave the cocoon they go 'ballooning', a fascinating feat which author Jean George describes in *The Amazing World of Nature*. She observed one grass spiderling make its way up a dried stalk, where 'it circled until it faced the wind. Then it threw up its hind feet and stood on its head like an acrobat. In this position it spun out two or three feet of ballooning thread, a dry and wide strand. Then it let go of the stalk, grabbed the silk with its front legs, and in the best circus tradition went flying through the air.

'Aided by the wind, it guided itself by pulling in on the streamer and then letting it out. As it billowed away, it struck the edge of the house and was stopped.

'There the spiderling reeled in its slender balloon and hurried to the porch roof to take off again. In this splendid manner it sailed out of sight.'

There are also trapping threads, which come in many shapes and sizes, ranging from the conventional and sometimes very beautiful orb of the garden spider to the crescent-shaped webs of tiny cave-dwelling species. Examine a trapping thread under a microscope and you will see something resembling a string of pearls. Each 'pearl' is a globule of sticky gum. An insect which touches one adheres to it, and in struggling to free itself contacts more globules – thereby becoming securely enmeshed. The rhythm of the struggling movements alerts the spider to the presence of its prey (spiders detect their prey through the vibrations of the thread). It rushes in, gives a poisonous bite to its victim, and binds it tightly in a swathing band – another kind of thread.

Some threads are used for receiving and sending warning or courting signals, for instance – and, in the case of the bolus spider, for 'fishing'. This nocturnal species spins out a single thread weighted at the end by a sticky ball, which it swings to and fro from a tree branch, on the off chance that it will connect with a passing insect.

The intricate silk threads and webs of a spider are therefore its eyes and ears, its voice, its livelihood and its chief weapon in the armoury of survival.

THE CAPE: THE GARDEN ROUTE

Above: Clouded skies are hazily reflected in the tranquil waters of the Keurbooms River Lagoon. **Right:** Abundant foliage forms a protective canopy for birds and insects in the Goudveld Forest, 25 km from Knysna. **Below:** A Cape grysbok (*Raphicerus melanotis*). This small antelope is mainly nocturnal.

units – one at Groenvlei Bush Camp and the other on the Buffalo Bay side of the reserve. If you have an angling licence you may fish in the reserve's waters.

The reserve is open throughout the year from 8 a.m. to 6 p.m. and is reached from the tarred road to Buffalo Bay. For further information, contact The Manager, Goukamma Nature and Marine Reserve, P O Box 331, Knysna 6570, telephone/fax (0445) 83-0042.

Groeneweide Nature Walk

The 10 km tarred road to the Saasveld Technikon leaves the N2 at the eastern approach to George. The technikon is the starting and finishing point of a 15 km circular walk, which has two shorter (7 km and 11 km) alternatives, through indigenous forest with some pine plantation. The walk is open from 6 a.m. to 6 p.m. Hikers should register in the visitors' book at the technikon. Maps can be obtained from the reception office there during office hours, or from the George Publicity Office. No dogs are allowed.

Grootvadersbosch Nature Reserve

In 1723 'Groot Vader' Roelof Oelofse was assigned a tract of forest, Melkhoutkraal, in the Langeberg. In 1896 the land was given to the state, and today the forest and surrounding wilderness are a nature reserve. The indigenous forest, covering some 250 ha, is one of the most noteworthy in the region and the largest remaining example in the Langeberg. Rising from it, clothing the foothills and slopes of the mountains, is the 14 200 ha Boosmansbos Wilderness Area (*see separate entry*) of mountain fynbos.

Bushbuck are abundant, and can be seen along the Bushbuck Trail that winds through dense and leafy vegetation known as Knysna high forest. The trail consists of a series of relatively easy day walks ranging in length from two to ten kilometres. Apart from bushbuck, Cape grysbok may be spotted in the forest fringes and the adjacent fynbos. Baboon, genet and porcupine may also be seen, while ornithologists will be entranced by the abundant birdlife, especially when viewed from the specially constructed hide. The forest is the only home of a subspecies of ghost frog, as well as the forest emperor butterfly. A gruelling 58 km mountain-bike route snakes through the conservancy and part of the reserve.

The reserve forms part of the Grootvadersbosch Conservancy, founded in 1992 by local farmers to protect the wildlife of the area. Boosmansbos makes up the larger part, Grootvadersbosch Nature Reserve the remainder.

Although it is unnecessary to book in advance, permits are required to enter the reserve. These can be obtained at the reserve itself for hikers intending to walk the Bushbuck Trail. Those wishing to walk through the wilderness, stay at the small campsite, or do the cycle route, will have to book in advance. Only 12 people per day are allowed into the reserve (except where prior arrangement has been made for larger groups). For further information, contact The Reserve Manager, Grootvadersbosch Nature Reserve, P O Box 109, Heidelberg 6665, telephone (02934) 2-2412, or fax 2-2838.

The reserve lies off the R322 travelling west from Heidelberg. Follow the signposted gravel road some 12 km from the town.

Huisklip Nature Reserve

This enchanting little reserve covers 321 ha of indigenous forest and fynbos to the west of Cape St Francis and Oyster Bay, on the banks of the Tsitsikamma River. Birds are plentiful, and careful observers may be lucky enough to catch a glimpse of small animals hiding in the undergrowth.

Entrance is free, but those wishing to take their 4x4 vehicles across the dunes (at recognised crossing points only) onto the beach must obtain a vehicle permit from the Western Region District Council in Humansdorp. All plant and animal life, as well as archaeological and historical features, are protected and may not be disturbed.

Kabeljousrivier Nature Reserve

A few kilometres north of Jeffreys Bay is a small (250 ha) reserve that is a pristine wilderness of

THE CAPE: THE GARDEN ROUTE

untouched coastal vegetation. Situated around the estuary of the Kabeljous River, the reserve is home to bushbuck, duiker, grysbok, and hosts of coastal birds. Colonies of seagull breed in the dunes, as do endangered African black oystercatcher, which are endemic to South Africa.

Visitors may walk through the reserve freely, although organised hikes, horse trails and bird-watching tours can be arranged. Book these through Aloe Africa Adventures, P O Box 921, Jeffreys Bay 6330, telephone (0423) 93-2313.

Keurbooms River Nature Reserve

For the most part, the Keurbooms River Nature Reserve is inaccessible to the general public, except by boat, which may stop at any one of the magnificent picnic spots dotted along the river banks.

The terrain is so rugged, with steep, sheer cliffs, that it is considered too risky for hikers but, from the safety of a boat on the river's calm waters, visitors may view the great milkwoods, yellowwoods and white stinkwoods typical of the Afro-montane forest.

The water and surrounding forests attract a wide variety of birds and small mammals, including bushbuck, blue duiker, vervet monkey, baboon and dassie. Bushpig and porcupine often root around in the gardens at night.

A canoe trail has proved popular, and guests may choose to stay over at a comfortable 12-bed hut situated 7 km from the estuary.

Within the boundaries of this 800 ha reserve, which embraces the Keurbooms River estuary some 8 km from Plettenberg Bay, is a pleasant public resort of about 28 fully equipped chalets, sites for 70 caravans, and 16 camping sites. The river has become a popular venue for anglers, waterskiers and boating enthusiasts.

The resort is on the west bank of the river and is signposted on the N2 from Plettenberg Bay. For reservations, write to The Manager, Aventura Plettenberg, Private Bag X1000, Plettenberg Bay 6600, telephone (04457) 3-2125 or 3-0322, or fax 9912.

Knysna Indigenous Forests

This wide strip of dense timberland, which includes Diepwalle Forest, Garden of Eden, Goudveld Forest, Groeneweide Nature Walk (*see separate entries*), and Jubilee Creek, covers a total of 60 500 ha on the southern slopes of the Outeniqua Mountains between Mossel Bay and the Krom River near Humansdorp.

Animals to be found in this forested wonderland include one last surviving cow belonging to the famous Knysna elephant herd, leopard, bushpig, baboon, vervet monkey, honey badger, bushbuck and blue duiker. But it is for their trees and the birdlife they support that these forests are most noteworthy. Species include stinkwood, kalander, kershout, hard pear, white pear, yellowwood, assegai and the pink-flowered Cape chestnut. The colourful Knysna lourie, the Narina trogon, wood owl, Rameron pigeon and Knysna scrub warbler are among the birds that live in the high forest canopy. The mountain buzzard, Cape eagle owl and crowned eagle can also be seen in the forests and surrounding mountains.

Three mountain-bike trails have been laid out, and hiking trails and nature walks are also available. There is a youth-group centre at the Harkerville Forest Station.

One of the best ways to discover the Knysna forests' 'Big Trees', picnic sites and nature walks is via a 48 km scenic drive starting and finishing at Knysna. It takes you along the Uniondale road (Prince Alfred's Pass) towards Diepwalle Forest Station. About 1 km after the sign to 'Elephant Walk' turn left into Kom-se-Pad, a dirt road that will take you to Gouna.

Enquiries and bookings for hiking trails and the youth-group centre can be made by writing to The Regional Director, Department of Water Affairs and Forestry, Private Bag X12, Knysna 6570, telephone (0445) 82-5466, or fax 82-5461. No bookings need be made for nature walks, although visitors are asked to register at certain points.

Knysna National Lake Area

The 15 000 ha Knysna Lagoon, dominated by the rocky bastions of the picturesque Knysna Heads, is an area of unsurpassed beauty and character. Tales of shipwrecks, gold, ivory and unlimited timber supplies lured many to this peaceful stretch of water in the early days.

Today, the lagoon area still attracts people – but now they come to enjoy watersports, such as sailing, cruising, boardsailing and angling. This playground is the country's second national lake area (Wilderness National Park is the first), and through careful management, such as zoning ecologically sensitive areas for specific uses, the National Parks Board aims to maintain a healthy balance between conservation and recreation.

The lagoon, characterised by sandbanks, salt marshes and reed beds, teems with life, providing food for countless organisms. One of the most peculiar and interesting creatures to be found here is the endangered Knysna seahorse (*Hippocampus capensis*).

Although no tourism facilities exist within the lagoon area, the town and its surrounds provide ample accommodation. Further information may be obtained from the National Parks Board office at the end of Thesen's Jetty; or contact The Park Warden, Knysna National Lake Area, P O Box 314, Knysna 6570, telephone (0445) 2-2095, or fax 82-5801.

Kranshoek Coastal Nature Walk

This fairly strenuous trail of some 9 km leads through indigenous coastal forest, fynbos and plantations clothing the heights above the Indian Ocean. The walk is reached via the Knysna/Plettenberg Bay road. Take the Harkerville turn-off 17 km outside Knysna and follow the signs to Kranshoek. The walk's starting point,

Left: Streams, waterfalls and freshwater pools provide welcome relief to sun-parched hikers along the 48 km course of the Otter Trail. The trail links up at Nature's Valley with the equally impressive Tsitsikamma Hiking Trail. Some hikers choose to walk both trails in succession.
Above: Sea anemones at low tide in the Tsitsikamma National Park.

picnic sites and a splendid viewing point are reached after about 5 km of winding gravel road through the beautiful Harkerville indigenous forest. The walk has interpretive signboards along the way.

Permits to follow the walk can be obtained from the kiosk on the Kranshoek road during holiday periods (school holidays). Out-of-season visitors must sign a self-issuing permit to enter the forest reserve. The walk, which is open from 6 a.m. to 6 p.m., should be undertaken only by the reasonably fit. No pets are allowed. Maps are available from the forestry office in Knysna.

Marloth Nature Reserve

Dramatic mountain scenery, evergreen forests, deep, cool valleys and a significant stretch of the Swellendam Hiking Trail are the main features of the 11 300 ha Marloth Nature Reserve, set on the southern slopes of the Langeberg range overlooking Swellendam.

The predominantly Cape fynbos vegetation comprises a wide variety of proteas, ericas and leucadendrons. In the deep pockets of indigenous forest, flowering trees such as wild gardenia and wild almond grow among the bigger stinkwood and yellowwood. Wildlife includes leopard, baboon and various antelope. There is also a rich birdlife, including raptors such as eagles and falcons. The reserve has a large variety of reptiles and amphibians, among them the rare ghost frog.

Within Marloth is the challenging 76 km, five- to seven-day Swellendam Hiking Trail, which starts at Koloniesbos, some 4 km from the Swellendam Forest Station. Six 16-bed huts accommodate hikers along the route. However, four of these have no fireplaces, so visitors should take their own camp stoves.

The terrain along the trail, which winds through both the southern and northern slopes of the Langeberg, is broken and mountainous, and a fair degree of physical fitness is needed, even on the shorter routes. For safety reasons, hikers must travel in parties of three or more. A permit is required for the trail which is open throughout the year.

To get to Marloth Nature Reserve, follow the signposts from Swellendam's Andrew Whyte Street. October to March is the best time to visit the reserve. Entry (during daylight hours) is by permit, available on weekdays from the office at the entrance between 8 a.m and 4 p.m. For reservations and further information, write to The Manager, Marloth Nature Reserve, P O Box 28, Swellendam 6740, telephone (0291) 4-1410, or fax 4-1488.

Noorsekloof Nature Reserve

This nature reserve in Jeffreys Bay, proclaimed in 1983, has as its focal point a small stream, with fern-fringed pools and distinctive slabs of shale, which can be followed all the way from the sea on a scenic 3 km path up the valley.

About 60 indigenous tree species may be found in the reserve, including the giant river euphorbia (*Euphorbia triangularis*). Invaders such as alien acacia are constantly being removed by conservation staff.

Wildlife sheltering in the Noorsekloof includes bushbuck, Cape grysbok, the common duiker, the little blue duiker, dassie and vervet monkey. It is also a haven for birds, from bulbul, shrike and the brilliantly plumaged sunbird, to African goshawk, gymnogene and raucous-voiced hadeda.

The 28 ha reserve is easily accessible from the town centre via Koedoe Street. For further information, contact Jeffreys Bay Tourism, P O Box 460, Jeffreys Bay 6330, telephone (0423) 93-2588, or fax 93-2227.

AN EQUINE ODDITY

The Knysna seahorse changes colour according to its surroundings.

With its uncannily horse-like head and heraldic posture it looks like a tiny creature of mythology, something dreamt up by the storytelling ancients. But in fact the seahorse is very real, and a true fish. It has gills, and a mouth which, although more of a tubular snout, is basically a fish's mouth. Through it, the seahorse sucks in the tiny marine organisms that make up its diet.

Timid and vulnerable to predators, the tiny seahorse (it is seldom over 12 cm long) rarely swims free, but is nearly always found hiding among the plantlife of tidal reaches, usually erect. It uses its prehensile tail as an anchor, and its head as a kind of hook to pull itself up and around clusters of seaweed. Like a chameleon, it can change colour to blend with its surroundings. Also like a chameleon, its eyes work independently of each other and provide all-round vision.

One of nature's curiosities, the seahorse's oddest feature is the brood pouch on the abdomen of the male, into which the female places her eggs. After this, she takes no more part in the breeding process. The eggs (as many as 600) are fertilised and develop in the pouch, hatch in 30-60 days, and the young are released by their father in a series of exhausting contortions that appear very much like birth pangs.

The five southern African species are found east of Mossel Bay. All are rare or endangered.

The Knysna seahorse (*Hippocampus capensis*) is constantly under threat by residential development and by human exploitation. Highly prized as an attractive aquarium oddity, sedentary and defenceless, it is a sad and declining victim of the skin-diving collector.

Otter Trail

This five-day trail traverses 48 km of the Tsitsikamma National Park (*see separate entry*), crossing ravines and rivers and winding up the sheer cliffs of the coastal plateau. It is a trail for fitter and more experienced hikers – and for those who are not afraid of heights. The trail starts at the Storms River Mouth rest camp, and leads westwards to Nature's Valley.

On the fourth day the trail climbs to the coastal plateau, then drops for the last time to reach the Groot River estuary at Nature's Valley. Energetic hikers can now also tackle the Tsitsikamma Hiking Trail (*see separate entry*), which starts in Nature's Valley and finishes at Storms River Forest Station – in all, a grand, virtually circular, tour. To reserve a place on the trails, write to the National Parks Board, P O Box 787, Pretoria 0001, or telephone them at

Left: Marooned by the tides, this sea snake – an air-breather, unlike eels – lies dying on the Tsitsikamma coast. The meeting of the warm Agulhas and cold Benguela currents along the coastline has resulted in a unique, colourful blending of tropical and cold-water species of marine flora and fauna.

(012) 343-1991, or fax 343-0905; or National Parks Board, P O Box 7400, Roggebaai 8012, telephone (021) 22-2810, fax 24-6211.

A maximum of 12 people per day may start the trail, though hikers are allowed to proceed singly. Hikers are required to obtain a permit at the reception area of the Storms River Mouth Rest Camp before starting. Firewood is usually available at the overnight huts, but a camp stove should be taken. A water bottle is essential. The shop at Storms River Mouth sells bread, fresh meat, 'long-life' milk, tinned foods, soft drinks and liquor. The licensed restaurant serves both à la carte and takeaway meals.

Outeniqua Hiking Trail

The full trail from Beervlei (north of Wilderness) to Harkerville (east of Knysna) is an eight-day adventure along 108 km of mountain track, through fynbos, forest and plantation. Hikers enjoy breathtaking views over the Garden Route and Indian Ocean. Shorter sections of the trail, lasting two or more days, can also be hiked.

Permits are needed and those wishing to follow the trail should book by writing to The Regional Director, Southern Cape Forest Region, Private Bag X12, Knysna 6570, or telephone (0445) 82-5466, fax 82-5461.

Outeniqua Nature Reserve

This 36 000 ha reserve comprises a number of sections, all of which were proclaimed on different dates, and each of which has its own special attraction. Attakwaskloof Nature Reserve, with its 9 800 ha of mountain fynbos, Ruitersbos Forest, Moordkuils Forest, Doringrivier Wilderness Area, Camferskloof Forest and Witfontein Forest provide visitors with a spectacular combination of scenic mountain views, striking fynbos, and the sheer tranquillity of the area – making this reserve popular with hikers.

Trails include the two-day Tierkop Hiking Trail, the two- or three-day Attakwaskloof Hiking Trail, a seven-day trail throughout the whole reserve (or parts of it), and a number of day hikes and walks. Trailists overnight at comfortable huts with beds and braai facilities, or at demarcated camp sites (bring your own tent). There is also a 4x4 trail, with two overnight stops, and a mountain-bike trail, which follows the same route.

Mammals likely to be spotted include klipspringer and bushbuck, while the Cape sugarbird, European golden oriole and black eagle are some of the bird species that may be seen.

The flora is mainly mountain fynbos, home to many species of erica which explode into colourful bloom during September and October. Occasional clumps of the rare black disa (*Disa bodkinii*) can be seen in the Attakwaskloof section.

To reach the reserve's main offices, follow the R29 from George towards Oudtshoorn. After some 5 km, turn right at the signpost marked 'Outeniqua Nature Reserve'. Look out for the reserve's signpost and wooden gates.

Enquiries and bookings for the trails should be directed to Outeniqua Nature Reserve, Private Bag X6517, George 6530, telephone (0441) 70-8323/70-8325, or fax 70-7138.

Pauline Bohnen Nature Reserve

Among the ravines and plains of this 150 ha reserve you will find a large display of limestone fynbos – shrubs and plants unique to the calcium-rich, calcrete soils to the west of Stilbaai. The reserve is named after Pauline Bohnen, an authority on southern Cape flora, who researched and compiled month-by-month lists of the flowering plants found within the reserve.

During springtime the display of flowers is particularly spectacular, and the strong fragrance of various species of pelargonium, blue daisy, painted lady and small granny bonnet attracts sunbirds and sugarbirds to the fynbos nectar. Large trees grow in the ravines, including the endangered bitter bush (*Euryops muirii*) and the protected white milkwood (*Sideroxylon inerme*). Grysbok, bushbuck, puff adder, mongoose, tortoise and rodent are common in the area.

For further enquiries, contact the Municipality, P O Box 2, Stilbaai 6674, telephone (02934) 4-1577, or fax 4-1140.

Plettenberg Bay Country Club

Some 67 ha of land around the Plettenberg Bay Country Club's golf course in the Piesang Valley, lying about 2 km from Plettenberg Bay, has been set aside as a municipal nature reserve. It features small areas of indigenous forest which shelter buck, monkey and other small animals. There are also numerous bird species. To reach the reserve, turn off the main road from Knysna at the Piesang Valley signpost. Another sign indicates the route to the country club, where visitors should seek permission to walk through the golf course. The reserve is open all year between sunrise and sunset.

Robberg Nature Reserve

Centuries ago, the 4 km long peninsula of Robberg ('Mountain of the Seal') was home to beachcombing Strandlopers, whose caves and middens can still be seen in this impressive 175 ha provincial reserve off the N2 at Plettenberg Bay. The walk from the car park to The Point and back takes about three hours to complete, although shorter alternatives can be taken. No pets or vehicles are allowed beyond the car park, and fires may be lit only in demarcated areas.

Visitors may fish, hike and picnic within the reserve, which is open during daylight hours throughout the year. Permits can be obtained at the entrance.

Above left: The burrowing rain frog, or blaasop (*Breviceps*), is a stocky, pugnacious-looking inhabitant of the Tsitsikamma Forest. Normally secretive, these frogs are active on the surface of the ground in rainy weather. The rain frog gorges itself on flying ants, earthworms and termites, and spends nine months of the year in suspended animation underground. When the frog is irritated or alarmed, it blows itself up into a round ball. **Above right:** A boat plies up the Touw River. The Wilderness Rest Camp, offering accommodation in chalets and at caravan and camping sites, lies on the banks of the river.

For further details, contact The Officer-in-Charge, Robberg Nature Reserve, Private Bag X1003, Plettenberg Bay 6600, telephone (04457) 3-2125 or 3-2185.

Seekoei River Nature Reserve

To reach this 66 ha provincial reserve, take the Jeffreys Bay turn-off from the N2, and then follow the Aston Bay road. It lies some 82 km west of Port Elizabeth. The reserve, which includes the estuary of the Seekoei and Swart rivers, was originally proclaimed as a sanctuary for waterfowl. In the areas of thick indigenous bush, you are likely to spot many of the smaller buck species, including blue duiker, grey duiker and bushbuck, while large populations of birds frequent the estuary. Bushpig, porcupine, caracal, spotted genet and mongoose species may also be seen.

Much of Seekoei River Nature Reserve is accessible by pontoon only, a charming form of transport which also gives access to a 3 km hiking trail. The reserve is open every day between 7 a.m. and 5 p.m.

For further details, write to The Manager, Seekoei River Nature Reserve, P O Box 1733, Jeffreys Bay 6330, or telephone/fax (0423) 92-0339.

Sinclair Nature Reserve

East of Knysna, in the Kruisfontein Forest, is this appealing biological reserve that extends over 1 828 ha through some of the southern Cape's most beautiful countryside. An impressive variety of indigenous shrubs and trees flourishes among the plateau's hillocks and ravines, among them Outeniqua yellowwood, red alder, witels, Cape redwood, real yellowwood, cherrywood and kamassi. Although there has not yet been a detailed study of its wildlife, the reserve is known to accommodate such animals as honey badger, leopard, grysbok, porcupine, and more elusive species such as bat, mouse, mole, shrew and mongoose. There is a large variety of birds, such as the Knysna lourie, fish eagle, crowned eagle and Knysna scrub warbler.

The reserve itself is not open to the public, but hikers can get a taste of it on the Harkerville Coast Hiking Trail. This two-day circular trail starts at Harkerville Forest Station (reached via a turn-off midway along the Plettenberg Bay/Knysna road) and leads through indigenous forest to the breathtaking Harkerville coastline.

Much of the trail involves clambering over rocks, and participants should be fit before attempting it. Overnight huts cater for parties of 12 hikers. Also passing through Sinclair is one of the Harkerville cycle routes, while anglers are permitted, on a day-permit basis, to fish on the Sinclair coast. Bookings are made via the Department of Water Affairs and Forestry, Private Bag X12, Knysna 6570, telephone (0445) 82-5466, or fax 82-5461.

Terblans Nature Walk

On this walk you can follow bushpig markers for two hours through the beautiful Gouna Forest – the domain of the last remaining Knysna elephant. The walk begins and ends at Grootdraai Picnic Site, 16 km north of Knysna on the Gouna road (Kom-se-Pad), and is open from 6 a.m. to 6 p.m. No pets are allowed.

While permits are not needed, hikers must register in the visitors' book at the start. For maps and more information, write to the Department of Water Affairs and Forestry, Private Bag X12, Knysna 6570, or telephone (0445) 82-5466, fax 82-5461.

Tsitsikamma Hiking Trail

The self-guided Tsitsikamma Hiking Trail can be started and completed at various points, such as the forestry stations of Bloukrans, Lottering and Kleinbos, at the Boskor Sawmill. But the full 64 km/five-day trip starts at Kalander in Nature's Valley, and ends at the Storms River Bridge. The shorter trips are suitable for weekend excursions.

The route takes in a wide range of indigenous trees, wild flowers, mountain streams and magnificent views. Stinkwood and yellowwood are commonly visible along the route which runs over low and high plateaus blanketed with the indigenous forest that is characteristic of the Tsitsikamma area. Trees are labelled with their national tree numbers for easy identification.

Large animals that once roamed the forests have unfortunately been exterminated, but surviving mammals include bushpig, vervet monkey, caracal, honey badger and otter. Approximately 70 bird species are commonly spotted.

Overnight huts can accommodate up to 20 people, the maximum number of hikers that may start the trail on any one day. Enquiries and reservations should be directed to SAFCOL, Private Bag X537, Humansdorp 6300, telephone (0423) 91-0393, or fax 5-2745.

Tsitsikamma Indigenous Forests

The Tsitsikamma Indigenous Forests form the eastern extremity of what could be called the southern Cape indigenous forest complex. Within the forests are a number of reserves, each with its own forest station. To the west are the forests of Groenkop, Woodville, Beervlei, Karatara, Farleigh and Goudveld (*see separate entry*), all of which are controlled from Farleigh Forest Station. Closer to Knysna are Gouna Forest, Diepwalle Forest (*see separate entry*), Ysternek Nature Reserve (*see separate entry*) and Harkerville Forest (including Sinclair Nature Reserve (*see separate entry*)) – all controlled from Diepwalle Forest Station.

To the east of these, starting at the Keurbooms River and lying about 8 km from Plettenberg Bay, is the Keurbooms Forest, followed by the forestlands of Bloukrans, Lottering, Storms River, Blueliliesbush and, in the extreme east, Witelsbos – a total of more than 11 000 ha controlled from the Tsitsikamma Forest Station at Storms River village. These eastern reserves are spread along the Tsitsikamma coastal plateau, a 10 km strip of land sandwiched between the Tsitsikamma Mountains and the Indian Ocean.

These dark and silent forests are popular with hikers, who regularly follow the trails that pass below the woody giants. The five-day Tsitsikamma Hiking Trail (see separate entry) traverses the southern flanks of the Tsitsikamma Mountains, passing through prime examples of mountain forest and fynbos. To the south, along the coast, is the famed Otter Trail (see separate entry), which winds from the Storms River Mouth to the estuary of the Groot River. A number of other walks have been laid out, and there is a mountain-bike route in the Storms River area. Worth visiting is the 'Big Tree', an ancient Outeniqua yellowwood standing taller than a ten-storey building. Here an interesting boardwalk route illustrates many of the forest's trees. Several large Outeniqua yellowwoods, estimated to be over 800 years old, dominate the site, and a platform has been erected over the remains of a fallen 'giant' that toppled on 31 December 1994.

Mammals and birdlife, although varied, are in no great abundance, as the forests have their roots in nutrient-poor soil. Small groups of bushpig (although these are rarely seen,) forage among the trees, and you may just be lucky enough to catch a glimpse of a bushbuck. Other animals include honey badger, chacma baboon, vervet monkey, lynx and leopard.

Birds that might be seen are Knysna lourie and Narina trogon, which is colourful, but very shy. Robins are found near the picnic sites and Cape batis hop around in the undergrowth. Visitors may also spot a mountain buzzard or, if extremely fortunate, a woodpecker.

Further information about Knysna's indigenous forests may be obtained by contacting the Department of Water Affairs and Forestry, Private Bag X12, Knysna 6570, telephone (0445) 82-5466, or fax 82-5461. Alternatively, contact The Forester-in-Charge, Tsitsikamma Forest, Private Bag X530, Humansdorp 6300, telephone (0423) 541-5448, or fax 541-1557.

Tsitsikamma National Park

From the placid lagoon at Nature's Valley, a rugged and unspoilt shoreline stretches eastwards for some 80 km to the mouth of the Groot River. This is the Tsitsikamma National Park, a narrow coastal plain bounded by cliffs and beaches, and extending 5 km into the sea, encompassing a total area of 54 000 hectares.

Tsitsikamma was the first marine national park in Africa, and below the heaving swells of the Indian Ocean is a wonderland of marine life equal in all respects to the verdant ravines and valleys of the landward segment.

The De Vasselot section, adjoining Nature's Valley, encapsulates the park's variety of vegetation, including sandy beaches, dense forest and fynbos. There are a number of interesting day trails through this section, and a beautiful camping and caravan site on the Groot River.

Storms River Rest Camp, close to the mouth of the river, offers a wide range of tourist accommodation, from fully equipped log chalets and beach cottages, to oceanettes (beach apartments), all close to the booming breakers of the ocean. There is also a picturesque and well-equipped camping area.

Angling is permitted only along a 2,8 km stretch of shore between Goudgate and the Waterfall. Spearfishing and the removal of bait organisms are strictly prohibited (bait is available from the shop). Indoor and outdoor exhibitions portray the biological diversity of the park, and several middens (refuse heaps containing shellfish and other remains) are visible evidence of the Strandlopers who once inhabited the caves along this shore.

Over and above the famous Otter Trail (see separate entry), a number of shorter trails exist. Walkers can choose to follow the hour-long Mouth Trail (with spectacular views of sea and coast), the three-hour Waterval Trail, the Loerie Trail, or, leading off it, the two-and-a-half-hour Blue Duiker Trail, which traces a winding path through coastal forests to join the Otter Trail (see separate entry).

More unusual are the underwater trails that have been marked out for diving enthusiasts. The snorkelling trail near the start of the Otter Trail is as popular as the Scuba Trail, which starts from the boathouse below the reception centre. Only divers who possess a valid SAUU (South African Underwater Union) certificate or recognised equivalent will be permitted to dive the Scuba Trail. The marine life is magnificent on both trails, and is typical of this section of the southern Cape coast.

TSITSIKAMMA NATIONAL PARK AT A GLANCE

When to go Rainfall is perennial but the driest months are generally in midwinter – June and July. The park is open every day from 5.30 a.m. to 9.30 p.m.

Reservations and information Enquiries and applications for accommodation (including camping and caravan sites and places on the Otter Trail) should be addressed to the National Parks Board, P O Box 787, Pretoria 0001, telephone (012) 343-1991, or fax 343-0905; or at P O Box 7400, Roggebaai 8012, telephone (021) 22-2810, or fax 24-6211. The National Parks Board publishes comprehensive guides to the trees, fishes and seaweeds of the parks.

Getting there The turn-off to the park is about halfway between Knysna and Humansdorp on the N2, 9 km west of the Paul Sauer Bridge over the Storms River.

Accommodation At Storms River Mouth there are fully equipped two-bedroomed beach cottages, a number of self-contained one-bedroomed (four-bed) cottages with kitchenette and bathroom, and one- and two-bedroomed oceanettes (beach apartments). There are also camping and caravan sites. Washing and ironing facilities are provided and there is a swimming pool.

The De Vasselot section has camping facilities, forest huts (two-bed) and caravan sites, while the Otter Trail has overnight huts.

Eating and drinking There is a restaurant, and a shop that sells groceries, perishables and liquor.

Getting around Several trails radiate from Storms River Mouth Rest Camp, the longest and most dramatic being the well-known Otter Trail, which leads 48 km west, over and around steep cliffs to Nature's Valley. Shorter trails include the Mouth, the Loerie, the Waterval and the Blue Duiker.

Swimmers, divers and underwater photographers can view the wonders of the sea on the Scuba Trail. There is also a snorkelling trail.

Fishing Anglers are restricted to a small area of the marine sanctuary. Bait-collecting and spearfishing are forbidden.

Special precautions There are strict regulations governing the lighting of fires. The Otter Trail demands forethought in equipping yourself, stamina (paths rise steeply to circumvent cliffs) and a head for heights.

THE CAPE: THE GARDEN ROUTE

Right: Separated from the Indian Ocean by a line of high, bush-grown dune, the Serpentine is a navigable link between the Touw River, near its estuary at Wilderness, and the saltwater Upper and Lower Langvlei, and Rondevlei.

Van Kervel Nature Reserve

This 9 ha reserve in George is situated near the railway level crossing in Caledon Street. It is open from sunrise to sunset and features a delightful selection of indigenous trees and shrubs. A number of flower species, including the George lily (*Cyrtanthus purpurea*), are also cultivated.

Wadrift Nature Reserve

This privately run 235 ha reserve offers nature walks, hiking trails and conveniently central accommodation from which to explore the lakes and dramatic coastline of the Garden Route. It lies in a rural area on the Bietou River, some ten minutes from Plettenberg Bay. The peaceful surroundings include a swimming pool and a children's playpark. Walks vary from a short 1,5 km stroll to an 18 km trail, and offer views of fynbos forest, small antelope and many birds.

To reach Wadrift, take the N2 leading from Plettenberg Bay to Port Elizabeth, cross the Bietou River and turn left at the Avontuur sign. The reserve is signposted some 4,5 km further on. To make bookings, write to The Manager, Wadrift Nature Reserve, P O Box 72, Plettenberg Bay 6600, or telephone (04457) 9425, fax 9453.

Whiskey Creek Nature Reserve

Exotically named, Whiskey Creek is a far more serene place than its name suggests, although it is more valued by botanists than the average day visitor (there are no facilities). No fewer than six soil moisture types – ranging from very wet to very dry – have produced a varied vegetation, including Karoo scrub, fynbos and forest. There are many keurboom or blossom trees (*Virgilia oroboides*) that produce a sweet-smelling mauve blossom in summer.

For further enquiries, contact Plettenberg Bay Tourism Association, P O Box 894, Plettenberg Bay 6600, telephone (04457) 3-4065, or fax 3-4066.

Wilderness National Park

Originally proclaimed in 1983 as South Africa's first National Lake Area, this unique wetland system creates an interconnected web of vlei, river and fen that covers 10 600 hectares. It stretches from the picturesque village of Wilderness eastwards up the coast to as far as the Goukamma Nature Reserve (*see separate entry*). The park includes the Touw River, Serpentine Channel, Eilandvlei, Langvlei, Rondevlei and Swartvlei (the largest of the five lakes in the area), and also embraces long stretches of rocky coastline. The national park is managed to ensure that conservation and recreation mix happily. Watersports are a feature of the region and range from angling and sedate canoe trips to the exhilarating speed of water-skiing and boardsailing.

Home to waterbirds in their thousands, the wetlands are also an ornithologist's paradise. Four kingfisher species are found, including the giant kingfisher, which is commonly seen skilfully skimming the water in search of its daily prey. There are bird hides at Langvlei, Swartvlei and Rondevlei.

A series of four Kingfisher trails, ranging in length from three to 12 km, explores the park's various attractions. The 3 km Giant Kingfisher Trail roams through the forest and emerges at boulder-strewn pools and a waterfall. The Brownhooded Kingfisher Trail follows the path of the Duiwe River, the Half-collared Kingfisher Trail winds through the forest, and the 12 km Pied Kingfisher Trail takes hikers across the floodplains of the Serpentine. A highlight of the Pied Kingfisher Trail is the 'boardwalk' – a walkway through the unspoilt intertidal zone of the Touw River and its reed-fringed banks. Also available is the 6 km circular Cape Dune Molerat Trail, which starts at the Rondevlei office and follows the dunes to the edge of Swartvlei.

The Wilderness Rest Camp on the bank of the Touw River offers chalets, and caravan and camping sites. There is also a reception office, as well as a shop offering basic commodities. The Ebb and Flow North Rest Camp, which provides more rustic accommodation further upstream, is connected to the Ebb and Flow South Rest Camp by a bridge over the Serpentine. Canoes may be hired for an unforgettable few hours' paddling on the lakes. Day visitors are not permitted during peak periods.

Wilderness National Park has been awarded Ramsar status, as its wetland area is regarded as being of international importance. (The name is taken from the Iranian village at which the wetland convention took place.) To make bookings and for further information, contact the National Parks Board, P O Box 787, Pretoria 0001, telephone (012) 343-1991, fax 343-0905; or P O Box 7400, Roggebaai 8012, telephone (021) 22-2810, or fax 24-6211.

The Rondevlei office, situated just off The Lakes Road within the park, is an important research and management centre. It serves as the head office for Southern Parks research and is also the starting point of the Cape Dune Molerat Trail.

Ysternek Nature Reserve

About 25 km north of Knysna, on the road to Avontuur, the 1 212 ha Ysternek reserve offers much to those who enjoy exploring the fynbos and evergreen indigenous forests of the southern Cape. However, the Knysna/Uniondale road (R339) is unfortunately not suitable for caravans and trailers.

Ysternek was created to conserve mountain fynbos and indigenous forest, part of which includes an area of typical wet mountain forest containing dense stands of tree fern. Inside this forest is a beautiful picnic spot known as the 'Dal van Varings' (Valley of Ferns). From this vantage point visitors can drive or walk up a steep, narrow road to a viewing site: to the south are the Knysna Forests and Plettenberg Bay; to the north the Buffelsnek Plantation, controlled by SAFCOL (South African Forestry Company Limited), reaches out to the deep and desolate ravines of the Outeniqua Mountains. To the east, on a clear day, the eye can follow the Tsitsikamma Mountains almost as far as Humansdorp, while to the west you will see dense forest containing tree ferns.

There is also a short walk from the picnic spot through the tree ferns. The birdlife is prolific; the mammal population includes leopard, bushbuck and bushpig. Yellowwood and stinkwood are among the tree species.

The best time to visit is from October to May. For further information, write to the Department of Water Affairs and Forestry, Private Bag X12, Knysna 6570, telephone (0445) 82-5466, or fax 82-5461.

Lure of the Little Karoo

There's nothing little about the Little Karoo. This broad, mainly arid, valley of fertile vineyards, fruit and ostrich farms is little only when compared with its big brother to the north – the Great Karoo. Some 300 km long and 100 km wide, the ochre-and-khaki Little Karoo, bounded on every side by mountains, receives an average of a mere 150 mm of rain a year, yet nature has endowed it with several blessings.

The valley is drained by the Olifants River, so named because when white men first set eyes on the 'Klein Karoo' (in 1689, Simon van der Stel led a party into the area) it teemed with elephant, lion, hippo, quagga, kudu, rhino and buffalo. Not a trace remains of these large mammals – except for leopard, which sun themselves in the remote areas, and baboon.

Another survivor is the ostrich – a primitive running bird that has earned fortunes for the farmers of this region (particularly in the late 1890s and early 1900s, when ostrich feathers were in great demand in Europe). Overnight, the Oudtshoorn farmers became 'feather barons', and their ornate and expensive mansions – 'feather palaces' – still bear testimony to the boom years.

The rugged Swartberg massif, with its beautiful red hues, has its own treasures. In its foothills are the world-famous Cango Caves – an intricate series of limestone caverns discovered in 1780 and later developed as a major tourist attraction.

Anysberg Nature Reserve

The 43 000 ha Anysberg Nature Reserve, established in 1987 to preserve the stark natural beauty of the Karoo and its wildlife, lies south of Matjiesfontein, about halfway between Ladismith and Laingsburg and some four hours' drive from Cape Town. The scenery is striking, ranging from tumbled hills to dramatic mountain gorges, and the varied plantlife encompasses Karoo veld, mountain fynbos and renosterveld, with beautiful proteas and drought-resistant succulents. Historic ruins, dating back to the 18th century, are dotted throughout the area, which is also rich in Bushman (San) rock art.

Cape Nature Conservation has recently purchased a farm, Touwsfontein, which adjoins the Anysberg Reserve. This 10 000 ha property is particularly rich in Karoo flora, with an estimated 500 species having been identified to date.

Wildlife includes steenbok, duiker and hare, as well as carnivores such as leopard, caracal and black-backed jackal. Birdlife is prolific, with raptors such as the black eagle and pale chanting goshawk wheeling across the (usually) cloudless skies, while waterfowl can be seen at the dams.

There are no formal hiking trails, but enthusiasts are welcome to hike through the reserve. However, an exciting two-day guided horse trail is offered over weekends (a maximum of ten riders per excursion). Riders camp overnight in a shelter or under the stars. Mountain-bike enthusiasts are also welcome but reservations must be made beforehand. For overnighters there are self-catering cottages (visitors must supply their own linen, food, cooking and eating utensils) and campsites.

For further information and to make reservations, contact Anysberg Nature Reserve, Private Bag X216, Ladismith 6655, telephone (02372) 1913.

Baviaanskloof Wilderness Area

Between the small towns of Willowmore in the west and Patensie in the east runs one of the most scenically beautiful drives in the Little Karoo – through the steep, thickly wooded Baviaanskloof ravine. Consisting of the forests of Baviaanskloof (68 532 ha), Cockscomb (52 740 ha) and Formosa (202 000 ha), the wilderness area is a wonderland of pristine wooded valleys dominated by the bare peaks of the Baviaanskloof and Kouga mountain ranges – long a favourite haunt of the hardier breed of climber and hiker.

The hills are studded with caves rich in Bushman (San) paintings and stone artefacts left by the prehistoric hunter-gatherers who frequented the area over 100 000 years ago.

Visitors may see chacma baboon, bushpig, klipspringer, rhebok, mountain zebra and the occasional leopard, as well as numerous birds.

Left: A flock of young ostriches on a farm near Calitzdorp. The ostrich can attain a weight of 156 kilograms. It has several features which distinguish it from other birds, including its long, powerful legs (capable of carrying it at speeds of up to 70 km/h), its oil-less feathers (which soak up water when it rains) and two-toed feet. **Above left:** Mating 'whites' (pierid) butterflies.

Above right: The rhombic skaapsteker is among the most beautiful of southern Africa's snakes. It is a curiously gentle reptile, and rarely bites humans – even given the strongest provocation. Growing to a length of about 90 cm, it lives on small animals such as mice, frogs and lizards.

THE CAPE: LITTLE KAROO

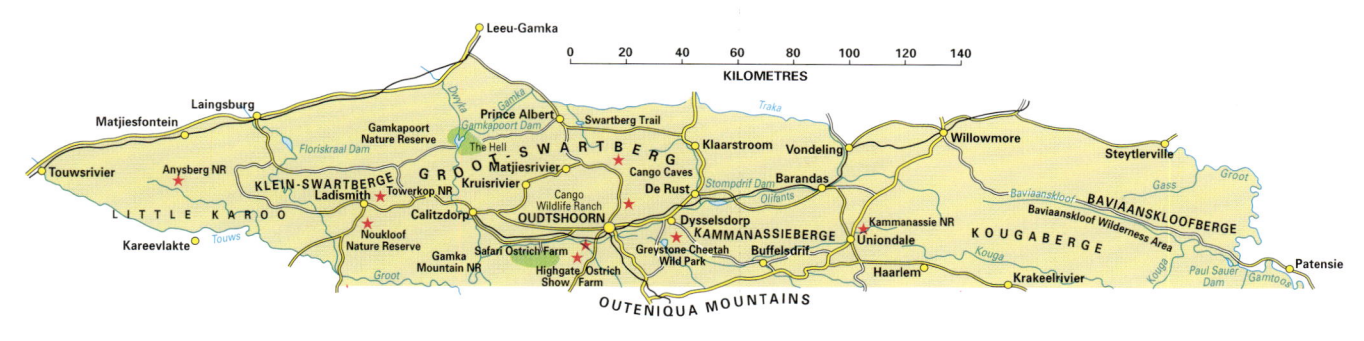

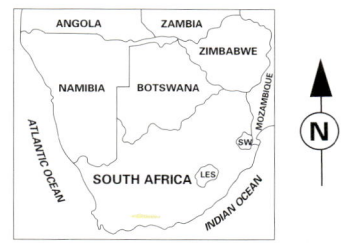

The access road meanders through the kloof, several times crossing the Baviaanskloof River in the west and the Witrivier and Grootrivier in the east with the result that, after heavy rains, the region is inaccessible to ordinary vehicles. There is, however, a self-guided motor trail, as well as two 4x4 trails. Varied accommodation is available.

For permits, write to The Regional Officer, Eastern Cape Nature Conservation, Private Bag X1126, Port Elizabeth 6000, or telephone (041) 390-2179, fax 33-7468; or The Reserve Manager, P O Box 218, Patensie 6335, telephone (04232) 3-0270, or fax 3-0382.

Cango Caves

In the southern foothills of the Groot Swartberge, 30 km north of Oudtshoorn, lies one of nature's most enchanting creations – the Cango Caves.

The process of their creation began countless centuries ago when limestone deposits shattered along a zone up to 90 m wide. Later, this fissure was sealed by calcite, and underground water spilled through the limestone bed to create the vast caverns.

Traditionally, the Cango Caves proper were found by a herdsman who had been sent by his employer, a farmer named Van Zyl, to look for missing cattle. The youngster stumbled across a gaping hole covered with brushwood in the mountainside. Curious to know what lay within, he persuaded a man named Barend Oppel (believed to be an itinerant sailor who

Right: The series of hairpin bends on the Swartberg Pass, just past the summit and descending towards the Great Karoo, has scarcely changed since the road was built in the 1880s. It was the work of Thomas Bain.

229

was working his way overland after jumping ship in Cape Town) to visit the spot. Oppel was so impressed that he called Van Zyl and eight helpers to plumb the hole's depths.

In time, the other chambers – leading westwards for nearly 2 km – were also explored. In 1972 two professional guides working at the cave broke through into what is now called the Wonder Cave. Further extensions to the Cango Caves have been found, but all (including the Wonder Cave) are closed to the public to prevent damage to the formations.

The caves have become a mecca for tourists: in 1995 there were 24 000 visitors. Unfortunately, Cango has not been left unscathed: the delicate limestone formations are under threat from the persistently raised temperatures associated with the large numbers of people passing through. A huge conservation area, encompassing the land above the caves as well as the surrounding mountain catchment area, is currently under negotiation.

There are sophisticated facilities near the cave entrance, including a licensed restaurant, a curio shop, toilets, showers, a large car park, kennels, and a crèche where parents can leave young children while they explore. The caves (proclaimed a national monument in 1938) are administered by the Oudtshoorn Municipality. They are well signposted from Oudtshoorn and all along the winding, tarred road through Schoemanspoort. Visitors may not enter the caves without a guide.

Tours are conducted every day (every hour on the hour from 9 a.m. to 4 p.m.). During the South African school holidays in December/January and over the Easter weekend period, tours are conducted from 8 a.m. to 5 p.m.

For more information, contact Cango Caves, P O Box 255, Oudtshoorn 6620, telephone (0443) 22-7410; or the Klein Karoo Marketing Association, P O Box 1234, Oudtshoorn 6620, telephone (0443) 22-6643, fax 22-5007.

Cango Wildlife Ranch

Crocodile, cheetah, jaguar and lion are among the fearsome stars of Oudtshoorn's Cango Wildlife Ranch – a ranch which has something for the whole family to enjoy.

On guided tours (conducted every 30 minutes), you'll see over 400 crocodile and the largest alligator population in South Africa. The crocs range from 30 cm to over four metres in length. The ranch and its attractions are brought to life by the talented and professional guides, who are able to converse in English, Afrikaans and German.

Once your tour of the crocs is over it is well worth exploring the ranch's well-stocked snake park and crocodile museum, while children will discover the delights of tame and interesting animals, including miniature horses, dwarf goats, wallabies, Winston the warthog, Tarka and Twinkle the otters, Herbert and Hilda the pygmy hippos, Claude the camel and a pair of emus from Australia.

Cheetahland, which was completed in 1988, is a novel concept for visitors. Its natural enclosures, which house cheetah, jaguar, puma and lion, are connected by an elevated walkway, which enables you to take once-in-a-lifetime photographs. Short talks are given by guides who stand within the enclosures. For a small fee (which is donated to the Cheetah Conservation Foundation, founded in 1990), visitors may experience the thrill of touching and cuddling the tame cheetah.

There is a well-stocked curio shop to tempt visitors, while refreshments are served at the 'Hot-Croc Cafe'.

The ranch is open daily from 8 a.m. to 5 p.m. in season and from 8 a.m. to 4.15 p.m. out of season. It overlooks the Swartberg range and is well signposted on the tarred road leading from Oudtshoorn to the Cango Caves.

Above: The world-famous Cango Caves, decorated over the ages with delicate dripstone formations.

THE CAPE: **LITTLE KAROO**

Left: A crocodile at the Cango Wildlife Ranch, which is home to more than 400 of these fearsome but fascinating reptiles.

dentally, about the same distance from its entrance. To get there from Oudtshoorn, follow the road to Calitzdorp and, after 10 km, turn left onto the old concrete road to Calitzdorp. This leads you to a sign reading 'Uitvlugt'. Take this route to the reserve gate, which is open between 7 a.m. and 5 p.m.

Limited accommodation is provided in a rustic, thatched bush camp at the foot of the mountain and at a campsite for hikers and 4x4 travellers on the mountain plateau. There is an information centre near the entrance gate.

Permits are obtainable from The Officer-in-Charge, Gamka Mountain Nature Reserve, Private Bag X21, Oudtshoorn 6620, telephone/fax (04437) 3-3367.

The Calitzdorp Spa, situated approximately 10 km further along the road past the reserve gate, has a restaurant, chalets, caravan park and swimming pool.

Gamkapoort Nature Reserve
This reserve, encircling the Gamkapoort Dam, is situated 38 km west of Prince Albert, at the confluence of the Dwyka and Gamka rivers, and extends into the northern foothills of the Swartberg range. It is one of the few Cape reserves featuring succulent Karoo veld, and has the most northerly distribution of false macchia veld. Other vegetation types include succulent mountain scrub, spekboomveld and karroid broken veld.

Gamkapoort, which extends for over 8 000 ha, is home to more than 100 bird species and numerous mammals. These include klipspringer, springbok, grey rhebok, kudu, bat-eared fox, caracal and black-backed jackal. A short walking trail has been laid out. Fishing and boating are permitted, and there is a picnic site for day visitors. For permits and directions to the reserve, write to Swartberg Nature Reserve, Private Bag X658, Oudtshoorn 6620, or telephone (0443) 29-1739, or fax 22-8110.

Highgate Ostrich Show Farm
Owned by the Hooper family, who came to South Africa from the London suburb of Highgate in 1850, this farm attracts a staggering 120 000 tourists a year. It boasts of being the oldest farm on earth to open its doors to the public – visitors were first welcomed in 1938. Today guests are met by multilingual guides who take them on a 90-minute tour (tours depart every 10 to 15 minutes) around the farm. One of the highlights of the tour is ostrich-riding. Highgate is open from 7.30 a.m. to 5 p.m. (including Sundays and public holidays). Refreshments are served on the porch of the impressive homestead and these are included in the tour price. The farm is clearly

For further information, write to Cango Wildlife Ranch, P O Box 559, Oudtshoorn 6620, or telephone (0443) 22-5593, fax 22-4167.

De Hoek Nature Walk
This seven-hour trail, which is part of the longer Swartberg Trail, takes hikers through the southern foothills of the Swartberg, near the Cango Caves. Hikers should be reasonably fit, as the 12 km route passes through some rugged territory.

Proteas, heaths, everlastings and a host of other fynbos species may be seen along the way, and the peaks and cliffs of the mountains provide a scenic treat that will long be remembered. Further information and maps of the trail are available from Cape Nature Conservation, Swartberg Nature Reserve, Private Bag X658, Oudtshoorn 6620, telephone (0443) 29-1739, or fax 22-8110.

Gamka Mountain Nature Reserve
The dwindling number of rare Cape mountain zebra (*Equus zebra zebra*) have found a sanctuary in this 9 428 ha reserve (part of the larger Swartberg Nature Reserve) situated in the Gamka Mountains, southwest of Oudtshoorn. Visitors are drawn by the beautiful scenery, and there are particularly good views from Bakenskop (1 105 m), the highest point in the reserve. There are four main vegetation types in the reserve, namely mountain fynbos, arid fynbos, succulent Karoo and riverine vegetation. Many interesting plants, including the recently discovered golden mimetes, a member of the protea family, occur here. The unexpected exuberance of the flowering plants in spring (August-September) makes this the best time to visit.

Roaming freely with the zebra are klipspringer, grey rhebok, grysbok, duiker, steenbok, dassie and baboon, with an occasional sighting of leopard and caracal. Some 132 bird species have been identified, including numerous resident pairs of black eagle.

By far the best way to see the reserve is on foot. A two-day trail winds through the sanctuary, while short day walks are also available. Other outdoor recreations are mountaineering, birdwatching, photography klooving, or simply relaxing and getting away from it all. Visitors can follow the approximately 60 km of newly opened 4x4 tracks. There is a picnic site with braai facilities.

Gamka reserve is signposted from both Calitzdorp and Oudtshoorn, which are, inci-

231

THE CAPE: LITTLE KAROO

Above: Ostrich chicks and unhatched eggs on a farm in the Oudtshoorn district. An ostrich egg weighs about 1,5 kg and is equivalent to 24 domestic hen's eggs in volume. The chicks are able to run within three days of hatching. **Right:** Gamkapoort Dam lies on the Dwyka River to the west of Prince Albert.

signposted on the road from Oudtshoorn to Mossel Bay, and is situated 10 km from the centre of Oudtshoorn. There is a large curio shop which offers ostrich eggs, leather goods, feather boas and other products of the industry.

For details, contact Highgate Ostrich Show Farm, P O Box 94, Oudtshoorn 6620, telephone (0443) 22-7115/6, or fax 29-2036.

Kammanassie Nature Reserve

Lying approximately 10 km north of Uniondale is a 48 000 ha wilderness of mountain fynbos and Karoo veld. Visitors may see a variety of antelope and, with luck, Cape mountain zebra. Hiking is a popular way to enjoy the rugged scenic beauty. The reserve is open all year, but there are no facilities, and a permit is required. Contact The Manager, Kammanassie Nature Reserve, P O Box 48, Uniondale 6460, telephone (044) 752-1110, or fax 752-1401.

Noukloof Nature Reserve

Although still to be fully developed, this reserve near Ladismith offers serious plant-lovers an opportunity to explore the wide variety of indigenous vegetation on some 2 800 ha of unspoilt Little Karoo veld.

The gates of Noukloof are usually kept locked, and prospective visitors must make arrangements to collect the keys from the Ladismith municipal offices between 8 a.m. and 5 p.m. The circular 12 km Klapperbos Trail affords hikers the opportunity to see eland and springbok, which have been introduced to the sanctuary. It is also home to duiker and steenbok. Noukloof is 5 km south of the town, on the road to Barrydale. Several gravel roads lead through the reserve.

For further information, write to Ladismith Municipality, P O Box 30, Ladismith 6655, or telephone (028) 551-1023, or fax 551-1766.

Safari Ostrich Show Farm

Ostrich farms in the Oudtshoorn district draw thousands of tourists from all over the world. Most of the farms offer comprehensive tours that give visitors a good idea of the habits of this huge bird (*Struthio camelus*). Among these is the Safari Ostrich Farm, about 5 km from the town centre on the road to Mossel Bay. It is clearly signposted on the left of the road.

Tours of the farm last about 90 minutes. Light refreshments are available from a kiosk (full meals are provided for booked tours only). The farm has its own 'feather palace' called Welgeluk – a national monument – with Burmese teak woodwork and Belgian roof tiles. It is open from 8 a.m. to 5 p.m. Further information is available from Safari Ostrich Show Farm, P O Box 300, Oudtshoorn 6620, telephone (0443) 22-7311/2, or fax 22-5896.

Towerkop Nature Reserve

Lying slightly north of Ladismith, the Klein Swartberg, with the split peak of its majestic Towerkop, looms protectively over this pretty Little Karoo town. Dominating it all is the Seven Weeks Poort (Seweweekspoort) Peak which, at 2 324 m, is the highest peak in the Western Cape. Nearby is the spectacular 50 064 ha Towerkop Nature Reserve, which falls under the control of Cape Nature Conservation, the main aims being to conserve and manage the mountain's water resources, to maintain the fynbos and to protect the soil against erosion.

Within the nature reserve is Besemfontein Camp, the starting point of two scenic hiking trails. One, the Klipkraal Trail, follows a circular 22,5 km route leading to the summit of the mountain. From here, the views over the surrounding countryside are superb. Hikers are likely to spot klipspringer and rhebok, while black eagles soar and the booted eagle makes its annual summertime appearance. The Verlorenhoek Trail (15,6 km return) leads to a cool pool shimmering below a series of impressive waterfalls.

The trails may be walked separately or combined as a two-day hike, with an overnight stop in a rock shelter. Besemfontein has two cottages sleeping a total of 30 visitors. Kitchen and braai facilities are provided. Hikers are expected to bring their own food, linen, wood and eating utensils.

Keen hikers might like to attempt the Elandsberg Hiking Trail, a 12,2 km circular route that follows the base of the Elandsberg, then ascends steeply to a point some 1 430 m above sea level. There are also facilities for education groups.

Within Towerkop is the Rooiberg Nature Reserve, a 25 163 ha sanctuary that is home to klipspringer, grey rhebok and baboon, as well as to a colourful array of protea and erica species. Rooiberg, which was proclaimed in 1973, has yet to be developed for visitors, and those wishing to find out more about its attractions should contact Towerkop Nature Reserve.

For more information, permits and a key to the camp, contact Towerkop Nature Reserve, Private Bag X216, Ladismith 6655, telephone (028) 551-1077.

THE CAPE: SOUTHERN CAPE

Rocky shores and green valleys

From the eastern curve of False Bay to beyond the most southerly tip of Africa – Cape Agulhas – there is a rugged, beautiful and largely uninhabited coastline. It is guarded by mountain ranges that descend through fertile foothills to coastal plains where ephemeral wild flowers cover fields and white, shining sands.

Behind these craggy peaks are wide valleys clothed in tapestries of blossom in spring. The passes through the Hottentots-Holland Mountains are the doorway to a wonderland of forested slopes that spill into clear trout streams; where herds of buck graze quietly.

Much of the land is protected in state or private reserves. There is a good reason: the Western Cape encompasses one of the floral kingdoms of the world, and in parts of it grow the greatest density and variety of flowers on earth. Great spaces have been exploited for industrial or farming purposes, but conservationists are working tirelessly in selected areas to restore the natural beauty that once existed.

Assegaaibosch Nature Reserve

Encircled by mountains and bisected by the Eerste River is the picturesque Jonkershoek Valley, named after an early settler, Jan de Jonker. It is here that Cape Nature Conservation established a nature reserve on the northern slopes of the Stellenboschberg in 1960.

Principally a fynbos sanctuary, the scenic 204 ha reserve rises steeply up the slopes of the mountain. About 5 ha of the reserve have been developed as a wildflower garden with predominant species of protea and erica, and indigenous trees like wild olive (*Olea africana*).

A circular trail of 7,3 km (which may be extended) follows two mountain streams and is a particularly pleasant, shaded walk in summer. The reserve is always worth a visit, but particularly from September to November when spring flowers add extra colour.

Birds, of which 135 species have been recorded, are the most conspicuous wildlife, but many reptiles, insects and smaller mammals – including a few very wary leopard – are also at home here.

The only facilities available are a picnic site, toilets and a car park about 50 m from the entrance. Assegaaibosch is open between 8.30 a.m. and 4.00 p.m. during the week and from 9 a.m. to 6 p.m. at weekends.

Permits to enter the reserve may be arranged during office hours by contacting Cape Nature Conservation, Private Bag X1, Uniedal 7612, telephone (021) 886-5858, fax 886-6575. To get there, follow the Jonkershoek road from Stellenbosch until you see the large green sign on the right indicating the reserve.

Boesmanskloof Trail

Situated in the picturesque Riviersonderend Mountains, this 14,1 km trail offers rugged mountain scenery, mountain fynbos and many large rock pools and waterfalls.

The hike may be started from just outside the village of Greyton, or 14 km south of McGregor at Die Galg. Since there is no road linking the two villages, the walk is usually done as a round trip, which takes from eight to ten hours. It is based on an old track that leads through the only gap in the mountains, giving stupendous views of the Greyton and McGregor valleys. A fair degree of physical fitness is essential, as the trail rises and falls continuously with the contours of the Boesmanskloof slopes. No fires may be lit, and no pets are allowed on the trail.

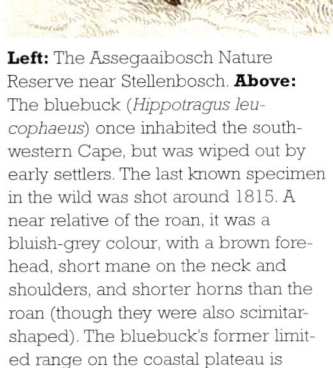

Left: The Assegaaibosch Nature Reserve near Stellenbosch. **Above:** The bluebuck (*Hippotragus leucophaeus*) once inhabited the south-western Cape, but was wiped out by early settlers. The last known specimen in the wild was shot around 1815. A near relative of the roan, it was a bluish-grey colour, with a brown forehead, short mane on the neck and shoulders, and shorter horns than the roan (though they were also scimitar-shaped). The bluebuck's former limited range on the coastal plateau is believed to be one of the major contributory factors to its demise. There is evidence that the bluebuck's last stronghold was the Soete Melk Valley near Swellendam. Mounted specimens are exhibited at museums in Vienna, Paris, Stockholm and Leyden. A pair of horns on display in the Albany Museum in Grahamstown is widely considered to be those of a bluebuck, and another pair was identified in Cape Town in 1995.

THE CAPE: SOUTHERN CAPE

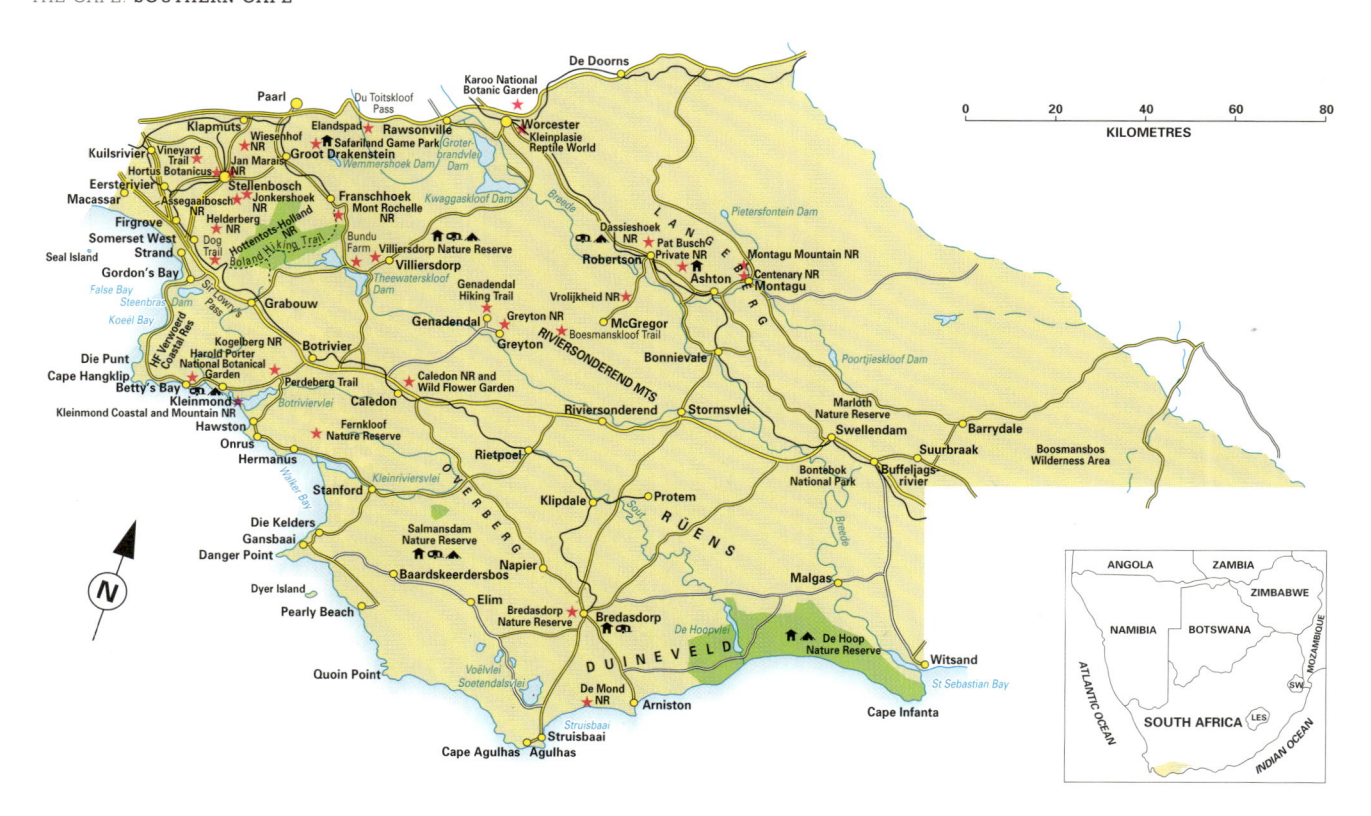

Above: A carpet of flowers transforms the Caledon Wild Flower Garden every spring, when visitors arrive in droves from Cape Town and further afield to view the display. Although the spectacular garden covers only 56 ha, the remaining 158 ha comprise indigenous fynbos and stunning mountain scenery that is traversed by a network of trails. **Right:** A cetoniid beetle feeding on a protea. Cetoniids can be extremely destructive, some species feeding on rose bushes and others on a variety of fruit.

The vegetation along the trail supports many small mammals, such as duiker, grey rhebok, baboon, caracal and genet, while birds include the malachite sunbird and Cape sugarbird. Leopard have also been seen.

To obtain a permit, write to The Manager, Vrolijkheid Nature Reserve, Private Bag X614, Robertson 6705; telephone (02353) 621/671, fax 674. Permits are also available on weekdays from the Greyton Municipality, telephone (028) 254-9620. Early booking for this very popular trail is essential.

Boland Hiking Trail: Hottentots-Holland Section

Cutting across the spine of the Hottentots-Holland and Franschhoek mountains, this 54 km trail, established in 1975, takes visitors through one of the wealthiest floral kingdoms in the world. There are about 1 300 species of indigenous plants along the route, many of them listed on the back of a comprehensive map available to prospective hikers.

All routes – they vary in length from 5 to 50 km or from one to three days – start at the Hottentots-Holland Nature Reserve office at Nuweberg, high on Viljoen's Pass between Grabouw and Villiersdorp. Overnight huts are fairly primitive, offering only bunks with thin mattresses, and water. Visitors bring their own food, bedding and cooking utensils. Because of the high risk of veld fires, fires are prohibited except at demarcated sites.

THE CAPE: SOUTHERN CAPE

Above: The moisture-loving *Wachendorfia paniculata* occurs in the Fernkloof Nature Reserve in the Kleinrivier Mountains, overlooking the seaside resort of Hermanus.

The route from Landdroskop to Jonkershoek Forestry Station is periodically closed and the Boegoekloof route is closed from April to September, so it is important to plan your trail well. Advance booking is essential (although bookings will not be accepted more than 12 months prior to your visit), particularly at weekends and during school holidays. The entire trail closes in July and August, because of severe winter conditions and for routine maintenance.

The weather in the Hottentots-Holland Mountains is unpredictable, and it is essential to follow instructions on protective clothing and other precautions. You have to be fit and well equipped to complete the full trail. For further information, or for bookings, contact Cape Nature Conservation, Private Bag X1, Uniedal 7612, telephone (021) 886-5858, fax 886-6575.

Bredasdorp Nature Reserve

An area of 800 ha has been set aside within the Bredasdorp municipal boundary for the preservation of local fynbos, with its dominant protea and erica families, and the birds and small mammals that live within it. Footpaths across the slopes of the 368 m hill in the reserve offer panoramic views of the town and surroundings. The reserve is open all year, and the best time to visit it is from mid-September to mid-October, when spring flowers are in abundance.

With the exception of a thatched rondavel, there are no facilities. However, a caravan park in the town has 30 sites and seven well-equipped bungalows. To reach the reserve from the Napier side, take Independent Road from the main road (turn right) and then turn right again into Van Riebeeck Road. The gates of the Bredasdorp Nature Reserve are at the end of this road and are well signposted.

For more information, contact The Town Clerk, Bredasdorp Municipality, P O Box 51, Bredasdorp 7280; telephone (02841) 5-1919, fax 5-1019.

Bundu Farm

This 160 ha area at the foot of the Villiersdorp Mountains is the base for Camp SOS and School in the Wilds. It offers outdoor education classes for youth groups, schoolchildren and trainee teachers.

Situated near the Theewaterskloof Dam, Bundu Farm lies in an area of rich fynbos and may be hired by private groups at weekends and on public holidays. The many facilities include dormitories, large halls, kitchens, hot and cold showers and a swimming pool. Guest groups have the use of these, but must organise their own activities. The farm is reached from a signposted turn-off (to SOS Camp) on the Villiersdorp/Grabouw road. For more information, write to SOS, P O Box 153, Villiersdorp 6848, or telephone/fax (0225) 3-1138.

Caledon Nature Reserve and Wild Flower Garden

Every spring, thousands of visitors, armed with cameras, make their way to Caledon to admire

---

A GRAIN OF POLLEN

Lobostemon fruticosus is found throughout the coastal districts of the Western Cape and extends to Namaqualand. The corolla may be pink or blue.

The origin of the natural vegetation of the Western Cape, commonly known as fynbos ('macchia' to the botanist) has been the subject of scientific debate for decades. How old is it, and what vegetation preceded it millions of years ago?

Clues to the answers were first provided in 1958, by the discovery of an exceptionally rich fossil bed at a phosphate mine near Saldanha Bay. In contrast to the immense age of the reptile and plant fossils of the Karoo (about 250 million years old), this fossil graveyard was only four to five million years old. Few plant fossils were found and botanists were obliged to speculate on the nature of the vegetation until another major clue was exposed. The evidence was derived from core samples that were taken from ancient peat bogs discovered on the Cape Flats. The pollen in the various levels of the peat gave an almost unbroken record of the Cape vegetation from the present right back into the mists of time.

The specialised study of pollen is known as palynology. Using pollen samples, palynologists have deduced that from about 35 million years ago the region experienced fluctuations in temperature, which in turn caused corresponding changes in the vegetation – from subtropical palm forests to cooler forests dominated by ancestral yellowwood trees.

The Western Cape, it appeared, enjoyed a summer rainfall and, despite the temperature fluctuations, the climate was warmer and wetter than it is today. However, about 12 million years ago the southern oceans began to cool. The increasing strength of the cold Benguela Current off the west coast of southern Africa introduced a drier and colder climate with winter rains.

The summers that followed caused the extinction of the remaining palm forests, and the yellowwoods survived only in the sheltering kloofs of the mountains.

Eventually, about 3,5 million years ago, the Cape macchia became the dominant flora of the Cape – hardy and able to withstand the rigours of wind, drought and periodic fire damage.

THE CAPE: SOUTHERN CAPE

Left: Cape mountain zebra in De Hoop Nature Reserve. **Above left:** *Helichrysum chlorochrysum* in De Hoop Nature Reserve near Bredasdorp. **Above right:** The *Peripatus* has long fascinated biologists. It is regarded as a link between worms and arthropods (a phylum that includes spiders, insects and crustaceans). The body is soft and contractile, like that of a worm, but the legs are tipped with claws, an insectean feature. Its only defensive weapon consists of slime papillae on either side of the mouth; these discharge a sticky substance which forms a tangled net of threads, also used in prey capture. Most of the African species are found at the southern tip of the continent (a blind species lives in the caves on Table Mountain).

the spectacular displays of Namaqualand daisies, gazanias, *Arctotis*, *Lampranthus* and *Dorotheanthus*. It is Caledon's modest boast that the land was granted for use as a park by command of Queen Victoria, in 1899.

The 56 ha cultivated section, which is also the venue for the annual Caledon Wild Flower Show (first held in 1892), takes up only a part of the sanctuary, which rises to the crest of Swartberg and covers an area of 214 ha.

The early morning (the garden is open from 7 a.m. to 5 p.m.) is a good time to spot duiker and other small mammals, but the middle of the day is the best time to see the flowers. At the top of a hill is Window Rock, from where visitors have a panoramic view of the surroundings. A 10 km hiking trail, which includes some fairly steep sections, takes from three to five hours to complete. Hikers are advised to take their own drinking water.

The garden, which was established in 1925 by a group of nature enthusiasts and is now administered by the Caledon Municipality, is open all year. During the peak spring season (from September to October) you can enjoy refreshments at the tearoom. The only other facilities provided are picnic sites and toilets, but there are hotels in town, including one at the site of the Caledon hot mineral springs. The garden is well signposted from the national road (N2) where it bypasses the town. Enquiries should be addressed to the Caledon Publicity Association, P O Box 258, Caledon 7230, telephone (0281) 2-1511.

Centenary Nature Reserve

Situated off Van Riebeeck Avenue in the southern part of the charming town of Montagu, this wildflower garden of 10 ha was established to preserve the indigenous vegetation. There are several footpaths leading through the reserve, which is open from sunrise to 5 p.m. Tea and cakes are served by the Horticultural Society every Tuesday morning from mid-June to the end of November.

Dassieshoek Nature Reserve

Dassieshoek, about 8 km north of the town of Robertson, is a sanctuary for fynbos – primarily members of the protea family. A pleasant feature is its picnic site near a dam, which attracts large numbers of birds. Several footpaths crisscross the reserve, offering visitors occasional glimpses of tortoises and bushbuck, and there are several waterfalls. While there is no accommodation in the reserve (it is open only from sunrise to sunset), the Robertson Municipality has a large resort (Silverstrand) nearby with caravan and camping sites tucked along the Breede River.

Silverstrand and the reserve are linked by the Dassieshoek Hiking Trail of 23 km (two days), which provides overnight accommodation in a hut situated near the entrance to the reserve. A four-day hike may be devised by combining this with the 23 km of the Arangieskop Trail, which rises to the summit of the Langeberg and returns to Dassieshoek Nature Reserve. Fine scenery, birdlife, fynbos and swimming places are among the highlights of both trails.

Permits are required to enter the reserve, and are available at the gate. Large groups should apply for a permit at least two weeks in advance as the reserve is open to only 100 people at a time. There are toilet and braai facilities. To get there, take Voortrekker Road from Robertson (heading north) and look for the signposts. For further information, write to The Head: Technical Services, Robertson Municipality, P O Box 52, Robertson 6705, or telephone (02351) 3112, fax 2426.

De Hoop Nature Reserve

This reserve has expanded considerably since it was originally established by the provincial authorities in 1956. Today it includes a nature reserve embracing some 36 000 ha between Cape Infanta and Koppie Alleen, and a fine 23 000 ha marine reserve that extends 5 km out to sea. The reserve also boasts a Cape vulture colony in the Potberg (the southernmost Cape vulture-breeding area in Africa), beautiful intertidal pools and Windhoek Cave – probably the most important bat cave in the Cape. The vulture-breeding area is, however, closed to the public.

Scenic drives along 20 km of gravel roads link points of interest in the reserve, and there are day walks along the Potberg Trail (8 km), the Vlei Trail (5,5 km) and the Coastal Walk (13 km). There is also a mountain-bike trail, for which booking is essential.

De Hoop's vegetation is classified as coastal fynbos with some 1 500 different species – of which 71 are regarded as rare or endangered. Since the reserve was established, 86 species of mammal (including 15 marine), 49 species of reptile and 14 species of amphibian have been recorded. The major game species present are bontebok, Cape mountain zebra, eland, grey duiker, steenbok, grey rhebok, grysbok and klipspringer. The vlei attracts great numbers of birds – 259 species have been recorded at De Hoop.

The marine section of the reserve contains at least 250 fish species, as well as marine

CAPE MOUNTAIN SPECTACULAR

The colourful *Leucospermum truncatum* (a pincushion).

One of southern Africa's richest and most beautiful natural kingdoms is that of the Western Cape mountains, a majestic and irregular sweep of peak and precipice stretching northwards from the Cederberg, then south to the Cape Peninsula and up to Port Elizabeth and the Eastern Cape.

The mountains are supreme recreational areas, and most are accessible by extensive but discreet footpaths. They are a paradise for rock-climbers and backpackers: the astounding combination of magnificent peaks, cool sparkling streams in well-wooded valleys and the floristic wealth is unsurpassed on earth.

This is the home of the 'Cape Floral Kingdom' or Fynbos Biome. The world is divided by botanists into six botanical kingdoms, of which the Cape is one. Although it covers only 0,04 per cent of the area of the earth (compared to the Palaeotropic Kingdom, which encompasses 35 per cent and includes the rest of Africa south of the Sahara), this floral kingdom, in botanical terms, is the richest area on the planet.

More than 8 500 plant species are found in the fynbos, of which 6 000 are endemic to specific areas. In a relatively small area of 10 000 ha in the Hottentots-Holland Mountains you may find as many as 121 different species. To put this into perspective, a nature reserve such as the Hottentots-Holland Nature Reserve (42 000 ha) contains more plant species than the entire British Isles.

Fynbos in its typical form has three distinctive elements – the proteoids (proteas, pincushions, mimetes and similar plants), ericoids (heaths and false heather), and restioids (reedlike sedges with beautiful brown flower heads). Many of our familiar garden plants, such as *Sparaxis*, *Ixia*, *Agapanthus*, *Watsonia*, blushing bride, heather, red-hot poker and others, grow naturally in the Western Cape mountains.

Outcrops of fynbos species are found as far north as Nieuwoudtville and become more common as you move south. To the south of the Cederberg lie the Kouebokkeveldberge – mostly privately owned, though several thousand hectares have been declared a mountain catchment area. The Citrusdal protea (*Protea mopina*) and the Bokkeveld ground protea (*Protea scabriuscula*) occur here. Immediately southwest of this area are the Groot Winterhoek Mountains, where a large wilderness area has been proclaimed.

South of the town of Tulbagh, the Elandskloof, Limietberg and Slanghoek ranges reach towards Wellington, where they become the Hawequas Mountains. This is the home of three lovely proteas: the mountain rose, a small protea with drooping flower heads; the very rare Kasteelskloof protea and the krantz protea. The historic Bainskloof Pass separates this range from the Du Toitskloof range, which stretches out towards Worcester and becomes Klein Drakenstein, Wemmershoek, Stettyns and eventually Hex River as it reaches De Doorns. Heaths, sedges, disas and many other flowers grow here in profusion.

The mountains of Drakenstein, Franschhoek, Jonkershoek, Simonsberg and Stellenbosch are equally beautiful. In these valleys are the wine routes and stately Cape Dutch homes.

Further south, the Hottentots-Holland range reaches towards Sir Lowry's Pass, on the other side of which is the Kogelberg. This is the richest of all the Cape mountains in terms of flora, with its very rare marsh rose, silver mimetes, Stokoe's protea and many other endemic species.

From Betty's Bay to Bot River, the Palmiet Mountains tower above the sea. Various trails can be followed here in the forests, home of a famous export protea – the Bot River protea (*Protea compacta*).

The most famous of all South African mountains is Table Mountain, with its attendants, Lion's Head, Devil's Peak, Twelve Apostles and Constantiaberg. This area offers a host of rewarding walks and climbs that vary in gradient and challenge to suit hikers of all fitness levels. The Riviersonderend range between Genadendal and the town of Riviersonderend also offers a variety of tracks and footpaths (maintained by the local nature conservator).

The Langeberg range extends from Worcester eastwards towards the Gourits River: the Little Karoo lies at its northern slopes and the Overberg to the south, presenting hikers with an ever-changing vista of farmlands. Historic towns and villages such as Swellendam, Montagu, Barrydale, Riversdale and Albertinia nestle at its feet.

Further north rise the austere cliffs of the Anysberg (Aniseed Mountain), Towerkop (Magic Peak) and Swartberg – home of the Towerkop snow protea (*Protea prumosa*). The nature conservator in this area controls large tracts of state land and privately owned catchment areas. It is a place of rare beauty – Gamkaskloof ('The Hell'), Seweweekspoort, Swartberg Pass, Meiringspoort and Huisrivier Pass are all well-known landmarks.

Even drier and more rugged, but equally beautiful are the Baviaanskloof, Kouga and Cockscomb mountains. This is a vast, undulating expanse of land, with breathtaking valleys, rugged peaks and countless twisting footpaths.

To the south is the Langkloof range. The southern valley wall is formed by the lush evergreen peaks of the Outeniqua and Tsitsikamma mountains – thousands of hectares of land protected by foresters. George Peak and Formosa Peak are well-known landmarks, as are the historic Montagu Pass, Prince Alfred's Pass, Bloukrans and Grootrivier. The forests on the southern slopes are famous for their yellowwood and stinkwood.

Most Western Cape mountains are managed as nature reserves, wilderness areas or mountain catchment areas by the provincial government.

mammals and invertebrates. Southern right whales can be seen in the waters from June to November.

Some of the most interesting inhabitants of this reserve are also the tiniest. These include *Peripatus*, which belongs to an archaic form bridging the evolutionary gap between worms and insects.

Environmental education is emphasised at De Hoop, and the Potberg Environmental Education Centre has been established to serve schoolchildren and youth groups. Educational programmes are readily available for adults on request.

There are six four-bed cottages, and one with 10 beds, as well as seven campsites. Visitors should bring their own bedding, cooking utensils and food. For day visitors, there are also picnic sites with braai areas. Organised educational groups can be accommodated at Potberg or Koppie Alleen.

De Hoop is signposted 6 km from Bredasdorp on the Swellendam/Bredasdorp road. This road leads to the main entrance to the reserve, which is about 50 km further on along a gravel road. Permits are issued at the gate and the reserve is open from 7 a.m. to 6 p.m.

For more detailed information, write to The Manager, De Hoop Nature Reserve, Private Bag X16, Bredasdorp 7280, or telephone (028) 542-1126.

De Mond Nature Reserve

On the long curve of Struisbaai or Struis Bay (ostrich bay), just east of Cape Agulhas, is the mouth (mond) of the Heuningnes River. This is the focus of the 1 580 ha reserve, with its prolific birdlife attracted by a wetland set amid profuse and varied fynbos growing close to the shoreline. There are also seabirds (such as Caspian tern and Damara tern) and there is a wealth of aquatic life.

Situated on an estuary about 23 km south of Bredasdorp (190 km east of Cape Town by road), the reserve is open daily from 7 a.m. to 6 p.m. Hiking a 6,7 km trail, angling and bird-watching are the most popular pastimes. Drinking water is available and there are toilets and picnic sites, but making fires is prohibited. Permits to enter the reserve may be obtained at the gate, which may be reached by following the signposts from the tarred road (R319) between Agulhas and Bredasdorp.

For more information, write to The Foreman-in-Charge, De Mond, P O Box 277, Bredasdorp 7280, or telephone (028) 542-1126.

Dog Trail

A short distance from where the Sir Lowry's Pass village road crosses the railway line is the start of a dog trail. It runs through 90 ha of fynbos between this secondary road and the N2, offering fine views of the Hottentots-Holland Mountains, the Helderberg and False Bay. There are some 7 km of circular paths, of which the longest may be completed in an hour – if dog and owner maintain a brisk pace. No permit is required. To reach the starting point, follow the signs for Sir Lowry's Pass village from the N2 or from Somerset West. For further information, write to Cape Nature Conservation, Private Bag X1, Uniedal 7612, or contact the local controlling reserve at telephone/fax (02823) 2-9425.

Elandspad River Kloofing Trail

This fairly strenuous scramble through the Elandspad River gorge is for those who are fit and agile. The start is at the parking area near the control point for heavy vehicles at the Du Toitskloof Pass (on the Worcester side), from where you follow the river upstream.

The trip takes you past sandbanks, a variety of riverine vegetation and dramatic rock formations, and there is also a waterfall that tumbles into a dark pool. If you have never tried kloofing, ask for advice on the correct footwear and how to waterproof your rucksack. Never explore the gorge in rainy or threatening weather – floodwaters quickly turn it into a potential deathtrap.

For day permits, write to Cape Nature Conservation, Private Bag X1, Uniedal 7612, or telephone (021) 886-5858, fax 886-6575.

Fernkloof Nature Reserve

Rising from 63 m to 842 m above sea level, Fernkloof Nature Reserve features a combination of montane coastal fynbos with several species of protea and at least 48 species of erica – an outstanding total for an area of only 1 446 ha. The wide and interesting diversity of species in the reserve is partly attributed to its elevation range, and to the efforts of conservationists who wage a continuous battle against alien vegetation.

The mixed fynbos at Fernkloof has no dormant season, so the reserve is interesting throughout the year. At the visitors' centre is a display of the prominent plants you are likely to see on your walks. Free walking sticks are provided and maps are available for a small fee. Radiating from the visitors' centre is a 40 km network of carefully maintained paths that traverse most of the reserve. Three gently sloping walks are marked, and take from 20 minutes to two hours to complete. All of the paths have spectacular views of Hermanus and the wide sweep of Walker Bay. The visitors' centre is about 500 m from the entrance, which is well signposted from the main road between Hermanus and Voëlklip.

Because this area has been protected for so long, there has been a remarkable resurgence of animals and birds. More than 100 bird species have been sighted, including two black eagles that nest in the Kleinrivier mountain range. Visitors may also see baboon, genet, mongoose, dassie, porcupine and small antelope. In the moist ravines are small areas of indigenous forest, where trees include Cape beech (*Rapanea melanophloeos*), wild olive (*Olea africana*), assegaai (*Curtisia dentata*), hard pear (*Olinia ventosa*) and the rooi-els (*Cunonia capensis*).

The botanical centre at the entrance to the reserve holds film shows, flower shows, plant

Left: *Phaenocoma prolifera* in the Fernkloof Nature Reserve. **Above:** The Cape dormouse, the largest dormouse in southern Africa, has thick, silvery grey fur with distinctive white and black patches on the face. This dormouse is usually found in the vicinity of rocks (its head is somewhat flattened, allowing it to squeeze into crevices), while other species live in abandoned birds' nests, bushes and even the thatched roofs of houses.

THE CAPE: SOUTHERN CAPE

Below left: A Cape gloxinia (*Charadrophila capensis*) in the Jonkershoek valley, near Stellenbosch. This small, herbaceous plant is extremely rare. **Right:** *Aloe striata* and brightly coloured *Dorotheanthus bellidiformis* (Bokbaai vygie) in the Karoo National Botanic Garden at Worcester. The daisy-like flowers provide a brilliant display in many parts of the south-western Cape. The plant received its botanical name from Professor Gustav Schwantes, who named it after his mother, Dorothea. **Below right:** An Egyptian goose. These birds will nest in a variety of places, ranging from ground level to the tops of tall trees. One enterprising individual built its nest in the belfry of the Grahamstown Cathedral. When the young hatched they fell into the street (30 m below) with no apparent injury.

and mountain bikes are also prohibited. The reserve is open from 7 a.m. to 6 p.m. in autumn and winter, and from 7 a.m. to 8 p.m. in spring and summer.

The reserve is clearly signposted from Somerset West's Main Street. When entering town from the west, turn left into Lourensford Road and, when approaching from the east, turn right into Gordon Road.

Hortus Botanicus

The Department of Botany at the University of Stellenbosch has a botanical garden (primarily for student research and study) in the centre of the town, on the corner of Van Riebeeck and Neethling streets. The garden confines one of the greatest concentrations of plant species from all over the world within the space of only 1,8 ha. There is a magnificent arboretum with examples of indigenous trees as well as exotics like Californian redwood and Chinese maidenhair tree (*Ginkgo biloba*).

Of special interest is the succulent house, where specimens of *Welwitschia mirabilis* (some more than 60 years old) of the Namib Desert have been successfully cultivated from seed for the first time in the world. Carbon dating has shown that these strange plants may reach an age of more than 1 000 years.

There is a tropical house, filled with insectivorous plants, orchids, crop plants like coffee, tea, ginger and vanilla, gigantic Brazilian ferns and eerie creepers from all over the world, as well as an outstanding collection of bonsai and aquatic plants. The collection also includes the sacred lotus flower of the east (*Nelumbium nucifera*), which has magnificent metre-high blooms that open early in the morning. The noise the blooms make when they open at dawn is audible enough to be recorded on tape. There is also an experimental herb garden where scientists are studying the medicinal, culinary and economic uses of the plants.

Hortus Botanicus is open on weekdays from 9 a.m. to 4.30 p.m. and on Saturdays from 9 a.m. to 10.30 a.m. Groups from schools, clubs and societies are admitted by appointment only. For further information, write to The Praefectus Horti, Hortus Botanicus, University of Stellenbosch, Stellenbosch 7600, or telephone (021) 808-3054, fax 808-4336.

Hottentots-Holland Nature Reserve

This large and impressive reserve (it covers 42 000 ha) stretches from Jonkershoek in the north to Grabouw in the south, and from Sir Lowry's Pass in the west to the Theewaterskloof Dam in the east. The only way to see the reserve is to hike through it on a section of the Boland Hiking Trail (*see separate entry*). Access is otherwise completely restricted. There are four overnight trails from Nuweberg, the starting point for the trails and the entrance to the reserve. There are also three day hikes and two kloofing trails. One of the day hikes, the Palmiet Blind Trail, covers 6 km in about two hours and is safe for blind and partially disabled people (but it is not suitable for wheelchair users).

The Hottentots-Holland Mountains harbour one of the richest and most diverse floral populations in the world. About 1 300 species have been recorded in the reserve, at least 37 of them threatened. Most of the indigenous forests that once covered the slopes have disappeared, but small remnants may be seen in the higher kloofs. The dominant vegetation, however, is mountain fynbos, so called for the great number of small-leaved shrubs such as heaths.

Leopard, caracal and jackal are seen occasionally, and other carnivores such as genet, grey mongoose and clawless otter, although present, are also rather elusive. Grysbok, grey rhebok and klipspringer exist in small numbers, and some 110 bird species in the reserve include sugarbird, sunbird and Victorin's scrub warbler.

Toilet and shower facilities are available at the entrance office. The overnight huts have bunks, mattresses and water.

Permits are required to enter the trails, and can be booked through Cape Nature Conservation, Private Bag X1, Uniedal 7612, telephone (021) 886-5858, or fax 886-6575. Information may also be obtained from The Manager, Hottentots-Holland Nature Reserve, Private Bag X27, Elgin 7180, telephone (0225) 4826, fax 4457. The entrance to the reserve lies off

THE CAPE: SOUTHERN CAPE

Viljoen's Pass on the road (R321) between Grabouw and Villiersdorp.

Jan Marais Nature Reserve

This botanical sanctuary of some 23 ha is almost in the centre of Stellenbosch, bounded by Marais Street and Cluver Road in the west, Jannasch Street in the east, Merriman Avenue in the north and the rear of Jonkershoek Road residences in the south. The main entrance is east of the junction of Marais and Victoria streets with Cluver Road.

The reserve features over 1 000 species of the rich fynbos that covered the area before the founding of the town. It is open every day from 7.30 a.m. to 6 p.m. between 1 April and 30 September, and from 7.30 a.m. to 8 p.m. between 1 October and 31 March. Admission is reserved by the Stellenbosch Municipality, which controls the reserve. There are footpaths leading through the reserve, and benches and toilet facilities have been provided. For more detailed information, write to The Chief, Department of Environment and Recreational Management, Stellenbosch Municipality, P O Box 17, Stellenbosch 7599, or telephone (021) 808-8453, fax 808-8200.

Jonkershoek Fish Hatchery

Established in 1893, the Jonkershoek Fish Hatchery in the attractive Jonkershoek Valley is the oldest field station of the Department of Nature and Environmental Conservation in the Western Cape.

At the reception area is an information centre and aquarium featuring typical freshwater fish such as indigenous yellowfish, Cape kurper, banded and Mozambique tilapia, and barbel, as well as exotic carp, bluegill sunfish, large-mouth bass and trout. Explanatory literature is available from the reception desk at the station and conducted tours can be arranged for groups of visitors.

The hatchery is just 9 km from Stellenbosch and is clearly signposted from Jonkershoek Road. It is open from 8 a.m. to 4 p.m. from Mondays to Fridays. For further information, write to the Jonkershoek Fish Hatchery, Private Bag X1, Uniedal 7612, or telephone (021) 887-0111 (changing to 889-1560).

Jonkershoek Nature Reserve

Forming a section of the Hottentots-Holland Nature Reserve (see separate entry), Jonkershoek's 9 800 ha are a year-round destination for those who enjoy flowers (spring), mushrooms (autumn), or waterfalls flowing from snowclad peaks (winter).

Four trails that traverse the mountain fynbos, which includes several extremely rare species, cover distances ranging between 6,8 km and 18,4 kilometres. Cycling is allowed on roads and within demarcated areas, while angling for trout is popular at Kleinplaas Dam, between 1 April and 15 October, when fishing permits are granted to 10 people daily.

Smoking and the lighting of fires are prohibited. Visitors and especially hikers are warned to take warm clothing as the weather may change rapidly. The reserve is open daily from 7.30 a.m. to 5 p.m., and is reached by taking Jonkershoek Road from Stellenbosch and passing through the Safcol plantations, after obtaining a permit at the gate.

For more information, write to Cape Nature Conservation, Private Bag X1, Uniedal 7612, or telephone (021) 886-5858, fax 886-6575.

Karoo National Botanic Garden

The largest collection of indigenous succulents in South Africa is housed in this regional garden curated by the National Botanical Institute. The garden was originally established near Matjiesfontein in 1921 but was transferred north of Worcester in 1945 to make it more accessible. Today it consists of a 10 ha cultivated area that draws hundreds of visitors in spring, when brilliantly coloured vygies and daisies are in bloom, and a natural veld reserve with low Karoo-type bushes and succulents covering an area of 144 hectares.

The garden sustains interesting collections of *Lithops*, *Conophytum*, *Drosanthemum*, *Lampranthus*, *Stapelia*, *Crassula*, *Haworthia* and *Aloe*. About 4 000 species of flowering plant grow here, 350 of them rare and endangered. There is a rich and varied birdlife in the area, and the reserve is used extensively by the local bird club and the Wildlife Society of Southern Africa.

Well-maintained trails link the developed garden with the reserve and present a spectacular view of the Breede River Valley. Starting from behind the office, the 1,7 km self-guided Shale Trail is an interesting introduction to flora, fauna (including busy insect life) and geology. The cultivated section contains a flora trail for the blind, with plant labels printed in Braille. As part of the garden's Namaqualand section, and showing how man formerly integrated with his environment, Bushmen (San) have built a typical 'skerm' or shelter. A wide selection of indigenous Karoo plants is available for sale on weekdays.

The garden, which is open throughout the year from 8 a.m. to 5 p.m., is situated on low hills about 3 km north of Worcester, and is well signposted from the N1 national road.

Kleinmond Coastal and Mountain Nature Reserve

A wonderful mixture of river, kloof and seashore, this 666 ha reserve was established to protect the area's fragile blend of coastal and mountain fynbos. Between 1 200 and 1 500 species occur here, including large stands of the rare *Mimetes hirtus* and *Erica patersonia*.

A feature of the coastal area is the milkwood scrub forest, while indigenous forest remnants occur on the banks of the Palmiet River (the whole estuary of this river lies in the western part of the reserve) and in the kloofs near Fairy Glen. More than 40 indigenous tree species have been recorded in the reserve. There is a variety of buck and small predators, and a resident troop of baboons.

Visitors can examine marine life in the rock pools and inlets along the spectacular 8 km coastal walk that links up with hiking trails throughout the reserve. Part of the walk near the hotel has been adapted for wheelchairs and less-adventurous walkers. A hut sleeping 10 has been built for overnight hikers – make

Left: The evergreen shrub known as the marsh rose is an extremely rare protea that grows only in a small area in the Hottentots-Holland. Each translucent, waxy flower has petal-like bracts that are folded over each other – much like a rose. **Above:** The ocellated gecko, one of the smallest found in South Africa.

Above left: A male South African pochard. **Above right:** The angulate tortoise (*Chersina angulata*) is the most common tortoise of the southern Cape. This specimen was photographed in the Salmonsdam Nature Reserve. It is recognised by its single gular shield (all other African tortoises have paired shields), which extends quite far beneath the neck, and the elongated carapace, which slopes steeply on the sides. The gular shield is used as an offensive weapon during the mating season, when the males butt each other and attempt to flip their adversaries onto their backs. **Right:** The Palmiet River meanders through the Kleinmond Coastal and Mountain Nature Reserve.

reservations through Cape Nature Conservation, Private Bag X1, Uniedal 7612, or telephone (021) 887-0111 (changing to 889-1560). There are two caravan parks and camping grounds in town.

Both the nature reserve and the coastal walk are open throughout the year from sunrise to sunset. Moderate winters afford pleasant conditions for hikes and walks, but the period from November to April is the best time to visit. If you want to stay in the vicinity overnight you should book well in advance, as this is a high-density summer resort.

For more information contact The Town Clerk, Kleinmond Municipality, Private Bag X3, Kleinmond 7195, telephone (02823) 4010, fax 2-9221; or telephone The Nature Conservation Officer at (02823) 2-9263.

Kleinplasie Reptile World

Rattlesnakes, mambas, leguans and crocodiles are some of the creepy creatures to be seen at this reptile park next to the well-known Kleinplasie Museum in Worcester.

Glass cases and secure cages house the dangerous snakes, while crocodiles and monitors stare unblinking from open-air pits. Newborn snakes and rare albino reptiles may also be seen, and educational talks and demonstrations are given.

For further information, contact Kleinplasie Reptile World, P O Box 1292, Worcester 6849, telephone/fax (0231) 2-6480.

Kogelberg Nature Reserve

One of the few reserves in South Africa that is managed in accordance with the internationally accepted principles of a biosphere reserve, Kogelberg lies some 90 km east of Cape Town and forms part of the Cape Floral Kingdom. Too rugged for cultivation, avoided by farmers and travellers for centuries, the area was declared a state forest in 1937 and then a nature reserve in 1987. It is now managed so that its *core area* of 18 000 ha is left wild, surrounded by *resilient areas* and by *transitional zones* that have a variety of uses, including recreation and forestry.

The reserve lies in the southern part of the Hottentots-Holland Mountains, between Gordon's Bay and Kleinmond, and is reached off the R44 at Oudebosch, near Kleinmond, where it is signposted. Its mountain fynbos boasts about 1 600 species, of which 150 are endemic. The endangered marsh rose (*Orothamnus zeyheri*) grows on its inaccessible peaks and it has the highest concentration of threatened *Mimetes* species in the country. The reserve shelters three pockets of the remaining indigenous forest, which contain yellowwood, stinkwood and boekenhout. The vegetation along the banks of the Palmiet River includes wild almond and Cape beech.

Small animals such as klipspringer, grysbok, baboon and Cape clawless otter may be seen, as well as raptors such as black eagle and fish eagle. Leopard are present but are rarely seen. A herd of wild horses roams the estuary of the Bot River.

Swimming and angling (with a valid licence) are permitted in the estuary, and there are several trails – including the overnight Highlands Trail. Between 1 June and 30 September, competent canoeists may take part in some Grade III white-water canoeing on the Palmiet River. Hikers and canoeists must book in advance.

For further information, write to The Manager, Kogelberg Nature Reserve, Private Bag X1, Kleinmond 7195, or telephone/fax (02823) 2-9425. Requests for reservations should be made by telephoning (021) 886-5858/6543, or fax 886-6575.

Mont Rochelle Nature Reserve

High above Franschhoek on the slopes of Franschhoek Mountain lies the Mont Rochelle Nature Reserve, 1 759 ha of unspoilt mountain fynbos, beautiful walks and spectacular views of the folded mountains of the Boland. It is particularly rich in fynbos – the mountains alone support more than 2 000 different species.

The heart of the reserve lies some 5 km out of Franschhoek on the Franschhoek Pass. On the second hairpin bend of this twisting road, look out for a road turning off to the left leading up to a gate, which is the start of numerous trails and walks. Northbound walks are very

THE CAPE: SOUTHERN CAPE

Far left below: The king protea (*Protea cynaroides*) is the largest of the proteas, with flowers that may measure 25 cm across (and more) when fully open. Its botanical name is derived from its resemblance to the artichoke. **Far left above:** A colour lithograph by George French Angas, entitled *Baviaans Kloof, the 'Glen of Baboons' near Genadendal*, from a 19th century book of travel at the Cape. **Left above:** A white mussel with its inhalant and exhalant siphons extended. These mussels dig into the sand beneath the surf extending their siphons into the water. The inhalant siphon admits organic particles (phytoplankton) on which the mussel feeds, using a fleshy lobe as a sieve. The water is then expelled through the other siphon. The small sand mussel *Donax sordidus* emerges from the sand periodically to allow itself to be moved by the tides. **Left below:** A malachite sunbird. This bird lives on nectar (it may often be seen hovering beside flowers much like a hummingbird), spiders, small moths and other insects. **Right:** Steenbras Dam, a large and beautiful body of water.

popular and lead to viewsites overlooking spectacular Wemmershoek Dam and Tygerkloof ravine and, if the weather is clear, a vista of distant Table Mountain.

For permits and more information, contact The Town Clerk, Franschhoek Municipality, P O Box 18, Franschhoek 7690, telephone (021) 876-2055 during office hours, or fax 876-3297.

Montagu Mountain Nature Reserve

Southern Africa is relatively well endowed with hot springs, where water, often richly mineralised, issues from the ground at a temperature above 25°C. There are at least 87 such springs in South Africa and 44 in Namibia, while in the whole of Australia there are only 25, and just two in the British Isles.

The hot springs at Montagu, now developed into a popular resort, lie on the edge of a 1 200 ha reserve of mountain fynbos that is particularly rich in protea species. Trails that lead from the baths area are Lovers' Walk (a level 2,2 km route along a riverbed to the other side of town) and the higher-rising and more scenic Cogmanskloof (12,1 km) and Bloupunt (15,6 km) trails.

Montagu is renowned for its attractive and historic buildings, and offers a number of other attractions, including wineries, farm excursions and an annual Muscadel Festival, as well as the Centenary Nature Reserve (*see separate entry*). Montagu lies on the R62 between Ashton and Barrydale.

The reserve is open all year. Bookings and enquiries should be addressed to The Information Bureau, Montagu Municipality, P O Box 24, Montagu 6720, telephone (0234) 42471. The Information Bureau is in Bath Street.

Pat Busch Private Nature Reserve

On the farms Bergplaas and Berg en Dal, in the foothills of the Langeberg and some 15 km from Robertson, this private reserve offers about 40 km of trails that wind through the valleys, giving glimpses of its rich birdlife and small antelope in fynbos rich in proteas, ericas, lilies and ferns.

The 2 000 ha reserve has comfortable, self-catering cottage and farmhouse accommodation, a dam for swimming, and fishing dams stocked with bass and trout, as well as bicycle trails through the vineyards and orchards. (There is also a 4x4 trail of approximately 10 kilometres.) To reach the reserve from the R62 between Ashton and Robertson, take the Klaasvoogds Wes turn-off and follow the signs to the farms Bergplaas and Berg en Dal.

For bookings, write to Pat Busch Private Nature Reserve, P O Box 579, Robertson 6705, or telephone/fax (02351) 2033.

Perdeberg Trail and Three Sisters Walk

The Perdeberg Trail is a rewarding one-day hike within the Kogelberg Nature Reserve (*see separate entry*) near Kleinmond, offering 15 km of easy walking, superb scenery and encounters with rare species of Western Cape fynbos.

The trail begins about 8 km from the office of the former Highlands Forestry Station (now Safcol, between Grabouw and Kleinmond), along a dirt road which is clearly signposted. There is ample parking at the starting point. This trail offers good views of the Palmiet River Valley and the Kogelberg Nature Reserve.

The shorter (10 km) Three Sisters Walk starts from near the parking area at the golf course behind Kleinmond, ascends a steep ridge and leads across streams and a rich growth of proteas before returning to the town. It may also be reached from Fairy Glen, near the mouth of the Palmiet River.

Permits for the trails may be obtained from Cape Nature Conservation, Private Bag X1, Uniedal 7612, telephone (021) 886-5858/6543, or fax 886-6575.

Safariland Game Park

Giraffe, wildebeest, eland, Burchell's zebra, springbok, warthog, ostrich, as well as several species of exotic animals, including camel, deer, llama and dwarf zebu cattle, roam freely

THE CAPE: SOUTHERN CAPE

the large sheet of water known as Steenbras Dam, a reservoir for the metropolitan area of Cape Town. It could be a postcard scene from Scandinavia, with crisp-edged islands, ranked pine forests rising from the water's edge and white, sandy banks washed, in windy conditions, by metre-high waves.

The Steenbras catchment area is 19 000 ha in extent, of which 1 000 ha is under pine plantation. Much of this area is out of bounds to the public, but there is a large recreation area near the dam wall. It is well stocked with trout (brown and rainbow). Fishing is the only recreational activity allowed (it must be done from the banks; no wading is permitted).

There are 21 bungalows in the recreation section, each sleeping four people. This accommodation is strictly functional, and visitors must supply their own bedding, crockery, cutlery, cooking and cooling appliances. Lighting is provided. No camping or caravanning is allowed, but there are several picnic sites.

Among the great attractions of Steenbras, which is administered by the Cape Town Metropolitan Council, are the magnificent gardens in the recreation area. Below the dam wall, for example, above the deep gully that stretches down to the Indian Ocean, is a particularly beautiful terraced garden with sandstone footpaths. The main conservation thrust at Steenbras is the preservation of fynbos endemic to the area.

Day permits are required to enter the area and these are available from the Cape Town Metropolitan Council as well as from several outlying municipal offices. Reservation forms and permits for use of the bungalows are available only from the Civic Centre in Cape Town.

Steenbras is open every day from 8 a.m. to 5 p.m. in winter and from 8 a.m. to 7 p.m. in summer. Areas accessible to the public are served by tarred roads that wind around the dam and are pleasantly shaded by flowering gums. The dam is worth a visit throughout the year but the fishing is particularly good in September and October.

The dam attracts a wide selection of birds, such as giant kingfisher, Egyptian goose and the occasional fish eagle. Several species of buck have been sighted (most of them in restricted areas) and officials stationed in the pine forests have spotted leopard spoor. Baboon inhabit the rocky promontories near the picnic site, and visitors are warned not to feed them.

Steenbras Dam is reached by taking the N2 from Cape Town towards Caledon. The northern entrance is clearly signposted at Sir Lowry's Pass; the southern entrance from the coastal road (R44) through Gordon's Bay is also signposted.

For further information, permits and reservations, write to The Civic Amenities Branch,

over this 200 ha piece of privately owned land near the town of Paarl.

Safariland Game Park, with its 10 km of good gameviewing gravel road, is a popular getaway. It has 12 bungalows equipped with everything the visitor could require, including fridges, stoves, kitchen- and tableware and linen (all you need to take is your food). There are also braai spots, swimming pools and a curio shop. The park is open daily throughout the year from 8 a.m. to 5.30 p.m.

To get there from Cape Town, take the N1 to Paarl, then take the Wemmershoek turn-off (exit 59), turn right at the stop street onto the R303 and follow the road for 8 km, from which point the park is signposted.

Reservations and further information may be obtained by writing to Safariland Game Park, P O Box 595, Suider-Paarl 7624, telephone (021) 864-0064, or fax 864-0065.

Salmonsdam Nature Reserve

The prime attraction of this 834 ha reserve to the southeast of Caledon is the superb mountain fynbos, which bursts into flower in spring.

There are also remnants of indigenous forest in the ravines.

Take a bakkie, 4x4 or mountain bike to explore the short road up Ravenshill, the highest point in the reserve, from where there are good views of the surrounding landscape. There are also three hiking trails of between 3 and 5 km to discover. You will see many birds and, if you are lucky, small mammals such as steenbok, klipspringer and bontebok.

The reserve is open daily between 7 a.m. and 6 p.m. and has picnic and braai facilities for day visitors. Three bungalows offer basic accommodation (it is necessary to take all provisions, bedding and cooking utensils) and there are caravan stands and campsites. To book accommodation or request further information on Salmonsdam, write to The Officer-in-Charge, Walker Bay Nature Reserve, Private Bag X13, Hermanus 7200, or telephone (0283) 77-0062, fax 77-1814.

Steenbras Dam

Cupped between the Hottentots-Holland Mountains and the rugged Kogelberg range is

245

THE STINGING NETTLE OF THE SEA

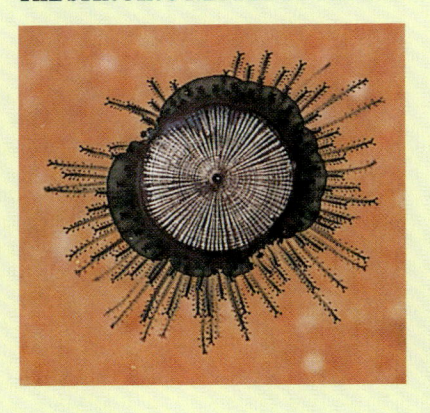

This raft-hydroid (*Porpita pacifica*) has a round, flat float that supports its fringe of dangling, stinging tentacles.

One of the most amazing creatures in the sea consists of little more than a bag of water. This is the jellyfish, a floating carnivore closely related to the familiar anemone. Jellyfish occur in a large variety of shapes and sizes, ranging from specimens only a few centimetres across to giants measuring 4 m in diameter – with a fringe of tentacles that can dangle 30 m beneath the surface of the sea. Some are harmless to humans, but others – such as the highly venomous sea wasp – can kill.

The sting of the jellyfish is delivered by the nematocysts (stinging cells) that line its tentacles. Some species produce a poison that raises a weal on the skin of the victim, whereas others inject their prey with a neurotoxin that attacks the nerves that regulate the involuntary muscles.

A typical jellyfish is umbrella-shaped (globular or cone-shaped), with tentacles dangling around the margin.

The mouth, leading to the digestive cavity, is beneath the umbrella and is equipped with four 'lips'. The feeding pattern differs widely: one jellyfish may sting and paralyse shrimps and fish before carrying them to the mouth; some trap planktonic animals with sticky mucus on the tentacles; a third type feeds like a sponge, sucking in its microscopic prey through thousands of 'mouths' on the elongated lips.

City Administrator's Department, Civic Centre, Hertzog Boulevard, Cape Town 8001, or telephone (021) 210-2507.

Villiersdorp Nature Reserve

A wildflower garden of about 36 ha lies at the foot of a mountain just outside the village of Villiersdorp and adjacent to the 500 ha Villiersdorp Nature Reserve. The garden is interesting all year, but is best seen between August and October, when wild flowers are blooming. Towards the end of this season a wildflower display is held.

About 60 species of protea grow here, including that with the biggest flowers of all – the giant king protea (*Protea cynaroides*), with a diameter of 25 centimetres. Another protea known as the mountain rose (*Protea acuminata*) is indigenous to the area and the garden features a good display of mountain fynbos, with many watsonias and ericas.

There is a network of footpaths through the garden, with thatched summerhouses for resting and picnicking. For the more energetic, the mountains are ideal hiking terrain, traversed by a scenic, four-hour trail. A camping, caravan and picnic area next to the reserve features seven huts, squash and tennis courts, bowling greens and a swimming pool. The reserve is open daily from 8 a.m. to 5 p.m.

On entering Villiersdorp from the Grabouw side, take the fourth turn to the left (watch for the signs) and follow this road directly to the reserve. For more detailed information, write to The Town Clerk, Villiersdorp Municipality, P O Box 23, Villiersdorp 6848, or telephone (0225) 3-1130.

Vineyard Trail

Winding through the beautiful vineyards west of Stellenbosch, this 24 km trail offers a pleasant and reasonably easy way of exploring the countryside. Hiking is permitted daily, but this scenic farmland trail is closed during the grape-harvesting season.

The route leads through privately owned estates and takes in a variety of terrain. You start at the cemetery in Stellenbosch and finish at a tarred road leading to Kuils River (from this point you return to Stellenbosch by train – remember to consult a timetable). The Stellenbosch Publicity Association will issue you with sketch maps of the route and also supplies the requisite permits.

For more information, write to the Stellenbosch Publicity Association, 36 Market Street, Stellenbosch 7600, or telephone their offices at (021) 883-3584/9633, or fax 883-8017.

Vrolijkheid Nature Reserve

The best time to see Vrolijkheid is in spring, when the mesembryanthemums (vygies) are in exuberant bloom. Some 20 km of gravel roads give visitors access to the various koppies in this 1 800 ha reserve, but walking will certainly provide a better opportunity to see the abundance of animals.

There are 40 species of mammal here, including the endangered honey badger and the ant bear. More common are the klipspringer, grey rhebok, duiker and the shy steenbok and grysbok. There is also a small herd of springbok that may be seen on the plains. A fascinating variety of some 180 bird species are found in the area, including ostrich, jackal buzzard, black eagle and the hadeda, while fish eagle can sometimes be spotted near the river. In the river itself lives one of the reserve's prize residents – the endangered Burchell's redfin minnow.

Two trails wind through the reserve – the 3 km Heron Trail, which leads to two dams, each with a bird hide, and the more strenuous 19 km Rooikat Trail. There are picnic sites near the offices, and self-issued permits for the trails may be obtained at the reserve entrance. The reserve is open daily from sunrise to sunset. Accommodation is available in the towns of McGregor and Robertson.

For further information, write to The Manager, Vrolijkheid Nature Reserve, Private Bag X614, Robertson 6705, or telephone (02353) 621/671, fax 674. The reserve is situated about 15 km south of Robertson on the way to McGregor, and is signposted.

Wiesenhof Private Nature Reserve

One of the most spectacular views of False Bay, Cape Town and the Boland mountain ranges can be obtained from a lookout tower on a hill in the Wiesenhof Reserve, about 40 minutes' drive from Cape Town. A variety of animals – including eland, wildebeest, cheetah and zebra – range freely in the 300 ha reserve.

There is a fine restaurant, a 10 ha picnic ground, a lake for small canoes, swimming pools and a roller-skating rink.

Wiesenhof is open to the public every day (except Mondays) from 9.30 a.m. to 6 p.m., and the animals are fed at 11 a.m. To get there, take the N1 to Paarl, turn off at the Klapmuts exit, drive under the highway and straight on after the stop street for approximately 3 km until you see the signposts. For more detailed information, you should contact Wiesenhof Private Nature Reserve, P O Box 50, Klapmuts 7625, or telephone (021) 875-5181.

Nature's showpiece

Attached to mainland Africa only by the sandy plain of the Cape Flats, the Cape Peninsula is a crooked spine of mountains extending north and south for some 56 km from Table Mountain to Cape Point, and is rarely more than 8 km wide. There is little level ground, except in the south, but the strips between beach and mountain slope are relatively densely settled.

This is the site of Cape Town and its suburbs, originating as a Dutch trading station in 1652 and now a major city experiencing an immense increase in population pressure. There can be few cities set against such a dramatically beautiful backdrop, and few city surroundings are more threatened.

Centuries of exploitation and muddled, indecisive management have taken their toll. In only a few remote gorges do remnants of dark green, indigenous forests survive. Fynbos clings tenaciously to all but the steepest, rockiest slopes, threatened or almost replaced by invasive alien vegetation. Surprisingly, perhaps, much remains, and bold plans for the future include restoration of a precious environment for its non-destructive enjoyment by increasing numbers of residents and visitors.

While most of the reserves on and adjoining the Peninsula are open to the public, admission to a few areas is restricted, invariably for ecologically sound reasons. The Peninsula's few offshore islands, including Duiker Island and Seal Island in False Bay, are rich in birdlife and seals, but can be visited only by scientists with a permit from the Directorate of Sea Fisheries. Most of Robben Island, the site of a former isolation hospital and a maximum-security prison in Table Bay, is open to visitors, although its future is still the subject of debate. For the rest, there are few restraints on exploring one of the world's floral kingdoms and its dramatic setting of sea and mountain.

Boulders Penguin Colony

African black-footed penguins have free rein at Boulders Beach, one of the Peninsula's toll beaches, just south of Simon's Town. From a few breeding pairs that waddled ashore in the late 1980s, the colony has increased to approximately 800 birds and has achieved international renown. Tourists from all over the world arrive to train their cameras and enjoy the spectacle of the birds mingling in an unfenced environment with human swimmers and sunbathers. To reach Boulders, turn seaward from the Cape Point road into Bellevue Road.

Cape Flats Private Nature Reserve

A great effort is being made by the University of the Western Cape to preserve the indigenous vegetation of the Cape Flats. The university has established a 21 ha reserve in which the indigenous flora and fauna are protected and studied. Rare and endangered plant species of related veld types are conserved by cultivation. Apart from its use by organised educational groups, the reserve is also open to the general public who should contact the Environmental Education and Resources Unit, University of the Western Cape, Private Bag X17, Bellville 7535, telephone (021) 959-2498 to arrange a visit.

Cape Flats Waste Waterworks

Also known as Strandfontein Sewage Works, the unprepossessing names belie the site's importance and the splendour of its birdlife. Situated between Baden-Powell Drive (which runs along the northern shore of False Bay)

Left: A ground orchid (*Disa cornuta*) near Cape Point. In many orchids, the pollen is packed into two large sacs joined by a harness. Insects transport these 'pollinia' from one flower to another. **Above:** Bontebok in the Cape of Good Hope Nature Reserve. This buck was once threatened with extinction by indiscriminate hunting, and was saved only by the foresight of a few private farmers. **Right:** The baboons in the Cape of Good Hope Nature Reserve are still – despite repeated pleas – fed by thoughtless visitors.

THE CAPE: CAPE PENINSULA

and Zeekoeivlei, the area is rated as the fifth most important waterbird habitat in South Africa. Compared to 12 Ramsar sites in the country, it is second in terms of bird numbers. (Ramsar sites are wetlands that have achieved international recognition in terms of a convention drawn up at Ramsar in Iran.) It has more abundant birdlife than the St Lucia wetland area, which is about 400 times larger, and it is widely known and highly regarded as a prime birdwatching site. Despite its importance, 'the works' has no official conservation status.

The waterworks is the main feeding ground for the birdlife of nearby Rondevlei and, indeed, for most of the Cape Flats birdlife as well. Flocks of up to 2 000 flamingoes may be seen in summer, among pelicans and thousands of other aquatic birds that include the rare red-necked phalarope and a number of endangered species such as the Caspian tern.

The aquatic habitat covers some 320 ha, and the terrestrial area, mostly alien vegetation and coastal dune scrub, measures 50 hectares. Grysbok, grey mongoose, water mongoose and Cape clawless otter are among other creatures found here.

Entry permits may be obtained at the Cape Town Civic Centre, telephone (021) 400-2203; Newlands Swimming Pool, telephone (021) 64-4197; and Muizenberg Pavilion, telephone (021) 788-7881. For an annual permit, write to The Manager, Drainage and Sewerage Branch, P O Box 1694, Cape Town 8000.

Cape of Good Hope Nature Reserve

Incorporating the southernmost tip of the Cape Peninsula is the Cape of Good Hope Nature Reserve, its 40 km of mostly rockbound coast extending from Smitswinkel Bay in the east to Schuster's Bay in the west. At first glance it appears a bleak and rather barren place, but in this 7 750 ha reserve are more than half of all the floral species found on the Peninsula, and as many as there are in the whole of the British Isles. Commonly known as fynbos, with the protea and erica (heath) dominant, this vegetation includes some 30 endangered or rare species, ten of them unique to the Cape Point area. Unfortunately, alien vegetation has invaded the reserve and staff are kept busy throughout the year weeding it out.

Small numbers of eland, bontebok, grey rhebok, grysbok and hartebeest are found here, together with mountain zebra, porcupine and ostrich – the great birds are often seen foraging along the beach. There are also troops of chacma baboon, unafraid and – despite prominent signs warning against it – frequently fed by thoughtless visitors.

The most sought-out spot in the reserve is Cape Point itself, with its sea cliffs (among the highest in the world) pounded by the restless tides. You can walk to the viewpoint (a steep climb on concrete paving) or take the funicular railway that starts from the parking area. From the top, a battered knife-edge of mountain dips to the sea where, according to popular but unscientific belief, the cold Benguela Current meets the warm Mozambique Current. Across the wide mouth of False Bay lies Cape Hangklip and the mainland of Africa, to which the Cape Peninsula is connected only by the low-lying, sandy corridor of the Cape Flats.

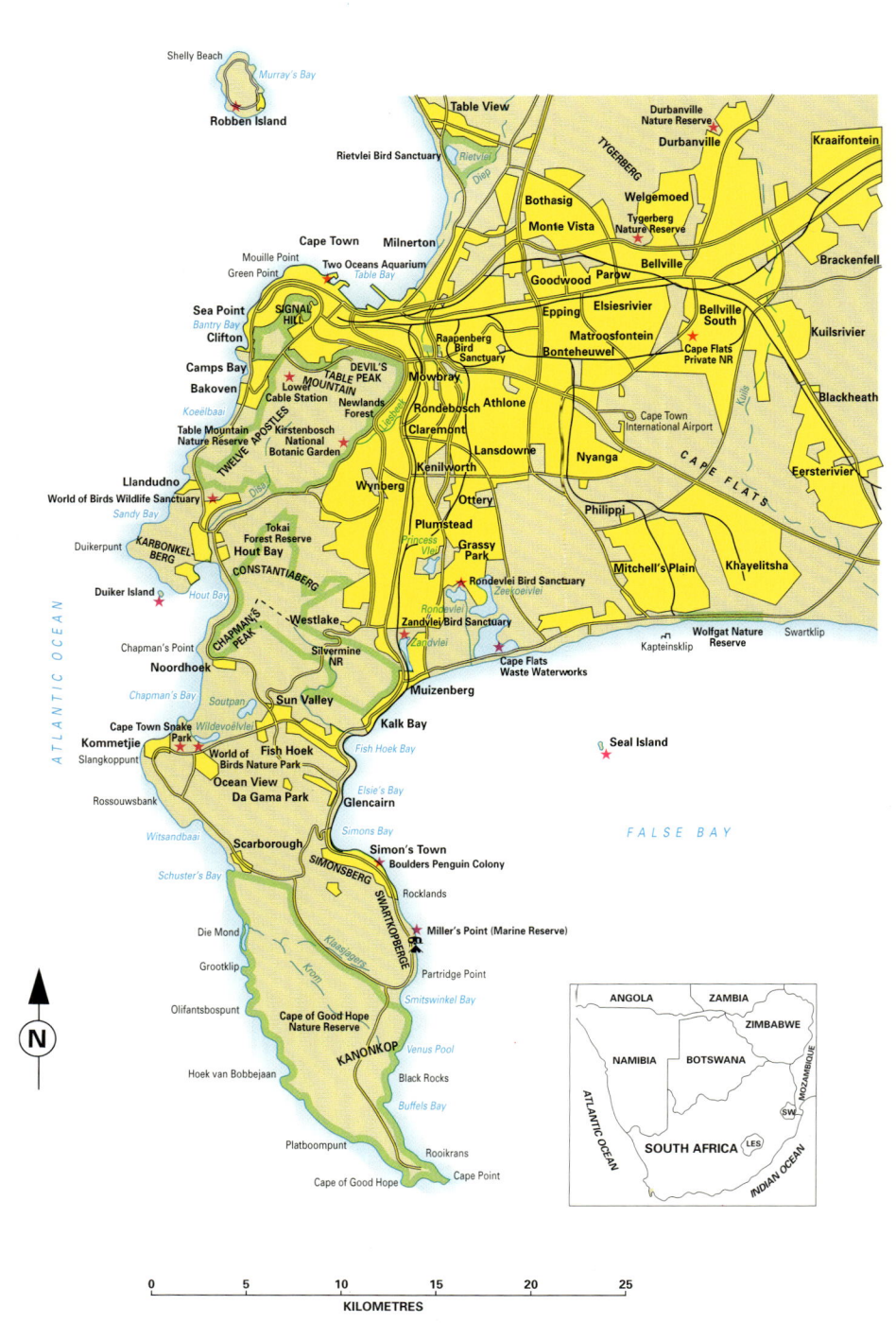

Among recreation areas, Bordjiesrif has a picnic area with toilets and fresh water, a tidal pool and a car park below a tall, stylised Portuguese cross – one of two erected to honour explorers who visited or sailed past this land five centuries ago. North of this is Black Rocks with its tidal pools, where an ancient lime kiln marks a vanished enterprise, Booi se Skerm (one of the few remnants of indigenous forest), and Venus Pool, a fine fishing and bathing spot.

South of Bordjiesrif, also on the False Bay side, is the Buffels Bay recreation area, with facilities similar to those at Bordjiesrif. Except in the marine reserve, extending north from the vicinity of Olifantsbos, there are signposted fishing spots along both the east and west coasts, the best known being Rooikrans, a cliff-side ledge where rock anglers drop their lines straight into deep water. Fishing permits may be obtained at the entrance gate. Visitors may walk anywhere, except in the sanctuary for black oystercatchers on the west side (Blaauwbergvlei is also closed to visitors). A brochure describing several trails may be obtained at the field museum, and guided walks are conducted on the third Sunday of every month, and every Sunday of the Western Cape school holidays. For details of the walks, telephone (021) 780-9204.

Many bird species can be seen, including fish eagle, black-shouldered kite, crowned plover and gannet. Marine life is abundant and visitors may spot shoals of tunny and snoek, as well as groups of the southern right whale (in winter and spring), seal, porpoise and shark from several viewsites on the shore. There is a restaurant, curio shop and information office at Cape Point and, further north, an information centre and field museum.

The reserve is open from 7 a.m. to 5 p.m. in winter, and from 7 a.m. to 6 p.m. in summer, with departure before sunset. There is no overnight accommodation, and camping is forbidden. The reserve is served by tarred roads on which the speed limit is 40 km/hour. Boats may be taken in and Buffels Bay has a launching ramp. No pets are allowed – telephone (021) 780-9050 to arrange day boarding – and fires may be made only in authorised places at Bordjiesrif and Buffels Bay. Swimming in the area is not forbidden, but visitors are warned that it is dangerous.

To reach the reserve from the city, take the M3 to Muizenberg. At the Westlake intersection, turn left and then right (it is signposted) to get to Muizenberg's Main Road. From there, follow the M4 Cape Point route. For more information, telephone (021) 780-9100 or 780-9526 during office hours.

Cape Peninsula Protected Natural Environment

In 1995 the provincial government of the Western Cape invited the National Parks Board to establish – subject to various conditions – a national park on the Cape Peninsula.

The latest plans visualise the addition of more land to that which has already been proclaimed as the Cape Peninsula Protected Natural Environment (CPPNE) and the creation of a consolidated Table Mountain and Cape Peninsula national park. Defined areas are set aside for special usage, including preservation zones to ensure the preservation of unique flora and fauna, remote areas buffered against the city by quiet areas, graduated leisure areas and areas of cultural or historical significance.

Once the approval of the national government has been obtained, moves would be made to have the area proclaimed a World Heritage Site in terms of the United Nations Environmental, Scientific and Cultural Organisation's World Heritage Convention. World Heritage Sites may be the most highly regarded examples of particular land forms, plant or animal communities, areas of great natural beauty, important habitats of threatened species and outstanding examples of the earth's evolutionary history. Before proclamation, a site must have been granted long-term protection and be large enough to be self-sustaining. The advantages of proclamation as a World Heritage Site include international recognition of the area's importance, as well as enhanced motivation for management and maintenance, and increased ecotourism.

The reasons that the Cape Peninsula qualifies as a World Heritage Site include its spectacular scenery and the fact that it forms a significant part of one of only six floral kingdoms in the world – its density of plant species is the highest in the world and it holds the highest number of both threatened and endemic plant species of any comparable area in the world. Among fauna, there are at least 111 invertebrates and one vertebrate (the Table Mountain ghost frog) that occur here and nowhere else in the world.

Cape Town Snake Park

Moving away from the old-fashioned 'snake-pit' concept to a more conservation-orientated approach, the park offers guided tours of its comprehensive collection of snakes and a unique collection of chameleons. Apart from African chameleons, there are many fascinating specimens from the island of Madagascar, while the snakes include a python believed to be the largest in southern Africa. Tortoises may

---

TABLE MOUNTAIN'S GIFT OF SILVER

'The Silver-tree', an engraving by William Burchell, from *Travels in the Interior of Southern Africa*.

Perhaps the loveliest of all southern Africa's indigenous trees grows naturally in just one secluded corner of the subcontinent – on the eastern slopes of Table Mountain and the Vlakkenberg. The flowers of the silver tree (*Leucadendron argenteum*) are attractive enough, but it is the leaves – lance-like, shimmering brightly in the wind – that give it its special beauty.

The leaves are covered with silky, silver hairs that protect the tree in the often harsh Cape climate, and especially from excessive transpiration (loss of moisture) in the dry, blustery months of the year. In summer, the hairs press down tightly against the leaves to keep the moisture in; in the moist winter the hairs are raised to allow air to circulate on the leaf's surface.

The silver tree looks fragile, but it is in fact a hardy species, able to withstand the buffeting of gale-force winds and to survive the devastating passage of mountain fires.

The wind plays an important part in the reproductive cycle of the silver tree. The female tree develops a cone (bearing a superficial resemblance to those of pines and firs) which contains the seeds. Unlike pines and firs, however, the cones remain upright; waiting for a strong wind in April and May to scatter the seeds onto the surrounding mountain slopes.

The tree was first recorded in 1620 by Augustin de Beaulieu, who found 'a great many trees . . . their trunks were straight, in shape like pear trees, the leaves small and whitish, the bark about 50 mm thick and reddish in colour . . .'

The silver tree is, in the words of the botanist Linnaeus . . . 'the most shining and splendid of all plants'.

also be seen and it is proposed to erect walk-through cages in which visitors can keep company with giant lizards from all over the world. The park, at Imhoff's Farm on the M65 near Kommetjie, on the west coast of the Peninsula, is open daily from 9 a.m. to 5 p.m. For information, telephone (021) 783-3573, fax 701-9075.

Duiker Island

Just west of the Sentinel at Hout Bay is Duiker Island, a small, rocky outcrop that is a reserve for seals and seabirds – mostly cormorants (*duikers*). The island is open only to marine scientists with permits, but visitors may have a close look from motor launches that leave Hout Bay harbour every day at 10.30 a.m. throughout the year. In high season the launches leave for the island every hour from 11 a.m. to 4 p.m.

The seals on Duiker Island come and go throughout the year, so there is never a static population. In summer as many as 4 000 seals have been seen there. To book a trip to the island, telephone Circe Launches on (021) 790-1040, fax 790-5722.

Durbanville Nature Reserve

Formerly a rural village, Durbanville, northwest of the Tygerberg hills, has become a part of greater Cape Town. In the 6 ha sanctuary are preserved several species of protea, leucadendron, erica and aristea (of the family Iridaceae). The best time to visit is from the beginning of April to the end of October.

Among the facilities are a car park, toilets (including toilets for the disabled), tables and benches, and a number of pleasant walks (including a short route for the disabled). By prior arrangement, a gazebo and up to 24 tables with chairs, and light refreshments, can be made available for up to 100 people. Picnics are permitted (no fires). The reserve is open from 9 a.m. to 4.30 p.m. daily.

To reach the reserve, turn off the N1 at the Durbanville exit between Cape Town and Paarl, and proceed along Durbanville Avenue, turn left into Tindale Road and then turn right into Race Course Road. From here the reserve is clearly signposted. Guided tours are available on request. For more information, write to The Curator, Durbanville Nature Reserve, P O Box 100, Durbanville 7550, or telephone (021) 96-3453, fax 96-6850.

Kirstenbosch National Botanic Garden

There is a granite Celtic cross in Kirstenbosch marking the grave of the garden's first director, Professor Harold Pearson, and it bears the inscription: 'If ye seek his monument, look around.' It is an apt and moving injunction – the grave is surrounded by one of the world's most famous reserves of indigenous flora.

Founded in 1913, Kirstenbosch lies on the eastern slopes of Table Mountain. It consists of landscaped gardens of indigenous plants and trees, watered by the Liesbeek River, as well as natural forest that extends up the lower slopes.

Kirstenbosch covers an area of 828 ha, 60 ha of which are cultivated; the remainder is a natural flora reserve. It is a living display featuring 4 700 of the estimated 20 000 species of indigenous South African flora, and close to 50 per cent of the Peninsula's floral wealth.

In the cultivated area, related plants are grouped together and radiate from the central lawns like the spokes of a wheel. Among the interesting sections here are the Cycad Amphitheatre, which hosts most species of these 'living fossils' found in southern Africa; the famed Protea Garden on the higher slopes with its profuse growth of silver trees (*Leucadendron argenteum*); the J W Mathews Rock Garden (named after the first curator) containing succulents of the genera *Crassula*, *Aloe*, *Lampranthus* and *Euphorbia*; the Erica Garden and the Pelargonium Koppie. Two streams cut through Kirstenbosch, both laced with *besembos*, red alder and hard fern.

Of historical interest is an avenue of camphor trees and fig trees planted by Cecil Rhodes in 1898, and a small section of wild almond (*Brabejum stellatifolium*) hedge planted by Dutch settler Jan van Riebeeck in 1660.

Within the grounds of Kirstenbosch are the headquarters of the National Botanical Institute that administers the national network of gardens and associated research institutes. One, the Compton Herbarium, is situated at the top of Camphor Avenue in Kirstenbosch itself.

Named after a former director, the Compton Herbarium is dedicated to research, particularly into Cape flora. It now preserves approximately 250 000 specimens, including its own collection and that of the South African Museum dating from 1825. As a data bank, the herbarium is of great historical interest internationally – its records include many rare plants and some that are now extinct.

All paths in the main section of Kirstenbosch are paved, but there are two gravel-surfaced routes to the higher parts of the garden. Smuts Track (used by the late General J C Smuts) leads through the mixed forest of indigenous trees up Skeleton Gorge to the summit of Table Mountain. The other route, Forest Walk, leads through leafy palaces of ironwood, yellowwood and red alder. There are two special routes along level, paved paths for wheelchairs, prams or the less agile. Known as the Weaverbird Walk and the Silver Tree Stroll, both are clearly signposted with the wheelchair sign. Three trails, Silvertree, Yellowwood and Stinkwood, provide more vigorous walks of up to 6 km or three hours.

Above: Silver trees (*Leucadendron argenteum*) shimmer in the Kirstenbosch National Botanic Garden on the eastern slopes of Table Mountain. These graceful trees can grow to a height of 16 metres.

THE CAPE: CAPE PENINSULA

Above: Sundew plants at the summit of Table Mountain. The leaves of this insectivorous plant are covered with sticky glands on stalks, which close over and entrap their insect prey.

The Braille Trail for the blind is a 470 m route that passes through natural Table Mountain forest and fynbos. The plants are clearly labelled with Braille and large-print labels. The Fragrance Garden, situated nearby, boasts a fine collection of indigenous aromatic plants, also labelled in Braille and large print, set out in a number of raised beds.

Kirstenbosch may be visited in spring and summer when the gardens blaze with Namaqualand daisies and other annuals, but winter is the best time to see proteas and ericas. The Kirstenbosch information kiosk is open from 8 a.m. to 7 p.m. in summer, and to 6 p.m. in winter. Visitors may purchase selected indigenous plants, books and souvenirs from the shop from 9 a.m. to 5 p.m. daily. There is a restaurant with an attractive outdoor section.

To get to Kirstenbosch from Cape Town, take the M3 towards Muizenberg. After passing Newlands Forest along Union Avenue, turn right into Rhodes Avenue and keep on this road until you see the sign directing you to the gates of the gardens. Picnics and fires are prohibited. Dogs are allowed if kept on a leash. For more information, telephone (021) 762-1166.

Miller's Point Marine Reserve

The reserve and resort area, on the western side of False Bay, are clearly signposted 8 km from Simon's Town, along the main road (M4) to Cape Point. The boundaries are the offshore Bakoven Rock in the north and Bobbejaansklip in the south. Fishing and spearfishing are prohibited within the reserve. However, snoek may be caught in season from licensed fishing boats. Swimming and diving are permitted and there is a boat-launching ramp. There are picnic sites, braai places, a campsite and caravan park, all under the management of the Cape Metropolitan Council.

For more information, contact The Resort Manager, P O Box 44, Simon's Town 7995, telephone (021) 786-1142.

Orange Kloof

The Disa River that flows to Hout Bay cuts down through the broad valley of Orange Kloof, some 285 ha in extent. The upper reaches form one of the last areas of indigenous forest surviving in the Cape Peninsula. Overexploitation and fire have destroyed almost all the rest, and only 85 ha of relatively undisturbed forest remain. Naturally occurring fauna includes grysbok, genet, caracal or lynx, Cape otter and Cape fox, and a number of small antelope species have been reintroduced.

Orange Kloof, which has been spared the ravages of fire for over six decades, is also noted for its fynbos which, because of its age, is of great scientific interest. Aerial photographs show that natural regeneration is increasing the area of the indigenous forest. All this, however, could be destroyed by a single fire, so Orange Kloof is not open to the public.

Entry is restricted to researchers, scientists and students, who are accompanied by officials of the City of Cape Town Parks and Forests Department, which manages the area. For more information, telephone The Forester or Law Enforcement Officer at Orange Kloof Forest Station on (021) 790-1023/4.

Raapenberg Bird Sanctuary

Despite being situated along the edge of the Black River Parkway, one of Cape Town's busiest freeways, this small (10 ha) wetland reserve provides a haven for a variety of freshwater and marine birds. Over 55 species have been recorded here, including kingfisher, stilt, heron, purple gallinule and yellow-billed duck. The reserve is popular with birdwatchers and photographers, and is to be extended by the addition of 5 ha of wetland along the Black River below the Vincent Pallotti Hospital.

While the southern section of the Raapenberg reserve is open, the northern part is fenced in and permits are needed to gain access to this ecologically sensitive area. Access is from Observatory Road (off Liesbeek Parkway) or from Black River Parkway. The reserve is open at all times.

For further information, write to The Director, Parks and Forests Branch, City Engineer's Department, P O Box 1694, Cape Town 8000, or telephone (021) 400-3823, fax 25-2685.

Rietvlei Bird Sanctuary

Situated at Milnerton, north of Cape Town, the Rietvlei wetland is the largest breeding area for waterfowl in the Western Cape. There are over 146 species, including flamingo, pelican, black-backed gull, fish eagle, Egyptian goose and migratory birds such as the Arctic tern.

Most of the vlei, which is reached from Otto du Plessis Drive and Pentz Drive in Milnerton, is privately owned and is maintained as a conservation and recreation area. Fed by the Diep River, the vlei dries up in summer – except for the deep-water area dredged for the Table Bay Harbour development, which is now used for recreation purposes. The vlei is linked to the sea by a large tidal lagoon, popular with canoeists and boardsailing enthusiasts. The reserve is open at all times.

Robben Island

There is no place out-of-doors on Robben Island where you can't hear the sea. For centuries its sound was a mocking reminder to lepers and lunatics, political prisoners, criminals, condemned felons and paupers that this was where they would probably die.

In a democratic South Africa, however, the role of Robben Island as a maximum-security prison has fallen away. Its future use has yet to be decided.

Robben Island was named for its seals (*robben* in Dutch). It covers 574 ha and lies 10 km north of Table Bay harbour and 7 km west of Bloubergstrand. Low-lying and sandy, the island is blasted by southeast gales in summer and, in winter, by the northwest storms that used to create havoc with shipping in the bay. The natural vegetation is of the west-coast Strandveld type, and the colourful spring display is impressive.

Animals thought to be indigenous to the island include rodents, lizards, snakes and one species of tortoise, as well as some 70 bird species. The island is an important breeding ground for seabirds. The European rabbit was

251

Above: This view of the fairest Cape from the summit of Table Mountain reveals a panorama of bush-covered mountains – composed of sandstone upon granite – rising from the almost encompassing sea.

introduced in 1654 and still survives. (Australia's problem rabbits are directly descended from Robben Island stock shipped by Captain Cook in 1772.) At various times small numbers of fallow deer, bontebok, eland, springbok and steenbok have been introduced and are still present. Because of the one-mile security zone around the island, submarine flora and fauna are left undisturbed and include abundant abalone (*Haliotis midae*) and rock lobster (*Jasus lalandii*). Also relatively undisturbed are the remains of at least 30 historic shipwrecks.

Intensive surveys are being undertaken to determine the island's new role, with the likelihood that it will become one of the country's major tourist attractions. Apart from the scenic magnificence of its position in the bay, attractions are cultural-historical and include a complete Victorian village, lighthouse, cemeteries and 20th century coastal defence artillery batteries. All this combined in a nature reserve, with the poignant past of the island, will require the most sensitive management.

At present, Robben Island is not generally open to tourists. Potential visitors should contact Captour, P O Box 1403, Cape Town 8000, telephone (021) 418-5214, fax 418-5227.

Rondevlei Bird Sanctuary

When Rondevlei, a wilderness of reeds, marshland and indigenous vegetation, was established in 1952 by the Divisional Council of the Cape of Good Hope, it was a quiet, rural area, a natural site for the conservation and protection of waterfowl and indigenous flora. The modern city, however, now reaches to the reserve's fences, but Rondevlei still maintains its purpose and provides one of the best birdwatching venues in the Peninsula. Some 228 species, including migratory birds from Europe, have been sighted in the 200 ha reserve.

From a narrow path that cuts through the reeds at the vlei's edge, with benches and lookout towers placed at strategic intervals, visitors have a general view of the birdlife, while discreet and well-constructed hides provide a field base for photography and close-up watching. The best time to visit Rondevlei is from February to May, although there is plenty to see throughout the year.

The reserve has developed into an important environmental education centre, complete with a small lecture theatre. Video programmes about the reserve are available for schools and other organised groups, and guided walks may be arranged.

The Leonard Gill Museum in the sanctuary has a comprehensive display of mounted birds, reptiles and mammals that occur at Rondevlei. Other inhabitants of the sanctuary include small numbers of steenbok, grysbok, mongoose, porcupine and hippopotamus.

Near the entrance gates is a small picnic area (no fires) and ornamental pond. The reserve is open every day of the year (except Christmas Day) from 8 a.m to 5 p.m. From December to February the gates close at 7 p.m. at weekends. Binoculars and a bird-identification book are essential aids.

To reach Rondevlei, turn off Prince George Drive at the Grassy Park sign and follow the signposts. For more information, write to The Reserve Manager, Rondevlei, Fisherman's Walk, Zeekoeivlei 7945 or telephone (021) 706-2404, fax 706-2405.

Seal Island

About 5 km off Strandfontein Beach in False Bay is a bald rock, about 2 ha in extent, named Seal Island. Apart from a population of about 50 000 seals, the island is also home to numbers of noisy bank cormorant and seagull.

Visitors are not allowed to land on the island, but boats from Kalk Bay and Gordon's Bay harbours make special trips around the island by arrangement. The best time to see the seals is in the summer months. Details of boat trips to the island can be obtained by telephoning (021) 788-5261.

Silvermine Nature Reserve

Some of the most attractive mountain scenery and indigenous flora of the Cape Peninsula can be seen in this high-lying 2 158 ha reserve, which extends from the Muizenberg and Kalk Bay mountains in the east to Noordhoek Peak in the west. A feature of the reserve is the Silvermine River, flowing through a forested gorge where it is joined by a tributary before creating a picturesque waterfall.

A network of tracks and paths provides breathtaking views of False Bay, Fish Hoek, Noordhoek and Simon's Town, as well as opportunities to glimpse grysbok, caracal, porcupine and genet. There are also two more-strenuous trails, of up to three hours' duration. The reserve contains fine specimens of protea, leucadendron and erica, which attract sugarbird, sunbird and Cape robin.

Many picnic sites are accessible by car, and those at the Silvermine Reservoir are only a few minutes' walk from the car park. Fires may be made only in the designated spots, and visitors should bring their own firewood. Swimming in the reservoir is prohibited. The reserve opens at 8 a.m. throughout the year and closes at 7 p.m. in summer (1 October to 31 March) and at 6 p.m. in winter (1 April to 30 September). The best times to visit are between October and December, and during March and April.

The Sunbird Environmental Centre caters for educational groups, and an environmental officer may conduct excursions on request. There is accommodation for 40 students.

To get there, take the M3 to Muizenberg, turn right at the Westlake intersection and then left onto Ou Kaapseweg (M64). Once on the plateau, signs mark the two entry points – one in the north, the other in the south. An entry fee is payable on the northern side of the reserve, where maps and pamphlets are available. Frequent visitors may apply for quarterly, half-yearly or annual permits.

For more information, write to The Reserve Manager, Silvermine Nature Reserve, P O Box 30223, Tokai 7966, or telephone (021) 75-3040/1/2/3, fax 75-1366.

Table Mountain Nature Reserve

Few, if any, of the world's cities have such a dramatic backdrop as Cape Town, nestled in a natural amphitheatre formed by its sheltering mountains. Table Mountain itself broods over town and bay, its face changing constantly – and often suddenly – with weather and season.

The mountain, a national monument (and parts of it a proclaimed nature reserve), is both unique and vulnerable. It has been used and abused by man for more than three centuries and much of the original fauna has been wiped out, though the flora – surprisingly – is in a reasonable state. A long-term strategy to preserve the mountain's character is being considered, and the authorities wage constant war against vandals, erosion, alien vegetation and fires.

The reserve covers an area of 2 904 ha, embracing Signal Hill, the northern face of the mountain, Van Riebeeck Park, portions of Devil's Peak, the upper and lower table, including Orange Kloof valley (a restricted area, where indigenous forest has regenerated) and Newlands Forest. It is open during daylight hours. The mountain summit is accessible by more than 500 routes, but the easiest and quickest method of getting there is by cable car. The lower cable station is situated on Tafelberg Road, which winds around the mountain at the 400 m mark.

There are several picnic spots in the area and well-marked walks (the contour path is one of the most popular) and climbs (a favourite is up Platteklip Gorge) from the road. Another route from Kloof Nek, turning sharp right as you arrive from the city centre, is Signal Hill Road, which takes you to the top of this small, rounded hill. Views – particularly at night – are spectacular.

At the summit of Table Mountain, at the upper cable station, is a kiosk, and a restaurant that serves lunches and teas. Apart from this, there are few organised facilities (fishing and overnight camping are prohibited, and braai fires are allowed only in designated places in the forest above Newlands).

Fauna in the reserve includes caracal, genet, dassie, mongoose, baboon and the odd grysbok. Velvet worms, belonging to an unusual and rare group of animals sharing both worm and insect characteristics, are found on the slopes. But the reserve is best known for its indigenous flora.

In the 1940s, the Cape Town City Council planted several species of pine on the eastern slopes of Table Mountain for their commercial value, but Newlands Forest is now used purely as a recreational area. It covers about 200 ha between Kirstenbosch and Devil's Peak. Newlands Forest is a favourite walking area for Capetonians, and offers a stunning view of the suburbs and the distant Hottentots-Holland range from many vantage points. It is open all year and no permits are needed.

Take the M3 to Muizenberg from the city and, on the Union Avenue section, watch for the Forestry Station sign on the right.

Above left: *Pelargonium cucullatum* in the Silvermine Nature Reserve on the mountainous spine of the Peninsula.
Above right: A cattle egret, photographed at the World of Birds Wildlife Sanctuary in Hout Bay. **Right:** White pelicans in the Rondevlei Bird Sanctuary. These birds sometimes feed in groups, driving schools of fish into shallow water where they can be seen and caught more easily. The pelican's plumage is tinged with pink in the breeding season. When in breeding condition, the female develops a longer crest, and the bald patch between the bill and the eyes becomes more swollen than in non-breeding birds.

Tokai Forest Reserve

Most of the higher parts of the 2 572 ha Tokai State Forest, which embraces Constantiaberg (including its western face), are devoted to the preservation of fynbos, indigenous forest and the area's once-abundant wildlife. Plantations of pine and eucalyptus (and even some North American redwoods) have been cultivated too.

The lowest-lying section of the plantation is a picnic area, with space for up to 1 000 people. Further up is the entrance to the reserve, where permits are issued during daylight hours.

Here is South Africa's first arboretum, in which the planting of trees – most of which are labelled – commenced a century ago, and it can be toured on a leisurely circular walk of just over one kilometre. A river, the Prinskasteel, flows by on its way to Princess Vlei on the Cape Flats. *Prinskasteel* – 'the prince's castle' – is an older name for the cave now more widely known as Elephant's Eye.

The start of the Tokai Walk is signposted, the route leading through the plantation and up the steep mountainside to Elephant's Eye. This large, open cave offers lovely views and is the junction of a number of paths. The Tokai Walk route is indicated by white elephant markers painted on rocks and tree-trunks, and it takes about three hours to complete. Although the Tokai Walk is the most popular, several other paths crisscross on Constantiaberg – some from Constantia Nek to Silvermine Reserve (*see separate entry*), while others go on to Hout Bay and Noordhoek Peak. The reserve is always worth a visit, but much depends on the weather, as it must be explored on foot.

To get there, take the M3 and turn off at the Tokai/Retreat sign, then turn right into Tokai Road, which leads directly to the reserve.

Two Oceans Aquarium

The two oceans – Atlantic and Indian – are popularly held to meet at Cape Point (although they actually meet further east, at Cape Agulhas), so Africa's largest and most technically advanced aquarium, at Cape Town's Victoria and Alfred Waterfront, is well named.

More than two million litres of sea water lap through immense tanks to create marine environments from intertidal zone to great ocean depths. Tree-like growths of kelp and weed shelter an entrancing array of life forms, some of which flit briefly in the shadows while others swim into the open to display feathery fins or silvery scales as, overhead, the large and ominous shape of a shark cruises silently by.

A single display shows an entire river ecosystem, following a drop of water from the river's source high in the mountains, all the way to the sea. The aquarium has a curio shop and a restaurant with panoramic views. It has been designed to be readily accessible to all and has a number of wheelchairs available. Classes and activities are organised for visitors of all ages – including adults. For more information, telephone (021) 418-4644.

Tygerberg Nature Reserve

Never the haunt of tigers, the hills to the north of Table Bay were named for the mottled appearance of their vegetation that reminded early Dutch settlers of the spots on a leopard – which they generally referred to as a *tyger*.

Although adjacent to residential areas, the 67 ha reserve is home to a surprising variety of animals and birds, including grysbok, porcupine, grey mongoose, dassie, spotted eagle owl, guinea fowl, pheasant and francolin. Grey-green fynbos thrives, with most flowers appearing in spring. The reserve offers numerous pleasant walks and picnic sites.

The main entrance is off Totius Street in the suburb of Welgemoed, and the reserve is open on weekdays from 8.30 a.m. to 4.30 p.m. and at weekends and on public holidays from 9 a.m. to 6 p.m. For further information, telephone (021) 918-2911.

Wolfgat Nature Reserve

This stretch of coastline between Mnandi and Monwabisi beaches, with its rugged calcrete-capped cliffs and wide views of False Bay, was proclaimed a nature reserve in 1986. It is the site of the largest mainland breeding colony of black-backed gulls in southern Africa, and its vegetation of Strandveld interspersed with pockets of coastal fynbos shelters grysbok, steenbok, Cape hare and tortoise. Bulbs and annuals make bright displays in spring.

The reserve is at the centre of a community project involving the residents of the nearby suburb of Mitchell's Plain. Alien vegetation has been cleared by unemployed members of the community; the reserve is used as an outdoor classroom; pupils not only clear the reserve of litter, but also sort and analyse the material they collect, to determine its source and try to devise ways of preventing future pollution.

Signposts direct the way to the reserve from Baden-Powell Drive. No entrance fee is charged and there are no facilities. Fences have been erected around the breeding area to protect the birds, but the remainder of the 248 ha reserve is open to the public.

For further information, write to The Director, Parks and Forests Branch, City Engineer's Department, P O Box 1694, Cape Town 8000, or telephone (021) 400-3823, fax 25-2685.

World of Birds Wildlife Sanctuary

Nestling in the Hout Bay valley is an extraordinary bird sanctuary – believed to be the largest in Africa – where visitors are offered the rare opportunity to explore 100 large and well-occupied walk-through aviaries.

There are more than 3 000 birds of 350 different species – both exotic and indigenous – together with small animals that include tortoise, meerkat, monkey, dassie and bushbaby. Some of the birds, like the African black-footed penguin, white pelican, Cape vulture, bald ibis, and brown-necked parrot, are on the endangered list.

The World of Birds is South Africa's foremost bird-breeding centre. Of special interest is a variety of ponds where swans, egrets, ibises, herons and cormorants live and breed under a fringe of willow trees.

The park is a photographer's paradise. Most of the birds are accustomed to humans and can be photographed close up with little difficulty to achieve excellent natural results.

There is an outside tea garden and cafeteria where light refreshments and curios may be bought, and an information centre. The sanctuary is open every day from 9 a.m. to 5 p.m. It can be reached from Hout Bay's main throughroad, where a sign at the intersection with Victoria Road directs you to Valley Road. For further information, telephone (021) 790-2730, or fax 790-4839.

The World of Birds Nature Park on the M65 at Ocean View, near Kommetjie, specialises in large flightless birds, including ostrich, emu, rhea and cassowary, and is a captive breeding centre for African cranes. There is a children's farmyard, and among the animals are eland and llama. Camel rides are available. The

Above: Various species of fish swim between the waving fronds of a kelp forest at the popular Two Oceans Aquarium, opened in 1995 on Cape Town's well-known Waterfront.

Nature Park is open daily from 9 a.m. to 5 p.m. For more information, telephone the sanctuary at (021) 783-2309.

Zandvlei Bird Sanctuary

The Zandvlei Bird Sanctuary covers about 20 ha of typical coastal marshland and is dotted with islands. A network of easily negotiated paths and bridges permits good viewing of pelican, wader, Cape teal and coot, and there are also small hides facing the vlei.

The gates are kept locked but permits are available from The Reserve Manager, telephone (021) 75-3040/1/2/3, fax 75-1366. During normal business hours, an environmental officer may conduct educational excursions if requested in advance. (Zandvlei and surroundings are the site of the Battle of Muizenberg, where half-hearted defence by the Dutch garrison allowed British invaders to advance to Cape Town in 1795.)

Adjoining the sanctuary is a large recreation area with picnic sites, braai places and a children's playground – an ideal spot for boardsailors and boating enthusiasts (there are launching ramps). The recreation area is open from sunrise to sunset. It can be reached from Muizenberg's Beach Road (there are signs). The sanctuary part of Zandvlei is reached by turning into Military Road from either Main Road or Prince George Drive and then turning south at Steenberg railway station.

THE CAPE: THE WEST COAST

Coastal wetlands and floral delights

For most of the year the west coast road (R27) from Cape Town to Saldanha Bay runs through flat and somewhat dull scrubby scenery. To the west, the landscape is relieved only by the occasional glimpse of the icy Atlantic rollers between the sand dunes. But, in spring, the landscape is transformed by a carpet of vibrant colour when swathes of indigenous flowers – particularly in the Darling area and around Clanwilliam – cloak the ground.

The west coast buckles into large pans of water that attract thousands of bird migrants. Langebaan lagoon is recognised by ornithologists as one of the great wetlands of the world. Islands, blessed with large breeding populations of seabirds, seals and other marine life, lie offshore. However, these are strictly controlled sanctuaries to which the general public has no access.

Inland is another visual treat – the Cederberg – a wonderland of grotesquely sculptured stone, cedars, waterfalls, sheer cliffs and gentle slopes. And in spring, it is clothed in flowers.

Bain's Kloof

Cutting through the Limietberg, Bain's Kloof Pass winds steeply for 16 kilometres to Ceres and the Breede River valley, and travellers are treated to ever-changing panoramas. This spectacularly scenic route dates from the 1840s, and honours its builder, Andrew Bain.

From the summit, a footpath (out of bounds without a permit from the Hawequas Forestry Station) leads to the upper Wit River valley. In spring, this Paradise Valley or Happy Valley is blanketed with flowers, and the river is punctuated by a series of pools.

Just beyond the road to Paradise Valley (at the summit), a picnic area is the start of a 6 km walk to Baviaanskloof, with several connecting paths that take hikers to gorges and waterfalls.

Further down the valley is Tweede Tol, a camping and picnic site on the banks of the Wit River. It marks the end of the Boland Hiking Trail's Limietberg section, and the start of shorter trails. For further information, write to the Boland District Office, Private Bag X1, Uniedal 7612, or telephone (021) 886-5858 or 886-6543, fax 886-6575.

Beaverlac Nature Reserve

East of Porterville lie the Olifantsrivierberge, famous for their striking rock formations and wild flowers. The privately owned Beaverlac Nature Reserve, based on the farm Grootfontein, is situated at the crest of Dasklip Pass. There are rivers with pools and falls, and Bushman (San) paintings in caves include a depiction of a ship (only two of this type are known).

The area is a sanctuary for fynbos and several small antelope species. Leopard may be glimpsed and lucky birding enthusiasts may spy a black eagle. There are pleasant scenic walks along the slopes, and visitors may also go kloofing, or follow the mountain-bike trails. Fishing for bass in the Olifants River is permitted, but is restricted because of the endangered, endemic yellowfish.

Accommodation is in a fully equipped farmhouse, two- and four-berth caravans, or a

Left: Colonies of Cape cormorant and Cape gannet on Bird Island, off Lambert's Bay. Most of the islands are inhabited by European rabbits – the descendants of those introduced to provide food for shipwrecked sailors. **Above:** *Dorotheanthus bellidiformis*, *Senecio elegans* (mauve) and *Dimorphotheca pluvialis* (white) brighten the veld near the pretty town of Darling. **Right:** A bat-eared fox (*Otocyon megalotis*). Its enormous ears can reach 13 cm in length and up to 10 cm around the base.

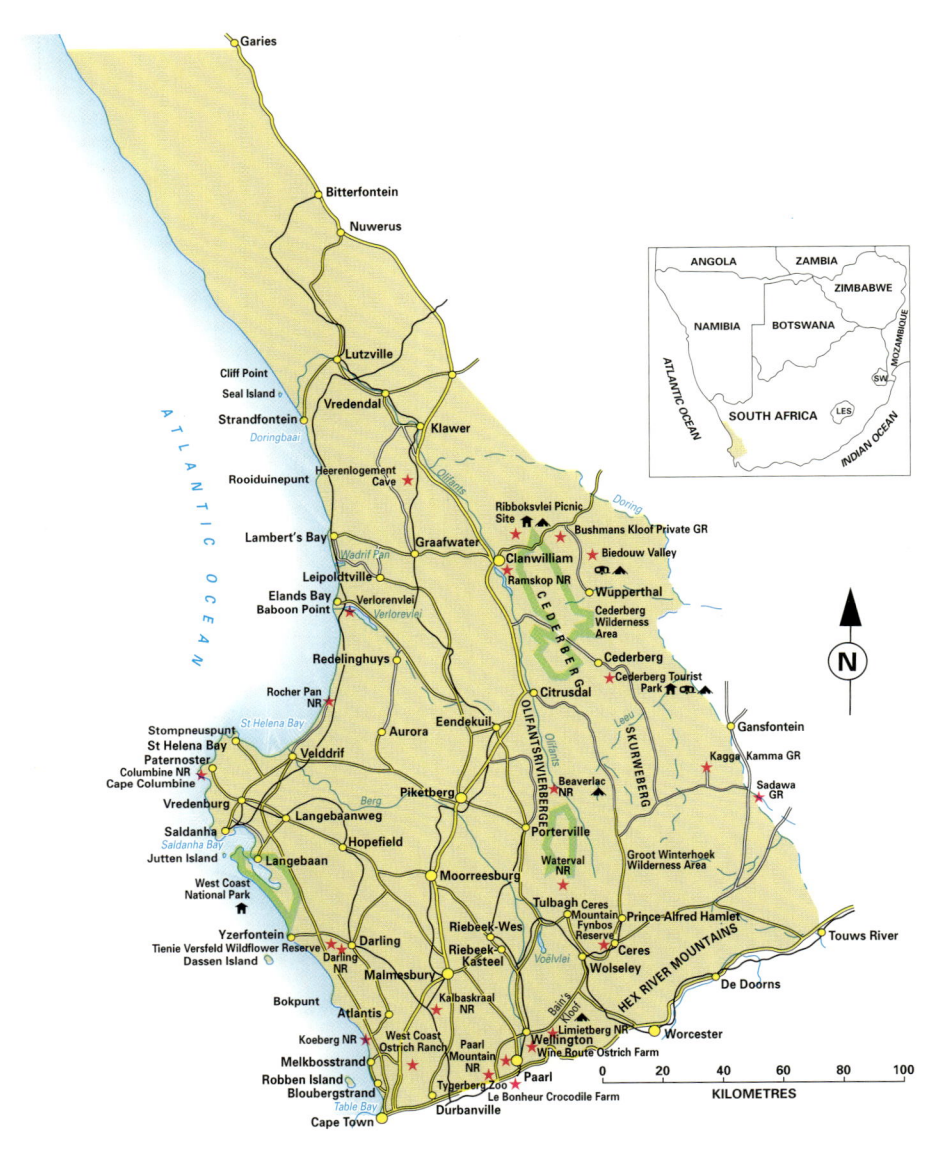

THE CAPE: THE WEST COAST

A fully catered lodge has ten double *en suite* bedrooms, and there are conference facilities, a swimming pool, library, sauna and curio shop. Game drives introduce visitors to the wildlife, and hikes – up to 10 km – meander along the Cederberg's rivers. Other activities are abseiling and mountain biking. For more information, contact Bushmans Kloof Private Game Reserve, P O Box 267, Clanwilliam 8135, telephone (027) 482-2627, or fax 482-1011.

Cederberg Tourist Park

This park near the southern end of the Cederberg wilderness forms part of the farm Kromrivier. There are 12 bungalows (with electric fridges, stoves and hot showers), ten campsites and 13 caravan sites, and the park serves as a base for exploring the mountains. A shop supplies milk, eggs, bread and basic necessities.

To visit Cederberg Tourist Park, take the road leading north from Citrusdal to Clanwilliam and, after some 23 km, turn right towards the Cederberg. Follow this road for about 57 km, then turn right at the 'Kromrivier' sign. To book accommodation, write to Mrs O Nieuwoudt, Kromrivier, P O Box 284, Clanwilliam 8135, telephone (027) 482-2807.

Next to Kromrivier farm is Sanddrif which, with its self-catering chalets and camping facilities, is an ideal base from which to hike the Cederberg. Permits may be obtained from Dwarsrivier, P O Cederberg 8136, telephone/fax (027) 482-2825. More information may be obtained from the Clanwilliam Tourism Association, P O Box 5, Clanwilliam 8135, telephone (027) 482-2024 or 482-2133, or fax 482-2361.

Cederberg Wilderness Area

Between Pakhuis Pass and Middelberg Pass is the craggy Cederberg, a weathered landscape of which 71 000 ha have been declared a wilderness area.

It is easy to reach: take the N7 north from Citrusdal and turn right at the Cederberg/Algeria sign. Cross the Olifants River, then the Nieuwoudt Pass, before reaching Algeria, where the required permits are issued.

The Cederberg is named for the rare Clanwilliam cedar tree (*Widdringtonia cedarbergensis*) that once covered the mountains, but many were burnt or felled, and only a few survive at the higher altitudes.

The flora of the Cederberg – varying from spring annuals to fynbos – is fascinating. The snow protea (*Protea cryophila*), found on the higher parts, occurs nowhere else in the world. The rocket pincushion (*Leucospermum reflexum*) also occurs naturally, while the large red disa (*Disa uniflora*) is found along some of the mountain streams.

The Cederberg is noted for its unique rock formations, and hundreds of rock overhangs shelter galleries of Bushman (San) paintings.

---

campsite with ablution blocks and braai facilities. A farm stall sells refreshments.

To get to Beaverlac, follow the road north from Porterville for 3 km. Turn right at the sign 'Cardouw' and drive for 10 km to the sign marking Dasklip Pass. Turn right again, then first left at the pine trees. Permits are not required, but it is essential to book in advance. Contact Beaverlac, P O Box 249, Porterville 6810, telephone/ fax (02623) 2945.

Biedouw Valley

To reach this valley at the entrance to Namaqualand, take the road east from Clanwilliam, over the Pakhuis Pass. About 40 km from Clanwilliam, turn right to Wupperthal. Follow this road for some 15 km until you reach the Biedouw Valley, a popular spot for viewing wild flowers in August and September.

Bushmans Kloof Private Game Reserve

East of Clanwilliam the Pakhuis Pass winds among the bizarre rock formations of the Pakhuis Mountains. South of the pass is situated the 75 000 ha Bushmans Kloof Private Game Reserve, opened in 1995.

Relatively abundant subterranean and surface waters nourish a varied flora that supports an impresssive number of large antelope species, Burchell's zebra and Cape mountain zebra. Lion and black rhino are to be introduced. Black eagle, martial eagle and African fish eagle are seen regularly.

Bushmans Kloof is a reminder of the Bushmen (San) who once roamed the Cederberg – over 125 rock art sites include some of the best preserved in the country. Cactus Canyon, in a remote corner of the reserve, is home to some 40 000 cacti from all over the world.

Above: *The Wolfberg section of the Cederberg is known for its challenging hikes and climbs, as well as for its eroded rock formations. A strenuous day's outing from Sanddrif might include the Wolfberg Arch and the equally spectacular Wolfberg Cracks.*

Among 30 or so mammal species, you may see baboon, klipspringer, grey rhebok, steenbok, duiker, grysbok, wild cat, caracal, Cape clawless otter, bat-eared fox and black-backed jackal. This is also a leopard conservation area.

Over 100 bird species include sugarbird, sunbird, Cape canary and francolin. Black eagle, rock kestrel and jackal buzzard are the main raptors. The Olifants River system contains several species of fish, including the rare Twee River redfin. Eight of the ten indigenous species of fish found here are endemic.

Hiking trails crisscross the Cederberg, and basic overnight huts are provided. Rock-climbers are welcome, provided the rock faces do not become damaged – the most popular sites are Table Mountain peak and Krakadouw.

At Algeria, a magnificent campsite beside the Rondegat River has some 46 caravan and camping sites with ablution blocks and hot and cold water. Visitors may swim in a natural river pool. Near the river, five chalets offer simple accommodation. Kliphuis campsite in the Pakhuis Pass – about 18 km from Clanwilliam – lies in a rich flower area, and offers ten shady sites. The campsites and hiking facilities should be reserved four months in advance by contacting the Citrusdal District Office, Private Bag X1, Citrusdal 7340, telephone (022) 921-2289, or fax 921-3219. Camping facilities and furnished bungalows may be hired on some farms bordering the wilderness area. Details are available from the Clanwilliam Tourism Association, P O Box 5, Clanwilliam 8135, telephone (027) 482-2024, or fax 482-2361.

Ceres Mountain Fynbos Reserve

As you enter Ceres from Michell's Pass, just before the Dwars River, the entrance to the Ceres Fynbos Reserve is on your left, under poplar trees and pin oaks.

It covers an area of 6 800 ha on the slopes of the Skurweberg, and was created for the preservation of local flora (principally protea and erica). Some plants, such as a subspecies of *Lithops comptonii*, are found nowhere else. There is a network of footpaths in the reserve, but there are no other facilities. It is open daily from 8 a.m. to 5 p.m., and is clearly signposted from the road. For more information, contact the Ceres Publicity Association, P O Box 563, Ceres 6835, telephone/fax (0233) 6-1287.

Clanwilliam Yellowfish Station

Established in 1976, this station serves as a hatchery where experimental programmes are undertaken to breed the rare Clanwilliam yellowfish (*Barbus capensis*) and seven other rare fish found only in the Olifants River system. All are threatened by the destruction of their habitat and by exotic predatory fish.

This is also a base from which the Olifants River system is studied. It can be reached by turning from the N7 to Clanwilliam. Just before you enter the town, a gravel road leads 500 m to the station (open from 8 a.m. to 4 p.m. on weekdays). Book in advance to ensure that someone is on hand to show you around. Contact The Officer-in-Charge, Clanwilliam Yellowfish Station, P O Box 83, Clanwilliam 8135, telephone (027) 482-2812, or fax 482-2404.

Columbine Nature Reserve

About 3 km south of the village of Paternoster is the Columbine Nature Reserve, covering an area of 263 ha, and protecting the local Sandveld fynbos. The reserve incorporates a number of tidal bays, the most popular being Tieties Bay, in an amphitheatre of sand dunes.

Spring, when the flowers are in glorious bloom, is the best time to visit. From Vredenburg, take the road to Paternoster, then continue south until you reach the reserve.

There are 60 campsites with rudimentary facilities. For bookings, apply in writing to Columbine Nature Reserve, Private Bag X12, Vredenburg 7380, telephone (02281) 75-2718. Columbine is accessible to campers and hikers all year round, but only postal bookings are accepted for the Easter holidays and from November to the end of January.

Darling Nature Reserve

A 3 km trail weaves through the fynbos and renosterveld of the Darling Nature Reserve, established in 1995 as a haven for the spring flowers that explode into vibrant colour every year. Its collection of mammals includes buck species, bush hare and porcupine. Situated 75 km from Cape Town and open all year, the reserve is best visited during September and October. Work sheets and brochures may be obtained from the Darling Field Studies Centre, Ye Olde Coffee Shoppe, 19 Main Road, Darling 7345, telephone (02241) 3155.

Groot Winterhoek Wilderness Area

The Vier-en-twintig River, noisily surging through shadowy ravines and cascading into a deep, cool basin, enchants visitors to Die Hel Valley – one of the most beautiful areas in the 19 200 ha Groot Winterhoek Wilderness Area (part of the greater 30 600 ha Groot Winterhoek Conservation Area).

Groot Winterhoek offers hikes of varying length and difficulty. Laid out in two zones – Kliphuis and Perdevlei in the east, and De Tronk and Die Hel in the south, the hikes penetrate the wilderness, winding below the rock formations so typical of the area and passing tempting rock pools. There are rudimentary shelters at Perdevlei and huts at De Tronk, or hikers may camp under the stars. It is advisable to accompany someone familiar with the area and to take a compass and map. Although summers are dry and hot, the temperature often drops to far below freezing point in winter, when heavy snowfalls are common on the prominent Groot and Klein Winterhoek peaks.

The beauty of the area is breathtaking – the diversity of the mountain fynbos is so great that locals say there is a different species in bloom every day of the year. Birdlife is prolific and includes raptors such as the peregrine falcon, rock kestrel and jackal buzzard. Among the smaller birds are Victorin's warbler, the protea canary and the Cape sugarbird. The rock formations consist of Table Mountain sandstone, and caves are decorated with Bushman (San) art dating back between 300 and 6 000 years.

The wilderness area is reached via the Dasklip Pass above Porterville. For bookings and enquiries, write to The District Manager, Cape Nature Conservation, West Boland District, P O Box 26, Porterville 6810, telephone (02623) 2900/7, or fax 2913.

Heerenlogement Cave

This cave (the name means Gentlemen's Lodging) lies about 32 km north of Graafwater, on the road to Klawer. It was once occupied by people of the Later Stone Age but, from about 1682, when the cave was stumbled upon by explorer Oloff Bergh, dozens of European travellers sheltered here.

Above: *Phaenocoma prolifera* in the Ceres district of the Boland. This attractive flower, also known as pink everlasting, is a perennial. **Right:** Spring in the Cederberg mountains, with *Euryops speciosissimus* in the foreground of the picture.

Of special interest is a Namaqua fig tree (*Ficus cordata*) – believed to be more than 200 years old – that grows from a fissure in the rocks and hangs over the top of the cave.

Kagga Kamma Game Reserve

Nestling below the stark slopes of the Cederberg, this magnificent 5 400 ha reserve is home to a group of former Kalahari Bushmen (San). They may demonstrate some of their skills and traditions to visitors, who can also view the beautiful rock paintings, many of which date back 6 000 years.

The reserve is richly populated with antelope, ostrich and zebra, while caracal, jackal and lynx hide in the rocky crevices, and the canyons echo with bird calls. Spring brings colourful brilliance as flowers swathe the land.

Hiking trails snake below the weather-beaten rock formations, and 4x4 guided game drives are available. Accommodation is provided in three camps: Rest Camp has three-bedroom chalets; Safari Camp has 65 twin-bed tents, and Bushmen Lodge has huts with twin beds, a restaurant and curio shop.

Kagga Kamma lies 260 km north of Cape Town. For more information, contact Kagga Kamma Game Reserve, P O Box 7143, North Paarl 7623, telephone (021) 863-8334, or fax 863-8383.

Koeberg Nature Reserve

When Koeberg Nuclear Power Station was built north of Melkbosstrand, a surrounding area of some 2 200 ha of west coast strandveld was set aside as a nature reserve and opened in 1992. Its main aims are to protect the indigenous species and to educate the public. Schools and universities use its facilities for research and educational purposes, while members of the public enjoy its two trails (the 4 km Grysbok Trail and the 13 km Dikkop Trail). Booking is essential for the longer trail.

Animals at Koeberg include antelope, caracal, African wild cat, porcupine, bat-eared fox and black-backed jackal. Over 150 bird species – mainly waterbirds – have been recorded. The waters offshore are visited in spring by large marine mammals, including southern right whale and the dusky dolphin.

For more information, contact Koeberg Nature Reserve, P O Box 53, Kernkrag 7441, telephone (021) 550-4021, or fax 553-1851.

Le Bonheur Crocodile Farm

Lying south of the picturesque town of Paarl is Le Bonheur Crocodile Farm, home to over 1 000 of these awe-inspiring reptiles. The farm is open every day from 9.30 a.m. to 4.30 p.m. Guided tours take place every 30 minutes and, afterwards, visitors may browse in the curio shop or visit the cafeteria to taste the farm's speciality, crocodile pie, or to buy crocodile meat. Contact Le Bonheur Crocodile Farm, P O Box 592, Suider Paarl 7624, telephone (021) 863-1142 for further details.

Limietberg Nature Reserve

In the Du Toitskloof mountains, with their stark cliffs and deeply shaded valleys, lies the new

THE CAPE: **THE WEST COAST**

Limietberg Nature Reserve. Stretching from Jonkershoek north to Voëlvlei Dam, Limietberg covers 117 000 ha, and is a major catchment area for both the Berg and Breede rivers.

There are no fewer than nine trails – ranging from 4,5 km to the 36 km/two-day Limietberg Trail (part of the longer Boland Hiking Trail) along Bain's Kloof (*see separate entry*). A pool is situated beside the overnight hut, which has four rooms and sleeps up to 24 people.

Hikers are likely to see dassie, klipspringer and baboon, with perhaps a glimpse of caracal and leopard. Look out for the Cape sugarbird, protea canary and raptors such as the black eagle. The vegetation comprises low mountain fynbos and a scattering of indigenous trees in the kloofs. In spring, bright orchids may be found in cool recesses near streams. Remember that lighting fires is strictly forbidden.

Bookings (by telephone only) and enquiries may be made by contacting the Boland District Office, Private Bag X1, Uniedal 7612, telephone (021) 886-5858/886-6543, or fax 886-6575.

Paarl Mountain Nature Reserve

Towering granite domes, like enormous pearls when they glisten with dew, are striking features of this 1 910 ha sanctuary west of the town of Paarl. Scenic drives offer breathtaking views of Paarl Valley and the Berg River to the east, and Table Mountain, False Bay and the Atlantic to the west. There are picnic sites, and fishing is permitted in the three dams on top of Paarl Mountain (a licence is required). The reserve also offers the two-hour Klipkers Hiking Trail, as well as a network of leisurely footpaths.

The reserve is open daily from 8 a.m. to 6 p.m. in winter, and 7 a.m. to 7 p.m. in summer. In Paarl, turn into Jan Phillips Mountain Road and follow the signs. The small Meulwater Wild Flower Reserve is situated within the Paarl Mountain Nature Reserve, and indigenous plant species number 200, with protea, erica, pincushion and gazania most prominent. For further information, contact Paarl Publicity Office, P O Box 47, Paarl 7622, telephone (021) 872-3829 or 872-4842, fax 872-9376.

Ramskop Nature Reserve

This 70 ha municipal reserve is the natural habitat of small mammals such as buck, hare and dassie, as well as several reptile species. No vehicles are allowed, but a circular footpath climbs to the highest point of the reserve, from where there are panoramic views of the Cederberg peaks, the Olifants River, Pakhuis Pass, the Clanwilliam Dam and the town itself. Situated within Ramskop is the 7,5 ha Clanwilliam Wildflower Garden, which features some 700 indigenous species. Every year, a five-day flower show is held in the 'old' Dutch Reformed church in Clanwilliam's main street, displaying the large variety of local species .

While there are no facilities in the reserve or garden, the adjoining Clanwilliam Dam has camping, caravanning and picnicking facilities. The reserve and garden, open every day, are clearly signposted on the N7. For more information, contact the Clanwilliam Tourism Association, P O Box 5, Clanwilliam 8135, telephone (027) 482-2024 or 482-2133, or fax 482-2361.

Riverlands Nature Reserve

Over 500 species of lowland fynbos occur at Riverlands Nature Reserve near Malmesbury. Of these, 20 are listed as rare – threatened by ploughing, development and the invasion of alien species. A programme is planned whereby members of the local community will help to clear the reserve of its ever-encroaching alien trees, and restore the natural fynbos.

The 1 297 ha reserve was proclaimed in 1994 and, while no facilities exist at present, visits can be arranged by contacting The Reserve Manager, Riverlands Nature Reserve, Private Bag X8, Malmesbury 7300, telephone/fax (0224) 7-7360.

Rocher Pan Nature Reserve

Rocher Pan Nature Reserve – over 900 ha in extent – encloses a seasonal vlei and wetland area, fed by the Papkuils River and full for seven months of the year. It attracts as many as 183 bird species, of which 70 are waterbirds. Cape teal, red-knobbed coot, yellow-billed duck, Egyptian goose and white pelican are often seen. Rocher Pan is one of the Cape shoveller's most important breeding and moulting sites, and is a sanctuary for the rare African black oystercatcher. Waders and seabirds also make their home here.

Left: White storks in the Tygerberg Zoo. Some years ago, white storks featured in a fascinating experiment on migratory habits. It was known that white storks in eastern Europe and central Asia flew southeast before entering Africa across the Suez Canal and Sinai Peninsula. In western Europe, however, they flew southwest before entering Africa over the western Sahara or west coast. These routes enabled both populations to avoid such obstacles as the Alps, the Sahara and the Mediterranean. Eggs from eastern storks were hatched and raised by foster parents in the west, and when the time came to migrate, their genetic memory caused them to fly southeast, where they encountered the Alps and became thoroughly disorientated. **Right top:** A grysbok in the Tygerberg Zoo. **Right above:** The Clanwilliam Wildflower Garden.

The adjacent section of the Atlantic Ocean is a marine reserve, and southern right whales may be spotted in its waters and along the coast in late winter and in spring. Small mammals such as duiker, steenbok, water mongoose and African wild cat also occur.

The best time to visit is in the spring, when wild flowers cover the ground and the bird population is at its densest. Visitors may follow the winding gravel track and make use of the two bird hides. Note that no vehicles may cross to the beach. There are also braai and picnic sites (but no camping facilities). The sanctuary is open daily from 7 a.m. to 5 p.m. between May and August, and between 7 a.m. and 6 p.m. for the rest of the year. To get to Rocher Pan, take the R27 leading north from Cape Town through Velddrif, Laaiplek and Dwarskersbos, 12 km beyond which is the reserve's signposted gate.

For permits and more information, write to The Manager, Rocher Pan Nature Reserve,

THE CAPE: THE WEST COAST

Left: Jackass (also known as African black-footed) penguins jump into the sea from Malgas Island in the vicinity of Saldanha Bay. Nearby Dassen Island is the breeding area for this species, which is the only endemic southern African penguin. **Above:** Verlorenvlei, a bird-rich paradise lying 5 km inland from Elands Bay.

P O Box 460, Velddrif 7365, telephone (02625) 727; or contact The District Manager, Cape Nature Conservation, West Boland District, P O Box 26, Porterville 6810, telephone (02623) 2900/7, fax 2913.

Sadawa Game Reserve

Encompassing some 16 000 ha of Karoo veld and fynbos 66 km northwest of Ceres, Sadawa was established in 1994 as a getaway for conference delegates and holiday-makers.

Its lush vegetation is home to 36 species of game, ranging from blesbok, red hartebeest, springbok, impala, eland and gemsbok, to leopard, caracal, Burchell's zebra, Cape fox, honey badger, striped polecat and aardwolf. Guided walks and drives are offered, and the reserve has an eco-route.

Accommodation is provided in six luxury chalets and six safari tents, and guests relax in the lapa and dine in the restaurant. A conference centre, swimming pool and laundry service are available. For further details, contact Sadawa Game Reserve, P O Box 228, Ceres 6835, telephone (0233) 2-2512, or fax 2-2483.

SAS Saldanha Nature Trail

Saldanha Bay, named after an early 16th-century Portuguese explorer, came into its own during the Second World War, and, since the 1950s, has been the home of the SA Naval Gymnasium. The entire area of 18 000 ha boasts fynbos and animal life representative of the west coast. Mesembryanthemums flower during winter, flame lilies (*Gloriosa superba*) and arum lilies (*Zantedeschia aethiopica*) bloom all year, while a highlight is the dainty yellow *Romulea saldanhensis* that is unique to the area.

A hiking trail, divided into four sections, traverses the reserve. The Red Route (14,5 km) is the longest, passing historical and geological sites, and Camp Klossie, where most of the game is kept. The 11 km Yellow Route follows a similar path, the 9,6 km Green Route encircles two large hills, from the top of which panoramic views may be had over Saldanha Bay, and the 4 km Blue Route explores military-historical aspects of the area.

Birdlife is plentiful, and there are many indications of the Later Stone Age people who frequented these shores. For further information, contact SAS Saldanha, Saldanha Bay 7395, telephone (02281) 4-2211 or 4-1131.

Steenbokfontein and Wadrif Pans

South of the tiny fishing village of Lambert's Bay, on the road to Leipoldtville, a chain of pans is host to countless birds including an impressive flamingo population.

Tienie Versveld Wildflower Reserve

This 22 ha piece of land near Darling was given to the then National Botanical Gardens of South Africa in 1956, to protect the flora of the Sandveld. Dominant species are bulbous plants like *Babiana*, *Spiloxene*, *Geissorhiza*, and several annuals, and the reserve is also known for its spring carpet of chincherinchee and insectivorous sundew (*Drosera*). There is a network of footpaths, but no other facilities exist. Although open 24 hours a day throughout the year, spring is the best time to see the wild flowers. For further information, contact Darling Publicity Association, 20 Pastorie Street, Darling 7345, telephone (02241) 3361.

Tygerberg Zoo

This privately owned zoo (a non-profit organisation administered by a trust) specialises in breeding endangered species such as chimpanzee and the rare Rothschild's mynah (only some 600 of these birds survive).

About 300 species include tiger, cheetah, and many other cats, European brown bear, dwarf crocodile, giant tortoise, and the Madagascan radiated tortoise. The layout of the zoo is informal, with lawns (a good picnicking area) and a car park with braai facilities. A tearoom serves refreshments.

The zoo, situated 40 km from Cape Town, is open every day from 9 a.m. to 5 p.m. To reach it, take the N1 highway towards Paarl, turn off at exit 39 to Stellenbosch/Klipheuwel, and follow the signs. For more information, contact Tygerberg Zoo, P O Box 524, Kraaifontein 7569, telephone (021) 884-4494, or fax 884-4238.

Verlorenvlei

Lying 5 km inland from Elands Bay, Verlorenvlei is a bird-rich haven (232 species have been identified). Although the 25 km vlei is owned by Cape Nature Conservation, the land surrounding it is privately owned, and permission must be sought to walk along its banks.

Waterval Nature Reserve

This reserve near Tulbagh is not yet open to the public, but hikers may explore its 13 km Jan du Toit's Kloof Trail, which may be tramped between April and December. Book at The District Manager, Cape Nature Conservation,

West Boland District, P O Box 26, Porterville 6810, telephone (02623) 2900/7, or fax 2913.

West Coast Islands

Soon after Jan van Riebeeck landed at the Cape, he dispatched a group of sailors to explore the west coast. They found many small islands – mostly off Saldanha Bay – teeming with seal and birdlife.

Dassen Island, the largest of the islands, has a population of some 60 000 penguin, and is also the breeding ground of pelicans. Other species found here include Egyptian goose, cattle egret, ibis, gull and various land birds.

There are six other islands in Saldanha Bay: Vondeling Island is a small, rocky outcrop just south of the entrance; in the entrance to the bay itself are three more islands (Jutten, Malgas and Marcus) and there are two more in the southern part of the bay – the Schaapen and Meeuwen islets. All provide safe nesting sites for over 750 000 seabirds, and all are closed to the public. Schaapen is home to one of the largest known colonies of southern black-backed gulls, while Malgas is sanctuary to 70 000 gannets.

The seals have disappeared from these islands, and only one protected colony (about 2 000 strong) remains on a small island called Robbesteen, just north of Melkbosstrand.

West Coast National Park

The rare vision of fields swathed in vivid flowers set against the sea draws thousands of visitors to the West Coast National Park's Postberg section for a brief period every spring.

For the rest of the year the focus shifts to Langebaan lagoon. This 16 km by 2,5 km expanse is one of the great wetlands of the world and teems with life. Tiny creatures that live in its mud, said to contain 60 million bacteria in every millilitre, are a vital food source for large numbers of birds. During summer, up to 60 000 birds arrive from places as distant as the Arctic, Siberia and Greenland to transform the lagoon into a birdwatchers' paradise. It is estimated that local bird populations consume some 150 tonnes of invertebrates annually (15 per cent of the annual invertebrate production of the lagoon).

The offshore islands (*see separate entry*) are bird sanctuaries in their own right, and large populations roost and breed here in safety. Public access is not permitted.

Fishing in the lagoon is good during summer, and its sheltered waters also offer good sailing, waterskiing, windsurfing and boating.

The lagoon and the islands of Malgas, Marcus, Jutten and Schaapen were proclaimed as Langebaan National Park in 1985. Subsequent additions, including Postberg Nature Reserve, have increased the park to 30 000 hectares. The park now forms a continuous strip of coast, lagoon and sandveld from the village of Langebaan to Yzerfontein in the south. It is being fenced and its animals (including red hartebeest, kudu, springbok, gemsbok, eland and mountain zebra), currently housed at Postberg, will be released to roam freely. It is hoped that black rhino will be reintroduced in the near future – the first time they will have roamed freely near Cape Town for 200 years or more.

The area around Langebaan contains some of the richest fossil deposits in South Africa.

West Coast Ostrich Ranch

All aspects of ostrich breeding and rearing may be seen at this ranch, one of the few places where you can be photographed astride an ostrich against the backdrop of Table Mountain. Guided tours begin every 30 minutes from 9 a.m. to 5 p.m., and there is a restaurant and a curio shop. The ranch is situated 20 minutes north of Cape Town. Contact the owners at P O Box 39, Tableview 7439, telephone/fax (021) 972-1905.

Wine Route Ostrich Farm

Travelling north along the N1 from Cape Town, turn at exit 55 onto the R45 to Malmesbury to visit the Wine Route Ostrich Farm, open daily between 10 a.m. and 6 p.m. Guided tours are held every 30 minutes. Emu and white ostrich are also on show. A restaurant specialising in ostrich dishes overlooks the paddocks. Casual visitors are welcome, but large groups should book in advance. Contact the farm at P O Box 7116, North Paarl 7623, telephone (021) 872-6023, or fax 872-3780.

WEST COAST NATIONAL PARK AT A GLANCE

When to go The park is open all year, but the Postberg section is open during August and September only (9 a.m. to 5 p.m.), when the spring flowers are at their best (watch the newspapers, or contact SATOUR, Cape Town, for information). Remember to choose a sunny day when the flowers will be open. Summer is the best time for bird-watching, boating and swimming in the lagoon.

Reservations and information For further information and enquiries, contact the National Parks Board, P O Box 787, Pretoria 0001, telephone (012) 343-1991, or fax 343-0905; or P O Box 7400, Roggebaai 8012, telephone (021) 22-2810, or fax 24-6211. There is a National Parks Board information centre at Langebaan – contact them at P O Box 25, Langebaan 7357, telephone (02287) 2-2144, or fax 2-2607.

Getting there Langebaan village is signposted on the West Coast road (R27) 122 km north of Cape Town. To reach Postberg turn left off the R27 at the West Coast National Park signpost, some 85 km from Cape Town. Turn left again at the Churchhaven/Postberg sign – follow this road to Postberg. An entrance fee is charged at the entrance gate of Postberg during the flower season, and also into the park at all times.

Accommodation A houseboat, sleeping a total of six, can be hired, and a limited number of moorings for yachts are also available for hire on a daily basis. Prior reservation is essential. The National Parks Board also has moorings for yachts at Kraalbaai. No camping is allowed in the park, but Langebaan village has caravan sites and beach bungalows.

Eating and drinking There are shops and restaurants in Langebaan, as well as at nearby Club Mykonos. The Postberg section has three picnic spots with braai and ablution facilities. Wood is available, but visitors must bring their own braai grids.

Getting around The reserve has approximately 30 km of hard gravel roads with demarcated areas where visitors may leave their vehicles. Two-day hiking trails penetrate the park, and hikers overnight at *Geelbek*, an old homestead built in 1860 and beautifully restored. Boating, boardsailing, sailing, and powerboating are popular lagoon activities. The lagoon is regulated by the National Parks Board, and is zoned into three areas for specific purposes (consult the information centre in Langebaan). Boat trips around the lagoon and to Malgas Island are offered, and canoes may be hired from the Parks Board headquarters. Boats may be launched at Langebaan Yacht Club, Club Mykonos or from the hard sand of Langebaan beach at the end of Alabama Street. Petrol is available at Langebaan.

Wildlife Some 55 000 birds may be found in the area. Among these are cormorant, gull, common and curlew sandpiper, sanderling, knot, turnstone, gannet and flamingo. Pelican, cormorant, penguin, tern and gannet breed on the islands. Postberg is stocked with bat-eared fox, zebra, eland, kudu, hartebeest, blue wildebeest, gemsbok, springbok, bontebok and others. Predators include caracal, African wild cat, genet and Cape grey mongoose. Various species of fish occur in the lagoon, with skate, ray, sand shark, white stumpnose and mullet commonly found.

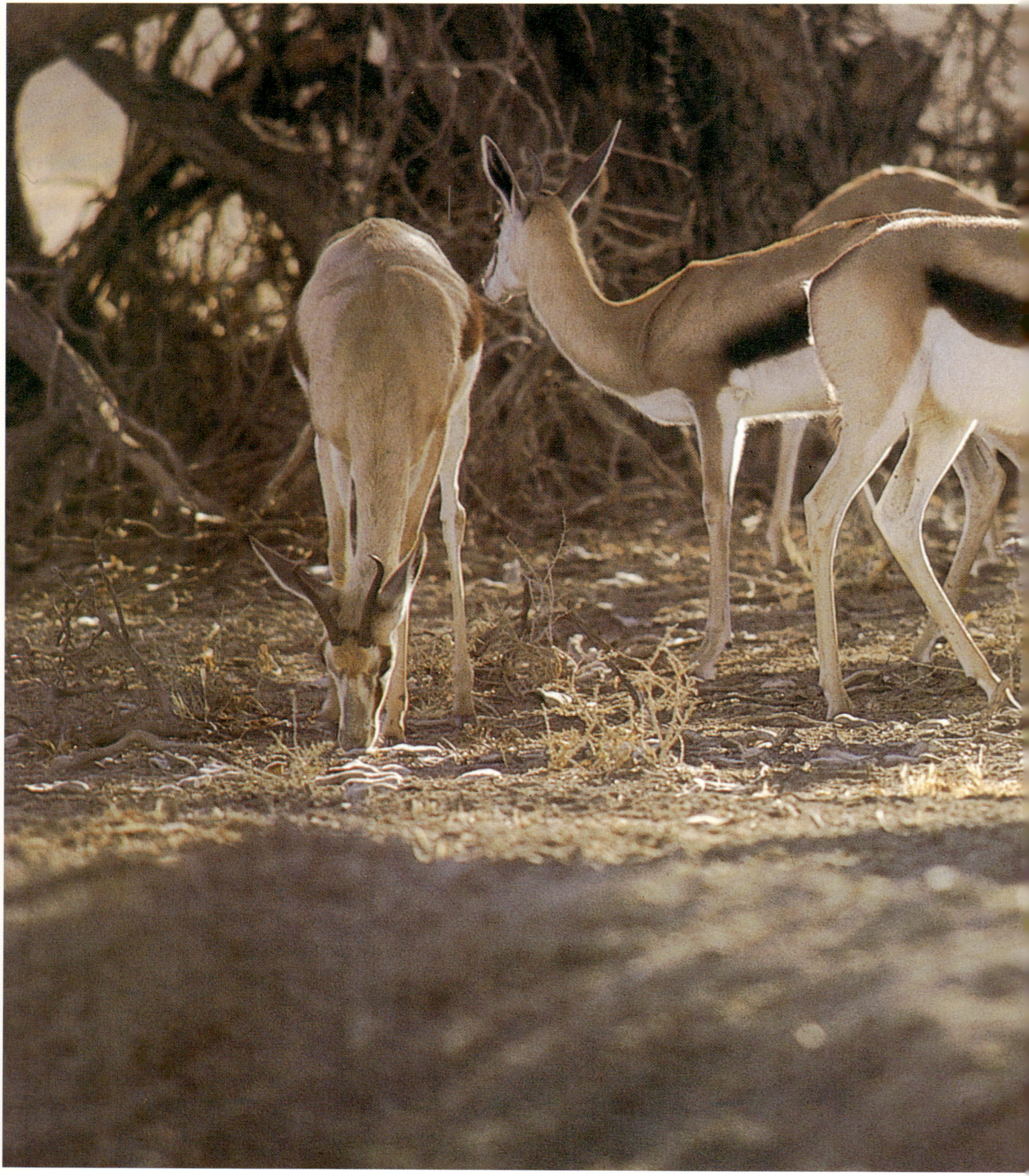

THE INTERIOR

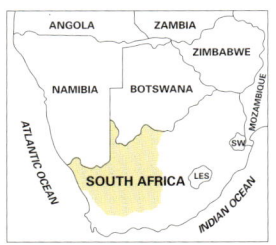

The Khoikhoi described the dry inland reaches of the country as the Karoo, meaning 'the thirstland'. Even more than the Little Karoo south of the Swartberg Mountains, the Great Karoo is a land of raw koppies, stony plains and a vegetation that is hardy enough to survive the baking heat of high summer and the frosty bite of winter nights. In earlier times the Karoo plains held large herds of game, but ruthless slaughter in the 19th century drove them to the edge of extinction.

Today, Karoo game is making a comeback on private farms and in several sanctuaries, in particular the Karoo National Park at Beaufort West and the Karoo Nature Reserve at Graaff-Reinet. More reserves are found in the Namaqualand region to the west, another near-desert, where the annual display of spring flowers is one of the marvels of southern Africa. North of Namaqualand lies the Richtersveld and its national park, a wildlife paradise of serene, never-ending plains extending to the banks of the Orange River.

Upstream, the river crashes and boils over the spectacular Augrabies Falls, centrepiece of a national park. To the north are the sandy plains of the Kalahari, another 'place of great dryness' in the language of the Khoikhoi. South Africa's famous Kalahari Gemsbok National Park adjoins a sister sanctuary in Botswana, and only a line of beacons separates them – allowing game to migrate back and forth across the international boundary as it has for millennia. In this place, at least, old Africa survives undisturbed.

Springbok graze on the arid veld of the Kalahari Gemsbok National Park. These graceful and strikingly coloured gazelle once swarmed in massive herds across southern Africa. The great springbok migrations or treks were described by awed early travellers as literally covering the veld to the horizon, although the motivation for these mass movements is uncertain.

Where rains herald a wildflower wonderland

Early travellers knew today's Namaqualand as 'Little Namaqualand', while 'Great Namaqualand' lay north of the Orange River in today's Namibia. For some, 'Little Namaqualand' embraced all the land between the Orange River and Garies, and even Vanrhynsdorp to the south, extending eastwards to a longitude beyond Calvinia.

More often, travellers divided the area into regions with names like 'the Roggeveld', 'the Sandveld' and 'the Richtersveld' in the north, and 'Bushmanland' to the east. Then, as now, the eastern reaches of this wilderness were flat and much more arid than the land further west.

In 1892, the legislature of the then Cape Colony proclaimed a large game reserve in Bushmanland – the first such reserve in southern Africa. Details are sketchy, but it is known that among those behind the establishment of the sanctuary was a Namaqualand magistrate, W C Scully, one of South Africa's earliest conservationists and a shrewd observer of nature.

A part-time game ranger named Andries Esterhuysen tried unsuccessfully to stamp out poaching in the reserve. The chief culprits were local farmers, who hunted the game ruthlessly and saw no purpose in the reserve, rather wanting it deproclaimed and shared among them. It is said that when they spotted Esterhuysen while poaching, they sent messages to one another by smoke signals. The slaughter continued – virtually unchecked – and thousands of animals died. After the game was wiped out, the reserve's land was whittled away, and the last fragment was deproclaimed in the late 1920s.

Today, fortunately, attitudes have changed considerably. Oorlogskloof, a 5 500 ha nature reserve near Nieuwoudtville, is a hiker's paradise with a rich history and a striking array of plants. The enchanting Skilpad Wildflower Reserve, situated in central Namaqualand near Kamieskroon, was proclaimed in 1993 to promote the conservation of the area's rich and varied flora.

Further north, bounded by a huge loop in the mighty Orange River, is the enormous (162 000 ha) Richtersveld National Park, which was established in 1991 as a cooperative venture between the National Parks Board and the indigenous communities. Other fascinating reserves, each with its own specific attraction, are dotted throughout this wild, magnificent and often lonely landscape.

Akkerendam Nature Reserve

The little town of Calvinia has two major attractions for those enamoured of nature. The first is the annual display of spring flowers, as vivid and dramatic as anywhere in Namaqualand. The other is Akkerendam Nature Reserve, proclaimed in 1962 and covering 2 301 ha of the spreading plains north of the town, as well as parts of the Hantam mountain range. Before becoming a municipal nature reserve, the area formed part of the farm Akkerendam, which was once owned by the South African Railways. Akkerendam's five boreholes provided the town's water and the farm was the obvious site for a town dam.

Today, Akkerendam and two other farm dams are attractive features of the nature reserve – which has become a bird and flora sanctuary. Nearby is a picnic area, and the reserve's 12 km of roads pass close to the

Left: The beautiful spread of wild flowers that attracts thousands of visitors to Namaqualand in spring. With an average annual rainfall of only 120 mm, Namaqualand is one of the driest regions of southern Africa. The spring flower bonanza begins in mid-July.
Above: In spring a sheet of colour spreads across wide stretches of Namaqualand, turning the once barren veld into a floral wonderland of almost every imaginable hue. These Namaqualand daisies (*Dimorphotheca sinuata*) are typical of the flowers in this region (though they are found in all parts of South Africa, with the exception of KwaZulu-Natal).

THE INTERIOR: **NAMAQUALAND**

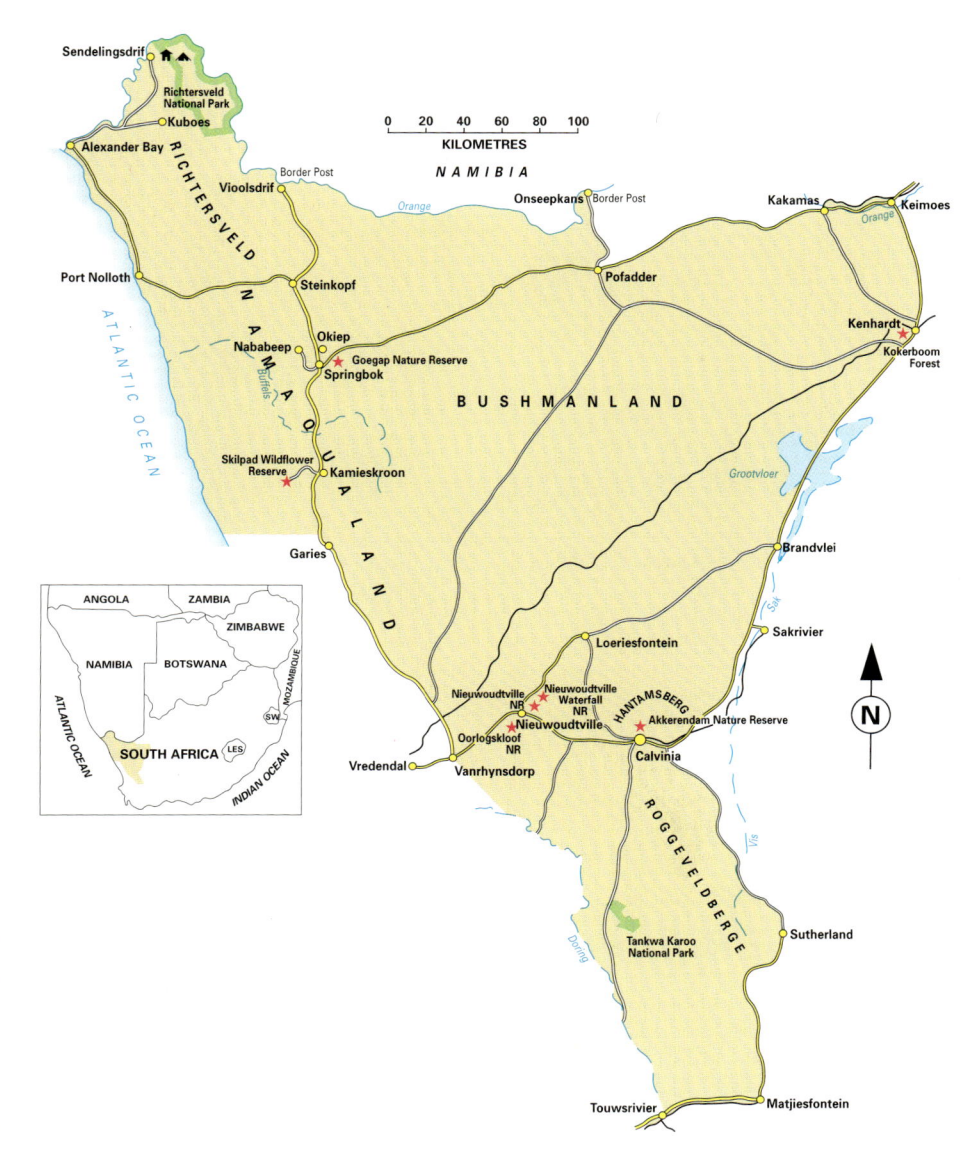

years later the copper company donated an additional 1 900 ha, to make an impresssive total of 6 500 hectares. In 1990 the adjoining farm 'Goegap' (the Nama name for a waterhole) was acquired, and the reserve's size was extended to approximately 14 860 hectares. The sanctuary, renamed Goegap Nature Reserve, encompasses sandy plains dotted with koppies, and is an excellent example of a wide range of Namaqualand habitats.

Goegap is well worth a visit during the spring months when the plains explode into a wonderland of wild flowers, covering the normally semi-arid landscape with a rainbow tapestry of vivid hues (581 plant species have been recorded). During the rest of the year, visitors can still enjoy the beautiful scenery – flat, scrubby plains interspersed with a tumble of rocky granite hillocks, their slopes dotted with the kokerboom or quiver tree (*Aloe dichotoma*). There is also an interesting display of Namaqualand succulents at the information centre. Plants and seeds may be purchased, and visitors are invited to watch the slide and video shows presented here.

Some 45 species of mammal, 25 species of reptile and three species of amphibian have been recorded in the reserve. Major game species represented are Hartmann's mountain zebra, Cape fox, aardwolf, honey badger, baboon, gemsbok, springbok, klipspringer and steenbok. Among the 94 bird species that have been recorded in the reserve are ostrich, black eagle, Cape eagle owl, pied barbet, Karoo korhaan, spotted dikkop and ground woodpecker. Plant and animal checklists are available.

A large portion of the reserve is inaccessible to visitors, but there is a circular 17 km flora- and gameviewing drive (on a good gravel surface). By far the best way to explore Goegap is on the Ian Myers Hiking Trail, which snakes for 7 km between the koppies from the parking area near the picnic site. Shorter routes may also be chosen. Also available are horse trails (you need to provide your own steed), a 4x4 trail, and a mountain-bike route. Picnic sites have been laid out and, although there are no overnight facilities within the reserve itself, the authorities can arrange limited accommodation on request.

The reserve is about 15 km from Springbok and adjoins the airport. It is signposted from the outskirts of the town and may be visited from 8.00 a.m. to 4.00 p.m. every day. For more information, contact Goegap Nature Reserve, Private Bag X1, Springbok 8240, telephone (0251) 2-1880, or fax 8-1286.

Kokerboom Forest

Bushmen (San) of Namaqualand, needing quivers for their poisoned arrows, cut branches from the picturesque 'tree aloe' that grows

dams, taking visitors to the higher ground that overlooks them.

The entrance to Akkerendam is a little more than 1 km from the centre of Calvinia and is signposted (visitors should leave the town by the road that passes the hospital). The reserve is open all year. Visitors are normally required to remain in their cars, but they may apply for permission to hike on one of two trails that penetrate the reserve.

The Kareeboom Trail along the Hantam mountain slopes is a 2 km/one or two hour hike that was designed with special consideration for the needs of senior citizens.

A longer and somewhat more strenuous route, the Sterboom Trail, takes some six to seven hours to complete. Both of these trails provide an ideal opportunity to discover the profuse and magical flora found only in the Hantam, including the orchid *Disperis purpurata* and the geophyte *Romulea hantamensis*.

For permits and more information, contact The Town Clerk, Calvinia Municipality, P O Box 28, Calvinia 8190, telephone (0273) 41-1011, fax 41-2750.

Goegap Nature Reserve

In 1960 the O'Okiep Copper Company of Namaqualand donated 4 600 ha of rugged farmland to the then Cape Provincial Administration to be developed as a wildflower sanctuary. The farmland lay some 15 km to the east of Springbok, and provided the ideal location on which to establish a fully fledged nature reserve, featuring a comprehensive variety of local flora and fauna.

In 1966 the administration proclaimed the area the Hester Malan Nature Reserve. Some

265

Right: *The Quahkah*, an aquatint by the artist and traveller Samuel Daniell, reproduced in *African Scenery and Animals* (published in two parts in 1804-5). Daniell's painting captures a distinctive feature of the old Karoo landscape that will never be seen again – large herds of the now extinct quagga. When the botanist William Paterson travelled through the Karoo in the late 1700s, the quagga was still one of the most common animals in the area. But within a century it had been hunted to extinction. Historical records indicate that the quagga was a gregarious animal, much like the zebra, and was often found in mixed herds along with black wildebeest (and even ostrich). The only specimen in Africa (there are several in Europe) is preserved at the South African Museum in Cape Town.

all over the western reaches of the Northern Cape and in southwestern Namibia. They hollowed out the branch's fibrous interior, sealed the bottom and attached a carrying strap. To this day the tree aloe is known as the 'kokerboom' or 'quiver tree'. The species (*Aloe dichotoma*) has been known to scientists since 1685, when it was discovered during Governor Simon van der Stel's expedition to Namaqualand in search of copper. This slow-growing tree, with its greyish-green leaves and yellow flowers, survives harsh conditions by soaking up water and storing it in the trunk.

Kokerboom trees were also once used for cooling primitive homes. People cut the trunks into squares and used them to construct walls. Water was then fed into the fibrous wood from a tank placed at the top.

Swarms of birds and locusts are drawn by the sweet nectar of the kokerboom flowers, and baboon have been known to strip off the blossoms in search of the liquid.

Individual quiver trees can be seen in many locations in Namaqualand and Bushmanland, including the Goegap Nature Reserve *(see separate entry)*. But close to the little town of Kenhardt is a 'kokerboom forest' consisting of at least 700 kokerboom 'trees' growing up to four metres high. Most stand on the slopes of a range of koppies that straddles the municipal boundary. To reach the forest, drive 7 km south from Kenhardt on the R27 to Brandvlei. The forest can be seen from the road, and offers visitors some attractive picnic sites and plenty of interesting walks.

Nieuwoudtville Nature Reserve

In 1973, the Nieuwoudtville Municipality set aside an area of some 115 ha, 2 km east of the village and adjacent to the R27 to Calvinia, for the establishment of a nature reserve. The reserve consists of two distinct halves – one of which is dominated by flat plains, while the other encompasses dolerite koppies that provide fine views of the surrounding Bokkeveld. Nieuwoudtville's chief pride is its unique spring flora and, in particular, some spectacular endemic species. It is open at all times, boasts an interpretation centre, ablution facilities, and a 3 km hiking trail for those wishing to explore. For more information, contact The Town Clerk, P O Box 52, Nieuwoudtville 8180, telephone (02726) 81052, fax 81316.

Nieuwoudtville Waterfall Nature Reserve

After heavy rains, the 90 m high Nieuwoudtville Waterfall is transformed from a trickle into a surging rush of water and a spectacular experience of sight and sound. The scenic falls are surrounded by a tiny 15,9 ha nature reserve, which was proclaimed in 1987, and which includes a wide variety of mountain fynbos and succulents.

The reserve lies on a plateau in the Bokkeveld Mountains, and the falls have their origin in general seepage in the area, combined with the waters of the Gras River and the Willems River, which join forces to plummet over the dramatic Maaierskloof into a deep circular pool. Colourful rocks, pitted by erosion, lie scattered over the riverbed.

The reserve, which has an interpretation centre and an ablution block, can be reached 6 km north of Nieuwoudtville on the R357 to Loeriesfontein. For further information on the reserve, write to The Town Clerk, P O Box 52, Nieuwoudtville 8180, or telephone (02726) 8-1052, fax 8-1316.

Oorlogskloof Nature Reserve

Bushman (San) paintings, breathtaking views and interesting rock formations are the main

---

ABSORBING WATER LIKE A SPONGE

In spite of its name, the Namaqua sandgrouse is found all over the western half of southern Africa and particularly in arid areas with short grass. You are most likely to see it at a waterhole in the Kalahari or Namib Desert where it announces its presence with the characteristic, melancholy *kelkiewyn* call. The dove-like sandgrouse feeds on small dry seeds on the ground. During the winter nesting period, it lays two or three eggs in a nest that is a mere scrape in the ground between the tufts of grass, and the male and female take turns to sit. The male performs his fatherly duties at night, while the female remains on the nest throughout the hot day: if she left her post the embryos would quickly be killed by the searing heat (surface temperatures can reach 50°C). She resists the heat by puffing up her feathers to create extra insulation between her body and the air outside.

Meanwhile, the male is free to join his fellows in a highly organised quest for water and food that may take them on a round trip of more than 80 kilometres. Starting after sunrise, small flocks of Namaqua sandgrouse fly to a favoured waterhole where they rendezvous with flocks from other areas. Two hours after sunrise, there may be a gathering of hundreds or even thousands.

When her chicks have hatched, the female rejoins the morning flight to water. The chicks need water too, and now it is the male who comes into his own.

Every morning at the waterhole he dips his belly feathers under the surface and allows them to absorb water like a sponge: each gram of feather can absorb up to eight grams of water. With his cargo complete, he flies back to the chicks, and they drink their water directly from his breast feathers.

attractions of the 5 577 ha Oorlogskloof Nature Reserve 10 km south of Nieuwoudtville, sprawled along the edge of the escarpment between the Karoo and the rugged Knersvlakte. This region is recognised as one of the richest botanical areas in the world.

Although there are no buildings or roads within the reserve, two four-day hiking trails (the 37,5 km Rameron Pigeon Route and the 46 km Rock Pigeon Route) cover areas suitable for camping. The trails are not for the feeble, but the effort needed bears rich rewards – the scenery is rugged and spectacular, filled with unsurpassed flora, as well as over 35 small species of animal and 130 bird species .

Access to the reserve is along rough, private farm tracks, so in order to arrange a visit first telephone The Officer-in-Charge, Oorlogskloof Nature Reserve on (02726) 81010 (before 9 a.m.) or 81159. (The latter number is also the fax number.) Remember to close farm gates behind you.

Above: *Conophytum intrepidum* flourishes on a mountainside near Port Nolloth. When not in flower, these hardy, dwarf succulents resemble a cluster of pebbles. **Right:** A puff adder (*Bitis arietans*) in the process of swallowing a meal.

Richtersveld National Park

Relatively unknown for many years, the Richtersveld covers vast, mountainous territory tucked into the northwestern corner of the Northern Cape. Bordered in the south by the R382 between Port Nolloth and Steinkopf, the area encompasses unique changes in environment. In the south, low rainfall gives rise to desert conditions, while the mountains in the central northwest experience a milder climate. The western reaches are tempered by coastal mists and, to complicate matters even further, receive their rainfall in the winter, while summer rains moisten the eastern sector. All these factors contribute to a rich diversity of flora, including numerous succulents.

Wedged into a loop of the Orange River in the far northern Richtersveld is a 162 445 ha national park, proclaimed in 1991 after some 18 years of negotiation between the National Parks Board and the local Nama population, who are largely pastoralists.

Richtersveld National Park is one of a new breed of sanctuaries. Called a 'contractual park', its focus is that of a community enterprise. Five representatives from the local communities collaborate with four National Parks Board members to manage the reserve area. The Nama people, who lease the land to the board for R80 000 a year, continue to live in and to graze their livestock in the area. They benefit from the jobs created and the tourist trade.

Richtersveld is home to grey rhebok, duiker, steenbok, klipspringer, kudu, Hartmann's mountain zebra, baboon, vervet monkey, caracal and leopard. Birdlife is prolific, and 650 plant species have been recorded (the Nama community have specific uses for some 150 of these species, ranging from medicinal and cosmetic to nutritional). Also peculiar to the Richtersveld is the world's largest diversity of succulents, including the unusual *halfmens*, a tall succulent plant that bears an uncanny resemblance to the human form when seen outlined against the skyline.

Canoeing, angling and bathing in the Orange River are allowed (although rather perilous – the river has claimed a number of lives over the years).

Three hiking trails offer visitors the opportunity to explore this deserted wonderland. Kodaspiek Trail, the easiest, covers 24 km in two days; the Lelieshoek-Oemsberg Trail is a three-day/23 km hike; and Venstervalle Trail, the most arduous, is a 42 km trek that takes four days to complete.

There are three fully equipped, self-catering guesthouses at Sendelingsdrif, as well as a number of camping sites (campers must be self-sufficient as these are simply sites with no facilities) dotted around the park. Outside the park, at Eksteenfontein, is a guesthouse run by the local community, while a campsite at Kuboes offers accommodation in *matjieshuise* (houses constructed of poles covered with grass mats), and a mobile toilet.

To get there, follow the N7 leading north from Springbok to Steinkopf, then turn west to Port Nolloth and take the coast road to Alexander Bay. From here, it's some 90 km to the park's headquarters at Sendelingsdrif. Safari vehicles are recommended.

Further details may be obtained from The Warden, Richtersveld National Park, P O Box 46, Alexander Bay 8290, telephone (0256) 831-1506, fax 831-1175.

Skilpad Wildflower Reserve

In the centre of Namaqualand a broken chain of mountains separates the low-lying Sandveld from the plateau region of Bushmanland. Lying on the edge of the mountainous escarpment, and to the west of Kamieskroon, is a charming 1 000 ha wildflower reserve. An executive committee controls Skilpad (the name means 'tortoise') with the specific aim of benefiting both conservationists and the local people, as well as the enthusiastic tourists, who numbered 22 000 in the spring of 1993. (In mid-1996 it was announced that control of Skilpad Nature Reserve would pass to the National Parks Board.)

Massed displays of wild flowers (some 335 species have been recorded) in the sandy central and eastern sections of the reserve include the orange *Ursinia cakilefolia* and *Dimorphotheca sinuata*, yellow *Cotula barbata*, blue felicias and yellow-and-mauve *Senecio*. The steep, mountainous western section is home to shrubs, some of which are adorned with enchanting flowers, while trees occur along the banks of annual streams.

Some 35 mammal species have made their home here, along with 25 reptile species and 89 recorded types of bird.

Skilpad is controlled by the World Wildlife Fund, South Africa, and is open between mid-July and September. It lies 11 km west of the N7, near Kamieskroon. Visitors approach along a gravel road with several farm gates and, once inside, can take short walks. No camping or braaiing is allowed.

Further details can be obtained from Kamieskroon Hotel, P O Box 19, Kamieskroon 8241, telephone (0257) 614 or 706, or (027) 672-1614 or 672-1706. The fax number is (0257) 675 or (027) 672-1675. A checklist of the animals is available.

Tankwa Karoo National Park

Despite covering large areas of South Africa, the sparse scrub that is so typical of the Karoo is not as hardy as it looks. Overgrazing and other bad farming practices have destroyed much of the original character of the area, often leaving only semi-desert in its wake.

In a bid to restore part of the Karoo to its original splendour, Tankwa Karoo National Park, a 27 064 ha area, 95 km south of Calvinia and 145 km north of Ceres, was proclaimed in

THE INTERIOR: NAMAQUALAND

Right: This view of the baking, inhospitable Richtersveld, looking north from Sendelingsdrif, must have intimidated many an early explorer. Those who persevered, though, found new and hardy strains of animals, plants – and people.

1986. However, it will take some years for the original vegetation to re-establish itself – and in the meantime there is little to attract the visitor except solitude and some smaller animals. No facilities have yet been built.

Tankwa is very dry and receives an average of only 50 mm of rain a year, with a maximum of 100 millimetres. When the occasional rains do fall, however, the park is transformed and the plains come alive with dazzling displays of colourful flowers.

Further information can be obtained from The Caretaker, Tankwa Karoo National Park, Private Bag X51, Calvinia 8190, telephone (0273) 41-2322.

NAMAQUALAND'S BRIEF SEASONS IN THE SUN

For most of the year, Namaqualand presents a landscape of almost unrelieved dryness. The night mists that swirl in from the cold Atlantic shores disperse long before they reach the central plains, where enormous, sun-baked boulders, stained with the greenish hues of dissolved copper salts, seem to be all that will grow from this hard and unpromising ground.

Rainfall is slight and unreliable, but winter showers – adding to a total that may be as little as 50 mm in a year – usually ensure the wonderfully colourful displays that erupt in spring. 'The very rocks have burst into flower' may not be entirely accurate, but it is a pardonable exaggeration during the all-too-brief days or weeks that Namaqualand is in brilliant flower.

Naturally, the spectacular transformation is not confined to parks and reserves, and the entire region becomes a vast showplace. Although it is relatively sparsely settled, Namaqualand has sufficient roads (most of them untarred) to enable the visitor to appreciate its brief floral glories.

Very roughly, Namaqualand may be said to extend from the Darling district north to the Orange River, and east from the coast to include Calvinia and Pofadder. There are several distinct areas, each with its own characteristics and dominant species.

In the south is the 30 km wide coastal strip called the Sandveld, including Lambert's Bay, where the dominant semi-succulent scrub derives most of its moisture from sea mists. Among the flora are the shining yellow *Grielum humifusum* or duikerblom, the mauve dew-flower (*Drosanthemum hispidum*) that fully opens its glistening petals only in the heat of noon, and silky, golden *Conicosia pugioniformis*, inelegantly known as pigs' root.

North of the Sandveld, and inland, is the area known vaguely to early Dutch settlers at the Cape of Good Hope as 'the copper mountains'. In 1685 the commander of the settlement, Simon van der Stel, led an expedition of discovery. Although it took place in late August and early September, flowers receive no mention in his diary, which does though, record lion and elephant, and the determined charge of a rhinoceros. The great beasts that Van der Stel saw have vanished from Namaqualand, but the flowers still return every year.

From the vicinity of Van der Stel's mine shaft near Springbok are seen fields of low-growing, glistening dew-flower (*Drosthanthemum*), of which Namaqualand has about 100 species. Especially plentiful here is the orange and brown double Namaqualand daisy, *Arctotis fastuosa*, and the white *Cheiridopsis denticulata*, a succulent of the mesembrythemum family. Among the brightest of Namaqualand's orange-yellow daisies is *Ursinia speciosa*, with the height of its stem determined by the amount of rain that fell in the period before flowering. After good rains, the flower heads may be carried as high as 20 cm above ground.

North of Springbok the rainfall diminishes, past Steinkopf, where a sprinkling of traditional beehive-shaped huts is to be seen among others made of more modern materials to angular designs. There are flowers here too, but this is a dry area, and drier still is the Richtersveld, now a national park (*see separate entry*).

No carpets of blooms soften the harsh outlines of the Richtersveld, but this is the landscape of curious succulents such as the eerily human-like halfmens, *Pachypodium namaquanum*, around which generations of local storytellers have woven rich skeins of legend.

Driving north from Cape Town, you see fields of spring flowers appear long before you reach Namaqualand. Darling and Biedouw, Clanwilliam and Calvinia, Cederberg and Knersvlakte – all are places where the sudden colours of spring are bright and dramatic. But nowhere is the effect on such a magnificent scale as on the plains and hills of Namaqualand where, dry and unsmiling for month after aching month, the lands bursts into brief, visible song.

Eye-catching twins of the Great Karoo

Fortunately for nature lovers, southern Africa's parks and nature reserves tend to have distinctive names and there are few problems in telling them apart. Of course, there are exceptions. The Eastern Cape has the Mountain Zebra National Park near Cradock and the Mountain Zebra Nature Reserve on the Gamka, while the Northern Cape's Kalahari Gemsbok National Park is easily confused with the adjoining Gemsbok National Park in Botswana. Adding to the confusion, there are three separate reserves named after the Karoo.

One of the three, the Karoo National Botanic Garden at Worcester, is in a class of its own. The others, the Karoo National Park at Beaufort West, and the Karoo Nature Reserve at Graaff-Reinet, are twins in more than name. Both came into being through the initiative of the SA Nature Foundation, a charitable trust backed by South African private enterprise and linked with the World Wildlife Fund. The foundation specialises in providing funds to help conserve endangered species and habitats.

Early in the 1970s, the foundation began campaigning for parks or reserves in the Great Karoo, which until then had been starved of conservation areas. The public response was so strong that the foundation arranged to help bring two such areas into being – one at Graaff-Reinet, controlled by Cape Nature Conservation, and the other at Beaufort West, under the able hand of the National Parks Board. The provincial reserve was proclaimed in 1975 and the national park in 1979.

The 'Karoo twins' have been friendly rivals from the beginning and keep a watchful eye on one another's activities. To the east, there are twins of a different sort: the provincial reserves Rolfontein and Doornkloof, which are near neighbours on the shores of Vanderkloof Dam (formerly P K le Roux) on the Orange River. In the heart of the Northern Cape, the Carnarvon and Victoria West municipalities support small but attractive reserves on their commonages.

Aalwynprag Nature Reserve

The smallest municipal nature reserve in the Northern Cape is on Strydenburg's 2 ha 'Aloe Mountain' – actually the eastern slopes of the prominent koppie divided by the national road as it bypasses the town. Proclaimed in 1977 and subsidised by Northern Cape Nature Conservation, the reserve contains a fine collection of Karoo aloes and other succulents. Unfortunately, Aalwynprag is currently in a state of neglect, but plans are afoot to restore it to its former floral glory in the near future. The reserve is located opposite Strydenburg's hotel, close to the southern exit from the national road. For details, contact The Town Clerk, Strydenburg Municipality, P O Box 60, Strydenburg 8765, telephone (053682) and ask for 16.

Aberdeen Nature Reserve

Springbok and kudu roam the koppie-studded plains of a 1 810 ha municipal nature reserve established on the fringes of the pretty Karoo town of Aberdeen in 1982. Waterbirds are also common, particularly around the reserve's

Below left: *Cliffortia arborea*, a hardy tree with needle-like leaves, growing in the Nuweveld Mountains, in the Karoo National Park. **Below right:** A pair of blesbok grazing in the Carnarvon Nature Reserve. The species mates between March and April, usually producing one active calf (the female reaches sexual maturity at about two and a quarter years). Its natural habitat is open grassland, where males will establish their own territory.

THE INTERIOR: GREAT KAROO

spring – where clean, clear water bubbles from the earth all year round. Picnic sites with braai facilities have been laid out in a shady area nearby.

Leading from the spring and passing through low acacia bush and scrub is a 15 km road, which provides a pleasant walk or drive. If you proceed quietly, you will have an excellent chance of spotting game. Besides springbok and kudu there are ostrich, gemsbok, eland, red hartebeest, steenbok, monkey and jackal in the area.

Accommodation is offered in a chalet sleeping up to six people. The reserve, which is signposted from the Willowmore/Graaff-Reinet road, lies some 300 m outside the town. For more information, contact The Town Clerk, Aberdeen Municipality, P O Box 30, Aberdeen 6270, telephone (049212) 14, or fax 174.

Carnarvon Nature Reserve

At the suggestion of the former mayor, Dr A P van Heerden, the Carnarvon Municipality set aside 670 ha of the town commonage for a nature reserve, which was proclaimed in 1971. Hartmann's mountain zebra, black wildebeest, eland, blesbok, springbok and ostrich were reintroduced and today the game population is so strong that each year the municipality sells surplus springbok to local farmers.

Roughly half of the reserve is low and flat, while the remainder consists of rough terrain at a higher elevation. Each species has its favourite habitat: the blesbok and springbok seek the plains while the black wildebeest lurk far off in the rocky gorges.

To reach the reserve, drive 1 km out of Carnarvon on the road to Loxton (R63). Most sections are served by good roads.

The reserve may be visited from 8 a.m. to 5 p.m. (seven days a week) by arrangement with the municipality. For more information, contact The Town Clerk, Carnarvon Municipality, P O Box 10, Carnarvon 7060, telephone (02032) and ask for 12.

Compassberg Hiking Trails

The towering Sneeuberg mountain range of the northeastern Cape, its upper reaches clad with a thick mantle of snow in winter, looms over hikers following the Compassberg Hiking Trails which snake and weave through its northern foothills.

Laid out on a farm near Nieu-Bethesda, the Compassberg trails, which may be hiked during a weekend, with one- and three-day alternatives, pass through these beautiful hills, revealing a wealth of birdlife (over 80 species have been identified) and mammals such as baboon, hare, lynx, jackal, steenbok, grey rhebok and kudu. Hikers undertaking the trail start out from a cottage, built in 1903 below Compassberg (the second highest peak in the

Left: *An armoured ground cricket feeding on a Karoo flower. These insects, which belong to the family Tettigoniidae, are omnivorous, feeding on both plants and other insects. They occur throughout South Africa, but are more frequently seen in arid areas. Although they offer no threat to humans, they may squirt strong-smelling blood from either side of the thorax as a defence mechanism.*

region), and overnight in a large farmhouse or stone shed. All cater for 12 people, with beds, ablution and braai facilities, and are warmed with fireplaces. The farmhouse also operates as a guest lodge, and is comfortably furnished. There is a reservoir at the shed, offering cool relief at the end of a hot day's trek!

For further information and to make reservations, contact The Valley, P O Box 205, Middelburg 5900, telephone (04924) 2-2418, or (04923) 667.

Doornkloof Nature Reserve

Like Rolfontein, Doornkloof was one of the Orange River farms bought by South Africa's Department of Water Affairs in the 1960s as it prepared to flood the valley of the Vanderkloof (formerly P K le Roux) Dam. Part of the old farm is today under water, but for years the higher ground was rented to neighbouring farmers as grazing land. Then, in 1980, the government handed Doornkloof to the Cape's Department of Nature and Environmental Conservation (it is now controlled by Northern Cape Nature Conservation), which prepared to turn it into a nature reserve.

Doornkloof's veld was allowed to recover from years of overgrazing. Then a gameproof fence was erected – a huge undertaking, for the reserve covers 9 400 hectares. Even before putting in any game, wilderness trails were established through Doornkloof, ranging from casual walks to the two- to three-day Doornkloof Hiking Trail. (Another way to explore this isolated, rugged terrain is on horseback – bring your own.)

Among the 41 species of mammal to be seen are kudu, eland and the gentle mountain reedbuck, while over 170 bird types have been recorded.

The veld in both Doornkloof and nearby Rolfontein is classified as False Upper Karoo, but it also contains vegetation typical of the Orange River broken veld (381 plant species have been identified). Wild olive, sweet thorn and karee can be seen in the kloofs; camphor bush, cabbage trees and swarthaak cover the mountainous ridges. More than 50 species of grass thrive on the plateaus and elsewhere in the area.

For further information, you should contact The Reserve Manager, Doornkloof Nature Reserve, P O Box 94, Colesberg 9795, telephone/fax (051) 753-1315.

Karoo National Park

In 1973 the National Parks Board decided to create a park in the Great Karoo, and began looking for a suitable site. The news was greeted enthusiastically throughout the region, and no fewer than 17 municipalities offered parts of their commonages to start the new park on its way. The board's researchers looked into all the possibilities and recommended that the park should be at Beaufort West, since it was surrounded by typical Karoo scenery. It was central, and easily accessible to visitors. 'Ideally, we wanted an area that was 80 per cent plains and 20 per cent mountains,' explained Bruce Bryden, the first warden of the Karoo National Park. 'That's the balance you find in the Karoo as a whole. But when I arrived there in 1977, all we had was the commonage

Above: A dusky sunbird, its head dusted with pollen, searches for nectar on an aloe in the Karoo National Park. **Right:** Renosterbos flourishes in the harsh climate of the Karoo, where little rain falls from year to year. Renosterbos (*Elytropappus rhinocerotis*), sour grass and shrubs such as harpuis are characteristic of the cooler southern slopes of the mountains in the Karoo National Park.

KAROO NATIONAL PARK AT A GLANCE

When to go The park is open between 5 a.m. and 10 p.m. throughout the year, but most visitors believe the best time to visit is during spring (October and November).

Reservations To make reservations for accommodation or the Springbok Hiking Trail, write to the National Parks Board, P O Box 787, Pretoria 0001, telephone (012) 343-1991, or fax 343-0905; or the National Parks Board, P O Box 7400, Roggebaai 8012, telephone (021) 22-2810, fax 24-6211.

Getting there The park is some five hours' drive from Cape Town and 12 hours from Johannesburg on the N1. The entrance gate is 6 km south of Beaufort West.

Accommodation A delightful rest camp consisting of Cape Dutch-style chalets and cottages, serviced and fully equipped, provides comfortable accommodation (some adapted for use by the physically disabled). A shop, restaurant and information centre may be found at the main complex. 'Ou Skuur', a beautiful historic building, houses various exhibits relevant to the park and its environs. There are a number of shady caravan and camping sites, each equipped with a power point.

Getting around A limited road system is provided, but for the most part the best way for the visitor to explore the park is on foot – on one of the four trails. Hikers on the Springbok Hiking Trail spend the night in huts consisting of two bedrooms with six bunks apiece and a kitchen area with water and a chemical toilet close by. A fair degree of physical fitness is recommended for this hike. The 4x4 trail offers one overnight hut with mattresses and toilet facilities.

Wildlife Cape mountain zebra, kudu, gemsbok, red hartebeest, black wildebeest, springbok, mountain reedbuck, grey rhebok, grey duiker, klipspringer, black-backed jackal, baboon and caracal can be seen. Black rhino may be spotted. At least 190 bird species have been recorded in the park, and reptiles include puff adder, the Cape cobra (in its different colour phases), as well as a variety of gecko and lizard.

---

donated by Beaufort West Municipality and the farm Stolshoek, bought for us by the SA Nature Foundation – a total of about 7 000 ha, and consisting chiefly of mountains.' A year later the Parks Board bought a small farm adjoining the commonage and afterwards another farm set in the mountains. The park's size was doubled, but the proportion of mountainous area to plains was still unacceptably high. Then, during 1981, three big manufacturing concerns

Above: An engraving of the trunk of a quiver tree (*Aloe dichotoma*) from a book (published in 1789) by the botanist William Paterson, entitled *A Narrative of Four Journeys into the Country of the Hottentots, and Caffraria.*

joined forces to sponsor an enormous fund-raising competition with the title 'Karoo 2000' – an effort aimed at buying more land for the park and restoration of the area to what it was like two centuries earlier. The money raised was then used to acquire land on the plains.

Bruce Bryden's first task was to tear down the old farm fences and remove alien vegetation. One consolation was the good condition of the veld on the commonage, as the area had lain fallow for five years. Bryden took a survey of small mammals in the park and began looking at birds and reptiles too. At the same time he did some research to establish which species had lived in the region previously. As a result of his studies springbok, black wildebeest, gemsbok, red hartebeest and Cape mountain zebra were reintroduced.

The people of Beaufort West were delighted by these developments but the farmers whose land bordered on the park saw it as a refuge for predators, especially caracal, and were convinced that their sheep would be raided. But their fears were not realised. The caracal's chief food is small mammals and, as the ground cover increased, so did the population of small mammals, and the caracal had no need to search for food beyond the park fences. The park staff also electrified the perimeter fence to deter the jackal and caracal from encroaching on neighbouring farms.

A GRAVEYARD FULL OF MISSING LINKS

Dicynodont skeletons found at Beaufort West. These herbivorous mammal-like reptiles lived about 230 million years ago.

To many a traveller the Karoo, with its dry, desert-like landscape stretching to the horizon, must seem one of the emptiest regions on earth. But a look at the same landscape through the eyes of a palaeontologist changes its character completely: suddenly it becomes a densely populated territory. In fact, the Karoo is one of the world's largest natural graveyards, containing an immensely rich collection of fossils from the Age of Reptiles. Scientists regard it as one of the great natural wonders of the world.

By far the most important fossils in this ancient treasure-house are those belonging to the order Therapsida, the mammal-like reptiles which link primitive reptiles with the first true mammals.

About 250 million years ago, the Karoo was a shallow depression covered by a thick sheet of ice. But, over the centuries, the climate grew warmer and the ice retreated, turning the depression into a large and generally swampy basin. With the passage of the millennia this extensive swampland became richly populated with primitive plants and reptiles, their remains settling into the sand or mud. Their skeletons were petrified as the layers of sediment gradually hardened into stone, and within 50 million years the original floor of this extensive and gradually sinking region had become carpeted with layer upon layer of fossil-bearing sandstone and mudstone – in places several thousand metres deep.

This fossil record lay imprisoned in stone for many more millions of years, but then immense forces beneath the planet's crust began to lift the ancient lowlands, pushing and coaxing the Karoo basin upwards until it formed a plateau. Then the process of weathering and erosion began. Over millions of years, the sun, wind and water began to cut deep valleys into this great layer cake, wearing away its softer layers to expose the long-hidden fossil treasure.

Although similar sequences of events have occurred elsewhere in the world, the Karoo is remarkable in that its rock strata contain a virtually unbroken record of species through a complete 50-million-year period (from 240 to 190 million years ago). This was a particularly important period because it saw the evolution of the first mammals.

Antelope species such as mountain reedbuck, grey rhebok, grey duiker and klipspringer have always inhabited the Beaufort West locality and are well represented in the park. The 64 mammal species represented here also include Cape mountain zebra, kudu, gemsbok, red hartebeest, eland, baboon, bat-eared fox, jackal and the elusive African wild cat. Over 190 bird species have been recorded, including some 20 breeding pairs of black eagle. There are also 59 species of reptile and eight types of frog.

The Karoo National Park consists of three topographical levels and the Nuweveld mountain range to the north of Beaufort West. It is an area of mountains, plains, koppies and chasms – features typical of the Great Karoo.

The park has three main vegetation zones determined by elevation – high, middle and low. The plains on the lowest levels bear typical Karoo vegetation of mixed grass and shrubs which include skilpadbossie, honey-thorn and sweet thorn, the well-known *Acacia karroo*. Sour grasses and renosterbos dominate the mountain slopes, and the plateau on the topmost level features a harsher sourveld, characteristic of Karoo mountains with their slightly higher rainfall.

As may be gathered from the type of vegetation, this is a dry, dusty land. Frequent and

THE INTERIOR: GREAT KAROO

reserve. These are especially interesting in that hikers do not have to follow set routes, but may choose their path according to their energy levels, or merely at a whim. Groups are limited to 12 people.

Rolfontein Nature Reserve

The original Rolfontein was one of the Orange River farms partly flooded by the P K le Roux (now Vanderkloof) Dam. In 1968, what remained of the farm was handed over to the Cape's then Department of Nature and Environmental Conservation to be developed as a reserve. For the next five years Rolfontein's largely mountainous terrain was left fallow, and then work started in earnest: a game fence was erected, a road system established – and animals reintroduced.

The aim was to restore the area's original character. Some species were already there: kudu, mountain reedbuck, duiker and steenbok. Early travellers' records were checked, and a variety of other species brought in, including eland, gemsbok, black wildebeest, red hartebeest, warthog (the reserve's logo), springbok, Burchell's zebra, white rhino and, later, cheetah and brown hyena.

Rolfontein, which was officially proclaimed a nature reserve in 1994 and falls under the authority of Northern Cape Nature Conservation, is a 6 200 ha expanse of windswept grassy flats, dolerite koppies and densely wooded mountain kloofs that will delight any visitor. Although the vegetation is classified as False Upper Karoo, it features vegetation types typical of the mountainous valley through which the Orange River flows. Karee, sweet thorn and wild olive may be seen in the kloofs, while cabbage trees, swarthaak, assegai grass, rooigras and camphor bush are distributed along the rocky ridges. Antelope feed on most of the area's more than 40 grass types. Over 160 bird species have been recorded.

The reserve was established to preserve a mountainous Karoo ecosystem, with all its animals and plantlife, and to provide facilities for outdoor education and recreation. One way of seeing Rolfontein and its game is through the windows of a car, but walking in the reserve is probably more rewarding. The 4 km/two hour Pied Barbet Trail winds through the shrubland, introducing hikers to the reserve's flora and fauna, especially the rich birdlife at the dam.

While working at Rolfontein, one of the conservation officers, Ken Coetzee, developed a

Right: An eland bull in the Victoria West Nature Reserve. These large animals (they may reach the size of an ox) were once distributed widely through southern Africa but are now found only in game parks and nature reserves. Mothers have been known to drive away predators such as hyena, leopard and cheetah when their calves were threatened.

ROLFONTEIN AND DOORNKLOOF AT A GLANCE

When to go The reserves are open to the public throughout the year, but are at their best in autumn (March and April) and spring (October and November). Hikers may visit either Rolfontein or Doornkloof at any time, but must make prior arrangements with the reserves' officers.

Reservations To arrange a hike along a wilderness trail at Rolfontein or Doornkloof, write to The Reserve Manager, Rolfontein Nature Reserve, P O Box 23, Vanderkloof 8771, telephone/fax (0536622) and ask for 160; or The Reserve Manager, Doornkloof Nature Reserve, P O Box 94, Colesberg 9795, telephone (051) 753-1315.

Getting there Rolfontein is close to Vanderkloof, the town built initially to accommodate workers at what is now the Vanderkloof Dam. To reach Vanderkloof, approach from Luckhoff in the Free State, or from Hopetown, De Aar or Hanover in the Northern Cape and follow the signs to the Vanderkloof Dam. From the centre of the town, drive 2 km east along the dam shore and follow the signs to the reserve's entrance gate, which is on a hillside.

Accommodation The only accommodation in the two reserves are overnight huts for Doornkloof and Rolfontein's hikers. Vanderkloof has a motel and municipal rest camp. There are picnic sites and braai facilities at both reserves.

Getting around There is a public road through Doornkloof, and Rolfontein has a comprehensive road network that takes in several lookout points and a picnic area. Wilderness trails are a speciality in both reserves. Trails may be organised at the convenience of the hikers. Visitors may hike within both reserves providing prior arrangements have been made.

Wildlife Numerous large game animals have been introduced, including eland, gemsbok, red hartebeest, Burchell's zebra, white rhinoceros, warthog, springbok and brown hyena. Species that already inhabit the area include mountain reedbuck, steenbok, grey duiker, bat-eared fox, baboon, vervet monkey, and aardvark. Over 160 species of bird have been recorded, among them fish eagle, blue crane, red bishop, malachite kingfisher and hamerkop.

Left: The secretary bird is a large and powerful bird found throughout southern Africa, though not in forest and mountain areas. Its feathered crest is reminiscent of the quill pens which secretaries tucked behind their ears in years gone by. It is a ferocious snake-killer. **Above:** A white rhino bull ambles across the Rolfontein Nature Reserve, a mountainous sanctuary alongside the Vanderkloof Dam. **Above right:** A bat-eared fox (*Otocyon megalotis*). These greyish-brown omnivores live on small animals, insects, birds and their eggs, fruit and various roots. Their large ears are so sensitive that they can detect the sounds of a beetle scrabbling in its burrow.

computerised 'data bank' to help monitor the various species, concentrating first on mammals, and then expanding the system to include birds and vegetation. He divided the reserve into 4 ha squares which were logged on a grid chart together with the three overall vegetation patterns – plateau, slope and riverine. Each species was given its own chart and, whenever it was spotted, its location was plotted on the grid. In this way a habitat preference and distribution pattern emerged.

As the data bank grew, observations became more sophisticated. 'For instance, if we come across a dead animal we analyse its stomach contents to see what it's been eating,' explained Coetzee. 'Its diet may vary greatly from season to season. A researcher may ask where the bat-eared fox goes in summer, or how vegetation re-establishes itself after a fire. Our data will help to provide answers.' Their success was gratifying. Added Coetzee, 'Other provincial reserves have adopted the idea and our combined data is stored in computer banks in Cape Town.'

Transkaroo Hiking Trail

Opened in 1993 on the farm Rietpoort near Middelburg, the three-day Transkaroo Hiking Trail explores the beautiful northern reaches of the Agter Renosterberg range, reaching elevations of up to 2 000 metres. The trail wanders past craggy kloofs, sparkling rivers and unusual rock formations, exposing panoramic views and introducing hikers to an overhang decorated with little-known ancient rock art, including a rare finger-painting of a white eland, thought to be approximately 500 years old.

Flora and fauna are diverse and fascinating. Hikers may spot mountain reedbuck, grey rhebok, blesbok, springbok, baboon, springhare and caracal (which have been adopted as the trail emblem). Birdlife is prolific, and includes red-eyed bulbul, Cape robin, pied crow, rock kestrel, black stork, and a nesting pair of black eagle above Visserskloof.

The trail, which consists of two separate loops, can accommodate groups of up to 12 hikers in overnight huts equipped with stretchers (no bedding), fireplaces, braai grids, water and firewood. A kiosk at the base camp sells firewood, eggs, milk and cooldrinks. Trailists should remember to carry extra water – at least one litre each per day. Watch out for Cape cobra, puff adder and skaapsteker.

For further information, contact Transkaroo Hiking Trail, P O Box 105, Noupoort 5950, telephone/fax (04924) 2-2112 or (04956) 2-1506.

Victoria West Nature Reserve

Just outside Victoria West, on the road to Loxton, are two attractive picnic sites overlooking the town dam – the haunt of flamingo, Egyptian goose and other waterbirds. The nearby Victoria West Nature Reserve accommodates Burchell's zebra, black wildebeest, eland, gemsbok, blesbok, springbok and ostrich. The game has done so well that the municipality has almost doubled the reserve's size: it now covers 664 hectares.

Permission to enter (and the key to the gate) may be obtained at the municipal offices. Alternatively, there are pleasant picnic spots outside the perimeter from which visitors can spot game.

There are plans to introduce a large variety of animals to the reserve, and to re-establish regular visiting hours. For details, contact the Municipality, P O Box 13, Victoria West 7070, telephone (053) 621-0193, or fax 621-0368.

stray branches of the river that have escaped the main stream. One of these branches goes underground near the northern lip of the gorge, then gushes from its side as the Bridal Veil. Another creates Klaas Island, which provides spectacular views of the main cascade, then enters the gorge via Twin Falls.

The quantity of water flowing over Augrabies varies greatly. In times of drought, it may diminish to a trickle. If there have been storms inland the river may rise and burst from its regular channel, hiding the whole of the end of the gorge behind a curtain of water. In 1974, so much water was on the move that the gorge was filled to the brim and the park headquarters on Klaas Island were marooned for 14 days. In 1988, the river came down in a deluge, engulfing the islands within its path, washing away the footbridge that linked the northern and southern sections and cutting off the rest camp for two weeks. The frequency of such floods has been reduced by the construction of major dams such as the Gariep and the Vanderkloof, on the Orange River.

Below the main falls, the stream froths and swirls down rapids at the bottom of the gorge. It can be seen to advantage at beauty spots such as Arrow Head, reached by an easy walk along a 2,5 km bridle path, or Oranjekom, which is accessible by road and offers a thatched lookout.

Many of those who visit Augrabies are content to admire the main falls and go on their way, but others find it worthwhile to drive through the park and explore its wild scenery and strange vegetation. At Moon Rock, visitors may clamber onto an immense granite dome that provides spectacular views across the whole park. At the Fountain, the attraction is a drink from a picturesque spring. And at Echo Corner on the river, they experiment with loud cries that produce a strong echo after a four-second delay.

Also offered within the park is the Augrabies Black Rhino Adventure, a day trip that involves setting off on a rubber dinghy, moored at Echo Corner, and being ferried to the northern bank to explore (in a 4x4 vehicle) the inselberg-studded plain for black rhino. This rare subspecies (*Diceros bicornis bicornis*) copes well with the arid conditions, having been imported from Namibia.

Of great appeal to hikers is the three-day/ 39,5 km Klipspringer Hiking Trail, which was designed to traverse all the major landmarks in the southern section of the park. Although regarded by some as a long hike, the schedule is, in fact, not too demanding. Overnight facilities on the route consist of two huts, each equipped with 12 bunks, mattresses, toilets, water, firewood and basic cooking utensils.

The trail takes its name from an animal that seems particularly well suited to the rocky Augrabies habitat – the klipspringer or 'rock-jumper'. This small antelope has near-perfect balance and is often seen perched motionless on a rock, with all four feet bunched together. The klipspringer is capable of phenomenal leaps and can scale almost sheer cliffs with great speed.

Another creature of the rocks, common at Augrabies, is the Cape red-tailed rock lizard (*Platysaurus capensis*). In fact, only the males have red tails – the females are a uniform grey-green in colour.

During 1775 a young Swedish-born soldier stationed at the Cape ran into trouble over gambling debts. The soldier's name was Hendrik Wikar and, to escape his problems, he deserted from the Dutch East India Company and headed into the interior. For the next four years he roamed the Orange River and kept a journal in which he recorded his impressions of Augrabies Falls: 'When the weather is favourable one can hear the noise like the roar of the sea from the distance of one stage away' (a day's journey by wagon).

Wikar mapped the falls and made many other discoveries on the Orange, as a result of which the Dutch East India Company agreed to overlook his desertion, and welcomed him back to Cape Town. But his achievements were forgotten until his journal was published in 1916. In the meantime, the credit for discovering Augrabies was given to a Cape Town merchant, George Thompson, who, after seing them in 1824, named them – in loyal colonial fashion – 'King George's Cataract'.

George Thompson was a man of many parts – one of his claims was that he was the first man in Cape Town to smoke cigarettes. He was an enterprising and well-informed explorer and his *Travels and Adventure in Southern*

AUGRABIES AT A GLANCE

When to go The park is open throughout the year, but the falls are most impressive between October and January. The Klipspringer Hiking Trail is open between 1 April and 30 September (the trail is closed for the rest of the year because of the excessive heat). The park's gates are open between 6.30 a.m. and 10 p.m.

Reservations and information Enquiries and applications for accommodation should be addressed to National Parks Board, P O Box 787, Pretoria 0001, telephone (012) 343-1991, or fax 343-0905; or National Parks Board, P O Box 7400, Roggebaai 8012, telephone (021) 22-2810, or fax 24-6211. Preference is given to bookings made 13 months in advance. Further information may be obtained by contacting Augrabies Falls National Park, Private Bag X1, Augrabies 8874, telephone (054) 451-0050, or fax 451-0053. An information centre tells the park's story and introduces some of its wildlife. Ask at the office for a map of the road system and Klipspringer Hiking Trail.

Getting there The falls are 120 km west of Upington and 40 km northwest of Kakamas. The access road is tarred.

Accommodation Augrabies offers air-conditioned accommodation in 59 serviced, self-contained bungalows. Family units have four beds and bedding, bathroom, living room and kitchen. Smaller chalets have one bedroom (two beds and double sleeper), kitchen and bathroom with shower. Two chalets have been adapted for the physically disabled. There is a large caravan and camping site with ablution blocks.

Eating and drinking The park cafeteria serves meals and refreshments (and is especially popular with day visitors). In front of the cafeteria is a garden containing about 100 species of aloe and other succulents. The park shop sells groceries, fresh and frozen meat, and firewood. There are braai facilities at the bungalows and at the caravan and camping site, and a picnic area with ablution and braai facilities.

Getting around The access road to Augrabies is tarred as far as the rest camp. Inside the park, a 30 km network of gravel roads takes visitors to major attractions like Oranjekom, Echo Corner, the Fountain and Moon Rock. Petrol is available in the park. The Klipspringer Trail in the southern section of the park has two overnight huts. For a less strenuous walk, take the 2,5 km bridle path from the caravan site to the Arrow Head.

Wildlife At Augrabies, rock and water take precedence over flora and fauna but the wildlife includes klipspringer, springbok, steenbok, Hartmann's mountain zebra, giraffe, dassie, porcupine, leopard, baboon and vervet monkey (a group of monkeys makes daily raids on the caravan site). A breeding herd of black rhino has been translocated to Augrabies from Etosha National Park. Some 186 bird species have been recorded.

Special precautions Visitors are advised to take precautions against malaria before and during their visit to Augrabies. Take binoculars and walking shoes – and stay behind the safety fences at all times.

Africa is one of the best books of its kind. In it he records that a party of Khoikhoi led him to the brink of the falls, even though 'the sight and sound of the cataract were so fearful, that they themselves regarded the place with awe, and ventured but seldom to visit it'.

Standing on a cliff opposite the top of the cascade, Thompson had a perfect view. 'The beams of the evening sun fell full upon the cascade, and occasioned a most splendid rainbow,' he wrote, 'while the vapoury mists arising from the broken waters, the bright green woods which hung from the surrounding cliffs, the astounding roar of the waterfall, and the tumultuous boiling and whirling of the stream below, striving to escape along its deep, dark and narrow path, formed altogether a combination of beauty and grandeur, such as I never before witnessed.'

'King George's Cataract' found its way onto maps and the name survived well into the 20th century – though local farmers usually talked of the 'Groot Waterval' and the traveller Guillermo Farini suggested the rapids and cascades should be named 'The Hundred Falls'. Meanwhile, local Khoikhoi continued to talk of 'Augrabies' just as their ancestors had done, and this is the name everyone uses today.

Strange tales are told of the great pool that lies at the foot of the main falls. Although its depth has never been plumbed, some authorities suggest that the water conceals a fortune in diamonds washed down the Orange River from sources far inland, but the sheer weight of water cascading down the cataract prevents them from investigating.

A severe drought occurred in 1934, exposing the pool at the bottom of the chasm. Some were tempted to explore it to test the diamond theory, but people became afraid when some cattle, desperate to quench their thirst, walked up the riverbed to drink at the pool. A strong wind came out of nowhere and blew them over the edge. They were never seen again.

The disappearance of the cattle reinforced an old legend. Local residents still believe the pool is the haunt of a terrifying 'water monkey' that is liable to emerge in search of food. Zoologists speculate that the 'water monkey' legend is prompted by sightings of giant barbel that are sometimes washed over the falls. Such fish grow to lengths of two metres or more, and their long 'whiskers' and hideous faces make them appear to be formidable monsters.

In spite of this explanation, local people are convinced that the 'water monkey' means business. During 1980 strange tracks were discovered around the Augrabies restaurant and there was near-hysteria as park employees reported that the monster had left the pool. Officials took photographs of the tracks and sent them to Pretoria for identification, but before the results came back the 'monkey' was identified as an otter.

The menace of the 'water monkey' may be a myth, but Augrabies itself has claimed many victims. Since the park was proclaimed in 1966 at least 20 people have died, most of them because they lost their balance on the lip of the gorge and tumbled to the river far below. Today a chest-high protective fence fronts the most popular vantage points on the south bank – but there are always foolhardy tourists eager to clamber over it.

In 1979 a Scandinavian visitor overbalanced on the lip of the gorge and tumbled over the edge. As he slid down the sheer rock face, the friction ripped off all his clothes – even his belt and underpants. The rock also badly lacerated his flesh, and when he hit the river several bones were broken. But the man was still alive and was able to scramble to a submerged rock, where he sat in 30 cm of water. A park employee was lowered and brought him to safety. However, after being released from hospital, he insisted on returning to find his wallet, which had been lost in the fall. Park officials scanned the cliffs with scant hope of any success but, to everyone's amazement, the wallet was spotted on a ledge. It was torn and flapping, but the money was intact.

Spitskop Nature Reserve

Upington's Spitskop is a spectacular granite koppie some 13 km north of the town, reached from a turn-off on the main route to the Kalahari Gemsbok National Park. In 1967 the municipality proclaimed a nature reserve on the sandy flats adjoining the koppie and introduced gemsbok, springbok, ostrich, eland, red hartebeest, Burchell's zebra and even a pair of camel brought from the Kalahari.

Above: The *Acacia karroo* occurs in the Augrabies area. It has many uses: the bark is used in tanning, the inner bark is used for ropes, the leaves, flowers and pods are useful fodder, the gum makes an adhesive, and the thorns are used as needles.

Originally the reserve covered 1 300 ha, but the animals flourished so well that it was enlarged to 5 641 hectares. Good gravel roads offer opportunities for gamewatching, and three trails of varying length penetrate its depths. There is an overnight hut for hikers. The reserve is open daily between 7 a.m. and 7 p.m. The Spitskop itself is surmounted by a sheltered lookout equipped with a telescope. At its foot is a picnic area. Camping facilities are available.

Further details may be obtained from Spitskop Tours and Safaris, P O Box 282, Upington 8800, telephone/fax (054) 2-2336; or Tourism Information Office, Upington Municipality, Private Bag X6003, Upington 8800, telephone/fax (054) 2-7064.

Tierberg Nature Reserve

Overlooking Keimoes is the squat bulk of Tierberg, the focus of a small municipal nature reserve covering some 160 hectares.

On Tierberg's summit is a sheltered lookout, and the slopes and surroundings are notable for a prodigious growth of aloes and other succulents. The most numerous species is *Aloe gariepensis*, named after the Gariep (the old Khoikhoi name for the Orange River). It blooms in August and September and produces vertical shafts of red flowers that bristle like spears. Tierberg is open all through the year and is accessible by a 4 km drive from the centre of Keimoes. Further details are available from Keimoes Municipality, P O Box 8, Keimoes 8860, telephone (054) 461-1016, fax 461-1230.

For years, this region was a land beyond frontiers. No government laid claim to it and the San were the only people who inhabited it. In fact, it was in this arid region that Regopstaan Kruiper, a Bushman (San) patriarch who died early in 1996 at the ripe old age of 96 years, was born. He later moved to the Kagga Kamma Reserve in the Cederberg, but told many tales of his early life in his beloved Kalahari Desert.

Finally, the region became attached to the then Cape Colony, which from 1897 began surveying large farms for white settlers. Even then, the region was largely a no-man's-land, and in 1904 the authorities in German South West Africa sent soldiers to blockade Nossob waterholes and force Khoikhoi rebels into submission. The ploy backfired and, at Grootkolk, an entire German patrol was slaughtered.

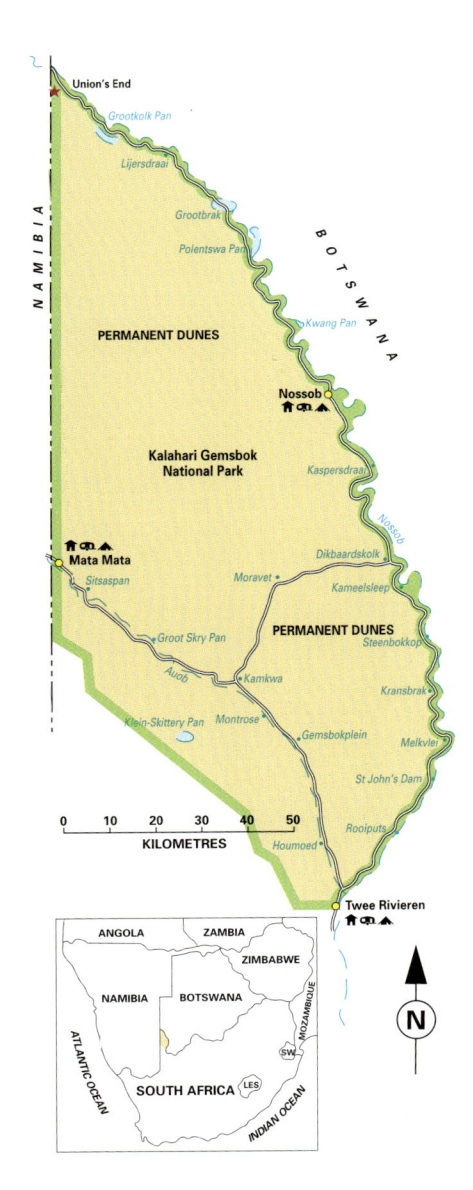

White settlers were slow to take advantage of the new farms in the north, so the Cape authorities gave them to coloured farmers instead. The farms had names like Kò Kò, Kameelsleep, Kasper's Draai and Kwang – many of them recalled in the names of today's park waterholes. Then, in 1914, South Africa went to war against Germany and prepared to invade German South West Africa. As part of the invasion strategy, the South Africans sank strings of boreholes for the benefit of soldiers and their mounts.

KALAHARI GEMSBOK AT A GLANCE

When to go The park is open year round but the best time for viewing game is from February to May. The rest camps are generally full during school holidays. The park's three rest camps open their gates at sunrise and close at sunset seven days a week.

Reservations and information Enquiries and applications for bookings should be addressed to: National Parks Board, P O Box 787, Pretoria 0001, telephone (012) 343-1991, or fax 343-9958; or National Parks Board, P O Box 7400, Roggebaai 8012, telephone (021) 22-2810, or fax 24-6211. For information and further details, contact The Warden, Kalahari Gemsbok National Park, Private Bag X5890, Gemsbokpark 8815, telephone (054) 561-0021, or fax 561-0026.

A small information centre at Twee Rivieren Rest Camp introduces the park's wildlife. Park officials at the three rest camps confer by radio each morning and evening and may be able to provide the latest information on the whereabouts of lion and cheetah. Otherwise, tourists themselves are the best sources – motorists approaching from opposite directions can flag one another down and compare notes.

Getting there The most popular approach route is a 288 km, largely tarred/partly gravel, road leading north from the tarred highway between Upington and Namibia. The turn-off is 63 km from Upington and fuel is available at Noenieput and Andriesvale. A second route approaches Andriesvale from the east by way of Kuruman, Hotazel and Vanzylsrus.

There are landing strips for light aircraft at the Twee Rivieren, Mata Mata and Nossob rest camps, but prior authority must be obtained for landing. Access is not permitted between the park and Namibia at Mata Mata and Union's End.

Accommodation There are rest camps at Mata Mata in the west, Twee Rivieren in the south and Nossob towards the north. All three camps offer comfortable family cottages (two double bedrooms, kitchen and bathroom); self-contained huts (up to four beds, kitchen and bathroom); and ordinary huts (up to four beds, with access to a shared kitchen and bathroom). Nossob and Mata Mata also have six-bed cottages. Bedding, towels, and cooking and eating utensils are supplied. Each camp has a camping and caravan site with braai sites, washing-up facilities and an ablution block.

Eating and drinking There is an à la carte restaurant at Twee Rivieren. The camps have shops selling groceries, but frozen meat, bread, butter and eggs are available only at Twee Rivieren. Beer, table wines and spirits are sold at all three camps. Firewood is sold by the bundle.

Getting around Seen from the north, the park's road system has the shape of a giant 'A', consisting of the two roads following the riverbeds and a dune road connecting unfenced 'halfway house' picnic spots. The roads are generally in good condition, but you are not permitted to leave them because you may get stuck in soft sand. Every evening, park authorities check on vehicles and conduct a search for any that are missing.

Fuel is available at all three camps.

Wildlife Species commonly seen include lion, cheetah, gemsbok, red hartebeest, blue wildebeest, steenbok, springbok, black-backed jackal, bat-eared fox, ground squirrel and suricate.

Lucky visitors may also see leopard, eland, spotted hyena, brown hyena, Cape fox, caracal and ratel. There are more than 200 species of bird.

Special precautions Park authorities advise visitors to embark on a course of anti-malaria pills before entering the park. When going for a drive, take water and emergency rations in case you have a breakdown. Stick to the route you have outlined on leaving the rest camp – if you encounter a problem the rangers will find you all the quicker.

Winter nights are cold, the temperature often falling to well below freezing point, but the days are usually warm. Summer days are usually hot and dry (the annual rainfall of some 200 mm is mainly between January and April).

Right: A gnarled tree overlooks the dusty bed of the Nossob River, in the Kalahari Gemsbok National Park. The discovery of Stone Age artefacts in the area indicates that the basin of the Nossob was once fertile. **Far right:** The tsamma melon is an important source of food, and especially moisture, in the Kalahari.

THE CUNNING GOSHAWK

Clem Haagner, a keen photographer who visited the Kalahari Gemsbok National Park so frequently that a borehole was named after him, told the story of a chanting goshawk that discovered a novel way to prey on sandgrouse. The bird used to sit on a telegraph pole near Twee Rivieren and wait until a flock of sandgrouse began drinking at a small pool next to a fence. Then the bird swooped – not with hopes of snatching sandgrouse on the wing, but to panic some of them into flying against the fence and knocking themselves senseless.

The chanting goshawk's light blue-grey feathers and long orange legs make it quite easy to identify, but it is only one of a large number of raptor species (birds of prey) that help to make the park a paradise for birdwatching. About one-sixth of the park's many bird species are raptors preying on insects, reptiles, smaller birds or small mammals. They range from martial and tawny eagles to white-backed and lappet-faced vultures, from secretary birds to giant eagle owls.

February, March and April are the park's best months for raptor-spotting, particularly if the rainfall has been better than average. Fortunately for visitors, the rain encourages rapid plant growth in the riverbeds and adjoining areas, and the whole food chain is stimulated.

The invasion went off without a hitch, and when it was over the South African government employed a number of 'borehole watchers' to keep an eye on the installations. The watchers, and indeed the farmers, were expected to live off the veld – with alarming consequences for the once-abundant game.

Biltong hunters from the south also made their mark. By the late 1920s a number of species were perilously close to extinction, and two Northern Cape conservationists invited the Minister of Lands, Piet Grobler, to inspect the region.

Piet Grobler had piloted the National Parks Act through parliament and played a major role in the proclamation of the Kruger National Park in 1926. His trip to South Africa's most remote corner convinced him that the area would make an ideal national park – not least because it was associated with the gemsbok, which, with the springbok, are featured on South Africa's coat of arms. He lobbied extensively in both Pretoria and Cape Town, and, as a result of his efforts, the Kalahari Gemsbok National Park was proclaimed in July 1931.

The new park's first ranger was Johannes le Riche, the son of a local trader. Le Riche and his family moved into a primitive hut vacated by one of the 'borehole watchers' who, like the few farmers in the park, were soon provided with new homes outside its boundaries. Hunting in the park was now strictly forbidden. The main task facing Le Riche and his assistant, Gert Januarie, was to intercept poachers and bring them before the magistrates.

For three years Le Riche and Januarie patrolled the park on horseback, but their efforts were hampered by a serious drought. Then, in 1934, came rains so abundant that both the Auob and Nossob came down in flood – the Nossob for the first time this century. The rains should have been cause for celebration – but they exacted a terrible penalty. Mosquitoes flourished in the area, Le Riche and Januarie contracted malaria, and both men died. A few

THE INTERIOR: **KALAHARI GEMSBOK NATIONAL PARK**

THE CHEETAH SHOW

Vehicles and people have become so commonplace in the Kalahari Gemsbok that many animals simply accept them as part of the environment. Motorists often find their path blocked by herds of springbok that show no inclination to break rank. Lion sometimes see cars as playthings, and may try to bite their tyres or swat their headlights with a massive paw. But the strangest reaction is that of the cheetah, which seems to turn a blind eye to people, and behaves as if they are not there.

There are only about 60 cheetah in the park, but these angular cats contribute some of the liveliest action that tourists are likely to see. Lion and leopard do most of their hunting at night, when visitors are in rest camps, but cheetah hunt by day, and because their favourite prey is the springbok they conduct their campaigns in the river valleys. The more fortunate tourists can watch them every step of the way, from the time they begin stalking until they make their run and knock a springbok into oblivion. Typically, the hunter will be a female cheetah who must satisfy her own needs as well as those of two (sometimes as many as five) cubs.

To begin with, her prey may be several hundred metres away. She will leave her cubs hidden as she prepares to take advantage of every scrap of cover. With her body flat and her ears laid back she inches closer to her prey – and it may be a matter of hours before she comes within range. Throughout that time her eyes remain fixed on her target, until finally, with a devastating sprint, she makes her attack.

Sometimes all goes to plan and she makes a kill. But more often the prey is too agile for her, and showing her resignation, she slows to a trot with her tail held high. On occasion she varies her prey and attacks the calves of larger antelope, or perhaps small mammals. But the existence of the cheetah and her family is precarious, for she is forced to compete with powerful predators, and without food her cubs will weaken and perhaps fall victim to spotted hyena or leopard.

---

various species they see, comparing tallies after each safari. Visitors often derive the most pleasure from spotting the smaller, less obvious mammals.

Gemsbok, red hartebeest, blue wildebeest and springbok are all fairly common in the riverbeds, whether as solitary bulls or rams rooted by breeding or by the territories they have marked out, or bachelor and breeding herds that are always on the move. Occasionally visitors see a group of eland, though the species tends to keep to the dunes and visits the riverbeds only in passing. The little steenbok is another creature of the dunes and may be spotted close to the gravel road connecting the 'halfway house' picnic sites.

Diminutive suricate and black-backed jackal are common, as are the little bat-eared fox often seen grubbing for insects in the late afternoon. Spotted hyena are rarely seen by day, and brown hyena are even more elusive. The Cape fox and caracal are real 'collector's items', and if a visitor reports seeing a leopard, impala or kudu, even park rangers sit up and take notice.

Running along the bed of the Nossob is a line of discreet beacons marking South Africa's border with Botswana. Otherwise there is no barrier between the two states, and the Kalahari's animals can roam from country to country as they please. Botswana's Gemsbok National Park (*see separate entry*) is even larger than South Africa's and together the great reserves comprise one of the least spoilt wilderness areas on the continent. This makes them extremely valuable to zoological researchers.

The best-known research project carried out in the Kalahari Gemsbok has been the University of Pretoria's study of the Kalahari lion – not a different species from the lion found in the Kruger Park and elsewhere, but certainly adapted to very different conditions.

The researchers found that a Kalahari lion may be expected to kill 47 animals a year – more than three times as many as its counterpart in the Kruger Park – even though prey is scarcer in the Kalahari, and the terrain makes it more difficult to catch.

The disparity is a matter of scale. As much as 50 per cent of a Kalahari lion's kill comprises small mammals, whereas in the Kruger Park the proportion is only one per cent. Given the opportunity, a Kalahari lion prefers to dine on ambitious fare such as gemsbok, blue wildebeest or red hartebeest. Sometimes, however, it is reduced to eating springhare, bat-eared fox and porcupine merely to stay alive (porcupine represent one-quarter of their prey).

A biologist named Gus Mills arrived at Kalahari Gemsbok in 1972 to gather material for a thesis on the little-known brown hyena (he later became full-time research officer). When the moon was full he drove through various sections of the park to observe the brown hyena on their solitary long-distance foraging expeditions. To make them easier to follow, several were fitted with 'radio collars' and located by mobile receiver.

'The first job was to home in on an animal with a radio-tracking kit,' explained Gus Mills. 'Once we'd found one, I put the radio kit away and followed the green lights on the back of the collar – I didn't need to use headlights. Probably the most interesting thing I discovered about the species was that it's the females who have territories. Their offspring can remain as long as food is plentiful, but males have the option of going off on their own. They wander from area to area until they find a female in heat. After mating they resume their nomadic existence, leaving the feeding of the cubs to the females and group-living males.'

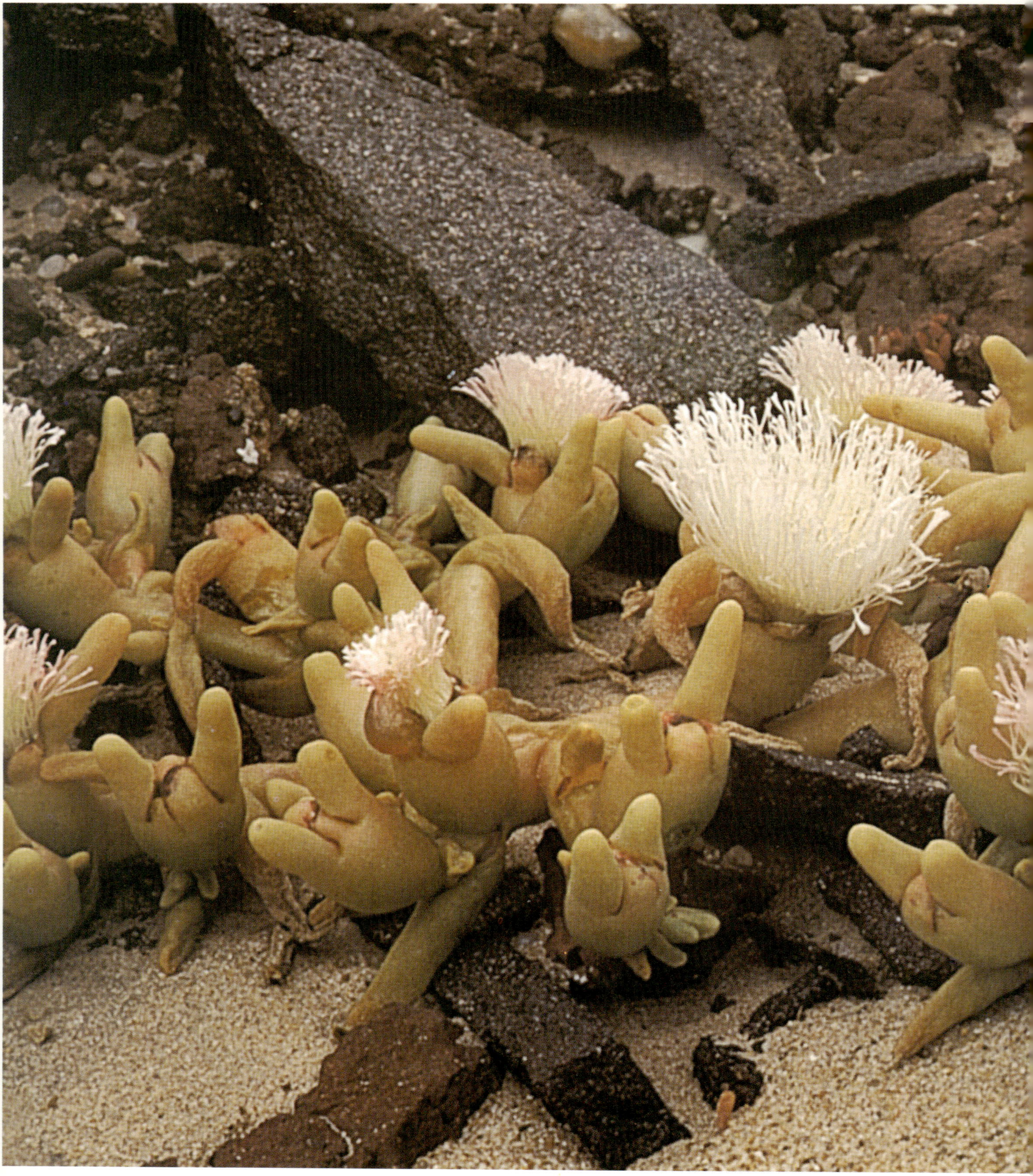

NAMIBIA

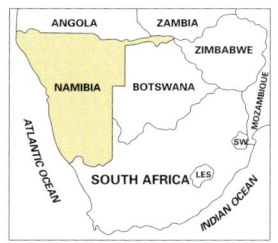

North of the Orange River is a vast tract of land, declared a German protectorate in 1900, transferred to South African control after the First World War and, finally, in 1990, gaining independence as the Republic of Namibia. Namib is a Khoikhoi word for a 'plain', and endless plains are the key to Namibia. Its Namib Desert is the oldest in the world, with extensive stretches of sand, gravel and rock. There are also grass-covered flats providing rich grazing, as well as typical savannah parkland with grass, trees and shrubs. In stark contrast are the country's tall, pastel-coloured mountain ranges and dry canyons cut deep into the barren rock – many of which conceal a gallery of ancient rock paintings.

As early as 1907, the German governor Friedrich von Lindequist set aside three large areas of Namibia to serve as game reserves. Two of them survive today as part of the vast Namib-Naukluft Park complex in the west (4 976 800 ha), and the Etosha National Park in the north – once the world's largest game reserve.

Although it has since been greatly diminished in size, Etosha's 2 227 000 ha make it larger than the Kruger National Park, and its devotees claim it is also more exciting to visit (though not nearly as much of it is open to visitors). Besides Etosha and Namib-Naukluft, Namibia offers gems like the Fish River Canyon in the south, the Skeleton Coast in the northwest, the Waterberg Plateau in the north and the Caprivi Strip in the northeast. Wildlife is abundant almost everywhere.

A cluster of *Halenbergia hypertrophicum* brightens the northern stretches of the Namib with an all-too-brief display of colourful blooms.

A journey through forbidding territory

One of the longest and most impressive rivers in Namibia is the Fish, which rises in the Khomas Hochland Mountains southwest of Windhoek and flows 800 km before it meets the Orange River far to the south. The river's last 161 km take it through a deep canyon that is counted among the geological wonders of southern Africa.

The Fish River Canyon is the setting of the most challenging hiking trail in Namibia, which ends at the Ai-Ais Hot Springs resort. The canyon is located in the centre of the vast plains typical of the Karas region and, further to the northeast – near Keetmanshoop – lies the strange Kokerboom Forest. To the west is the 'Sperrgebiet', the 'forbidden territory' that has been closed to visitors since the days of German administration to protect the coastal diamond industry.

Offshore is forbidden territory of a different sort – the bird-rich paradises of the Namibian government-owned offshore islands.

Ai-Ais Hot Springs
Although the 'discovery' of the hot spring at Ai-Ais is often attributed to a 19th-century Nama herdsman looking for straying cattle, it is likely that the spring was already known thousands of years earlier to the Stone Age people who lived in the canyon. When the pastoral Khoikhoi arrived, they named the spring *ai-ais*, which is Nama for 'scalding hot'. Like many other such springs, Ai-Ais was soon credited with medicinal properties and invalids went there in hope of a rapid cure.

Step by step a little spa developed at the spring, and during the First World War the German authorities took over Ai-Ais, building a rest and recuperation camp for sick and wounded soldiers. Today, Ai-Ais is one of the most visited spas in southern Africa – not least because it is located at the bottom of the Fish River Canyon (at its southern tip) and provides an excellent base from which to explore the surrounding region.

Set beneath towering peaks, the resort is popular with a large variety of visitors, ranging from those who come to ease their rheumatism and nervous disorders in its salubrious thermal baths, to the hiking enthusiasts who begin and end the Fish River Hiking Trail here. The sunburnt backpackers celebrating the end of the long hike through the canyon traditionally complete their trek by leaping into the large outdoor pool to cool off, followed by a thirst-quenching ice-cold beer.

Even the winter sun makes Ai-Ais uncomfortably hot (although nights can be extremely chilly). In summer, because of the intense heat and the risk of flooding, the resort closes its doors from the end of October to the second Friday in March.

Although the heat in December and January (Ai-Ais' hottest months) can be devastating, February and March can pose an even bigger problem. That's when the floods may come, although, fortunately, it's not a regular occurrence. The Fish and its tributaries drain about a quarter of Namibia's surface area, and all that water rushes down the canyon past Ai-Ais.

Occasionally the Fish River comes down in a real fury, sweeping aside whatever comes in its path. In March 1972 the flood was of a phenomenal magnitude, and the raging river swamped the terrace at Ai-Ais, washing away the field kitchens and ablutions and burying

Left: The double-banded courser, with its pale plumage, may easily be overlooked by visitors to Namibia, and often it is spotted only when it runs. This species feeds on termites and ants, and is usually found on open grassland or sandy veld. It lives in pairs or small flocks. **Above:** The magnificent Fish River Canyon, or 'Groot Kloof' as it is known to local farmers, is a deep maze of gorges and multilayered outcrops representing aeons of relentless erosion.

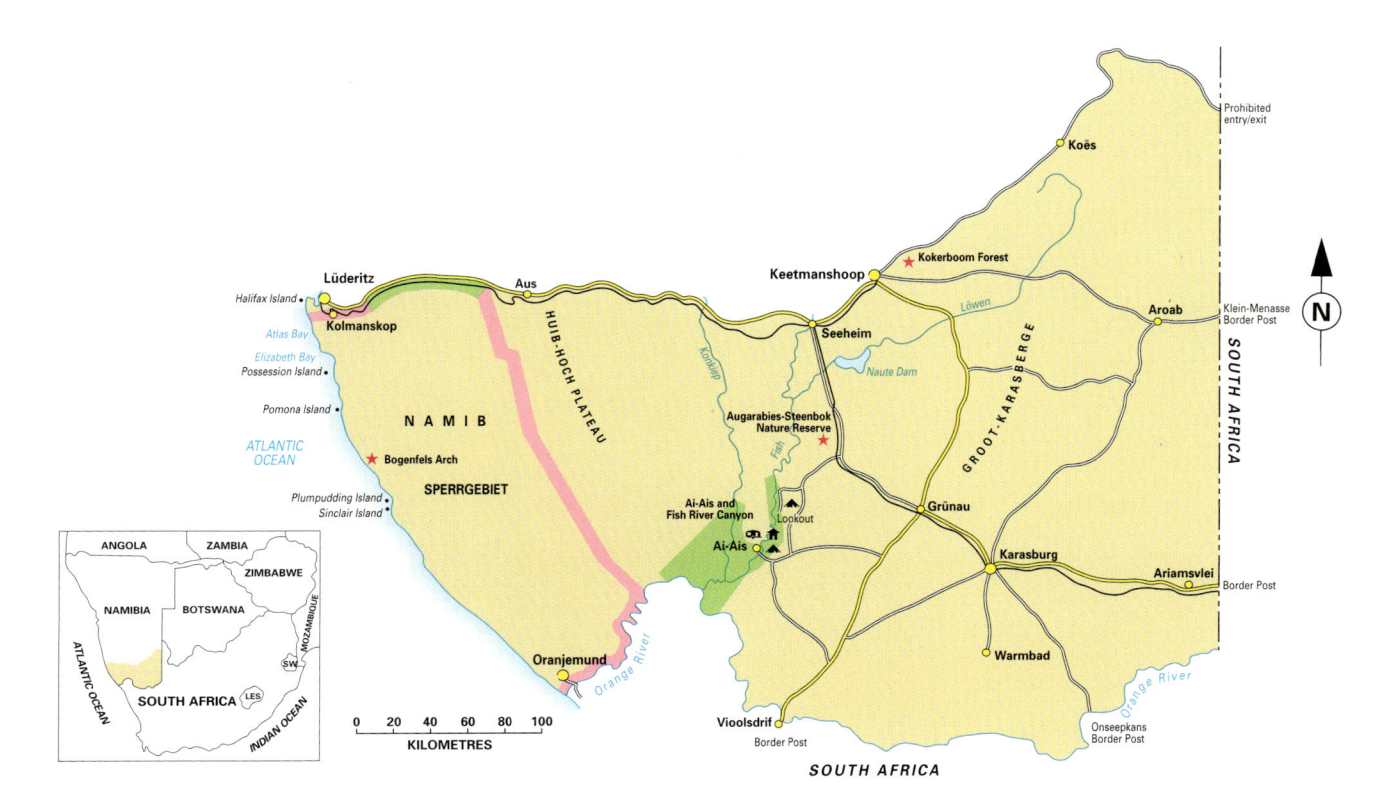

the swimming pool in evil-smelling mud. Two years later Ai-Ais was battered by another flood. It then escaped the wrath of the river for 14 years before it was flooded once again. In some years, however, such as 1982 and 1995, the river didn't flow at all, and there were only a few scattered pools in the riverbed.

Augarabies-Steenbok Nature Reserve

This tiny reserve, almost unnoticed by visitors intent on reaching the Fish River Canyon, lies some 69 km to the northwest of Grünau. It was created as a sanctuary for steenbok, gemsbok, Hartmann's mountain zebra and klipspringer. The only facilities for visitors are toilets, but camping is allowed. There is no admission fee. To reach Augarabies-Steenbok, follow the C12 northwest from Grünau for 59 km, then turn left and continue for a further 10 km to the reserve's entrance.

Fish River Canyon

Ai-Ais is not the only hot spring in the bed of the Fish River. About 65 km upstream, a spring with a strong smell of sulphur surfaces at the base of the canyon slopes and runs through dense reeds to a large pool in the riverbed. During the First World War two German prisoners who had escaped from the internment camp at Aus hid at the spring for several months, and the story goes that one was cured of skin cancer and the other of asthma. The men lived partly on dates and thoughtfully planted the stones, so today there is a small grove of palm trees in that spot.

The sulphur spring and its shady palms provide a welcome oasis in the Fish River Canyon, which extends 161 km from the falls north of the main lookout to its junction with the Orange River. In places the gorge reaches a width of up to 27 km, but for most of its length it is much narrower, its course a crazy, zigzag meander between steep cliffs.

Its steep, rocky walls are a geologist's peepshow, offering glimpses of varying strata, the lowest levels of which were laid down more than 2 500 million years ago.

For the first 65 km of its course towards the Orange, the Fish River's gorge is really a canyon within a canyon. An earlier version of the present river cut a wide swathe through the soft sediments of the Nama Series. The rift was enlarged when earth movements created cliffs to the west, and a geological fault had a similar effect to the east. The land tilted against the force of the stream, and in retaliation the Fish began to cut a deep channel in the bed of the original trough – much deeper, narrower, and more spectacular.

In places the canyon's floor reaches a depth of some 550 m below the level of the plateau. Usually it is a silent world of placid pools and mighty boulders strewn across beds of sand, with little evidence of vegetation or wildlife.

Only rarely does the river come down in flood, but when it does the flow is so violent that rock is smashed against rock, gradually deepening and reshaping the canyon with the passing of the centuries.

Before the 1960s the Fish River Canyon was little known and seldom visited, but in 1962 it was made a national monument and the area surrounding it was proclaimed a nature reserve. Since then its reputation has attracted an ever-increasing number of visitors, some content to gaze on its ancient contortions from the security of the main lookout, but others wanting closer contact by descending to its rocky floor.

The hiking trail from the northernmost lookout near Hobas southwards to Ai-Ais has become known as one of the most challenging in southern Africa. The enchanting 85 km route following the rivercourse (which usually flows between March and June) descends steeply into the canyon, crosses boulder-strewn fields and deep sand, fording the river several times. It's hard going, but the journey does become easier the further south one walks, and the breathtaking views are well worth the effort.

Kokerboom Forest

Early in the 1960s an extensive stand of 'quiver trees' (*Aloe dichotoma*) on the farm Gariganus, 14 km northeast of Keetmanshoop, was fenced off and proclaimed a national monument. The

AI-AIS AND FISH RIVER CANYON AT A GLANCE

When to go The hot-springs resort is open for overnight visitors from the second Friday in March to 31 October, but day visitors are welcome out of season. Hobas campsite is open throughout the year from sunrise to sunset. The main lookout over the canyon can be reached all year round but in the summer months it is best to visit it early in the morning. Hiking through the canyon is permitted only from the beginning of May to the end of September. During the season the resort gates are open 24 hours a day, while out of season they are open between sunrise and sunset. Dogs and other pets are banned and so are motorcycles.

Reservations To make reservations and to apply for hiking permits, contact the Directorate of Tourism and Resorts, Ministry of Environment and Tourism, Private Bag 13267, Windhoek, telephone (09264) 61 23-6975/6/7/8, fax 22-4900. For further information, contact the Directorate of Tourism and Resorts, Ministry of Environment and Tourism, Private Bag 13346, Windhoek, telephone (09264) 61 284-2111, fax 22-1930.

Getting there From the south, take the gravel D316 branching northwest from a turn-off on the Vioolsdrif/Keetmanshoop road (B1), 39 km north of Vioolsdrif (Ai-Ais is 84 km from the turn-off and the lookout is another 68 km to the north). From the east (the best approach) take the gravel C10 branching off the main (B1) highway, 31 km southwest of Grünau (Ai-Ais is 73 km away and the lookout is 55 km from a turn-off 23 km east of the resort). From the north, approach from Seeheim on the Keetmanshoop/Lüderitz road (B4). Follow the C12 towards Grünau for 77 km, turn right onto the D601 and, after 30 km, turn right again onto the D324. Ai-Ais is 67 km from the turn-off and the main lookout is 14 km further on. There are signposts.

Accommodation There are campsites, ablution facilities and a swimming pool at Hobas close to the canyon lookout, but most visitors stay in the resort itself. Luxury flats (one double, two single beds), flats (four beds) and huts (four beds) are available. In all cases bedding and towels are supplied but not cooking utensils, crockery or cutlery. There is also a large caravan and camping site, with ablution blocks. A maximum of one caravan/tent, two vehicles and eight persons is permitted per site.

Eating and drinking The resort's licensed restaurant serves meals and refreshments. A shop next door sells frozen meat, bread, butter and other groceries, and also beer, wine and spirits. There are several field kitchens at the site for the use of caravanners and campers. There are braai facilities at the resort and at the canyon lookout. Visitors staying at Hobas must be self-sufficient, as there is no restaurant, only a kiosk which sells basic necessities.

Getting around There is a pleasant drive from Ai-Ais to the main canyon viewing point 78 km away, and two other lookouts are easily reached. Fuel is obtainable at Ai-Ais. No permits are necessary for the many short walks in the riverbed and mountains close to Ai-Ais. The long hike from the lookout to Ai-Ais along the canyon floor involves 85 km of walking and arduous scrambling over boulders and through deep sand, and takes four to five days (though some parties travel faster). Individual hikers are banned, the rules stipulating parties of at least three but no more than 40 people. The hike must be booked in advance and permits obtained from the Directorate of Tourism and Resorts, Ministry of Environment and Tourism, Private Bag 13267, Windhoek, telephone (09264) 61 23-6975/6/7/8, fax 22-4900. Medical certificates issued within 40 days prior to the hike must be handed in at Hobas before commencing the trail.

Scenic highlights The canyon is a place of rock and water but many plants have found a foothold. These include reeds and rushes in the riverbed and camelthorn and sweet thorn trees on the banks. Watch out for the kokerboom (quiver tree), Namaqua fig and the noorsdoring (*Euphorbia virosa*) on the canyon walls and rocky slopes. Clumps of melkbos (*Euphorbia gregaria*) are conspicuous on the plains above the canyon.

Wildlife Klipspringer are sometimes seen in the canyon but most visitors spot only baboon and rock dassie, as well as the spoor of leopard and Hartmann's mountain zebra. On the plains at Hobas, visitors may see mountain zebra and springbok. Birdlife includes ostrich (on the plains), hamerkop, grey heron and black eagle.

Special precautions When starting the hike, ensure you have enough food (including emergency rations). Despite its muddy appearance the water of the Fish River is drinkable but, if you want peace of mind, take water purification tablets with you. (If there is no water in the river, it is impossible to do the hike.) It is best to begin walking early in the morning, then stop at 11 a.m. and rest until about 3 p.m. Darkness falls rapidly, so allow time to choose a campsite.

Above: The stark beauty of the southern Namib coastline. **Top:** The 'desert rose', its 'petals' formed of gypsum crystals, is a familiar sight in the Namib.

aim was obviously to conserve the 'forest' for posterity – but unfortunately the move backfired. Visitors went to Gariganus not merely to admire the trees; they wanted to dig up a 'quiver tree' (commonly known as a kokerboom) and take it home with them. By 1981 people had removed more than 200 young trees, ignoring the threat of heavy penalties. Fortunately, strict access control subsequently put an end to this situation and enough of these trees remain to make a visit worthwhile. There is an entrance fee which also entitles visitors access to the Giant's Playground, a collection of bizarre natural rock formations created by the erosion of sedimentary material and the exposure of basalt rock laid down some 170 million years ago.

Camping and accommodation (single and double rooms) are available at the farm. Contact the owners at (09264) 638 1-1302/3.

NAMIBIA: **FISH RIVER CANYON**

A RAUCOUS GLUTTON

Above: A large colony of cormorants inhabits Sinclair Island, off the Namib coast. The Cape cormorant, distinguished by its yellow throat and dark plumage, is by far the most abundant of the four species found on the southern African coast. In a study conducted between 1977 and 1981, the breeding population was estimated at 314 000 birds at 24 breeding sites along the Namibian coast. The South African population was estimated at 212 000 birds breeding at 27 localities. Cormorants feed on a variety of small fish, supplementing their diet with crabs and squid. **Right:** An engraving of Ichaboe, one of the most important offshore islands, from Charles Andersson's book, *The Okavango River*.

Off the southern African coast, the islands that are home to colonies of Cape gannets are said to be among the noisiest, most crowded spots on earth (they are also rich repositories of guano, a natural fertiliser sought all over the world).

Gannets live in colonies of thousands, guarding their small nesting sites with startling ferocity: an encroaching bird is driven off with screeches and slashes of razor-sharp beaks. Because the colonies are so crowded, gannets have developed a few protective devices. Landing is as precise as possible, even though a descending gannet has difficulty halting the fall of its relatively heavy body – with tail widespread, webbed feet forward, body vertical and wings beating furiously to counter its momentum.

When a bird arrives at its colony, it immediately points its blue-grey bill skywards, indicating to the other gannets that it is not about to attack. It is then allowed access to its nest.

Phenomenal speed and great diving skill are among the gannet's many accomplishments. It hovers effortlessly above the sea on the lookout for fish (the eyes are so placed that it can look down while in level flight), plunging into the water after its prey like a feathered arrow. Such is its momentum that it descends many metres beneath the surface.

Most gannets feed on the teeming fish stocks of the Benguela Current, which runs along the west coast of southern Africa, sometimes following the sardine run up the east coast in June and July. They generally prey on surface fish such as mackerel, pilchard and mullet.

The Offshore Islands

The Fish River meets the Orange some 70 km south of Ai-Ais and its waters are carried to the sea. There it falls under the influence of the Benguela Current, the nutrient-rich stream that originates among Antarctic icebergs and fosters an abundant growth of plankton. The plankton feed hosts of fish and in turn the fish feed large colonies of seabirds, including gannet, cormorant and penguin, that breed on a long chain of rocks and islands off Namibia's shore. Seafarers of old knew the perilous landfalls as the Isles of Dead Ned.

The secret of Ned's identity and how he met his death may be lost forever, but the isles that bore his name saw one of the strangest booms in commercial history. During the 1840s British merchants became aware that the islands held huge accumulations of seabird droppings or guano, a substance that had only recently become valuable after scientists had pointed out its qualities as a fertiliser. On one of the islands (Ichaboe), to the north of Lüderitz, the guano was found to be deeper than seven metres in places. Ships raced south to recover as much of the guano as they could find.

As the months passed, many hundreds of ships anchored off Ichaboe. Thousands of men camped on its shores and laboured in guano pits that were pegged like mining claims. What happened to the displaced birds is not clearly recorded, though miscreant humans are known to have been pelted with dead penguins. By the middle of 1845 Ichaboe was stripped to the bare rock, and the process was repeated at other islands, including Roast Beef, Plumpudding, Pomona and Possession.

The boom faded as rapidly as it had begun and the ships and men sailed away. For two years the Isles of Dead Ned were left in peace.

KEETMANSHOOP'S FLYING SNAKE

Late in 1941, strange tales circulated in the lonely sheep-farming country between Keetmanshoop and Aroab to the east. Owambo shepherds reported seeing a giant snake 'as thick as a man's thigh' that 'flew from cliff to cliff' and frightened the sheep. Another man said he had been out hunting with dogs when a huge snake attacked one of them, rolled itself into a ball and 'flew up into the cliffs', taking the dog with it. Local farmers heard the stories but dismissed them with a smile.

Then early in 1942 a farmer's son, 16-year-old Michael Esterhuise, was watching sheep near a remote koppie when he saw a large reptile peering at him from a crevice. He thought it was a leguan or monitor lizard and threw a stone at it, upon which the creature 'growled like a dog', puffed up its throat and inflated 'fins' on the side of its head. Thoroughly alarmed, the boy rounded up the sheep and went home to tell his family.

A few days later Michael Esterhuise saw the 'thing' again, this time stretched on a ledge with its head and tail overhanging each end. It was more than seven metres long. He left it alone, but the following Tuesday, while he was watching his sheep near another koppie, he heard a sound 'like wind blowing through a pipe'. Looking up, he saw the reptile 'rolled up like a cartwheel' and flying at him from the top of the koppie. Its head protruded from the bottom and the 'fins' were extended.

The boy threw himself to one side, and with a great thud the snake landed where he had been sitting. The snake skidded on the gravel, then unfurled and straightened as the boy scrambled frantically to escape.

The huge snake lashed out twice with its tail, then curled it towards its head and with 'two short jerks' shot up into the air, cleared a five-metre tree and sped back to the top of the koppie. The boy was terrified. He ran for 200 m but collapsed behind some bushes, where his father later found him.

News of Michael Esterhuise's encounter spread through the district like wildfire, and a group of farmers formed a shooting party. Pat Honeybone, in command at Keetmanshoop police station, led the hunt. He and the farmers examined the spoor at the koppie and subsequently found many traces of the snake over a large area, sometimes alongside animal bones. But the reptile itself was not seen again, and the story was gradually forgotten.

Then a Cape Town merchant wondered if the birds were producing more guano – and found they were. From that time on, men have looked upon guano as a renewable resource, allowing the birds to breed on the islands and keep up their numbers.

Since 1866 the guano 'factories' have been under various forms of government protection. They were first proclaimed British territory in 1867 and then, in 1874, became part of the Cape Colony. Subsequently they were administered by South Africa until their reintegration (together with Walvis Bay) into Namibia on 1 March 1994. The smaller islands in this group, including Black Sophie, Sparrow-Hawk, Dumfudgeon, Eighty-Four, Boat Rock and Marshall Reef, were not annexed by Britain and have therefore always been considered Namibian territory.

The Isles of Dead Ned stretch for 350 km, from Sinclair (once known as Roast Beef Island) between Oranjemund and Lüderitz to Hollam's Bird Island, which lies 160 km south of Walvis Bay. All but two fall within a strip of 100 km from Sinclair Island to Ichaboe. Some are no more than rocks poking from the sea, but at the other end of the scale there is Possession, with a surface area of 90 hectares. Perhaps the strangest of all is Mercury, which is so honeycombed by erosion that it vibrates when hit by a large wave.

The Isles of Dead Ned are tantalising, but access to them is strictly controlled to protect the birds, including the African black-footed penguins, from human disturbance. The islands were proclaimed nature reserves by Cape Nature Conservation in 1988. The closest most visitors can come to the offshore islands is at Lüderitz, from where they may train binoculars on Halifax Island – only 90 m from the mainland. Penguin and Seal islands, with areas of 36 ha and 44 ha respectively, are clearly visible in Lüderitz Bay.

The Sperrgebiet

A large area of the southern Namib was decreed the *Sperrgebiet* (German for 'forbidden territory') in 1908 to protect the coastal diamond industry from theft and illegal prospecting. 'Diamond Area 1' originally stretched from the Orange River to the 26th parallel and was policed by the concession-holders, CDM (Pty) Limited of Oranjemund. Access was severely restricted and the only part that could be seen by the general public was the narrow strip that straddles the main road between Aus and Lüderitz. In 1990 the western half of Diamond Area 1, north of the

Aus/Lüderitz road, was incorporated into the Namib-Naukluft Park and four years later De Beers announced that it would relinquish about half of its remaining concession area in Diamond Area 1 to the state.

Also active in the area is the Namibian Minerals Corporation (NAMCO) which, in 1994, was awarded offshore diamond-mining concessions at Lüderitz and Hottentots Bay by the Namibian government. Diamonds are also prospected around the offshore islands.

Though the Sperrgebiet has shrunk considerably, security remains as tight as ever and even VIPs are not allowed in without an escort of diamond security officials. The section of Diamond Area 1 which now forms part of the Namib-Naukluft Park likewise remains forbidden to tourists, although the reason for this is the extreme fragility of the desert environment.

To open up some of the Sperrgebiet's attractions, CDM introduced tours to the ghost mining village of Elizabeth Bay in 1990. Three years later the tours were privatised and are now run by the Kolmanskop Tour Company. In addition to excursions to Kolmanskop and Elizabeth Bay, tours are also conducted to the Atlas Bay seal colony and the dramatic Bogenfels Arch, exploring the ghost mining village of Pomona en route.

Opposite page: A colony of Cape fur seals frolics along the coast of the southern Namib. The male reaches sexual maturity at two years (three years for the female), but becomes a fully active herd bull only three or four years later. **Above:** Plumpudding Island, one of more than three dozen islands that occur along the coast of Namibia. Guano, a valuable fertiliser, is deposited there by the large colonies of seabirds – mainly cormorant, gannet and penguin – that nest on the islands. Since these birds live on fish and other sea creatures, their droppings are especially rich in phosphorus and nitrogen.

PLANTS OF THE DESERT

Sarcocaulon patersonii (Bushman's candle)

The plants of the Namib are remarkable for the ways in which they have adapted to desert conditions, not merely surviving but actually thriving in the hostile environment.

Because the Namib receives very little rain and the heat quickly evaporates surface moisture, the indigenous plants have evolved many methods of storing water. Some species have developed small leaves (thus reducing the rate of transpiration and increasing the rate of cooling), some have leaves that drop off, and others have no leaves at all. The mesembryanthemums have converted their leaves into water storage tanks enclosed in leathery skin, while the *Ammocharis* lilies hoard their precious water supply in large underground bulbs.

One of the most common Namib plants, *Arthraerua leubnitziae*, lives through long periods of drought by shrinking. But one of the most fascinating survival methods is that employed by the so-called 'ephemerals', which pack their entire life cycle into the brief spell of good growing conditions following a rare desert shower. The seeds lie dormant during the dry period, but suddenly spring into life with the rain, burst into bloom, and release new seeds – all within a matter of days.

Fenestraria rhopalophylla (window plant)

Lithops (stone plant)

Mesembryanthemum (vygie)

Sarcocaulon crassicaule (Bushman's candle)

NAMIBIA: FISH RIVER CANYON

THE SCORPION THAT SQUIRTS ITS POISON

Parabuthus villosus, one of southern Africa's largest and most venomous scorpions, is shown above with its paralysed victim. This species produces a venom sufficiently powerful to kill a child, and has the ability to squirt its poison for a considerable distance when alarmed: if struck in the eyes, its victim may be blinded.

Scorpions are arachnids, not insects, although both are arthropods. They have a capacity for survival under extremely harsh conditions. Desert species of the genus *Parabuthus* are so resilient that they may be kept alive in a laboratory without food or water for as long as 12 months – as long as they are given a good meal at the start!

Although a relatively primitive life form, the scorpion is lethally efficient. Its large, claw-like pedipalps hold its prey while the segmented tail is brought over the head and down to deliver the sting. The two poison glands in the bulbous sting are surrounded by a muscular sheath which is compressed to inject the venom through two openings near the sharp tip. The dead or paralysed prey is chewed with the chelicerae (or jaws), while its soft parts are consumed in semi-liquid form.

The female scorpion, which is generally larger than the male, gives birth to 40 or more live young – each a colourless miniature of the adult, and already equipped with a gland charged with venom. The moment they are born, she gently lifts them with her pincers and places them in rows on her back, where they remain for some weeks while the mother feeds them with partly chewed portions of her prey.

All southern African scorpions belong to one of two families. Firstly there are the Scorpionidae, which have large pincers and small tails. This family relies mainly on its pincers for catching prey, and its tail sting is not especially dangerous.

The second family is that of the Buthidae, or 'stinging scorpions', which have relatively small pincers but a much larger tail, and a far more potent sting.

Reservations are essential, as both Elizabeth Bay and Bogenfels lie within the Sperrgebiet. Since mining is still practised at Elizabeth Bay, children under 14 years of age are not allowed on the tour. For additional information and to make reservations for the tours, contact Kolmanskop Tour Company, P O Box 357, Lüderitz, telephone (09264) 6331 2445, or fax 2526.

Because man has interfered so little with the land here, virtually the whole of the Sperrgebiet is an unspoilt wilderness, and conservationists see it as one of the most interesting areas in Namibia. As in much of Namibia, it is a stark, dry and sometimes searingly hot stretch of territory that would daunt even the boldest explorer. Daytime bathes its gravel plains in a relentless light, while nights can be icy. However, in spite of the harsh surroundings, brown hyena, black-backed jackal, gemsbok, springbok and ostrich seem to thrive in the area (as do seal colonies along the coast). One herd of gemsbok has even turned opportunist and each night steals into the outskirts of Oranjemund to graze on the diamond town's well-watered lawns.

Above: The black-backed gull is primarily a coastal seabird and is rarely seen far out to sea, though it frequently follows fishing trawlers and other vessels in the hope of picking up scraps of food. **Top:** The kokerboom (quiver tree) of Namibia was first recorded by Simon van der Stel in 1685. He noted that Bushmen (San) made quivers from its branches.

A land God made in anger

Bushman (San) hunters wandering through Namibia's harsh and inhospitable interior used to say: 'When God made this land, he must have been very angry.' Yet even in his anger God endowed the parched land with a gift of great and dramatic beauty. Much of Namibia's stark grandeur still remains intact in a select group of state-owned game parks and in many private reserves where man's influence has been little felt.

The largest of the state-owned parks in the central interior is attached to Hardap Recreation Resort and Game Park northwest of Mariental, which is also the home of the state-run Freshwater Fish Institute. Daan Viljoen Game Park – fascinating for its wealth of both flora and fauna – lies in the highlands some 24 km to the northwest of Windhoek. Close to Okahandja are the beauty spots of Gross-Barmen Hot Springs and Von Bach Recreation Resort, the latter sited around a dam that supplies the greater portion of Windhoek's water.

The small, privately owned Tsaobis Leopard Nature Park, popular with hikers, lies in the hilly Chuos Mountains, approximately 140 km west of Windhoek.

Auas Game Lodge

Encircled by the low mountains of the Windhoek Bergland, Auas Game Lodge takes its name from the mountain range which lies to the south of Windhoek.

In addition to kudu, warthog and a variety of small predators resident in the area when the sanctuary was proclaimed, herds of plains animals roam this large 10 000 ha private nature reserve. Among these are blue wildebeest, gemsbok, eland, springbok, red hartebeest and Burchell's zebra. Other mammals reintroduced include Hartmann's mountain zebra, giraffe, waterbuck and blesbok, while the dainty Damara dik-dik is also found. Crocodile are kept in a dam near the lodge and in a crocodile enclosure built in a setting closely resembling this mighty reptile's natural habitat.

The savannah is dominated by a variety of acacias, shepherd's tree, buffalo-thorn and wild olive, while conspicuous in the rivercourses are tall camelthorn and sweet thorn trees.

Guests can follow a self-guided walk, lasting between 60 and 90 minutes, to a dam near the lodge. From the hide overlooking its waters they can view the game as they come to drink, as well as a variety of waterbirds. Guided game drives in open vehicles are conducted both in the early morning and late afternoon – the latter usually incorporates sundowners at a prominent vantage point. From time to time guests are invited to enjoy sundowners at a sunset lapa, situated at the highest point in the reserve, from which a bird's-eye view may be had of the surrounding plains and undulating hills. Afterwards, guests are served a traditional braai before returning to the lodge – their vehicle fitted with a spotlight to seek out nocturnal creatures.

The lodge offers accommodation in 16 double rooms with *en suite* bathroom facilities, and one luxury suite. There is also a dining room, bar, reading room, swimming pool and thatched poolside area. It is conveniently situated close to Windhoek and the Windhoek International Airport. From the city, travel south on the B1 for 22 km and turn left onto the D1463 at Aris. Continue for a further 22 kilometres. Approaching from the airport, travel towards Windhoek for 15 km, turn left onto the C23 and, after 33 km, right again onto the D1463. Continue for a further 16 kilometres.

Left: Visitors enjoy the lush surroundings of the rest camp at Daan Viljoen.
Above: Ostriches wander among the rondavels at the rest camp in the Daan Viljoen Game Park, near Windhoek. Visitors have become used to seeing a variety of animals in the camp, which is built around a dam in the rolling hills of the Khomas Hochland. Because no large predators occur in the area, visitors are encouraged to explore the park on foot. As in most reserves, there is a prohibition on domestic pets, and dogs must be left in kennels at the entrance gates.

NAMIBIA: THE CENTRE

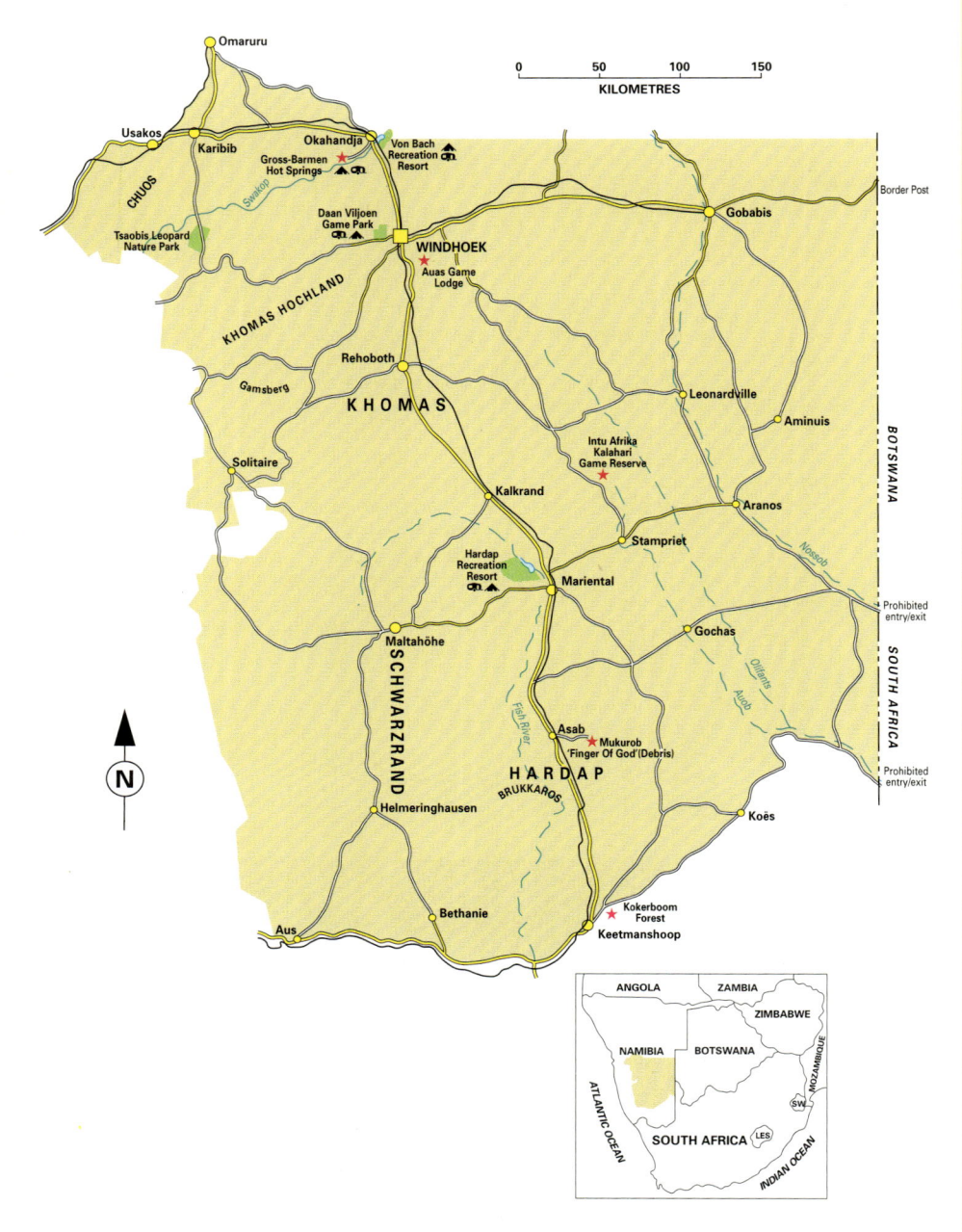

DAAN VILJOEN AT A GLANCE

When to go The park is open year round, but the best time to visit is between April and September. Try to avoid school holidays and long weekends. The park's gates open at sunrise and day visitors must leave by 6 p.m. Tourists staying in the park are allowed to enter until midnight.

Reservations and information To apply for accommodation, contact the Directorate of Tourism and Resorts, Ministry of Environment and Tourism, Private Bag 13267, Windhoek, telephone (09264) 61 23-6975/6/7/8, fax 22-4900. More information may be had from the Directorate of Tourism and Resorts, Ministry of Environment and Tourism, Private Bag 13346, Windhoek, telephone (09264) 61 284-2111, fax 22-1930.

Getting there The park is reached from Windhoek via a turn-off on the C28 through the Khomas Hochland to Swakopmund, and lies 21 km from the capital. From the turn-off there is a three km drive to the gates of the park.

Accommodation Daan Viljoen's rest camp has two-bed rondavels equipped with washbasins and kitchenettes. Bedding and towels are supplied, but not cooking utensils, crockery or cutlery. Breakfast is included in the price of the rondavels. There are communal ablution facilities. The large caravan and camping site has field kitchens and ablution blocks.

Eating and drinking A licensed restaurant serves meals and refreshments, while the kiosk next door stocks cooldrinks and sandwiches. There are braai facilities beside the bungalows, in the caravan and camping site, and at picnic places above the Augeigas Dam.

Getting around A 6,5 km gravel road takes visitors through the prettiest parts of the park. Many interesting paths cross its hills and ravines, and visitors are encouraged to pick their own routes. There is also a two-day overnight trail.

Special attractions Among the park's many attractions are the large swimming pool (at the rest camp), Augeigas Dam with its weeping willows and thatched 'umbrellas', a ruggedly beautiful setting of ravine and precipice, and a rich variety of shrubs, trees and other flora.

Wildlife The park accommodates eland, gemsbok, kudu, red hartebeest, blue wildebeest, Hartmann's mountain zebra and springbok. More than 200 bird species have been recorded.

For information and reservations, write to Auas Game Lodge, P O Box 80887, Windhoek, telephone (09264) 61 24-0043.

Daan Viljoen Game Park

It is difficult to say who is more appreciative of Daan Viljoen – the people of Windhoek, or those who come from far away to visit its attractions. Windhoek's inhabitants see it as a playground on their doorstep and flock there over weekends and during school holidays. Out-of-town visitors often stay at the rest camp in preference to hotels in the city. They sleep in cosy rondavels, eat in a well-run restaurant, enjoy the gamespotting and cool off in a large pool.

The Daan Viljoen Game Park is set in the Khomas Hochland, a topsy-turvy world of rolling hills and deep ravines. The reserve covers just under 4 000 ha at the eastern end of the highlands, and not the least of its attractions is a fine view of Windhoek – particularly impressive at sunset. With the capital so close, it is no surprise that the park's name honours the former Administrator of what was then called South West Africa, who was largely responsible for its establishment.

From a conservation point of view, Daan Viljoen is very important because, except for the Von Bach Recreation Resort, it is the only conservation area in the Khomas Hochland (classified as one of the 15 main vegetation zones in Namibia). In places the hills support thornscrub, but for the most part they are open and grassy with a few scattered trees. The ravines have richer vegetation, and so does the Augeigas, a seasonal stream that runs close to the western boundary of the park and is dammed and landscaped at the rest camp.

Daan Viljoen's game population is made up of the species that were always common in the Khomas Hochland area: Hartmann's mountain zebra, kudu, impala, gemsbok, eland, red hartebeest, blue wildebeest and a few springbok. The animals roam freely all over the park – even in the rest camp, which they enter in the late afternoon and by night to graze on the well-watered lawns.

Tourist roads are confined to a mere 600 ha of the park and the remainder is a wilderness closed to vehicles, not least because gradients are too steep for most cars. Tourists are not restricted to their vehicles, however, and are free to wander throughout the reserve. Two short trails, the easy 3 km 'Wag 'n bietjie' (Wait a minute) Trail, especially suitable for families with children, and the 9 km circular Rooibos Trail have been laid out for anyone wishing to explore further. The two-day/32 km Sweet Thorn Hiking Trail takes hikers over undulating hills and along scrubby river valleys in the north of the park (this area is closed to vehicles). A basic shelter is provided at the end of the first day's hike (take everything you need, including firewood).

Visitors who want a change from mammals can look out for the over 200 bird species that have been reported in the park – among them the rare Damara rockjumper, Monteiro's hornbill and the beautiful crimson-breasted shrike, sometimes known as the 'Reichsvogel' because its red, black and white feathers recall the colours of Imperial Germany.

The park is open all year. Overnight visitors with reserved accommodation may enter the camp until midnight. Day visitors are admitted from sunrise, but must make prior arrangements (telephone (09264) 61 22-6806) and leave the camp before 6 p.m. Apart from the rondavels, there are also campsites and picnic areas. For further information, contact the Directorate of Tourism and Resorts, Ministry of Environment and Tourism, Private Bag 13446, Windhoek, telephone (09264) 61 284-2111, or fax 22-1930.

To book accommodation and a place on the hiking trails, contact the Directorate of Tourism and Resorts, Ministry of Environment and Tourism, Private Bag 13267, Windhoek, telephone (09264) 61 23-6975/6/7/8, fax 22-4900.

Gross-Barmen Hot Springs

In 1977 this handsome spa was unveiled on the site of an old Rhenish mission station, 24 km southwest of Okahandja. Visitors are able to pamper themselves in a large thermal pool enclosed in a glass-walled hall, or cool off in the outdoor swimming pool which is also fed from the spring. The spa's modern camp offers bungalows, a restaurant, shop, and a caravan and camping site.

There are long walks along a riverbed running past the caravan and camping site, and rambles among stony koppies that overlook the resort may lead to encounters with baboon, warthog, or even a kudu or two. Gross-Barmen's reed-surrounded dam is considered a must for birdwatchers.

The resort, reached from a turn-off lying 1,7 km south of Okahandja, is open throughout the year. Overnight visitors with reserved accommodation may enter the resort at any time, but day visitors are admitted from sunrise and must leave the resort before 6 p.m. Day visitors must also make prior arrangements to visit by telephoning (09264) 621 50-1091.

Enquiries and applications for accommodation should be addressed to the Directorate of Tourism and Resorts, Ministry of Environment and Tourism, Private Bag 13267, Windhoek, telephone (09264) 61 23-6975/6/7/8, or fax 22-4900. For further information, contact the Directorate of Tourism and Resorts, Ministry of Environment and Tourism, Private Bag 13346, Windhoek, telephone (09264) 61 284-2111, or fax 22-1930.

Hardap Recreation Resort and Game Park

When Hardap Dam filled with water in 1963, one of the islands created provided an unexpected windfall for Namibia's white pelicans – a protected breeding place. At times up to 800 birds congregate on the island and, with up to 100 breeding pairs, it is the largest permanent colony of its kind in Namibia, and the only artificial wetland in southern Africa supporting a breeding colony of this species.

Classified as rare, the only other permanent breeding colony of pelican in Namibia is on the Bird Rock guano platform to the north of Walvis Bay, which supports some 60 breeding pairs. Sporadic breeding also occurs when large areas of Etosha Pan and the more northerly Lake Oponono are filled with water after rains. In South Africa there are only two breeding colonies – one on Dassen Island, which lies approximately 58 km northwest of Table Bay, and at Lake St Lucia on the northern KwaZulu-Natal coast.

Above: Cyphostemma juttae (wild grape) is an attractive and hardy succulent which produces its brightly coloured clusters of 'grapes' near the end of summer. The papery skin around the thick trunk peels off continuously as the plant grows. *Right:* A black-headed heron peers across tall grass near the Hardap Dam, haven for a large variety of waterfowl.

HARDAP AT A GLANCE

When to go The resort and game park are open throughout the year. Overnight visitors with reserved accommodation may enter the resort at any time, but day visitors are admitted only from sunrise and must leave the park by 6 p.m.

Reservations and information For reservations, contact the Directorate of Tourism and Resorts, Ministry of Environment and Tourism, Private Bag 13267, Windhoek, telephone (09264) 61 23-6975/6/7/8, fax 22-4900. For further information, contact the Directorate of Tourism and Resorts, Ministry of Environment and Tourism, Private Bag 13346, Windhoek, telephone (09264) 61 284-2111, fax 22-1930.

Getting there The park is reached along the B1 leading north from Mariental to Windhoek. The Hardap Dam turn-off is signposted and, from the B1, it is 6 km to the entrance gate.

Accommodation The resort offers fully furnished luxury 'flats' (actually bungalows, with five beds in two bedrooms, kitchenette, shower and carport); ordinary 'flats' (three beds in one bedroom, kitchenette and shower); and dormitories (intended for youth groups, with ten beds and a supervisor's room). In all cases towels and bedding are supplied, but not cooking utensils, crockery and cutlery. There are also caravan and camping sites.

Eating and drinking There is a restaurant above the dam. A shop and a kiosk (selling cooldrinks and takeaways) are also available. There are braai facilities at the bungalows, in the caravan and camping site and at picnic sites, but not in the reserve.

Getting around Inside the reserve are 82 km of gravel roads leading to a lookout and other special features. Beware of dongas caused by floods and do not leave the road, or you may get stuck in sand. Fuel is available at the entrance gate.

Special attractions An aquarium adjoining the resort office has specimens of the fish stocking the dam and a pictorial introduction to the species found in Namibia.

Wildlife Visitors may see kudu, gemsbok, red hartebeest, Hartmann's mountain zebra, eland, springbok, steenbok, black rhino and some 260 bird species.

Fishing There is a special area for fishing from the dam shore, but many anglers go out in boats or fish in the river below the dam. Angling licences are available at the rest camp.

Above: The Cape wolf snake has sharp wolf-like teeth which enable it to maintain a firm grip on smooth-scaled lizard prey.

Lying mostly on the southern side of the dam, across the water from the smart Hardap Recreation Resort, is the 25 000 ha game park. The resort was established in 1964 and the game park was proclaimed four years later, the result of the merging of several farms. Today it accommodates healthy populations of kudu, gemsbok, red hartebeest, eland, Hartmann's mountain zebra and springbok, as well as Namibia's southernmost population of black rhino. There was once a large cheetah population which exploded beyond control with the rich pickings available and was, as a result, relocated to other parks. Over 260 bird species have been recorded.

Most Namibians visit Hardap simply to relax (the resort has tennis courts and a swimming pool) or to pursue watersports – freshwater angling (for barbel, mudfish, tilapia and yellowfish), boardsailing and boating. Foreign visitors, on the other hand, are primarily interested in exploring the game park and its attractions across the water.

The road to Hardap runs along the top of the dam wall and, once inside the game fence, it enters a world of stone and thorn, a challenging landscape of rocky koppies and deep dongas created by heavy floods of the past. The road takes visitors on an 82 km circle through the park, and from a lookout high on a plateau they may see the great dam as a ribbon of blue on the horizon. The more adventurous leave their cars there and blaze their own hiking trail through the park to reach the dam's shores. There is a 15 km loop walk through the northern end of the reserve. A short cut across its middle converts it into a 9 km hike for those feeling the strain. Take care, however, as the route is sometimes indistinct in places. For more information, contact the Directorate of Tourism and Resorts, Ministry of Environment and Tourism, Private Bag 13346, Windhoek, telephone (09264) 61 284-2111, or fax 22-1930. To make reservations, contact the Directorate of Tourism and Resorts, Ministry of Environment and Tourism, Private Bag 13267, Windhoek, or telephone (09264) 61 23-6975/6/7/8, fax 22-4900.

Intu Afrika Kalahari Game Reserve

Few people realise that the red sands of the Kalahari extend up to 230 km westwards into Namibia. Situated northeast of Mariental, on the edge of this mighty desert, is the Intu Afrika Kalahari Game Reserve – an unspoilt tract of land dominated by undulating dunes, sandy plains and magnificent camelthorn trees.

Large game species, such as the eland, gemsbok, springbok and blue wildebeest typical of the Kalahari, as well as giraffe, kudu and Burchell's zebra, have been resettled in this 15 000 ha reserve. Predators include the bat-eared and Cape fox, caracal, African wild cat and a pair of leopard which are housed in a 1 ha enclosure. Among the approximately 120 recorded bird species are the pygmy falcon, giant eagle owl and both the kori and Ludwig's bustards. Synonymous with the Kalahari and unlikely to escape the visitor's attention are the enormous communal nests of the sociable weaver (*Philetairus socius*).

About 40 Bushmen (San) people from the Gobabis district were settled on the reserve early in 1996 and guests may meet them in their traditional village and learn a little about their age-old traditions. Other activities at Intu Afrika include walks lasting between one and two hours, under the expert guidance of a Bushman (San) tracker, night drives (available on request), and two- to three-day accompanied walking trails.

The lodge comprises a lounge, restaurant, bar, swimming pool and boma where visitors dine. Accommodation ranges from luxury twin-bed rooms to equally well-appointed two-bed chalets – all with *en suite* facilities. The open-plan chalets, comprising one bedroom and a lounge, are widely spaced to ensure privacy, and are discreetly tucked below shady trees. A short distance from the lodge is a tented camp with communal ablutions.

To reach the reserve from Windhoek, turn left onto the C21 at Kalkrand and continue for 44 km to the D1268. Turn right and continue for about 22,5 km to the reserve entrance. From Mariental, travel north for some 7 km and turn right onto the C20. After about 20 km turn left onto the D1268. The entrance to Intu Afrika lies some 45 km along this road. The lodge lies a few kilometres beyond the entrance along a road suitable for ordinary vehicles. For further information, contact Intu Afrika Kalahari Game Reserve, P O Box 40047, Windhoek, telephone (09264) 61 24-8741, or fax 22-6535.

Tsaobis Leopard Nature Park

During 1969 a Swiss conservationist, Dr August Juchli, established a sanctuary for leopards on a 35 000 ha farm in the Chuos Mountains south of Karibib. Although free-ranging leopard do roam in the park (the oldest in Namibia), visitors are warned that they are elusive and hard to spot. Several animal species, including leopard, are kept in enclosures at the rest camp. Among these are cheetah, wild dog, aardwolf, caracal, Hartmann's mountain zebra and gemsbok. Since the animals are either hand-reared or bred in captivity, they are extremely tame, and offer excellent opportunities for photography. As far as is known, Tsaobis is the only centre which has succeeded in breeding aardwolf in captivity, and it is the first in Namibia to breed cheetah under the same conditions.

Although there are no demarcated walks, visitors are encouraged to explore the park on foot. In addition to the abundant birdlife, trailists may also spot kudu, Hartmann's mountain zebra, springbok, giraffe, klipspringer and a variety of smaller animals in the wild. Since the roads are not suitable for sedan vehicles, guests may book guided 4x4 trips lasting from four to seven hours.

The park's attractive rest camp offers self-catering two-bed bungalows with separate living and sleeping quarters. There is also a swimming pool. Enquiries and applications for accommodation should be made direct to Tsaobis Leopard Nature Park, P O Box 143, Karibib, telephone (09264) 6-2252 and ask for Karibib 1304.

To reach Tsaobis from Karibib (it is open throughout the year), drive south on the C32 for 68 km to the signposted turn-off. The rest camp is 10 km from the turn-off.

Von Bach Recreation Resort

Like Hardap Dam to the south, the attractive Sartorius von Bach storage dam just outside Okahandja is popular with aquatic sport enthusiasts, including yachtsmen, waterskiers and fishermen.

Fish found in the dam include blue kurper, large-mouth bass and small-mouth yellowfish. Permits are needed, and these may be purchased at the entrance gate.

This hilly resort is 4 285 ha in extent and provides sanctuary for numerous kudu as well as eland, Hartmann's mountain zebra, springbok, and baboon, as well as numerous bird species. Accommodation is available in a two-bed hut (no bedding is provided), and there are also caravan and camping sites for overnight visitors. There are no cooking facilities, except braai places. Picnic sites are available for day visitors and there are communal ablution blocks.

Von Bach Dam is reached from a turn-off 1 km south of Okahandja on the road to Windhoek. It is open throughout the year, from sunrise to sunset. Pets are not allowed.

Day visitors must make prior arrangements by telephoning (09264) 621 50-1475. For more detailed information, contact the Directorate of Tourism and Resorts, Ministry of Environment and Tourism, Private Bag 13346, Windhoek, or telephone (09264) 61 284-2111, fax 22-1930. To make reservations, write to the Directorate of Tourism and Resorts, Ministry of Environment and Tourism, Private Bag 13267, Windhoek, or telephone (09264) 61 23-6975/ 6/7/8, fax 22-4900.

A DEMOLISHED DEITY

The spectacular rock formation known as 'Mukurob' – popularly known as 'the finger of God' – was one of Namibia's most evocative natural symbols. A vertical column of sandstone and shale strata, it stood 34 m high and perched precariously on a pedestal of Karoo slate. Nature had gradually formed it in the course of some 60 million years. Then, on 8 December 1988, it was instantly toppled from its throne – probably by a combination of creeping weathering and fracturing of the thin mudstone neck, which caused the formation to collapse under its own weight. It has also been suggested that the demise of Mukurob could have been hastened by an earthquake that occurred in Armenia the previous day. Great was Mukurob's fall!

Etymologists disagree with the popular translation 'finger of God'. To the ancient Quena, or Khoikhoi, Mukurob (accent on the second syllable: mukoorob) was quite simply a term for the 'creator' or 'highest god'. It stood at the centre of Quenaland and was a religious symbol of enormous significance to the local people.

To view the shattered remains of this demolished deity, turn east onto a gravel road at Asab, on the highway between Mariental and Keetmanshoop, and drive for 24 kilometres. In 1955 the bulbous 'finger' was declared a national monument.

Mountains and a sea of sand

In 1965 the American space capsule Gemini V orbited Earth for eight days with astronauts Gordon Cooper and Pete Conrad at the controls. The men circled the globe 120 times and were able to take hundreds of remarkable photographs of its surface, some so detailed that they showed the wake of ships at sea and the course of roads and railways. One of the most revealing was taken from above the dry Kuiseb River, and scanned a large area of the central Namib Desert.

In the photograph, Walvis Bay's fine harbour appears as a hook of land grappling with the blue Atlantic to the west. About 48 km to the south, the shifting sandspit that closes Sandwich (known also as Sandvis) Harbour is a faint ribbon of pink with a large lagoon trapped behind it. Wave after wave of red dunes run parallel with the coast, forming a sea of sand that stretches 120 km inland. Yet to the north, the dunes are cut off by the Kuiseb River and give way to gravel plains.

As the photograph showed, the Kuiseb bisects the Namib, which is one of the oldest and driest deserts in the world, to demarcate sharply the dune sea and gravel plains. Periodic floods washed away the northern tentacles of dunes before the sand had a chance to 'walk' across the riverbed and overwhelm the other bank. Today the lower Kuiseb is a part of the Namib-Naukluft Park, which contains vast areas of the desert as well as the Naukluft Mountains, stronghold of Hartmann's mountain zebra. The park's total area is 4,9 million hectares. The richest vegetation is to be found in the beds of the Kuiseb and Swakop rivers: even the dunes support several plant species.

Because the park is so large it can be divided into three areas. The Namib section in the north includes the beds of the Swakop and Kuiseb rivers, Welwitschia Plains (a home of the plant *Welwitschia mirabilis*), Sandwich Harbour and the Kuiseb River Canyon.

The sand section from the Kuiseb southwards includes the dramatic Sesriem Canyon and Sossusvlei – which lies among the world's highest dunes. The Naukluft section, once a separate reserve, has some spectacular mountain formations and beautiful valleys with perennial springs. To the west of the park lies Walvis Bay with its variety of birdlife in the bird sanctuary and at the lagoon which lies on the outskirts of the town.

Namib-Naukluft Park

Although Namibia's largest park was proclaimed only in 1979, most of its components have enjoyed conservation status for much longer. The Namib section in the north was proclaimed 'Game Reserve 3' by Governor Friedrich von Lindequist in 1907, which makes it a contemporary of Etosha National Park. The dune sea in the south was part of the Sperrgebiet for half a century before being incorporated into the park. Naukluft in the east was originally a farm that was bought by Namibia's administration in 1966 to provide a refuge for mountain zebra.

The administration steadily enlarged the 'Naukluft Mountain Zebra Park' by acquiring more farms, eventually linking the reserve with the dunes of the Namib by opening a 30-km-wide corridor. Today Namib-Naukluft is one of the three largest conservation areas in Africa (the other two are Selous Game Reserve in Tanzania and the Central Kalahari Game Reserve in Botswana). Springbok and gemsbok can now migrate freely from the Naukluft section of the park to the spreading plains and dune sea of the west. North and south of the corridor are the only two major rivers south of the Kuiseb, the Tsondab and the Tsauchab. From their origin in the mountains, they flow westwards into the dune sea until they are eventually trapped among the dunes.

The rivers end at Tsondabvlei and Sossusvlei respectively, both clay-floor pans in a

Left: Goanikontes, an oasis on the Swakop River (47 km from the town of Swakopmund). The oasis, situated in a deep ravine flanked by dark-coloured hills, is a popular picnicking and camping spot. **Above left:** 'The dancing white lady.' This unusual spider, seen here digging a burrow, owes its name to its habit of rearing up aggressively when threatened. However, it is possibly even better known for its method of descending a Namib dune: it folds its legs inwards and launches itself down the slope like a tiny, furry cartwheel. The dancing white lady hunts mainly during the night, sometimes capturing prey larger than itself. **Above right:** The sidewinding adder (*Bitis peringueyi*) has developed an unusual way of crossing the loose sand of the Namib, moving in a series of thrusts which leave the distinctive trail of parallel lines. This small adder can achieve a surprising speed with its seemingly awkward method of locomotion.

NAMIBIA: **THE NAMIB**

cul-de-sac of sand that at Sossusvlei towers more than 350 m above the riverbed. Geographers believe that the rivers once flowed to the sea, and there is evidence that the Tsondab's water still seeps some considerable distance through the sand to emerge at Conception Bay on the coast. Tsondabvlei has a rich growth of trees which provide a haven for lappet-faced vultures, and for this reason it is closed to all visitors except scientific researchers.

Sossusvlei, which is the most accessible part of this huge sand sea covering over 3,2 million ha of western Namibia, provides visitors with their closest view of the Namib's desert sands. At different times of day the dunes appear ivory-white, golden, ochre, orange or maroon. Sesriem (six thongs) campsite is the gateway to the spectacular Sossusvlei. The nearby canyon was so named because early travellers found that, to draw water from the bottom with a bucket, they needed to knot together six harness thongs (*osrieme*). From the campsite the road traverses the gravel plains and then follows the valley swept clean by the Tsauchab River when it occasionally comes down in flood. The first 60 km are negotiable in ordinary sedan cars, but the final 5 km demand a 4x4 vehicle. Wildlife found here includes springbok, gemsbok and ostrich.

In spite of the rivers and the corridor, the Naukluft is inevitably the incongruity in the Namib's *mélange* of ecosystems. One geologist has described it as 'a mass of rock that once formed the top of a range of mountains. But somehow it slipped sideways and travelled at least 70 km to reach its present position, riding over softer formations or crumpling them up and pushing them from behind. You can see the folds in the rock.'

The small Naukluft campsite is the starting point of the 120 km/eight-day Namib-Naukluft Hiking Trail and shorter alternatives (*see separate entry*). Also within the park is the Naukluft 4x4 Trail, opened in 1995 and the first of its kind in a conservation area in Namibia. It starts near the Naukluft campsite and is a 73 km/two-day test of driving skills across the plateau, forging some of the steepest off-road routes in southern Africa. Trailists overnight in A-frame shelters on the plateau at Tjeriktik. On winter mornings zebra can be seen sunning themselves on the slopes, standing broadside to the sun, whereas in warmer conditions they almost always face away from the sun.

A former chief of research employed by Namibia's conservation authority, Dr Eugene Joubert, spent three years studying the species as part of his doctorate in wildlife management. He explained that the reason for the zebra's preferred stance was that the dark stripes on their coats absorbed more heat than the lighter-coloured areas.

He noted that a Hartmann's zebra, standing broadside on, displayed a body surface with a light to dark ratio of 1:3, whereas the ratio changed to 3:1 when it faced away, thus reducing the exposure of areas which absorbed the most heat. This fact, combined with the difference in total body surface when viewed laterally and posteriorly, made the orientation of body surfaces to physical stimuli an important factor in the adaptation of the Hartmann's zebra to its environment.

Dr Joubert made equally fascinating discoveries about the zebra's social life. He described a typical family unit, consisting of an adult dominant stallion, one or more mares and their foals. The stallion was nominally the head of the group's social organisation, wrote Dr Joubert, but played no conspicuous role in the daily social organisation of the family unit. Its role was rather more outwardly directed, protecting its family group against predators and other encroaching stallions. Anyone in the family group – most often it is a mare – gives the alarm when danger threatens. The male then usually takes up a position between the source of danger and the rest of the family group.

When the family group takes flight the dominant stallion shows a tendency to bring up the rear. The advantage of this behaviour to the survival of the species is clear. It allows the mares who are important for breeding purposes a greater margin of safety.

The pecking order is most obvious at a dustbath, where the mares take turns to wallow, in strict order of seniority. But in spite of the occasional bad feeling, it takes more than an encroaching stallion to split the family. A young stallion was once observed making a successful challenge for a group of four mares. It forced out the stallion that had formed the family, but was interested only in two of the mares, and tried to lose the others. They refused to leave and the young victor ended up having to accept all four.

Namib-Naukluft: Gobabeb
The lower reaches of the Kuiseb River have been the desert home of the Topnaar Khoikhoi for many generations. They are livestock farmers, keeping mainly goats and small numbers of cattle, and form a permanent population in the Namib-Naukluft Park. Their numbers are

Above: Flamingoes make their graceful way over the tall dunes at Sandwich. These beautiful birds, with their wings tinted red and black, and their black-tipped, pink bills, provide an unforgettable sight as they soar in formation over the desert. Sandwich was visited twice by ships of the Dutch East India Company in the 1670s, and two centuries later (between 1904 and 1906) was used to route smuggled arms to Khoikhoi and Herero rebels.

not great, but their stamp on the Namib is indelible. Part of their rich heritage is evident in the scores of curious place names like Gobabeb, 'the place of the fig tree'. They refer to the moaning west wind as 'soo-oop wa'.

In 1960 Gobabeb was selected as the site for a permanent research station, as it has access to the central Namibia's three main ecosystems – dunes, riverbeds and gravel plains. The complex was opened in 1963.

Today the Namib Research Institute, with its small staff of scientists and conservationists, attracts researchers in many fields from all over the world. They live here in bungalows and caravans clustered around a block containing offices and laboratories. At the heart of this community is the Desert Ecological Research

Unit, established in 1966 through the foresight of a famous Austrian entomologist, Dr Charles Koch. Originally funded by South Africa's Council for Scientific and Industrial Research (CSIR) and the Transvaal Museum, the institute now derives its funding from research and education grants, donor funds, a membership organisation and other sources. However, the physical infrastructure of the institute is maintained by the Ministry of Environment and Tourism in Windhoek.

The unit's director, American-born ecologist Dr Mary Seely, arrived at Gobabeb as a research biologist in 1967 and became director after the death of Dr Koch in 1970. She is a world authority on arid-land ecology, and has done much to make Gobabeb world-famous.

Gobabeb has a resident staff of about 20 people, attached to the Desert Ecological Research Unit of the Desert Research Foundation of Namibia, and the Namib Research Institute. Visiting scientists – among them geologists studying the dunes, archaeologists looking for signs of ancient humans, ornithologists, zoologists and entomologists – stay at Gobabeb for up to a year.

To avoid unnecessary disruption of the research work in progress, Gobabeb is out of bounds to casual visitors. However, the centre does hold one or two 'open days' each year. These feature self-guided nature trails, lectures, field excursions and educational demonstrations by the Topnaar community. For details, contact The Director, Desert Research Foundation of Namibia, P O Box 20232, Windhoek, telephone (09264) 61 22-9855, or fax 23-0172; or Friends of Gobabeb, P O Box 6063, Windhoek, telephone as above.

Early research focused mainly on various aspects of the Namib, including the astonishingly rich variety of animal life that is one of the Namib's chief attractions – life in miniature, so varied and abundant that scientists regard the Namib as one of the most fascinating deserts in the world. However, in more recent years, the focus has shifted to research into arid and semi-arid environments, research training, environmental education and the establishment of a database on combating desertification internationally.

In many ways, the sand environment has more in common with the sea than with conventional solid ground. When disturbed by the wind, the sand flows and ripples like water, and the cloud of sand 'smoke' sometimes blown from the top of a dune resembles a cloud of spray. Many desert creatures have webbed feet or paddles that help them 'swim' through the sand, and even the food chain that supports them is like the chain in the sea: wind-blown detritus takes the place of plankton, primary feeders (insects) eat the detritus, while the predators eat the primary feeders.

NAMIB-NAUKLUFT AT A GLANCE

When to go In view of the Naukluft's popularity and the limited number of campsites (there are only four), advanced reservations are essential. Likewise, sites at Sesriem should also be booked ahead. The Namib Research Institute at Gobabeb may not be visited without special permission from The Director, Desert Research Foundation of Namibia, P O Box 20232, Windhoek, telephone (09264) 61 22-9855, or fax 23-0172; or Friends of Gobabeb, P O Box 6063, Windhoek, telephone as above.

Permits and information If you stay on the proclaimed main roads you may drive through the park without a permit. If you want to see more, apply for a permit from the Directorate of Tourism and Resorts, Ministry of Environment and Tourism, Private Bag 13267, Windhoek, telephone (09264) 61 23-6975/6/7/8, or fax 22-4900. For further information, contact the Directorate of Tourism and Resorts, Ministry of Environment and Tourism, Private Bag 13346, Windhoek, telephone (09264) 61 284-2111, or fax 22-1930. You may also apply to the Ministry offices in Swakopmund, as well as some filling stations in Swakopmund and Walvis Bay. The Ministry issues a sketch-map of the Namib section of the park: ask for it in Swakopmund or Windhoek.

Getting there From Windhoek, the most popular approach is by the main road to Swakopmund, but a more scenic route crosses the Gamsberg Pass before continuing through the park to Walvis Bay. To reach Naukluft, drive via Solitaire (249 km from Windhoek) to Büllsport. Alternatively, travel via Klein Aub and Rietoog to Büllsport, continue along the D854 for 9 km, turn right and follow the road for 12 km to reach the Naukluft office. To reach Sesriem and Sossusvlei from Solitaire, continue south along Route 36 for 71 km, turning right onto the D826 and continuing for 12 kilometres.

Accommodation There is no hutted accommodation in the park (though Walvis Bay and Swakopmund are nearby), but there are 11 official overnight camping sites scattered throughout the Namib section. Facilities are basic, with picnic tables, braai sites and toilets. The sites include Homeb (in the bed of the Kuiseb River); Ganab (near a watering point that is a good place to watch game); Welwitschia Plains (best known for the fascinating *Welwitschia mirabilis*); Naukluft and Sesriem,

which has 18 camping sites and two ablution blocks. Fuel, wood and a small shop selling basic provisions are available at Sesriem. No camping is allowed at Sossusvlei. There is a swimming pool at Sesriem. The Sossusvlei Karos Lodge, situated just outside the Sesriem entrance gate, offers 45 *en suite* bedrooms under canvas, a restaurant, bar and swimming pool. For information and reservations, contact Karos Central Reservations, P O Box 87534, Houghton 2041, telephone (011) 484-1641, or fax 484-6206.

Eating and drinking Take all the food and water (extremely important) you will need, and emergency supplies in case your vehicle breaks down. You should also pack your own firewood (you are not allowed to collect firewood in the park).

Getting around Fuel is available at Sesriem, Büllsport and Solitaire, but otherwise motorists should fill up at Walvis Bay or Swakopmund.

The 120 km Namib-Naukluft Hiking Trail takes eight days, although it can be hiked in shorter sections. Hiking is permitted between 1 March and 31 October. Groups must comprise a minimum of three to a maximum of 12 persons. Only water, toilet facilities and basic shelter are provided. Written bookings are accepted up to 18 months in advance, but are confirmed only 11 months prior to the reservation date. Telephone bookings can be made 11 months in advance. Day trails through the Naukluft include the seven-hour Waterkloof Trail and the five-hour Olive Trail. The four-hour Welwitschia Trail can be explored by drivers using a brochure, which corresponds with numbered beacons at points of interest along the way. The 4x4 trail takes two days to complete, with overnight facilities available for 16 people.

Fishing Angling spots may be found down the coast between Walvis Bay and Sandwich (but you will need a 4x4 vehicle to reach them). Permits to visit Sandwich are obtainable from the Environment and Tourism Ministry's offices in Swakopmund or from certain filling stations in Swakopmund and Walvis Bay. However, no fishing is allowed south of the fence at Sandwich.

Wildlife Gemsbok, springbok and ostrich are the most visible species on the gravel plains. Hartmann's mountain zebra abound in the Naukluft. In the dunes and near the Kuiseb, watch for beetles and listen for the barking gecko at sundown.

THE ENTERPRISING ANT

Ants of the species *Camponotus detritus*.

Studies of desert ants have revealed that they are one of the most abundant and ecologically important groups of animals. In fact, in almost all terrestrial ecosystems, social insects such as ants, wasps, bees and termites are frequently the ecologically dominant animals.

It is a remarkable but little-known fact that, in terms of biomass and food consumption, the social insects exceed all the vertebrates (mammals, reptiles and birds) put together. In other words, the weight of all the lions, elephants, antelope, rodents, lizards, snakes, eagles, owls and sparrows, to mention but a few of the vertebrates that occur in a natural ecosystem such as Etosha Pan, would fall short of that of all the social insects in that area! The possible importance of ants in the Namib Desert has resulted in two scientists devoting their sojourn at Gobabeb to the study of ants.

While studying the ecology of the Namib dune ant for her master's degree, Barbara Curtis (who now runs Etendeka Mountain Camp (*see separate entry*) with her husband Dennis Liebenberg) found that *Camponotus detritus* was the predominant species in the dunes. It is a large ant that lives in colonies of up to 20 000 individuals, and is found at the base of sand dunes, where it spends much of its time climbing the typically sparse vegetation of that zone (usually grass) in search of scale insects. These insects secrete a sugar-rich fluid known as honeydew, and this forms the ant's staple diet.

It is an aggressive species of ant, sometimes biting and squirting formic acid at creatures which happen to disturb it. Excavating nests to determine the number of individuals is consequently an uncomfortable experience for the investigating scientist. The ant is also highly aggressive towards rival colonies of its own species and stray ants are frequently waylaid and killed, literally by being torn to pieces.

The gravel plains are the habitat of some 30 ant species, and in some areas up to 12 species live together. How can so many species coexist and find sufficient food in this apparently barren and harsh habitat? Research by Dr Alan Marsh has shown that their coexistence can be attributed to differences in their activity patterns and diets. While some are active during the early mornings and late afternoons, others forage during the heat of the day, and yet others emerge only after sunset. Their diets are, likewise, different, ranging from mainly seed and plant material to arthropod remains and the honeydew secretion of scale insects.

From the west comes a breeze cooled by the Benguela Current off the coast and, with it, frequent fogs that creep inland and blanket the dunes. The fog brings moisture that, in the right conditions, condenses into tiny droplets on detritus, sand grains, the sparse vegetation, even the desert creatures, and many of them have evolved special methods of capturing it. The most inventive are four species of beetle. Three of the species belong to one genus, *Lepidochora* (sometimes referred to as 'flying saucers'). Normally they remain below the surface of the dune until sunset, when they emerge to search for detritus, but on a foggy morning they appear in great numbers and plough a narrow trench – up to a metre in length – in the damp sand. On either side is a ridge which catches extra moisture and the beetles then extract this moisture from the damp ridges. The beetles bide their time until droplets form, then move down the trench and gather the moisture.

The most celebrated Namib beetle is *Onymacris unguicularis*, which has been described as a living condensation unit. During the night it shelters in the slip-face of a dune, but on a foggy morning it climbs slowly to the top and virtually does a handstand, with its head facing down and its back near vertical and facing the wind to collect moisture. The fog condenses and little droplets roll down the beetle's back, eventually reaching its mouth. Then the beetle drinks its fill.

Namib-Naukluft: Hiking trails

The Naukluft is one of the most varied areas of Namibia, and most visitors to the park come to hike one of two day walks, Waterkloof Trail and Olive Trail. Bookings need not be made but, if you wish to overnight at the Naukluft campsite, make reservations well in advance. Waterkloof Trail is a seven-hour/17 km loop which begins at the Naukluft campsite, passes natural pools formed by the Naukluft River, crosses a plateau with panoramic views over the surrounding undulating hills and valleys, and descends a waterfall before returning to the starting point. Olive Trail, which takes its name from the olive trees that grow along it, is a 10 km loop that climbs onto the plateau overlooking the rugged mountainscape, descends a deep canyon (chain-assisted in one difficult spot) and returns along a jeep track.

The Naukluft Hiking Trail can be hiked either as a 120 km circular route over eight days, or two four-day linear routes of 58 and 62 km each, with an option of a 63 km/four-day circular route. Hikers booked for the last four-day route must inform the conservation officer at Naukluft beforehand (telephone (09264) 6638 and ask for Nudaus 4131).

Most of the terrain covered by both the trails crosses the mountain plateau, affording beautiful views across the multihued desert plains below. Water is available at the overnight stops, but on each day's hike it is advisable to carry at least two to three litres of water per person, as the springs and windmills along the trail could dry up during periods of drought. Also be sure to take enough food – if you can't carry enough supplies for the eight-day hike, leave a supply cache at the Tsams-Ost Shelter before you leave. Animals likely to be seen include baboon, Hartmann's mountain zebra, kudu and a variety of reptiles.

Hiking is permitted only between 1 March and 31 October because of soaring summer temperatures and potentially heavy rainfall. Groups must consist of a minimum of three to a maximum of 12 people, each of whom needs to have obtained a doctor's medical certificate

Left: Hartmann's mountain zebra in the Namib-Naukluft Park. **Above:** A white-backed vulture, the most common vulture in Namibia. This species builds its nest in a tree, laying only one egg which is incubated by both parents for about two months. Like other vultures, this (summer-nesting) species does not require rain as a stimulus for breeding. The adult vulture is distinguished by its white back and wing-coverts, which are darker than those of the widely spread Cape vulture.

issued less than 40 days before the hike. For more information, contact the Directorate of Tourism and Resorts, Ministry of Environment and Tourism, Private Bag 13346, Windhoek, telephone (09264) 61 284-2111, or fax 22-930.

To make reservations, contact the Directorate of Tourism and Resorts, Ministry of Environment and Tourism, Private Bag 13267, Windhoek, telephone (09264) 61 23-6975/6/7/8, fax 22-4900.

Namib-Naukluft: Kuiseb River Canyon

About 70 km northwest of the Naukluft is another geological phenomenon, the great canyon of the Kuiseb River. Like the Fish River in the south, the Kuiseb must once have been far more powerful than it is today – it has gouged a deep trough in the soft rock of the interior plateau. Seen from above, the inside of the canyon is a bewildering hotchpotch of domed hills and long ridges that enshrine a kaleidoscope of eroded sediments. Far below, the present riverbed meanders along the bottom as a narrow ribbon of sand and vegetation. In a good year, the river may reach Gobabeb but, further to the west, the water simply seeps into the sand. Drinking water for Walvis Bay is pumped from this underground supply.

The canyon, with walls so broken and precipitous that there are few tracks to the bottom, could hardly be more desolate. At the outbreak of the Second World War in 1939, two German geologists named Henno Martin and Hermann Korn decided to use the loneliness to their advantage. If they stayed in Windhoek, they reasoned, they might well be interned as aliens. By hiding in the desert, they could live as they liked while the world went mad around them.

In his book, *The Sheltering Desert*, Henno Martin tells how they loaded a truck with petrol and supplies and set off on a circuitous route to the canyon, hoping to confuse possible pursuers. Once there, they found to their surprise that carp had populated a shallow pool in the riverbed, and deduced that floods had washed them from sources far upstream. They located a rock overhang high up the canyon wall which they named 'Carp Cliff' in recognition of their good fortune. With their few possessions dispersed around the hideaway, they planted vegetables beside the pool and went out hunting for the pot.

For more than two years the two men lived as Robinson Crusoes of the desert, surviving off the land and its wildlife and facing drought, flood, hunger and illness with equanimity. A radio kept them abreast of the latest war news, but throughout they were nagged by the worry that the authorities would come looking for them. They went to elaborate lengths to construct traps for trucks (nearly falling victim with their own vehicle). Twice the resourceful fugitives changed their abode to make detection even more difficult for their pursuers. The nastiest moment of the long sojourn came when they found fresh 'Man Friday' footprints in the sand of the riverbed. They were certain the intruders had spotted their vegetable patch and were sure they would be reported, but then realised the strangers must have passed by night, and could not have seen anything. After some time Korn fell seriously ill, and Martin persuaded a farmer to take him to Windhoek. Martin wanted to remain in the desert, but Korn believed that his friend could not survive on his own, and revealed his whereabouts to the police.

This desolate region is not home to a large number of animal species, but the canyon does support chacma baboon, dassie, spotted hyena, klipspringer, springbok, Hartmann's mountain zebra and the occasional leopard.

Namib-Naukluft: Welwitschia Trail

This self-guided drive to Namib-Naukluft Park's Welwitschia Plains lets you discover fascinating specimens of this unusual plant. To get there turn off the tarred Swakopmund/Karibib road (B2), just beyond the Martin Luther steam engine, into the Khomas Hochland road (C28) and, after 15 km turn left at the signposted turn-off onto Welwitschia Drive. Continue to the first of 13 numbered stone beacons. Four hours will leave you time to explore the area around all the beacons with the aid of a brochure.

NAMIBIA: THE NAMIB

Left: The Kuiseb River Canyon. **Top:** Beetles of the genus *Lepidochora* dig a trench in the desert sand to catch condensed moisture from the periodic fogs so typical of the Namib. **Above:** White pelicans in a Namib Desert coastal vlei. These birds, their wingspan stretching an impressive three metres, can soar and glide at heights of some 1 000 metres.

Permits are necessary and are obtained by writing to the Ministry of Environment and Tourism, Private Bag 13267, Windhoek, telephone (09264) 61 23-6975/6/7/8, or fax 22-4900. Permits can also be obtained in person at the Ministry's tourist office in Swakopmund (corner of Kaiser Wilhelm and Bismarck streets), as well as at certain filling stations in Swakopmund and Walvis Bay.

NamibRand Nature Reserve

In the late 1980s a well-known Windhoek businessman, Albi Brückner, became increasingly concerned about the wholesale slaughtering of herds of springbok and gemsbok on the farms neighbouring his own. He decided to put an end to the carnage by purchasing the surrounding farms – which now combine to form the nucleus of what is the largest private reserve in Namibia.

Bordering on the Namib-Naukluft Park for almost 100 km, the NamibRand Nature Reserve encompasses a 150 000 ha mosaic of stark gravel plains, rugged island mountains or *inselbergen* and windswept sand dunes. The main attraction of this desertscape doesn't lie in its wildlife, but rather in its awesome scenic beauty, solitude and sweeping, open spaces. Along its western boundary the red sands of the Namib dune sea spill onto grassy plains which in turn are replaced by stony gravel plains further inland. Rising from these flat plains are island mountains – erosional relics from the distant past.

The most abundant large mammals are gemsbok and springbok, but red hartebeest, Burchell's zebra, various predators and a variety of smaller mammals also occur. Far more prolific is the birdlife and the amazing diversity of smaller creatures adapted to surviving the harsh desert conditions – lizards, geckoes, snakes, beetles and spiders.

There are two tourism concessionaires within NamibRand offering balloon safaris and 4x4 safaris from the Wolwedans Dune Camp.

Before a balloon flight, visitors are accommodated overnight at Camp Mwisho, a small tented camp with *en suite* facilities. Flights take off just after sunrise (weather permitting) and, after floating silently above the desert for about one hour, a champagne breakfast is served at the landing site.

From Wolwedans Dune Camp, a secluded hideaway in the centre of the reserve, guests can explore the Namib. Scenic and game drives, ranging in length, are conducted by experienced guides, while the more energetic can set off on an escorted walk. Visitors can travel to Wolwedans in their own vehicles or book a fly-in safari. The entire camp is elevated on wooden decks and walkways, and has at its heart a lounge, dining area and sundowner deck. Guests stay in tents equipped with *en suite* showers and toilets, and a verandah offering magnificent vistas.

NambiRand, which lies some 360 km from Windhoek, can be reached by travelling down the scenic Spreetshoogte Pass to Solitaire and Sesriem. From here continue on the D826 for 44,3 km to the signposted turn-off to Camp Mwisho and about 24 km further to the turn-off to Wolwedans Dune Camp, continuing for another 20 km to the office. Alternative routes from the north are via Kalkrand and Maltahöhe, or via Rehoboth, Klein Aub and Büllsport. From the south, access is through Maltahöhe along Route 36, the D827 and the D826.

For information on balloon safaris and to make reservations, contact Namib Sky Adventure Safaris, P O Box 197, Maltahöhe, telephone (09264) 61 6632 and ask for 5703. For further information on Wolwedans Dune Camp, write to NamibRand Safaris, P O Box 5048, Windhoek, telephone/fax (09264) 61 23-0616.

Sandwich Harbour

The Kuiseb leaves the Namib-Naukluft Park about 100 km downstream of the canyon and, south of Walvis Bay, loses itself in a wide sandy delta that is very seldom filled with water. Over millions of years a vast subterranean reservoir formed in this delta, but abstraction to supply water to the towns of Walvis Bay and Swakopmund, as well as Rössing's uranium mine at Arandis, has resulted in an alarming decrease in the level of the groundwater. This necessitated the investigation of alternative sources, including desalination. Yet some of the water continues to flow in the old bed beneath the dunes and eventually seeps into the lagoon at Sandwich (also known as Sandwich Harbour or Sandvis). Until the early 1980s the northern section of the lagoon comprised a mosaic of salt marshes, water channels and reed-fringed freshwater pools. However, since 1982, the lagoon has undergone profound geomorphological changes and the northern freshwater wetlands have disappeared completely.

> ### THE NARA PLANT
>
> Of all the intriguing items in the Namib's natural larder, the one that has proved among the most precious to man since the earliest times is surely the remarkable nara plant (*Acanthosicyos horrida*). Many Khoisan people must surely have owed their survival at one time or another to the life-saving supply of water stored within its hard and knobbly outer shell.
>
> The nara, a member of the cucumber family, survives in the desert by sending its twisted root deep down through the sand to a hidden reserve of water, while up above, in the sunshine, the adult plant minimises the loss of water through evaporation by simply growing a multitude of thorns instead of leaves. It seems that these thorns (and the stems on which they grow) contain all the green chloroplast cells that the plant needs for photosynthesising its food from the carbon dioxide absorbed from the air. This essential function is normally performed by the leaves. Throughout its life the plant resembles a great tangle of grey-green barbed wire. It is dioecious (separate male and female plants) and, while the male plant bears yellow-green flowers for most of the year, the female flowers for only a few months. The melon-like fruit has the tough outer skin typical of its kind, but inside it is a fairly bitter, watery pulp with a taste reminiscent of cucumbers. When dried, the plant's seeds have a taste much like that of almonds.
>
> Although successful as a desert plant, underground water is vital to the existence of the nara, and their demise is a sure sign that water levels are alarming low.

In the 18th and 19th centuries, Sandwich was a well-known refuge on the dangerous Atlantic coast and many ships anchored there to shelter and refit after storms. According to an old story, a sailing ship carrying a great treasure was stranded in the lagoon in 1770 and abandoned to the sand.

But in spite of frequent searches neither the ship nor the treasure has come to light. In the 19th century the bay was used by whalers, and from 1910 to 1947 it was exploited by several guano concessionaires.

The concessionaires exploited the guano deposited on a group of small, artificial islands in the lagoon, but the entrance silted up periodically and the water inside became much shallower. Fewer fish were able to enter the lagoon, with the result that the bird population decreased considerably.

In 1941, even before guano-digging came to an end, Sandwich was made part of Game Reserve 3. The reserve was proclaimed to keep out independent fishermen. To protect this pristine stretch of coastline, the entrance to the lagoon has been fenced off. No vehicles are allowed and this haven may be visited only on foot (with a permit). As a result of the natural changes, the rich diversity of waterfowl and wading shorebirds which were once attracted to the northern wetlands no longer occur here.

However, in summer, flocks of flamingo and pelican still visit the lagoon, and then the southern mudflats (inaccessible to tourists) support up to 135 000 wetland birds, making Sandwich one of the most important coastal wetlands on the African continent.

Sandwich is also the breeding ground of vast numbers of fish. This attracts large flocks of birds that live off the young fish trapped in shallow waters by the outgoing tide. Open from 6 a.m. to 8 p.m. daily, there are no visitor facilities. Permits are needed.

Walvis Bay bird sanctuaries

Walvis Bay (with an area of 112 400 ha), was administered by South Africa for several

Above: Various seabirds congregate at Walvis Bay Lagoon. Up to 60 000 greater and lesser flamingoes congregate on the lagoon at times.

decades until its integration with the independent Republic of Namibia on 1 March 1994.

The Walvis Bay coast and wetlands are noted for their abundant birdlife, of which over 170 species have been identified. Many of these birds migrate from inland pans such as Etosha, while others, including Arctic tern and sandpiper, fly great distances from Russia and Siberia. Although shorebirds such as the white pelican, greater flamingo, marsh and curlew sandpiper, sandplover, dabchick, moorhen and sanderling, as well as cormorant, tern (Caspian, swift and white-winged all visit) and hordes of wheeling gull, are found all along the 30 km beach between Walvis Bay and Swakopmund, up to 60 000 greater and lesser flamingo and large flocks of pelican use the Walvis Bay wetlands, where over 105 000 birds have been recorded at a single count. Each of its three components – the lagoon, adjacent intertidal areas and the saltworks – supports at least a third of the wetland birds at some stage in the tidal or annual cycle. In addition to providing a habitat for the birds, the wetlands are also a sanctuary area for several rare and endangered species.

The second bird sanctuary in the area is known as the 'Bird Paradise' – a series of small ponds between the dunes adjoining the sewage disposal works.

The sanctuary's waterbeds, fringed with reeds, attract pelicans, flamingoes and various other bird species. Several gravelled access roads have been built, and an elevated bird hide in the centre of the sanctuary provides fine views over the surrounding ponds.

Also worth visiting are the Salt Works, lying to the southwest of the lagoon. These pans, from which salt is procured from the sea water by evaporation, are also visited by hosts of migratory birds each year. Tours can be arranged. Remember to take your binoculars and camera with you.

STUMBLING ACROSS THE WORLD'S ODDEST PLANT

In 1860 the explorers James Chapman, a photographer, and Thomas Baines, an artist, teamed up to travel from Walvis Bay to the Victoria Falls. They were not far up the sandy Swakop riverbed when they came upon a large plant which resembled nothing they had seen before.

The two men were fascinated: Baines promptly sat down to sketch the plant, and later sketched himself sketching, while Chapman set up a stereoscopic camera to capture a double image that through a special viewer would appear in three dimensions.

The plant was a *Welwitschia mirabilis*, hailed by Charles Darwin as 'the platypus of the Plant Kingdom'. This strange plant, which can live for over a thousand years, produces only two leaves in its lifetime. They grow continuously, but the sun and wind-driven sand wither and shred the outer tips.

The plant order to which the welwitschia belongs has representatives in the tropical parts of Africa, as well as in the North American deserts. Although it has a taproot with side branches, some scientists believe that the leaves are able to absorb moisture from fog.

A plant dug up by Baines and Chapman weighed more than 100 kg and had a single long taproot (though today's botanists say the roots are branched). Baines packed sketches and some specimen cones in a box and forwarded them to Kew Gardens in London. It was months before they arrived and by then the cones were rapidly decomposing. Even so they were eagerly examined by Sir William Hooker, director of the Gardens, and Britain's leading botanist.

Hooker later described the plant as 'the most wonderful, in a botanical point of view, that has been brought to light during the present century'. But he had a feeling that it might be the same as a specimen described in a letter he had just received from an Austrian-born botanist working in southwestern Angola. Further enquiries showed that this was the case. The Austrian was Friedrich Welwitsch and, as he was technically the first to report the wonderful plant, it was named *Welwitschia mirabilis* in his honour.

Coastal fog and mountain dew

Few places in southern Africa sound more forbidding than the Skeleton Coast, that lonely stretch of shore between Swakopmund and the Kunene River on Namibia's border with Angola. The Skeleton Coast is the graveyard of many fine ships – and the men who sailed them. Relics of one wreck have been dated to the 15th century, and more recent victims include passenger liners.

Even a few aircraft have met their end on these shores and, despite modern navigation equipment, fresh additions to the grim list of maritime casualties still occur.

For the mariner, the Skeleton Coast is a nightmare, but it can also be a revelation for those who want to share nature's secrets. The barren coastline's mood seems to change continually as fog battles with sunshine and the wind plays games with the sand. Wide horizons delight the eye and the desert's solitude and tranquillity are treats for the soul. That is the essence of Skeleton Coast Park, a strip of land roughly 40 km deep that hugs the shore from the mouth of the Ugab River to the Kunene in the north.

Inland from the coast are the mountains of the huge, untamed regions of the Kaokoveld, comprising the area between the Ugab and Kunene rivers within the Kunene Region (formerly Damaraland and Kaokoland). Linking the interior to the sea are a number of usually dry riverbeds. Wildlife, including elephant, giraffe and the occasional lion, use the riverbeds as corridors when they move from east to west and back again in their search for food and water. This pattern of migration has probably continued unchanged for centuries.

All of the Kaokoveld is beautiful, but a few sites have a special status. The Brandberg, with its over 40 000 ancient rock paintings, is one of these. Twyfelfontein's rock engravings of rhino and other species are said to be among the finest in Africa. The Petrified Forest near Khorixas, with fossil remains dating back some 260 million years, is also well worth a visit. Back on the coast, the Cape Cross Seal Reserve, situated 78 km south of the Ugab River, is another interesting area.

Left: The impressive Brandberg, on the eastern edge of the Namib Desert. Relics such as stone tools, grinding stones, fragments of pottery and arrowheads have been found on the Brandberg, indicating that Stone Age man once lived there. **Above:** Ancient rock paintings on a cave wall on the slopes of the Brandberg. The curiously named 'White Lady' is the striding figure at centre right. Despite its name, the figure is thought to be neither white nor female. **Right:** A colourful display of blooms on the Namib edelweiss (*Helichrysum roseo-niveum*), an annual with thick, downy leaves.

NAMIBIA: SKELETON COAST

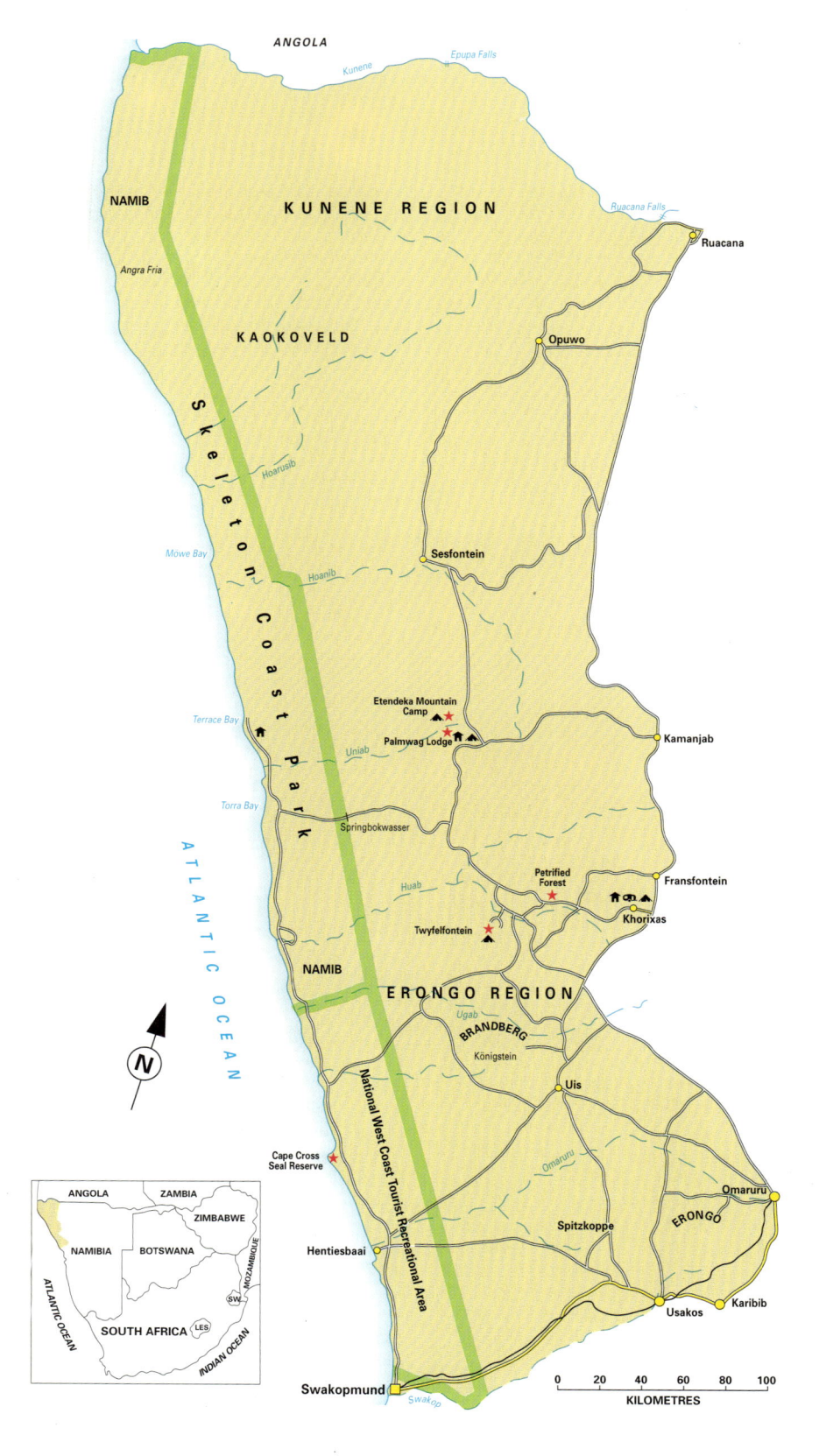

KAOKOVELD AT A GLANCE

Note: The Kaokoveld's attractions are spread over a large area but many visitors devise a 'grand tour', basing themselves in Khorixas, an important tourism centre.

When to go The attractions may be visited all year round, but the months from November to March are extremely hot. Khorixas Rest Camp is open all year.

Reservations Enquiries and applications for bookings at Khorixas Rest Camp should be addressed to Khorixas Rest Camp, P O Box 2, Khorixas, or telephone (09264) 65712 196 or 111, fax 388. For details about Etendeka Mountain Camp, contact P O Box 21783, Windhoek, telephone (09264) 61 22-6979, fax 22-6969. To make reservations at Palmwag Lodge, contact Desert Adventure Safaris, P O Box 339, Swakopmund, telephone (09264) 64 40-4459 or 40-2434, or fax 40-4664.

Getting there Khorixas can be reached from the north, south, east and west. From Windhoek or the Etosha National Park, drive to Outjo, then 132 km to the west. From Skeleton Coast, drive 238 km east from Torra Bay. From Walvis Bay and Swakopmund, drive via Hentiesbaai and Uis. The rest camp is 4 km from the centre of the town.

Accommodation Khorixas Rest Camp offers self-contained rondavels with linen, and a caravan and camping site with ablution block. Fuel and supplies are available. For more detailed information, contact The Directorate of Tourism and Resorts, Ministry of Environment and Tourism, Private Bag 13346, Windhoek, telephone (09264) 61 284-2111, or fax 22-1930.

Eating and drinking The licensed restaurant at Khorixas Rest Camp serves meals and refreshments. Shops are few and far between in the Kaokoveld and campers should stock up at Khorixas, Uis, Omaruru or Opuwo.

Getting around Most of the Kaokoveld's roads are rudimentary at best, so visitors should prepare themselves for clouds of dust and long stretches of corrugations. Petrol can be obtained at Khorixas, Palmwag, Uis and Omaruru.

Wildlife The northern Kaokoveld still has a significant population of lion, desert elephant, black rhino, leopard, large antelope and Hartmann's mountain zebra, but in the southern farmlands only antelope and zebra are common.

Left: A black rhino and her calf on the rugged plains of the Kaokoveld. This species has a gestation period of about 15 months and the single calf is suckled for at least a year. Black rhino live for up to 40 years.

company, Olympia-Reisen, for a period of ten years. Louw Schoeman died shortly afterwards, but the company he founded is now run by his sons who operate fly-in safaris to Terrace Bay and to camps in the Kaokoveld.

For more information, contact The Directorate of Tourism and Resorts, Ministry of Environment and Tourism, Private Bag 13346, Windhoek, telephone (09264) 61 284-2111, or fax 22-1930. To make reservations, contact Olympia-Reisen, P O Box 5017, Windhoek, telephone (09264) 61 26-2395, fax 21-7026; or Skeleton Coast Fly-in Safaris, P O Box 2195, Windhoek, telephone (09264) 61 22-4248, or fax 22-5713.

Twyfelfontein

'Doubtful Spring' (its flow has always been erratic) is set in a long shallow valley flanked by boulder-strewn hills. The hills contain more than 2 400 rock engravings, comprising the richest such collection in Africa. The delicately etched engravings have been chipped out of hard rock, perhaps with a quartz hammer. Experiments using one of these crude tools have shown that a typical engraving would have been completed in as little as 30 minutes.

A staff archaeologist at the State Museum in Windhoek has pointed out that Twyfelfontein's engravings have a different emphasis from the rock paintings found in the Brandberg and, indeed, from engravings found in South Africa. The most numerous of the larger animal species depicted are giraffe, rhino, zebra and ostrich, while smaller mammals and humans feature less frequently. There are also engravings of animal spoor and a mystifying series of patterns, circles and dots – believed by some to represent the hallucinations experienced during a trance.

Twyfelfontein's engravings were discovered in the early 1900s, but it is only since the 1970s that they have become a tourist drawcard. To view this ancient and fascinating art, follow the signs from turn-offs on the road between Khorixas and the sea. The two turn-offs are situated some 46 km and 78 km respectively from Khorixas.

The community campsite on the banks of the Aba-Huab River is the ideal base from which to explore Twyfelfontein and nearby Burnt Mountain – a red-brown shale formation that glows with a rainbow of colours when caught in the light of early morning or late afternoon. The camp's amenities include shady campsites, running water, braai facilities, rustic open-ended A-frame shelters and hot- and cold-water ablutions.

with views of the surrounding mountains. It is located 42 km west of Khorixas, on the road to the sea, and is signposted.

Skeleton Coast Park

Not only ships have come to grief along the 550 km-long Skeleton Coast. For decades men have dreamed of uncovering great storehouses of diamonds like those at the mouth of the Orange River – and they have failed. Certainly, diamonds have come to light, and small mines have been established – but in at least three cases these have been dismal failures. One of the mines was situated at Terrace Bay, between the Uniab and Hoanib rivers. When the company concerned went bankrupt, it surrendered its buildings to the country's administration.

The windfall could not have been more welcome. The Skeleton Coast Park had been in existence since 1971, but all it could offer in the way of tourist accommodation was a camping site at Torra Bay to the south, open only in December and January and catering for fishermen and their families. Terrace Bay had the makings of a first-rate tourist camp, and nature conservationists had visions of a brisk stream of appreciative visitors who would be drawn to the park by its beauty and by the curious fulfilment it offered.

However, visitors to Terrace Bay are restricted to a narrow strip along the coast, stretching 14 km north and 10 km south of Terrace Bay. Here they may be lucky enough to catch a glimpse of elusive lion which appear intermittently in the dry riverbeds as they follow their prey, whose movements in turn are dictated by grazing conditions in the interior. They lie in wait at waterholes, secure in the knowledge that their next meal must appear sooner or later. However, when good rains ensure plentiful grazing further inland, the lion have been known to feed on seals found on the beaches.

As yet, visitors heading for Terrace Bay and Torra Bay must keep to the road, thereby missing many of the beauty spots along the way. However, some fascinating areas are open to hikers, including the 6 km trail at Uniab River Delta, where a waterfall lies hidden in a canyon. Hikers undertaking the three-day Ugab Trail (which departs on the 2nd and 4th Tuesday of every month) are led by a conservation officer along the Ugab River, which forms the southern boundary of the park.

Besides these pockets which are open for exploration the only 'wilderness experience' offered in the Skeleton Coast Park has been the result of private enterprise. Explains an official: 'A part of the wilderness concept is the knowledge that you or your group are alone in a vast territory. This aspect would be lost if all sorts of additional areas are opened to tourists. This is why only one firm has been allowed to operate safaris – despite pressure for more.'

The Skeleton Coast owes much of its popularity to the Schoeman family, pioneers of ecotourism in Namibia. Louw Schoeman, a Windhoek lawyer, had business interests in the Skeleton Coast for years, and in 1977 was given permission to organise fly-in safaris. From his camp in the bed of the Khumib River, 35 km inland from the coast, trips were undertaken north to the seal colony at Angra Fria, the clay castles of the Hoarusib Canyon and the roaring dunes to the south, and the lichen-clad plains lying to the east. The emphasis of his safaris was on the ever-changing landscape and the fascinating variety of smaller creatures inhabiting this inhospitable tract of land.

In 1993 the tourism concession for the area was awarded to a German-based tourism

The lake of a mother's tears

An old San legend tells of a party of strangers that strayed into Hai//om territory. A band of hunters surrounded the intruders and killed the men and children, but allowed the women to live. One young mother was inconsolable. She sat under a tree and rocked her dead infant in her arms, weeping so bitterly that her tears formed a huge lake. The sun dried the tears, leaving the ground covered in salt. That, say the Hai//om, was the real origin of Etosha Pan – lake of a mother's tears.

The San-speaking Hai//om (widely known as the 'Bushmen') have lived in the area for more than 1 000 years. Their forebears were hunters and gatherers, preying on the huge herds of antelope that fed on the savannah plains around the pan and drank at the perennial springs that oozed through cracks in its rim. They were familiar with the three seasons of Etosha's year: four cold and dry months, four hot and dry months, and four hot months wet with the tears of the grieving mother.

Until the 1890s the Hai//om and their game were undisturbed. But then came the outbreak of rinderpest that affected all southern Africa, killing both game and domestic cattle. In an attempt to contain the disease, the German authorities in Windhoek quickly developed a stock-free zone along the southern edge of the pan. Several small military detachments were sent to enforce the stock ban and prevent cattle-smuggling, and two of them were based at the remote locations named Okaukuejo (pronounced 'O-ka-kwi-yoo') and Namutoni, where the men were housed in cramped forts.

In 1907 Governor Friedrich von Lindequist proclaimed three large game reserves. One was north of Grootfontein, another covered a large area of the Namib Desert, and the third, the 'Etosha Game Park', included the area around the pan and much of the Kaokoveld.

Once, the park covered 9 952 600 ha (it was the largest conservation area in the world), but in 1967 it was cut back to make room for tribal homelands, and became the Etosha National Park – one of the best-known and most fascinating natural sanctuaries in the world. The park's present area is 2 227 000 hectares.

NAMIBIA: ETOSHA NATIONAL PARK

HIGH SOCIETY

A lithograph by Sir Andrew Smith depicts the sociable weaver against a background of somewhat stylised nests.

Most birds are fairly discreet in building their nests, and few visitors manage to locate them. One exception is the sociable weaver (*Philetairus socius*), whose nest could not be more obvious. The weaver's home is a vast edifice of straw resting on the sturdy branches of certain acacia trees or in a fork of *Aloe dichotoma*. These are, quite possibly, the work of generations of weavers that kept it in a fine state of repair and steadily added to it as their colony grew. The large communal nest keeps the birds warm in winter and cool in summer.

To build such a home, adult weavers begin by pushing individual twigs into cracks and crevices in the bark of the acacia (or in the aloe's forked stem). Before long, the twigs are packed together so tightly that they provide an anchor for more straw, or light sticks, and gradually the weavers thatch a roof. Meanwhile, some of the birds begin to make rounded nesting chambers – suspended from the roof but thatched together to form a solid mass. Each chamber has a near-vertical tunnel connecting it with the underside of the nest.

In the breeding season, each pair of sociable weavers has a nesting chamber to itself, but sometimes several (non-breeding) birds share a chamber. The arrangement seems to suit them well, for weavers like living together. Every morning, the birds leave the nest to feed. Towards midday they all return, and later they go feeding again. At dusk they disappear into their nesting chambers, which serve as their homes all year, whether or not they are breeding.

Like most thirstland birds, the weaver will not breed unless there have been adequate rains. When rain occurs, the drive to reproduce is accompanied by an urge to build new nesting chambers, and the colony's home may be greatly extended. But on occasion these winged engineers make mistakes: sometimes the nest becomes waterlogged and too heavy for the branch that supports it, and parts of it, or even the whole structure, may crash to the ground. When that happens, the weavers simply begin all over again, possibly using the original straws and ferrying them one by one to a fresh site.

Sociable weavers at work on their elaborate communal home (viewed from below).

Top: The graceful steenbok is monogamous, and pairs for life (though the male and female occasionally separate for short periods). The adult male marks out his territory with a system of dung heaps and secretions from a throat gland – unique to the steenbok. **Above:** *Moringa ovalifolia* is one of Etosha's most fascinating trees. Its bark, stem and roots are eaten by a number of animals.

'And so the chain goes on,' says a researcher. 'In the past, the lion would have gone hungry during the wet season and many of their cubs would have died. Now they thrive, and their growing population is competing with cheetah for living space, robbing them of their prey, and killing the young cheetah when they find them. As a result, we have a greatly reduced cheetah population.' It became obvious that the lion numbers would have to be contained but that it would not help to shoot them. 'Nature has a way of over-compensating in retaliation,' the researcher claimed.

Instead, the conservation officers undertook an experiment that was the first of its kind in the world. In the early 1980s, ten of Etosha National Park's lionesses were implanted with time-release contraceptive capsules. They were monitored closely and showed no side effects or behavioural changes. When the contraceptives were removed, they fell pregnant within less than seven weeks. However, no other lionesses have been treated, because the park's lion population fell from an estimated 500 animals in 1981 to about 250 in 1985, through natural causes and the killing of stock-raiding lions on farms to the south of Etosha.

Ongava Game Reserve

This 30 000 ha private game reserve shares its 32 km northern border with Etosha National Park. In addition to the gameviewing opportunities offered by the reserve, it is ideally situated for those seeking to use its luxurious lodge as a base from which to explore Etosha.

Ongava, a Herero word meaning 'rhinoceros', is a sanctuary for white rhino, as well as for rare species such as the black-faced impala and the roan. Other animals have been reintroduced, including giraffe, red hartebeest, gemsbok, eland, blue wildebeest and springbok, as well as Burchell's and Hartmann's mountain zebra.

Predators include lion, leopard, black-backed jackal and bat-eared fox. There are also numerous smaller mammals, and more than 200 recorded bird species.

Prior to its establishment, the land comprising the reserve was prime cattle-ranching country. Today, one of its best-known inhabitants is 'Brutalis', an ill-tempered white rhino bull that was acquired by the owners of Ongava from Givskud Zoo in Denmark. His aggressive and destructive temperament led to a decision to have him put down, but fortune intervened and he lives on, still grumpy, but in safety, at the reserve.

Like much of Etosha, the vegetation at Ongava is dominated by mopane woodlands with a sprinkling of red bushwillow, leadwood and purple-pod terminalia trees. On the slopes of the dolomitic outcrops are marula, white seringa and paperbark.

The reserve's luxurious lodge, built in the foothills of the Ondundozonanandana ('mountain where the boy took the calves') range, comprises a main building with reception area, lounge, dining room and bar with views over a small waterhole and the vast expanse of the reserve. There are ten thatched bungalows with *en suite* facilities, air-conditioning and a swimming pool. There is also a tented camp situated a short distance from the main lodge. Activities include early morning game drives, night drives to track down elusive nocturnal animals, and ranger-led walks. There are two gameviewing hides.

The reserve is reached via Outjo and is signposted at Etosha's Andersson Gate. The lodge lies some 7 km further along on a gravel road. There is a landing strip, and Air Namibia has two scheduled flights per week.

Left: Giraffe at the Klein Namutoni waterhole. **Above:** A yellow mongoose surveys his small slice of Etosha territory. This species is very similar to the slender mongoose.

East to the water country

Attached to the northeastern corner of Namibia is the odd panhandle of land known as the Caprivi Strip, 450 km from west to east and at no point wider than 100 kilometres. The strip is named after a former Imperial Chancellor of Germany, Count Leo von Caprivi – but those who live in the area know it as Linyandi, the Water Country.

Since Namibia achieved independence in 1990 and military forces were withdrawn from the area, the Caprivi's tourist potential has soared and a number of reserves have been established on both banks of the magnificent Kavango River.

In the early 1970s it was decided to proclaim the Waterberg Plateau Park as a refuge for Namibia's fast-dwindling eland population and to serve as a breeding centre for rare and endangered species. Visitors to the park stay in Bernabé de la Bat Rest Camp, from where gameviewing tours are conducted. Here the bushy savannah vegetation is much like that of the Caprivi (though not as rich) and the summit of the plateau makes a perfect sanctuary, not only for these animals, but also for other threatened species. Waterberg's game population ranges from buffalo to rhino, and from giraffe to roan.

The plateau's water manifests itself in the form of contact springs that bubble from the sandstone walls (a contact spring is formed by a top layer of porous material through which rainwater seeps until it makes contact with an impervious layer of rock. The water finds its way to the edge of this layer, where it gushes out in the form of a spring). These springs have long made the Waterberg an important focus of settlement. The impressive Lake Otjikoto, a large, water-filled dolomite sinkhole, lies 170 km to the north.

In remote eastern Kavango the Khaudum Game Park offers a pristine wildlife experience. The park, which can be reached only by 4x4 vehicle, has two rustic bush camps, Sikereti and Khaudum.

Various private resorts in northern Namibia offer visitors accommodation as well as a personalised introduction to the area's wildlife.

Caprivi Game Park

In 1966 the ecologist Ken Tinley was asked to appraise the western Caprivi for Namibia's administration. Was it a good idea to open the area for agricultural settlement, as was happening in eastern Caprivi?

After analysing the soils, Tinley advised against it, instead recommending that western Caprivi should be left in its natural state as a haven for wildlife, and as a homeland for the indigenous Bushman (San) hunter-gatherers. The West Caprivi Game Park was proclaimed in 1963 and, in 1968, virtually the entire strip was proclaimed as the Caprivi Game Park. Covering 57 157 ha, the park encompasses floodplains, dune belts, riverine forest and acacia woodland.

Because of its strategic location, the Caprivi Strip was militarised by the South African Defence Force during Namibia's liberation struggle, and the park became totally out of bounds to visitors until after independence in 1990. Although much of the park is still closed to visitors, an area along the Kwando border,

Left: A lone boatman punts his mokoro along the reed-fringed Linyandi waterways. **Below:** Oxpeckers swarm over a wild donkey in Caprivi. These birds live mainly on blood-gorged ticks. Their sharp claws, stiff tail feathers (used to prop themselves against their host's body) and flattened bills are well suited to their feeding habits.

NAMIBIA: THE NORTHEAST

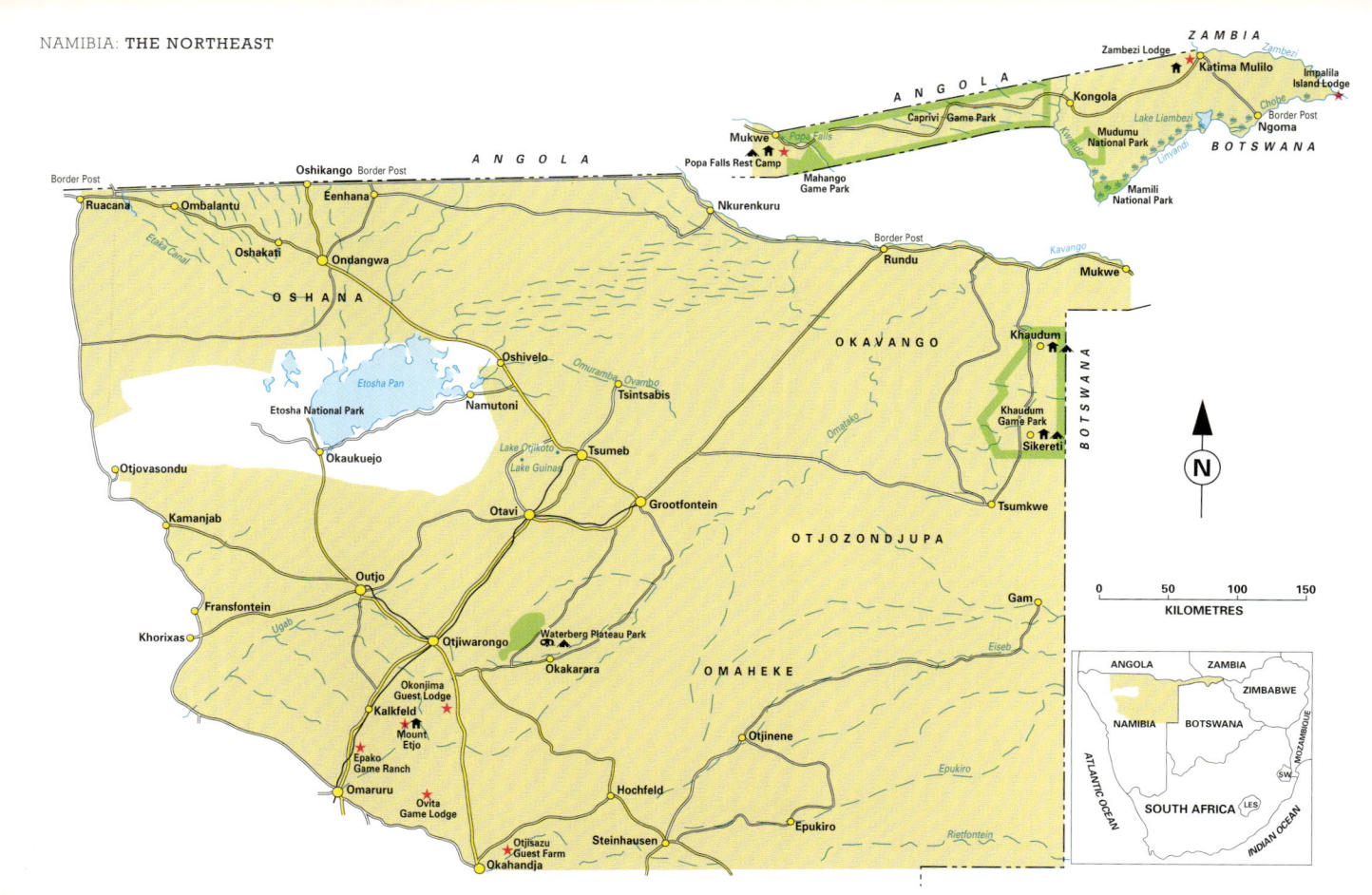

Above: A strangler fig clasps a mopane tree in an unbreakable grip that may eventually kill the tree. The strangler fig grows from a seed (dropped by a bird or mammal) in the branches of the host tree. When the seeds germinate, they extrude long 'roots' that wind around the tree-trunk.
Right: A white-headed vulture. This carrion-eater (it also feeds on live birds and mammals) is found in savannah bushveld across southern Africa.

which forms its eastern boundary, has been opened for tourism.

Visitors stay in one of two campsites within the park: Nambwa in the southeast and Chisu further north, both on the Kwando River. There are no facilities, and a 4x4 vehicle is essential. Gameviewing and birdwatching are excellent here. Visitors can expect to see elephant, hippo, buffalo, crocodile, lechwe, sable, roan, reedbuck and a host of waterbirds.

The road running from west to east along the strip is expected to be fully tarred by the end of 1999. For more information, contact the regional office of the Ministry of Environment and Tourism at Katima Mulilo, telephone (09264) 677 3027, or fax 3187/3341. To make reservations, contact the Directorate of Tourism and Resorts, Ministry of Environment and Tourism, Private Bag 13267, Windhoek, telephone (09264) 61 23-6975/6/7/8, fax 22-4900. For further information about Caprivi, contact the Directorate of Tourism and Resorts, Ministry of Environment and Tourism, Private Bag 13346, Windhoek, telephone (09264) 61 284-2111, fax 22-1930.

Epako Game Lodge

Epako, a Herero name meaning 'the corner of a mountain range', covers 11 000 ha of flat plains studded with rocky mountain outcrops.

Northeast of Omaruru, the acacia savannah veld surrounding this exclusive lodge supports elephant, white rhino and giraffe, as well as herds of gemsbok, eland, blue wildebeest, impala, springbok and Burchell's zebra. Among the other species to be seen are kudu, waterbuck and warthog, while the larger predators are represented by cheetah and leopard. Birdlife includes a variety of raptors and many colourful species such as the lilac-breasted roller.

To enable guests to discover Epako's rich variety of wildlife and its magnificent landscape, guided gameviewing drives are conducted, on which visitors may also view age-old rock engravings and rock paintings. Sundowner drives, with breathtaking views of the Brandberg and Spitzkoppe, may be arranged by special request.

Built against the slopes of a hill, the lodge overlooks the Epako River. Accommodation consists of 21 luxury double bedrooms with *en suite* facilities and air-conditioning. Other amenities include a lounge, bar, terraced restaurant overlooking an illuminated waterhole, a swimming pool and tennis court. Epako is well known for its outstanding cuisine – a combination of traditional Namibian fare and French cooking.

To reach Epako from Omaruru, follow the C33 towards Kalkfeld for some 22 kilometres. Further information may be obtained from Epako Game Lodge, P O Box 108, Omaruru, telephone (09264) 64 57-0551, or fax 57-0553.

Impalila Island Lodge

Two mighty rivers and a myriad reed-lined channels merge with floodplains and woodlands in the extreme northeastern corner of Namibia to form an island few people have heard of – Impalila. Situated at the confluence of the Zambezi and Chobe rivers, it has aptly been described as 'the one island in Africa where four countries meet', and lies at the junction of the international boundary between Namibia, Botswana, Zambia and Zimbabwe.

Here the waters of the Zambezi River reputedly offer some of the finest tigerfishing in southern Africa, and the diverse habitats make this a birding paradise (some 400 species have been recorded). Two much sought-after species – the African skimmer and the rock pratincole – may be spotted, and other species found here include western banded snake eagle, Pel's fishing owl, tropical and swamp boubous, and the violet widowfinch.

Shaded by large baobabs and lush riverine forest, Impalila Island Lodge overlooks the Mambova Rapids in the Zambezi River. Guests stay in thatch-and-timber chalets (with *en suite* facilities), elevated on stilts above the rapids. There is also a central lounge and dining area under thatch, as well as a swimming pool.

Left: An early representation of Lake Otjikoto in Charles Andersson's book, *Lake Ngami*. **Below:** A modern view of Lake Otjikoto. 'So effectually [sic] is it hidden,' wrote Andersson, 'that a person might pass within fifty paces of it without being aware of its existence.' He could not resist investigating further. With his companion, Francis Galton, he swam into a cavern. 'In this mysterious spot, two owls, and a great number of bats, had taken up their abode. On approaching some of the latter, which I saw clinging to the rocks, I found, to my surprise, that they were dead; and had probably been so for many years...'

One of Impalila's main attractions is its excellent tigerfishing, and guests may either fish from boats or fly-fish from a 'mokoro' (dugout canoe). Visitors may also explore the waterways by mokoro and walk on the islands under the watchful eye of a guide. Impalila borders on Botswana's famed Chobe National Park (*see separate entry*) and, during a boating trip on the Chobe River, it is possible to see hippo, large herds of elephant and a variety of other game.

Although Impalila is situated in Namibia, access by road is through Kasane in Botswana. From Katima Mulilo, travel via the Ngoma border post to Kasane, from where it is a 20-minute transfer by boat. There is an airstrip on the island, and there are airports at Kasane and Victoria Falls, 70 km to the east. A visit to Impalila can also be combined with a trip to Kalizo Lodge, some 90 km upstream.

For further information and to make reservations, write to Impalila Island Lodge, P O Box 70378, Bryanston 2021, telephone/fax (011) 706-7207.

Khaudum Game Park

Despite its out-of-the-way location in northern Namibia, on the Botswana border, the rich wildlife and beauty of the 38 000 ha Khaudum Game Park are still within the reach of adventuresome outdoor enthusiasts.

Two rustic bush camps, Sikereti and Khaudum, have timber-and-thatch huts, campsites and ablution facilities. The camps are linked by tracks which cross Kalahari sand dunes and fossil drainage lines, locally called

EXPLORING A HELL ON EARTH

Even today, a land journey from the coast of Namibia eastwards to Lake Ngami is not lightly undertaken. Back in the 1850s it was the nearest thing to hell on earth.

The mysterious 'Great Lake' Ngami had been a lure to explorers since missionary David Livingstone's sighting of its waters a few years previously. Livingstone had travelled north from near Kuruman, and the search for a route from the west captured the imagination of numerous explorers.

On 20 August 1850, two explorers – Charles Andersson (above left), a Swede, and Francis Galton (above right), an Englishman – landed at Walvis Bay determined not only to find a way to the lake, but also to 'fill in the empty space on the map between the Cape Colony and Portuguese settlement in the west'.

Enlisting the help of a local missionary, the explorers and their party headed east through the dangers of wild animals and crushing heat. Windhoek was reached before the party turned north, to discover Lake Otjikoto at Tsumeb, and Owambo. Further travel was then blocked by the paramount chief Nangoro and the party returned to the coast.

Undaunted, Galton and Andersson set out again, this time reaching beyond present-day Gobabis. But again Lake Ngami eluded the pair – Galton returned to Cape Town and England, leaving Andersson alone to unlock the secret of a westerly route to the lake in 1853. Both men left extensive records of their adventures, particularly of the wild animals that once roamed the Kalahari.

In *The Narrative of an Explorer in Tropical South Africa*, Galton recalled his near brush with a lion that suddenly appeared, crouching, a few feet above his head on a rocky outcrop. 'I did feel queer, but… I walked steadily down the rock, looking very frequently over my shoulder; but it was not till I came to where the men stood that I could see the round head and pricked ears of my enemy, peering over the ledge under which I had been at work.'

Heat was another problem. On a hunting expedition, Andersson began to feel giddy and realised he was suffering from heatstroke – the temperature was 69°C.

Above: A grove of *Lonchocarpus capassa* (apple leaf), a typical tree of the region. It produces sprays of pale blue, violet or lilac flowers in December and January.

'Omiramba' (singular 'Omuramba'). There are numerous waterholes and seasonal pans, which are the most advantageous spots from which to view game, throughout the park. During the dry season (June to October), the waterholes are frequented by lion, elephant, giraffe, gemsbok, wildebeest, eland, kudu and wild dog.

Khaudum's vegetation is quite different from other parks in Namibia. In the dry woodland savannah areas there are leadwood and acacia, while the dunes are dotted with kiaat, Rhodesian teak and false mopane.

The park is about 60 km north of Tsumkwe, where fuel is usually available. The park may also be reached from the north via a signposted turn-off on the Rundu/Divundu road. Because of sandy roads, driving is slow and plenty of time should be set aside to complete your journey. The most rewarding routes are those that run along the courses of the ancient – now dry – rivers in which there are a few spring-fed waterholes. Visiting groups must have at least two 4x4 vehicles and be well equipped with fuel, water and food.

To make bookings, write to the Directorate of Tourism and Resorts, Ministry of Environment and Tourism, Private Bag 13267, Windhoek, or telephone (09264) 61 23-6975/6/7/8, fax 22-4900. For further information, write to the Directorate of Tourism and Resorts, Ministry of Environment and Tourism, Private Bag 13346, Windhoek, or telephone (09264) 61 284-2111, fax 22-1930.

Lake Otjikoto

In his book, *Lake Ngami*, the explorer Charles Andersson described Lake Otjikoto as 'the most extraordinary chasm it was ever my fortune to see'. He and fellow traveller Francis Galton arrived on its cylindrical brink during 1851 and, having plumbed its depths to some 55 m, astonished their Owambo guides by plunging in headfirst. They swam into a half-submerged cavern that sparkled like crystal in the reflected sunlight: 'The transparency of the water, which was of the deepest sea-green, was remarkable.'

The travellers' exploration of Otjikoto was free of incident, but later it was said the lake was haunted: when retreating German soldiers dumped war materiel, including a Krupp ammunition wagon, into the water in 1915, a trooper was snagged in a harness line and drowned. It was also suggested that the lake was bottomless, and hid a treacherous whirlpool – in 1927 the Tsumeb postmaster dived in and was never seen again. Today such tales are discounted, and it is accepted that the lake is a classic dolomite sinkhole.

NAMIBIA: THE NORTHEAST

For scientists, Otjikoto's chief attraction is its population of fish. Charles Andersson commented on the large numbers of dwarf bream, whose descendants now live on the lake's rubbish-strewn bottom. They have been driven there by an alien species somehow imported from a larger sinkhole named Lake Guinas, 19 km to the west.

The *Tilapia guinasana* have multiplied enormously in their new home, so much so that they are now known as 'Otjikoto cichlid'. In 1980, Mozambique or blue tilapia were introduced (illegally) into Otjikoto. They too multiplied rapidly, with the result that the lake's population of Otjikoto cichlids has been reduced.

Lake Otjikoto has been a national monument since 1972, and for many years its water has been used to irrigate local farmland (which explains the quaint pumping platform that hangs from the rim). The lake has been fenced to control access and is open daily between 8 a.m. and 6 p.m. You can also view the lake from several viewing points on the cliffs situated on its northern side. To reach the site, drive northwest from Tsumeb on the road to the Etosha National Park (*see separate entry*). The lake lies near the road, some 20 km from the town.

For more information, contact Tsumeb Tourism Centre, P O Box 779, Tsumeb, telephone (09264) 671 2-0728, or fax 2-0916.

Mahango Game Park

The wide, lushly vegetated plains of the Kavango River are the setting for the idyllic 25 000 ha Mahango Game Park. Wild dates and huge baobabs thrive in the fertile soil of the floodplains and provide a dense habitat for a profusion of birds and other animals.

Gameviewing is best during the dry season (August to October). Besides elephant, visitors may see lion, buffalo, kudu, bushbuck, reedbuck, tsessebe, sable, roan, wildebeest, waterbuck and warthog, as well as the rare red lechwe and sitatunga. Despite the heat, summer is the best time for birdwatching – there are over 450 species, including large numbers of raptors such as Dickinson's kestrel, African fish eagle and the majestic bateleur. Fishing is not permitted.

Mahango is bisected by two roads, both of which begin about one kilometre south of the main gate. The first, a gravel road leading past two picnic sites and a floodplain, is suitable for all road vehicles, while the second, through the western section of the park, is to be used only by 4x4 vehicles.

Visitors are permitted to picnic at two sites that have been established on the river bank, but be cautious at all times. Do not be tempted to swim – although the shimmering water looks inviting, it shelters crocodile and hippo. If you look out over the far side of the river you

Above: The small (about 1 cm) fruit of a wild fig in Caprivi. This widely distributed species may vary in size (it has been known to reach almost 20 m in height). **Right:** Open-billed storks migrate to southern Africa from the African tropics. This stork has a gap between its closed mandibles, and this is believed to be an adaptation to its staple diet of freshwater mussels. It has been seen to carry mussels from the water into the hot sunlight and wait until they open.

might see a herd of elephant from Caprivi Game Park (*see separate entry*) converging on the bank to drink their fill. There are no overnight facilities, but Popa Falls Rest Camp (*see separate entry*), which has a campsite and bungalows, is located 15 km north of the entrance. Reservations may be made by contacting the Directorate of Tourism and Resorts, Ministry of Environment and Tourism, Private Bag 13267, Windhoek, telephone (09264) 61 23-6975/6/7/8, fax 22-4900. For further information, contact the Directorate of Tourism and Resorts, Ministry of Environment and Tourism, Private Bag 13346, Windhoek, telephone (09264) 61 284-2111, fax 22-1930.

Mamili National Park

In the far northeastern corner of Namibia is a tract of land unlike any other in the country, the Linyandi Swamps.

Described as a microcosm of Botswana's renowned Okavango Delta, Linyandi is a wonderland of meandering waterways, lily-covered lagoons, floodplains and extensive reed beds. Adding to the scenic beauty of the landscape are stately fan palms and patches of magnificent forests, dominated by tall jackalberry, waterberry and sausage trees.

Until the early 1970s this area was a wildlife paradise but, since no land in the eastern Caprivi enjoyed formal conservation status, the region's wildlife suffered heavily at the hands of poachers. To ensure the survival of the rich diversity of wildlife, Mamili National Park and nearby Mudumu National Park (*see separate entry*) were proclaimed in 1990.

Covering 31 992 ha of the Linyandi Swamps, including Nkasa and Lupala islands, Mamili is the largest wetland area enjoying protection in Namibia. Fed by the Kwando/Linyandi River which rises on the central Angolan highlands, up to 80 per cent of the park becomes inundated when the floods peak around June, leaving only Nkasa and Lupala and a few smaller, high-lying islands dry.

Hippo, crocodile and otter inhabit the waterways, while red lechwe and waterbuck occur on the adjacent floodplains. The park is also a sanctuary for one of southern Africa's most elusive antelope – the sitatunga – a species confined to papyrus swamps. One of Namibia's largest populations of buffalo can be seen, as can elephant, reedbuck, impala and warthog. Carnivores include lion, leopard, spotted hyena and wild dog, as well as a variety of smaller predators. Birdlife is prolific, with over 400 species being recorded. The bird list includes several species with a limited distribution in southern Africa. Among these are the lesser jacana, pink-throated longclaw, wattled crane and swamp boubou.

A 4x4 vehicle is needed to visit Mamili, and a sense of adventure is also a prerequisite, as

Above: The widely occurring dassie, or rock hyrax, is an outstanding climber, being able to scramble up and down trees and rocks with surprising rapidity. It us-ually sunbathes in the morning. **Right:** Carmine bee-eaters nesting on a bank of the Chobe River in Caprivi. This attractive bird (the young have pink or pale bluish throats) eats beetles, grasshoppers and other insects.

the roads are mere tracks (not signposted) and some of the channels are waterlogged well into the dry season. Facilities are basic and limited to three designated camping areas – clearings without any amenities, but plans are afoot to develop the park for tourists.

Mamili is situated approximately 130 km southwest of Katima Mulilo, the regional capital of Caprivi, and is approached through the village of Sangwali. Parties should consist of a minimum of two vehicles and must be self-sufficient.

The regional office of the Ministry of Environment and Tourism at Katima Mulilo, where permits are obtainable, will assist visitors with information, advice and directions. Telephone them on (09264) 677 3027, or fax 3187/3341.

Mount Etjo Safari Lodge

Conservationist Jan Oelofse owns a private nature reserve that boasts an abundant wildlife, including white rhino, elephant, lion, black rhino, hippo and giraffe.

The savannah and woodland areas of this reserve are dotted with numerous waterholes and dams, ensuring an almost constant parade of wildlife, and the past is evocatively conjured up by caves that were once the dwelling-place of the hardy Bushman (San).

Mount Etjo Safari Lodge nestles in this spacious reserve, east of Kalkfeld, on Route 2483. Visitors can view game from open safari vehicles, on foot or – most leisurely of all – at a hide beside a waterhole. At one of the hides, fortunate visitors may enjoy close-up views of lion feeding during the early hours of evening.

The safari-lodge complex includes a restaurant, swimming pool and conference facilities, and there is an airstrip for guests who arrive by plane (Windhoek is 250 km away). All bedrooms have their own bathrooms. There is also a fully serviced, rustic camp comprising seven two-bed, stone-and-thatch huts situated near a waterhole with a gameviewing hide.

For further information and to make reservations, write to Mount Etjo Safari Lodge, P O Box 81, Kalkfeld, or telephone (09264) 651 4462/3, or fax 4035.

Mudumu National Park

Like nearby Mamili National Park (*see separate entry*), Mudumu was proclaimed in 1990 to protect the fast-dwindling numbers of game in the eastern Caprivi.

Covering approximately 11 000 ha of mainly mopane woodlands and extensive silver cluster-leaf woodlands, interspersed with patches of grassland, the park is bounded in the west by the Kwando River with its reed-lined channels, placid lagoons and magnificent riverine vegetation.

The waterways of the Kwando River support healthy populations of hippo, crocodile and otter, and small numbers of red lechwe frequent the floodplains. Sitatunga also occur, but since this species is confined to papyrus swamps, it is rarely seen. The short grasslands and floodplain margins are home to oribi, while large numbers of elephant, buffalo, kudu, roan, sable, impala and Burchell's zebra roam the woodlands.

Even more enriching than gameviewing is the park's wilderness atmosphere and profuse birdlife. Among the more than 400 bird species recorded are several 'specials', including slaty egret, cuckoo hawk, long-toed plover, red-winged pratincole and Arnot's chat, as well as a number of sunbirds.

Being a relatively young park, a management plan is still in the making. Except for the proclaimed road that passes through the park, the road network is limited to sandy tracks, and amenities are restricted to hutted accommodation at Lianshulu Lodge and a campsite (no facilities) at Nakatwa. In 1995 a concession was granted to the Lianshulu community to develop tourism facilities near the park's southern boundary. However, once the management plan has been drawn up, more amenities will be provided.

Lianshulu is an exclusive lodge set among green lawns and indigenous vegetation overlooking the Kwando River. It comprises a reception area, lounge, bar and dining room under thatch. Guests are accommodated in charming two-bed, A-frame chalets with *en suite* showers and toilets.

The emphasis here is on the wilderness rather than the game, and activities include nature drives, walks, boat trips and a sunset cruise on a double-decker pontoon. All activities are conducted by experienced guides.

Lianshulu is accessible by family sedan, but the sandy tracks within Mudumu require 4x4 vehicles. Visitors camping at Nakatwa must be self-sufficient. To reach Lianshulu, follow the Sangwali road turn-off, signposted about 7,4 km west of the Kongola River, on the main road between Rundu and Katima Mulilo. The northern boundary of the park (no entry control) is reached after about 36 km, and the lodge lies some 3,2 km further on. There is also a private airstrip. Nakatwa Camp is a few kilometres further south.

The regional office of the Ministry of Environment and Tourism at Katima Mulilo, where permits are obtainable, will assist visitors with information, advice and directions. Telephone them on (09264) 677 3027, or fax 3187/3341. Enquiries and reservations for Lianshulu Lodge can be made at The Namib Travel Shop, P O Box 6850, Windhoek, telephone (09264) 61 22-5178, or fax 23-9455; or Lianshulu Lodge through Walvis Bay Radio, telephone (09264) 64 20-3581 code 277, and the lodge will return your call.

Okonjima Guest Lodge

West of the Waterberg Plateau Park (*see separate entry*), the vast plains are occasionally broken by remnants of the Etjo sandstones that once covered large areas of northern Namibia. Set among one of these rugged geological relics, the Omboroko Mountains, is Okonjima Guest Lodge – its Herero name means 'place of the baboons'.

To participate in the variety of activities offered at this small, privately run lodge, a two-night stay is recommended. It is a particularly fine spot from which to get really close-up views of cheetah and leopard. Okonjima's three tame cheetah – Ching, Caesar and Chui – roam freely around the garden at teatime. Another permanent inhabitant of the lodge is Elvis, a fully grown male baboon that joins guests for brunch.

Okonjima is the home of the Africat Foundation, a non-profit organisation established in 1992 with the aim of conserving and protecting Namibia's large cats, especially cheetah and leopard. Trapped, injured and orphaned animals are cared for and rehabilitated, with a view to returning non-problem animals to the wild. Their numbers vary between 12 and 20, and guests are able to see aspects of the programme at work, and to watch the wild cheetah being fed in the afternoon. Okonjima's several wild leopard – there are usually at least two – are fed separately, and guests may look on from the comfort and safety of a hide.

Another unusual and exciting activity is viewing nocturnal animals, such as porcupine, from a hide close to the lodge. A visit to the hide is especially rewarding in the winter months when honey badger are frequently seen, while caracal also visit from time to time.

During the day the hide, which overlooks a small waterhole, is ideal for birding; among the more than 300 bird species on record are several Namibian endemics. Among these are Hartlaub's francolin, Monteiro's hornbill, white-tailed shrike and rockrunner.

Guests may take sundowner walks (depending on the feeding times of the cats) and early-morning guided walks. The Bushman Trail highlights the way of life and philosophies of the Bushman (San) people. Several other trails are also available. Accommodation comprises ten luxury double rooms with *en suite* facilities. There is also a dining room under thatch, and a swimming pool.

Approaching from the south along the B1, take the turn-off onto the D2525, about 130 km

---

MUSCLE, TOOTH AND CLAW

Although the lion is usually looked upon as the king of the carnivores, it certainly is not the bravest. Some believe that this title should be reserved for the mighty little bundle of energy that goes by the name of honey badger, or ratel (*Mellivora capensis*).

Although a small mammal, seldom reaching more than 75 cm from the tip of its nose to the base of its stubby tail, the honey badger is very powerfully built – a compact 12 kg of muscle, tooth and claw. It is easily identified by the light-coloured band that runs along the length of its body.

This gutsy creature, which is classified as a carnivore, actually eats a variety of roots, bulbs and fruit, as well as insects, rodents, scorpions, frogs, lizards and snakes. Its long, curved claws are perfectly designed for flipping over stones and ripping the bark off dead tree-trunks in search of insects. These formidable claws are also useful for 'burgling' the nests of wild bees, for the honey badger, as its name implies, has a particular fondness for honey. The bees attack it ferociously when it tears open their nests, but its thick hide provides almost complete immunity against their stings. This taste for honey has apparently led the ratel into an habitual association with a bird known as the honeyguide, which leads it to bees' nests with its chattering displays, and then eats the titbits exposed when the nest is broken open.

NAMIBIA: THE NORTHEAST

Above left: *Hibiscus calyphyllus,* found on the Waterberg. **Top:** Blister beetles, with their striking coloration, are members of the fascinating family Meloidae. Their blood contains a poisonous substance, cantharadin, which is widely believed to be an aphrodisiac (it is the basis of 'Spanish Fly'). However, doctors point out that cantharadin merely irritates the urinary tract – and can be extremely dangerous. The beetles were also used to a limited extent in medicine, in cases where it was thought necessary to cause blisters on the patient's skin. **Above right:** *Belenois aurota,* a common butterfly in the Waterberg Plateau Park and elsewhere in southern Africa. It has a wingspan of four to six centimetres.

north of Okahandja. Travelling from the north, the turn-off is signposted about 48 km south of Otjiwarongo. From the turn-off onto the D2525, it is about 24 km on a gravel road to the lodge.

For more information and to make reservations, contact Okonjima Guest Lodge, P O Box 793, Otjiwarongo, telephone (09264) 651 4563, or fax 4565.

Otjisazu Guest Farm

Otjisazu has been a landmark for weary travellers ever since the German missionary, Jacob Irle, built a mission station in the upper reaches of the Swakop River Valley in 1878. A Herero name meaning 'Land of the Red Cattle', Otjisazu later became one of the first guest farms in Namibia.

Blesbok, red hartebeest and kudu can usually be seen drinking at the watering place close to the guest-farm complex in the early mornings. There are also gemsbok, steenbok, warthog and a variety of smaller mammals, as well as a rich diversity of birds.

Despite the presence of game, Otjisazu's owner points out that the major appeal of the place lies in its unspoilt and contrasting landscapes and its long history of hospitality. The farm covers some 8 000 ha, and the scenery ranges from riverbeds lined with stately camelthorns to flat acacia savannah, dotted with rocky outcrops and mountains rising nearly 200 m above the plains.

Visitors may explore the farm by joining nature drives and sunset excursions in an open 4x4 vehicle. Other options for the more adventurous include guided nature walks, mountain biking and horse riding.

The guest farm is centred on the historic mission station, and the main complex, consisting of the dining room, lounge and bar, is accommodated in the old mission house.

There is also a swimming pool (especially appreciated in summer), and a poolside restaurant and bar under thatch. Accommodation consists of 12 double rooms and a family room, all with *en suite* facilities, a luxury suite and honeymoon suite. Otjisazu's traditional German and African cuisine and its game specialities are well known.

To reach Otjisazu, travel north from Windhoek to Okahandja and, just before reaching Okahandja, take the signposted turn-off onto the D2102, continuing for 27 kilometres. The farm has a landing strip for air transfers.

For information and reservations, write to Otjisazu Guest Farm, P O Box 149, Okahandja, telephone (09264) 621 50-1259.

Ovita Game Lodge

Ovita Game Lodge, northwest of Okahandja, encompasses 10 000 ha of large, open plains of acacia savannah, rocky outcrops of red granite and basalt, and sandy riverbeds. Established 20 years ago, Ovita was one of the first farms to be set aside as a private game reserve, and it is still run by the original owners, the Nebe family. Its varied landscape, including numerous dams and waterholes, provides a diversity of habitats for large herds of game and a prolific birdlife.

Game species found here include elephant, leopard, cheetah, giraffe, Hartmann's mountain zebra, Burchell's zebra, crocodile and ostrich. Among the 17 species of antelope are the rare and endangered roan, as well as Damara dik-dik, eland, waterbuck and nyala.

Birdlife is abundant and the reserve's bird list of over 300 species includes endemics such as Hartlaub's francolin, rockrunner, white-tailed shrike, Monteiro's hornbill and Carp's black tit. A feeding programme aimed at supporting the endangered Cape, white-backed and lappet-faced vultures has led to a relatively stable population at Ovita.

In addition to abundant wildlife there are numerous sites of archaeological interest. Stone tools and rock engravings provide evidence that Early Stone Age people and Later Stone Age ancestors of the Bushmen (San) once lived in the region.

Two three-hour activities are offered daily, with a choice of guided walking trails or game drives. For those who want to spend more time watching game, there are several gameviewing hides at prime spots in the reserve.

The central part of the lodge consists of dining rooms and a reading room, as well as a bar. Accommodation is provided in five double rooms (with *en suite* facilities) leading onto a terraced swimming pool and shady gardens. Elephant are frequent visitors to the two adjacent dams where crocodile, a variety of waterbirds and as many as ten species of game may be seen at times.

There is also a secluded bush camp, built of natural timber and thatch, in the Leopard Hills on the reserve's western boundary. Close by is a gameviewing hide overlooking a waterhole and ancient rock engravings.

To reach Ovita from Okahandja, travel towards Otjiwarongo and turn onto the D2110 at the western outskirts of the town. After 55 km turn right onto the D2121. The lodge lies 20 km further on.

For information and reservations, write to Ovita Game Lodge, P O Box 104, Okahandja, or telephone/fax (09264) 621 50-3882.

Popa Falls Rest Camp

Rapids, rather than falls, would be the best way to describe this stretch of white water on the Kavango River. But don't be disappointed – a feast of activities caters for every taste, from serene and beautiful sunsets and inspiring walks, to the ultimate thrill in freshwater angling – tigerfishing.

The water level drops during the dry season, allowing you to reach some of the smaller islands in the river via two footbridges, and by using the exposed rocks as stepping stones. Walk a short distance upstream to get a good view of the river before it churns and tumbles over the rapids.

The islands are well worth exploring – their forests are home to innumerable birds, and are threaded by the distinctive paths steamrollered by hippo during their nocturnal wanderings in search of food. Crocodile are occasionally seen in the main section of the river, so be on the lookout for them, especially near the water's edge.

Besides its own varied attractions, Popa is an excellent base from which to explore Mahango Game Park (*see separate entry*).

Accommodation comprises four-bed, rustic wood-and-thatch huts, a caravan site with ablution facilities, a field kitchen and braai sites. Nearby a private safari camp arranges fishing expeditions and offers meals. There is a kiosk that sells cooldrinks, tea, coffee and some basic foodstuffs such as tinned foods.

Access is via a tarred road from Rundu in the west, to the Divundu Bridge that crosses the Kavango River into the Caprivi Game Park. Just before the bridge, take the right fork and follow a gravel road along the river to Popa Falls, a distance of some five kilometres.

To make reservations, contact the Directorate of Tourism and Resorts, Ministry of Environment and Tourism, Private Bag 13267, Windhoek, telephone (09264) 61 23-6975/6/7/8, or fax 22-4900.

For further information, write to the Directorate of Tourism and Resorts, Ministry of Environment and Tourism, Private Bag 13346, Windhoek, or telephone (09264) 61 284-2111, fax 22-1930.

WATERBERG PLATEAU PARK AT A GLANCE

When to go The park is open all year, but bear in mind that it is very hot in summer. It is increasingly popular during school holidays and over long weekends. The office is closed between 1 p.m. and 2 p.m. No pets are allowed.

Reservations Enquiries and applications for accommodation should be addressed to the Directorate of Tourism and Resorts, Ministry of Environment and Tourism, Private Bag 13267, Windhoek, telephone (09264) 61 23-6975/6/7/8, fax 22-4900.

Getting there To reach the park, turn off the Windhoek/Otjiwarongo road some 27 km south of Otjiwarongo, and drive a further 42 km east on the C22 to a second turn-off to the northeast. Drive another 17 km to the park entrance.

Accommodation The Bernabé de la Bat Rest Camp (named after Namibia's first director of conservation) has luxury five-bed chalets, three-bed bungalows and two-bed 'bus quarters' or 'tourisettes'. Take your own crockery and cutlery. A restaurant, bar, shop, filling station and swimming pool are provided. There is also a large caravan/camping site with ablution facilities and field kitchens.

Getting around Private vehicles are not allowed on the plateau's rudimentary road system, but reservations for guided 4x4 tours can be made at the office. Numerous trails have been laid out around the camp's large grounds and beneath the plateau cliffs. A guided three-day wilderness hiking trail leaves on the second, third and fourth Thursday of each month between April and November. There is also a self-guided 50 km hiking trail, open between April and November, which takes four days to complete. This trail should not be taken lightly – buffalo and rhino might be met.

Wildlife Below the plateau you may find kudu, steenbok, klipspringer, dassie, dik-dik, warthog and rich birdlife, including the rare Bradfield's hornbill, paradise flycatcher and Hartlaub's francolin. On the plateau itself visitors may see a variety of game, including leopard, caracal, cheetah, brown hyena, giraffe, white rhino, black rhino, buffalo, eland, roan, sable, red hartebeest, blue wildebeest, tsessebe and smaller species, including impala and duiker. The sandstone cliffs accommodate Namibia's only breeding colony of Cape vulture, a threatened species. Ask at the reception office when the vulture restaurant will be open.

Waterberg Plateau Park

The Waterberg Plateau, like Mount Etjo to the southwest, is an erosional relic of the Karoo Sequence that once covered large areas of Namibia. The plateau's hard, red sandstone rises up to 250 m above the surrounding plain, and on three sides there are near-vertical cliffs that impose natural boundaries on the Waterberg's treasured wildlife species. Only in the north is there any need for a fence, for there the plateau gradually widens and dips until it becomes one with the plain.

The vegetation of the plateau is fairly similar to that of the Caprivi, with notable species including the silver cluster-leaf and Kalahari apple-leaf trees, while enormous common cluster (sycamore) figs are conspicuous near the springs on the lower slopes of the plateau.

Even before the plateau became a park it held an impressive population of eland (the largest of southern Africa's antelope) and several other species of buck. Since the country's eland population was declining rapidly, however, it was decided to establish a sanctuary that could serve as a breeding centre for eland, as well as for other rare and endangered game species. To ensure that the only animals reintroduced would be those that had occurred in the area historically, researchers examined the descriptions given by early travellers such as Francis Galton and Charles Andersson.

Giraffe were brought from the north, blue wildebeest from Daan Viljoen Game Park, duiker from around Tsumeb, and red hartebeest from a local farm. White rhino and impala came from KwaZulu-Natal, and buffalo from Addo Elephant National Park in the Eastern Cape. In two cases, animals were received only after periods in quarantine near Etosha's Otjovasondu – roan from Kavango in northeastern Namibia, and sable and tsessebe from Caprivi. In 1989 black rhino were relocated here from Etosha and Damaraland to safeguard them against poachers and to establish new populations elsewhere in the country.

Today over 90 mammal species inhabit the 41 000 ha park. There are also over 200 recorded bird species. Viewsites at the vulture restaurant are open to the public whenever a carcass is available for these threatened birds – usually once a week. Enquire at the rest-camp reception office.

Bernabé de la Bat Rest Camp is a modern, well-equipped complex accommodating visitors in bungalows and campsites. It is the start of a network of trails of varying lengths.

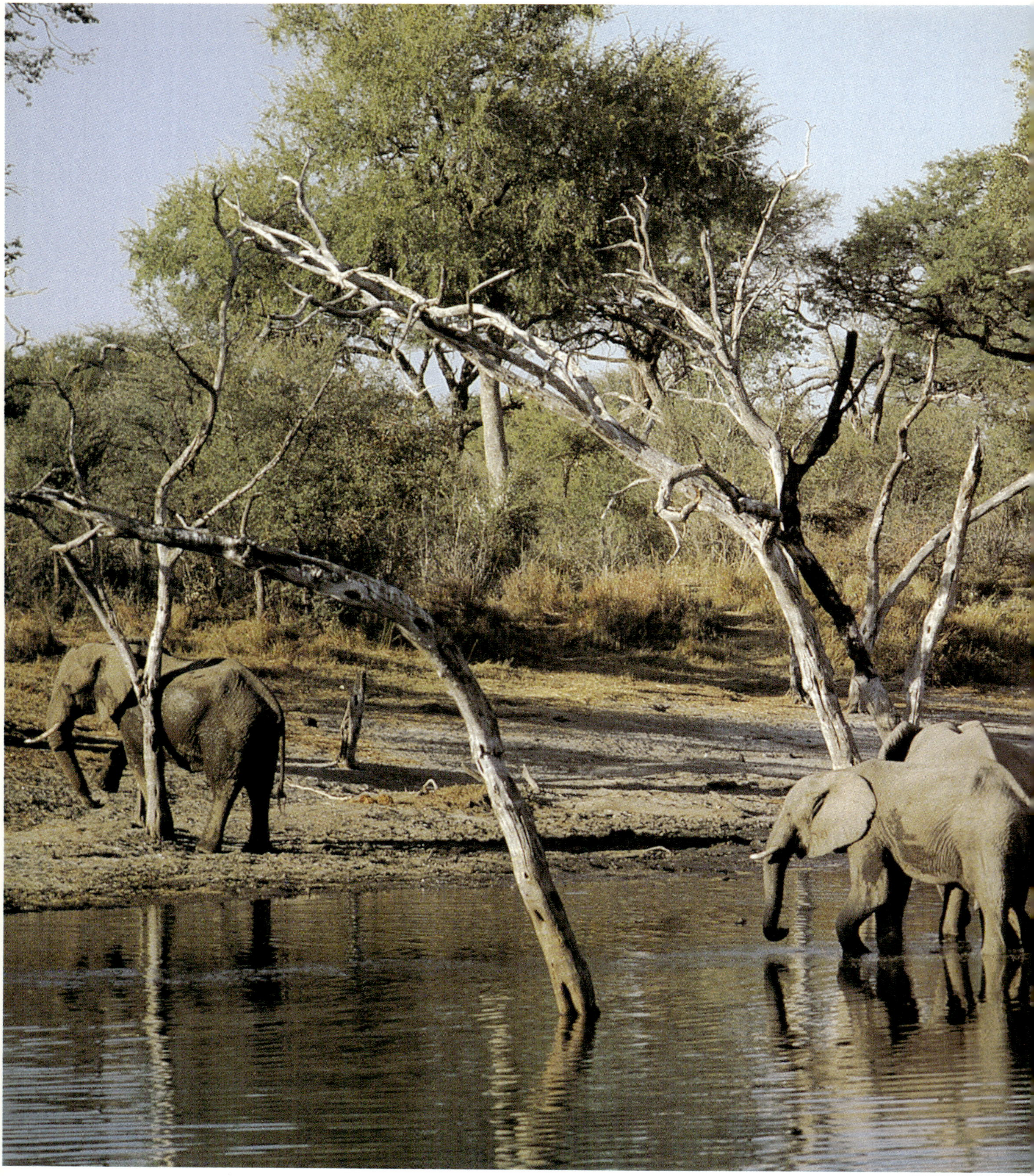

BOTSWANA

Botswana is southern Africa's largest and most authentic wilderness, a country of harsh contrasts and matchless beauty: once seen, it will never be forgotten. This is the country of Sir Laurens van der Post, a parched expanse of sand, sweet grass and teeming game that conjures up a hundred adventure stories.

Once the exclusive haunt of indigenous peoples, hunters and adventurers, Botswana is today an exciting mixture of cultures and lifestyles. The lean, sunburnt hunters still exist, but they rub shoulders and share sundowners with more conventional tourists – and sometimes with conservationists, a multitalented body of people dedicated to the preservation of the Kalahari's wildlife heritage.

There are many privately owned lodges and camps throughout Botswana, and facilities and accommodation vary widely. Some are basic and relatively cheap, while others are unabashedly luxurious and expensive. Visitors may fly in and explore the country in 4x4 vehicles and, in the vast and beautiful Okavango Delta, they may navigate the shallow channels in dugout canoes.

Whatever the medium of transport, however, it should be remembered that Botswana is big, untamed and potentially dangerous. Do not attempt to explore its sandy wastes in a conventional vehicle (in some areas the authorities recommend two 4x4 vehicles as a precaution), and do not stray from the roads and tracks.

Elephants drinking in the Savuti Channel, an abrupt offshoot of the Linyandi River, in Botswana's Chobe National Park. Wildlife is drawn as if by a magnet when the channel is in flood.

Wild and misty waterways

In the waterways of the Okavango, one of the world's last great wildernesses, scented water lilies, yellow, white, pink and lilac, shimmer on the water. A dragonfly hovers and a jacana bird hops across the lily leaves in search of its food. At water level in a nearby water-rooted fig, where the sacred ibis, cormorant, darter and egret huddle, spiders weave delicate filigree webs and cocoons of incredible complexity. On and around islands of tufted grass, snakes keep company with turtles and thousands of colourful, noisy frogs. As the dugout canoe cuts its way silently through the reeds, the lily leaves – green to the sun and red to the tigerfish below – trail on long stalks.

On a floating papyrus bed, a tiny crocodile basks open-mouthed in the sun, its hide glistening, needle-sharp teeth bared in unconscious menace. Round the next bend – and there are many bends in the labyrinthine meanderings of the delta – a scrum of hippo huff, snort and lower their corpulent bodies beneath the water. When the flood comes in midwinter, the water is crystal clear and fast-running; later, the current may be barely discernible over the flats, making navigation difficult for the inexperienced explorer. Water creeps down the dry riverbeds and across the dusty floodplains, obliterating stagnant pools and dispersing the thousands of animals which concentrated upon them in the drier times.

Born in the uplands of western Angola, the Okavango is a great and troubled river (the third largest in southern Africa). It flows, not to the sea, but east into the fiery heart of the Kalahari Desert – and there, in a fragile, tremor-shaken depression, it slows, stretches and dies. But its grave is a delta extending for 15 000 km – a natural symphony of rivers, lagoons, islands and forests. To those who have been there, it is beautiful beyond words.

Protected by the presence of tsetse fly and by its very size, the delta has until recently remained largely unconquered by man's rifles, ever-expanding habitations and herds of cattle.

The large variety of game in the delta includes some 20 000 buffalo and the elusive sitatunga, whose splayed, elongated hoofs enable it to walk through the swamps and reed beds without getting bogged down.

There are numerous safari camps (of which we describe a selection), some accessible only by air from outside the delta. Maun is the main springboard to the delta and services some of the camps by road and air. The road between Maun and Shakawe on the delta's panhandle is tarred, and the 380-odd km journey can be covered in about five hours (before the road was tarred it used to take some 12 hours in a 4x4 vehicle). The normal route from Namibia is via the border post of Mamuno to the cattle centre of Ghanzi. This 200 km stretch of bone-jarring road also used to take some 12 hours in a 4x4, but the road surface has been improved. It forms part of the system known as the Trans-Kalahari Highway, and is scheduled for tarring. Visitors entering Botswana from Namibia through Mamuno, or the Mohembo border post near Shakawe, should note that Namibian Winter Time (first Sunday in April to first Sunday in September) is one hour behind South African Standard Time, and they should time their border crossings accordingly.

There are flights from Johannesburg to Gaborone which link up with internal flights to Maun. For further information, write to Maun Office Services, P O Box 448, Maun, telephone

Below left: A bird's-eye view of the delta and its waterways. The Okavango is the third largest of southern Africa's rivers. **Below right:** A nymphal foam grasshopper belonging to the family Pyrgomorphidae. Although it possesses wing pads, this family has flightless adults. For self-protection, these large grasshoppers, or bush locusts, depend very much on their bold 'warning' colours, which advertise their toxic nature to vertebrate predators. In response to an attack by a predator they release foul-smelling, poisonous fluids from various points on their bodies. Some species propel the fluid in a jet from special glands; others produce a foam composed of irritants mixed with their own blood.

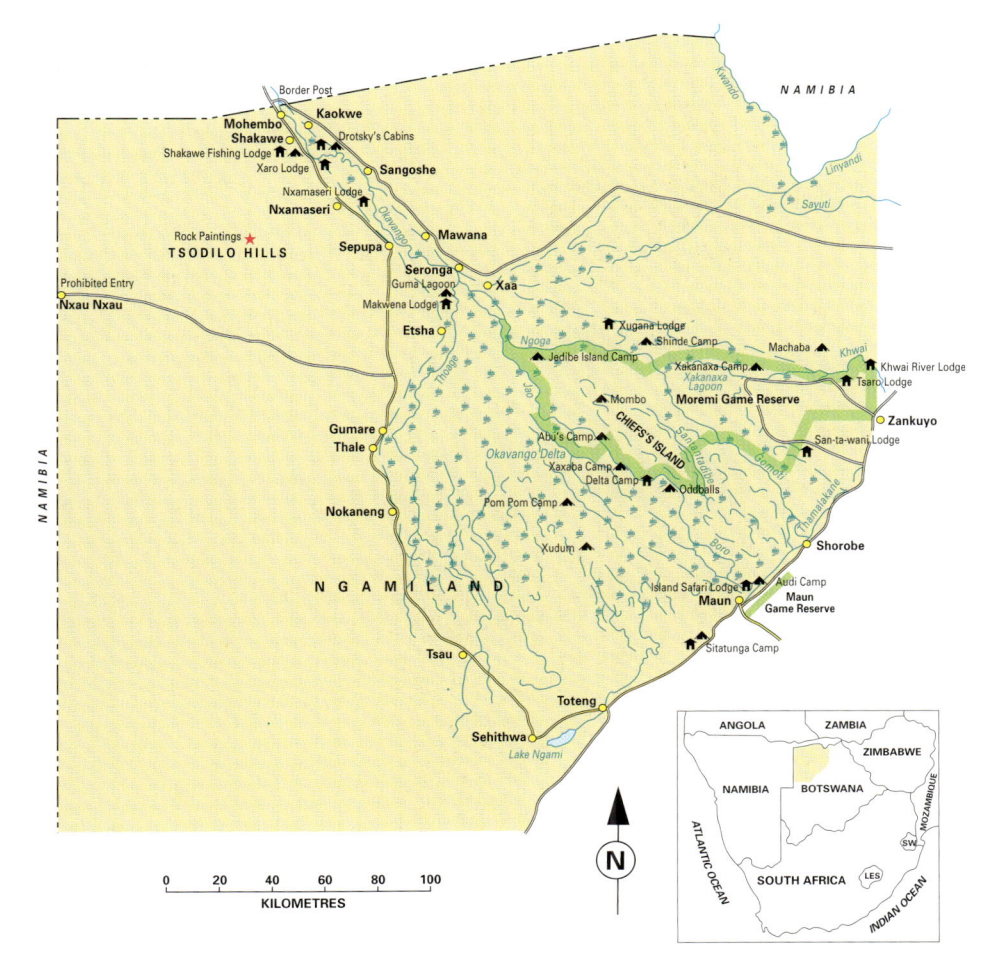

BOTSWANA: OKAVANGO

(09267) 66-0222, fax 66-0205; Travel Wild, P O Box 236, Maun, telephone (09267) 66-0822/3, fax 66-0493; or the Department of Tourism, Private Bag 0047, Gaborone, telephone (09267) 35-3024, fax 37-1539.

Audi Camp

Situated on the banks of the Thamalakane River, some 12 km north of Maun, alongside the road to Moremi Game Reserve (*see separate entry*), Audi Camp caters for the budget traveller. Facilities include campsites with communal hot-water ablutions, two-bed tents, a restaurant, bar and swimming pool. Reasonably priced day trips are conducted to Moremi and Nxai Pan, while overnight trips further afield are also undertaken. Also on offer are self-catering day and overnight mokoro (dugout canoe) trips. For more information, contact Audi Camp, Private Bag 28, Maun, telephone (09267) 66-0599, or fax 66-0581.

Chief's Island

Named after Moremi, chief of the Tawana people who used to hunt here, Chief's Island in the Okavango Delta is a great tract of woodland and savannah rich in game, hidden waterways and birdlife. The arid interior of the island is covered with mopane woodland and acacia thornscrub, home to large herds of buffalo. One hundred kilometres long and 15 km across its widest point, the island is flanked by two of the delta's largest rivers, the Boro and the Santantadibe, both of which flow into the Thamalakane River, not far from Maun. It forms a good third of the Moremi Game Reserve (*see separate entry*). No camps or human habitations are permitted on the island and, as a result, the sense of wildness is complete.

There are several (tented) safari camps fringing Chief's Island – all accessible from Maun by small aircraft (it is 70 km by air to these camps). The distance by river is about 80 kilometres. For further details, write to Maun Office Services, P O Box 448, Maun, telephone (09267) 66-0222, or fax 66-0205; Travel Wild, P O Box 236, Maun, telephone (09267) 66-0822/3, fax 66-0493; or contact the Department of Wildlife and National Parks, P O Box 131, Gaborone, telephone (09267) 37-1405, or fax 31-2354.

Delta Camp

Situated on Noga Island just outside the southern boundary of the Moremi Game Reserve (*see separate entry*), and accessible only by light aircraft from Maun, Delta Camp is a well-shaded, rustic bush camp accommodating 25 people (the accommodation includes a four-bed family chalet). The camp is also a week's lazy travel (by water) from Shakawe, and is rendered especially appealing by the fact that powerboats are prohibited from entering the

Right: Little bee-eaters huddling together at night in the depths of an Okavango reed bed. Although these birds are (for obvious reasons) unpopular with apiarists, bee-eaters do in fact feed on many types of flying insect other than honeybees.

area. This is the haunt of hosts of birds and mammals, including barred owl, bearded woodpecker, baboon and porcupine.

One of the first camps in the delta, Delta Camp dates back to the early 1970s when it was built as a family retreat by Lothar Swoboda. It was purchased in 1982 by Peter Sandenburgh, who also owns Oddballs Camp (see separate entry). Situated on the southern banks of the Boro River, the camp offers mokoro trips, excellent opportunities for birding and fishing (tigerfish, bream and barbel). Their address is Okavango Tours and Safaris, P O Box 52900, Saxonwold 2132, telephone (011) 788-5549, fax 788-6575.

Drotsky's Cabins

Owned by the extremely hospitable Jan and Eileen Drotsky, this shady camp lies high on the banks of the Okavango River some 5 km from Shakawe.

With a bird list of some 370 species (including such rarities as Pel's fishing owl, African skimmer and white-backed night heron), birding is the main attraction. Fishing is also rewarding, and guests can hire four-berth cruisers (with drivers) for leisurely tours of the panhandle.

Accommodation is provided in thatched A-frame chalets and tents, and there is a large area for campers. A restaurant and bar complete the creature comforts.

For reservations, contact Drotsky's Cabins, P O Box 115, Shakawe, telephone (09267) 67-5035, or fax 67-5043.

Elephant Safaris

Viewing the world perched on a howdah atop an African elephant is a wonderfully exhilarating experience. Your presence goes almost unheeded by other members of the animal world, and you have an unhindered view across the landscape.

Some years ago the American conservationist/biologist, Randall Jay Moore, brought a group of trained elephants from the United States and established them on an island in the southern Okavango Delta. The star bull, a huge tusker named Abu (after whom the camp on the island is named) is the leader of the herd of six adult and eight young elephant.

The safari (each lasts a few hours at a time over a period of at least four days) sets out from the camp and rocks and sways beneath beautiful Okavango trees and alongside lily-filled waterways. Each of the adult elephants used is fitted with a howdah seating two guests and a *mahout* or professional elephant trainer.

Overnight accommodation at Abu's Camp consists of five 'Out of Africa'-style tents with private bucket showers and toilets, and the attentions of an expert chef. For details or to make reservations, contact Elephant Back Safaris, Private Bag 332, Maun, telephone (09267) 66-1260, or fax 66-1005.

Guma Lagoon

Guma Lagoon, recognised as one of the most beautiful in the delta, is the perfect base from which to explore the fish-rich waters of nearby Etsatsa. Other activities include birdwatching, mokoro trails and gameviewing walks on neighbouring islands.

Visitors are accommodated in tents with private ablution facilities. For further information, contact Guma Lagoon, P O Box 66, Maun, telephone (09267) 66-0351, fax 66-0571.

Jedibe Island Camp

Located deep in the heart of the delta, perched on an island surrounded by a maze of waterways, Jedibe Island Camp is a popular and extremely attractive lodge. From here guests can explore the surrounding lagoons, floodplains and streams in a mokoro, or wander around one of the many palm-fringed islands in the area. Rich aquatic life – including the ever-popular tigerfish – and the prolific birdlife are added attractions. Sitatunga and red lechwe may be spotted.

Visitors stay in comfortable tents with private ablution facilities. For more information, contact Wilderness Safaris, P O Box 651171, Benmore 2010, telephone (011) 884-1458, or fax 883-6255.

Khwai River Lodge

The Khwai River (in the northeast of the Okavango Delta) is one of the major rivers of the delta, though it occasionally all but dries up, leaving a few hippo pools to await the fresh waters of the new season. It forms the northern border of the Moremi Game Reserve (see separate entry) and is host to several lodges and photographic safari camps, among them the Khwai River Lodge (operated by the Orient Express group) near the reserve's northern entrance gate.

The lodge, sheltered beneath spreading camelthorn and knobthorn acacia shade trees and huge sycamore figs, its thatched chalets, pool and patio overlooking the river and Moremi forest, was built in 1966 by Ker, Downey and Selby – professional hunters. A herd of red lechwe gallops through the reed beds in the early morning, pauses to browse, then gallops away. The nocturnal 'chorus' includes hyena,

Left: A sharp-eyed Pel's fishing owl (*Scotopelia peli*) watches the Okavango waters for signs of its prey. One of the rarer species of owl (though fairly common in the wetlands of Botswana), it has bare legs and long, strong claws. **Opposite page above left:** A semi-aquatic antelope related to the waterbuck, the red lechwe lives mainly in the floodplains of the Okavango, western Zambia and southern Zaïre. Water is both its sustenance and its defence: the species feeds on wetland grass and aquatic plants, retiring to deeper water (slow-footed on land, it is a competent swimmer) when threatened. Lechwe are gregarious animals, sometimes gathering in herds of a thousand and more. **Opposite page above right:** *Nymphaea caerulea*, a delicately attractive species of water lily that thrives in the Okavango area. **Opposite page below:** Tsessebe in the Moremi Game Reserve. Normally these antelope live in small groups of eight to ten (though single bulls are occasionally seen in the company of other species such as blue wildebeest and zebra), but come together in herds of up to 200 in the dry season. Not only is the tsessebe the swiftest of all southern Africa's buck, but it also has stamina to match its speed – it can maintain its full pace for anything up to five kilometres.

BOTSWANA: OKAVANGO

breeding pelicans, gulls, storks, greater and lesser flamingoes, herons and many other species throng the shallows. October to March is the best time to visit. Ornithological safaris are operated to the lake from Maun.

Machaba

At Machaba it is not unusual to see large herds of elephant walking past the camp on their way to the Khwai River. The sycamore fig-sheltered camp lies on the northern banks of the river, just outside the Moremi Game Reserve (see separate entry), and attracts a never-ending stream of game. Among these are lion, leopard, buffalo, waterbuck, tsessebe, sable and roan. Accommodation is provided in seven 2-bed tents with *en suite* facilities, with a central lounge, dining room and bar overlooking the river, and a swimming pool. For further information, contact Ker and Downey, P O Box 612, Green Point 8051, telephone (021) 434-1954, or fax 434-0489.

Makwena Lodge

The enchanting reed chalets of Makwena Lodge are clustered on a floodplain island, opening onto a papyrus-fringed lagoon, at the southernmost end of the Okavango Delta's 'panhandle'. It's a place for surveying the abundant birdlife – fish eagle, slaty egret, Pel's fishing owl, African skimmer, swamp boubou and many others – or for boating in mekoro (dugout canoes) or powerboats through clear waters that are home to bream and tigerfish, not to mention the occasional hippo. Water-loving lechwe and the elusive sitatunga inhabit the area's floodplains.

The camp takes up to 16 guests in chalets with *en suite* washing facilities. Its beautifully situated lookout bar offers wonderful sunset views, and the occasional glimpse of animals grazing on the island across from the lagoon. Further enquiries can be made to Okavango Wilderness Safaris, P O Box 66, Maun, telephone (09267) 66-0351, or fax 66-0571.

Maun

Patched-up safari vehicles, compressed sand, floodplains and whisky: this was Maun in the 1970s and 1980s – an appealing anachronism whose residents (some of them, anyway) appeared to have walked out of the pages of a Wilbur Smith novel. Today, however, the picture is different. The tarring of the road to Nata has changed the face of this once-dusty town. Tarred roads, modern shopping complexes and a burgeoning number of tourists have brought Maun firmly into the busy 1990s.

Maun is the centre from which enthusiastic lovers of the outdoors springboard into the Okavango. There are several companies with which most of the safari operators deal: Merlin Travel, telephone (09267) 66-0635, or

lion, baboon and crickets, but is inevitably dominated by the grunting and snorting of hippo – hardly tuneful, but certainly authentic Africa. Birdlife is plentiful, with saddle-billed stork, wattled crane and numerous raptors, including the giant eagle owl.

The lodge offers morning and afternoon gameviewing drives and walks, night drives, and cultural visits to local villages.

From Maun it is 140 km or four hours to Khwai River Lodge (the road along the east bank of the Thamalakane River is tarred as far as Shorobe, from where a 4x4 vehicle is needed). The lodge is 6,5 km east of Moremi's north gate. There is an airstrip nearby. From the Kazungula border post on the Zambezi, 70 km from the Victoria Falls, visitors face a rough drive of approximately 280 km to Khwai River Lodge. For further information, write to Gametrackers Botswana, P O Box 2608, Cape Town 8000, telephone (021) 23-1054, or fax 23-1060.

Lake Ngami

The legendary Lake Ngami is like a great mirage on the edge of the dry grassland of the Okavango Delta, about 70 km from Maun. This lake attracted (among others) David Livingstone in 1849, and its shores are now the home of Yei fishermen and colourful Herero pastoralists. In some years it is a dustbowl, but for decades on end can be a shallow lake 45 km long and up to 16 km wide.

Countless birds wheel, dive and feed in the water, in the air and on the shores; colonies of

347

OKAVANGO AT A GLANCE

When to go The best time to visit this rugged and beautiful area is from late May through to October, when the Okavango River floods the delta. December to February is the wet season, and not recommended. The Moremi Game Reserve in the delta is open year round, except when the rains occasionally necessitate closure of some of the roads. The later in the year (before the onset of the December rains), the better the gameviewing.

Reservations and information To reserve accommodation in the two camps at Khwai River and San-ta-wani (on the eastern fringe of the delta), write to Gametrackers Botswana, P O Box 2608, Cape Town 8000, telephone (021) 23-1054, fax 23-1060.

The travel contacts in Maun are: Merlin Travel, telephone (09267) 66-0635, fax 66-0036; Travel Wild, telephone (09267) 66-0822, fax 66-0493; Okavango Tours and Safaris, telephone (011) 788-5549, fax 788-6575; and Bonaventure Botswana, telephone (09267) 66-0503 or 66-0502. You can also contact Maun Office Services, P O Box 448, Maun, telephone (09267) 66-0222, or fax 66-0205.

For information on the Okavango Delta, you should write to the Department of Wildlife and National Parks, P O Box 131, Gaborone, telephone (09267) 37-1405, or fax 31-2354.

Getting there Maun is the springboard for most trips in the delta. It is accessible by road and by air.

Accommodation There are government camping sites in the Moremi Game Reserve, and numerous (privately run) fishing and birdwatching safari camps in the Okavango. Nearly all offer all-inclusive camp facilities.

Eating and drinking All foodstuffs and drink are supplied at safari camps. Because the Okavango is a true wilderness, there are no shops or fuel stations. Visitors intending to camp should bring their own food, fuel, spares and water. Maun is the nearest shopping area.

Getting around Aircraft are an obvious form of transport in the Okavango Delta, and air charters can be booked through office services and travel agencies. Although some of the main routes are tarred, 4x4 vehicles are essential to explore areas off the beaten track. Vehicles can also be hired in Maun. Various companies operate safaris into the Okavango, and they usually include the Savuti Channel area of the Chobe National Park in their itinerary. There is a rustic bus service from Francistown to Maun.

Special attractions A trip on a mokoro at Xaxaba, Xakanaxa, Xugana or from Shakawe is an unforgettable experience. The limestone Drotsky's Caves (also known as the Gcwihaba Caverns), 150 km west of the delta, are worth a detour. The Tsodilo Hills, 50 km west of the Okavango, and rising 400 m above the surrounding Kalahari plains, are studded with endless small samples of prehistoric rock art.

This is the only place left in southern Africa where Bushmen (San) still live near the rock art of their forefathers.

Wildlife Hippo, crocodile, python, lion, elephant, lechwe, baboon, wildebeest, buffalo, warthog, bat-eared fox and hundreds of bird species are represented in the Okavango Delta.

Fishing The Okavango is not a swamp. Its waters are crystal clear and teem (at its fringes) with bream and tigerfish. The best fishing is from September to February (tackle can be hired in the camps). Fishing licences or permits are not required in the delta, but they are necessary in the game reserves.

Special precautions Anti-malaria precautions and a snake-bite kit are essential. Use mosquito nets at night. A first-aid kit should be carried. Swimming is inadvisable unless a 'safe' spot has been pointed out by a local guide. Slow-flowing water in Maun may be infested with bilharzia-carrying snails. There is tsetse fly in the delta, but sleeping sickness is rare. The public camping sites in Moremi are unfenced and visitors should under no circumstances sleep under the stars. Food should be packed away to avoid nasty encounters with inquisitive monkeys, baboons and hyenas.

---

fax 66-0036; Travel Wild, telephone (09267) 66-0822/3, or fax 66-0493; Wilderness Safaris, telephone (011) 884-1458, fax 883-6255; and Bonaventure Botswana, telephone (09267) 66-0503 or 66-0502, or fax 66-0502. Riley's Garage (Private Bag 19, Maun, telephone (09267) 66-0203, fax 66-0556) and Riley's Hotel (P O Box 1, Maun, telephone (09267) 66-0204, fax 66-0580) are more or less 'national monuments'. Maun is one hour by air from Victoria Falls, and three hours from Lanseria Airport in Johannesburg.

Apart from Riley's Hotel, there are several other lodges and camps: Okavango River Lodge, telephone/fax (09267) 66-0298; Crocodile Camp, telephone (09267) 66-0265, or fax 66-0793; and Island Safari Lodge, telephone/fax (09267) 66-0300. All are on the Thamalakane River (just north of Maun) and all feature thatched chalets and campsites. Activities include wildlife and Okavango Delta safaris (visitors travel in 4x4 vehicles and boats). Boats may be hired, and guides are available. You can drive a normal sedan car the entire (tarred) distance from Francistown (on the Cape/Zimbabwe highway) to Maun.

For further information, contact Maun Office Services, P O Box 448, Maun, telephone (09267) 66-0222, fax 66-0205, or any other travel agent.

Maun Game Reserve

Botswana's first educational game park lies alongside the Thamalakane River near Maun. At the entrance gate, a board informs visitors that this sanctuary, 2 km long and 1 km wide, was established to teach people about wildlife conservation and management. It embraces vegetation typical of the area at the confluence of the Okavango and Kalahari rivers, and supports numerous antelope species, including kudu, impala, red lechwe, as well as giraffe, Burchell's zebra and warthog.

The park is ten minutes by car from Riley's Hotel in the village. For further information, write to the Department of Wildlife and National Parks, P O Box 131, Gaborone, telephone (09267) 37-1405, fax 31-2354.

Mombo Camp

Mombo Camp is famous for its wild dogs and hyena – a large segment of the classic documentary on these nocturnal predators, 'Sisterhood', was filmed here. This remote, tented camp is set beneath large shady trees on Mombo Island, at the northern tip of Chief's Island, and is situated within the Moremi Game Reserve (see separate entry). In addition to morning and afternoon game drives, guided walking trips are conducted. A trails camp, lying about 1 km from Mombo Camp, caters for visitors keen to explore the delta on foot. Mombo offers a dense concentration of

Left: A flight of squacco herons on the papyrus-lined Okavango River – a fairly rare sight because, although the species is common in the wetter regions of southern Africa, it tends to be a solitary bird, spending much of its time standing almost motionless among the marsh reeds. **Above left:** The blood lily brings a splash of strident colour to the delta countryside. **Above right:** The nocturnal scrub hare is larger (the males weigh up to 2 kg) and longer-eared than other southern African hares. The species thrives throughout the subcontinent – though it tends to avoid forest – and, in many areas, encroaches destructively on cultivated lands.

wildlife, including large and small predators, elephant, buffalo, giraffe, blue wildebeest and numerous birds – notably waterbirds.

Mombo Camp sleeps 20 and the trails camp a maximum of eight. For further information, contact Wilderness Safaris, P O Box 651171, Benmore 2010, telephone (011) 884-1458, fax 883-6255.

Moremi Game Reserve

Botswana is a magnet for hunters, and has been so for centuries. It was the decimation of the game that prompted naturalists Robert and June Kaye to rally the Batawana people into declaring 180 000 ha of their land in the Okavango Delta a game reserve. Proclaimed in 1963, Moremi's expanse has been increased to 487 200 hectares. Its floodplains offer a rich variety of game, magnificent mopane forests, islands of tall fan palms, crystal-clear Okavango waterways and practically every wildlife habitat. Even a short drive into the reserve results in a dozen sightings: impala, roan, lion, tsessebe, kudu, elephant, buffalo, lechwe, warthog and legions of baboon.

Huge strangler figs, with roots resembling snakes, enmesh the sausage trees, while in the distant vlei hundreds of tsessebe graze. The birdlife in Moremi is rich to the point of extravagance: roller, hoopoe, kingfisher, owl and woodpecker are the most common, while a bend in the Khwai River offers a view of birds such as wattled crane, spur-winged goose, saddle-billed stork and heron.

For further information on Moremi, write to the Department of Wildlife and National Parks, P O Box 131, Gaborone, telephone (09267) 37-1405, fax 31-2354. For campsite reservations, contact Parks and Reserves Reservations, P O Box 20364, Boseja, Maun, telephone (09267) 66-1265, fax 66-1264.

Nxamaseri Lodge

Activities at Nxamaseri Lodge include fishing, birding, mokoro trails and motorised boating trips, as well as outings (lasting two or three days) on board the luxury riverboat *Kubu Queen*. Overnight excursions to the Tsodilo Hills can be arranged. Accommodation is in brick-and-thatch chalets with a private wooden deck and *en suite* facilities, and amenities that include a dining room, lounge and bar under thatch, and a boma. Nxamaseri lies some 55 km south of Shakawe – the 380 km road from Maun to Shakawe is tarred, but transfers to the camp must be arranged. For further information, contact General Safari Company, P O Box 41567, Craighall 2024, telephone (011) 880-8466, fax 880-6136. The best time for fishermen to visit the lodge is between the months of June and September.

Oddballs

Situated alongside the Boro River on Noga Island, Oddballs was the Okavango's first budget camp. Visitors are brought to Oddballs from Maun, about 50 km away, by air. Once there, the waterways of the delta and its fauna can be explored at leisure by mokoro (dugout canoe) for as long as you wish. Facilities include campsites with hot-water ablutions and non-perishable groceries.

For further information, write to Okavango Tours and Safaris, P O Box 52900, Saxonwold 2132, telephone (011) 788-5549, fax 788-6575.

Pom Pom Camp

This remote camp in the heart of the Okavango offers a combination of excellent birding, gameviewing drives and mokoro trips along the delta's reed-lined waterways. Accessible

Right: The sun rises over the Okavango, washing its waters with a rosy orange-pink. The wooden mokoro, or dug-out canoe, is perfectly designed for negotiating the waterways. It was introduced to the Okavango by the Yei and Mbukushu, expert fishermen who came from the Zambezi River area.

only by air (some 35 minutes from Maun), a maximum of 14 guests at a time can be accommodated in its 2-bed tents with *en suite* facilities. Hippo are frequently spotted in the pool in front of the camp, and safari drives reveal a wealth of game. For more information, contact Ker and Downey, P O Box 612, Green Point 8051, telephone (021) 434-1954, fax 434-0489.

San-ta-wani Lodge

San-ta-wani is named after a mythical fox (as opposed to the bat-eared fox, symbol of Botswana's Department of Wildlife and National Parks), whose footprints are, according to legend, purple in the dew. Take the 'great north track' towards the Chobe National Park (*see separate entry*) and Victoria Falls, passing through Shorobe – from here the tracks are accessible only to 4x4 vehicles. Turn left just beyond the village of Shukumukwa, continuing for about 29 kilometres.

There is an airstrip beside a nearby lagoon formed by the Mogogelo River, and the game-viewing is excellent: visitors are likely to spot elephant, wildebeest, kudu, zebra, hyena, buffalo and myriad birds of many species.

The Orient Express Hotels group manages San-ta-wani Lodge, which was closed for extensive refurbishment in 1996 (scheduled for reopening in late 1997/early 1998). Game-viewing drives are conducted along the Khwai River and in the Moremi Game Reserve (*see separate entry*).

For more information, write to Gametrackers Botswana, P O Box 2608, Cape Town 8000, telephone (021) 23-1054, fax 23-1060.

Shakawe Fishing Lodge

Shakawe is a sprawling conglomeration of huts, reeds, dugout canoes and ant hills, situated in the far northwest corner of Botswana, some 15 km from the Caprivi Strip. Perched beside the Okavango River, the lodge, which opened its doors in 1969, was the first such tourist facility in the area. It offers fishing (best between June and September), motorised boating, excellent birding, riverine forest nature walks, and optional excursions to the Tsodilo Hills. Accommodation consists of thatched chalets with *en suite* facilities. There is also a restaurant, bar and swimming pool, as well as a campsite with communal hot-water ablutions, flush toilets and firewood. The lodge lies about 10 km south of Shakawe – the 380 km road between Maun and Shakawe is tarred, but visitors must arrange transfers to the lodge in advance. For further information, contact Shakawe Fishing Lodge, P O Box 12, Shakawe, telephone (09267) 66-0822, or fax 66-0493.

Shinde Camp

Located on a remote island in the permanently flooded area of the northern delta, Shinde Camp is situated on the edge of the lagoon after which it has been named. Visitors can explore the waterways surrounding the island in mekoro (dugout canoes) or powerboats – trips can also be arranged to the nearby Gcodikwe heronry. Other activities include gameviewing walks and fishing for tigerfish and bream. The area's varied game includes sitatunga, red lechwe, reedbuck, elephant, giraffe, lion, leopard and wild dog. Guests are accommodated in twin-bed luxury tents with *en suite* bathrooms, and are flown in and then transferred to the camp by boat. For further details, contact Private Bag 47, Maun, telephone (09267) 66-0570, fax 66-0258.

Sitatunga Camp

Situated 12 km south of Maun on a mostly tarred road (the last 2 km are on gravel which is negotiable by ordinary sedan vehicle), is the budget-priced Sitatunga Camp. Facilities at the shady campsite, which lies on the banks of the Thamalakane River, include power points, braai sites and communal hot-water ablutions. There are also two self-catering chalets, a shop and a liquor outlet. Sitatunga is located on a farm where crocodiles are bred for their skins, and visitors are allowed to view these fearsome reptiles. For further enquiries, write to Private Bag 47, Maun, or telephone (09267) 66-0570, fax 66-0258.

Tsaro Lodge

Tsaro is a luxurious safari camp on a 6 ha floodplain island on the northern border of the Moremi Game Reserve (*see separate entry*), situated near Khwai River Lodge. It lies some 160 km from Maun, near the reserve's northern gate. Brick-and-thatch rondavels (split-level and with a sunken bath) and a number of cottages have been built beneath giant trees, including motshaba figs, leadwoods, crotons and knobthorns, overlooking the Khwai River. It is the sister camp to Xugana Lodge (*see separate entry*).

Left: A herd of red lechwe in the Moremi Game Reserve. These delicate creatures are in perfect harmony with their surroundings, timing their breeding season to coincide with the delta's seasonal floods.
Above: Xugana Lodge nestles beneath shady trees on the shores of an oxbow lagoon.

For more information on Tsaro, contact the owners at Private Bag 48, Maun, telephone (09267) 66-0528, or fax 66-1806.

Xakanaxa Camp

Fifty kilometres from Khwai River Lodge and 140 km from Maun, in the north of the Moremi Game Reserve (see separate entry) along a sandy road through dense forests of mopane, is Xakanaxa – a crescent-shaped and crystal-clear lagoon on the Moanachira River. Here, on the permanent water of the Okavango (as opposed to the floodplains), safari operators Tony Graham and Dougie Skinner established Xakanaxa Camp, the first private camp within Moremi Game Reserve. Huge sausage trees overhang the safari tents at the water's edge, and an elevated thatch-and-reed dining room and bar overlook the lagoon.

Xakanaxa (pronounced Ka-Kan-A-Ka) is one of the few camps offering water-based activities and gameviewing throughout the year. These activities include boating on the waterways, guided walks on nearby islands, gameviewing drives in the reserve, fishing, and excellent birding (by special arrangement, trips are conducted to the Gcodikwe heronry). The landing strip is a 15-minute drive from the camp, which caters for 24 people. For further information, contact Moremi Safaris, P O Box 2757, Cramerview 2060, telephone (011) 465-3842, fax 465-3779.

Two other lodges in close proximity to Xakanaxa are Camp Moremi (Private Bag 19, Maun, telephone (09267) 66-0564), in a savannah setting, and Camp Okuti (Private Bag 47, Maun, telephone (09267) 66-0570, or fax 66-0258), which offers accommodation for 14 in thatched, brick-walled bungalows.

Xaro Lodge

An ideal retreat for anglers, Xaro Lodge lies on a peninsula jutting out into the fast-flowing Okavango River, on the western side of the delta's panhandle. There are bird- and game-watching too; while an unusual attraction is an outing – by road or air – to the nearby Tsodilo Hills, where more than 2 500 rock paintings are to be found. The area is still inhabited by Bushmen (San).

Xaro Lodge sleeps 12, in luxury double tents, with en suite facilities. The lounge and dining room are under thatch, African style. To make enquiries, write to P O Box 66, Maun, telephone (09267) 66-0351, or fax 66-0571.

Xaxaba Camp

Shaded by magnificent riverine forest trees, Xaxaba lies 8 km from Chief's Island on the southern banks of the Boro River, just outside the Moremi Game Reserve (see separate entry). The camp is 67 km (by air) from Maun, and is closed in January and February. Xaxaba flies all its visitors in to the camp, which can accommodate up to 25 guests. Motorboat and mokoro trips, sundowner barge cruises, guided walks and visits to local villages are offered.

Reservations for Xaxaba, which forms part of the Orient Express Hotels portfolio, can be made by contacting Gametrackers Botswana, P O Box 2608, Cape Town 8000, telephone (021) 23-1054, fax 23-1060.

Xudum

Located in the southwestern corner of the delta, the island on which Xudum nestles is enclosed on three sides by seasonal lagoons. One of the delta's most luxurious camps, Xudum offers accommodation in tents with en suite facilities, as well as a lounge and dining area under canvas. Activities include game drives, walks with trained elephants, mokoro trips and guided walks. Walking trails, accompanied by Bushman (San) trackers, are also on offer, and horseback safaris are a favourite way to explore the region. For further information, contact The Legendary Adventure Company, P O Box 411288, Craighall 2024, telephone (011) 327-0161, or fax 327-0162.

Xugana Lodge

The word xugana, which means 'kneel down and drink', was given by the ancient Bushmen (San) to one of the most idyllic and secluded locations in the northern reaches of the Okavango Delta. This beautiful camp on the shore of an oxbow lagoon offers raised luxury wooden chalets within a vault of wild fig, garcinia and mokutshumo trees. The showers, toilets, bar and dining room are of brick-and-thatch construction.

Xugana lies to the north of the Moremi Game Reserve's north gate (by air, 115 km north of Maun). Guests fly to the private airstrip, and are then ferried, by boat, the remaining 1 km to the camp.

For further information, write to Okavango Explorations, Private Bag 48, Maun, telephone (09267) 66-0528, or fax 66-1806.

A sunburnt wilderness

There is no such place as the lost city of the Kalahari – but it is all too easy to lose yourself in this vast grassland. The Kalahari is a flat, seemingly endless expanse of land where the days are scorching and the nights sometimes very cold. Four of Africa's most remote game areas are here: the Central Kalahari, Khutse, Mabuasehube and Gemsbok.

At 6,5 million ha these regions cover a land area three-quarters the size of KwaZulu-Natal. Here you'll find lion, leopard, cheetah, caracal, wild dog, bat-eared fox, gemsbok, herds of wildebeest several thousand strong – and practically no water. It is a harsh, unforgiving land, where only the strong and the resourceful are able to survive.

The Kalahari is one of the last strongholds of the hunter-gatherers of southern Africa, the San (also known as the Bushmen). There are around 45 000 San in Botswana (with possibly another 55 000 in neighbouring territories) – remnants of a once-prolific population that, in the Later Stone Age, hunted game and gathered the fruits of the earth and sea throughout the southern African subcontinent.

Negroid migrants swept down from the north, mixed and cohabited with the San and their pastoralist Khoikhoi cousins. Much later, white men from the south occupied the fertile lands, forcing into the inhospitable regions of the interior the survivors of these distinctive people whose lives so closely harmonised with the land and its creatures.

The San way of life, then, was adaptable even to their new and harsh environment. Superb tracking skills, combined with spears, knobkerries and, most feared and lethal, bow and poison-tipped arrows, were usually successful, providing the food and clothing needed for survival. The shaft behind the arrowhead was smeared with lethal poison derived from the plants of the semidesert, from the beetle *Diamphidium*, and from various spiders. The poison worked slowly, and the prey usually rejoined the herd, which was then shadowed by the hunters, perhaps for three days or more. When the animal became too weak to keep up with the herd, the patient San closed in for the kill. They killed only what they needed, and left no scars on the land.

These are the San, whose tenure of remote places once seemed so assured. Today, however, many have been displaced again – by later wars – and are caught in the conflict between their traditional culture and the demands of an industrialised society with its unprecedentedly large-scale commercial farming. Few San are able to pursue the old way of life in an increasingly crowded world of dwindling natural resources.

Many of the San are at the crossroads – still mobile, but owning a few goats and chickens and trade-bought goods such as cooking pots and knives. Thousands of others have settled on farms and are becoming integrated with the modern rural economy.

Central Kalahari Game Reserve
Passing through wetter and drier periods, the Kalahari has steadily become drier over the last million years. Even the name, sometimes spelt 'Kgalagadi', means 'the great drying up' or 'thirst' in the dialect of the Tswana people. Rainfall is sporadic, although twice in the last half-century it has been known to snow.

There is water to be found under the vast wilderness of savannah, dry grassland and fossil riverbeds, but most of it is heavily mineralised and undrinkable.

The Central Kalahari Game Reserve was established in 1961 as a sanctuary for the desert's migratory herds of eland, blue wildebeest, red hartebeest, springbok and zebra, to safeguard the area against development, and

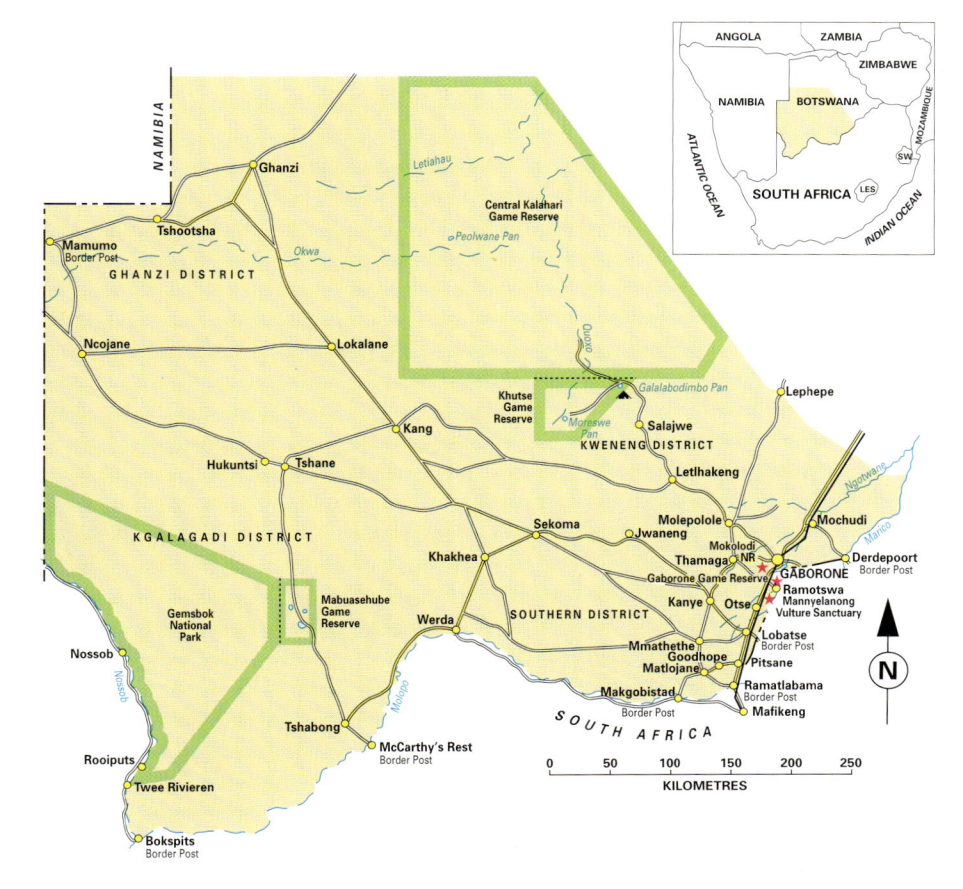

BOTSWANA: **KALAHARI DESERT**

to protect the main hunting ground of the Bushmen (San) – ensuring the continuation of their nomadic life as hunter-gatherers.

In the late 1980s, because of pressure from conservationists and changes in San social structures, the government tried to persuade them to leave the reserve to the animals. The San, backed by an international organisation campaigning for the rights of indigenous peoples, have resisted the move and still inhabit the area – the largest settlement – with clinic, school and borehole – is at Xade near the reserve's western boundary. The Botswana government has pledged not to remove them against their will.

The Central Kalahari Game Reserve covers 5,18 million ha (the second largest protected area in the world), and is an important haven for the threatened herds. By a miracle of nature they can exist without rivers or waterholes – by feeding at night from plants wet with dew, and from succulents that gain moisture from deep root systems. The swollen underground parts of plants such as wild cucumber and aloe are favourites. After a veld fire, the herds feed on tender young shoots.

The Bushmen (San) also survive on some unlikely plants and animals in this harsh land. Virtually any creature is a potential meal, as Guillermo Farini discovered during his travels. In his book *Through the Kalahari Desert*, he describes how his companion, Kert, 'went into a transport of joy at finding some "Bushman's rice" – the immature stages of certain species of termite or white ant, with broad black heads and long fat bodies.... Taking a handful of these he poured them into his mouth and chewed them with the greatest gusto, smacking his lips as they disappeared down his throat.'

The beautiful Deception Pan, located in the northwestern corner of the reserve's northern Deception Valley, is part of the course of an ancient river that flowed through the Kalahari until about 16 000 years ago. The flat bed is now grass-covered, dotted with stands of trees and home to impressive numbers of game. There is a campsite here, and an airstrip – built by Mark and Delia Owens who researched brown hyena in the area in the 1970s.

A danger to the great herds in the reserve is the construction of fences that have been erected over great areas of the Kalahari – including most of Botswana, parts of Angola and Namibia, and South Africa south to the Orange River. Intended to demarcate borders and to prevent the spread of foot-and-mouth disease among cattle, these fences now pose a threat to the wild herds, cutting them off from traditional grazing grounds.

They also have a devastating effect on game migration patterns, especially during droughts – more than 300 000 blue wildebeest, 250 000 red hartebeest and 60 000 zebra died in

Opposite page left: A family of spotted hyena rests up during the heat of the day in the Gemsbok National Park. The species is probably best known for its lunatic laughter – the cry of triumph after a successful hunt – but it has many other calls. Fully 17 distinctive sounds have been recorded, ranging from a high-pitched howl when gathering for the hunt to an angry scream when competing for a carcass.

Opposite page right: A 'dust devil', or small whirlwind, whips its erratic way across one of the park's pans.

Right: A porcupine. This nocturnal animal spends most of the daylight hours inside its burrow, emerging occasionally, as this one has, to sunbathe. Porcupines have a highly developed defence mechanism and few natural enemies. When a predator – perhaps a particularly hungry leopard or lion – does attack, their needle-sharp quills rise and they either jump backwards against their assailant, driving home the quills or, if chased, stop abruptly, causing the pursuer to impale itself. The porcupine does not 'shoot' its quills.

BOTSWANA: KALAHARI DESERT

KALAHARI AT A GLANCE

When to go The winter months of June, July and August are the best time to visit the Kalahari region.

Reservations and information To visit the Kalahari and all the national parks and game reserves in Botswana, a permit is necessary. More information about all reserves, permits and the fees payable may be obtained from The Director, Department of Wildlife and National Parks, P O Box 131, Gaborone, telephone (09267) 37-1405, or fax 31-2354; or The Director, Tourism Division, Private Bag 0047, Gaborone, telephone (09267) 35-3024, or fax 37-1539.

For campsite reservations, contact the Department of Wildlife and National Parks, Parks and Reserves Reservations, P O Box 20364, Boseja, Maun, telephone (09267) 66-1265, fax 66-1264.

Getting there There are scheduled flights into Gaborone from Johannesburg, Harare, Windhoek and Lusaka, and into Maun and Francistown from Windhoek and Gaborone. Safari operators – situated mostly in Maun – offer 4x4 vehicles, light aircraft and guides. Both the Gemsbok and the Mabuasehube reserves are best approached from the south; Khutse from Gaborone, and the Central Kalahari Game Reserve from Ghanzi in the west (via D'kar) or Francistown (via Orapa) in the east.

Accommodation There is no hutted accommodation in any of the game parks. Camping is permitted but facilities are non-existent or minimal.

Eating and drinking Visitors should bring their own food supplies and sufficient water for the duration of their stay. About eight litres of water are needed per person per day for drinking and washing.

Getting around Topographical maps, a compass or, even better, a GPS (Geographical Positioning System) should be taken. For safety, take two 4x4 vehicles.

Wildlife Practically every species of game, with the exception of elephant, can be found in the Kalahari (there are 3 000 giraffe in the Central Kalahari Game Reserve alone). Thousands of wildebeest, hartebeest and springbok gather at the pans, attracting a variety of predators.

Special precautions A trip into the Kalahari must be carefully planned. Two 4x4 vehicles are necessary, and you should take all the motor spares, food and water you may require. Start a course of anti-malaria tablets before you leave.

Remember that it is normal desert etiquette in Botswana to assist a vehicle or its passengers stranded in the Kalahari or other outback areas.

Botswana during the prolonged drought of the 1980s because their traditional migratory routes were unyieldingly blocked by fences.

Until the early 1990s the reserve was closed to the general public, but permits are now obtainable on arrival, and a fee is charged if you wish to enter or camp within its boundaries (camping is permitted at Deception Valley, Sunday Pans and Piper's Pan). Water may be obtained from Matswere Game Scouts Camp in the north. For more information, contact The Director, Department of Wildlife and National Parks, P O Box 131, Gaborone, telephone (09267) 37-1405, or fax 31-2354. To make campsite reservations, contact the Department of Wildlife and National Parks, Parks and Reserves Reservations, P O Box 20364, Boseja, Maun, telephone (09267) 66-1265, or fax 66-1264. This area includes some of the harshest territory in Botswana, so if you do intend visiting it, remember to take special precautions.

Gaborone Game Reserve

A good place to see two white rhino is in the heart of Botswana's capital city, at the small Gaborone Game Reserve. While the rhino are kept securely in a special enclosure, the other game in this educational reserve can roam quite freely within 500 ha of fenced-off plains. Along the reserve's eastern boundary is the heavily forested Ngotwane River.

Among the reserve's impressive array of animals are eland, gemsbok, wildebeest, impala, springbok, warthog, kudu, and many species of bird and reptile.

For more information, contact The Director, Department of Wildlife and National Parks, P O Box 131, Gaborone, telephone (09267) 37-1405, or fax 31-2354.

Gemsbok National Park

There are two Gemsbok parks: the Kalahari Gemsbok National Park in South Africa, and the larger Botswana section, the 2,6 million ha Gemsbok National Park, separated by the ancient bed of the Nossob River.

The entrance to the Kalahari Gemsbok National Park is at Twee Rivieren, while visitors approaching the Gemsbok National Park from the south should pass through the border post at Bokspits, continuing north to the Botswana side of the border (suitable for sedan vehicles), to the park's southern entrance gate (also known as Twee Rivieren).

An alternative route is via the road to Tshabong, from where a rather sandy track – on which a 4x4 is needed – is followed in a northwesterly direction to the Mabuasehube Game Reserve (see separate entry) and the adjoining Gemsbok National Park.

The road along the ancient bed of the Nossob River – which may not flow for ten years at a stretch – is used by visitors to both parks and is negotiable by sedan car. Visitors can also follow a sandy 4x4 track along the park's southern boundary to or from the Mabuasehube Game Reserve, but must inform the Department of Wildlife and National Parks officials at the point of departure, indicating whether they intend camping out en route, and their estimated time of arrival. A circular 4x4 trail, which will link up with these tracks in the Mabuasehube Game Reserve, is planned.

Game to be seen includes springbok, hartebeest, gemsbok, eland, wildebeest, ostrich and kudu, with predators such as lion, cheetah, brown hyena, leopard and wild dog. This is also one of the best places in the subcontinent for raptors, including secretary bird, pale chanting goshawk, greater kestrel, lanner

BOTSWANA: **KALAHARI DESERT**

Far left below: A Cape fox beside its den in the Gemsbok National Park. This is the only true fox found in southern Africa. The species has extremely good sight and hearing. **Left above:** The brown hyena is smaller, shyer, and more solitary than its spotted cousin. It lives in rock fissures and thickets but most often in a burrow, which is easily recognised by the bones and feathers – the remains of many meals – that litter the immediate surroundings. **Above:** The fork-marked sand snake, a quick-moving, diurnal species which is sometimes preyed on by its traditional enemy – the snake eagle. **Left below:** A herd of springbok on the move along the banks of the Nossob River.

and pygmy falcon, tawny, black-breasted and martial eagle, as well as numerous species of owl and vulture. In all, over 260 bird species have been recorded, including yellow canary, lilac-breasted roller, kori bustard and korhaan. Sociable weavers are common, with their huge nests housing up to 300 birds, each in its own individual compartments.

There are no designated campsites within the park, but plans are afoot to establish one at Rooiputs on the Nossob River, and more along the 4x4 route. In the meantime, visitors may choose their own camping spots, but must take great care not to cause veld fires, and must remove all their refuse. They must also be completely self-sufficient, making sure they have food, firewood, water and medical supplies. General supplies may be purchased at the camps on the South African side. Contact The Director, Department of Wildlife and National Parks, P O Box 131, Gaborone, telephone (09267) 37-1405, or fax 31-2354 for further details. To make campsite reservations, contact the Department of Wildlife and National Parks, Parks and Reserves Reservations, P O Box 20364, Boseja, Maun, telephone (09267) 66-1265, fax 66-1264.

Khutse Game Reserve
Fifteen thousand years ago, the complex of seasonal Kalahari pans that forms the Khutse reserve was probably part of a (now long-dead) river system that flowed north to the Makgadikgadi. Khutse is next to the Central Kalahari Game Reserve and is connected to it by a dirt road.

Khutse may be reached by 4x4 vehicle after a 240 km drive from the Botswana capital of Gaborone, via Molepolole – the road is tarred

355

Left: Trees in the Gemsbok National Park are cast into stark silhouette by the dying rays of the setting sun. **Above:** Ochre sand dunes at Twee Rivieren, southern entrance to the Gemsbok National Park.

to Letlhakeng. However, sufficient fuel should be carried for at least 650 km, to allow for touring the 259 000 ha reserve – which has one circular road – and to return to Gaborone. Maps are available at the Game Scouts Camp at the gate. There are no lodges or permanent camps within Khutse, but visitors may stay at a number of public campsites, notably those at Galalabodimbo and Moreswe pans (note, however, that facilities are limited). The camp at the gate is the only one that offers showers (cold water) and toilet facilities.

This is a rewarding area for those seeking absolute peace and tranquillity. Some 60 white, sandy pans interrupt the vast, scrubby savannah plains, while the gentle grasslands, woodlands, fossil dunes and riverbeds support a wealth of game.

In this true desert environment you may see a surprising variety of large and small antelope – often clustered in small herds around the pans. Ostrich stalk purposefully across a shimmering landscape that conceals predators such as caracal, lion (fairly common), cheetah, brown hyena and spotted hyena, and there are mongoose, black-backed jackal, bat-eared fox, ground squirrel and porcupine.

More than 250 seasonal bird species have been recorded, including lark, kori bustard, greater kestrel, chanting goshawk and white-backed vulture.

For further information, write to The Director, Department of Wildlife and National Parks, P O Box 131, Gaborone, or telephone (09267) 37-1405, fax 31-2354.

Mabuasehube Game Reserve

The Mabuasehube (place of red earth) reserve lies in the Kalahari Desert approximately 100 km north of the South African border post of McCarthy's Rest near Kuruman.

The 179 200 ha reserve encompasses six large pans (and numerous smaller ones) with a good variety of game. It lies adjacent to and east of the Gemsbok National Park (*see separate entry*). Large herds of eland, hartebeest, springbok and gemsbok can be seen, and predators such as lion, brown hyena, caracal, Cape fox, leopard, and wild dog are active at night, when a spotlight can reveal a 'laager' of animals around the camp. There are no formal lookout platforms, but naturally good game-viewing points are dotted around the pans. The landscape is stark and stunning, with sparsely vegetated dunes (some reaching heights of up to 30 m) and grassy pans, which attract hosts of animals when rains cover their clay surfaces with water.

Birdlife includes species typical of the area, such as kori bustard, secretary bird, black korhaan and numerous raptors. Other species commonly spotted are red-eyed bulbul, pied barbet, crimson-breasted boubou, capped wheatear and red-capped lark.

Visitors should note that, at Tshabong, which lies 21 km inside Botswana, there is a store selling food and other essentials, and fuel can be purchased. Here the tarred road gives way to a sandy track, negotiable only with a 4x4 vehicle, and it is strongly recommended that people travel in groups of no fewer than two vehicles. The best time to visit Mabuasehube is from September/October to April/May. There is one campsite within the reserve, at the Game Scouts' Camp (ensure that you are self-sufficient). For further information, contact The Director, Department of Wildlife and National Parks, P O Box 131, Gaborone, telephone (09267) 37-1405, or fax 31-2354.

Mannyelanong Vulture Sanctuary

Mannyelanong, about 40 km south of Gaborone near the tiny village of Otse, means 'the place where vultures defecate' – and is today one of the few remaining nesting grounds of the Cape vulture (*Gyps coprotheres*). There were 300 pairs in 1963; by 1980 there were only about 100, swooping and diving above the Mannyelanong Hill face. The current population is approximately 90 pairs.

There are few predators left in this part of Botswana, and strenuous efforts are being made to save the Cape vulture. Mannyelanong Vulture Sanctuary has been established to protect them from being eradicated, and the birds are well cared for in this breeding colony. The best time to visit the sanctuary is between the end of May and September/October. A small fee is payable.

Mokolodi Nature Reserve

Situated in the bushveld some 15 km south of Gaborone, the 3 000 ha Mokolodi Nature Reserve was established in 1994 as a joint conservation effort by the residents of Gaborone and the Mokolodi Wildlife Foundation.

The reserve is beautifully situated and features ample game, ranging from white rhino and giraffe to zebra, eland, kudu and mountain reedbuck. Hippo have been released into the dam and there are four young elephant orphans, ranging in age from four to six years. Birdlife is plentiful, and a checklist is currently being compiled.

Visitors are welcome, and the reserve offers safe and comfortable accommodation in five fully equipped self-catering cottages (take your own food), all of which overlook a busy waterhole. There is also a charming thatched restaurant and bar facilities. The Mokolodi Environmental Education Centre accommodates up to 80 students in dormitories, and here they learn about the environment and the wildlife in a unique, hands-on way. Budget travellers or hitchhikers may also use the dormitory accommodation when the centre is not in use, and it may also be hired for functions.

Visitors may arrange specialist walks (with the elephants, if desired), on rhino tracking safaris, guided nature walks or on gameviewing drives in safari vehicles. Sundowner bush braais are a popular event.

For further details, contact Mokolodi Nature Reserve, P O Box 170, Gaborone, telephone (09267) 35-3959, or fax 31-3973.

Remote and burnished grassland

In the early 19th century the area around the Boteri River, in central Botswana, was one of several regions of the country that served as sanctuary to an awesome number and variety of wild animals. Early travellers trekking across the edge of the dusty Kalahari and the Makgadikgadi region told of countless herds of wildebeest and zebra.

Then came the hunters and traders, greedy for furs, skins, feathers and, above all, ivory. During the two years following Lake Ngami's discovery in midcentury, 900 elephant were shot in the Boteri River area alone. Author Alec Campbell, in his *Guide to Botswana*, estimated that 'it would be a fair guess to say that each year from 1865 onwards approximately 5 000 elephant, 3 000 leopard, 3 000 lion, 3 000 ostrich, 250 000 small fur-bearing animals and probably another 100 000 meat animals were slaughtered, mainly for trade. In ten years the country could have been stripped had it not been for the difficulty of penetrating some of the major wildlife areas.'

The very remoteness of this huge land, combined with the introduction of expensive hunting licences before the turn of the century, prevented the extermination of Botswana's magnificent living heritage.

The 1,2 million ha Makgadikgadi is a wilderness of dry saltpans (supposedly the largest in the world), sweeping grass plains and herds of ever-moving game. There are few roads and there is usually no water. About 2 million years ago, this ancient lake was almost certainly filled by the Zambezi, Cuando, Kavango and Okwa river systems, but today only severe storms deposit enough water in the pans to attract the flamingoes.

Two roads loop around the pans and link Francistown in the east and Maun on the fringe of the Okavango Delta in the west. There are two main pans, the Sowa (or Sua) and the Ntwetwe. The two game reserves of the Makgadikgadi, the Nxai Pan National Park and the Makgadikgadi Pans National Park further to the south, although two separate parks, are treated as a single entity for the purposes of management and administration. Blue wildebeest, springbok, zebra and other antelope graze on the grassy plains, and visitors may also see lion, bat-eared fox, hyena, as well as bateleur and a host of other bird species.

Below: Selous' mongoose (seen here beside its hole in the Makgadikgadi Pans National Park). This small, slender mongoose is mainly nocturnal, though it may be seen in daylight. **Right top:** Very enlarged antennae are a characteristic of this paussid beetle, found (usually in ants' nests) all over Botswana. Ants may often be seen clustered around this beetle, stimulating it into producing secretions of which they are particularly fond. **Right below:** The shallow waters of the Makgadikgadi Pans are a magnet to waterfowl of many species. Although once an immense sheet of water, much of the area has dried up, leaving stretches of salt-encrusted sand as far as the eye can see. There is evidence that the pans of Makgadikgadi are all that is left of a huge lake which reached a depth of 945 m and an area of 6 million ha – including a large part of the area now occupied by the Okavango Delta. Boreholes sunk in the area have revealed sedimentation of up to 100 m in depth, while beaches of tumbled quartz mark its old shoreline. Man occupied the area of the pans in very ancient times, and many Stone Age artefacts have been found.

BOTSWANA: MAKGADIKGADI

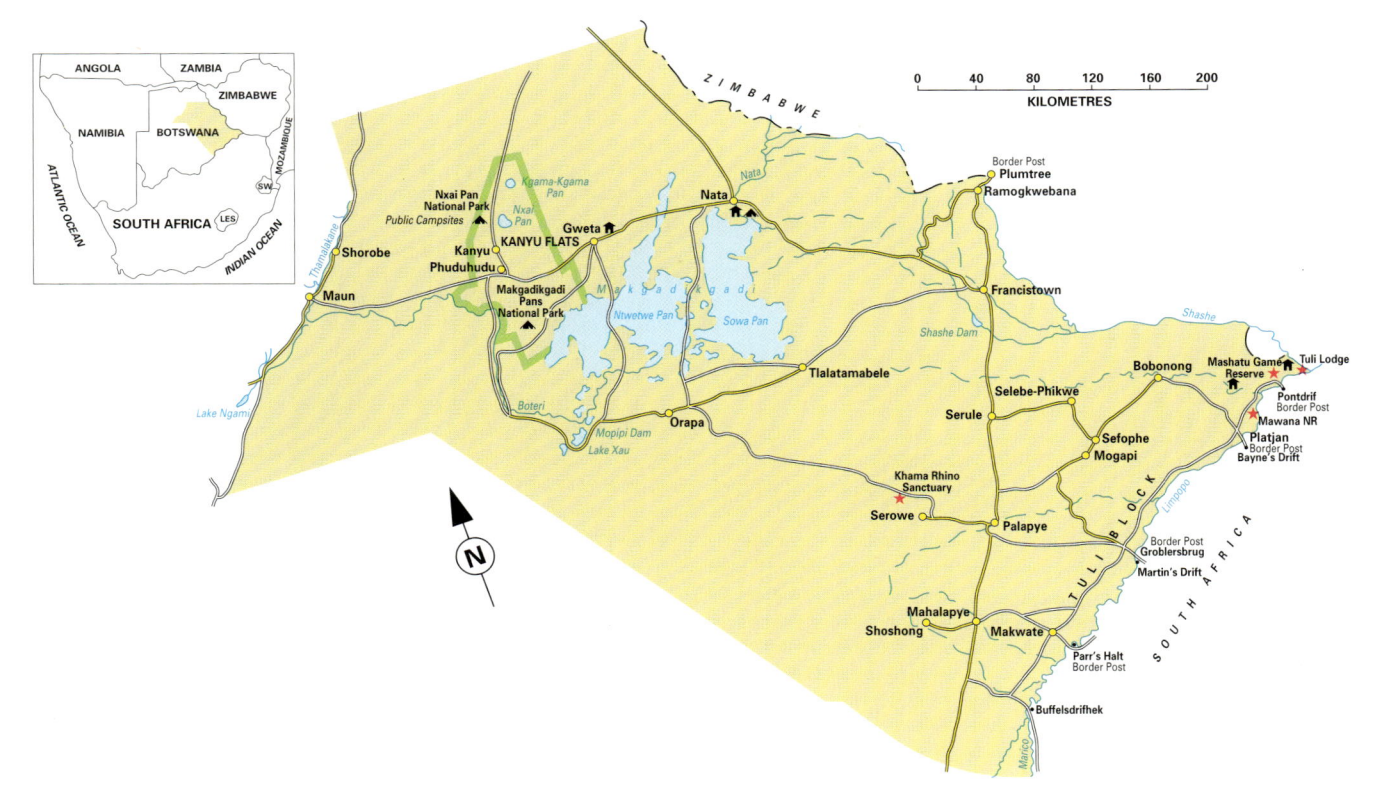

Gweta Rest Camp

A little more than halfway along the main road from Francistown (via Nata) to Maun lies the rural village of Gweta, set among tall palms. The well-signposted rest camp comprises thatched brick cottages, a restaurant, a lively bar well patronised by the local community, a shop and a swimming pool. Limited camping facilities are also available. Fuel can be obtained at the village, but there are no facilities for vehicle repairs.

To the south of Gweta are the Makgadikgadi saltpans – all that remain of a once great lake that covered much of northern Botswana. From the Gweta Rest Camp visitors can explore these vast expanses by taking a trip to the edge of the pans from where they set off on four-wheeler bikes for a three to four-hour ride across the plains.

For further information about Gweta Rest Camp, write to P O Box 124, Gweta, telephone/fax (09267) 61-2220.

Khama Rhino Sanctuary

An aerial survey, conducted in northern Botswana in September 1992, established that all but a handful of the country's white rhino had been wiped out by poachers.

Left: Vegetable ivory (*mokolwane*) palms at Makgadikgadi. Each tree produces up to 2 000 fruits, popular with baboon and elephant.

To save the species from becoming extinct, the Khama Rhino Sanctuary was established near Serowe in 1993. Four animals were captured in the Chobe National Park and translocated to the sanctuary (one, unfortunately, died), where they could be closely guarded. Their numbers were strengthened by further specimens donated by the Pilanesberg National Park in the North-West Province.

The sanctuary has also been stocked with Burchell's zebra, blue wildebeest, red hartebeest, kudu, steenbok and ostrich, while predators include the occasional leopard, brown hyena and bat-eared fox.

The sanctuary, which lies some 30 km northwest of Serowe on the road to Orapa, is open daily from 8 a.m. to 6.30 p.m.

Lake Xau

Lake Xau was once a large, shallow lake fed by the Boteri River, which flows out of the Okavango Delta east for 500 km into the Kalahari, carrying the last of the Okavango's water. Today, with the waters trapped at the Mopipi Dam (itself originally a pan), Lake Xau is usually as dry as its sister pans of the Makgadikgadi, on whose southern edge it lies. The reeds still line the lake shore, but are less luxuriant. Khoikhoi oral history relates that the lake dried up in about the year 1800 when thousands of fish, crocodile and hippo were reported to have died and rotted on the bed of the lake.

In the main, the area's wildlife stays further north and west on the grasslands between the Boteri River and the Ntwetwe Pan of the Makgadikgadi, while ever-present vultures hover in the sky. When the lake fills, however, an abundance of birdlife still flocks to its waters.

A sand and gravel road south of the Makgadikgadi Pans stretches 350 km from Francistown to Lake Xau (240 km to Orapa). There are no facilities, fuel stations or accommodation, and a 4x4 vehicle is essential. The road that runs parallel to the Boteri River from Lake Xau to Maun comprises 140 km of 'choose-your-track' that eventually becomes the main Maun/Nata road.

For further information, write to The Senior Tourism Officer, Private Bag 0047, Gaborone, telephone (09267) 35-3024, fax 37-1539; or to the Department of Wildlife and National Parks, P O Box 131, Gaborone, telephone (09267) 37-1405, fax 31-2354.

Makgadikgadi Pans and Nxai Pan national parks

At a point 350 km from Francistown, the main road to Maun crosses the migratory path of blue wildebeest and zebra, separating two adjoining national parks – Makgadikgadi Pans National Park to the south, and Nxai Pan National Park to the north of the road. In the early 1990s, the former Makgadikgadi Pans Game Reserve grew by some 100 000 ha, and its status was elevated to that of a national park, while Nxai Pan National Park was extended southwards to include the well-known Baines' Baobabs. Today the two parks cover 490 000 ha and 250 000 ha respectively but, for administrative and management purposes, they are controlled as a single entity.

The parks' 550 000 ha of game-rich grasslands include the northwest section of Ntwetwe, one of two giant saltpans that together form the Makgadikgadi pans – reputed to be the largest in the world. In the shimmering heat of midday the pans become blinding mirages of make-believe water surrounded by burnished grasslands. When rains fill the shallow depressions to a depth of a few centimetres, they attract countless flamingoes, waders, pelicans and other waterfowl.

There are animals in profusion: gemsbok, zebra, springbok, wildebeest, ostrich, lion, jackal, hyena and cheetah. In the palm trees and thickets, silhouetted against the pale sky, are doves, rollers and eagles.

North of Ntwetwe Pan are huge grassy plains and strikingly beautiful (especially in a dusty African sunset) groves of *mokolwane* palm trees (in some parts of the country people extract, ferment and drink its juice as wine, or distil it to create a powerful spirit). This tree produces vast quantities of spherical, orange-brown fruit, which contain white seeds known

MAKGADIKGADI PANS AND NXAI PAN NATIONAL PARKS AT A GLANCE

When to go April to July are the best months for the Makgadikgadi area, when nights are cool and gameviewing is at its best, but the grasslands of Nxai Pan teem with game in the rainy months between December and April. The parks are open throughout the year.

Reservations and information For further information, contact the Department of Wildlife and National Parks, P O Box 131, Gaborone, telephone (09267) 37-1405, or fax 31-2354. To make campsite reservations, contact the Department of Wildlife and National Parks, Parks and Reserves Reservations, P O Box 20364, Boseja, Maun, telephone (09267) 66-1265, or fax 66-1264.

Getting there There are scheduled air services from Harare and Johannesburg to Gaborone, which in turn is linked to Francistown and Maun. The only airstrip in the parks lies between the two campsites in the Makgadikgadi section. The 350 km road from Francistown is tarred, but 4x4 vehicles are essential to enter the park.

Accommodation There is no organised accommodation in the pans, and the nearest lodges are at Gweta Rest Camp and Nata Lodge (*see separate entries*). There are, however, various public campsites – two in the Makgadikgadi section at Kumaga and Njuca Hills (the first with a cold-water ablution block and the second with pit latrines), and two in the Nxai Pan section, both with ablution blocks and borehole water. Makgadikgadi Camp accommodates up to eight guests in tents equipped with bucket showers and basic toilet facilities. For reservations, contact Makgadikgadi Camp, P O Box 124, Gweta, telephone/fax (09267) 61-2220.

Eating and drinking Visitors should take sufficient provisions and water for the duration of their trip.

Getting around Driving in the pans (the roads are only tracks) can be treacherous. Visitors should travel with two 4x4 vehicles. Essential equipment includes a puncture-repair kit, extra fuel in metal (not plastic) jerry cans, at least 20 litres of water, motor oil, jacks, spanners, fan belts, inner tubes, a pump, spare coil, rotor, fuel-pump kit, regulator, condenser, plugs, points, radiator hose, nylon tubing, clips and sand ladders, or other vehicle aids, as well as a compass. Fuel is available at Nata, Gweta, Maun, Rakops and Francistown. A guide is necessary if you desire to explore the pans outside the park boundaries.

Also available are four-wheel motorbike safaris. Contact Gweta Rest Camp, P O Box 124, Gweta, telephone/fax (09267) 61-2220 for details.

Wildlife Wildebeest and zebra live and migrate between the Boteri River and the northwest corner of Ntwetwe Pan, and northwards to Nxai Pan. They tend to move north and east during the rainy months to feed on the grassy plains and then, as the surface water decreases in volume, they return once more to the Boteri – followed by lion and other predators. The Nata River flows out of Zimbabwe and eventually dries up in a delta at the northeastern tip of the Sowa Pan, the smaller of the two Makgadikgadi pans. Here, you can sometimes see flamingoes lining the shore for many kilometres. One sighting was estimated at over a million.

Fishing There is good fishing (bream) in the Nata and Boteri rivers (the best time is September to April). Fishing permits are required.

Special precautions Visitors are advised to start a course of anti-malaria tablets (available from pharmacies) before embarking on a trip to this region.

BOTSWANA: MAKGADIKGADI

Left: An aardwolf at Nxai Pan. At first glance the aardwolf resembles a small striped hyena, with its slender legs, mane from neck to tail, and vertical stripes. However, it is noticeably smaller than the scavenger.
Above: The bateleur (*Terathopius ecaudatus*) is one of the best-known raptors of the African savannah: it is easily recognised by its characteristic straight-line flight across the veld, rocking from side to side as it flies. It has been suggested that this peculiar characteristic may stem from the instability caused by the bird's short tail.

as vegetable ivory. These are of decorative value, and are used to create necklaces, trinkets and curios, including the ornamental heads of carrying sticks.

In the dry season and in times of drought, wildebeest and zebra roam the open country between the Boteri River and the northwestern edge of the pan. When the rains come they migrate to the northern plains, returning to the waters of the Boteri for the duration of the dry winter months.

To the north, the area around Nxai Pan consists mainly of forest and savannah woodland. The pan itself is a fossil lake bed some 14 km wide, and covered with short grass (dotted with small islands of trees). There are many giraffe, which may be seen in herds of up to 60, scattered across its surface.

This is also the playground of bat-eared fox, which scamper from one ant hill to the next. These endearing animals are omnivorous (wild fruits, rodents and reptiles feature in their diet) but termites, locusts and beetles are their staple food. Their outsize ears are sensitive to the sounds of insect movement beneath the surface and, once located, the prey (sometimes colonies of termites) is swiftly dug up, even from the hardest ground, and devoured. A colloquial Afrikaans name for the species is *draaijakkals* (turning jackal), descriptive of its nimbleness – it can turn and double back on its tracks at speed. It has a fluid, twisting way of running that helps it both to evade predators and to catch small, elusive prey.

During the rainy summer months (December to March), large herds of wildebeest and zebra concentrate at water-filled depressions in Nxai Pan.

The smaller Kgama-Kgama Pan, where King Khama III once had a cattle post, lies 35 km to the north of Nxai Pan, while south are the Kanyu Flats, a 'billiard table' of miniature pans on the eastern fringe of which stand Baines' Baobabs (also known as the Seven Sisters), a group of baobabs painted by artist-explorer Thomas Baines over 130 years ago, and hardly changed since.

On the edge of Ntwetwe Pan, just outside the boundary of the park, is Makgadikgadi Camp, which accommodates up to eight guests in tents equipped with bucket showers and basic toilet facilities. Activities offered include four-wheel motorbike trips, game-viewing, night drives and walks.

To make reservations, contact Makgadikgadi Camp, P O Box 124, Gweta, telephone/fax (09267) 61-2220. For further information about both parks, contact the Department of Wildlife and National Parks, P O Box 131, Gaborone, telephone (09267) 37-1405, fax 31-2354. To make campsite reservations, contact the Department of Wildlife and National Parks, Parks and Reserves Reservations, P O Box 20364, Boseja, Maun, or telephone (09267) 66-1265, or fax 66-1264.

Mashatu Game Reserve and Tuli Safari Lodge

In the populated eastern section of Botswana, the Limpopo forms the boundary with the Northern Province. The river forms the rounded 'hat' of South Africa as it flows first north then east to the Indian Ocean. At its crown, not far to the west of Messina and Beitbridge, it links up with the Shashe River.

In the watered mopane woodlands between the Shashe and the Limpopo is a complex of privately owned ranches and farms forming a part of the Tuli Block, approached from South Africa on roads leading from Nylstroom, Potgietersrus, Pietersburg, Louis Trichardt and Messina. The countryside is wild and beautiful mopane woodland, broken up by koppies and granite outcrops, and interlaced with acacia- and *mashatu*-lined rivers.

Two major attractions of this remote wilderness area are Mashatu Game Reserve and the Tuli Safari Lodge.

One of the largest privately owned game reserves (46 000 ha) in southern Africa, Mashatu (the vernacular for the nyala tree) offers morning game drives in 4x4 open vehicles, night drives and game walks, accompanied by rangers and trackers. There's no shortage of game here – Mashatu provides refuge for the largest single population of African elephant on private land in the world – more than 700 animals. You can also see cheetah, zebra, giraffe, eland, impala, leopard, lion, kudu, bushbuck, baboon and more than 350 species of bird.

The reserve's main camp offers accommodation in air-conditioned, *en suite* chalets or rondavels, set in beautiful indigenous gardens. Guests may make use of the swimming pool, elevated lounge, open-air bar and dining terrace overlooking the floodlit waterhole, as well as a palm-walled dining boma. Conference facilities are also available.

In the remote northern corner of the reserve lies the luxury Mashatu Tented Camp, with seven insect-proofed double tents that have *en suite* toilet and shower facilities. There is also a clear plunge pool, an open-sided deck under thatch for dining, and a boma. The main camp accommodates a maximum of 34 guests, and the tented camp a maximum of 14.

You can reach Mashatu by road (five and a half hours from Johannesburg) or by chartered aircraft from most parts of southern Africa. For more information, contact Mashatu Game Reserve, P O Box 2575, Randburg 2125, telephone (011) 789-2677, or fax 886-4382; or P O Box 136, Alldays 0909, telephone (09267) 84-5321, fax (01554) 458.

The luxurious Tuli Lodge, surrounded by 7 500 ha of bush and savannah plains, is also a five-and-a-half-hour drive from Johannesburg, or one and a half hours by air from Lanseria Airport. Here no fences restrict your movement while you track elephant, lion, leopard, giraffe, Burchell's zebra and blue wildebeest in the bush.

Accommodation in the main camp, with its park-like lawns stretching down to the Limpopo River, is in luxury thatched chalets with *en suite* bathrooms. Amenities include a bar (built around a 500-year-old nyala tree), a cosy boma, a lounge, curio shop, and swimming pool (built in a natural rock setting). Adjacent to the main camp is a fully serviced guesthouse with three bedrooms. Located less than 100 metres from the Limpopo River is a tented camp, with four fully serviced double tents with shower facilities, a kitchen and a braai area. Guests staying in the guesthouse and the tented camp may use the main camp's facilities. Two game drives in open 4x4 vehicles and a guided game walk are included in the daily tariff, which also includes three fine meals a day.

For further information and to receive their brochures, contact Tuli Safari Lodge, 17 Eton Road, Parktown 2193, telephone (011) 482-2634, or fax 482-2635.

Mawana Nature Reserve

Covering some 10 000 ha of bushveld wilderness and stretching 12 km along the Limpopo River, Mawana Nature Reserve offers striking scenery and a rich animal life. The trees, both those on the plains and those that line the river banks, support a rich birdlife, while game to be found includes elephant, zebra, leopard, warthog, blue wildebeest, kudu, klipspringer (observed on the reserve's numerous granite koppies), steenbok, hippo and crocodile. Guided walks and drives introduce visitors to the reserve's wildlife.

Accommodation is offered at Koro Bush Camp, with its five, self-catering 2-bed tents. These are served by a fully equipped kitchen tent with a gas stove, freezer, refrigerator, crockery and cutlery, and ablutions comprising flush toilets and showers (with wood-fired geysers). Visitors must bring their own food, beverages, sleeping bags and towels.

Access to the reserve from South Africa is via the Platjan border post and along 22 km of gravel road to the entrance. Remember that you must enter Botswana before 6 p.m., and you will need a passport. For more information, contact Jacana Country Homes and Trails, P O Box 95212, Waterkloof 0145, or telephone (012) 346-3550/1/2, fax 346-2499.

Nata Lodge

Set close to the edge of the Makgadikgadi saltpans, Nata Lodge is 10 km from Nata, on the tarred road to Maun. The birdlife in this remote, yet beautiful area is diverse and abundant, and the lodge is the ideal base from which to explore Nata Sanctuary and the Sowa (Sua) Pan. Other attractions are its bar, swimming pool, restaurant and accommodation: thatched A-frame cottages and safari tents in a setting of palms, marulas and tall thorn trees. There's also a campsite. Sundowner trips and birdwatching outings to the Makgadikgadi pans can be arranged. Fuel is available.

If you wish to take your break during the holiday season, prior booking is essential. Write to Nata Lodge, Private Bag 10, Francistown, telephone/fax (09267) 61-1210.

Lying some 20 km to the south of the lodge is Nata Sanctuary, established by a committee in Nata Village as a preserve for the spectacular birdlife (especially flamingo) attracted to the pan when rains fall. A wooden lookout offers wide views across the pan and its flurry of feathered inhabitants.

The sanctuary, which includes the mouth of the Nata River, is accessible through a thatched gateway, near which are the remains of an old baobab that was once used as a shelter by many travellers. It toppled in 1992.

Above: Pelicans take to the air from the Nata River. The Nata flows only when there is rain, and empties into Sowa (Sua) Pan, forming a shallow inland delta of a few hundred square kilometres.

Havens of the north

Chobe National Park, on Botswana's northern border, is one of Africa's great national parks. Rolling grassy plains, dusty mopane woodlands, the fossil lake-bed of the Mababe Depression and the lush floodplains of the Linyandi and Chobe rivers – they join the Zambezi at Kazungula, meeting point of four nations – offer a variety of habitats for the herds of elephant, buffalo and zebra for which this park is world renowned.

The game provides ample feeding ground for predators such as lion, leopard, cheetah, hyena and wild dog. Tigerfish and bream lure fishermen to the papyrus-fringed waterways of the Linyandi.

The winter sunsets at Savuti are spectacular, while the pans in the east are host to a variety of wildlife that includes lion and elephant. The riverine forests of the north, watered by the Chobe, reveal myriad multicoloured birds, bushbuck, lechwe, sable, giraffe, crocodile, hippo, baboon, eland, tsessebe, kudu and buffalo. Some of the 80 km of road along the river are suitable for family cars, while Africa's greatest spectacle, the Victoria Falls, is only an hour's drive away.

Chobe, Kasane, Kazuma, Maikaelelo and Sibuyu forest reserves

Kasane, Kazuma and Sibuyu forest reserves stretch one after another north to south along the Zimbabwe and Hwange National Park borders, and – together with Maikaelelo and Chobe forest reserves to the west – they constitute the only natural timber forests occurring in all of Botswana.

Access is by tarred road leading south from Kasane village to Nata and Francistown – an old ivory trail to the Zambezi, known as Mpandamatenga. The Mpandamatenga border post is 100 km south of the crossing at Kazungula and 5 km from the Zimbabwe border, at a point that connects with a dirt road through the Matetsi Safari Area, adjoining Zimbabwe's famous Hwange National Park. This road branches north to Matetsi and the tarred Bulawayo road (65 km), and south to Robins Camp, in the Hwange National Park (48 km). Chobe Forest Reserve can be explored along the road to Savuti via Kachekabwe.

There are many tree species in Botswana. Larger specimens occurring in the forest reserves include Zambezi teak and mukwa (or kiaat). A wide variety of game (both herbivores and predators) moves between the forest reserves, the mopane woodlands and the unfenced Chobe National Park, and the birdlife is rich and colourful.

There are no facilities in any of the forestry reserves, and camping is not permitted. However, a master plan on the multiple use of forestry areas was drawn up in 1993, and there is a possibility that they may be more accessible once the plan has been approved.

For more information, write to the Department of Crop Production and Forestry, Private Bag 003, Gaborone, or telephone (09267) 35-0684, fax 30-7057.

Chobe National Park: Kasane and Serondela

Much of Botswana consists of various floodplains, sandy depressions, grasslands and Kalahari-type desert. Chobe National Park, with an area of 1,1 million ha, is a combination of all of these – a spectacular, game-rich wilderness interspersed with patches of swampland and stands of mopane, kiaat, teak and acacia woodland. It takes its name from the Chobe River, known by other names further upstream, which forms an irregular boundary between Botswana and Namibia's Caprivi Strip. The river, running west to east, starts as the Cuando which, like the Okavango, rises in Angola. (It is known as the Kwando in Namibia.) It soon becomes the Linyandi, then Itenge, and finally the Chobe – which, in turn, is a major tributary of the Zambezi.

Kasane village, 13 km west of the Kazungula border post, is primarily known for its rewarding fishing and its proximity to Serondela, which is an extremely popular section of the park. Facilities at Kasane include an airstrip, a butchery, a number of general stores, a bookshop, bakery, service station, bottle store and bank, as well as a number of lodges. Visitors will be intrigued by two baobab trees in the centre of the town. One was used as the kitchen for the women's prison until quite recently, and the second served as an unusual holding place for prisoners.

The northern section of Chobe offers 35 km of river frontage as far as Ngoma. It has gravel

Left: The magnificent Chobe River at sunset. **Above:** A stalk-eyed fly. This bizarre insect, with eyes and antennae at the end of stalks which may be as much as 12 mm apart, is commonly found along rivers. It feeds largely on decaying plants. **Opposite page:** A young sitatunga in dense papyrus beside the Linyandi River – a typical habitat for this small, shy buck. The sitatunga's hooves are adapted for running across swamps.

BOTSWANA: CHOBE NATIONAL PARK

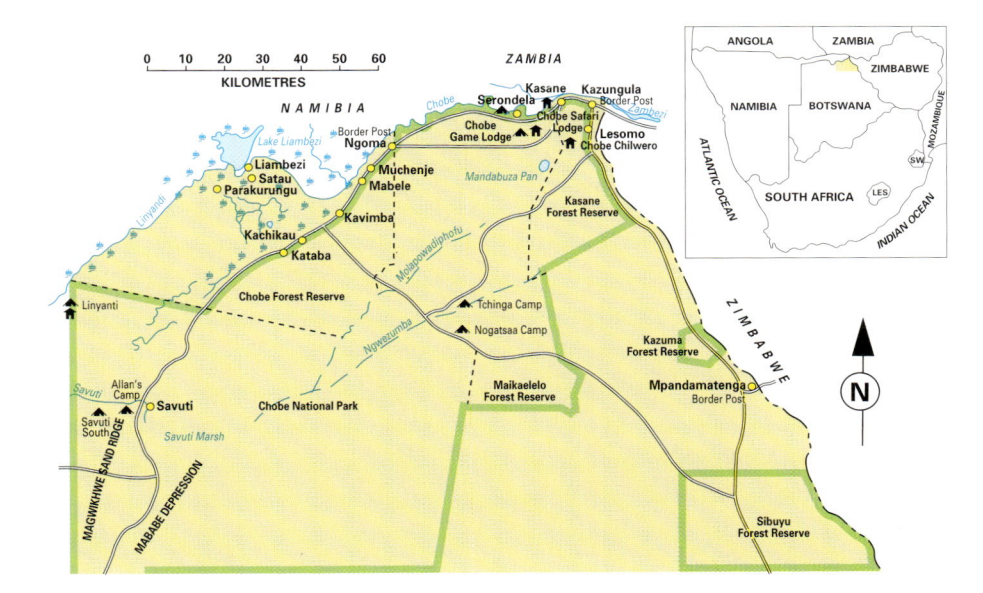

roads suitable only for 4x4 vehicles, which can also be used to explore the forests and riverside paths. The animals, which come down to drink at the river from about 3 p.m., include elephant (breeding herds of up to 300 come to the waterhole in winter), buffalo, sable, bushbuck, waterbuck, tsessebe and baboon. Visitors may also see hippo and crocodile, and there are lion, leopard (very rarely seen), rhino, warthog and a variety of birds that includes fish eagle, bateleur, egret, Egyptian goose, marabou stork, sacred ibis, and a colony of carmine bee-eaters nesting in burrows excavated into the sheer banks of the Chobe River. An astonishing 460 species have been recorded in the park.

A public camping site at Serondela (some 15 km from Kasane) has ablution facilities in the form of showers and toilets. Kasane itself offers a number of accommodation alternatives, catering for all pockets and preferences (see box).

There is good fishing in the river (bream, barbel and tigerfish). Entry and fishing permits are available at the Chobe Gate, and at Mababe Gate, if you are travelling from Maun village. A 4x4 vehicle is always necessary for travelling in this part of Botswana. The best time to visit is from June to October. From December to April (the wet season), access is limited by washed-out roads and extensive mudholes. Reservations for campsites must be made in advance by writing to the Department of Wildlife and National Parks, P O Box 20364, Boseja, Maun, or telephone (09267) 66-1265, fax 66-1264.

Chobe National Park: Nogatsaa

A cluster of eight large pans, surrounded by open grassland, mixed deciduous forest and mopane woodland, forms this section of Chobe National Park. One of the most underdeveloped and exciting areas within Chobe, Nogatsaa lies 70 km south of the Chobe River and the Serondela campsite, on the alternative eastern route (4x4 vehicles only), via Nantanga Pans, to Savuti.

The pans, including the Cwikampa, Mandabuza and Mapororo, usually contain water in varying amounts – but it is at the beginning of the wet season that they are host to herds of buffalo and elephant. Oribi, eland, gemsbok and roan can be seen on the grassy plains.

There are two campsites, Nogatsaa (with shower and toilet) and Tchinga (no facilities). Nogatsaa has a lookout over the pan. There are also four bungalows which, during the 1992 drought, were damaged by elephant trying to reach the water in the bathrooms. They were due to be rebuilt in 1996.

At Tchinga, take care not to camp too close to the pan, or the animals will be unlikely to come down to drink. You should write to the

CHOBE AT A GLANCE

When to go The park is open all year – with the exception of the Mababe Depression and Savuti Channel area, which may be closed during the rainy season (1 December to 31 March). The rains create large mudholes, and travel during this period is risky. March to July is a good period in which to view game.

Reservations and information Entry permits are available at the gates, but campsite reservations must be made in advance by contacting the Department of Wildlife and National Parks, P O Box 20364, Boseja, Maun, Botswana, or telephone (09267) 66-1265, fax 66-1264.

Getting there There are landing strips for light aircraft at Kasane, Savuti and Linyanti (to the west of the park). Numerous operators conduct all-inclusive safaris, one of the longest-established being Gametrackers, which has two permanent camps at Savuti, the most densely (game) populated area of the park. The normal overland route into Chobe is via the good 69 km road from Victoria Falls in Zimbabwe to the Kazungula border post. Kasane village is 13 km west of Kazungula. There is a sand road from Maun (4x4 vehicles only). Before setting off you are advised to get information on the condition of the road from the Department of Wildlife and National Parks.

Accommodation There are luxury tented camps at Savuti and Linyanti, chalets and camping at the Chobe Safari Lodge at Kasane, and public campsites at Savuti in the west, Serondela in the north and Nogatsaa in the east. Chobe Safari Lodge, P O Box 10, Kasane, Botswana, telephone (09267) 65-0336, fax 65-0437, offers rondavels, rooms and camping facilities overlooking the Chobe River. Cresta Mowana Lodge, contacted through Cresta Hotels, Central Reservations, P O Box 200, Gaborone, Botswana, telephone (09267) 35-3631, fax 35-1840, offers beautiful luxury accommodation. Chobe Chilwero Lodge, P O Box 22, Kasane, Botswana, telephone (09267) 65-0505, fax 65-0352, lies some 3 km from the park gate and consists of thatched bungalows. Chobe Game Lodge, P O Box 32, Kasane, Botswana, telephone (09267) 65-0340, fax 65-0280, is located inside the park and caters for the fabulously wealthy. Buffalo Ridge Camping Site, near Ngoma Gate, offers campsites with hot-water ablutions and flush toilets. Reservations are generally not necessary, but can be made by contacting Buffalo Ridge, P O Box 109, Kasane, Botswana, telephone (09267) 65-0430, or fax 65-0881.

Eating and drinking Tariffs at the luxury camps are inclusive of all meals. Visitors planning to camp must be self-sufficient as there are no shops in the Chobe National Park. Supplies can be purchased in Kasane, Maun or Victoria Falls.

Getting around A 4x4 vehicle is a definite advantage, but the family car will be more than adequate for the road between Chobe Game Lodge and Kasane. Kasane has food stores, fuel, banks and a post office.

Special attractions The elephant at Savuti, the carmine bee-eaters along the Chobe River, the forests and the papyrus waterways of Linyanti will delight the eye. The bush sunsets in the dry dust of winter are unforgettable.

Wildlife There are few places in the world that can equal Chobe's enormous variety of big game and birdlife. The aristocrats of the wild – buffalo, elephant, giraffe, lion, impala, sable and fish eagle – are all here.

Fishing Tigerfish, bream and barbel are the principal fish caught in the Linyandi-Chobe river systems.

Special precautions A course of anti-malaria tablets should be started before visiting Chobe. Because nights tend to be chilly, a warm jacket should be packed in with other essentials. A mosquito repellent would be useful and a hat is essential during the hot daylight hours. As in Botswana's other parks and reserves, the public campsites in Chobe are unfenced, and under no circumstances should visitors sleep out under the stars. Food should be packed away to avoid unpleasant encounters with monkey, baboon and hyena.

---

warden at Kasane before visiting this section of the Chobe National Park.

Intending visitors should make reservations for campsites and bungalows by contacting the Department of Wildlife and National Parks, P O Box 20364, Boseja, Maun, or telephone (09267) 66-1265, fax 66-1264.

Chobe National Park: Savuti

The Mababe Depression, lying to the south of Savuti, is the remnant of the massive Lake Makgadikgadi that once covered most of northern Botswana. Enclosed within this enormous tract of endlessly flat grassland is the Savuti, an area of 5 000 square kilometres.

The Savuti Channel intermittently carries the overspill of the Kwando/Linyandi floodwaters through the Magwikhwe Sand Ridge and into the Savuti Marsh at the northern tip of the Mababe Depression (this usually occurs between June and December). The plains of Savuti, home to dozens of baboon, stork and cormorant, had been recorded as dry for a century or more when, in 1957, it flooded and drowned the giant trees that now stand stripped of their bark, grey and dead in midriver. In 1966 the waters dried up again, but started flowing once more the following year until, in 1981, the flow diminished and, in 1982, it stopped completely.

Late afternoon at one of these bends in the river is like a line-up for Noah's Ark. The crocodile lie motionless, jaws agape. Downstream, a dozen hippo yawn, twitch and snort. A line of elephant and their young emerge from the dusty mopane scrub to splash playfully in the water, and to drink. Sable, impala, warthog, guinea fowl and giraffe all seem to find a favourite spot. In the distance, from the direction of the Savuti Marsh comes the chilling grunt of a lion on the prowl. Birding enthusiasts are well rewarded: Savuti boasts almost 300 bird species, including kori bustard, secretary bird, red-billed francolin and lilac-breasted roller, and a number of summer migrants from northern Europe.

The Savuti Marsh is anything but a marsh in the dry season: it is a treeless and seemingly uninhabited grass plain stretching to the horizon. But, when flooded, it is a magnet for game: zebra, buffalo, sable, wildebeest, tsessebe, elephant and impala – literally thousands of animals venture onto the plains.

Several safari operators provide tours of Savuti, and there are two camps operated by a safari firm called Gametrackers: Savuti South and Allan's Camp. Savuti South features luxury tents, electricity, game drives in padded safari vehicles, and candlelight dinners. Allan's Camp has thatched A-frame chalets, *en suite* facilities, a lounge, dining room and bar under thatch. Unlike other Gametrackers camps, this camp caters for self-drive visitors, and no gameviewing drives are offered. Each caters for up to 16 people. For further information, write to Gametrackers, P O Box 2608, Cape Town 8000, South Africa, telephone (021) 23-1054, fax 23-1060. Lloyd's Camp, owned by Lloyd and June Wilmot, is also worth a visit. Its private waterhole and hide ensure close encounters with the prolific game. Accommodation is provided in comfortable tents with shared external facilities. Early morning game drives are a speciality. For details, contact Lloyd Wilmot Safaris, P O Box 2490, Fourways 2055, South Africa, telephone/fax (011) 462-5131.

A public campsite at Savuti has three ablution blocks and water taps. However, before

Right: Sable in the Victoria Falls National Park. These elegant antelope, with their long, scimitar-shaped horns, generally live in groups of up to 15 individuals. A breeding herd is led by a territorial male.

facilities (guests must bring their own crockery and cutlery) and communal ablution blocks. There are also camping and caravan sites. There is a store in the camp, and petrol and diesel are available. The ground floor of the old concrete tower now does convivial duty as the Hyaena Restaurant and Bar. The tortuous game drive to Crocodile Pools on the Deka River is rewarding. There is a gameviewing platform at Big Toms vlei and a hide at Little Toms. Allow a full day to travel from Robins Camp through the park to Main Camp.

Hwange: Sinamatella Camp

Situated on a boulder-strewn ridge 55 m high overlooking the Sinamatella valley, the camp is 48 km from the town of Hwange on a gravel road via Mbala Lodge in the Deka Safari Area. There are lodges, cottages and chalets (visitors have to bring their own food, crockery and cutlery), and a number of camping and caravan sites. The camp has a restaurant, bar, a shop selling basics only, and petrol pumps.

The bush, with grassy vleis, is thicker here than at Main Camp, Sinamatella being north of the watershed which drains into the Zambezi. Several dams, including Detema, halfway to Robins Camp, Mandavu (both with picnic sites) and Masuma provide good gamewatching. Impala, warthog, klipspringer and leopard are more numerous here than at Main Camp.

The famous Beadle croc, raised in the former Chief Justice's goldfish pond and later transferred to Nyamandhlovu Pan near Main Camp, is probably the most photographed predator ever. Several game drives include the popular Lukozi River loop. Visitors must leave Sinamatella by 2 p.m. to reach Main Camp at dusk and by 3 p.m. to reach Robins Camp.

Hwange Safari Lodge

Part of the Zimbabwe Sun hotel group, Hwange Safari Lodge is a luxury hotel of 200 beds, situated some 4 km from the Hwange Park airport (follow the signposts) and just a few kilometres from the park's main entrance.

There is a swimming pool (from which bathers can watch elephant at the nearby drinking hole) and activities include guided walks and game drives. Diners on the patio also have a fine view of the pan, which is well patronised by many species both by day and by night, and from hides nearby you can practically touch the elephant. Lion have killed within camera range.

Hwange Safari Lodge is the unofficial gateway to Hwange National Park, where guides and visitors find one another. For further information, address enquiries to Zimbabwe Sun Hotels Central Reservations, P O Box CY 1211, Causeway, Harare, or telephone (09263) 4 73-6644/5, fax 73-6646.

Accommodation in the vicinity includes the Baobab Hotel in Hwange town, about one hour's drive from the park. Write to The Manager, Baobab Hotel, P O Box 120, Hwange, or telephone (09263) 81 2323, fax 3481.

The Gwaai River Hotel has a riverside setting on the main Victoria Falls/Bulawayo road and has become well known over some 50 years. For more information, write to The Manager, Gwaai River Hotel, P O Box 9, Gwayi, or telephone (09263) 18 355, fax 268.

Halfway House Hotel at Gwayi on the main Victoria Falls/Bulawayo road offers *en suite* and chalet accommodation as well as camping facilities. Vehicles and guides are available for drives to Hwange or on Chimwara Estates. For further information, write to The Manager, Halfway House Hotel, P O Box 6, Gwayi, or telephone/fax (09263) 89 281.

Hwange area: Camp Selous

Formerly known as Jabulisa, Camp Selous is a few kilometres from Gwayi and offers accommodation in twin chalets (or a honeymoon chalet). Lion, kudu, waterbuck, bushbuck and birdlife are among the highlights. Resident guides and safari vehicles are available. For further information, write to Camp Selous, P O Box 20, Gwayi, or telephone (09263) 18 2306/2101/295, fax 295.

Hwange area: Chimwara Tented Camp

Adjoining Hwange National Park is Chimwara Estate of 12 140 ha, its camp only 40 minutes' drive from Hwange's Kennedy Gate. There are seven tents, all luxuriously furnished and with *en suite* facilities.

For more detailed information, write to Run Wild (Pvt) Ltd, P O Box 6485, Harare, or telephone (09263) 4 79-5841, fax 79-5845.

Hwange area: Chokamella Lodge

Adjacent to Hwange National Park, Chokamella's thatched bungalows are set on cliffs overlooking a river and its extensive floodplain. The peak gameviewing season is during the dry months, from May to October, when animals gather at several nearby boreholes. Guests have options of walks and drives, and there are resident guides. For further information, you should write to Central Reservations, Landela Safaris, P O Box 66293, Kopje, Harare, or telephone (09263) 4 73-4046, fax 73-1229; or write to Chokamella Lodge, P O Box 61, Dete, or telephone/fax (09263) 18 398.

Hwange area: Detema Safari Lodge

With accommodation in tree houses or in standard thatched chalets, the lodge is less than 1 km from Dete, on the edge of Hwange National Park. Several open safari vehicles are available and there are resident guides to show visitors the area's varied game, which includes elephant, giraffe, lion, cheetah, leopard, buffalo and plains antelope.

For further information, you should contact Detema Safari Lodge, P O Box 69, Dete, telephone (09263) 18 256/7, fax 269.

Hwange area: Ganda Lodge

The lodge overlooks Ganda Pan, floodlit at night, a few kilometres off the road between the main Victoria Falls/Bulawayo route and Hwange National Park. Game drives and walks are offered and there are resident guides. For more detailed information, direct enquiries to Ganda Lodge, P O Box 25, Dete, or telephone (09263) 18 413.

Hwange area: Gwaai Valley Safaris and Nyati Lodge

Although most safaris are to Hwange National Park, there are also many thousands of hectares of privately owned land nearby that offer excellent gameviewing and birdwatching. Nyati Lodge overlooks the valley of the Shangani River which, with the Gwayi River, offers rewarding fishing.

For further information, write to Gwaai Valley Safaris, P O Box 17, Gwayi, or telephone (09263) 18 3401, fax 268.

Hwange area: Ivory Lodge

The Red Waterhole, overlooked by 10 tree houses, offers exciting, close-up gameviewing at this 'family camp', situated on 26 000 ha some 15 minutes' drive from Hwange Airport. Safari vehicles and guides are available.

For more detailed information, you should write to Ivory Lodge, P O Box 55, Dete, or telephone (09263) 18 224, fax 9 6-5499.

Hwange area: Jijima

Accommodation is in airy tent-under-thatch chalets with unobstructed views of Jijima vlei and waterhole on the eastern boundary of Hwange National Park. Jijima is an excellent gameviewing area off the main tourist route, and is also known for its birding safaris. For further information, you should write to Jijima Reservations, P O Box 15, Gwayi, or telephone (09263) 13 4219, fax 4349.

Hwange area: Kalambeza Lodge

A turn-off at the 239 km peg on the road from Bulawayo leads for 4 km to A-frame chalets overlooking the Gwayi River on a 12 140 ha private game ranch. Safari vehicles and guides are available.

For further information, write to Kalambeza Lodge, P O Box 28, Gwayi, or telephone (09263) 18 2107, fax 4644.

Hwange area: Kanondo Tree Camp

Six tree houses and an open, communal dining room are situated close to a waterhole in an area of good gameviewing adjoining Hwange Safari Lodge and the park. An interesting aspect of conservation applied here – as part of the measures to preserve the natural environment – is that private vehicles are not allowed on the estate. For further information, you should write to Touch the Wild, Private Bag 6, Bulawayo, or telephone (09263) 9 4-4566/7, or fax 4-4696.

Hwange area: Katshana Tree Lodge

New and luxurious, Katshana has six teak-and-thatch lodges, and an open entertainment area, all just 30 m (and a discreet electrified fence) away from a waterhole that is floodlit at night. Katshana is located 8 km from Hwange Safari Lodge and, as at Kanondo, no private vehicles are allowed on the estate.

For further information, write to Touch the Wild, Private Bag 6, Bulawayo, or telephone (09263) 9 4-4566/7, fax 4-4696.

Hwange area: Malindi Station Lodge

Three restored railway carriages, unobtrusively sheltered by thatch, sleep 12 guests who enjoy mixing their gamewatching with the grandeur of an almost-vanished style of travel. Two waterholes close to the carriages and in easy view on this 2 428 ha reserve are regularly visited by big game, including elephant, buffalo, lion and sable.

For further information, write to Malindi Station Lodge, P O Box 2728, Harare, or telephone (09263) 4 70-5551/2, fax 70-5554.

Hwange area: Sable Valley Lodge

Located in the Dete Vlei area near Hwange Safari Lodge, Sable Valley is a small, luxurious estate in an area abounding with game. Activity at a nearby waterhole may be watched from the spacious lodges or from a raised observation platform (with bar).

For further information, write to Touch the Wild, Private Bag 6, Bulawayo, or telephone (09263) 9 4-4566/7, fax 4-4696.

Hwange area: The Hide

Guests sleep in tents under thatch near the 'Dete straight' – a 120 km length of railway track that is the fourth-longest railway straight in the world. Livelier attractions are the varied plains antelope and big game that gather at the waterhole close by. A ground-level hide at the waterhole is a special attraction. Safari vehicles and guides are available.

Left above: The white-crowned shrike, found throughout the Hwange National Park, has a habit of perching on the outermost branches of trees – particularly baobabs. **Right above:** 'The smoke that thunders': swathed in the permanent mist of its plummeting waters, the Zambezi surges through the gorge at the base of the Victoria Falls.

For further information, write to The Hide, P O Box GD 305, Greendale, Harare, or telephone (09263) 4 49-8548/ 5650, fax 49-8265.

Hwange area: Umkombo Safari Lodge

Thatched lodges on stilts accommodate guests at Umkombo, at the entrance to the Gwayi Conservancy on the border of Hwange, near Halfway House. The waterhole in front of the lodge attracts a good variety of game, while birding and guided walks in the conservancy are specialities.

For further information, write to Umkombo Safari Lodge, P O Box 10, Gwayi, or telephone (09263) 18 321, fax 268.

Kazuma Pan National Park

Hwange National Park, Deka Safari Area, Matetsi Safari Area, Kazuma Pan National Park, the Zambezi National Park and the Victoria Falls National Park form a continuous south to north belt in the northwestern corner of Zimbabwe. They differ widely. The Kazuma Pan National Park in the far west of the Matetsi Safari Area is a 31 200 ha reserve where a series of natural pans is seasonally flooded, attracting wildfowl.

The game, which includes gemsbok, cheetah and giraffe, tends to concentrate in the more watered and tree-covered western section, the east being open grassland. Gameviewing on foot is permitted but there are no facilities, and 4x4 vehicles are essential in this remote area.

To get to the park from Victoria Falls, turn right at the Matetsi Safari Area signpost and ask at the Matetsi Headquarters for directions to the Pandamatenga road, which runs parallel to the Zimbabwe/Botswana border, to Kazuma Pan. Prior permission must be obtained from Matetsi Safari Area Headquarters.

For more information, write to the National Parks Central Booking Office, P O Box CY 826, Causeway, Harare, or telephone their offices at (09263) 4 70-6077, fax 72-6089.

Victoria Falls National Park

The Victoria Falls National Park is the 2 340 ha area surrounding the falls and stretching some 500 m back from both falls and river's edge. The spray of *Mosi-oa-Tunya*, or the 'smoke that thunders', reaches as high as 450 m and has on occasion been seen from 80 km away.

The great throb of the falls and the seething cauldron below dominate the whole area – pulling one like a magnet. In the flood season, the Zambezi River pours over the falls at the staggering rate of 545 million litres a minute.

David Livingstone, Victorian explorer, missionary and the first white man to have recorded seeing the falls, approached them on 16 November 1855 from upriver, in a canoe paddled by Kololo clansmen. They landed him on Kazeruka Island (now Livingstone Island) which is perched on the very lip. It was from here, lying full-length, that he first peered over. He later wrote: 'Scenes so lovely must have been gazed upon by angels in their flight'. He carved his name on a tree – 'a weakness', as he put it, that he only once indulged in. It is almost certain that Portuguese traders saw the falls centuries before Livingstone, but it is his record that is the best known.

David Livingstone's statue today gazes over the savage spectacle of Devil's Cataract.

A walk, with steps cut into the cliff, descends a third of the way down to a viewing platform, and there are several viewsites along the length of the falls.

A rain forest fringes the chasm, and in this fairyland of ferns, orchids and blood-lilies, the falls appear as a tumultuously moving mosaic behind a screen of spray. Vervet monkeys and the occasional scarlet-breasted sunbird chatter in the vines that loop the wild fig and the palms, the moss-covered African ebony and sausage trees.

A hand-laid path traces the edge of the cliff and meanders through the sun-speckled and perpetually drenched forest. There is always at least one rainbow, and the gossamer spray is tinted soft pink and gold in early morning and evening. To see the rare lunar rainbow at night is an entrancing experience.

Nearby, Victoria Falls village has some splendid hotels and a casino. Commercial activity at the falls has increased, and includes bungee jumping among the options open to tourists.

The entrance to the park is reached just before the border post with Zambia. The park is open from sunrise to sunset. There are the usual border formalities, but once they are negotiated, viewing is possible from the bridge and Zambian bank. For more detailed information, you should write to the National Parks Central Booking Office, P O Box CY 826, Causeway, Harare, or telephone (09263) 4 70-6077, fax 72-6089.

Zambezi National Park

Zambezi Drive starts at the Victoria Falls and, tracing the river bank, ends 46 km upstream at the Zambezi National Park's western boundary. The park, stretching south from the river in a wedge of the Zambezi basin 26 km deep, is 56 010 ha in area.

Along the drive are some delightful picnic sites and fishing spots (tigerfish, bream and vundu can be caught). No fishing licence is required. There are six-bed lodges on the banks of the Zambezi River. Fishermen are also well accommodated in the Kandahar, Mpala-Jena and Sansimba fishing camps.

Two other roads traverse the park: the main route to Kazungula on the Botswana border, and the Chamabonda Drive, some 6 km from the Victoria Falls on the Bulawayo road. This drive follows the small Masuwe River, with its thick vegetation opening out into large, treeless vleis where herds of up to 200 sable have been seen.

Other large mammals in the park include buffalo, waterbuck, kudu, impala, elephant, zebra, lion, leopard and cheetah. Visitors are more than likely to see crocodile and hippo in the river, and should not venture close.

For further information and reservations, write to the National Parks Central Booking Office, P O Box CY 826, Causeway, Harare, or telephone (09263) 4 70-6077, fax 72-6089.

VICTORIA FALLS AND ZAMBEZI NATIONAL PARKS AT A GLANCE

When to go Spray can obscure the falls during the peak-flow winter months, and visitors find the period between August and November the best time for photography. The Zambezi National Park's gates are open during daylight hours only, and the road is closed during the wet season (1 November to 30 April). The camps, which remain open, are then accessible only by canoe.

Reservations Bookings for the two lodges and five exclusive camps (one party at a time) in the Zambezi National Park and for the Kandahar, Mpala-Jena and Sansimba fishing camps should be made through the National Parks Central Booking Office, P O Box CY 826, Causeway, Harare, Zimbabwe, telephone (09263) 4 70-6077 or fax 72-6089. Visitors who wish to book cottages, chalets, camping and caravan sites at the rest camp in Victoria Falls town should write to Victoria Falls Town Council, P O Box 41, Victoria Falls, Zimbabwe, or telephone (09263) 13 4210.

Getting there The falls are 439 km from Bulawayo by road, and there is also a daily train from the city. Air Zimbabwe has daily non-stop flights from Harare and others via Kariba and Hwange National Park. International flights arrive from Namibia, Botswana and South Africa and there are daily buses from Hwange town and Bulawayo. The Zambezi National Park is about 6 km from Victoria Falls town (take the road running alongside the Zambezi River and past the crocodile ranches).

Accommodation The Zambezi National Park has two fully equipped lodges (sleeping six persons each) on the banks of the Zambezi and five exclusive camps (each for one party of up to 12 people at a time). The basic but appealing fishing camps in the Zambezi National Park may be booked by parties of up to ten people. Each has a central sleeping shelter and ablution block. The facilities at the rest camp in Victoria Falls town include cottages and chalets (visitors supply their own crockery and cutlery). There are camping spots in the town and caravan sites further upstream. The town has an impressive range of hotels.

Eating and drinking As with most national parks in Zimbabwe, there are no restaurants or bars within the reserves. The hotels and restaurants at and near Victoria Falls, however, provide this region's many visitors with excellent facilities.

Getting around There are launch cruises up the Zambezi and flights (known as 'the flight of angels') over the falls. More adventurous visitors can board rafts to shoot the rapids in the Boiling Pot below the falls. Canoes and kayaks, motor scooters and bicycles are also for hire. The Zambezi National Park can be explored by driving along the picturesque Zambezi Drive or taking either of the two other roads traversing the park.

Special attractions The Victoria Falls area features a crocodile ranch with 5 000 specimens, a snake park, tribal dancing at the Victoria Falls Hotel and an Ndebele craft village. Fishing cruises are available and bungee jumping from the Zambezi Bridge is a recent option.

The inland ocean of Kariba

Dawn creeps across the mist-shrouded waters of Lake Kariba. The ghostly skeletons of long-dead trees play mournful host to egret and darter. In a giant leadwood tree, a fish eagle hunches and surveys its world. As the sun appears, a buffalo heaves itself out of the mud; a Goliath heron breaks and glides away. The sun clears the tree-line, its rays skim over the Matusadona Mountains and catch a malachite kingfisher spraying rainbow droplets in its morning bath. The mists swirl and vanish, and another day begins.

At Kariba on the Zambezi, where for thousands of years only the elephant and warthog paused to drink, there now stands one million cubic metres of concrete and 11 000 tons of reinforcing steel. This is Kariba Dam. Some 126 m high and 617 m wide, the wall holds back one of Africa's greatest rivers in a lake 282 km long. This inland ocean is the size of Wales – a wilderness of tigerfish and sudden storms that is unique in southern Africa. The dam is the focal point of the Mana Pools, Matusadona and Chizarira national parks, the Chete and Charara safari areas, and a host of smaller wildlife safari resorts.

Bumi Hills Safari Lodge

Bumi is a wild haven on the edge of Matusadona National Park where, say visitors, each day begins like the dawn of creation and ends in an Armageddon of blazing blood-red sky. The luxury lodges and rooms of Bumi Hills Safari Lodge are poised on a ridge overlooking the southern shores of Kariba, with the lake stretching in an arc far below.

Guided bush walks, game drives, fishing and watersports are offered, with the real chance of seeing the 'Big Five' and a good selection of the 300 bird species recorded in the area. Close photographic encounters, especially with elephant, are almost assured.

Bumi's spacious and ultra-luxurious Katete Lodge, 5 km to the west, evokes a romanticised atmosphere of early colonial days. Their nearby Water Wilderness Camp on a tributary of the Ume offers accommodation in houseboats tethered to half-submerged trees. A twin-engined aircraft flies guests to Bumi's strip from Kariba. Road access is limited to 4x4 vehicles via a long, poorly maintained track and there is a weekly ferry from Kariba town. Bumi is open year round.

Visitors to the area should take precautions against malaria. For reservations, contact Bumi Hills Safari Lodge, P O Box 41, Kariba, Zimbabwe, telephone (09263) 61 2353, fax 61 2354; or Zimbabwe Sun Hotels Central Reservations, P O Box 8221, Causeway, Harare, telephone (09263) 4 73-6644, fax 4 73-6646.

Charara Safari Area

Extending over 170 000 ha from the outskirts of Kariba village, Charara has a network of gravel roads (4x4 vehicles only) and there is good gameviewing, particularly in the late afternoon

Left: Kariba at dusk. The huge lake (it has an area of over 5 100 km^2) is retained by a massive concrete arch, 617 m wide, 126 m high and 21 m thick. An estimated 50 000 people and countless animals were displaced by the rising waters of the dam. **Top:** *Combretum mossambicense* along the Zambezi. **Above:** A waterbuck ram beside Lake Kariba, in the Bumi Hills region.

Here you will see carmine bee-eaters, their nests burrowed into the river bank, rare nyala and sacred ibis, while colourful dawns and sunsets will be among sights and experiences that will remain with you always.

Once threatened with inundation by a dam subsequently abandoned, Mana Pools National Park and adjoining Chewore Safari Area have been designated a World Heritage Site. Mana means 'four', after the four pools near the park headquarters – Long, Main, Chine and Chisambik. Long Pool rarely disappoints the game-watcher, who is likely to see crocodile, hippo, elephant, zebra and a variety of antelope. Birdlife is stunning in its variety and profusion.

Apart from Nyamepi Camp near the park headquarters, there are six camps and two eight-bed lodges. Campsites may be used only during the dry season – May to October. Also within the park are two luxury lodges operated by private enterprise. Both campers and day visitors are admitted to the park, but the number of people and vehicles allowed in at any one time is strictly controlled. There are no shops or restaurants in the park.

Mana Pools is one of the few Zimbabwe game parks where visitors are allowed to leave their cars and explore on foot, between 6 a.m. and 6 p.m. However, you are urged to exercise a certain degree of caution. Mana's hinterland – a quarter of a million hectares extending from the Zambezi escarpment, down through mopane woodland, then *jesse* bush, and eventually the floodplain and river – is there primarily for the animals. There are no fences, and if an elephant bumps your tent at night or steps over your sleeping bag, the ranger is likely to express the hope that the elephant was not upset!

If not upset, elephants are certainly attracted by the smell of fresh fruit – especially citrus. Use of this weakness was made in the Addo Elephant National Park (*see separate entry*) near Port Elizabeth, where oranges from nearby plantations used to be dumped to lure the elephants from the thick bush for the benefit of camera-toting visitors. In the end, it worked too well: the elephants became aggressive and neurotic, and the practice has long been discontinued. So when you're out in Mana, or in any elephant country, make sure that fresh fruit is left behind, preferably well sealed.

The Zambezi here is a fisherman's dream, with tigerfish, barbel, bream and vundu, but there are other aspects of this region that visitors will find less appealing.

The temperature can reach a suffocating 46°C; precautions against malaria are essential; drinking water must be boiled; this is a tsetse fly area. You should also note that the Zambezi is definitely not, as a sarcastic lady once wrote in the visitors' book, 'such nice, safe water for the children to bathe in'.

A fishing camp, Nyamuomba, is situated some 53 km from Marongora by dirt road, and access is allowed only to 4x4 vehicles, and then only between 1 May and 31 October. During the rainy season, access by boat is permitted from Chirundu, some 40 km away. Boats must be off the water by sunset and may not be launched before dawn.

Marongora, where Mana Pools entry permits must be obtained before 3.30 p.m., is 16 km north of Makuti (the last petrol stop) and 312 km from Harare on the road to Zambia. Leaving Marongora, turn right onto a gravel road 6 km further north, at the foot of the escarpment; drive 30 km to Nyakasikana Gate, and then 42 km to Nyamepi Camp. The road is rough, but can be managed without a 4x4 vehicle. There is an airstrip.

Visitors intending to stay over may book through National Parks Central Booking Office, P O Box CY 826, Causeway, Harare, telephone (09263) 4 70-6077, fax 4 72-6089. For information about the private lodges, telephone Acacia Hotels, Harare, on (09263) 4 70-7438.

Matusadona National Park

You can get to Matusadona by road, but you'll have to wait for the dry season before tackling the jolting 468 km from Harare, and you'll need a 4x4 vehicle. It's easier to take a boat or the weekly ferry from Kariba village, or to arrive by light aircraft at the strip at Sanyati, the park headquarters.

Matusadona sprawls across 140 700 ha between the Ume and Sanyati rivers, its tumble of wooded mountains falling down from the uninhabited plateau to the little bays, creeks and islands of Kariba. The Sanyati Gorge is particularly dramatic. Once the hot, narrow valley through which the Sanyati uncoiled from the mountains to the Zambezi Valley, it has been transformed into an African fjord navigable for 12 kilometres.

All camps are close to the shoreline, the main ones being Tashinga and Sanyati West, both with showers, baths, toilets and laundry basins. Camping equipment may be hired at these camps. In addition, there are three exclusive (one party at a time) camps, each accommodating up to ten people for a minimum of seven days. Each camp has two fully equipped, two-bedroomed units with bathroom and toilet, kitchen, dining area and store. There are no shops in the park, but petrol and diesel are usually available at Bumi harbour, 14 km from Tashinga.

Visitors should remember to take precautions against the malarial mosquito and tsetse fly, and drinking water must always be purified. Consult your doctor or chemist for advice. The camps are open from sunrise to sunset throughout the year. Bumi, Fothergill, and Spurwing safari lodges are three privately run

AN EAGLE FALLS

Lake Kariba's fish eagle (*Haliaeetus vocifer*) are in danger of extinction as a result of the pesticide DDT. This pesticide, extensively used in crop spraying and in tsetse and malarial mosquito control, is not banned in Zimbabwe as it is in many other countries. It affects birds' reproductive processes. Eggshells become thinner, vulnerable to excessive moisture loss, and too weak to support the weight of the brooding parent. This was discovered when national parks rangers were lowered by helicopter onto fish eagle nests atop the dead trees of Kariba's shoreline to collect clutches of eggs for analysis.

The American bald eagle population began declining when eggshell thinning reached ten per cent: at Lake Kariba it exceeds 16 per cent. The peregrine falcon (*Falco peregrinus*) will, however, probably be the first bird to disappear, as it did in the eastern USA. Others on the death list if immediate action is not taken (there are several alternative, safer pesticides) are the heron, cormorant, black sparrowhawk and rare fishing owl. The lake's huge fish population is also threatened.

offshore Matusadona base camps. A fourth, Sanyati Lodge, is situated 300 m from the spectacular Sanyati Gorge. Guided walks with armed game scouts may be undertaken from Tashinga, while longer trips are organised by several private safari companies.

Elephant, hippo, buffalo and crocodile are among the most visible of Matusadona's animals, black rhino having suffered from the attentions of poachers armed with war-surplus assault rifles. (Remember, if you come across a hippo on land, that it will probably make for the nearest river, so try to stay out of its line of retreat.) Zebra and assorted antelope, lion, leopard and spotted hyena are also seen. Fishing is a big attraction, especially in September and October, when the international tigerfishing contest is held.

Kariba Dam has not entirely suppressed the instincts of the elephant and buffalo, which still try to follow the old migration routes to the north, the buffalo pushing to the very edge of the land and the elephant actually swimming to Starvation Island, north of Bumi Hills.

In January 1982, a pair of elephant following these ancient routes swam the entire 40 km across Lake Kariba, spending some 30 hours in the water. Both effort and determination were prodigious, and profoundly moved those humans who witnessed this response to a call that they could neither hear nor understand.

ZIMBABWE: LAKE KARIBA

Below left: A lone baboon surveys the shores of Kariba from the safety of a high branch. By day these gregarious animals comb the ground for fruit, roots, bulbs, insects and other food, but when night falls they invariably seek high places such as precipices, where they huddle together until morning. In flat country, they climb to the topmost branches of tall trees. Once settled in their refuge, they are reluctant to leave, and even an attack by a leopard will not prompt a mass flight. **Left:** A cluster of flowers of *Stereospermum kunthianum* (pink jacaranda). The seed pods of the tree are sometimes used as a cough remedy (they are chewed with salt). **Below right:** Saddlebill stork wade through the shallows at the edge of Lake Kariba. This is the largest of the African storks.

Exhausted, the elephants helped each other along, the one in front inflating his lungs for buoyancy and being pushed by the one behind. National Parks staff in boats, led by the warden, came to the intrepid elephants' rescue, eventually guiding them gently ashore near Kariba village.

Enquiries and reservations should be made through National Parks Central Booking Office, P O Box CY 826, Causeway, Harare, telephone (09263) 4 70-6077, fax 4 72-6089.

Matusadona Tented Safaris

Variations on the theme of a guided safari on foot include daily walks from a permanent camp, backpacking between camps erected by a backup team, or backpacking and setting up camp yourself.

The emphasis is on walking – through the savannah woodland area of Matusadona National Park – with all safaris starting and ending at Fothergill Island.

For further information and to make bookings, contact Zimbabwe Sun Central Reservations Office, PO Box CY 1211, Causeway, Harare, telephone (09263) 4 73-6644/5, fax 4 73-6646; or Fothergill Safari Lodge, Private Bag 2081, Kariba, telephone (09263) 61 2253, fax 61 2240.

Nyamasowa Camp

Set in the Kuburi Wilderness Area bordering both the Zambezi River and Lake Kariba, Nyamasowa consists of five large, insectproof, two-bed tents under thatch. Guided gameviewing is available on foot or from vehicles, and canoeing and hiking trips are also offered.

For more information, telephone or fax (09263) 4 70-7675.

Sanyati Lodge

After dark at Sanyati Lodge, on the edge of the isolated Matusadona National Park, there's not even an electricity generator to intrude on the peace and the natural night-time sounds, for energy is provided by solar power. The lodge is on the shore of Lake Kariba, and a mere 300 m from the Sanyati Gorge. The area abounds with birdlife and other animals; the angler is well provided for too.

There is a small camp, with accommodation in well-spaced stone-and-thatch chalets, with bathrooms. Meals are taken on a patio that overlooks the entire Kariba Eastern Basin.

For more information and to make bookings write to Sanyati Lodge, P O Box 66293, Kopje, Harare, or telephone (09263) 4 73-4043/6, fax 4 70-6366.

Sijarira Lodge

West of Chizarira National Park is Sijarira Forest Reserve, where picturesque lodges on the lake are built – in the practical Batonka style – on stilts. In all, the eight lodges of Sijarira can accommodate up to 16 people. A white sandy beach, unusual at Kariba, frames the lake and the distant blue mountains of Zambia.

Sijarira is a fisherman's paradise and lines may be cast from the lake shore or from a boat. In the private Sijarira Forest Reserve, game drives are conducted in open safari vehicles, by boat or on foot with professional guides.

Road transfers are available from Hwange airport to Binga and thereafter by boat from Binga to the Sijarira reserve. For further information and bookings, write to Touch the Wild Safaris/Nagamo Safaris, Private Bag 5, Hillside, Bulawayo, or telephone (09263) 9 7-4589 or 4-4566/7, fax 9 22-9086).

Spurwing Island

On an island in one of Africa's most spectacular lakes and overlooked by the majestic Matusadona Mountains, Spurwing Island is an excellent base for the wildlife enthusiast and holiday-maker alike. Accommodation includes ten large tents, six cabins and three larger chalets. The dining room and two-storey thatched pub overlook the lake.

Game drives on the open expanses of the lake shore provide opportunities for close-up photography. Elephant, lion and large herds of buffalo are sighted regularly and impala, waterbuck and zebra are among the more common inhabitants of the surrounding bush. With luck, the elusive leopard and cheetah may also be seen. The area around Spurwing Island is a birdwatcher's delight and more than 200 species have been recorded, while the local waters support Kariba's claim to be one of the best freshwater angling sites in Africa.

Visitors arrive by launch after a 45-minute trip from Kariba Breezes Marina, or by charter aircraft via Fothergill Island.

For further information, contact Spurwing Island, P O Box 101, Kariba, telephone (09263) 61 2466, or fax 61 2301.

The ancient land of the Shona

The imposing Mashonaland plateau of Zimbabwe is a parkland of rolling *msasa* woodlands between the Zambezi and Limpopo rivers. Some 600 km wide, the plains and great grassy vleis are littered with granite, castle-like koppies, whale-back domes called *dwalas* and impressive nests of balancing rocks, some as old as 3 000 million years.

This, the land of the Shona, is rich in small-game species, in birdlife and in a thousand-year history of Iron Age agriculture, trade and conquest. The evenings are always cool and the summer daytime temperatures average 27°C. The rainy season is from November to March. The winter months of June and July can bring frost at night.

The northeast of Zimbabwe encompasses much of the plateau and the nation's capital, Harare. None of the country's great concentrations of big game are here, but there are numerous parks, recreational areas and sanctuaries, usually around man-made dams. Features such as the Chinhoyi Caves, Lake Chivero's Bushman (San) paintings, Ewanrigg's aloe rockeries and Epworth's balancing rocks have been complemented by an increasing number of private game reserves, by botanical gardens, the Larvon Bird Gardens and innumerable bream-fishing waters.

Adequate, inexpensive accommodation is provided in the main recreational areas by the Department of National Parks and Wildlife Management, and access is usually via tarred roads. There is also an increasing number of privately owned reserves with various grades of accommodation. A stay of three to five days in and around Harare, en route from Beitbridge to Lake Kariba, or perhaps from Bulawayo's Matobo Hills to the Eastern Highlands, can be thoroughly rewarding.

Ballantyne and Blair parks

These twin Harare suburban parks, with their miniature lakes, weeping willows and wild duck, are open throughout the year from 10.30 a.m. to 4.30 p.m. (closing at 1 p.m. on Sundays). To reach the parks, take the Borrowdale road, drive past the racecourse, turn first right into Whitwell Road and keep straight on down Addington Lane (the parks border this road). Children, who should not be allowed to paddle in the water, are entertained by duiker, rabbit, guinea fowl and peacock while their parents fish for bream. The parks, which are some 8 km from the city centre, are home to spur-winged geese, migratory teal, Egyptian geese and many other waterfowl.

Bally Vaughan Game Park

Two main sections make up this attractive reserve just 44 km from Harare (take Enterprise Road and, on the outskirts of the city, turn left onto the Shamva road). The bird park and animal orphanage may be visited daily, except Mondays, between 9 a.m. and 5 p.m. Prior bookings must be made for day trips through the game-park section, which start at 9 a.m. Diversions include lunch in a tree-house, a canoe trip and an afternoon game drive –

Left: The Chinhoyi Caves, once a refuge for warring tribesmen, are now a favourite tourist attraction. The main cave at Chinhoyi penetrates 45 m into the limestone rock at the base of which is the 'Sleeping Pool'. The pool is 102 m deep, and divers from all over the world have plumbed its crystal-clear depths. **Above:** The botanical reserve in the Mtoroshanga Pass was created especially for this flame-red species of aloe (*Aloe ortholopha*), which grows only in the chrome-rich Great Dyke in Zimbabwe. **Right:** The balancing rocks at Epworth, Harare, form a natural sculpture 58 m high.

ZIMBABWE: HARARE AND THE NORTHEAST

the 23 game species include elephant, buffalo and giraffe. A lodge provides overnight accommodation, there is a snack bar in the bird park, and a restaurant in the game park is open for lunch on Sundays. For further information, contact Sunlink International, P O Box HG 529, Highlands, Harare, telephone (09263) 4 78-6521, fax 78-6556.

Chinhoyi Caves National Park

A sinkhole (or collapsed limestone cavern) and the haunt of spirits or a legendary serpent, Chinhoyi Caves' Sleeping Pool, 10 km beyond Chinhoyi town on the main road to Kariba, is a fairytale sight, whether viewed from ground level 46 m above the water, from the Dark Cave, or from the steps of the Sloping Passage.

The Shona know the place as *Chirorodziva*, or 'pool of the fallen'. This may refer to the collapsed roof of the cave, to the unfortunate victims of the wide-ranging Zulu army in the 1830s, or perhaps to the murderous traits of the later outlaw Nyamakwere, who once made the caves his stronghold. Divers have explored the pool, now stocked with goldfish, to a depth of about 100 metres. People lived in or near the labyrinth of caves and tunnels for 1 500 years. Chief Chinhoyi used to retreat into them to avoid Ndebele raids more than 100 years ago. Today the Chinhoyi Caves National Park has suitable camping and caravan facilities and picnic sites for day visitors. There is also a motel with a restaurant.

The caves are open all year, from sunrise to sunset. For further information, write to the National Parks Central Booking Office, P O Box CY 826, Causeway, Harare, telephone (09263) 4 70-6077, fax 72-6089.

Domboshawa

A huge whale-backed rock that takes some 15 minutes to climb, Domboshawa (red rock) comes complete with caves, Bushman (San) paintings, blasted heath-like trees halfway up, and windy, panoramic views from the summit. It is situated 35 km north of Harare on the Domboshawa road and 2 km from Domboshawa village. There is a 15-minute walk from the car park and museum to the cave with its many paintings. The site is open daily until 5 p.m. The surrounding Chinamora area has many other examples of rock art, the next most accessible being Ngomakurira.

Epworth Balancing Rocks

Piled haphazardly one upon the other like huge kitchen platters, these great granite slabs are the result of millions of years of heat, storms and freezing nights – erosion that crumbled the surrounding soil, leaving the boulders stark against the blue sky – an imposing sight and an occasionally frustrating challenge to the photographer. Some formations have acquired fanciful names, and the group known as The Banknotes has been depicted on Zimbabwean currency. This delightful giant's playground is 10 km southeast of Harare's city centre. Take Robert Mugabe Road East and turn right into Chiremba Road, which passes the site, open from sunrise to sunset. There are many other examples of this form of weathering in the immediate vicinity.

Ewanrigg Botanical Garden

A 286 ha garden park of brilliant aloes and prehistoric cycads set in natural woodland 40 km northeast of Harare on the Shamva road, and open during daylight hours throughout the year, Ewanrigg is a floral feast of colour, particularly from June to August. Farmer Basil Christian named it after his brother Ewan, who was killed in the First World War ('rigg' is Welsh for ridge), and bequeathed it to the nation in 1950.

It has been enlarged to include cacti, fuchsia, Barberton daisy and bougainvillea sections, a water garden, a bamboo and palm dell, and a filigree network of footpaths through the woods, lawns and rockeries. Ewanrigg is a popular weekend resort for the people of

Eastwards to the frontier highlands

Zimbabwe's eastern highlands form a natural frontier with Mozambique. They sweep 300 km from Nyanga, south through the Bvumba Mountains near Mutare, to the Chimanimani range and Chipinge, to end south of the Chirinda Forest in a tumble of green slopes.

The most striking feature of this part of the country's Highveld is probably Mount Nyangani. From its summit, 2 593 m above sea level (it is an easy two-hour, three-stage climb), you look back to the lakes and forests, and to range after purple range stretching to the distant horizon. A gentle prospect, but deceptive – turn the other way and you realise you are perched on a great granite shelf. At your feet, Africa's central plateau has come to an abrupt break in an awe-inspiring avalanche of fallen rock and craggy peak.

Bridal Veil Falls

Bridal Veil Falls in California drop 189 m and vaporise. At 50 m, Chimanimani's Bridal Veil Falls are nowhere as grand, but the cascades of water gently descending from one level to the next make up in beauty what they lack in size. The falls – 5 km from the village – are within the Chimanimani Eland Sanctuary (*see separate entry*) on a tributary of the Nyahodi River.

The spot is surrounded by spray-fed ferns and shady trees that make it an ideal picnic spot. The falls are accessible by road, but care is needed with low vehicles. There is a wide range of accommodation within the Chimanimani area.

The twisting Skyline section of the main road linking Chimanimani to the mountain village of Chipinge is one of the most beautiful in the highlands. Trek leader Tom Moodie's grave is by the side of the Skyline road, and the 'Ponte Italia' bridge, built by Italian prisoners during the Second World War, is another feature of the dramatic pass.

For more information and reservations, contact ChiVuNya, Bhadella Arcade, 91 Herbert Chitepo Avenue, P O Box 534, Mutare, Zimbabwe, telephone/fax (09263) 20 6-5165.

Bunga Forest Botanical Reserve

Central to the Bvumba – high-lying ground south of Mutare on Zimbabwe's eastern border – are its botanical gardens and forest reserves. Footpaths and dappled, damp foliage are reminiscent of the Knysna forests of the Western Cape, and both regions possess a jealously guarded wealth of dense, indigenous evergreen vegetation.

There are paths that lead to waterfalls and to viewsites but, apart from these – and an access road from Mutare originally built in 1917 – the environment is undisturbed.

To drive from Mutare (one of the most beautifully situated towns in all of Africa) to the forest is a memorable experience. The road winds up and through the densely wooded, often misty, granite heights of the Bvumba Mountains, and the views are breathtaking. After

Left: Bridal Veil Falls, near the town of Chimanimani. **Above:** The long-necked darter, found near rivers and other stretches of water throughout southern Africa, may often be seen perched on stumps or dead trees. These birds swim with their gracefully proportioned bodies almost completely submerged. They feed on fish and frogs. **Right:** Autumn colours on the firebush (*Hymenodictyon floribundum*). This thin-barked tree is very susceptible to fire, and is often found growing in fissures in rock and other spots where fires are unlikely to affect it.

ZIMBABWE: THE EASTERN HIGHLANDS

9 km there is a turn-off leading to the 75 km scenic drive through the Burma Valley, taking you past scattered coffee, cotton and banana plantations. Apart from the abundance and variety of flora, there is also a profusion of birds, butterflies and, for those with patience, the shy, small antelope and other wildlife of the forests.

Accommodation in the Bvumba is limited to around 300 beds, so it is advisable to book early. There are hotels, a guesthouse and places offering budget accommodation for backpackers. The Manicaland Publicity Association, P O Box 69, Mutare, Zimbabwe, telephone (09263) 20 6-4711, keeps a list of cottages and can also supply current accommodation rates. Bookings may also be made through ChiVuNya, Bhadella Arcade, 91 Herbert Chitepo Avenue, P O Box 534, Mutare, Zimbabwe, telephone/fax (09263) 20 6-5165.

Bvumba Botanical Gardens

Once a private estate, Bvumba is an interesting contrast to the nearby Bunga reserve of indigenous forest and flora. Bvumba's glories are its exotics, such as ferns, azaleas, roses, fuchsias, aloes and cycads that flourish in the slightly acid soil of this cool, humid refuge.

The total area is 201 ha, of which 42 ha form the indigenous botanical reserve, while the remainder has been set aside as a garden. Of this generous area, 32 ha of garden have already been developed. A superb collection of flowering plants is supplemented by a herb garden which, with its mix of the indigenous and the exotic, demonstrates the many uses to which herbs are put in different cultures.

Many of the Bvumba's bird and butterfly species may be seen while simply walking about the gardens, and some of the larger animals, such as the rare blue duiker, may be glimpsed from the discreet paths that lead through the 42 ha of unspoilt forest of the Bvumba Botanical Reserve.

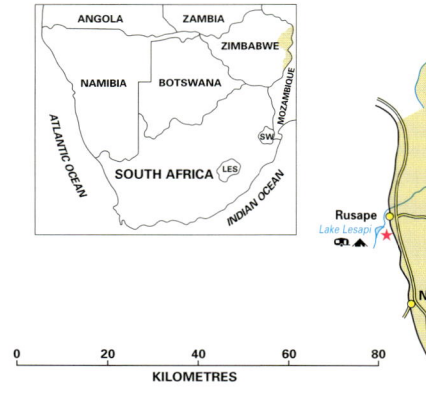

THE IMPREGNABLE LAIR OF THE BIRD OF DOOM

The hamerkop – to many rural people a bird of evil omen – is often seen standing in shallow water, deep in concentration as it watches for fish and frogs. It is said that to disturb it will bring disaster. A displeased hamerkop will cry as it flies over a homestead, a signal that tragedy will soon strike.

This so-called 'bird of doom' is, however, one of nature's cleverest architects. Its monumental nest is virtually impregnable and is so well disguised that many potential enemies never realise it is there. Usually sited on a ledge or in a tree, it resembles a haphazard heap of sticks and rubbish. Inside, though, there is a neat dome roof plastered with mud – so strong that it can bear the weight of a person. It has three chambers, one for the parent birds, one for fledgelings, and a reception area reached by a concealed outside entrance.

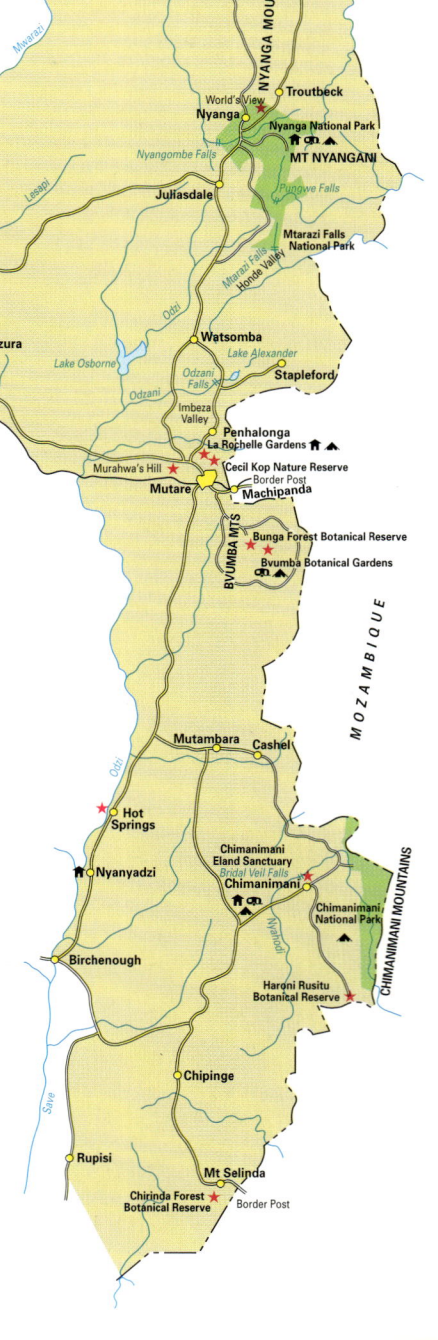

388

Left: The Bvumba Botanical Gardens, situated in an extensive woodland reserve, attract many visitors with its multicoloured display of flora and its network of footpaths that wind through beautiful countryside. **Right:** *Bauhinia galpinii*. This plant is also commonly known as camelsfoot – a name derived from the belief that its leaves (when laid flat) resemble the footprint of a camel.

A privately run tearoom (open daily from 10 a.m. to 4.30 p.m.) provides refreshments and there is a camping and caravan site nearby with ablution blocks and a swimming pool. To reserve sites, write to the National Parks Central Booking Office, P O Box CY 826, Causeway, Harare, Zimbabwe, telephone (09263) 4 70-6077, fax 4 72-6089.

Cecil Kop Nature Reserve and Thompson's Vlei

Cecil Kop Mountain overlooks Zimbabwe's eastern gateway city of Mutare. The game reserve is 1 740 ha of natural mountain grassland, forest, open woodland and vlei, only 3,5 km from the city centre.

Phase one of the three-stage development brainchild of the Wildlife Society of Zimbabwe was the fencing of a 400 ha gamewatching area overlooking a waterhole. The game in this Tiger's Kloof section includes elephant, giraffe, buffalo, zebra, sable, eland, tsessebe, wildebeest and, at the dam, Egyptian goose, cormorant, grey heron, darter and numerous other species of waterfowl. Many of the larger mammals are in the habit of gathering at the dam at around 4 p.m. to be fed. Visitors see the game from outside the fence – an elevated area on which there are two viewing platforms.

There is a road to the more distant Thompson's Vlei where there is another (unfenced) pan with a gameviewing platform. The western half of the reserve consists of a wilderness section, in which paths are currently being laid out. Visitors should keep away from the boundary with Mozambique in the east, where land mines were sown during the independence war or *chimurenga*.

A tea kiosk operates daily from 9.30 a.m. The reserve, which is open daily from 7 a.m. to sunset, is reached by driving north along Herbert Chitepo Avenue and into Arcadia Road.

For more information contact the Manicaland Publicity Association, P O Box 69, Mutare, Zimbabwe, telephone (09263) 20 6-4711.

Chimanimani Eland Sanctuary

The 1 800 ha eland reserve is adjacent to the village of Chimanimani. There have always been wild eland in the forests of the area, the species being the only large antelope to adapt to the artificial environment of pine plantations. They ceased their normal migratory habits and learned to feed off the buds and bark of the young pine trees. Much damage was caused, so the buck were captured and placed in the reserve, funds for which were provided by the small Chimanimani community and the Conservation Trust of Zimbabwe.

Eland are Africa's largest antelope, weighing up to 900 kg and standing nearly two metres high. Their meat is comparable to lean beef. The Department of National Parks has developed an experimental herd at Mushandike near Masvingo, as the species has potential for domestication. There are a few eland left in the Chimanimani sanctuary, but you are more likely to see waterbuck and zebra. The road that leads into the reserve twists up Pork Pie Mountain or *Nyamzure*. Although 1 992 m above sea level, its summit is only some 120 m above the surrounding plain.

The eland reserve has no facilities. Several interesting drives start from the village of Chimanimani, including the 70 km scenic drive to the farming community of Cashel. It passes the Chimanimani gap through which the Musapa River flows, and there are some magnificent msasa forests on the way.

Chimanimani National Park

Of all mountains of Zimbabwe, the Chimanimani are probably the loveliest. Raw beauty on a vast scale, they extend some 48 km to form the southern bastion of the eastern highlands.

The Portuguese were not the first outsiders to make their way through what must have been a daunting barrier. Centuries earlier, Arab traders used the Chimanimani gap, or 'pincers', through the range to reach the interior and Great Zimbabwe. The original name for the Chimanimani may have been *chimwenjemwenje*, after the flashes of sunlight sparkling off their heights.

The eastern highlands, backbone of Zimbabwe, are part of that seemingly endless series of mountains fringing Africa's plateau, a range stretching from the ancient uplands of Ethiopia through to the rugged Drakensberg of KwaZulu-Natal. Geologists refer to it as the Frontier System. The Chimanimani section, 2 440 m at its highest, came into being some 1 600 million years ago when the white quartzite massif was forced against the plateau, shattering in folds over its leading edge.

The 17 100 ha of the Chimanimani National Park is subject to sudden storms and mists that highlight a startling landscape of scarred and splintered rock, twisted in shape and multihued with lichen. But just as suddenly the great humped range is bathed in sunlight that seeks out the shadowed green folds and glistening wet rock faces.

Ferns and orchids grow in profusion beside the streams. In the foothills and valleys, proteas and wild fig trees abound, mingling in the evergreen forest with cedars and yellowwood, Howman's cliff aloe, wild sweet pea, mountain hibiscus, traveller's joy and the familiar Zimbabwe creeper.

No roads spoil the tranquillity of the Chimanimani. The mountains are a haven for bird and other wildlife and, of course, for the mountaineer, the nature enthusiast and the explorer.

There are mountain lakes, and rivers with trout pools and waterfalls, one of the loveliest being near the Outward Bound School. Another is the 120 m high Martin's Falls on the eastern side. Eland, sable, bushbuck and blue duiker are seen regularly; klipspringer and leopard less often. The birdlife includes purple-crested louries, malachite sunbirds, laughing doves, trumpeter hornbills and francolins.

Zimbabwe's Department of National Parks operates a base camp and information office at

Mutekeswane, where there is a campsite and parking area for visitors' cars. From Chimanimani village, drive along the road in front of the Chimanimani Hotel for 14 km, ignoring both the Orange Grove and Tilbury turn-offs, and, at the Outward Bound School fork, turn right and continue for a further 4 km until you reach the camp entrance. In summer, the ranger's office is open on weekdays from 6 a.m. to noon and from 2 p.m. to 5 p.m. (winter times are 7 a.m. to noon and 2 p.m. to 4 p.m.). On Saturday, the office is open from 8 a.m. to 12.30 p.m. All visitors must report here before entering the park.

The most popular walk from Mutekeswane is one of three hours (it's known as Bailey's Folly) that brings you to a rustic cabin overlooking the Bundi River valley. Camping is allowed in the park, and many caves and rock shelters are cosy and easily accessible.

For further information, write to the National Parks Central Booking Office, P O Box CY 826, Causeway, Harare, Zimbabwe, telephone (09263) 4 70-6077, fax 4 72-6089.

Chirinda Forest Botanical Reserve

The Chirinda Forest Botanical Reserve, of 949 ha and with more than 100 tree species, is a good example of primeval subtropical forest and is an entomologists' mecca. The name means 'place of watching' or 'refuge': many years ago, local inhabitants would hide in the forest from raiders and keep a watch from the trees, one of which is the country's tallest – a 1 000-year-old red mahogany (*Khaya nyasica*) that stands 58,5 m high and measures 16 m in circumference at the base of the trunk.

The forest is 32 tarred km south of Chipinge, Zimbabwe's tea- and coffee-farming centre; 183 km from Mutare and 230 km from Masvingo. Turn into the forest just before the American Mount Selinda Mission.

It is a whisper-world of ironwoods, parasitic creepers, figs, ferns, butterflies (including lilac beauty), the rare pink or lilac orchid (*Calanthe natalensis*), samango monkey and the occasional cough of a leopard.

Features include the 'Valley of the Giants', a picnic site, and a memorial tablet to the British naturalist Charles Swynnerton, who lived in the forest at the turn of the century and happily recorded its wonderland of insects, squirrels, birds and butterflies.

Haroni Rusitu Botanical Reserve

You need a detailed map and the assistance of the Forestry Commission to reach this 150 ha area of low-altitude dense forest, 50 km due south of Chimanimani on rough gravel roads. There are no facilities at all, but if you are a botanist or admirer of butterflies, you will enjoy being here.

This is the only lowland rainforest in Zimbabwe and the trees are magnificent. Unusual orchids and unique types of fern are seen, with many rare species of bird and amphibian. During the dry season a pick-up truck (*bakkie*) will have no problem navigating the rough roads, but it is advisable to use a 4x4 vehicle for easier accessibility.

For directions and further information, write to the Chimanimani Rural and District Council, P O Box 20, Chimanimani, Zimbabwe.

Hot Springs Resort

These mineral springs are situated at Nyanyadzi, on the main Mutare/Birchenough Bridge Road. Attractive thatched accommodation is available.

Birchenough Bridge was designed by Ralph Freeman, who also designed Sydney Harbour Bridge, and it is the largest single-span steel suspension bridge in southern Africa. There is not much to see around the bridge, although photographic opportunities towards dusk are very good.

For further information, contact The Manager, Hot Springs Resort, P O Box 190, Nyanyadzi, Zimbabwe, telephone (09263) 26 2361.

Lake Lesapi

Completed in 1972, the dam on the Lesapi River supplies irrigation water to estates along the Save River 200 km downstream. The 80 ha park surrounding the dam lies just outside the town of Rusape, 'the place of sandy soil', 170 km east of Harare on the Mutare road, the best route to the Nyanga National Park (*see separate entry*).

There is an attractive campsite and caravan park situated among koppies and balancing rocks, and the fishing (bass and bream) in the 615 ha dam is excellent.

The shoreline has numerous coves, while near the dam wall scenic walks lead to landscaped gardens. Some magnificent rock paintings can be seen on Diana's Vow Farm, some 30 km from Rusape off the Nyanga road. A reproduction of these paintings may be seen in the Mutare Museum.

Left: The La Rochelle Gardens near Mutare provide visitors with a wealth of flowers, trees and shrubs (both indigenous and exotic). **Above:** The giant kingfisher (*Megaceryle maxima*) is a widely dispersed species that frequents lagoons, rivers, streams and coastal pools. Its long bill aids the kingfisher in holding its slippery prey which is turned head first before it is swallowed. **Right:** The msasa tree has several practical uses: tannin is extracted from the bark, a substance in the roots is used to alleviate the symptoms of dysentery, and the wood is widely used as fuel.

For information and to reserve campsites, write to the Department of Water Resources and Development, P O Box 229, Rusape, Zimbabwe, or telephone (09263) 25 28-1515.

La Rochelle Gardens

A fanciful white tower dominates the beautiful La Rochelle Gardens, the 14 ha former estate of the late Sir Stephen and Lady Courtauld, in the green, wooded Imbeza Valley of Penhalonga, 13 km north of Mutare.

The landscaped gardens are a blaze of formal colour, exotic trees, rare orchids and ornamental shrubs among the waterfalls, fountains and ponds. There is also a Braille trail for the blind through the botanical gardens.

The imposing main house has been turned into a country hotel, several self-catering cottages are available on the estate, and there is also a campsite.

The colourful gardens are open all year from 8 a.m. to 5 p.m. and a tearoom is open from 9.30 a.m. to 4.30 p.m.

For further information, write to The Manager, La Rochelle, P O Box 38, Penhalonga, Zimbabwe, telephone (09263) 20 5 22250.

Penhalonga was named after one of the several aristocratic Portuguese adventurers who came to Manicaland in the late 19th century in search of gold. Nearby are Lake Alexander (Mutare's water supply and watersport venue), the Odzani Falls and Stapleford Forest Reserve.

Murahwa's Hill

One of two breaks in the eastern highland range is at Mutare. It was through this gap, up the hot, steaming valley, that Portuguese traders came in search of gold 400 years ago.

Hidden in a bowl of wooded hills, Mutare, 262 km east of Harare, straddles the access route to Beira on the coast. Novelist Evelyn Waugh once said of the place: 'There is neither snow nor sea, but there is everything else.' On the northwestern outskirts of the town is a small nature reserve known as Murahwa's Hill, named after a Nyika subchief. It has a great diversity of indigenous trees: more than 100 have been identified. It also has some rock paintings and the remains of an Iron Age village, and is an ideal habitat for birds, butterflies and wild orchids. The entrance is near the showgrounds on Magamba Drive.

Nyanga National Park

'Nyanga is much finer than you described,' Cecil John Rhodes wrote to his agent James McDonald. 'Before it is all gone, quickly buy me up to 100 000 acres.' In terms of his will, Rhodes bequeathed this spectacular piece of land to the nation.

Nyanga and the Mtarazi Falls National Park, some 28 900 ha and 2 495 ha respectively, are administered as one unit, a giant 2 000 to 2 300 m high plateau of downs, heather-scented air, lakes, evergreens, waterfalls and rippling streams on Zimbabwe's eastern border mountains. Much of Zimbabwe's fruit (apples in particular) is grown in the vicinity of the reserve. The air is bracing, and cosy nights are spent in thatched lodges tailor-made for roaring log fires.

Well-tended gravel roads link the many mountain viewsites with the Nyangwe (Mare), Nyanga and Udu dams, which are all well stocked with rainbow, brown and brook trout.

Just outside the park, 5 km west of the main Nyanga road past Udu Dam, are the two stages of the attractive Nyangombe Falls. They lie on the Claremont estate (John Moodie, renegade member of the 1892 Gazaland Trek, named his farm Claremont, after his wife's former home near Cape Town). There are two paths to the falls – a gentle walk and a steep climb over rough terrain. The ground around the falls is often steep and slippery, and the rocks near the water may be treacherously slimy. If you visit during the rainy season, it is advisable not to allow children to climb on the rocks.

Nyanga's high plateau is the birthplace of many rivers. The Pungwe, Odzi and Gairezi

NYANGA AT A GLANCE

When to go The park is open to visitors throughout the year (from sunrise to sunset), but Nyanga can be bitterly cold during the short winter months. Summer days can be extremely hot, though the nights are generally cool.

Reservations and information Enquiries and applications for accommodation should be addressed to the National Parks Central Booking Office, P O Box CY 826, Causeway, Harare, Zimbabwe, telephone (09263) 4 70-6077, fax 4 72-6089.

Getting there The park is 275 km of tarred road eastwards from Harare, via Rusape; 99 km north from Mutare.

Accommodation There is one hotel in the park and there are several others nearby. A private holiday cottage to rent in Nyanga is a much sought-after prize, and it would be worth your while to locate one. There are a few self-catering cottages just outside the park — contact Manicaland Publicity Association, P O Box 69, Mutare, Zimbabwe, telephone (09263) 20 6-4711; or ChiVuNya, Bhadella Arcade, 91 Herbert Chitepo Avenue, P O Box 534, Mutare, Zimbabwe, telephone (09263) 20 6-5165. National Parks offer fully equipped and serviced lodges at the Nyanga, Nyangwe and Udu dams. Park accommodation should be booked well in advance. There is a caravans-only site at the Mare River, and a campsite and caravan park at Nyangombe River on the Nyanga village road, 2 km past the Nyanga Dam turn-off.

Eating and drinking Meals are available at the hotel in the park. Visitors must supply their own food for braais and picnics.

Wildlife Nyanga is essentially a mountain-scenery area. You may, however, see kudu and smaller antelope.

Special attractions Mount Nyangani, on the circular drive, is well worth ascending (it's not really a climb) for the magnificent view from its summit — unless of course the weather is cloudy, in which case it would be unwise to attempt the walk. Scattered throughout the park are the ruins of scores of stone enclosures, popularly believed to have been 'slave pits' (in reality they were probably small cattle pens, built by long-ago Karanga people who, like modern tourists, were attracted to the area). Guided horse trails, lasting from one and a half to six hours, explore the Nyanga Dam archaeological sites. There is swimming at Nyangombe rock pool.

Fishing The park is very popular among trout-fishermen. Trout licences are available from the Udu, Mare and Nyanga offices. These dams are open throughout the year, and rowing boats can be hired. Purdon Dam and Lake Gulliver are open between 1 October and 31 July, while the reserve's 80 km of rivers are accessible to anglers from 1 October to 31 May.

Special precautions There is no bilharzia at Nyanga, but tiny ticks in the park's long grass during winter can be an irritant.

---

are situated at the car park 200 m from the final walk to the falls, and there is also a National Parks campsite.

Just beyond the Rhodes Nyanga Hotel in the Nyanga National Park, a scenic drive through rolling mountain moorland, wattle and pine plantations, past the Pungwe Falls and Honde View sites, leads to the Mtarazi Falls.

The view of the falls from the semi-tropical Honde Valley far below is just as spectacular as the view from the top.

For all accommodation in the Nyanga National Park, contact the National Parks Central Booking Office, P O Box CY 826, Causeway, Harare, Zimbabwe, telephone (09263) 4 70-6077, fax 4 72-6089.

Nyanga: Nyamziwa Falls and Pungwe Falls

What might be the perfect picnic spot can be found on the banks of the Nyamziwa River in Nyanga, within earshot of the sparkling falls of the same name.

Among its attractions are riverside walks and the sweeping vista of distant Mount Nyangani — at 2 593 m Zimbabwe's highest mountain. It lies 11 km from the Nyanga Dam tourist office, en route to the mountain.

The viewsite overlooking the Pungwe Falls balances on the edge of a precipitous drop, enabling photographers to capture the full, breathtaking beauty of the huge cascade of water winding its way seaward through the jungle-green gorge.

A 20 km scenic drive, starting at Rhodes Nyanga Hotel, leads to the Pungwe. The river rises at the foot of Mount Nyangani in the national park and, joined by the Matenderere and at least two other tributaries, slices through highland for 30 km before plunging 240 m into the 10 km gorge. After its long, winding journey, the Pungwe River reaches the Indian Ocean near Beira. Two riverside National Parks lodges are sited at the Pungwe Drift near the falls.

World's View

Bracken and heather moorland surround the Connemara Lakes en route to World's View, the northernmost edge of the Nyanga range, with a drop of some 1 000 metres. World's View is part of a 92 ha National Trust estate.

The cliff-edge paths offer windswept picnic spots and, of course, spectacular views. Turn left just before the Troutbeck Inn for the 11 km drive to the summit. After passing through the golf course, the road becomes steep with sharp corners, and is very slippery during the rainy season. Drive slowly and watch out for approaching vehicles.

The westward slopes of the Nyanga park support msasa trees that turn the mountains red and gold during spring.

---

start here as gently bubbling streams beneath the marsh grass. And some, such as the Pungwe, Nyangombe and Mtarazi, leap off the plateau in spectacular waterfalls.

In the Mtarazi Falls National Park a narrow track parallels the plateau rim to the point where the river cascades in a ribbon of silver 762 m down the cliff face and into the Honde Valley. It is converted into glistening mist and spray en route, and moistens a luxuriant rainforest, home of the rare blue duiker, immediately beneath it. Picnic sites and braai places

The place of the elephant

Defeated by Shaka in 1819, the Zulu-speaking Ndwandwe fled north in the direction of Delagoa Bay under their generals Nxaba, Zwangendaba and Soshangana. Soshangana proved the most militarily efficient, turning on his rival generals and subjugating the Tsonga people of Gazaland, across the Limpopo. Part of the territory he captured is today Zimbabwe's second largest national park, the 496 400 ha Gonarezhou (Place of the Elephant) National Park, stretching for over 100 km along the country's southeastern Lowveld boundary with Mozambique.

Masvingo, 296 km from Beitbridge and close to the ruins of Great Zimbabwe and Lake Mutirikwi, is the centre for this area.

Bangala Recreational Park

The southeastern Lowveld, nourished by a network of irrigation canals and dams such as Mutirikwi, Bangala and MacDougall, is the granary and sugar storehouse of Zimbabwe. The Mutirikwi River near Great Zimbabwe is dammed by the Mutirikwi Dam and, further south, by the Bangala Dam, to create a still-undeveloped 2 800 ha park where boating and fishing are permitted. From the Esquilingwe weir on the Mutirikwi, a system of canals carries water 55 km to sugar and fruit estates at Triangle and Hippo Valley. The park is 147 km south of Masvingo and the road is tarred all the way. Take the Mutare road, turn right for Triangle/Chiredzi, and turn right again for Bangala Dam. There are no facilities in the park, which is open 24 hours a day.

Chilo Gorge Safari Lodge

Opened in 1996 and based on the concepts of ecotourism and of the Communal Areas Management Programme for Indigenous Resources (CAMPFIRE), the lodge consists of 14 luxury, two-bed thatched bungalows set on cliffs high above the Save River adjoining Gonarezhou National Park. Local Shangaan people played a part in the development of the project and are involved in its administration. Guests are transferred by safari vehicle from an airstrip just 5 km away, and a coach service into the area, via Great Zimbabwe, has recently been introduced. Guides take guests on game walks and drives, and on photographic and birdwatching safaris.

For more detailed information, write to Zimbabwe Sun Central Reservations, P O Box CY 1211, Causeway, Harare, or telephone (09263) 4 73-6644/5, fax 4 73-6646.

Chiredzi River Conservancy

Conveniently sited between Great Zimbabwe and Gonarezhou National Park, the 81 000 ha Chiredzi River Conservancy is nevertheless an exciting destination in its own right.

Elephant, buffalo and black rhino have been reintroduced, and most other Lowveld species are present and increasing in number, while more than 250 bird species have been recorded. Accommodation is provided in a pleasant stone-and-thatch lodge set on the banks of the Mungwezi River.

For further information and to make reservations, contact Mungwezi Adventure Safaris, P O Box 297, Chiredzi, or telephone (09263) 31 2865/2640, fax 31 3026.

Gonarezhou National Park

This park is wild, hot, remote and full of game – particularly elephant, which have become somewhat cantankerous thanks to the activities of hunters and poachers before the area was declared a reserve. Tsetse-fly control operations in surrounding areas took a heavy toll of the park's game population, and some 55 000 animals were shot, including 12 000 kudu and 15 000 duiker. After becoming a game reserve in 1968 and a national park seven years later, the area improved immensely. More recently, though, poaching, war and prolonged drought have taken a heavy toll.

Gonarezhou is some 40 km wide and forms a natural migratory triangle, together with the

Left: The Save River, one of the crucial arteries in Zimbabwe. Animals are drawn by the thousand to its verdant banks. **Above left:** The 19th-century hunter and explorer William Baldwin. He came to colonial Natal in 1851, and made several hunting trips to Zululand before travelling to the Transvaal and further north. He met David Livingstone at the Victoria Falls in 1860, and claimed to be the second white man to reach the falls. Baldwin covered vast distances on his trips through southern Africa. **Above right:** The Zimbabwe creeper (*Podranea brycei*) is fairly widely distributed throughout that country, and differs from the South African species (Port St Johns creeper) in that the corollas are slightly compressed at the mouth.

ZIMBABWE: THE SOUTH

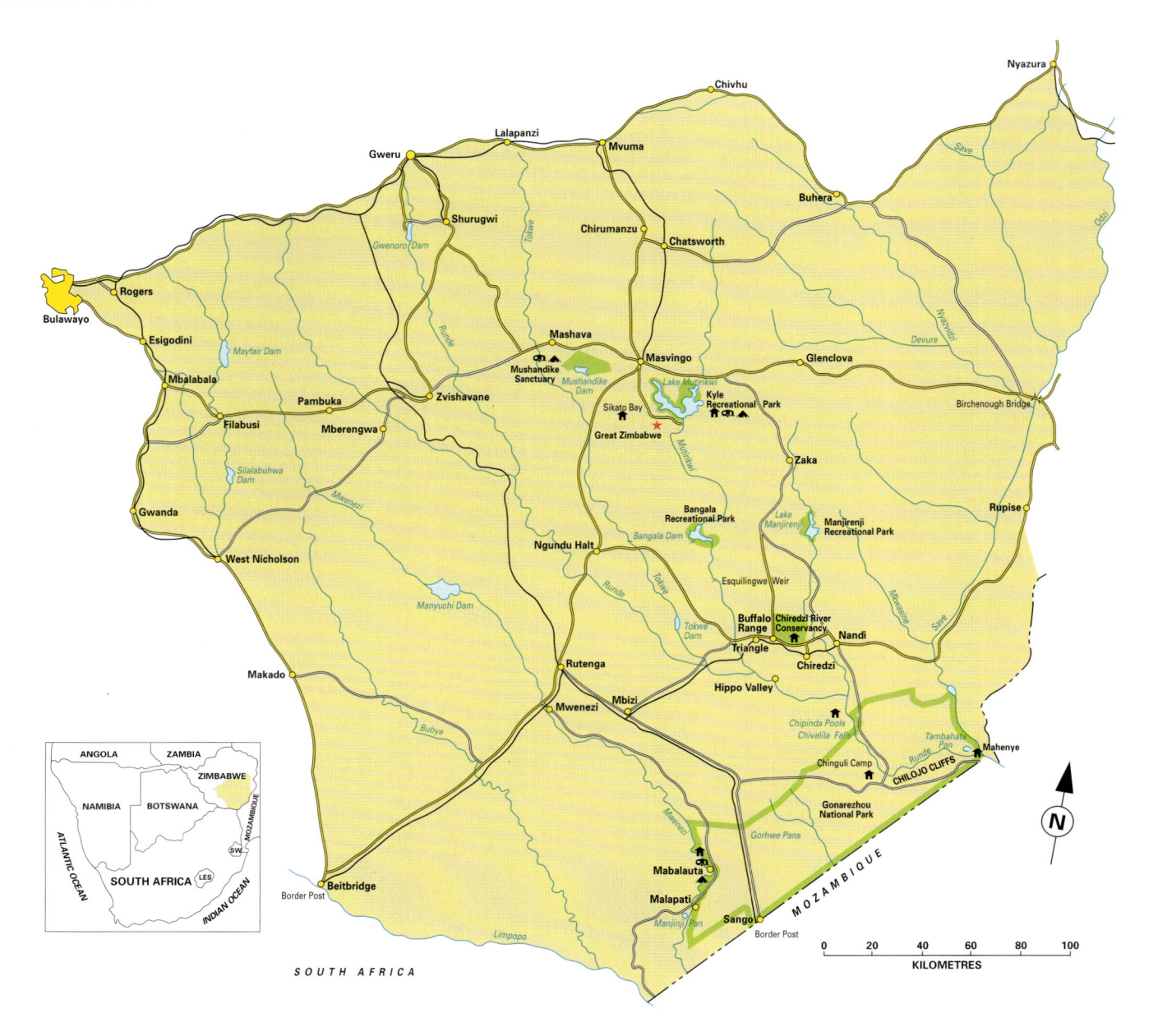

Kruger National Park in South Africa and the Mozambique game area bordering on Gonarezhou. Some 800 Kruger Park eland are known to have crossed into the Gonarezhou region, as well as several herds of elephant. There are kudu, lion, leopard, hippo, the rare nyala and many other species.

The park is divided into the rugged Save-Runde subregion in the north, and the southerly Mwenezi subregion. There is no road (within the park) linking them and the vast central section is an untouched wilderness area.

The park is open in the dry season (1 May to 31 October), from 6 a.m. to 6 p.m. From November to April, visitors are admitted only to Chipinda Pools in the northern section, and to Mabalauta and Swimuwini in the south. For more information and for bookings, contact the National Parks Central Booking Office, P O Box CY 826, Causeway, Harare, telephone (09263) 4 70-6077, fax 4 72-6089.

Gonarezhou: Chivalila Falls

Two kilometres south of the Chipinda Pools tourist office, the Runde River has carved a path along a rocky gorge through which the water courses in a series of 10 m drops. This is Chivalila Falls, one of the many attractive Runde River campsites in the park.

Fishing is permitted only at designated campsites and for a distance of 500 m on either side of those sites. Only people who are overnight occupiers of a campsite are allowed to fish, and there are strictly enforced rules relating to the number of fish that may be caught or removed from the park. It is recommended that prior permission should be obtained before attempting to go fishing in any river in the park.

Gonarezhou: Gorhwe Pans

This series of at least four pans is situated in the wilderness area some 30 km north of Mabalauta, between the railway line and the Guluene River in the Gonarezhou National Park. They are accessible only by 4x4 vehicle along an old tsetse 'cut' (with the permission of the Department of National Parks). Elephant and many other species of game are attracted to the pans when they are filled with water.

Gonarezhou: Mabalauta
The Mwenezi River marks the southern boundary of the 200 000 ha Mwenezi subsection of the Gonarezhou National Park. Mabalauta is the Shangaan name for the local *Ficus capreifolia* tree, the leaves of which are sufficiently rough to have been used by hunters as sandpaper for smoothing down the wood of their bows and arrows. This is the land of the big elephant, some with tusks weighing up to 45 kg each.

The park rest camp, Swimuwini (the place of baobabs), is sited on a cliff overlooking the Mwenezi River's Buffalo Bend which, in the dry season, is a vast, snake-like sweep of yellow sand. The camp's chalets are named in Latin, after trees in the area (*Trichilia, Albizia*), and all are sited beneath giant baobabs.

The park's wildlife is very much in evidence: visitors invariably speak of hearing lions roaring near the camp at night. The park's tourist office, to which all visitors must report on arrival, is situated 8 km away. Five camping and caravan sites have been opened along the river, and two airstrips serve the area.

A half-hour's drive at midday can easily result in close-up sightings of a dozen species of game, including nyala, black-backed jackal, waterbuck and elephant, while in the evening lion may be seen stalking the jostling herds of antelope that amble down the many game trails to the water.

You can leave your car at any of the four viewpoints overlooking the Mwenezi River. One of these, a thatched shelter perched on a cliff edge, looks right down on the Mwatombo crocodile pools. Fishing in the river is not permitted. There are over 180 km of game drives, including Soshangana, named after the old warrior chief, and half a dozen pans – the best of which is probably Manyanda.

Gonarezhou: Manyanda Pan
Piped water ensures a good count of animals even during the dry season, and a viewing platform, flush toilet and washbasin provide some ease for the human visitor.

Manyanda Pan, in the southern subsection, is accessible to most types of vehicle if reasonable care is taken. It is a one-group camp accommodating up to ten people. Water intended for drinking should be boiled or treated chemically.

Gonarezhou: Save-Runde subsection
In summer it is uncomfortably hot (40°C) and humid at Chipinda Pools. The pools, on the Runde River, form a series of water havens for hippo and crocodile. Chipinda is also the site of the park offices for this northern subsection.

Access is via Chiredzi, 59 km distant (and the last point for fuel and stores) on a manageable but often badly corrugated gravel road. There are a number of campsites spread out over 100 km of the Runde River. Those at Chipinda Pools itself and Chinguli Camp have an open-air dining rondavel and ablution facilities. The other bush camps are for single parties (up to ten persons), and have no facilities other than a primitive lavatory, rubbish pit and braai area. The furthest is 30 km distant, at Chilojo Cliffs, the spectacular red sandstone bluffs along the Runde. A 4x4 vehicle is recommended on most of the 200 km of game drives and to reach the bush camps. There are several picnic sites suitable for day visitors. Anti-malaria precautions should be taken. The river is infested with bilharzia.

The Save-Runde subsection is a good fishing area (tigerfish and black bream). Game includes lion, giraffe, elephant, buffalo, Lichtenstein's hartebeest and nyala. There is also rich riverine birdlife, although birdwatching can be difficult because of the thick bush. The bush further south at Mwenezi offers easier access to birdwatchers.

Gonarezhou is the only Zimbabwe game park situated astride a major river. The Runde links up with the Save River at the border with Mozambique to form the Tambahata Pan, which stretches 8 km between the two rivers in times of flood. On the Save River are impressive falls, which can be approached only on foot. Permission is needed to visit the area. For further information and bookings, contact the National Parks Central Booking Office, P O Box CY 826, Causeway, Harare, telephone (09263) 4 70-6077, fax 4 72-6089.

Above: A gorgeous bush shrike (*Telophorus quadricolor*), photographed in lower-lying country south of Mutare. This beautiful bird builds its nest with twigs, arranging them loosely in the form of a shallow bowl and lodging the structure low down in a bush or tree. Because of its retiring nature, the gorgeous bush shrike is rarely seen. The young of this species has a yellow throat and green tail.

Great Zimbabwe
The sheer size of Great Zimbabwe is awe-inspiring. These great *dzimba dzemabwe*, or houses of stone, 30 km southeast of Masvingo, were built by the Karanga, ancestors of today's Shona, between the 11th and 15th centuries, as the royal capital of a state that dominated the central plateau and the gold trade to the coast.

Great Zimbabwe occupies an area of some 720 ha, and the city itself may have had a population of 30 000 people.

A solid stone conical tower akin to a giant grain bin, symbol of the king's largesse and repository of tribute, forms the centrepiece of a huge elliptical building, a wall-and-hut complex. The outer wall is 249 m in circumference and, in parts, over 10 m high and 5 m thick.

Some 8 km by road from Lake Mutirikwi's shores, Great Zimbabwe is set in a rugged koppie-strewn valley with a site museum and 4 ha of colourful aloe gardens. This national monument – related to the history of human occupation and development rather than to natural history of the area – is open until 5 p.m. every day. There is a wide range of accommodation close to the site.

For further information, write to The Director, National Museums and Monuments, P O Box CY 8540, Causeway, Harare, or telephone (09263) 4 70-7202.

Left below: A brown-hooded kingfisher. Unlike some other species of kingfisher in southern Africa, this bird hunts insects in bush country. **Left above:** Lake Mutirikwi (also known as Mutirikwi Dam), the second largest body of water in Zimbabwe, is one of the country's most popular tourist spots. **Above:** *Anomatheca grandiflora*, photographed in the Kyle Recreational Park. **Right:** A female grey duiker. The males of this species are very pugnacious, marking their territory (with the preorbital gland's secretions) on the tips of twigs, and defending it with vigour.

Gwenoro Dam

The dam is 40 km from Gweru off the Bulawayo road (the turn-off is 6 km south of Gweru). Gwenoro Dam is noted for its bass- and bream-fishing, and is also popular with yachtsmen – many from the nearby chrome mine, which operates a club on the shore. Caravanning and camping facilities are available among the rolling hills of Ferny Creek, 2,5 km from the town of Shurugwi. Near Gwenoro Dam is the newer Amanpongokwe Dam, the largest of the area's three dams. Picnicking and fishing are allowed.

Kyle Recreational Park

A river with crocodiles is ecologically balanced, a display inside the Kyle park's wildlife museum informs visitors. Lake Mutirikwi, Zimbabwe's second largest stretch of water (formerly Lake Kyle), at the confluence of the Mshagashe and Mutirikwi rivers, certainly has crocodiles. In recent years, four confirmed man-eaters, including the infamous 'Cripple Koos', have actually lived among less notorious relatives in the park's crocodile pond.

The lake is part of the 16 900 ha Kyle Recreational Park, 13 km east of Masvingo on the Birchenough Bridge/Mutare road. The park, on the northern shore of the lake, offers white rhino, reedbuck, tsessebe, giraffe, oribi, nyala and many other species. Visitors may explore the park on foot or by pony, and the lake is renowned for its bass-fishing.

The hills of Great Zimbabwe can be seen from the ten fully equipped lodges overlooking the lake. There are two caravan parks and campsites (the site on the west bank at Sikato Bay is reached via the Masvingo/Great Zimbabwe road). The park is open throughout the year between 6 a.m. and 6 p.m. There are holiday hotels on the lake shore offering chalets, lodges and camping.

For more detailed information, write to the Publicity Bureau, P O Box 340, Masvingo, or telephone (09263) 39 6-2491. Bookings and enquiries should be addressed to the National Parks Central Booking Office, P O Box CY 826, Causeway, Harare, or telephone their offices at (09263) 4 70-6077, fax 4 72-6089.

Mahenye Safari Lodge

Examples of ecotourism as practised at Mahenye, adjoining Gonarezhou National Park, include use of solar power and the limiting of guests to a maximum of 16, to preserve the unspoilt nature of the area. In addition, local people benefit from financial income generated by the lodge, and find opportunities for employment.

Mahenye Safari Lodge is a group of cool, Shangaan-style thatched buildings in the shade of indigenous trees along the bank of the Save River.

The lodge lies close to Tambahata Pan, which offers outstanding birdwatching (around 400 species recorded) and animal life. For more detailed information, write to Zimbabwe Sun Central Reservations, P O Box CY 1211, Causeway, Harare, or telephone their offices at (09263) 4 73-6644/5, fax 4 73-6646.

Manjirenji Recreational Park

Boating and fishing are permitted in this scenically attractive and remote 3 500 ha park, which encompasses Lake Manjirenji (formerly MacDougall), a Lowveld wheat-irrigation dam on the Chiredzi River.

Tom MacDougall is a legendary Lowveld figure who pioneered sugar-farming here with the use of irrigation tunnels, one of which, in the Triangle area, burrows 472 m through a granite hill (it is now a national monument). The park is situated 65 km north of Chiredzi on the Zaka/Nandi road, and is open 24 hours a day throughout the year.

Mushandike Sanctuary

There are only camping and caravan facilities (with an ablution block) in Mushandike, a 12 900 ha park surrounding the small (417 ha) mountain-ringed Mushandike Dam, 26 km west of Masvingo on the Zvishavane/Bulawayo road. The access roads and internal (gravel) roads can be negotiated by all types of vehicle, although the internal routes may be subject to seasonal flooding. Prospective visitors are advised to ask the warden's advice.

Game includes a number of white rhino, leopard, sable, waterbuck, wildebeest, zebra, impala and grysbok. Waterfowl in the dam area include red-billed teal, Egyptian goose, knob-billed duck, heron and cormorant. Fishing is permitted in the dam, and anglers may catch black bass, tilapia and barbel. The sanctuary is open all year from sunrise to sunset. However, the eland research station within the park is closed to the public. Bookings should be addressed to The Warden, Mushandike Sanctuary, Private Bag 9036, Masvingo, or telephone (09263) 39 29-4513.

Save Valley Conservancy

The conservancy is believed to be the largest privately owned game reserve in the world, and covers some 326 000 ha in the southeastern Lowveld of Zimbabwe, north of Chiredzi.

Extending for 100 km between the Masvingo/Birchenough Bridge road in the north and the Mkwasine River in the south, the conservancy has the Save River forming most of its eastern border.

A lodge at Senuko near the southern end of the conservancy, about 70 km from Chiredzi, is built on a granite koppie with individual lodges nestling among the boulders. Humani Turgwe Camp, near the centre of the conservancy, offers a range of accommodation and activities from horse riding to foot safaris. A waterhole has been built below the camp, close enough to the dining area to offer good gameviewing in safety. Many animals, including black rhino, wild dog, elephant, giraffe and plains antelope, have been moved here from Gonarezhou National Park. There is also a large variety of birds, both at the waterhole and on the veld.

For more information and for bookings, contact Zimbabwe Sun Central Reservations, P O Box CY 1211, Causeway, Harare, telephone (09263) 4 73-6644/5, fax 4 73-6646.

The story of 'development' in the Save Valley is typical of the clash between the requirements of commercial farming and those of the natural environment. It does, though, have a happy ending.

Until 1920, when this area of Zimbabwe's Lowveld was proclaimed as 'commercial agricultural land', man's impact here had been slight. Then, after the introduction of beef herds, many changes followed. Water was pumped long distances, and traditional watering places dried up. The erection of fences prevented wildlife from ranging to seek the best pastures. Pastures themselves suffered under herds of coarse-grazing cattle. Selective grazers, already denied water sources, were the first to move away.

Predators that threatened cattle were eradicated. Large animals that interfered with the domesticated herds – elephant or rhino, for instance, that broke fences – were likewise destroyed. Biodiversity of both plants and animals declined, and soil erosion increased. After a little more than 50 years in the Save Valley, the end was in sight for the profitability of cattle-ranching.

In 1991, with the urgent need for a refuge for the much-threatened black rhino, ranchers of the Save Valley decided to establish a conservancy with no internal fences throughout an area large enough to carry, in time, more than 100 rhino. This meant a complete switch of the economy, from ranching to the tourism-based utilisation of wildlife. In this sense, and in the broadest possible sense, utilisation here may be equated with sustainable conservation.

MABALAUTA AT A GLANCE

When to go The park is open only from 1 May to 31 October, the local dry months. Visitors should arrive not later than 5 p.m.

Permits Visitors to all areas of Gonarezhou, including Mabalauta, should note that it is essential to check with the booking office before undertaking a visit as restrictions apply and sometimes temporary closures are enforced.

Reservations and information Reservations should be made through the National Parks Central Booking Office, P O Box CY 826, Causeway, Harare, Zimbabwe, telephone (09263) 4 70-6077, fax 4 72-6089.

Getting there Access to Mabalauta is by road from Ngundu Halt (on the Beitbridge road) to the sugarcane town of Chiredzi, and then along a 160 km gravel road which follows the western edge of the park. There is also an untarred road (116 km) leading from Mwenezi.

Accommodation There are five chalets at the Swimuwini rest camp, with a total of 21 beds. Each chalet has a refrigerator/deep freeze, cooking utensils and linen, but no crockery or cutlery.

Eating and drinking There are no restaurants, shops or bars at Mabalauta. Visitors in chalets or at the campsites should bring their own supplies.

Getting around All visitors should report on arrival to the tourist office, situated 8 km to the north of the rest camp. Private aircraft charters are available (write to Cane Air, P O Box 20, Chiredzi, Zimbabwe, or telephone (09263) 31 2643. There are many game drives, and there are plans to introduce wilderness trails. There are no fuel pumps, and visitors should make allowance for this when planning their routes.

Special attractions These include a shelter offering a bird's-eye view of the crocodile pool and a gamewatching platform at Manyanda Pan.

Wildlife Visitors may see a wide variety of game, including elephant, lion, black-backed jackal, waterbuck, nyala and several other antelope.

Fishing You may not fish in the Mwenezi River.

Special precautions Visitors should proceed with caution when encountering elephant – they are unpredictable creatures. You should take a course of anti-malaria tablets before entering the area. These are available from any chemist without prescription. However, because specific precautions may be necessary for certain strains of the disease, intending visitors should seek medical advice. There is bilharzia in the Mwenezi River. Most family cars should reach Swimuwini without difficulty, but some game drives require a pick-up or 4x4 vehicle to get through the sandy areas. Visitors must be in camp by sundown.

Brooding land of the 'hill of spirits'

Zimbabwe has some of the oldest rock formations in the world, and some of the most interestingly exposed. Especially dramatic are those in the 43 000 ha Matobo National Park, 34 km from the country's second largest city, Bulawayo, where Lobengula, the second Ndebele king to reign north of the Limpopo, built his own residence in the 1870s.

Here, horizon follows horizon of granite domes and giant balancing rocks – an immense and brooding place which, it is said, is haunted by the spirits of the ancients, their words of wisdom and warning spoken through the unseen oracle of Malindidzimu, 'hill of the spirits'.

Lobengula's predecessor, King Mzilikazi, referred to the hills, somewhat whimsically perhaps, as Amatobo, 'the bald-headed ones'. White settlers rendered this as 'Matopo', but the correct version has been reinstated.

The Matobos, in fact, are by far Bulawayo's most impressive wilderness attraction, and southwest Zimbabwe's only game park other than the Tuli Safari Area (reserved for hunting) on the Botswana border.

Bulawayo is served by Air Zimbabwe to and from Johannesburg and major Zimbabwean centres, including Harare, Victoria Falls and Hwange National Park. There are similar rail links. Express Motorways operate daily coaches to and from Harare and Johannesburg. Other companies operate daily services between Bulawayo and Hwange, Victoria Falls, Masvingo and, except on Sundays, Francistown and Gaborone in Botswana.

There is a fully tarred road of 316 km from the Beitbridge border post.

The city has pleasant hotels and motels, and there is a beautifully situated campsite and caravan park in the municipality's Central Park. Write to P O Box 2034, Bulawayo, or telephone (09263) 9 6-3851 for information.

Centenary and Central parks

Southeast of Bulawayo and within walking distance of the city centre is a green belt through which the small Matsheumhlope River runs.

This pleasant space stretches from the Hillside Dams 6,5 km away, through the Bulawayo golf course to the National Library, the municipal caravan park and the twin Central and Centenary parks, divided from east to west by Leopold Takawira Avenue, which becomes the main road to Beitbridge.

Covering an area of 45 ha, these two parks, three if one includes the tiny Princess Park, with their lily pond, superb gardens, fountains, bougainvillea, giant date palms and evergreens are among the best city gardens in Zimbabwe (after the National Botanical Garden in Harare). Central Park has a swimming pool on Samuel Parirenyatwa Street.

Centenary Park has an aviary, a miniature railway for children (open weekends) and an open-air amphitheatre in which concerts are held. The Natural History Museum of Zimbabwe, which contains exhibits illustrating the country's history, mineral wealth and wildlife, is situated in the park.

The displays include the second largest mounted elephant in the world. The approximately 75 000 specimens of mammal and 60 000 specimens of bird make it the largest collection in the southern hemisphere, and it is a magnet to ornithologists and research scientists the world over.

It is open daily, including Sundays and public holidays (except Christmas Day and Good Friday), from 9 a.m. to 5 p.m. Exercise caution when walking in the remoter parts of the parks and between the parks and the city centre. For

Left: A black eagle (*Aquila verreauxii*) with its month-old chick high up in Zimbabwe's Matobos. These hills accommodate one of the densest eagle populations in the world. **Right above:** Spectacular blooms on a broad-leaved *Erythrina*. The bark of this tree is used in traditional medicine; it is burnt, reduced to a powder and used to treat open sores. **Right below:** Veld violets sometimes form a dense mat on the surface of the ground. **Below:** A blue-eared glossy starling. In Zimbabwe this species breeds from September to January.

MATOBO AT A GLANCE

When to go The park, including Whovi Wilderness Area, is open all year, from sunrise to sunset. High season is from the beginning of May to the end of October.

Reservations Arrangements should be made through the National Parks Central Booking Office, P O Box CY 826, Causeway, Harare, Zimbabwe, telephone (09263) 4 70-6077, fax 72-6089.

Getting there Follow Bulawayo's Robert Mugabe Way south to get onto the main road to the Matobos. An alternative route is the Plumtree road: turn left at the 28,5 km peg onto the gravel-surfaced Cyrene Mission road to reach the park at the 48,5 km peg. Operators in Bulawayo organise day tours and longer visits.

There are campsites, lodges (including the luxury Black Eagle and Fish Eagle lodges) and chalets at Maleme Dam. The lodges are fully equipped, but visitors to the chalets must take their own cutlery and crockery. Visitors supply their own food. There are camping and caravan facilities at five other sites within the park. Private accommodation of various standards is available in several places just outside the park's borders.

Eating and drinking There are no restaurants. Basic supplies only may be bought at Maleme.

Getting around There are tarred roads to the main entrance and to Maleme Dam. Most of the other roads have a gravel surface and are usually in good condition. Walking is permitted everywhere except in the Whovi Wilderness Area. At White Waters, near the entrance to Whovi, and at Maleme, 90-minute guided horseback rides are available.

Wildlife Visitors may spot buffalo, black rhino, white rhino, leopard, giraffe, eland, impala, zebra, hippo and a large variety of small mammals. There are also crocodiles in the park.

Fishing Angling and boating are allowed on the dams in the park, and anglers may catch bass, bream, barbel and Hunyani salmon.

Special precautions Visitors should take a course of anti-malaria tablets (available, with instructions, from any pharmacy) before entering the area. All water in the park should be regarded as being infested with bilharzia.

---

visionary, instigator of the Rhodes scholarships at Oxford, prime minister of the Cape Colony and founder of Northern Rhodesia and Southern Rhodesia, wrote in his will: 'I admire the grandeur and loneliness of the Matopos in Rhodesia, and therefore I desire to be buried in the Matopos on the hill "Malindidzimu" which I used to visit and which I called the "View of the World", in a square to be cut in the rock on the top of the hill, covered with a brass plate with these words thereon: "Here lie the remains of Cecil John Rhodes".'

On 10 April 1902, to the salute of *'Bayete'* from assembled Ndebele elders, his final – and simple – request was honoured.

Buried nearby are Rhodes' friend and doctor, L S Jameson, Charles Coghlan, who was the first prime minister of Southern Rhodesia, (later called Rhodesia and, briefly, in the 1970s, Zimbabwe-Rhodesia) and the remains of British South Africa Company troopers who, under Major Allan Wilson, were killed in battle against the Ndebele on the banks of the Shangani River in 1893.

The turn-off to the huge granite dome of World's View, with its panorama of range after range of hills, lies 44 km from Bulawayo within the Matobo National Park. There is an easy climb to the summit from the car park, where there are braai sites and a pictorial history of Rhodes.

For further information, contact The Warden, Matobo National Park, Private Bag K5142, Bulawayo; or the National Parks Central Booking Office, P O Box CY 826, Causeway, Harare, or telephone (09263) 4 70-6077, fax 72-6089.

Mazwi and Nguza nature parks

These two recreational parks are being developed close to Bulawayo. Mazwi is 20 km west of the city centre down 11th Avenue, and offers walking and cycling, while horse trails are also being laid. Nguza offers walking and cycling, and is 15 km from Bulawayo on the Victoria Falls road.

Both parks have facilities for picnics. For further information, contact The Director, Bulawayo Publicity Association, P O Box 861, Bulawayo, telephone (09263) 9 6-0867.

N'tabazinduna Lodge and Trails

Nestling on N'tabazinduna Hill, in a private game reserve, is Chiefs Lodge, a family-run, six-bedroom guesthouse within easy driving of the Matobos, ancient ruins such as Kame, Dhlodhlo and Naletale, Chipangali Wildlife Orphanage (*see separate entry*) and Bulawayo. Offering lovely views across the surrounding countryside, N'tabazinduna is 16 km from Bulawayo on the main Harare road.

For further information, write to N'tabazinduna Lodge and Trails, P O Box 7, Bulawayo, or telephone (09263) 9 6-2553, fax 9 7-6558.

Above: A zebra *(Uquus burchellii)* in the grassland of the Matobo National Park. Plainly visible are the 'shadow stripes' between the black stripes on the hindquarters. Like human fingerprints, no two zebra have stripe patterns that are quite the same.

Sondelani Private Game Reserve

Some 25 000 ha form this private game reserve at West Nicholson, 195 km from Bulawayo on the Beitbridge road. The lodge has facilities for 14 visitors and the homestead for eight. The chalets consist of one family unit and five *en suite* twin units. Facilities include game drives, birdwatching, fishing, walking, horse trails, hide visits and educational safaris. For further information, contact Sondelani, P O Box 1472, Bulawayo, telephone (09263) 9 6-8739, or fax 6-4997.

Tshabalala Sanctuary

About 8 km out of Bulawayo on the Matobo road (an extension of Robert Mugabe Way) is the 1 215 ha Tshabalala Game Sanctuary – a reserve for non-dangerous game such as zebra, wildebeest, tsessebe, giraffe, kudu, warthog, sable, impala and a variety of smaller mammals. Tshabalala is run by the Department of National Parks as an interpretive educational sanctuary and as a recreational area for the people of Bulawayo. You may walk, cycle or drive your car along its roads, and horses may be hired for riding as well. It is open from 6 a.m. to 6 p.m. in summer and from 8 a.m. to 5 p.m. in winter.

Umzingwane Dam

This small (1 200 ha) park has no facilities apart from a dam and the unspoilt rural charm of its surroundings. It is situated 55 km south of Bulawayo and 267 km north of Beitbridge (near the main highway). Fishing and scenery are its principal attractions, and it is open 24 hours a day throughout the year.

Index

A

Aalwynprag Nature Reserve 269
aardvark 23, 164, 240, 278
aardwolf 360
Aasvoëlkop 126
Aba-Huab River 323
abalone *see* perlemoen
Abe Bailey Nature Reserve 94
Aberdeen 269
Aberdeen Nature Reserve 269
Abu's Camp 346
Acacia karroo 188, 286
Acanthosicyos horrida (nara plant) 315
acrae, spotted 34
adder
   Gaboon 161, 166
   puff 267
   sidewinding 308
Addo Elephant National Park 206, 209, 379
   at a glance 208
Adenium swazicum (impala lily) 55
Africat Foundation 339
Agter Renosterberg 276
Ai-Ais Hot Springs 296
   at a glance 298
Akkerendam Nature Reserve 264
albatross 160
Albert Falls Resources Reserve 144
Alexandria State Forest 205
Alfred Park 172
Algeria 257
Algoa Bay 211
Aliwal North 190
Allan's Camp 364
Alldays 31
Alldays Lodge 31
Allemanskraal Dam 117, 126
Aloe
   albida 108
   chortolirioides 108
   dichotoma (quiver tree) 266, 272, 297
   gariepensis 286
   marlothii 148
   ortholopha 381
   striata 241
   thorncroftii 108
   vryheidensis 108

Aloe Ridge Game Reserve 95
Aloe Ridge Hotel 95
Alsophila dregei (tree fern) 75
Amalinda Fisheries Station and Nature Reserve 195
Amanita muscaria (mushroom) 70
Amanpongokwe Dam 396
Amanzimtoti 172, 175
Amanzimtoti Bird Sanctuary 172
Amatikulu Nature Reserve 166
Amatikulu River 166
Amatola Hiking Trail 195, 196
Amatole Mountains 195, 199, 201, 202
Amphitheatre 134, 141
Anas undulata (duck) 110
Andersson, Charles 321, 327, 335, 336
Andoni Plains 330
Andover Game Reserve 41
Andries Vosloo Kudu Reserve 203
Andriesbergen 188
anemone, sea 222
Angas, George French 159, 244
Angra Fria 323
Anomatheca grandiflora 396
ant, desert 312
antlion 194
Anysberg 237
Anysberg Nature Reserve 228
Aonyx capensis (otter) 191
Apies River 81, 87
Apple Express (train) 210
aquarium
   East London Aquarium 198
   F C Braun Aquarium 71
   Hardap (Namibia) 306
   Hartbeespoort Aquarium 98
   Port Elizabeth Oceanarium 206, 210
   Pretoria Aquarium and Reptile Park 87
   Two Oceans Aquarium (Cape Town) 253
Aquila verreauxii (black eagle) 92, 398
Arabie Dam 91
Arctotis fastuosa (Namaqualand daisy) 268
Aroab 300
Arrow Head (Augrabies) 285

Arthraerua leubnitziae 301
Askham 279
Assegaaibosch Nature Reserve 233
Aster perfoliatus (plant) 138
Asthanasia acerosa (plant) 63
Atherstone Nature Reserve 76
Atlas Bay 301
Attakwaskloof Nature Reserve 224
Auas Game Lodge 303
Auckland Nature Reserve 195
Audi Camp 345
Augarabies-Steenbok Nature Reserve 297
Augeigas Dam 304
Augeigas stream 305
Augrabies Falls 283
Augrabies Falls National Park 277, 283, 328
   at a glance 285
Auob River 288, 290
Austin Roberts Bird Hall 78
Austin Roberts Bird Sanctuary 76
Aventura Badplaas 108
Aventura Blydepoort Resort 62, 64
Aventura Eiland Resort 32, 33
Aventura Kareekloof Resort 115, 116
Aventura Midwaters Resort 119
Aventura Swadini Resort 62, 64
Aventura Tshipise Resort 33
avocet 114, 116

B

Baakens River 212
baboon 16, 247, 248, 380
badger, honey (ratel) 339
Badplaas 107
Bailey, Sir Abe 94
Bain, Andrew 198, 255
Bain, Thomas 229
Baines, Thomas 316, 360
Baines' Baobabs 359, 360
Bain's Kloof 255
Bainskloof Pass 237, 255
Bakenskop 231
Bakkersberg 126
Bakubung Lodge 88, 89

Baldwin, William Charles 370, 393
Balearica regulorum 186
Ballantyne Park 381
balloon safaris *see under* safaris
Bally Vaughan Game Park 381
Balule Rest Camp 13, 14, 15, 29
Bambata Cave 400
Bambatha 170
Bamboesberg 188
banana tree, wild 182
Bangala Dam 393
Bangala Recreational Park 393
Bankberg 192
Bankfontein 192
Banzi Pan 163, 164, 165
baobab (tree) 36, 37
Baobab Hotel 371
Barberspan Nature Reserve 96
Barberton 107, 108, 112, 114
   flora reserves 108
Barberton Indigenous Tree Park 108
Barbus capensis (fish) 257
Barkly West 277, 281
Barrow, Brian 291
Basil Maskew Miller Herbarium 240
Basotho Cultural Village 123
bat, horseshoe 74
bateleur 360
Bateleur Bushveld Camp 14, 15
Bathurst 205
Battle Cave (Injasuti) 137, 138
Bauhinia galpinii (camelsfoot) 389
Baviaanskloof Forest 228
Baviaanskloof Mountains 209, 228, 237
Baviaanskloof River 229
Baviaanskloof Wilderness Area 228, 255
Baya Camp 161
Baynes, Joseph 144
Baynesfield Estate 144
Beachwood Mangroves Nature Reserve 172
Beaufort West 269, 271
Beaverlac Nature Reserve 255
bee, leaf-cutter 96
bee-eater 55, 345
   carmine 19, 338, 365

European 76
  swallow-tailed 277
Beervlei Forest 225
beetle
  blister 340
  cetoniid 118, 234
  Christmas 138
  desert 312, 314
  dung 129, 206
  fruit 151
  ladybird 121
  Lampyridae 142
  leaf 204
  longhorn 192
  paussid 357
  scarab 129
  tortoise 119
Belenois aurota (butterfly) 340
bell flower 125
Ben Alberts Nature Reserve 78
Ben Lavin Nature Reserve 60
Benoni 111
Berg Nature Reserve 188
Bergdeel Private Nature Reserve 117
Berg-en-dal Rest Camp 11, 14, 16, 22, 24, 25
Bergh, Oloff 258
Berlin Forest Station 67
Bernabé de la Bat Rest Camp 333, 341
Bestershoek Valley 190
Bethlehem 127
Bethulie 122, 126
Betty's Bay 239
Bewaarkloof Nature Reserve 61
Bezuidenhout Park 109
Bhanga Nek 160
Bhangazi Bush Camp 156
Bhubesi Camp 54
Biedouw Valley 256, 268
Bietou River 227
Big Cave Camp 400
Biggarsberg Conservancy 145
Biggarsberg range 145
Binga 375, 378
Birchenough Bridge 390
Bird Island
  Eastern Cape 205
  West Coast 255
  Wild Coast 185
Bird Paradise 316
Bird Rock guano platform 305
Bisley Nature Reserve 145
Bitis (adder)
  arietans 267
  peringueyi 308
Biyamiti Bushveld Camp 11, 14

Blaauwkrantz Nature Reserve 196
Blaauwkrantz River 196
Black Eagle Lodge 401
Black Eagle Nature Reserve 188
Black Hills 33
Black Mbuluzi River 53
Black River 251
Black Rock 279
Black Rocks (Cape Peninsula) 248
Blair Park 381
Blanco Guest Farm 196
blesbok 96, 84, 88, 269, 277
Blesbokspruit 111
Blinkwater Nature Reserve 146
Bloemfontein 117, 119
Bloemfontein Zoological Gardens 117
Bloemhof 94, 103
Bloemhof Dam 96, 117, 124
Bloemhof Dam Nature Reserve 96, 105
Blouberg mountain range 70
Blouberg Nature Reserve 61, 70
Bloukrans 226, 237
Blouswawelvlakte 68
bluebell, wild 125
bluebottle 158
bluebuck 233
Blueliliesbush 226
Bluff Nature Reserve 172, 173, 178
Blyde Dam 64
Blyde River 52, 60, 62, 64, 65, 72
Blyde River Canyon 60, 64, 69, 73
  at a glance 62
Blyde River Canyon Hiking Trail 62, 63, 66, 70
Blyde River Canyon Nature Reserve 60, 62, 63
Blydepoort dam 62
Bobs River 72
boerboon 209
Boesmanskloof Trail 233, 239
Bogenfels Arch 301
Bohnen, Pauline 224
Bokkeveld 266
Bokkeveld Mountains 266
Boland Hiking Trail 234, 241, 255, 259
Boler, Stephen 281
Bonamanzi Game Park 154
Bongami Lodge 45
bontebok 216, 247

Bontebok National Park 216, 218
  at a glance 218
Bonwa Phala Game Lodge 78
Booi se Skerm 248
Boophone disticha (plant) 112
Boosmansbos Wilderness Area 218, 221
Borakalalo National Park 78
Bordjiesdrif 248
Boro River 345, 346, 349, 351
Bosberg Hiking Trail 189
Bosberg Nature Reserve 189
Bosbokstrand Private Nature Reserve 197
Bosele Camp 88, 89
Boskop Dam 96
Boskop Dam Nature Reserve 96
Bot River 243
botanical gardens
  Bvumba Botanical Gardens 388
  Durban Botanical Gardens 173, 174, 175
  Ewanrigg Botanical Gardens 381, 382
  Free State National Botanical Garden 117, 119
  Harare National Botanical Garden 385, 386
  Harold Porter National Botanical Garden 239, 240
  Johannesburg Botanical garden 98
  Karoo National Botanical garden 241, 269
  Kirstenbosch National Botanical Garden 250
  Lowveld National Botanical Gardens 41, 44
  Natal National Botanical Garden 151
  Pretoria National Botanical Garden 90
  Witwatersrand National Botanical Garden 105
Boteri River 357, 358, 359, 360
Botlhaba Camp 97
Botsalano Game Reserve 97
Botshabelo Nature Reserve and Museum 79
Botswana
  central 357
  Chobe 362
  Kalahari 352
  Makgadikgadi region 357
  northern 362
  Okavango 344
botterboom 321

bottle tree 321, 322
Boulders Beach 247
Boulders Penguin Colony 247
Boulders Private Camp 14, 15
Bourke's Luck Potholes 60, 62, 63, 64, 65
Bow Hunters Camp 45
Bowler, T W 195
Braamfontein Spruit 109
Braamfontein Spruit Trail 108, 109, 111
Bracken Hill Falls 218
Brackenridgea Nature Reserve 31
Brackenridgea zanguebarica (tree) 31
Brak River 35
Brand, Dr D J 79
Brand, Peter 319
Brandberg 317, 319, 335
Brandwag Lodge 120
Bredasdorp 216, 235, 238
Bredasdorp Nature Reserve 235
Breede River 216, 218, 236
Brenton Island 211
Breuil, Abbé 319
Breviceps (frog) 225
Bridal Veil Falls
  Augrabies 283, 285
  Sabie area 69
  Zimbabwe 387
Bridle Drift Dam Nature Reserve 197
Bristow, Ossie 384
Bronkhorstspruit 106
Bronkhorstspruit Dam 106
Bronkhorstspruit Dam Nature Reserve 106
brood parasites 139
Broom, Dr Robert 104
Brückner, Albi 314
Bryden, Bruce 16, 271
buffalo 28, 47
Buffalo Bay 218
Buffalo Camp 43
Buffalo Ridge Camping Site 364
Buffalo River 148, 197, 202, 205
Buffalo Valley Game Farm 218
Buffels Bay 249
Buffelspruit Nature Reserve 190
bug
  coreid 66
  Pyrrhocorid 24
  shield 48
  stink 48
Bulawayo 398
Bulungu Gorge 55

403

Bulwer 134, 143
Bulwer Cattle/Game Project 64
Bumbusi Camp 371
Bumi Hills Safari Lodge 374, 375, 377, 379
Bundi River valley 390
Bundu Farm 235
Bunga Forest Botanical Reserve 387, 388
bungee jumping 373
Burchell, William 211, 249
Burchellia (gardenia) 211
Burgersdorp 188
Burman Bush Nature Reserve 173
Burnt Mountain 323
Bush Camp (Londolozi) 48
Bush Lodge 48
bushbaby 37, 57
bushbuck 27, 159, 213, 378
Bushbuck Walk 209
Bushlands Game Lodge 154
Bushmanland 264, 267
Bushman's candle 301
Bushmans Kloof Private Game Reserve 256
Bushman's Nek 131, 136
Bushman's Point (Lake Chivero) 385
Bushmans River (Eastern Cape) 199
Bushman's River (KwaZulu-Natal) 136, 150, 153
Bushmen (San) 138, 258, 307, 324, 348, 352, 353
bustard, Kori 325
Butha-Buthe 130
Buthidae (scorpion) 302
Butimba (traditional hunt) 53
butterfly
  African monarch 82, 279
  joker 17
  milkweed see African monarch
  sulphur 45
  whites (pierid) 228
Bvumba (town) 388
Bvumba Botanical Gardens 388
Bvumba Mountains 387
Byblia ilithyia (joker butterfly) 17
Byseewah Safari Lodge 326

C

C N Mahlangu Lodge 91
cabbage tree 100
Cactus Canyon 256
Calanthe natalensis (orchid) 390
Caledon 235
Caledon Nature Reserve (Free State) 118
Caledon Nature Reserve and Wild Flower Garden (Western Cape) 234, 235
Caledon River 118, 126
Calvinia 264, 267, 268
Camdeboo Conservation Education Centre 273, 274
Camel Rock 178
camelsfoot (plant) 389
Camferskloof Forest 224
Camp Moremi 351
Camp Mwisho 315
Camp Okuti 351
Camp Selous 371
Camp SOS and School in the Wilds 235
Campbell, Alec 357
Camponotus detritus (desert ant) 312
Cango Caves 228, 229, 231
Cango Wildlife Ranch 230, 231
Canteen Koppie Nature Reserve 277
Cão, Diego 320
Cape Cross Seal Reserve 317, 320, 322
Cape Flats 235, 247, 248
Cape Flats Private Nature Reserve 247
Cape Flats Waste Waterworks 247
Cape Floral Kingdom 237
Cape Hangklip 248
Cape Henderson Nature Reserve 197
Cape of Good Hope Nature Reserve 247, 248
Cape Peninsula 247
  proposed national park 249
Cape Peninsula Protected Natural Environment 249
Cape Point 248
Cape Recife Nature Reserve 209
Cape St Francis 218, 221
Cape St Francis Nature Reserve 218
Cape Town 247, 252
Cape Vidal 155, 158
Cape Vidal State Forest 157
Caprivi Game Park 333, 338
Caprivi Strip 333, 350
caracal 188, 291
Carissa bispinosa (shrub) 206

Carnarvon Estates 188
Carnarvon Nature Reserve 269, 270
Carolina 112, 115
carrot tree 39
Cashel 389
cat, black-footed (small-spotted) 188
caterpillar
  hawk-moth 68
  looper 106
Cathedral Peak 136
Cathedral Peak Hotel 136
Cecil Kop Mountain 389
Cecil Kop Nature Reserve 389
cedar tree 256
Cederberg 255, 258, 268
Cederberg Tourist Park 256
Cederberg Wilderness Area 256
Centenary Nature Reserve 236, 244
Centenary Park 398
centipede-eater, Cape 202
Central Kalahari Game Reserve 352, 354, 355
Central Park 378
Central Wilderness Area (Matobo) 400
Centurion 113
Cercopithecus aethiops (monkey) 173
Ceres 258, 267
Ceres Mountain Fynbos Reserve 257
Cetshwayo 169, 170
Ceylon Forest Station 69
Chamberlain Bird Sanctuary 79
chameleon
  Bradypodion 239
  Cape dwarf 239
  Chamaeleo 239
  flap-necked 42, 279
Chapman, James 316
Chapungu Lodge 49
Charadrophila capensis (Cape gloxinia) 241
Charara Safari Area 374, 377, 378
Charters Creek 158, 159
chat, Herero 321
cheetah 293, 319, 325
  king 79, 80
Cheetahland 230
Cheilomenes lunata (ladybird) 79
Cheiridopsis denticulata (mesembryethemum) 268

Chelmsford Nature Reserve 146
Chersina angulata (tortoise) 243
Chete Gorge 378
Chete Safari Area 374
Chewore Safari Area 379
Chief's Island 345, 348, 351
Chief's Lodge 401
Chilo Gorge Safari Lodge 393
Chilojo Cliffs 395
Chimanimani (village) 389, 390
Chimanimani Eland Sanctuary 387, 389
Chimanimani mountain range 387, 389
Chimanimani National Park 389
Chimwara Estate 371
Chimwara Tented Camp 371
Chinamora area 382
chincherinchees 216
Chine Pool 379
Chinese lantern 156
Chinguli Camp 395
Chinhoyi Caves 381, 382
Chinhoyi Caves National Park 382
Chinhoyi Caves Sleeping Pool 381, 382
chinks see chincherinchees
Chipangali Wildlife Orphanage 399, 401
Chipinda Pools 394, 395
Chipinge 387, 390
Chiredzi 395, 397
Chiredzi River 397
Chiredzi River Conservancy 393
Chirinda Forest 387
Chirinda Forest Botanical Reserve 390
Chirundu 379
Chisambik Pool 379
Chisu campsite 334
Chitwa Chitwa Game Lodge 46
Chivalila Falls 394
Chivhu 386
Chizarira National Park 374, 375, 377, 378, 380
Chizarira Wilderness Lodge 375
Chobe Chilwero Lodge 364
Chobe Forest Reserve 362
Chobe Game Lodge 364
Chobe National Park 335, 348, 362
  at a glance 364

Kasane and Serondela 362
Savuti 364
Chobe Reptile Park 365
Chobe River 335, 338, 362, 363
Chobe Safari Lodge 364
Chokamella Lodge 371
Christiana 94, 104
Christmas bells 146
Chuos Mountains 303, 307
cicada 138
Clanwilliam 255, 257, 259, 268
Clanwilliam Dam 259
Clanwilliam Flower Garden 259
Clanwilliam Yellowfish Station 257
Clarens 127
Clausena anisata (tree) 209
Clematopsis scabiosifolia (shrub) 111
Cliffortia arborea (tree) 269
Cobham 137
Cockscomb Forest 228
Cockscomb mountains 237
Coega River 211, 212
Coetser, Captain J J 25
Coetzee, Ken 275
Coffee Bay (Mqanduli) 186, 187
Coleford Nature Reserve 134
Columbine Nature Reserve 257
Combretum mossambicense 374
Commando Drift Dam 190, 194
Commando Drift Nature Reserve 190
Compassberg Hiking Trails 270
Compton Herbarium 250
Conception Bay 309
Confidence Reef gold-mine shaft 99
Conicosia pugioniformis (pig's root) 268
Connemara Lakes 392
Conophytum intrepidum (succulent) 267
Constantiaberg 253
coot, red-knobbed 31, 94
cormorant 299
Cape 255
cosmos 101
courser, double-banded 296
crab
fiddler 172
Crabtree, Iain 71
Cradock 192, 194

crane
crowned 75, 143, 185, 186
wattled 74, 139, 142, 143
crane flower 199
creeper
lucky-bean 50
Port St Johns 393
Zimbabwe 393
Cresta Mowana Lodge 364
cricket
armoured ground 270
long-horned 100
mole 170
tree 108
crocodile, Nile 18, 19, 30, 158, 231
Crocodile Bridge 11, 20
Crocodile Bridge Rest Camp 11, 14, 17
Crocodile Camp 348
crocodile farm
Crocworld 173
Greater St Lucia Wetland Park 156, 158, 159
Kwena Gardens Crocodile Paradise 82
Le Bonheur Crocodile Farm 258
Victoria Falls 373
Crocodile Pool (Kruger) 27
Crocodile Pools (Hwange) 370
Crocodile River 10, 12, 17, 22, 27, 44, 98, 99
Crocodile River valley 78
Crocodylus niloticus (Nile crocodile) 30, 158
Crous, Ranger 29
crow 124
black 124
pied 124
white-necked 124
Crystal Dam 136
Crystal Springs Mountain Lodge 65
Cuando River 362
cuckoo, striped 139
cucumber bush 24
Curtis, Barbara 312
cushion bush, Zuurberg 209
Cussonia paniculata (tree) 100
Cwebe 182
Cwikampa Pan 363
cycad 35, 37, 39, 55, 66, 67, 73, 170, 173, 175, 197, 198, 200, 209
Cycad Nature Reserve 197, 200
Cycad Valley 75
Cyphostemma
currorii (botterboom) 321
juttae (wild grape) 305

Cyrtanthus contractus (lily) 148
Cythna Letty Nature Reserve 108

D

Daan Viljoen Game Park 303, 304
at a glance 304
daisy
Barberton 107
Namaqualand 264, 266
Damaraland *see* Kunene Region
Danaus chrysippus (butterfly) 82
dancing white lady (spider) 308
Daniell, Samuel 191, 266
Darling 255, 260, 268
Darling Nature Reserve 258
Dart, Professor Raymond 104
darter, long-necked 387
Darville Bird Sanctuary 146
Dasklip Pass 255
Dassen Island
Namibia 305
West Coast 261
Dassieshoek Nature Reserve 236
Dassieskraal Mountain 213
Dawidskraal 239
De Hoek Nature Walk 231
De Hoop Nature Reserve 236
De Kaap valley 108
de Laporte, Cecil 13
De Mond Nature Reserve 238
De Vasselot 226
De Wildt Cheetah Research Centre 79
Debengeni Falls 67
Deception Pan 353
Deception Valley 353, 354
deer, Mauritian sambar 176
Deka River 370
Deka Safari Area 371, 372
Delareyville 96
Delosperma herbeum (vygie) 134
Delta Camp 345
Delta Environmental Centre 109
Delta Park 108, 109
Dendrohyrax arboreus (dassie) 199
Desert Ecological Research Unit 310

desert rose 298
Dete 369, 371
Dete Vlei 372
Detema Dam 371
Detema Safari Lodge 371
Devil's Knuckles 112
Devil's Tooth 134
dew-flower 268
Dhlodhlo Ruins 401
Diana's Vow Farm 390
Diceros bicornisse bicornis (rhino) 281, 285, 328
Dichrostachys cinerea (plant) 156
Dicoma zeyheri (daisy) 57
Dicynodon bainii (dinosaur) 198
Die Bos Nature Reserve 277
Die Hel Valley 258
Die Oog see Eye of Kurman
Diep River 251
Diepwalle Forest 218, 222, 225
Diepwalle Forest Station 219
Dierama (iris) 117
dik-dik, Damara 330
Dilatris pillansii 239
Dimorphotheca (Namaqualand daisy)
pluvialis 255
sinuata (Namaqualand daisy) 264
Dingane, King 169
Dinizulu Camp 154
Dinosaur Park 74
Dionychopus amasis 182
Diospyros lycioides (tree) 111
Disa cornuta (orchid) 247
Disa Gorge 240
Disa River 251
Disselboom Farm 100
Djuma Bush Lodge 41, 47
Dlinza Forest Nature Reserve 166, 167
D'Nyala Nature Reserve 80
dog, wild 22, 41
Dog Trail 238
Domboshawa 382
Donax sordidus (mussel) 244
Doorndraai Dam 76
Doorndraai Dam Nature Reserve 80
Doornkloof Nature Reserve 269, 271
at a glance 275
Doreen Clark Nature Reserve 147
Doringberg 126
Doringrivier Wilderness Area 224
dormouse, Cape 238

405

Dorotheanthus bellidiformis (vygie) 241, 255
Double Drift Game Reserve 196, 197, 203
Douglas Mitchell Centre 151
Dr Hamilton Protea Reserve 112
draaijakkals (turning jackal) *see* fox, bat-eared
dragonfly 147
Drakensberg 31
   Cape 191
   Eastern Cape 184
   Escarpment 60, 75, 106
   foothills 147, 148, 153
   Free State 124
   KwaZulu-Natal 134
Drakenstein Mountains 237
Drosanthemum hispidum (dew-flower) 268
Drotsky, Jan and Eileen 346
Drotsky's Cabins 346
Drotsky's Caves 348
Du Toitskloof Pass 238
Du Toitskloof range 237, 258
duck, yellow-billed 110
Dugandlovu Camp 156
duiker
   blue 219, 388, 392
   grey 166, 396
Duiker Island 247, 250
duikerboom 268
Duiwelskloof 35, 37, 39
Duke, Thomas 13
Dukuduku Forest Nature Reserve 166
Dullstroom 65
Dullstroom Dam Nature Reserve 65
Dundee 148
Durand, Dr Francois 18
Durban 172
Durban Botanical Gardens 173, 174, 175
Durbanville Nature Reserve 250
dwarf tree 202
Dwesa-Cwebe Reserve 182, 187
Dwyka River 231

E

eagle
   American bald 379
   black 92, 398, 400
   fish 85, 379
   martial 92
earwig 32

East London 195, 197, 198, 199, 202, 205
Eastern Shores Nature Reserve 157
Ebb and Flow rest camps 227
Ecca Nature Reserve 198
Echo Caves 65
Echo Corner (Augrabies) 285
Ecowa Trail 191
edelweiss, Namib 317
Eden Park campsite 158
Eerste River 233
egret, cattle 54, 253
1820 Settlers Wild Flower Garden 198
Eilandvlei 227
Eileen Orpen Dam 22, 29
Eksteenfontein 267
eland 112, 122, 136, 275, 389
Elands Bay 260
Elands River 72, 86, 91, 141
Elandskloof range 237
Elandskrans Hiking Trail 106
Elandskrans Holiday Resort 106
Elandspad River Kloofing Trail 238
elephant 14, 16, 25, 28, 162, 165, 206, 330, 368, 379
   Addo 207
   Asian 150
   desert-dwelling 322
   Knysna 207, 218, 219
   Mafunyane 16
Elizabeth Bay 301
Ellisras 80, 86
Elytropappus rhinocerotis (renosterbos) 271
Emaweni Game Lodge 81
Embuleni Nature Reserve 107
emKhambathini 153
Emmarentia Dam 98, 109
eMolweni River 175
Empisini Nature Reserve 173
Encephalartos (cycad)
   caffer 197, 200
   dyerianus 35
   ferox 175
   friderici-guilielmi 198
   humilis 66
   longifolius 209
   transvenosus 37, 39, 67
   umbeluziensis 55
   woodii 170, 173
Engelhard Dam 20, 22
eNjesuthi peaks 138
Enseleni Nature Reserve 167
Entumeni Nature Reserve 167
Eobacterium isolatum (fossil) 108

Epako Game Lodge 334
Epako River 335
ephemeral (desert plant) 301
Epworth (balancing rocks) 381, 382
Equus
   burchelli 81, 401
   zebra zebra 192
Erfenis Dam 119
Erfenis Dam Nature Reserve 119
Erica perspicua (heath) 239
Erythrina (tree) 99, 399
Eshowe 166, 167
Estcourt 148, 151, 153
Esterhuysen, Andries 264
Etendeka Mountain Camp 318, 320
Etosha National Park 324
   at a glance 326
Etosha Pan 305, 324, 327, 329
Etsatsa River 346
Euphorbia 20
   damarana (melkbos) 322
   grandicornis 168
Euryops speciosissimus 258
Euskelosaurus (dinosaur fossil) 18
evening flower 143
everlasting 128, 143, 258, 321
Ewanrigg Botanical Garden 381, 382
Eye of Kuruman 277, 280
Ezulwini Valley 56

F

Faan Meintjies Nature Reserve 97
Faerie Glen Nature Reserve 81, 87
Falco peregrinus (peregrine falcon) 379
falcon, peregrine 379
False Bay 247
False Bay Park 156
Fanie Botha Dam *see* Tzaneen Dam
Fanie Botha Hiking Trail 62, 66
Fanies Island 158, 159
Fann's Falls 62
Farini, Guillermo 353
Farleigh Forest 225
farmer's bean 209
Fauresmith 120
F C Braun Aquarium 71
Featherbed Bay Beach 219
Featherbed Nature Reserve 219

Fenestraria rhopalophylla (window plant) 301
fern, tree 75
Fernkloof Nature Reserve 235, 238, 239
Ferny Creek 396
fever tree 26
Ficus (tree)
   capreifolia 395
   cordata 258
   salicifolia 93
Fiestaland recreational area 99
fig
   namaqua 258
   strangler 334
   wild 93, 337
finch (bird) 139
firebush 387
firefly 142
fish, buoyancy of 158
Fish Eagle Camp 79
Fish Eagle Lodge 401
Fish River 296
Fish River Canyon 296, 297
   at a glance 298
Fish River Hiking Trail 296, 297, 298
fishing
   Allemanskraal Dam 127
   Bloemhof Dam 96
   Bontebok National Park 216, 218
   Boskop Dam 96
   Cape Vidal 155
   Caprivi region 335
   Chobe 364
   Giant's Castle 137
   Hardap (Namibia) 306
   Hartbeespoort Dam 98
   Kariba 377
   Kosi Bay 160
   Makgadikgadi region 359
   Matobo 401
   Nwanedi (Northern Province) 37
   Nyanga (Zimbabwe) 392
   Okavango Delta 348
   Royal Natal National Park 140
   Sandwich Harbour (Namibia) 311
   Skeleton Coast (Namibia) 320
   Sodwana Bay 158
   Tsitsikamma National Park 226
   Wild Coast 183, 184, 185
   Zambezi (Zimbabwe) 373
FitzPatrick, Sir Percy 64, 110
Fitzsimons, Frederick 174

Fitzsimons Snake Park 174
Flagstone Lodge 92
flamingo 279
　greater 113, 114, 310, 316, 328, 359
　lesser 310, 316, 328, 359
flatworm 154
Flintstone Lodge 92
Flora Nature Reserve 66
Florence Bloom Bird Sanctuary 108, 109
fly
　bluebottle 156
　stalk-eyed 362
fly-in safaris *see* safaris
Fomothini Pan 154
Fontainebleau Camp 39
Fordyce, Colonel 191
Forest Falls 66
Forest Falls Nature Walk 66
Forest Lodge 164
Formosa Forest 228
Formosa Peak 237
Fort Fordyce Nature Reserve 191
Fort Merensky 79
Fort Pato Nature Reserve 198
Fortuna Mine Hiking Trail 108
fossils
　Barberton 108
　footprints (Lesotho) 128
　Kaokoveld (Namibia) 317
　Karoo 272
　Kruger National Park 18
　Langebaan 261
　Moyeni 128
　Saldanha Bay 235
　Sterkfontein Caves 104
Fothergill, Rupert 376
Fothergill Island 376, 380
Fothergill Island Safari Lodge 376, 377, 379
Fountains Valley Recreation Resort 82
4x4 trails
　essential equipment for 359
　Karoo National Park 271, 273
　NamibRand (Namibia) 314
　Naukluft (Namibia) 309
　Qwa-Qwa Park 123
Fouriesburg 122, 127
fox
　bat-eared 255, 276, 360
　Cape 192, 355
francolin, crested 28
Franklin Nature Reserve 119
Franschhoek Mountains 234, 237, 242
Franschhoek Pass 242
Fraser, Major A A 13

Free State National Botanical Garden 117, 119
Freeman, Ralph 390
Freshwater Fish Institute (Hardap) 303
Frithia pulchra (vygie) 100
frog
　rain 225
　reed 159, 169
　river 197
Fyfe, Percy 88
fynbos 235, 237, 247, 248
Fynbos Biome 237

G

Gaborone 354, 356
Gaborone Game Reserve 354
Gache Gache 377
Gairezi River 391
Galalabodimbo Pan 356
Galton, Francis 327, 335, 336
game rangers (Kruger) 14
Game Valley Estates 147
Game Valley Lodge 147
Gamka Mountain Nature Reserve 231
Gamka Mountains 231
Gamka River 231
Gamkapoort Dam 231
Gamkapoort Nature Reserve 231
Gamkaskloof 237
Gamtoos Coastal Nature Reserve 209
Ganab campsite 311
Ganda Lodge 371
Ganda Pan 371
gannet, Cape 255, 299
Ganspan Waterfowl Sanctuary 278
Garcia Forest 219
Garden Castle Reserve 137, 138
Garden of Eden 219, 222
Garden Route 216
Gardenia spatulifolia (shrub) 48
Gariep Dam 119, 126, 193
Gariep Dam Nature Reserve 119
Gariganus Farm 297
garrick 200
Gazebo Game Lodge 41
Gcodikwe heronry 350, 351
Gcwihaba Caverns *see* Drotsky's Caves
Geelhout Trail 147
Geelkrans Nature Reserve 219

geese
　Egyptian 125, 144
　spur-winged 125
gemsbok 35, 280, 292, 325
Gemsbok National Park 293, 352, 354, 356
Gemsbokspruit Dam 85
Genadendal Hiking Trail 239
George 221, 227
George, Jean 220
George Peak 237
Germiston 106, 114
Gerrands Dam 127
Ghio Wetland Reserve 199
Giant's Castle 134, 136, 138
　at a glance 137
Giant's Castle Camp 137
Giant's Castle Game Reserve 136, 139, 141
Giant's Cup Hiking Trail 136
Giant's Playground 298
Gilbert Reynolds Memorial Garden 56
Ginn, Peter 383
Giraffa camelopardalis (giraffe) 51
giraffe 45, 51, 332
Giyani 36
Glaucus atlanticus (nudibranch) 158
Glen Reenen 120
Glendale Farm 147
glow-worms 142
gloxinia, Cape 241
Glynis and Elna falls 69
gnu
　brindled *see* wildebeest, blue
　white-tailed *see* wildebeest, black
Goanikontes 308
Gobabeb 310
God's Window 62, 64, 66
Goegap Nature Reserve 265, 266
Gold River Game Reserve 81
Golden Gate Highlands National Park 117, 120, 121, 127
　at a glance 120
Golden Rhino Passport 135
Goldfields Environmental Centre 20
Gonarezhou National Park 393, 396, 397
　at a glance 397
Gonubie Nature Reserve 199
Gonubie (Gqunube) River 199, 201
goose, Egyptian 241

Gorhwe Pans 394
gorilla 108
Goro Game Reserve 66
goshawk, chanting 290
Goudveld Forest 220, 221, 222, 225
Goukamma Nature and Marine Reserve 220, 227
Goukamma River 218, 220
Gouna Forest 225
Graaff-Reinet 269, 273, 274
Graafwater 258
Graham, Tony 351
Grahamstown 198, 202, 204
grape, wild 305
Gras River 266
Graskop 62, 63
grass
　ncema 158
　torpedo 377
grasshopper
　foam 344
　toad 284
Gray, 'Gaza' 13
Great Brak River 216
Great Fish River 196, 197, 200, 202
Great Fish River Reserve 196, 203
Great Fish River Wetland Reserve 200
Great Letaba River 13, 20, 23
Great Usutu River 55
Great Zimbabwe 393, 395, 396, 399
Greater Kuduland 31
Greater St Lucia Wetland Park 155, 162
Green Belt Trails 147
Greyton 233
Greyton Nature Reserve 239
Greytown 150, 152
Grielum humifusum (duikerblom) 268
Grimwood, Ian 54
Griqua people 135
Griquatown 280
Grobler, Piet 290
Groblersdal 85
Groblershoop 282
Groendal Dam 209
Groendal Wilderness Area 209
Groeneweide Nature Walk 221, 222
Groenkloof Nature Reserve 81
Groenkop Forest 225
Groenvlei 220
Groot River (Tsitsikamma) 226
Groot Swartberge 229

407

Groot Winterhoek Conservation Area 258
Groot Winterhoek Mountains 209, 237
Groot Winterhoek Wilderness Area 258
Grootberg 320
Grootberg Pass 321
Grootbosch Nature Reserve 66, 69
Grootrivier (Karoo) 229, 237
Grootvadersbosch Conservancy 221
Grootvadersbosch Nature Reserve 218, 221
Gross-Barmen Hot Springs 303, 305
Grünau 297
grysbok 259
  Cape 221
  Sharpe's 25, 368
Gubalala Pan 369
Gudzani Dam 26
gull, black-backed 302
Gulu Nature Reserve 199
Gulu River 199
Gulubahwa Cave 400
Guluene River 394
Guma Lagoon 346
Gumbandebvu Hill 25
Gustav Klingbiel Nature Reserve 67
Gwaai River Hotel 371
Gwaai Valley Safaris 372
Gwayi 371
Gwayi Conservancy 372
Gwayi River 369, 372
Gwenoro Dam 396
Gweru (town) 383, 396
Gweru Antelope Park 383
Gweta Rest Camp 358, 359
Gweta village 358
Gxwaleni River 185
Gypaetus barbatus (bearded vulture) 130
Gyps coprotheres (Cape vulture) 102, 356

H

H F Verwoerd Coastal Reserve 239
Ha Baroana cave 128, 129
Ha Khotso 129
Haagner, Clem 290
Haga-Haga 197
Hai//om people *see* Bushmen (San)
Halali Rest Camp 326

halfmens 267, 268
Halfway House 116
Halfway House Hotel 371
Haliaeetus vocifer (fish eagle) 379
Halifax Island 300
Hall-Martin, Dr Anthony 16
hamerkop 388
Hangklip 72
Hans Merensky Nature Reserve 31, 32
  at a glance 33
Hans Strijdom Dam *see* Mokolo Dam
Hantam mountain range 264
Happy Rest Nature Reserve 67
Happy Valley Bird Sanctuary 178
Harare 381, 390
Hardap Dam 305
Hardap Recreation Resort and Game Park 303, 305, 328
  at a glance 306
hare, scrub 191, 349
Harkerville Coast Hiking Trail 225
Harkerville Forest 223, 225
Harkerville Forest Station 222
Harold Johnson Nature Reserve 174
Harold Porter National Botanical Garden 239, 240
Haroni Rusitu Botanical Reserve 390
Harris, William Cornwallis 98, 151, 274
Harrismith 122, 123, 125
Harry's Camp 48
Hartbeespoort Dam 94, 97, 98
Hartbeespoort Dam Nature Reserve 97
Hartbeespoort Snake and Animal Park 96, 98
Harts River 96
Harvey Nature Reserve 109
Hawaan Forest Reserve 174
Hawequas Mountains 237
Hazelmere Resources Reserve 174
heath, Prince of Wales 239
hedgehog 40
Heerenlogement Cave 258
Heia Safari Ranch 98
Heidelberg 115, 221
Helderberg 240
Helderberg Nature Reserve 240
Helichrysum
  adenocarpum 143
  chlorochrysum 236

  ecklonis 128
  roseo-niveum (Namib edelweiss) 317
  squamosum 138
Hella-Hella 147
Helpmekaar Forest 69
herbarium
  Basil Maskew Miller Herbarium 240
  Compton Herbarium 250
  Moss Herbarium 112
  Natal Herbarium 173
  National Herbarium 90
Herero people 347
Hermann Eckstein Park 110
Hermanus 235, 238
heron
  black-headed 305
  night 94
  squacco 349
Hesperantha (flower) 143
  schelpeana 141
Hester Malan Nature Reserve *see* Goegap Nature Reserve
Heuningnes River 238
Hex River 237
Hibiscus
  calyphyllus 340
  tiliaceus 184
hibiscus, tree 184
Highgate Ostrich Show Farm 231
Highmoor 139
hikes and trails
  Akkerendam Nature Reserve 265
  Alexandria Hiking Trail 205
  Amatola Hiking Trail 195, 196
  Augrabies Falls National Park 285
  Biggarsberg Conservancy 145
  Black Eagle Nature Reserve 189
  Blinkwater Nature Reserve 146
  Blyde River Canyon Hiking Trail 62
  Boesmanskloof Trail 233, 239
  Boland Hiking Trail 234, 241, 255, 259
  Bontebok National Park 218
  Boosmansbos Wilderness Area 218
  Bosberg Hiking Trail 189
  Botshabelo Nature Reserve and Museum 79

Bushbuck Walk 209
canoe (Keurbooms) 222
Cape Vidal 155
Cathedral Peak 136
Cederberg 257
Chimanimani National Park (Zimbabwe) 390
Compassberg Hiking Trail 270
Daan Viljoen Game Park 305
De Hoek Nature Walk (Karoo) 231
De Hoop Nature Reserve 236
Dog Trail 238
Doornkloof Hiking Trail 271, 275
Drakensberg 134
Drakensberg Hiking Trail 137
Dullstroom Dam Nature Reserve 65
Ecowa Trail 191
Elandskrans Hiking Trail 106
Elandspad River Kloofing Trail 238
Empisini Nature Reserve 174
Enseleni Nature Reserve 167
False Bay Park 156
Fanie Botha Hiking Trail 66
Featherbed Nature Reserve 219
Fish River Canyon (Namibia) 296, 297, 298
Forest Falls Nature Walk 66
Fort Fordyce Nature Reserve 191
Fortuna Mine Hiking Trail 108
Garcia Forest 219
Geelhout Trail 147
Genadendal Hiking Trail 239
Giant's Cup Hiking Trail 136, 137, 138
Goegap Nature Reserve 265
Golden Gate Highlands National Park 120
Goudveld Forest 220
Green Belt Trails 147
Groeneweide Nature Walk 221
Groot Winterhoek (West Coast) 258
Grootvadersbosch Nature Reserve 221
Hans Merensky Nature Reserve 32, 33

408

Harkerville Coast Hiking Trail 225
Hluhluwe-Umfolozi Park 168
Holkrans Hiking Trail 148
Honnet Nature Reserve 34
Jan du Toit's Kloof Trail (Tulbagh) 260
Johannesburg and Sandton urban trails 109
Kaapschehoop Hiking Trail 67
Karoo National Park 271, 273
Karoo Nature Reserve 273, 274
Katberg 201
Kirstenbosch National Botanic Garden 250
Klaserie Private Nature Reserve 43
Knysna Forest 219
Kogelberg Nature Reserve 243
Kosi Bay 160
Kowie canoe trail 205
Kranshoek Coastal Nature Walk 222
Kromdraai Conservancy 99
Kruger National Park 11, 13, 14, 15, 30
Leon Taljaard Nature Reserve 281
Limietberg (West Coast) 259
Loerie Walk 69
Mabuda-Shango Hiking Trail 36
Magoebaskloof Hiking Trail 69
Manyeleti Game Reserve 44
Maria Moroka Park 122
Mkhaya Trail 169
Mkuzi Game Reserve 162
Moreleta Spruit Nature Trail 87
Mountain Zebra National Park 193
Namib-Naukluft Park (Namibia) 309, 311, 312
Ndzalama Wildlife Reserve 37
Ngele Nature Reserve 143
Okonjima (Namibia) 339
Oorlogskloof Nature Reserve 267
Otter Trail 222, 223, 226
Outeniqua Hiking Trail 224
Outeniqua Nature Reserve 224
Perdeberg Trail 245
Platberg Hiking Trail 123
Porcupine Hiking Trail 124
Prospector's Hiking Trail 66, 72
Qwa-Qwa Park 123
Rhebuck Trail 120
Rhino Bushveld Eco Park 90
Richtersveld National Park 267
Rietvlei Nature Reserve 113
Robertson area 236
Rolfontein Nature Reserve 275
Rooikat Nature Walk 72
Royal Natal National Park 141, 142
Rustenburg Nature Reserve 103
SAS Saldanha Nature Trail (West Coast) 260
Shipwreck Trail 203
Silvermine Nature Reserve 252
Skeleton Coast (Namibia) 323
Skip Norgarb Trail 124
Soutpansberg Hiking Trail 72
St Lucia Estuary 158
Sterkfontein Dam Nature Reserve 125
Strandloper Trail 197, 203
Suikerboschfontein Hiking Trail 115
Suikerbosrand Nature Reserve 114, 115
Swartberg Trail 231
Swellendam Hiking Trail 223
Table Mountain 253
Terblans Nature Walk 225
Tewate Wilderness Area 157
Three Sisters Walk 245
Towerkop Nature Reserve 232
Transkaroo Hiking Trail 276
Tsitsikamma Hiking Trail 222, 223, 225, 226
Tsitsikamma National Park 226
Tussen-die-Riviere Nature Reserve 126
Uitsoek Hiking Trail 74
underwater (Tsitsikamma) 226
Vineyard Trail 246
Vrolijkheid Nature Reserve 246
Waterberg (Namibia) 341
Weenen Nature Reserve 153
West Coast National Park 261
Wild Coast Hiking Trail 187
Wilderness National Park 227
Windy Brow Game Farm 93
Wolhuterskop Hiking Trail 127
Woodcliffe Cave Trails 194
Zwartkops Valley Nature Reserve 213
Hillside Camp 137
Hillside Dams 398, 399
Hilltop Camp 168
Himeville 135, 143
hippo 17, 18, 57, 158
  pygmy 90
Hippo Pool 25, 26
Hippo Pools Camp 386
Hippocampus capensis (seahorse) 223
Hippotragus leucophaeus (bluebuck) 233
Hlamalala plains 26
Hlamvu Dam 27
Hlane Royal National Park 53, 55, 57
Hlomo Hlomo Game Reserve 167
Hluhluwe 154
Hluhluwe Game Reserve 154, 158, 168
Hluhluwe River 158, 168
Hluhluwe-Umfolozi Park 165, 166, 168, 170, 171
  at a glance 168
Hluleka Nature Reserve 183
  at a glance 184
Hlumuhlumu Mountains 107
Hoanib River 321, 322, 323
Hoarusib Canyon 323
Hobas campsite 298
Hobas viewpoint 297
Hobatere Lodge 326
Hoedspruit 41, 42, 52
Hoedspruit Research and Breeding Centre 42
Hoedspruit Safari Park 42
Hogsback 195, 199, 201
Hole in the Wall 182, 187
Holkrans Hiking Trail 148
Hollam's Bird Island 300
Holland Dam 212
Homeb campsite 311
Hone Valley 392
honeybee 122, 240
honeyguide (bird) 139, 152
Honeyguide Safari Camp 45
Honnet Nature Reserve 33
hoopoe, African 55
Hoopstad 124
Hopefontein Nature Reserve 31, 35
hornbill 327
  ground 23
  Monteiro's 321
  yellow-billed 176
horse trails
  Anysberg (Karoo) 228
  Nyanga (Zimbabwe) 392
horsefly 10
Horseshoe Falls 185
Hortus Botanicus 241
Hot Springs Resort (Nyanyadzi) 390
Hotazel 279
Hottentots-Holland Mountains 233, 234, 237, 240, 241, 242
Hottentots-Holland Nature Reserve 234, 237, 241
Houghton 116
Hout Bay 250, 253, 254
Houtbosloop River 66, 75
Howick Falls 144, 148, 152
Hudson Ntsanwisi Dam *see* Nsami Dam
Huisklip Nature Reserve 221
Huisrivier Pass 237
Humani Turgwe Camp 397
Humansdorp 218
Hunyani Rowing Club 385
Hwange (town) 369
Hwange area 371
Hwange National Park 362, 368, 378
  at a glance 369
Hwange Safari Lodge 369, 371
Hydrocynus vittatus (tigerfish) 378
hyena
  brown 20, 293, 322, 355
  spotted 16, 20, 353
Hymenodictyon floribundum (firebush) 387
Hyperolius tuberlinguis (frog) 169

I

ibis
  bald 73, 139
  wood *see* stork, yellow-billed
Ichaboe (island) 299
Idube Game Lodge 46
Ifafi 98
Igoda River 199
Ilanda Wilds Nature Reserve 175
Imbeza Valley 391
Imire Game Park 383

impala 21, 154, 376
Impalila Island Lodge 335
Impatiens sylvicola (plant) 68
Impofana Nature Reserve 139
Inanda Dam 175
Inanda Resources Reserve 175
Ingeli Forest Lodge 143
Ingwavuma 156
Inhluzana hills 150
Injasuti Camp 138
Injasuti River 138
Injasuti Valley 138
Intu Afrika Kalahari Game Reserve 306
Inungu Guest House 400
Inyati Game Lodge 41, 47
iNzinga Reserve 137
Iphika Tented Camp 152
Iphiva campsite 158
Ipomoea 26
Irle, Jacob 340
Iron Age settlement
  Kruger National Park 12
  Mapungubwe 40
  Melville Koppies 111
  Murahwa's Hill (Zimbabwe) 391
  Songimvelo Nature Reserve 114
Iron Mask hills 385
Isaac Edwin Stegmann Nature Reserve 104
Isibindi Eco-Reserve 148
Isibindi Lodge 149
Isipingo Estuary 178
Island Safari Lodge 348
Island State Forest, The 209
Isles of Dead Ned 299
Itala Game Reserve 149, 151
Ivory Lodge 372
Iwaba 383

J

J G Strijdom Dam *see* Jozini Dam
J L de Bruin Dam 188
Jabiru Fountain 211
jacaranda, pink 380
jackal, black-backed 322
Jackalberry Lodge 49
Jahleel Island 211
Jakkalsbessie Bushveld Camp 11, 14
James and Ethel Gray Park 111
Jameson, Robert 107
Jan du Toit's Kloof Trail 260
Jan Kempdorp 278

Januarie, Gert 290
Jedibe Island Camp 346
Jeffreys Bay 221, 223
jellyfish 245
Jericho Dam Nature Reserve 106, 109
Jijima 372
Joan Muirhead Nature Reserve 200
Jock of the Bushveld Private Camp 11, 14
Jock of the Drakensberg 64
Johannesburg 99, 108, 109, 110, 111
  urban trails 109
Johannesburg Botanical Garden 98
Johannesburg Lion Park 99
Johannesburg Zoological Gardens 108, 110
Jonker, Jan de 233
Jonkershoek Mountains 237
Jonkershoek Valley 233, 241
Joubert, Dr Eugene 309
Jozini Dam 151, 164
Jubaeopsis caffra 184
Jubilee Creek 220, 222
Jukskei River 109
Jutten Island 261

K

Kaapschehoop Hiking Trail 67
Kabeljous River 222
Kabeljousrivier Nature Reserve 221
Kaemferia rosea (rose ginger flower) 368
Kagga Kamma Game Reserve 258
Kalahari
  Botswana 352, 357
    at a glance 354
  Namibia 306
  South Africa 277
  Zimbabwe 370
Kalahari Desert 35, 344, 356
Kalahari Gemsbok National Park 277, 278, 279, 286, 288, 354
  at a glance 289
Kalahari Raptor Rehabilitation Centre 278
Kalahari Raptor Route 278
Kalahari River 348
Kalambeza Lodge 372
Kalkfeld 338
Kalkfontein Dam Nature Reserve 120

Kamanassie Nature Reserve 232
Kamanjab 321, 326
Kambaku Game Lodge 41, 50
Kamberg 134, 139
Kame (Khami) Ruins 399, 401
Kamfersdam 279
Kamieskroon 264, 267
Kandahar fishing camp 373
Kanniedood Dam 27
Kanondo Tree Camp 372
Kanyu Flats 360
Kaokoland *see* Kunene Region
Kaokoveld 317, 324, 328
  at a glance 318
Kap River 200
Kap River Nature Reserve 200
Kapama Game Reserve 42
Kapama Guest House 43
kapenta 378
Kapupuhedi waterhole (Etosha) 325
Karas region 296
Karatara Forest 225
Kariba area 368, 374, 379
  at a glance 377
Kariba Dam 374, 379
Kariba Heights 378
Kariba village 374, 376, 378
Kariba weed 377
Karibib 307
Kariega Park Game Reserve 200
Kariega River 200
Karkloof Falls 147, 149
Karkloof Nature Reserve 149
Karnmelks River 191
Karnmelkspruit Vulture Reserve 191
Karoo 192, 267
  Great 229, 269
  Little 228, 237
Karoo National Botanic Garden 241, 269
Karoo National Park 269, 271, 328
  at a glance 271
Karoo Nature Reserve 269, 273
  at a glance 273
Karoo Rest Camp 273
Kasane Forest Reserve 362
Kasane village 362
Kaswiswe Camp 375
Kat River 203
Katberg 193, 200
Kate's Hope Game Lodge 31, 35
Katete Lodge 374
Kathu Nature Reserve 279
Katshana Tree Lodge 372

Kavango region 333
Kavango River 333, 337, 341
Kaye, Robert and June 349
Kazuma Forest Reserve 362
Kazuma Pan National Park 372
Kazungula 362, 365
Keetmanshoop 296, 297, 300
Kei River 186
Keimoes 283, 286
Keiskamma River 197
Kenhardt 266
Kenneth Stainbank Nature Reserve 172, 175
Kenton on Sea 200
Ketane Falls 130
Kettlespout waterfall 196, 199
Keurbooms Forest 226
Keurbooms River Lagoon 221
Keurbooms River Nature Reserve 222
Keyter, Bernie 116
Kgama-Kgama Pan 360
Kgokong River 82
Khama Rhino Sanctuary 358
Khami Ruins *see* Kame (Khami) Ruins
Khaudum bush camp 333, 335
Khaudum Game Park 333, 335
Khaya nyasica (red mahogany) 390
Khoikhoi, Topnaar 310
Khoikhoi people 198
Khoka Moya Game Lodge 44
Khomas Hochland Mountains 296, 303, 304
Khorixas 317, 318, 323
Khorixas Rest Camp 318
Khumib River 323
Khutse Game Reserve 352, 354, 355
Khutse Game Scouts Camp 356
Khwai River 346, 347, 349, 350
Khwai River Lodge 346, 348, 350, 351
King Nehale waterhole (Namutoni) 326
King William's Town 202
kingfisher
  brown-headed 396
  giant 205, 391
Kings Camp 41, 50
King's Pool Lodge 365
Kipling's 377
Kirkman's Camp 48
Kirstenbosch National Botanic Garden 250
Klaarwater Nature Reserve 280
Klaas Island 285

Klaserie Private Nature Reserve 41, 43, 50
Klaserie River 43, 45, 49
Klein Drakenstein 237
Kleinmond 244
Kleinmond Coastal and Mountain Nature Reserve 242
Kleinplasie Reptile World 243
Kleinrivier Mountains 235
Klerksdorp 94, 97
Klingbiel, Gustav 67
Klip River 124, 149
Kliphuis campsite 257
Klipriviersberg Nature Reserve 110
klipspringer 28, 39, 285
Klipspringer Mountain Pass 273
Klipvoor Dam 78
Kloof Falls 175
Kloofendal Nature Reserve 99
Knersvlakte 267, 268
Knysna 218, 219, 227
Knysna Forest 216
Knysna Heads 219, 222
Knysna Indigenous Forests 219, 220, 222
Knysna Lagoon 219, 222
Knysna National Lake Area 216, 222
Koch, Dr Charles 311
Koeberg Nature Reserve 258
Kogelberg 237
Kogelberg Nature Reserve 243, 244
Kok III, Adam 135
kokerboom *see* quiver tree
Kokerboom Forest
  Namaqualand 265
  Namibia 296, 297
Kokstad 136
Kolmanskop 301
Kolo 129
Kolobe Lodge 82
Kologha Forest 201
Kololo Safari Camp 88, 89
Kolver, Hans 19
Komati Gorge 54
Komati River 114
Komati River Lodge 114
Kommandonek 98
Königstein 319
Koos Ras Nature Reserve 192
Koppies Dam Nature Reserve 120
Korannaberg 277, 281
korhaan, Rüppell's 321
Korn, Hermann 313
Koro Bush Camp 361

Korsman Bird Sanctuary 111
Kosi Bay Coastal Forest Reserve 160, 161
Kosi Bay Estuary 160
Kosi Bay Nature Reserve 160
Kosi Fountain 211
Kouebokkeveldberge 237
Kouga mountain range 228, 237
Kowie Nature Reserve 201
Kowie River 201, 205
Kraai River 190
Kransberg 78
Kranshoek Coastal Nature Walk 222
Krantzkloof Nature Reserve 172, 175
Kromdraai Conservancy 99, 102
Kromrivier Farm 256
Kroonstad 120
Kruger National Park 10, 31, 32, 36, 41, 42, 43, 47, 49, 50, 57, 394
  central 15, 20, 22, 23, 24, 26
    at a glance 13
  northern 22, 25, 27, 31
    at a glance 15
  southern 14, 16, 17, 20, 22, 28
    at a glance 11
  tips for visitors 12, 14
Kruger, Paul 11, 164
Krugersdorp 94, 99, 100, 105
Krugersdorp Game Reserve 100
Krugersdrift Dam 124
Kruiper, Regopstaan 289
Kruisfontein Forest 225
Kuboes 267
Kuburi Wilderness Area 380
kudu 10, 327, 385
  greater 10
  lesser 10
Kudu Bush Camp 45
Kuiseb River 308, 310, 313, 315
Kuiseb River Canyon 308, 313, 314
Kumaga campsite 359
Kunene Region 317, 321
Kunene River 317, 321
Kuruman 277, 278, 279, 280, 282
Kuruman Bird Sanctuary 280
Kuruman Nature Reserve 277, 280
Kuruman River 278
Kwa Maritane Lodge 88, 89
Kwalata Game Ranch 82

KwaMalibala 162
KwaMehlenyati Reserve 137
Kwando Island Camp 365
Kwando Lagoon Camp 365
Kwando River 333, 338, 339, 362, 364, 365
KwaNtula Camp 149
Kwekwe 383, 384, 380
Kwelegha Nature Reserve 201
Kwelegha River 201
Kwena Gardens Crocodile Paradise 82
Kyle Recreational Park 396

L

La Rochelle Gardens 390, 391
lacewing larva 111
Ladismith (Karoo) 232
Lady Grey 191
ladybird 121
  lunate 79
Ladysmith (KwaZulu-Natal) 149, 152
Lake Alexander 391
Lake Amanzimnyama 160
Lake Bhangazi 156
Lake Chivero 381, 383
Lake Chivero Recreational Park 383
Lake Fundudzi 36
Lake Guinas 337
Lake Kariba 374, 375, 376, 377, 380
Lake Kyle *see* Lake Mutirikwi
Lake Lesapi 390
Lake MacDougall *see* Lake Manjirenji
Lake Makhawuleni 160
Lake Manjirenji 397
Lake McIlwaine *see* Lake Chivero
Lake Mpungwini 160
Lake Mutirikwi 393, 395, 396
Lake Ngami 336, 347, 357
Lake Ngoboseleni 158
Lake Nhlange 160, 161
Lake Oponono 305
Lake Otjikoto 333, 335, 336
Lake Sibayi 160, 161
Lake Sibayi Freshwater Reserve 160
Lake St Lucia 154, 155, 156, 158, 161, 165, 305
Lake Xau 358
Lakes Road 216, 227
Lalapanzi Camp 154
Lambert's Bay 255, 260, 268

Lammergeier Nature Reserve 192
lammergeyer *see* vulture, bearded
Lammergeyer Hide 137
Lancaster Hill 153
Lang Elsieskraal 216
Langebaan lagoon 255, 261
Langebaan National Park 261
Langeberg 216, 218, 219, 221, 223, 236, 237, 244, 277
Langjan Nature Reserve 31, 32, 34, 35
Langkloof range 237
Langvlei 227
Lapalala Wilderness 82
Lapalala Wilderness School 82
lark, rufous-naped 203
Larvon Bird Gardens 381, 384
Latrodectus indistinctus (black widow spider) 386
Lavin, Ben and Molly 60
Lawrence de Lange Nature Reserve 188, 192
Le Bihan Falls *see* Maletsunyane Falls
Le Bonheur Crocodile Farm 258
le Riche, Joep 292
le Riche, Johannes 290
le Vaillant, Francois 216
Leadwood Lodge 46
lechwe, red 346, 351
leervis 200
Leeukop Mountain 146
Lekgalameetse Nature Reserve 68
Leon Taljaardt Nature Reserve 280
leopard 23, 27, 33, 34, 46, 291, 307
Leopard Hills 341
Leopard Rock Bush Camp 38
Lephalala River 82
Lepidochora (desert beetle) 312, 314
Leqooa River 131
Leribe 129
Lesapi River 390
Lesheba Wilderness 68
Lesotho 128
Leswena Nature Reserve 83
Letaba Rest Camp 13, 14, 20, 22, 23
Letaba River 22, 33
Letsitele Valley 72
Leucadendron argenteum (tree) 249, 250
Leucospermum truncatum (pincushion) 237

411

Lianshulu Lodge 339
lichens 60, 319
Lichia amia (fish) 200
Lichtenburg 94
Lichtenburg Game-Breeding Centre 101
Liebenberg, Dennis and Barbara 321
Liesbeek River 250
Lillie Flora Nature Reserve 31, 35
lily
　Ammocharis 301
　blood 349
　chincherinchees 216
　fire 148
　impala 12, 55
　water 346
Limietberg 237, 255
Limietberg Nature Reserve 258
Limnothrissa miodon (kapenta) 378
Limpopo River 10, 13, 18, 39, 93, 360, 361, 381
Lindanda flats 21, 22
Lindanda memorial 22
Linksfield Ridge 109
Linnaeus, Carl 69
Linyandi River 338, 362, 364, 365
Linyandi Swamps 333, 338
Linyanti 365
lion 21, 26, 29, 45, 329, 332, 384
　Kalahari 288, 293
　Skeleton Coast 323
　white 29, 50, 52
Lion Cavern (mine) 54
Lion Dam (camp) 43
lion parks
　Harare Lion Park 384
　Johannesburg Lion Park 99
　Natal Lion and Game Park 150
Lithops (stone plant) 211, 301
　comptonii 257
　lesliei 96
Little Mhlatuzana River 175
Livingstone, David 336, 347, 373, 393
lizard
　Cape red-tailed rock 284, 285
　crag 273
　flat rock 86
Lloyd's Camp 364
Lobedu people 37

Lobengula, King 398
Lobostemon fruticosus (plant) 235
Loch Athlone 127
locust, milkweed stink 281
Loerie Dam Nature Reserve 209
Loerie Walk 69
Lolamontes Dam 83
Londolozi Private Game Reserve 41, 46, 47, 48
Lone Creek Falls 66
Lone Hill Tor 109
Long Pool 379
Longhill Nature Reserve 188, 192
Loskop Dam 76, 84
Loskop Dam Nature Reserve 32, 82, 83
Loteni Reserve 139, 140
Loteni River 140
Lotlamoreng Dam 101
Lotlamoreng Nature Reserve 101
Lottering 226
lotus flower 241
Louis Trichardt 33, 36, 38, 60, 67
Louw, Adriaan 18
Louw Geldenhuys Viewsite 111
Louwsberg 149
Lower Sabie Rest Camp 11, 14, 20, 24
Lower Zivagwe Dam 384
Lowhills Private Game Reserve 43
Lowveld 31
Lowveld National Botanical Gardens 41, 44
Lubombo Escarpment 164
Lubombo Mountains 55, 162, 163, 164, 165
Lüderitz 300
Lukosi Camp 371
Lupala Island 338
Luphephe River 38
Lusikisiki *see* Msikaba (Lusikisiki)
Luvuvhu Gorge 30
Luvuvhu River 17, 18, 24, 25, 26
Lydenburg 67, 68, 70, 71

M

Maaierskloof 266
Mababe Depression 362, 364, 365

Mabalauta (Gonarezhou) 394, 395
　at a glance 397
Mabibi Coastal Camp 161
Mabolo Camp 375
Mabuasehube Game Reserve 352, 354, 356
Mabuda-Shango Hiking Trail 36
Mabula Game Lodge 84
Mabusa Nature Reserve 84
MacDougall, Tom 397
MacDougall Dam 393
Machaba 347
Maclear 194
Mac-Mac Falls 6
Mac-Mac Pools 66
Madeira Mountain 192
Maden Dam 201
Madikwe Game Reserve 84
Madikwe River Lodge 84
Madonna and Child waterfall 196, 199
Madoqua kirkii (Damara dik-dik) 330
Mafeteng 128
Mafikeng 101
Mafunyane 16
Magaliesberg 69, 87, 94, 97, 98, 100, 101, 102, 103
Magaliesberg Protected Natural Environment 101
Magdalena Game Ranch 169
Magoebaskloof 60, 66, 68, 69, 75
Magoebaskloof Hiking Trail 67, 69
Magwegwana (Selinda) Spillway 365
Magwikhwe Sand Ridge 364
Mahai campsite 141
Mahango Game Park 337, 341
Mahemane area 163
Mahenye Safari Lodge 396
Mahlabatini Park 175
mahogany, red 390
Mahovohovo waterfall 36
Mahulungwane Falls 54
Maikaelelo Forest Reserve 362
Main Camp (Hwange) 369
Main Camp (Londolozi) 47
Main Caves (Giant's Castle) 137, 138, 140
Main Pool (Mana Pools) 379
Maitland, Sir Peregrine 210
Maitland Nature Reserve 210
Maitland River 210
Makahane, Chief 30
Makalali Private Game Reserve 70

Makgadikgadi Camp 359, 360
Makgadikgadi Pans 357, 358, 359, 361
Makgadikgadi Pans National Park 357, 359
　at a glance 359
Makgadikgadi region 355, 357
Makhutswi River 68, 70
Makonjwa mountain range 108
Makuya Park 36
Makwassierante Conservation Area 101
Makwena Lodge 347
Mala Mala Game Reserve 41, 47, 48, 51
Mala Mala Main Camp 48
Malandeni 149
Malati Park Nature Reserve 84
Malebocho Nature Reserve 70
Malekgonyane (Ongeluksnek) Nature Reserve 184
Malelane 43, 44
Malelane Bushveld Camp 11
Malelane Gate 11, 16, 22, 41
Malelane Rest Camp 14, 22
Maleme Dam 401
Maleme Wilderness Area 400
Maletsunyane Falls 128, 130
Malgas Island 261
Malibamatso River 130
Malindi Station Lodge 372
Malindidzimu 398, 401
Malmesbury 259
Malolotja Falls 54
Malolotja Nature Reserve 53, 54, 57
Maloti Mountains 117, 120, 122, 128
mamba
　black 400
　green 142
Mambova Rapids 335
Mamili National Park 338
Manala Camp 85
Man'ombe Nature Reserve 36
Mana Pools National Park 374, 376, 377, 378
Mandabuza Pan 363
Mandavu Dam 371
mangrove 172
Manjirenji Recreational Park 397
Mankelekele Mountain 74
Mankwe Bush Camp 88
Mankwe Dam 88, 89
Mannyelanong Vulture Sanctuary 356
mantis, praying 37
　Wahlberg's 85
Mantrombi Nature Reserve 85

412

Mantuma Hutted Camp 162
Manyame Recreational Park 384
Manyane Camp and Caravan Park 88, 89
Manyeleti Game Reserve 41, 44, 45
Manzimtoti River 175
Manzini 56
Manzituba Camp 375
Manzou Lodges 384
Mapelane 155, 157, 158, 159
Maphutseng 129
Mapororo Pan 363
Mapulaneng Nature Reserve 70
Mapungubwe 40
Maputaland Marine Reserve 159
Maputo (Usutu) River 154
Maqoma, Chief 191
Marais, Eugene 35
Marakabei 128
Marakele National Park 85
Marble Hall 91
Marcus Island 261
Maria Moroka Park 122
Maria Ratschitz Mission 145
Mariannwood Nature Reserve 175
Marico River 84
Mariental 303, 306, 328
Mariepskop 64, 70
Marievale Bird Sanctuary 106, 111
Marloth Nature Reserve 223
Maroela Rest Camp 13, 14, 24
Marongora 379
Marsh, Dr Alan 312
Martin, Henno 313
Martin's Falls 389
Marula Camp 76
Masebe Nature Reserve 85
Maseru 128
Mashatu Game Reserve 360
Mashatu Tented Camp 361
Mashava Hills 386
Mashikiri plateau 26
Mashonaland 381
Mashushe Shongwe Game Reserve 44
Masinda Camp 168
Masqobe Camp 41
Masuma Dam 371
Masuwe River 373
Masvingo 389, 390, 393, 395, 396, 397
Mata Mata Rest Camp 289, 292
Matenderere River 392

Matetsi Safari Area 362, 372
Matjiesfontein 228
Matjulu Spruit 16
Matlabas Camp 85
Matobo Dam 400
Matobo Hills 400, 401
Matobo National Park 398, 399
  at a glance 401
Matsheumhlope River 398
Matswere Game Scouts Camp 354
Matumi Game Lodge 41, 45
Matusadona Mountains 374, 376, 377, 380
Matusadona National Park 374, 376, 379
Matusadona Tented Safaris 380
Maun 344, 345, 347, 349, 350, 351
Maun Game Reserve 348, 351
Mawana Nature Reserve 361
Mawewe Cattle Game Project 45
Mazoe Citrus Estate 384
Mazowe Dam 384
Mazowe River 386
Mazowe Valley 384
Mazwi Nature Park 401
Mbabane 56
Mbala Lodge 371
M'bali Camp 51
M'bali Dam 51
Mbanyana River 182
Mbashe River 182, 186
Mbilo River 177
Mbizo Bush Camp 149
Mbukushu people 350
Mbuluzana River 54
Mbuluzi River 56, 57
McGregor 233
Mdala Nature Reserve 85
Mdedelelo Wilderness Area 138, 141
Mdwala Nature Reserve 176
Meerhof 98
meerkat, grey 190
Meeuwen Island 261
Megaceryle maxima (giant kingfisher) 391
Meiringskloof Nature Park 122
Meiringspoort 237
Meldrani Wildlife Reserve 86
melkbos 322
Mellivora capensis (honey badger) 339
Meloidae (beetle) 340
melon, tsamma 290
Melrose Bird Sanctuary 109, 111

Melville Koppies Nature Reserve 106, 109, 111
Memel 124
Mercury (island) 300
Mesembryanthemum (vygie) 268, 301
Messina 36, 38
Messina Nature Reserve 31, 37
Metswedi Safari Camp 88, 89
Metzer, Dr Woody 79
Meulwater Wild Flower Reserve 259
Meyerspark Bird Sanctuary 87
Mfabeni 155, 157
Mfazana Pans 156
Mfihlwini corridor 165
Mfolozi River 157, 168
Mfula Lodge 165
Mgamazi Lodge 150
Mgeni River 145, 149, 150, 152, 172
Mhlangamphepha Valley 54
Mhlangeni Bush Camp 149
Mhlatuzana River 176
Mhlopeni Private Nature Reserve 149
Mhondoro Game Park 385
Mica 35
Middelburg 76, 79
Midmar Dam 146, 150
Midmar Historical Village 150
Midmar Public Resort Nature Reserve 150
Millais, John Guille 126, 385
Miller's Point Marine Reserve 251
Mills, Gus 293
Millstone Lodge 92
Millwood 220
Milnerton 251
Mimetes (plant) 243
Mingerhout Dam 20
minnow, Burchell's redfin 246
Mitchell Park Aviary 176
Mitchell's Plain 254
Mkambati Nature Reserve 184
  at a glance 185
Mkambati River 185
Mkangoma Hill 177
Mkhaya Nature Reserve 53, 55
Mkhaya Trail 169
Mkhomazi River (Mkomazi) Valley 143, 152
Mkhomazi Wilderness Area 137, 139
Mkhombo Dam Nature Reserve 85, 86
Mkomazi River 137, 147
Mkuze River 158, 162
Mkuze swamps 155

Mkuzi Game Reserve 154, 155, 158, 162, 164, 165
  at a glance 162
Mkwasine River 397
Mlambonya Wilderness Area 137, 141
Mlawula Nature Reserve 53, 55, 57
Mlawula River 56
Mlazi wetland 177
Mlibizi River 378
Mlilwane Wildlife Sanctuary 53, 54, 56
  at a glance 56
Mlumati Valley cycad forests 57
Mndindini Bush Camp 168
Mngazi River Mouth 187
Moanachira River 351
Modder Dam 124
Modjadji (Rain Queen) 37, 198
Modjadji Nature Reserve 37
Modjadji palm 37, 39, 75
Moffat Mission 278
Mogobe Camp 97
Mogobe Dam 97
Mogogelo River 350
Mohlapitse River 75
Moholoholo Forest Camp and Wildlife Rehabilitation Centre 70
Moholoholo Mountain *see* Mariepskop
Mokolo Dam 86
Mokolo Dam Nature Reserve 86
Mokolo River 86
Mokolo River Private Nature Reserve 86
Mokolodi Environmental Education Centre 356
Mokolodi Nature Reserve 356
Mokolodi Wildlife Foundation 356
mokoro 333, 335, 348, 350
Mokuti Lodge 326
Moletsi Nature Reserve 86
Molimo Nthuse Lodge 128
Molopo Nature Reserve 281
Molopo River 281, 288
Mombo Camp 348
Mombo Island 348
Mome Gorge 170
mongoose 192
  banded 370
  dwarf 174
  Selous' 357
  yellow 332
monkey, vervet 22, 66, 173, 205
monkey's tail 106

413

Monk's Cowl 141
Mont Rochelle Nature Reserve 243
Montagu 236
Montagu Mountain Nature Reserve 245
Montagu Pass 237
Mont-aux-Sources 141
Montello Safari Lodge 150
Monticola rupestris (thrush) 208
Montloatse Setlogelo Dam 122
Monwana River 49
Moodie, John 391
Moodie, Tom 387
Mooi River 96, 139
Mooi River (town) 140
Moor, Sir Frederick 150
Moor Park Nature Reserve 150, 153
Moordkuils Forest 224
Moore, Randall Jay 346
Mopani Rest Camp 14, 15, 22, 25
Mopipi Dam 358
Moraea (plant)
  polystachya 194
  spathulata 70
Moratele Camp 78
Moratele River 78
Moreleta Spruit Nature Trail 87
Moremi forest 346
Moremi Game Reserve 345, 346, 347, 348, 349, 350, 351
Moreswe Pan 356
Morija 129
moringa (tree) 321, 331
Moringa ovalifolia (moringa tree) 321, 331
Moringa waterhole (Halali) 326
morning glory 151
Moss Herbarium 112
Mostert, Peter 49
moth
  Cape tiger 182
  pine 240
Motshane (Motjane) 54
Motswari Game Lodge 51, 52
Motswari-M'bali 41, 51
Mount Anderson Ranch 66, 71
Mount Currie Nature Reserve 135
Mount Etjo Safari Lodge 338
Mount Everest Game Reserve 122
Mount Nyangani 387, 392
Mount Sheba 71

Mount Sheba Nature Reserve 71
Mountain Lodge 164
Mountain View Rest Camp 273
Mountain Zebra National Park 188, 192
  at a glance 193
mousebird, speckled 28
Mouton, Gert 292
Moyeni 128, 129
Mpala-Jena fishing camp 373
Mpama River 109
Mpambanyoni River 178
Mpenjati Nature Reserve 176, 177
Mpenjati River Mouth 176
Mphaphuli Cycad Reserve 37
Mphongolo stream 27
Mpila Camp 168
Mpofu Game Reserve 193
Mpumalanga Parks Board and Development Facility 71
Mqanduli see Coffee Bay (Mqanduli)
msasa tree 391
Mshagashe River 396
Msihlengeni Falls 169
Msikaba (Lusikisiki) 186
Msikaba River 184
Msunduzi River 162, 163
Msuthlu River 48
Mswati III, King 53
Mtamvuna River 185
Mtarazi Falls 392
Mtarazi Falls National Park 391, 392
Mtata River Mouth 187
Mtentu River 184
Mthethomusha Game Reserve 41, 45
Mthomeni Bush Camp 44
Mtoroshanga Pass 381
Mtunzini 171
Mudumu National Park 338
Mukurob 307
Mukuvisi Woodlands 385
Muldersdrift 95, 98
Mungwezi River 393
Munyati River 383
Murahwa's Hill 391
Musape River 389
museum
  Albany Museum (Grahamstown) 233
  Anglo-Boer War Museum (Spioenkop) 152
  Botshabelo Nature Reserve and Museum 79

Bushman Site (Giant's Castle, Drakensberg) 137, 138, 141
Kleinplasie Museum (Worcester) 243
Leonard Gill Museum (Rondevlei, Cape Town) 252
Loteni Settlers Homestead Museum (Drakensberg) 140
Masorini Museum (Kruger National Park) 12, 13
Midmar Historical Village (Midmar Dam) 150
Museum of Man (Echo Caves) 65
Mutare Museum (Zimbabwe) 390
Natural History Museum (Bulawayo) 398
Robert Broom (Sterkfontein Caves) 104
State Museum (Namibia) 323
Suikerbosrand farm museum 115
Transvaal Museum (Pretoria) 78
Tsonga Museum (Hans Merensky Nature Reserve) 33
Mushandike 389
Mushandike Dam 397
Mushandike Sanctuary 397
Mushroom Rocks 117
mussel
  sand 244
  white 244
Mutale River 36
Mutare 387, 389, 390, 391, 395
Mutekeswane 390
Mutirikwi Dam see Lake Mutirikwi
Mutirikwi River 393, 396
Mvelase Lodge 150
Mvoti River 152
Mwatombo crocodile pools 395
Mwena Game Park 386
Mwenezi region (Gonarezhou) 394, 395
Mwenezi River 395
Mynhardt Game Reserve 122
Myrothamnus flabellifolius (plant) 71
Mzilikazi, King 169, 398
Mzimkulu Wilderness Area 138
Mzinti River 44

N

Naboomspruit 76, 80, 85, 88
Nagle Dam 150
Nagle Resources Reserve 150
Nakatwa Camp 339
N'Kaya Lodge 49
Naletale Ruins 401
Nama people 267
Namaqualand 256, 264
  wild flowers 264, 268
Nambwa campsite 334
Namib Desert
  Namib-Naukluft Park 308
  north coast 319, 322
  plants of 301
  southern coastline 298
Namib Research Institute 310, 311
Namib-Naukluft Hiking Trail 309, 311, 312
Namib-Naukluft Park 301
  at a glance 311
Namibia
  Caprivi region 333
  Etosha National Park 324
  Namib Desert 308
  northeast 333
  offshore islands 296, 299
  Skeleton Coast 317
  southern 296
NamibRand Nature Reserve 314
Namutoni Rest Camp 324, 326
Nantwich Camp 369, 370
nara plant 315
Nata Lodge 359, 361
Nata River 359, 361
Nata Sanctuary 361
Nata village 361
Natal Drakensberg Park 134, 136
Natal Herbarium 173
Natal Lion and Game Park 150
Natal National Botanical Garden 151
Natal Parks Board (accommodation) 143
Natal Sharks Board 176
Natal Zoological Gardens 76, 151
National Botanic Garden (Harare) 385, 386
National Herbarium 90
national parks 49
National Parks Board 49, 76
National Zoological Gardens (Pretoria) 87, 89, 101
Nature's Valley 222, 226
Naudes Nek 194

Naukluft campsite 311
Naval Hill 119
Ndawana River 134
Ndebele craft village 373
Ndedema Gorge 141
Ndlovu Camp 54
Ndugulu Camp 45
Ndugulu Game Farm 45
Nduli Nature Reserve 185
Ndumo Game Reserve 151, 154, 163, 165
  at a glance 163
Ndumo Wilderness Camp 163, 164
Ndwandwe people 393
Ndzalama Wildlife Reserve 31, 37
Ndzindza Nature Reserve 55
Nels River 44
Nels River Falls 44
Nelshoogte Nature Reserve 112
Nelspruit 73, 74
Nelspruit Cascades 44
Nelspruit Nature Reserve 41, 46
Nelumbium nucifera (lotus flower) 241
New Agatha Forest 72
New Chum Falls 62
New Formosa Nature Reserve 151
New Germany Nature Reserve 176
New Muckleneuk 76
New Oxbow Lodge 128, 130
Newcastle 148
Newlands Forest 253
Ngala Private Game Reserve 41, 51
Ngele Nature Reserve 143
Ngezi Dam Recreational Park 386
Ngoma 362
Ngomakurira 382
Ngome Forest 169
Ngotwane River 354
Ngoye Forest Reserve 169
Nguza Nature Park 401
Ngwangwane River 134
Ngwenya iron-ore mine 54
Nhlonhlela Bush Lodge 162
Nieu-Bethesda 270
Nieuwoudtville 237
Nieuwoudtville Nature Reserve 266
Nieuwoudtville Waterfall Nature Reserve 266
Nigel 106, 112
Nigel Nature Reserve 112

Njuca Hills campsite 359
Nkandla Forest Reserve 170
Nkasa Island 338
Nkomati Bushman (San) paintings 57
Nkombe Tented Camp 48
Noetzie River 218
Noga Island 345, 349
Nogatsaa 363
Nogatsaa campsite 363, 364
Nooitgedacht 101
Nooitgedacht Dam Nature Reserve 112
Noorsekloof Nature Reserve 223
North Park Nature Reserve 176
Northern Wilderness Area (Matobo) 400
Nossob Rest Camp 289, 292
Nossob River 288, 290, 354, 355
Notten's Bush Camp 46
Nottingham Road 140, 143
Notuli Hutted Camp 144
Noukloof Nature Reserve 232
Nsami Dam 36
Nseleni River 167
Nselweni bush camp 168
Nshawu Dam 27
Nsumo Pan 162
Nswatugi Cave 400
Ntabathemba Tribal Reserve 201
N'tabazinduna Hill 401
N'tabazinduna Lodge and Trails 401
Ntendeka Wilderness Area 169
Ntenjwa Rustic Camp 152
Ntshondwe Camp 149
Ntshongweni cliffs 177
Ntwetwe Pan 357, 359, 360
nudibranch 158
Numbi Gate 11, 24
num-num shrub 206
Nuweberg 234
Nuweveld Mountains 269, 272, 273
Nwanedi Nature Reserve 38
  at a glance 37
Nwanedi River 38
Nwanetsi Private Camp 13, 14, 22
Nwanetsi River 22
Nxai Pan 345, 359, 360
Nxai Pan National Park 357, 359
  at a glance 359
Nxamaseri Lodge 349

Nxaxo Mouth 186
Nxwala 163
Nyahodi River 387
nyala 19, 20, 40, 170
Nyamandhlovu Pan 368, 369, 371
Nyamasowa Camp 380
Nyamepi Camp 379
Nyamithi Pan 163, 165
Nyamuomba Camp 379
Nyamziwe Falls 392
Nyamziwe River 392
Nyamzure (Pork Pie Mountain) 389
Nyanga (town) 387
Nyanga Dam 391, 392
Nyanga National Park 390, 391
  at a glance 392
Nyangombe Falls 391, 392
Nyangwe (Mare) Dam 391
Nyanyadzi 390
Nyanyana Camp 375, 377, 378
Nyanyana River 375
Nyati Lodge 372
Nyengelezi rustic camp 179
Nyl River 88
Nylstroom 81, 82
Nylsvley Nature Reserve 88
Nymphaea caerulea (water lily) 346
Nyoni River 166
Nzhelele Dam 38
Nzhelele Nature Reserve 38
Nzhelele River 35

O

O P M Prozesky Bird Sanctuary 102
Oberon 98
Ocean View Game Park 170
Octocyon megalotis (bat-eared fox) 255, 276
Oddballs Camp 346, 349
Odendaalsrus 125
Odzani Falls 391
Odzi River 391
Oelofse, Jan 338
Oelofse, Roelof 221
Ohrigstad 64, 65
Ohrigstad Dam Nature Reserve 68, 71
Ohrigstad River 71
Okahandja 303, 305, 307, 340
Okaukuejo Rest Camp 324, 326, 328
Okavango Delta 344, 357
  at a glance 348

Okavango River 344, 346, 348, 349, 350, 351, 365
Okavango River Lodge 348
Okonjima Guest Lodge 339
Old Camp 76
Oldenburgia arbuscula (cushion bush) 202, 209
Olifants Rest Camp 13, 14, 15, 20, 23, 24, 26
Olifants River 13, 15, 23, 26, 29, 52, 83, 91, 228, 257
Olifantsrivierberge 255
Olive Trail 312
Olivier, Louis 19
Omaruru 320, 335
Omboroko Mountains 339
Ondundozonanandana range 332
Ongava Lodge and Game Reserve 326, 332
Ongeluksnek *see* Malekgonyane (Ongeluksnek) Nature Reserve
Onymacris unguicularis (desert beetle) 312
Oorlogskloof Nature Reserve 264, 266
Operation Genesis 89
Operation Noah 370
Oppel, Barend 229
orange, black monkey (tree) 41
Orange Kloof 251, 253
Orange River 117, 126, 264, 267, 268, 269, 275, 277, 284, 293, 296, 297
Oranjekom (Augrabies) 285
Oranjemund 302
orchid
  disa 240
  ground 247
  pink or lilac 390
Oreodaimon quathlambae (fish) 131
oribi 148, 202, 204
Oribi Gorge Nature Reserve 172, 177, 178
  at a glance 177
ornithogalum (lily) 216
Orothamnus zeyheri (marsh rose) 243
Orpen Gate 13, 26, 41, 42
Orpen Rest Camp 13, 14, 24
Oryx gazella (gemsbok) 280
osprey 209
ostrich 80, 228, 232
Otjikoto cichlid 337
Otjisazu Guest Farm 340
Otjiwarongo 328

Otjovasondu 330
Otse 356
otter, Cape clawless 191, 210
Otter Trail 222, 223, 226
Oudtshoorn 228, 229, 232
Outeniqua Hiking Trail 224
Outeniqua Mountains 220, 222, 237
Outeniqua Nature Reserve 224
Outward Bound Centre (Lesotho) 130
Outward Bound School (Chimanimani) 389
Overberg 237
Oviston (town) 193
Oviston Nature Reserve 193
Ovita Game Lodge 340
Owambo region 328
Owen, Captain W F W 160
Owens, Mark and Delia 353
owl
   barred 38
   pearl-spotted 384
   Pel's fishing 346
oxpecker 333
Oyster Bay 221

P

P K le Roux Dam *see* Vanderkloof Dam
Paarl 258, 259
Paarl Mountain Nature Reserve 259
Pachypodium
   lealii (bottle tree) 321, 322
   namaquanum (halfmens) 268
   succulentum 195
padrão (Cape Cross) 320
Pafuri Gate 15
Pafuri Rest Camp 15, 18, 20, 25
Pakhuis Mountains 256
Pakhuis Pass 256, 257
palm
   makalani 322
   Mkambati 184
   Modjadji 37, 39
   vegetable ivory (*mokolwane*) 358, 359
Palmiet Mountains 237
Palmiet Nature Reserve 177
Palmiet River 242, 243
Palmwag Lodge 318, 320, 322
Pamuzinda Safari Lodge 386
Panicum repens (torpedo grass) 377
Panorama Route 63
Papkuils River 259

Parabuthus villosus (scorpion) 302
Paradise Camp 64
Paradise Valley 255
Paradise Valley Nature Reserve 177
Pat Busch Private Nature Reserve 244
Paternoster 257
Paterson, William 266, 272
Paul Kruger Gate 11
Pauline Bohnen Nature Reserve 224
Peacehaven Nature Reserve 112
Peak Road Nature Reserve 378
Pearson, Professor Harold 250
peat 124
Pelargonium cucullatum (plant) 253
Pelea capreolus (rhebok) 218
pelican 361
   white 158, 161, 253, 305, 314
penguin, black-footed (jackass) 210, 211, 239, 247
Penguin Island 300
Penhalonga 391
Pephricus livingstonei (bug) 66
Percy Fyfe Nature Reserve 88, 90
Perdeberg Trail 245
perdepis (tree) 209
Peripatus 236, 238
petrel, giant 160
Petrified Forest 317, 319, 322
Phaenocoma prolifera (plant) 238, 258
Phalaborwa Gate 12, 13, 15, 20, 22
phantom tree *see* moringa (tree)
pheromones 240
Philetairus socius (sociable weaver) 307, 331
Philothamnus natalensis occidentalis (snake) 153
Phinda Resource Reserve 164
Phongolo River 149, 151, 169
Phophonyane Nature Reserve 53, 57
Phudufudu Camp 79
Phumangena Zulu Umuzi 95
Pienaar, Dr Tol 29
Pienaars River 90
Piesang Valley 224
Pietermaritzburg 144, 147, 150, 151
Pietermaritzburg Bird Sanctuary 151
Pietersburg Game Reserve 88

pigeon, Rameron 77
Pigeon Valley Park 177
pig's root 268
Piggs Peak 57
Pilanesberg National Park 76, 89
   at a glance 88
Pilgrim's Rest 65, 72
Pilgrim's Rest Nature Reserve 72
pincushion 237
Pinetown 176
Pinnacle, The 63, 64, 66
Pintado Fountain 211
Pioneer Dam 22
Piper's Pan 354
Pirie Forest 201, 202
Pirie Trout Hatchery 202
Pitjane Camp 79
Platberg 123
Platberg Nature Reserve 123
Platberg Wildflower Gardens 123
Platysaurus capensis (lizard) 284, 285
Plettenberg Bay 222, 224, 227
Plettenberg Bay Country Club 224
Plumpudding Island 301
pochard 243
Podocarpus falcatus (yellow-wood) 219
Podranea brycei (Zimbabwe creeper) 393
Pofadder 268
Polemaetus bellicosus (martial eagle) 92
Pom Pom Camp 349
Pomona 301
Pomongwe Cave 400
Pongola Bush Nature Reserve 151
Pongola floodplain 154
Pongola Game Reserve 149
Pongola River 161, 164
Pongolapoort Biosphere Reserve 164
Pongolapoort Dam *see* Jozini Dam
pony, Basotho 128
pony-trekking 128, 130
Popa Falls Rest Camp 338, 341
popgun tree 39
poplar 201
porcupine 353
Porcupine Hiking Trail 124
Pork Pie Mountain 389
Porpita pacifica 245
Port Edward 176

Port Elizabeth 206, 209
   Oceanarium 210
   Snake Park 174, 210
Port Shepstone 143
Portulacaria afra (tree) 206
Possession (island) 300
Postberg 261
Postberg Nature Reserve 261
Postmasburg 282
Pot River 194
Potberg 236
Potberg Environmental Education Centre 238
Potchefstroom 96, 102
Potgietersrus 93
Potgietersrus Nature Reserve and Game-Breeding Centre 89
Potlake Nature Reserve 72
Potter's Pass Wildflower Reserve 202
prawn
   penaeid 158
Pretoria 76, 79, 81, 87, 93, 113
Pretoria National Botanical Garden 90
Pretorius, Major P J 206
Pretoriuskop Rest Camp 11, 14, 24, 26, 28
Prieska Koppie Nature Reserve 281
Prince Albert 231
Prince Alfred's Pass 216, 237
Princess Park 398
Prinskasteel River 253
Prionium serratum (plant) 177
Prospector's Hiking Trail 66, 72
protea 237, 246
   king 244, 246
   mountain rose 246
   snow 256
Protea 69
   acuminata 246
   caffra 69
   comptonii 69
   cryophila 256
   cynaroides 198, 244, 246
   gaguedi 69
   laetans 69
   roupelliae 69, 112
   rubropilosa 63, 69
Prutzer, Timothy 116
Pseudocordylus microlepidotus 273
Pseudocreobotra wahlbergi (praying mantis) 85
Pseudocrenilabrus (dwarf tilapia) 278
puku 365

Pumalanga Nature Reserve 164
Punda Maria Gate 15
Punda Maria Rest Camp 14, 25, 27
Pungwe Falls 392
Pungwe River 391, 392
Pycnoporus sanguineus (fungus) 216
Pyrgomorphidae (grasshopper) 344

Q

Qaba 128
Qalo 129
Qolora Mouth 186
quagga 266
Queen Elizabeth Park Nature Reserve 151
Queen's Park and Zoo 202
Queenstown 192
quiver tree 266, 272, 297, 302
Quthing district 129
Qwa-Qwa Park 120, 123

R

Raapenberg Bird Sanctuary 251
rabbit, European 251
Rabelais Dam 24
rafting
 Buffalo River 149
 Palmiet River 243
 Swaziland 55
Rainbow Trout Farm 100
Ramskop Nature Reserve 259
Rana angolensis (frog) 197
Raphicerus melanotis (grysbok) 221
raptors 62
ratel (honey badger) 339
Rattray, Michael 71
raven, Cape 124
Recurvirostra avosetta (bird) 116
Red Hill Nature Reserve 166
Red Waterhole 372
Redunca fulvorufula (reedbuck) 97
reedbuck 157
 mountain 97, 103
Reich, Allen 22
Reilly, Ted and Liz 55, 56
Renoster River 122
renosterbos 271
resurrection plant 71

Reunion Rocks 178
rhebok, grey 122, 203, 218
Rhebuck Trail 120
rhino
 black 25, 27, 168, 323, 328, 376
 desert-dwelling 281, 285, 322
 white 25, 27, 56, 84, 89, 97, 168, 170, 203, 211, 276, 332, 354, 358
Rhino and Lion Nature Reserve 99, 102
Rhino Bushveld Eco Park 90
Rhino Camp 82
Rhodes, Cecil John 400
rhombic skaapsteker (snake) 228
Ria Huysamen Garden 281
Ribaneng Falls 130
Richards Bay Game Reserve 171
Richmond 153
Richtersveld 264, 268
Richtersveld National Park 264, 267
Rietvlei 106
Rietvlei Bird Sanctuary 251
Rietvlei Nature Reserve 112, 113
Riley's Hotel 348
River Lodge 48
Riversdale 219
Riviersonderend Mountains 233, 237, 239
roan 12
Roan Camp 88
Robben Island 247, 251
Robberg Nature Reserve 224
Robbesteen Island 261
Robert Jameson Rose Park 176
Roberts, Austin 78
Robertson 236, 244
Robins, Herbert 370
Robins Camp 369, 370
Rocher Pan Nature Reserve 259
rock art
 Baviaanskloof (Karoo) 228
 Beaverlac (West Coast) 255
 Bushmans Kloof (West Coast) 256
 Cederberg 256
 Chinamora (Zimbabwe) 382
 Commando Drift Dam (Eastern Cape) 194
 Groot Winterhoek (West Coast) 258
 Ha Baroana 128, 129

Kaokoveld (Namibia) 317, 319, 321, 323
KwaZulu-Natal Drakensberg 137, 138, 141
Lake Chivero (Zimbabwe) 385
Matobos (Zimbabwe) 400
Murahwa's Hill (Zimbabwe) 390
Okavango Delta 348
Rusape (Zimbabwe) 390
rock hyrax *see* dassie
Rock Lodge (Touchstone Game Ranch) 92
Rocklodge 49
rockrunner 321
Rocktail Bay Lodge 161, 165
Roggeveld 264
Rolfontein Nature Reserve 269, 275
 at a glance 275
roller
 lilac-breasted 281, 329
 purple 365
Romulea saldanhensis 260
Rondebult Bird Sanctuary 106, 113
Rondegat River 257
Rondevlei
 Cape Peninsula 248, 252
 Garden Route 227
Rondevlei Bird Sanctuary 252, 253
Roodeplaat Dam 90
Roodeplaat Dam Nature Reserve 90
Roodepoort 99, 105
Roodewal Private Rest Camp 13, 14, 24, 26
Rooiberg mountain range 117, 121, 122
Rooiberg Nature Reserve 232
Rooikat Nature Walk 72
Rooikrans 249
Rooiputs 355
Root, William and Catherine 140
Rose, Dr Walter 184
rose, marsh 243
rose ginger flower 368
Rosetta 140
Roundhill Oribi Reserve 202
Royal Natal National Park 134, 141, 142
 at a glance 140
 rules for hikers 140
Royal Natal National Park Hotel 140, 141
ruff 199
Rugged Glen 142

Ruiterbos Forest 224
Runde River 394, 395
Rusape 390
Rust de Winter 86
Rust de Winter Dam 91
Rust de Winter Nature Reserve 91
Rustenburg 94
Rustenburg Nature Reserve 100, 101, 103
Rustfontein Dam 123
Rustfontein Dam Nature Reserve 123

S

S A Lombard Nature Reserve 103
S J Mabena Educational Centre 85
S S Skosana Nature Reserve 84, 91
Sabi Sabi Game Reserve 48, 51
Sabi Sand Private Nature Reserve 41, 44, 48
Sabie area 60, 69
Sabie Bridge 28
Sabie Game Reserve 12, 13, 26, 164
Sabie River 12, 19, 20, 21, 25, 27, 28, 48
sable 85, 98, 370, 371
Sable Camp 88
Sable Lodge 383
Sable Park 384
Sable Valley Lodge 372
Sadawa Game Reserve 260
safaris
 balloon (NamibRand) 314
 elephant (Botswana) 346
 fly-in safaris (Skeleton Coast) 323
 operators (Maun) 347
 rhino-tracking (Namibia) 321, 322
 walking (Matusadona) 380
Safari Lodge 49
Safari Ostrich Show Farm 232
Safariland Game Park 245
Saldanha Bay 260, 261
Salmonsdam Nature Reserve 242
Salt Works 316
Salvinia molesta (Kariba weed) 377
Sam Knott Nature Reserve 196, 202

San people *see* Bushmen (San)
Sand River 47, 48, 126
Sand Spruit 111
Sanddrif 256
Sandenburgh, Peter 346
Sandersonia aurantiaca (plant) 146
sandgrouse, Namaqua 266
Sandile, Paramount Chief 202
Sandringham Private Nature Reserve 49
Sandton (urban trails) 109
Sandveld 264, 267, 268
Sandveld Nature Reserve 96, 117, 124
Sandwich Harbour 308, 310, 311, 315
Sani Top 131
Sansimba fishing camp 373
Santa Lucia (launch) 158
Santantadibe River 345
San-ta-wani Lodge 348, 350
Sanyati Gorge 379, 380
Sanyati Lodge 377, 379, 380
Sanyati River 378, 379
Sanyati West Camp 379
Sarcocaulon (Bushman's candle)
  crassicaule 301
  patersonii 301
Sardinia Bay Nature Reserve 211
SAS Saldanha Nature Trail 260
Satara Rest Camp 13, 14, 20, 22, 24, 26, 28, 29
Save River 390, 393, 395, 396, 397
Save Valley Conservancy 397
Save-Runde region (Gonarezhou) 394, 395
Savuti Bush Camp 365
Savuti campsite 364
Savuti Channel 348, 364, 365
Savuti Marsh 364
Savuti region 362, 364, 365
Savuti South Camp 364
Schaapen Island 261
Schoeman, Louw 323
Schoemansville 98
Schotia (tree) 209
Schuinsdraai Nature Reserve 91
Schwantes, Professor Gustav 241
Scorpionidae (scorpion) 302
Scotopelia peli (Pel's fishing owl) 346
Scully, W C 264
Sea Lion (ferry) 378
Sea Vista 218

Sea World, Durban 177
seabird, desalination mechanism of 160
seahorse, Knysna 222, 223
seal, Cape fur 96, 301, 319, 320
Seal Island
  Namibia 300
  South Africa 247, 252
Seaview Game Park 212, 213
Sebakwe Dam Recreational Park 386
Sebungwe River 378
secretary bird 276
Seekoei River 225
Seekoei River Nature Reserve 225
Seekoeivlei Nature Reserve 124
Seely, Dr Mary 311
Sehlabathebe National Park 128, 131, 136
Selati Lodge 48
Selby, Paul 26
Selinda Camp 365
Selinda Spillway *see* Magwegqana (Selinda) Spillway
Selous (village) 386
Selous, Frederick Courteney 19, 126, 163
Semonkong 128, 130
Semonkong Lodge 130
Sendelingsdrif 267, 268
Senecio elegans (flowers) 255
Sentinel, the 141
Senuko 397
seringa, Indian 77
Serondela 362
Serondela campsite 363, 364
Serondella Lodge 49
Serowe 358
Serpentine Channel 227
serval 370
sesame bush, Herero 321, 322
Sesamothamnus querichii (Herero sesame bush) 321, 322
Sesriem campsite 309, 311
Sesriem Canyon 308, 309
Settlers Dam 204
Settlers' Park Nature Reserve 212
Seven Sisters *see* Baines' Baobabs
Seven Weeks Poort 232, 237
Seweweekspoort *see* Seven Weeks Poort
Shabeni Hill 24
Shakawe 344, 345, 346, 349

Shakawe Fishing Lodge 348, 350
Shamwari Game Reserve 203
Shanati Bush Camp 38
Shangaan people 37
Shangani River 372
shark, Zambezi 18
Shashe River 39, 40, 360
Shazibe Lake 158
Sheba's Breasts 56
Sheldrake Camp 39
Sheldrake Game Ranch 38
shell, blue-raft 158
Shimuwini Bushveld Camp 14, 15
Shinde Camp 350
Shinga Camp 46
Shingwedzi Game Reserve 13
Shingwedzi Rest Camp 14, 15, 20, 25, 27
Shingwedzi River 27
Shipwreck Trail 203
shipwrecks
  Eastern Cape 211
  Skeleton Coast 317, 321
  Wild Coast 187
Shisha stream 27
Shongweni Resources Reserve 177
shrike
  bush 395
  crimson-breasted 305
  long-tailed 46
  white-crowned 372
Shurugwi 396
Sibuyu Forest Reserve 362
sickle bush 156
Sihadla River 160
Sijarira Forest Reserve 380
Sijarira Lodge 380
Sikereti bush camp 333, 335
Silaka Nature Reserve 185
Silozwane Cave 400
silver tree 249, 250
Silverglen Nature Reserve 178
Silvermine Nature Reserve 252, 253
Silvermine River 252
Silverstrand 236
Simes Rustic Cottage 140
Simon's Town 247
Simonsberg 237
Simunye 56
Sinamatella Camp 369, 370
Sinclair Island 299
Sinclair Nature Reserve 225
Singita Private Game Reserve 41, 49
Siphiso Camp 56
Siphiso Valley 55

Sir Lowry's Pass 237
Sir Lowry's Pass village 238
Sirheni Bushveld Camp 14, 15
Sishen 279
sitatunga 338, 344, 362
Sitatunga Camp 350
Skeerpoort 101
Skeleton Coast 317, 321, 322
  at a glance 320
Skeleton Coast Park 317, 321, 322, 323
Skilpad Wildflower Reserve 164, 267
skink, Wahlberg's 376
Skinner, Dougie 351
Skip Norgarb Trail 124
Skukuza Rest Camp 11, 14, 22, 24, 28
Skurweberg 257
Skurwerant Peak 74
Skyline Nature Reserve 178
Slanghoek range 237
snail, giant land 16
snake
  black-headed 202
  flying 300
  green 153
  mole 33
  Natal black 184
  sand 355
  sea 224
  spotted bush 383
snake park
  Cape Town Snake Park 249
  Fitzsimons Snake Park 174
  Hartbeespoort Dam Snake and Animal Farm 98
  Kleinplasie Reptile World 243
  Port Elizabeth 174, 206, 210
  Pretoria Aquarium and Reptile Park 87
  Transvaal Snake Park 116
  Victoria Falls 373
Sneeuberg 270, 274
snow skiing 130
Soada Forest Nature Reserve 152
Sobhuza II, King 53, 55, 57
Sodwana Bay 155, 164
Sodwana Bay National Park 157, 165
Soetdoring Nature Reserve 117, 124
Soete Melk Valley 233
Sohelbele River 51
Somerset West 240
Sondelani Private Game Reserve 401
Sondeza Mountain 57

418

Songimvelo Nature Reserve 106, 114
Sontuli Bush Camp 168
Soshangana 393
Sossusvlei 308, 309
Sossusvlei Karos Lodge 311
Sotho prehistoric settlement 126
South Africa
   Amatola region 195
   Augrabies Falls 283
   Bushveld 76
   Cape Peninsula 247
   Free State 117
   Garden Route 216
   Great Karoo 269
   Highveld 94, 106
   Kalahari 277
   Kalahari Gemsbok National Park 288
   Kruger National Park 10
   KwaZulu-Natal interior (Zululand) 166
   KwaZulu-Natal Midlands 144
   KwaZulu-Natal south coast 172
   Little Karoo 228
   Lowveld 41
   Maputaland 154
   Namaqualand 264
   national parks 49
   north eastern Cape 188
   Northern Province 31
   Port Elizabeth area 206
   southern Cape 233
   Transkei 182
   West Coast 255
   Western Cape 233
Southern Coastal Park (proposed) 178
Soutpansberg 31, 35, 36, 38, 60, 67, 68, 70, 72
Soutpansberg Hiking Trail 72
Sowa (Sua) Pan 357, 359, 361
Spandau Kop 273, 274
spekboom 206
Sperrgebiet 296, 300, 308
spider
   black widow (button) 386
   ground 220
   jumping 146
   threads and webs 220
Spioenkop Public Resort Nature Reserve 152
Spitskop 192
Spitskop Nature Reserve 283, 286
Spitzkoppe 335
spoonbill 172
springbok 196, 274, 282, 355

Springbok 265, 268
Springbokwasser Gate 320
Springside Nature Reserve 178
Spurwing Island 376, 380
Spurwing Island Lodge 379
squirrel, Cape ground 123
St Croix (island) 205, 210, 211
St Croix Island Nature Reserve 211, 212
St Francis Bay 209
St Lucia Estuary 158, 159, 165
St Lucia Game Reserve 158
St Lucia Marine Reserve 159
St Lucia Park 159
St Lucia Resort 159
St Lucia village 158
Stapleford Forest Reserve 391
star-chestnut, African 321
starling, blue-eared glossy 398
stars of Bethlehem *see* chincherinchees
Starvation Creek Nature Reserve 72
Starvation Island 376, 379
steenbok 168, 240, 331
Steenbokfontein Pan 260
Steenbras Dam 244
Steenkampsberg plateau 74
Steganotaenia araliacea (carrot tree) 39
Steinkopf 268
Stellenbosch 233, 241, 245
Stellenboschberg 233, 237
Sterculia africana (African star-chestnut) 321
Stereospermum kunthianum (pink jacaranda) 380
Sterk River 80
Sterkfontein Caves 104
Sterkfontein Dam 125
Sterkfontein Dam Nature Reserve 125
Sterkspruit Nature Reserve 73, 75
Sterkstroom 188
Stettyns 237
Stevenson-Hamilton, James 12, 28, 29
Stevenson-Hamilton Memorial Library 22, 28
Stilbaai 219
Stilbaai Forest 220
Stone Age sites 54, 317, 340
   Kalahari Gemsbok National Park 290
   Melville Koppies 111
   Saldanha Bay 260
   Wonderkloof Nature Reserve 75

Stone Camp 55
stone plant 301
Stony Point Penguin Reserve 239
stork
   marabou 27
   open-billed 337
   saddlebill 380
   white 259
   yellow-billed 18, 83
Stormberg 188
Storms River 226
Storms River Mouth 226
Storms River Rest Camp 226
Strandfontein Beach 252
Strandfontein Sewage Works 247
Strandloper Trail 197, 203
Strandlopers 203, 220, 224
Strelitzia
   nicolai (banana tree) 182
   reginae (crane flower) 199
Striga elegans (plant) 114
Struben Dam 87
Struisbaai 238
Strydpoort mountain range 61, 75
Stutterheim 201
Sua Pan *see* Sowa (Sua) Pan
Subeng 129
Sudwala Caves 73
   bats of 74
Sugarloaf campsite 158
Suikerboschfontein Hiking Trail 115
Suikerbosrand Nature Reserve 69, 106, 114, 115, 116
   at a glance 115
Suku River 182
Summerton, Thomas 199
Sun City 82
sunbird
   dusky 271
   malachite 244
   Marico 171
Sunbird Environmental Centre 252
Sunday Pans 354
sundew plant 251
Sungulwane Game Lodge 165
suni 165
Sunnyside Cottage 135
Suricata suricatta 190
suricate 190
Swakop River 308
Swakop River Valley 340
Swakopmund 317, 319
swallow, blue 68
Swallowtail waterfall 199

Swamp Nature Reserve, The 143
Swart, Dick 28
Swart River 225
Swartberg 228, 231, 236, 237
Swartberg Nature Reserve 231
Swartberg Pass 229, 237
Swartberg Trail 231
Swartfontein Pleasure Resort 280
Swartkop Mountain 102
Swartkops Hills 95, 98
Swartkops River 209
Swartkrans Cave 104
Swartvlei 227
Swaziland 53
Swellendam 216, 218, 223, 233
Swellendam Hiking Trail 223
Sweni River 22
Swimuwini 394, 395, 397
Swoboda, Lothar 346
Swynnerton, Charles 390
Sylvic Nature Reserve 211

T

T C Robertson Nature Reserve 178
Table Bay 247
Table Mountain 236, 237, 249, 250, 251, 252
   proposed national park 249
Table Mountain (KwaZulu-Natal) 153
Table Mountain Nature Reserve 252
Talamati Bushveld Camp 13, 14
Talmage Pan 166
Tambahata Pan 395, 396
Tamboti Bush Camp 62
Tamboti Rest Camp 13, 14, 24
Tanda Tula Game Lodge 41, 52
Tankwa Karoo National Park 267
Tarka River 190
Tashinga Camp 379
Tau Game Lodge 84
Tchinga campsite 363
Telophorus quadricolor (bush shrike) 395
Tembe Elephant Park 154, 163, 165
Tembe fishermen 160
Tendele Camp 140, 141
Tendele Lodge 141
Tendele Valley 141

419

Terathopius ecaudatus (bateleur) 360
Terblans Nature Walk 225
termite 39, 45, 94
Terrace Bay 320, 322, 323
terrapin 205
tetraselago wilmsii (plant) 75
Tettigoniidae (cricket) 270
Tewate Wilderness Area 155, 157
Thaba 'Nchu 122
Thabana-Ntlenyana 128, 131
Thabazimbi 76, 78, 90
Thabina Falls 75
Thalu Bush Camp 149
Thamalakane River 345, 348, 350
Thathe Vondo Forest 36
Thathe Vondo plantation 36
The Hide 372
The Horseshoe 191
The Wilds 116
Theewaterskloof Dam 235
Theronia Pan Nature Reserve 125
Thesen, Hjalmar 218
Thilachium africanum (cucumber bush) 24
Thomas Baines Nature Reserve 202, 203, 204
Thompson, George 285
Thompson's Vlei 389
Thorncroft Nature Reserve 108
Thornybush Game Reserve 41, 49, 51
Thornybush Main Lodge 49
Thorp, Ernest 173
Three Rondavels, The 60, 62, 64
Three Sisters Walk 245
thrush, Cape rock 208
Thukela Biosphere 153
Thukela River *see* Tugela River
Thunberg, Carl 198
Tienie Louw Nature Reserve 108
Tienie Versveld Wildflower Reserve 260
Tierberg Nature Reserve 283, 286
Tieties Bay 257
tiger 29
tigerfish 378
tilapia
 dwarf 278
 Mozambique 161
Tilapia guinasana (Otjikoto cichlid) 337
Timbavati Private Nature Reserve 31, 39, 41, 43, 50

Timbavati River 24, 26, 49
Tinley, Ken 333
Tobias, Professor Phillip 104
Tokai Forest Reserve 253
Torra Bay 320, 323
tortoise, angulate 243
Touchstone Game Ranch 92
Touw River 225, 227
Towerkop 237
Towerkop Nature Reserve 232
Trachypetrella andersonii (toad grasshopper) 284
Trafalgar Marine Reserve 178
Tragelaphus angasii (nyala) 40
Transkaroo Hiking Trail 276
Transvaal Snake Park 116
Trappes' Valley 202
Treasure Beach Project 178
Tree Camp (Londolozi) 49
Tree House Camp 45
Tree Lodge (Bonamanzi) 154
treehopper 40
Treur River 60, 64, 65
Tribulus terrestris (herb) 279
Tritonia lineata (plant) 82
Triumfetta sonderi (plant) 90
Trollope, Harold 207
trout, rainbow 71
Tsaobis Leopard Nature Park 303, 307
Tsaro Lodge 350
Tsauchab River 308, 309
Tsende River 20
tsessebe 19, 80, 85, 346
Tsessebe Camp 88
Tshabalala Sanctuary 401
Tshabong 356
Tshakuma Catchment Area 39
Tshakuma Dam 39
Tshatshingo potholes 36
Tshihovhohovho Falls 37, 38
Tshipise 31, 33
Tshipise Lodge 32
Tshokwane 23, 29, 30
Tshukudu Camp (Pilanesberg) 88
Tshukudu Game Lodge 41, 52
Tsikoane 129
Tsisab Ravine 319
Tsitsikamma Forest 216, 219, 220, 225
Tsitsikamma Hiking Trail 222, 223, 225, 226
Tsitsikamma Indigenous Forests 225
Tsitsikamma Mountains 226, 237
Tsitsikamma National Park 222, 223, 226
 at a glance 226

Tsitsikamma River 221
Tsodile Hills 348, 349, 350, 351
Tsoelike River 131
Tsolwana Game Park 201, 204
Tsondab River 308
Tsonga Kraal and Open-Air Museum 33
Tsonga people 33, 36
Tsumkwe 336
Tswalu Lodge 281
Tswalu Private Desert Reserve 281
Tugela Gorge 141, 142
Tugela River 141, 152, 174
Tulbagh 260
Tuli Block 361
Tuli Safari Area 398
Tuli Safari Lodge 360
tulp, blue 194
Tundazi Mountains 395
turtle, leatherback and loggerhead 157, 158, 160
Tussen-die-Riviere Nature Reserve 117, 126
Twee Rivieren (Botswana) 354, 356
Twee Rivieren Rest Camp (South Africa) 289, 292
Tweede Tol 255
Twin Falls (Augrabies) 285
Twyfelfontein 317, 321, 323
Tygerberg Nature Reserve 254
Tygerberg Zoo 259, 260
Tyler's Park Nature Reserve 212
Tyume Valley 199
Tzaneen 31, 35, 60, 72
Tzaneen Dam 32, 39

U

Ubizane Game Reserve 171
Udu Dam 391
Ugab Gate 320
Ugab Hiking Trail 323
Ugab River 317
Uitenhage Nature Reserve 212
Uitsoek Forest 74
Uitsoek Hiking Trail 74, 75
Ulusaba Game Reserve 49
Umbabat Private Nature Reserve 41, 52
Umbeje Khumalo 169
Umbogavango Nature Reserve 178
Ume River 374, 377, 378, 379
Umfolozi Game Reserve 154, 158, 168

Umfolozi Wilderness Area 168
Umfurudzi Safari Area 386
uMgeni River *see* Mgeni River
Umgeni River Park 178
Umgeni Valley Nature Reserve 152
Umhlanga 176
Umhlanga Lagoon Nature Reserve 179
Umhlanga Ponds 179
Umhlanga River 174
Umhlanga River floodplain 174
Umkomaas Valley *see* Mkhomazi River Valley
Umkombo Safari Lodge 372
Umkumbi Bush Camp 162
Umlalazi Nature Reserve 166, 171
Umlalazi River 171
Umlani Bush Camp 41, 52
Umngazi River Bungalows 187
Umtamvuna Nature Reserve 179, 185
Umtiza listerana (tree) 205
Umtiza Nature Reserve 198, 205
Umvoti Vlei Conservancy 152
Umzingwane Dam 401
Underberg 143
Uniab River 322, 323
Uniab River Delta Trail 323
Uniondale 232
Union's End 288
University of Port Elizabeth Nature Reserve 213
Upington 281, 283, 286
Ursinia speciosa (Namaqualand daisy) 268
Usutu (Maputo) River 154
Uvongo Bird Park 179
Uvongo River Nature Reserve 179
Uzi Swamp 165

V

Vaal Dam 116
Vaal River 104, 105, 124, 277, 281
Vaal Spa Game Reserve 104
Vaalbos National Park 281, 328
Vaalkop Dam 92
Vaalkop Dam Nature Reserve 92
Valley of a Thousand Hills 149, 150, 153
Valley of Desolation 273, 274
Van der Stel's mine 268
van Dyk, Ann and Godfrey 79

Van Kervel Nature Reserve 227
van Niekerk, Hugo 16
Van Riebeeck Karoo Gardens 194
Van Riebeeck Nature Reserve 87, 113
Van Ryneveld's Pass Dam 273, 274
Van Stadens Pass 213
Van Stadens River 213
Van Stadens Wild Flower Reserve and Bird Sanctuary 213
Vanderkloof (town) 275
Vanderkloof Dam 269, 271, 275, 276
Vanzylsrus 279
Varty, John and Dave 47
Venda people 30, 33, 36
Venus Pool 248
Verdoorn Dr Inez 35
Vergelegen Nature Reserve 137, 143
Verlorenvlei 260
Verlorenvlei Vallei Nature Reserve 74
Vernon Crookes Nature Reserve 172, 179
Vet River 124
Vhembe Nature Reserve 39
Victoria Falls 362, 368, 372, 373
Victoria Falls National Park 371, 372, 373
  at a glance 373
Victoria Falls village 373
Victoria West Nature Reserve 269, 275, 276
Vier-en-twintig River 258
Viljoen's Pass 234
Villiersdorp 245
Villiersdorp Mountains 235
Villiersdorp Nature Reserve 246
Vineyard Trail 246
violet, wild 398
Virginia Bush Nature Reserve 179
Vivo 35, 61
Vlakkenberg 249
Von Bach Dam 307
Von Bach Recreation Resort 303, 304, 307
von Caprivi, Count Leo 333
von Lindequist, Governor Friedrich 308, 324
Vondeling Island 261
Voorburg Camp 39
Voorburg Dam 39
Vorstershoop 281
Vrolijkheid Nature Reserve 246
Vryburg 280
Vryheid 153, 169
Vryheid Hill Nature Reserve 153
Vulovedu mountains 35
vulture
  bearded 130, 184, 192
  Cape 20, 102, 184, 191, 236, 340, 341, 356
  lappet-faced 20, 340
  white-backed 20, 168, 281, 313, 340
  white-headed 334
vulture restaurant 102
  Free State 122
  Hartbeespoort Dam 98
  KwaZulu-Natal 162
  Moletsi Nature Reserve 86
  Swaziland 56
vygie 134, 301
  Bokbaai 241

W

Wachendorfia paniculata (plant) 235
Wadrif Pan 260
Wadrift Nature Reserve 227
Wagendrift Dam 150, 153
Wagendrift Nature Reserve 153
Wahlenbergia (plant) 125
Walvis Bay 305, 308, 315
  bird sanctuaries 315
Walvis Bay Lagoon 316
Warmbaths 78, 84, 92
Warmbaths Nature Reserve 92
warthog *see* aardvark
wasp, cuckoo 65
Water Wilderness Camp 374
Waterberg 35, 76, 78, 80, 81, 82, 84, 85, 86, 92
Waterberg Plateau Park 328, 333, 339, 340, 341
  at a glance 341
waterbuck 24, 48, 374
Waterbuck Lodge 50
Waterfall Bluff 184
Waterkloof Trail 312
Waters Meeting Nature Reserve 205
watersports
  Albert Falls Resources Reserve 144
  Boskop Dam 96
Chelmsford Nature Reserve 146
Commando Drift Dam 190
Hartbeespoort Dam 97
Hazelmere Resources Reserve 174
Inanda Resources Reserve 175
Midmar Dam 150
Wagendrift Dam Resort 153
Waterval Nature Reserve 260
Waterval-Boven 106
weaver
  lesser masked 41, 43
  sociable 307, 331
Wedza (Hwedza) area 383
Weenen Nature Reserve 153
weevil, broad-nosed 50
Welbedacht Dam 118
Welkom 125
Welwitsch, Friedrich 316
Welwitschia mirabilis 241, 316
Welwitschia Plains 308, 313
Welwitschia Plains campsite 311
Welwitschia Trail 313
Wemmershoek 237
Wemmershoek Dam 244
West Caprivi Game Park 333
West Coast National Park 261
  at a glance 261
West Coast Ostrich Ranch 261
West Nicholson 401
Whiskey Creek Nature Reserve 227
White Lady (rock painting) 317, 319
White Waters 401
white-eye, Cape 105
Whovi Wilderness Area 400, 401
whydah (bird) 139
Whyte, Ian 26
Widdringtonia cedarbergensis (cedar tree) 256
Wiesenhof Private Nature Reserve 246
Wikar, Hendrik 285
Wild Coast 182, 184, 186
  shipwrecks along 187
Wild Coast Hiking Trail 187
wild flowers 264
Wild Geese, The (film) 35
wildebeest 23, 24, 26, 291
  black 104, 116, 126
  blue 24, 53, 126, 329, 330
Wilderness 227
Wilderness Leadership School 175
Wilderness National Park 216, 222, 227
Wilderness Rest Camp 225, 227
Willem Pretorius Game Reserve 117, 126
  at a glance 127
Willems River 266
Wilmot, Lloyd and June 364
Wilton Valley Game Reserve 92
Windhoek 303, 304
window plant 301
Windy Brow Game Farm 93
Windy Ridge Game Park 171
Wine Route Ostrich Farm 261
Winterberg 188, 196, 200
Winterskloof 147
Winterton 152
Wit River 255
witchweed 114
Witelsbos 226
Witfontein Forest 224
Witpoortjie Falls 105
Witrivier 229
Witsand 282
Witsand Nature Reserve 282
Witteberg 117, 191, 192
Witvinger Nature Reserve 93
Witwatersrand National Botanical Garden 105
wolf snake, Cape 306
Wolfgat Nature Reserve 254
Wolhuter, Harry 13, 21
Wolhuterskop Hiking Trail 127
Wolhuterskop Nature Reserve 127
Wolkberg Caves 75
Wolkberg Wilderness Area 68, 69, 75
Wolmaransstad 102
Wolwedans Dune Camp 314
Wolwespruit Nature Reserve 105
Wonder Cave 100
Wonderboom Nature Reserve 93
Wonderkloof Nature Reserve 75
Wonderwerk Cave 282
Woodcliffe Cave Trails 194
Woodville Forest 225
Woody Cape Nature Reserve 205
Worcester 241, 243, 269
World of Birds Nature Park 254
World of Birds Wildlife Sanctuary 253, 254
World's View (Nyanga) 392

World's View (Pietermaritzburg) 153
worm, velvet 253
Wurmbea krausii (plant) 134

X

Xade 353
Xakanaxa Camp 348, 351
Xaro Lodge 351
Xaxaba Camp 348, 351
Xerophyta retinervis 106
Xudum 351
Xugana Lodge 348, 350, 351

Y

Yei people 347, 350
yellowfish, Clanwilliam 257
yellowwood, Outeniqua 219, 226
Yellowwoods Nature Reserve 213
Yssel, Tom 19
Ysternek Nature Reserve 225, 227

Z

Zambezi National Park 372, 373
   at a glance 373
Zambezi River 335, 338, 362, 368, 373, 374, 379, 380, 381
Zandvlei Bird Sanctuary 254
Zangozolo Bush Camp 166
zebra 81, 401
   Burchell's 81, 104
   Cape mountain 81, 188, 192, 231, 236
   Hartmann's mountain 309, 313
Zibadianja Lagoon 365
Zimbabwe
   eastern highlands 387
   Harare and northeast 381
   Hwange and Victoria Falls 368
   Kariba 374
   southeast 393
   southwest 398
Zithabiseni Holiday Resort 84
zoo
   Bloemfontein Zoological Gardens 117
   Hartbeespoort Dam Snake and Animal Farm 96, 98
   Johannesburg Zoological Gardens 108, 110
   Natal Zoological Gardens 76, 151
   National Zoological Gardens (Pretoria) 87, 89, 101
   Queens Park and Zoo 202
   Tygerberg Zoo 259, 260
Zosterops pallidus (bird) 105
Zuurberg 209
Zwartkops River 213
Zwartkops Valley Nature Reserve 213
Zwartrand Camp 39
Zwelabo Lodge 85